PROCLAIMING CHRIST

In the Power of the Holy Spirit

OPPORTUNITIES
& CHALLENGES

Explore These Other Empowered21 Titles

Global Renewal Christianity: Spirit-Empowered Movements Past, Present, and Future. Vinson Synan, Amos Yong, general editors.
> Volume 1: Asia and Oceania.
> > ISBN:978-1-62998-688-3
> Volume 2: Latin America with Miguel Álvarez, editor.
> > ISBN: 978-1-62998-767-5
> Volume 3: Africa, with J. Kwabena Asamoah-Gyadu, editor.
> > ISBN: 978-1-62998-768-2
> Volume 4: Europe and North America.
> > ISBN: 978-1-62998-943-3

The Truth About Grace: Spirit-Empowered Perspectives. Vinson Synan, editor.
> ISBN: 978-1-62999-504-5

Human Sexuality & The Holy Spirit: Spirit-Empowered Perspectives. Wonsuk Ma, Kathaleen Reid-Martinez, Annamarie Hamilton, editors.
> ISBN: 978-1-950971-00-8

PROCLAIMING CHRIST
In the Power of the Holy Spirit

OPPORTUNITIES
& CHALLENGES

Edited by

Wonsuk Ma *and* **Emmanuel Anim**
Rebekah Bled, *Associate Editor*

ORU
PRESS
Tulsa, Oklahoma USA

Cover design by Jiwon Kim
Composed by Angela Sample at Pressbooks.com using the Clarke design
Design & Production Editor: Mark E. Roberts

ISBN: 978-1-950971-03-9 (softcover)
ISBN: 978-1-950971-05-3 (ebook)

Printed in the United States of America

Contents

Part II. Proclaiming the Uniqueness of Christ in the World

Foreword

Pentecostals and charismatics have long regarded Acts 2 as more than a picture of the early church. It is, instead, a paradigm for ministry in every age. That paradigm includes three components:

The first component is *charisma*. Acts 2 begins with the dramatic outpouring of the Holy Spirit on the Day of Pentecost (verses 1–13). Through his Holy Spirit, God empowered the church to "speak in other tongues" (verse 4), indicating that God's people had a prophetic mission oriented toward proclaiming the gospel throughout the world. Throughout Acts, this baptism of the Holy Spirit certified that God himself welcomed all people into his family: "in Jerusalem, and in all Judea and Samaria, and to the ends of the earth" (1:8).

Christ himself is the second component of the Acts 2 paradigm. Pentecostals and charismatics are often described as "people of the Spirit," and there is much truth to that. But Peter's Pentecost sermon keeps the focus on Jesus throughout, showing how his death, resurrection, and ascension both fulfills biblical prophecy, and inaugurates the new age of the Spirit in which we now live. "God has made this Jesus, whom you crucified, both Lord and Messiah" (2:36). The Holy Spirit charismatically empowers our proclamation of the gospel, but the focus of that proclamation is always Christ Jesus. Spirit-empowered people are thus "Jesus people," first and foremost.

The third component of the Acts 2 paradigm is community. Verses 42–47 describe the daily life of the Jerusalem church, but they also set an agenda for all other churches. Through the Spirit, Christ calls individuals to follow him, but he never calls them to follow him alone. He calls us to follow him in a Spirit-filled community. The devotion to apostolic doctrine, fellowship, the ordinances, and prayer which these verses describe are universal in scope, but they also take into account local context. This accounts for the cultural variation we see across the churches established in the book of Acts.

The book you hold in your hands demonstrates the persistence of these three components of the Acts 2 paradigm in today's Spirit-Empowered Movement (SEM). Most of the individual chapters emerged from the May 2018 Johannesburg Consultation jointly organized by the

Empowered21 Global Council and African Congress. The scholars who contributed to this consultation addressed the following three issues: 1) affirmation of the uniqueness of Christ as Savior, 2) challenges arising from social contexts, both global and local; and 3) the work of the Holy Spirit manifested in SEM ministries. The result is a fascinating look at the theology and practice of Spirit-filled Christianity worldwide.

I encourage you to learn from these scholars by reading these essays. More than merely learning information from them, however, I pray that your theology and practice will be renewed as a result. May our lives and ministries continue to be powered of the charisma of the Spirit, to be centered on the good news of the kingship of Christ, and to result in communities that, like the first Pentecostal congregation, bring praise to God, enjoy society's favor, and continuously add members to the company of the redeemed!

Dr. George O. Wood
Chairman, World Assemblies of God Fellowship
Global Co-Chair, Empowered21

Preface

The book began its life with the eleven studies presented at the 2018 Scholars Consultation in Johannesburg. The lively spiritual atmosphere of the African continent, and the close engagement of the church with tumultuous social changes in South Africa provided a rich environment for the reflections. Then, the editorial team commissioned eleven new studies for the book.

In a work of this nature, the Editors are immensely indebted to countless hands serving the Consultation, editorial work, and the publishing process. Our sincere thanks go to the various authors. Some participated in the Johannesburg Consultation, and others responded to our invitation to make contributions to this volume. We are so grateful for every effort and commitment to this project.

The editorial team would also like to acknowledge our indebtedness and gratitude to the Global Council of Empowered21, whose foresight, encouragement, and funding were indispensable in making this project a success. The International Co-Chair of Empowered21, Dr. William Wilson, joined the Consultation at its opening session and summarized the vision and initiative of Empowered21.

We are also grateful to the E21 Executive Director, Ossie Mills, and Africa Region Co-Chairs, Rev. Dr. Frank Chikane and Apostle Prof Opoku Onyinah for their encouragement and support. We also appreciate with much gratitude, Dr. Michael Rakes, the Global Council Liaison to the Scholars' Consultation, who launched the session with a soul-searching devotion. Thanks also go to Dr. Mark Roberts, who ably facilitated the Consultation by making the Digital Showcase of the Oral Roberts University the online management tool.

Through the editorial process, two friends assisted the editors with their skills and commitment. Mr. Lemuel Jezreel Godinez, an MDiv student at Oral Roberts University, worked closely with the editors to process the commissioned studies. Then Mrs. Rebekah Bled joined the process as Associate Editor to copyedit each chapter through close coordination with the authors. She kept every one of us on our toes and ensured that we reached our goal in such speed and alacrity, which only a few could do. This manuscript is vastly improved because of the two friends with their comments and attention to detail. The production stage calls for the professional hand of the ORU Press. We remain ever grateful to all the hands that generously offered different gifts to make this book possible. The book, therefore, is a product of Spirit-empowered minds and skills.

May the Lord, the Holy Spirit, empower his Church!

The Editors
May 2020

I

Establishing the Foundation

Introduction

Wonsuk Ma and Emmanuel Anim

Two Edinburgh Conferences at the Backdrop

The first World Missionary Conference held at Edinburgh, Scotland in 1910 marked a decisive paradigm in the history of global Christian mission. During this period, Europe and North America were generally recognized as Christian heartlands, while Africa and Latin America were considered the least evangelized continents. Asia also was yet to have a strong Christian presence. A century later, at Edinburgh in 2010, the story was different as the global South was noted to have tipped the balance of Christian presence. This demographic shift also presents to us the complex nature of contemporary Christian mission, where the Western world now grapples with the challenge of making the message of the gospel relevant in the midst of the secular humanism and religious pluralism which characterizes Western societies. We are in recent times also witnessing a reverse mission, where Christians from the global South continue to migrate to the northern continents, not only as economic migrants or refugees, but also becoming principal bearers of the Christian faith.

On June 6, 2010, representatives of world Christianity from the Catholic, Orthodox, Protestants, and Pentecostals (an emerging and fast-growing denomination) gathered in the Church of Scotland Assembly Hall in Edinburgh, not only to commemorate the historic World Missionary Conference of 1910, but also to reflect and review the nature of global Christian mission, and the way forward in accomplishing the Great Commission of our Lord Jesus Christ. The Edinburgh 2010 Call was put together by a working group which affirmed, among other things, the belief in the church as "a sign and symbol of the reign of God." The church has the divine mandate to witness to Christ today by sharing in God's mission of love, peace, and justice through the transforming power of the Holy Spirit. The Common Call affirmed, "Trusting in the Triune God and with a renewed sense of urgency." It continues in the first paragraph that, "we are called to incarnate and proclaim the good news of salvation, of forgiveness of sin, of life abundance, and of liberation for all poor and oppressed. We are challenged to witness and evangelize in such a way that we are a living demonstration of love, righteousness, and justice that God intends for the whole world."

The second paragraph of the Edinburgh 2010 Call also drew attention to, "remembering Christ's sacrifice on the cross and his resurrection for the world's salvation, and empowered by the Holy Spirit, we are called to authentic dialogue, respectful engagement, and humble witness among people of other faiths #8212; and no faith #8212; to the uniqueness of Christ."[1] The Common Call emphasizes the significant role of "the Holy Spirit, who blows over the whole world at will, reconnecting creation and bringing authentic life, are called to become communities of compassion and healing. . . ."[2] It is in this light that the vision of Empowered21 finds its deepest meaning and expression, thereby inspiring hope and zeal for Christian mission in our contemporary world in the power of the Holy Spirit.

2018 Johannesburg Consultation

From May 14–15, 2018, the Scholars Consultation was held in the heart of Johannesburg with a group of scholars and mission practitioners. Although the Consultation is a global program, the Global Counsel decided to host its global meetings in this city where the African regional congress was meeting. With a robust theological program in the African Congress, the regional council nominated its fine scholar to join the organizing team of the Consultation, and subsequently serve as the co-editor of the book. The theme was close to the heart of the African Spirit-empowered churches: "Proclaiming Jesus Christ as the Only Savior in the Power of the Holy Spirit to the Challenges of Today's World." The theme was set in the context of secular humanism, universalism among fellow Christians, religious pluralism, and issues of gospel and culture, and the challenges of syncretism and human flourishing. These, among others, present the socio-religious context in which Christ is preached as the only authentic and God's accredited Savior of the world.

The metropolis of Johannesburg was vibrant in cultural diversity, historical experiences, and its engagement with contemporary issues. The painful memory of the apartheid era and the ensuring struggle to bring equity, peace, and reconciliation are either still fresh or currently progressing. Although the nation claims to have the Christian majority, its diverse cultural landscape and rapid social change challenge the church to reinvent itself. Acting as the most prominent convening power in the continent, South Africa hosts a large number of refugees and immigrants, especially from the trouble-ridden neighboring states. Religiously rich in belief and practice, South African Christianity serves as a creative religious laboratory. There are several well-organized churches, including the Reformed Church and the Apostolic Faith Mission. Then, there are a plethora of African Initiated churches, most of which exhibit Pentecostal/Charismatic belief and worship, but with a varying degree of contributions from their indigenous religiosity. Even within the historic churches, for example, the Apostolic Faith Mission, there is a rich diversity depending on the location, demography, and social context. On top of these challenging diversities, the whole society grapples with the haunting memories and implications of the pain of apartheid experiences, the widening gap between the have's and have-not's, corruption charges in the government system, deepening poverty, the fast secularizing trend, and many more issues. The church finds itself as a shining beacon to these bewildering circumstances. It takes the church to embrace the Holy Spirit's creativity in its theology, life, and mission, to rise above the challenge as a prophetic voice and hope. God's people are called to witness in life, word, and deed to proclaim Christ as the only Savior in the face of global and local challenges. More than anything, the church needs to receive the empowerment of the Holy Spirit.

The African regional council had already been working with local hosts to plan its own theological program. Some speakers, thus, served both the African and global gatherings. The Consultation, therefore, took full advantage of the African contributions. There were six (of the eleven) presentations from the African continent. They were augmented by other regional studies (an Asian and a European), various foundational studies (such as two biblical, a historical, and a theological). The group also spent the time to visit a local theological institution to learn about their work. Rev. Frank Chikane, the leader of the local host committee, enriched the Consultation group with the story of his life-threatening experience under the apartheid government, and his involvement in the subsequent government's program through the Truth and Reconciliation process.

With the full support of the Global Council of the Empowered21, Dr.

Michael Rakes ably served the Consultation as the Council's liaison. The Consultation team consisted of the two organizers (now serving as the editors), Dr. Mark Roberts of Oral Roberts University, who managed the Digital Showcase site for the Consultation's digital space and online presentations, and Ms. Kristin Towles of the Empowered21 Office to handle logistics.

During the short two-day Consultation, the participants expressed the value of rewarding fellowship with fellow Spirit-filled and empowered scholars from various parts of the world. At the same time, they voiced concerns that more women scholars should join the program, and the desire to see an ongoing collaboration between the Consultations. With the first successful utilization of an online presentation, the Consultation saw a high possibility to bring in more voices to the forum who may not be able to travel to be physically present in a Consultation. The participants unanimously agreed to convey their warm appreciation to the Global Council for "valuing the service of Spirit-empowered scholarship" and for "expressing their value by scheduling and funding the annual Consultations."[3]

Theme Description

To aid the presenters, the organizing team developed an elaboration of the Consultation theme as follows:

> Chosen through carefully surveying world leaders of the Spirit-Empowered Movement (hereafter "SEM"), this theme invites scholars in this movement (and others wishing to help) to help SEM members proclaim the distinctiveness of Jesus Christ as the only Way, Truth, and Life. As this consultation takes place in Africa and is jointly organized by the Empowered21 Global Office and the African host, the Consultation can offer to the world the gift of experiences, reflections, and lessons gained by African SEM. They will be joined by outsiders who can bring similar reflections but from different contexts.

The following description of the theme aims to inform E21 leaders of how the Consultation intends to approach the topic and to suggest to scholars how broadly the Consultation views the theme, so they may offer scholarship that aligns with it. Through this Consultation, E21, as a movement, wishes to affirm Jesus Christ as the only Way, Truth, and Life. The Consultation also intends to be a space for mutual learning. Case studies are actively encouraged to bring lived-out experiences in specific socio-cultural contexts for deeper reflection. The studies would also identify challenges that are at work in each context. The result of the Consultation all participants seek is a deeper understanding of such issues to promote effective Spirit-empowered ministry.

Each study may include part or all of the following elements:

Affirmation of the Uniqueness of Christ as the Savior

The biblical affirmation of Christ as the only Savior is the foundation for Christian life, discipleship, and witness, and this conviction is shared broadly throughout Christian confessional families. This shared foundation, however, is experienced by Spirit-empowered believers or churches in distinct ways. Two elements may be worthy of investigation. One is the role of religious expectations in the shaping and strengthening of one's belief. For example, in some parts of the world, healings, dreams, visions, and casting out demons are expected regularly, regardless of one's religion. In this context, a Christian believer would be more open to the work of the Holy Spirit than in a sociocultural context where religions, including Christianity, do not carry such expectations. The second is one's religious experience. Healing often comes as the most common and life-changing experience. The question is how these and other unique features of Spirit-empowered life have contributed to the theological shaping of the uniqueness of Christ as the only Savior.

Challenges Arising from Social Contexts, both Global and Local

The second part identifies, from the contemporary context, challenges to the proclamation of the uniqueness of Christ as the only Savior. Some challenges are universal, while others are only local. The former would include the threats of religious pluralism, increasing secularism, universalism, liberal theology, and postmodernity. The latter would include specific political, sociocultural, economic, and religious elements. This part emphasizes identifying and elaborating key challenges and their effect on society and the church, particularly on its proclamation of Christ as the only Savior.

Work of the Holy Spirit Manifested in the Ministries of SEM

This third part brings the first two discussions together and explores how

Spirit-empowered communities communicate, demonstrate, and live out Spirit-empowered faith in real-life situations. The role of the Holy Spirit will be important in his empowerment through the exercise of gifts (both "natural" and "supernatural"). Whether the study is theoretical or empirical (such as a case study), the question to be asked is: "How are the Spirit-empowered communities responding to the challenges identified in the second section, both global (e.g., pluralistic tendencies) and local (e.g., traditional religions)?" For the latter, the issue of syncretism may merit attention when the community engages with traditional religions. Another question may follow: "What difference does this Spirit-empowered approach make, both to the authentic witness to Christ as the only Savior and also to other churches in the area?"

Growing into a Book

The transition to the book process has brought ten additional studies. Assessing the missing topics and regions, the editors are grateful to the contributors. Some of them represent exciting areas of research. For instance, the Castellanos-Harding couple from Colombia contributes a chapter on reaching the youths in Latin American. Equally important is the study, prepared by the Paul and Paul father-daughter team from Pakistan. Given the challenging socio-religious circumstance, it took their courage to raise the Christian voice and share with the world. In addition to the two more Asian contributions, the editors are also pleased to strengthen the European perspectives (now three), North American experiences (now two), and the biblical studies (now two). The editors are equally pleased to have a good number of female contributions (now five) and the strength of African scholarship. On the other hand, we regret the weak presence of Latin America and no voice from the Oceania-Pacifics.

The book contains twenty-two main chapters, arranged in two parts. The first part establishes the foundation and context for our reflections. It brings together two biblical, two theological, one historical, and one philosophical chapters. The second part, "Proclaiming the Uniqueness of Christ in the World," brings together various reflections and practical engagements in the process of proclaiming Christ in the postmodern world. The chapters, by both practitioners and academics, are arranged by continents: Africa, Asia, Europe, Latin America, and North America. The authors carefully identify salient issues and challenges in Christian mission from different parts of the globe. While certain events and developments depict a gloomy picture, there emerge examples of vitality and hope in people's response to the demands of the gospel of Christ as people all over the world begin to experience a fresh wind and fire of the Holy Spirit which offers hope in the face of the crisis in human experience.

The editorial team offers a prayer of commitment to make the vision of Acts 1:8 come alive: "But you will receive power when the Holy Spirit comes on you; and you will be my witnesses in Jerusalem, and in all Judea and Samaria, and to the ends of the earth" (NIV).

Notes

1. "The Edinburgh 2010 Common Call," http://www.edinburgh2010.org/fileadmin/Edinburgh_2010_Common_Call_with_explanation.pdf, accessed March 15, 2020.
2. "The Edinburgh 2010 Common Call."
3. Scholars Consultation, "Report of Scholars Consultation, May 14–15, 2018, Johannesburg" (2018).

1.

The Name of Jesus in Luke-Acts with Special Reference to the Gentile Mission

James B. Shelton

Abstract

Peter declares, "There is no other name . . . by which we must be saved" (Acts 4:12); yet later he says, "Truly I understand that God shows no partiality, but in every nation, anyone who fears him and does what is right is acceptable to him" (Acts 10:34–35a). Are there then those among the Gentiles who follow God without hearing the name of Jesus, or are all who have not heard the name are lost? The question, often posed in "either/or" discourse terms, fails to understand the meaning and scope of the name of Jesus and the urgency of the mandate to proclaim the gospel to every person. God is able to reveal himself to whomever he wills; yet every culture and creature therein need Jesus in his fullness. This divine-human synergy can only be approached as a mystery, a paradox juxtaposing sovereignty and the missional mandate given to the church.

Key words: "holy name of God," "name of Jesus," Gentiles, salvation, *Nomina Sacra*

How Luke presents the name of Jesus throughout Luke-Acts — one-quarter of the New Testament — sheds light on the question of the state of the Gentiles who have not heard the name. The name of Jesus is more than a moniker for the gospel message proclaimed and involves divine workings that are not solely dependent upon the witness of the church. Nevertheless, the urgent state of the masses of humanity compels the Church to proclaim the name and message of Jesus all the more. How Luke understands "the name" provides a solution to either/or impasse.

The name of Jesus figures prominently in the Acts of the Apostles, and its function has varied applications. Its meaning, however, is seated in the authority, power, and person of Jesus, the Christ, in both his humanity and his divinity. Like other humans, Jesus relies on the power and direction of the Holy Spirit, but he is more than a Spirit-empowered human being. His presence, emblematic in his name, is also a divine enabling. This name, will, and authority play an essential role in the gospel, which is for all people. The name transcends the divide between those who have heard the name and accepted salvation through it and those who have never heard the name. The way the question has been posed suffers from a too-narrow understanding of the power of the name of Jesus and the person behind it and a too broad and vague assessment of those who know nothing of him.

A second question arises: What is the significance of the name of Jesus in the mission of carrying the gospel to the nations? What does the authority of the name demand from them and their cultures? To use Niebuhr's terms, what does the name of Jesus say of Christ "in culture," and what does it say of Christ "against culture"?[1]

To understand what Luke means when he uses the name of Jesus, one must look at uses of the concept of a name in contemporary Hellenistic, in the Old Testament, and in the rest of the New Testament, especially in Luke's Gospel, which is the prequel to Acts. Most significant is the concept of the name of God.

Greek Use of the Concept of Name

An exhaustive analysis of "name" in the Greek literature will not be offered here, but concepts and uses that shed light on Luke's understanding of "the name of Jesus" will be considered. The name was a constituent part of a person. The Greek word for "name" (*onoma*) could mean "to have a reputation," because to know a name was to know the person.[2] It could also refer to the rights and obligations of an individual in a contract.[3] The practice of using the name of a god, spirit, or demon in magic stretched far back in antiquity and persisted in the era contemporary with the early church.[4] Names had a binding or controlling quality on a spirit or god obligating or forcing it to do what the petitioner wanted. The name made the signified spirit/divinity and its power accessible to humans. Magic, though prohibited by Roman law,[5] was pervasive in the Empire.[6] As Luke describes in Acts 19:13–20, practitioners readily used names from various cults and religions. Magicians often relied on foreign names (*onomata babarika*) and readily used the Jewish and Christian *nomina sacra*.[7] Luke makes a clear distinction between Hellenistic magic and supernatural activity in Christianity.

The Concept of Name in the Old Testament

The primary Hebrew word for name is *šēm*, usually translated as *onoma* in the Septuagintal Greek. It implies ownership; the giving of a name "establishes a relation of dominion and possession" towards the one receiving the name. For example, God the Creator "determines the number of the stars; he gives to all of them their names" (Ps 147:4).[8] Similarly, God says to his people, "He who created you, O Jacob, he who formed you, O Israel: do not fear, for I have redeemed you. I have called you by name, you are mine" (Isa 43:1). Adam in his exercise of delegated dominion gives names to the animals (Gen 2:19).

In the Ancient Near East, the names of gods were used to leverage favor or control of the deity; however, the God of the Hebrews does not give his name to be manipulated and answers such demands with "Why is it that you ask my name?" (Gen 32:30; Judg 13:17–18). Manoah's request of the name receives the added answer, "It is too wonderful (*pl'y*)." Even when Moses asks for God's name, the response is elusive, *yhwh* referring to God's undeniable existence in the wake of astounding, fearful miracles. Clearly, God is in charge. Though God does give a name for himself, the power resides with him. He reveals himself in his miraculous intervention (Gen 17:1; Ex 3:14; 6.2). Clearly, the initiative and prerogative lie with God; it is he who gives his name in revelation (Ex 6:1–2). "Thus the name of Yahweh is not an instrument of magic; it is a gift of revelation."[9] In revealing his name, he reveals himself, his will, and his power; he does not self-identify to allow humans to control him.

"The name" is often qualified by "holy" (*qdš*). By inference, the holiness refers to separateness, which means not being profane.[10] "His holy name" is used in the context of worship, in parallel with the *yhwh*, the Tetragrammaton, the four-letter name of God, the name that was not to be uttered. Thus "his holy name" is a reverential reference to the Tetragrammaton (e.g., 1 Chron 16:35; Ps 145:21). Profaning the name also involves improper behavior and disobedience; the goal of this sacralizing is reciprocal: "You shall keep my commandments and observe them: I am the LORD. You shall not profane my holy name, that I may be sanctified among the people of Israel: I am the LORD; I sanctify you" (Lev 22:31). The holiness does not lie in utter separation between God and his people but in their covenant relationship.[11] To use God's name implies a covenant relationship by which the user honors

God's sovereignty and will. It follows that false prophets and diviners who used God's name in magical ways or swore falsely by the name of the Lord for gain would be condemned (Ezek 13:1–16, esp. vs. 6, 9). One dare not speak in the name of the Lord something contrary to God's will.[12] God gives his name to the Hebrews, a name that simultaneously gives access to his aid and requires accountability to his will. This name is based on his ultimate beingness, which cannot be vitiated by human will.

God's name signifies God's presence and is similar to the concept of his "face" (*pānîm*), the presence of God (*penê yhwh*), God present in person (e.g., Jer 10:6; Mal 1:11; Ps 54:8; Prov 18:10). The name and the face of the Lord appear together; to profane the name of God in ritual is to risk being cut off from the Lord's presence (*pāni*, Lev 22:2–3). In even stronger language the name and face appear in a prohibition of infant sacrifice: "I myself will set my face (*pāni*) against them, and will cut them off from the people because they have given of their offspring to Molech, defiling my sanctuary and profaning my holy name (*šēm qādĕši*)" (Lev 20:1–3).

The holy name is often paired with the glory and might of God (e.g., Isa 12:4; Zech 14:9; Ps 8:2, 10; 20:2). God's manifold power is evident in his name: "Our Redeemer — the LORD of hosts is his name — is the Holy One of Israel" (Isa 47:4). He is the Lord of armies (*ṣĕbā'ôt*, see also Isa 48:2; 54:5). The name of God then, should be understood as God manifesting himself in history and creation in glory and power.[13]

The name sometimes appears somewhat distinct from God, approaching something akin to a distinct presence since God builds a temple to house his *šēm* (2 Sam 7:13; 1 Kings 3:2; 8:17). According to Schmidt, "The presence of the *šēm* in the temple denotes terminologically distinctive from the proximity of God from the standpoint of salvation history. The *šēm* guarantees God's presence in the temple in clear distinction from Yahweh's throne in heaven."[14] The name speaks of God's immanent presence.

The name of God is so close to "the hypostatization of the *šēm* standing over against Yahweh in greater independence," it is as though God and his name have become two distinct things.[15] This distinctness of the name connotes the immanence of God. Yet Besnard cautions, "It is vain for us to ask if we are in the presence of *Deus revelatus* or *Deus absconditus*. We are before a divine dialectic more profound than this alternative." When God reveals his name in theophany one must acknowledge the noetic nature of the intervention. "[O]ne must do justice to the *mystery* which God always surrounds his theophanies."[16] The name and the revelation of the same are mysteries revealed but not mysteries completely comprehended; his sovereignty is always intact.

The name is God present replete with his power. For example, the revelation of the name to Moses at Horeb not only presents the inscrutable mystery of the name, but also the presence of God's power in the miracles of the burning bush, the rod turned into a snake, and the leprous hand healed (Ex 3:1–4:7). In this theophany, the angel of God (*mal'āk yhwh*), God, and the name of God are all present (3:2, 4, 13–14). The name works like the "hand of God," in that it creates, works miracles, defends, and destroys (e.g., Ex 6:1; 9:15; 15:3; 1 Sam 5:6, 7, 9, 11; Ps 78:42; Isa 41:20). Often the hand of the Lord and his name appear together: "The Lord is a warrior; The Lord is his name. . . . Your right hand, O Lord, glorious in power — your right hand, O Lord, shattered the enemy" (Ex 15:3,6). In Exodus 9:15–16, hand, name, and power are linked together as the means of the Hebrews' deliverance and the destruction of Pharaoh's lands and people. His name, *yhwh*, not only refers to his existence but also his actions.[17] Often the arm of God and his hand are mentioned together as the powerful agent of both creation and destruction, with the latter bringing simultaneously judgment and salvation.[18]

The Name of God/the Lord in Luke-Acts

The title Lord (*kyrios*), which occurs 205 times in Luke-Acts, almost always refers to God or Jesus.[19] Luke follows in the OT understanding of the name of God. In the *Magnificat*, Mary's hymn in response to the Annunciation, she repeats the worshipful phrase, "holy is his name," which is frequently found in praise to God in the OT (Luke 1:49). Mary is praising the God of Israel. The context provided in Mary's hymn (Luke 1:46–53) reflects the aspects associated with the "name of the Lord" in the OT. She calls God "Lord" (*kyrion*) in verse 46, "God, the Savior" (verse 47), and "the mighty One" (*ho dynatos*, v. 49). In verse 50, Mary proclaims that the Holy One is merciful yet to be approached with reverential fear, leaving no room for presumption. God reveals his strength in his arm (*kratos en brachioni autou*, v. 51) to judge the haughty and powerful, raise the humble, and mercifully provide help for the needy (vs. 52–53). In the *Magnificat*, "the Powerful One" (*ho dynatos*) does great things for Mary. "Holy is his name" (*kai hagion to onoma autou*) means that God's name is unique, powerful, and accomplishes his will. Mary describes God's program of salvation, which is the will of God inherent in the name of the Lord, as resulting in a miraculous deliverance and great reversal, shaking the foundations of the world order.

Luke uses similar language in his version of the Lord's Prayer (Luke 11:2–4). The name of the Father is hallowed (*hagiasthētō to onoma sou*). Here the parallelism shows how to hallow the name of God: to call for and work for the coming of God's kingdom. His sovereignty must be acknowledged. Matthew's version equates "hallowed be thy name" with "thy will be done" (Matt 10:6b). One cannot presume to invoke the name of the Lord apart from carrying out his program and agenda (similarly with God's will, *thelēma*, Luke 22:14).

The next use of the name of God occurs in Luke 13:31–35 in the context of Jesus' prophecy that Jerusalem would reject him and that he would die there: "I tell you, you will not see me until the time comes when you say, 'Blessed is the one who comes in the name of the Lord'" (Luke 13:35). Jesus says it to the Pharisees. His words have an eschatological ring of judgment.

In the previous context, Jesus answers the question as to whether many or few will be saved by indicating the latter (Luke 13:23–24). We hear again the refrain, "Blessed is the king who comes in the name of the Lord," at his Triumphal Entry (Luke 19:38). But the adulation is short-lived, for after being rejected by many, Jesus will die, and the destruction of the city will follow in a few decades. For Luke, for Jesus to "come in the name of the Lord" means that he is the acknowledged agent of God, particularly at the Triumphal Entry as the messianic king as per Matthew, Mark, and John (Matt 21:9; Mark 11:9–10; John 12:13). Luke notes that the people acclaim, "Peace (*eirēnē*) in heaven and glory in the highest," the latter, a *passivum divinum*, the former reflecting the meaning inherent in the Hebrew, *šālôm* of "completeness." The divine will and plan begin their completion with the arrival of King Jesus in Jerusalem: "As Jesus enters the city he presents himself as the king who brings the nation's eschatological hope."[20] In Luke, his message and miracles are also affirmed: "in the name of the Lord," for of the Gospel writers only Luke says that "the whole multitude of the disciples began to praise God joyfully with a loud voice for all the deeds of power that they had seen" (Luke 19:37b). His works confirm his words (Luke 5:24).

A Calculated Ambiguity

"And it shall be that all who should call on the name of the Lord shall be saved" (Acts 2:21).[21] Here, in Luke's account of Pentecost, Peter is quoting from Joel 2:28–32 who relates that God will pour out his Spirit on "all flesh" in the midst of an eschatological apocalypse, culminating in salvation (Acts 2:17–21). On the face of it, Peter's audience would understand "the name of the Lord" (*onoma kyriou*) as referring to God. Here God promises to pour out his Spirit, even as he did upon Jesus (Luke 3:21–22; 4:1, 14, 18; Acts 10:38). Here God empowers, enlightens, and saves.[22] By the time Peter concludes his Pentecost Sermon, he is obviously referring to the name of Jesus: "Peter said to them, 'Repent, and be baptized every one of you in the name of Jesus Christ so that your sins may be forgiven; and you will receive the gift of the Holy Spirit'" (Acts 2:38). Between verses 21 and 38 Luke place a quotation from Psalm 110:1, "The Lord said to my Lord, 'Sit at my right hand, until I make your enemies your footstool.'" So, in effect, there are two "Lords." Next, Peter identifies Jesus as the one whom God has made "both Lord and Messiah" (Acts 2:35), who is also the dispenser of the Holy Spirit (Acts 2:34). Between verses 21 and 38, Luke creates a calculated ambiguity between the name of God and the name of Jesus. This subtle shift makes a crucial point: the prerogatives of God the Lord are the prerogatives of Jesus the Lord; they are the same.

Larry Hurtado does think the "Lord'" refers to Jesus: "[T]he exalted Jesus is identified as (or associated with) the "Lord" in places in the biblical texts where God (Heb. *Yahweh*) was the original referent (Acts 2:20–21, 25)."[23] But he does so cautiously:

> I express some uncertainty here because the texts exhibit some ambiguity in this matter. On the one hand, Jesus is linked with, and identified as, the *Kyrios*, but on the other hand God can be referred to as the *Kyrios* by the same authors (e.g., 2:39; 3:22, the Lord our God;" 4:26, "the Lord . . . and his Christ;" 4:29, "Lord [*Kyrie*], look at their threats;" cf. 4:24, "Sovereign Lord [*Despota*]"). It is also clear that the author of Acts, along with all other Christians whose faith is reflected in the New Testament writings, thought of God and Jesus as distinguishable and yet also as linked/associated in astonishingly direct and close ways. This is, of course, especially apparent in the functions of God that are shared by Jesus. In the discussion of Pauline Christianity, I noted that already in Paul's letters there is this association of Jesus with biblical texts that refer to *Yahweh*.[24]

In the first account of Paul's conversion in Acts Luke emphasizes Jesus and his name and his title as Lord (Acts 9:5, 13–17, 27). Paul says when overcome by the intense light, "Who are you Lord?" and receives the response, "I am Jesus, whom you are persecuting" (Acts 9:5). Ananias relates to Paul that *Jesus* sent him to pray for his healing and Paul's infilling with the Holy Spirit (Acts 9:17). But the interaction between Ananias and the Lord after Paul's encounter and before he visits the afflicted Paul resemble the structure of an Old Testament theophany. The "Lord" approaches Ananias in a vision calling his name and he answers, "Here I am Lord" (Acts 9:10). This vision and the disciple's response are quite reminiscent of Samuel's encounter with God as well as that of Abraham, Moses, and Isaiah (2 Sam 3:4–8; Gen 22:11; Ex 3:4; Isa. 6:8). "Here I am" is the appropriate response to a divine visitation. The "crime" Paul wants to eliminate is the Christian calling upon the name of Jesus (Acts 9:14). But the language of the next verse that Ananias hears sounds like divine language: "Go, for he is an instrument whom I have chosen to bring my name before the Gentiles, and kings and before the people of Israel." This calling sounds like that of the prophet Jeremiah: "I appointed you a prophet to the nations" (Jer 1:5). Eventually Luke lets his readers know that it was Jesus who appeared to Ananias as "Lord" later when he later visits Paul (Acts 9:17). Again, the line between God and Jesus is not so clear.

The pattern of ambiguity continues in the descriptions of the precedential visit of Peter to the Gentile Cornelius. Cornelius is a devout Gentile who feared God and "prayed constantly to God" (Acts 10:1–2). In a vision "[an] angel of the Lord" (*angleon tou theou*) appeared to Cornelius. This is theophanic language and he addresses the celestial visitor as "Lord." The visitor does talk of God as third person in that Cornelius' prayers and alms are a "memorial before God;" but it still has the markings of theophany. The visitor is called [a] holy angel (*angelou hagiou*) in v. 22 which may weaken the theophanic sense.

The next day, Peter has his vision in which he addresses the voice as "Lord" (Acts 9:14). The voice says, "What God has made clean, you must not call profane" (see also Acts 11:7–9). This does sound like a personage separate from God, but when Peter relates the event to Cornelius he says, "God has shown me that I should not call anyone profane or unclean" (Acts 10:28b; see also 10:34). With the Spirit directing Peter to go with Cornelius' messengers (Acts 10:19) and Peter calling Jesus Christ "Lord of all" (Acts 10:36), the delineation between Jesus and God is not so clear-cut. Later, at the Jerusalem Council, James says "Simeon has related how God first looked favorably on the Gentiles, to take from among them a people for his name" (Acts 15:4). Here, the message to Peter is being described as coming from God and for the sake of his name and next he cites Amos 9:11–12 and Jeremiah 12:15 as evidence for the inclusion of non-Jews: "so that all other peoples may seek the Lord — even all the Gentiles over whom my name has been called" (Acts 15:17). Yet these Gentiles were "baptized in the name of Jesus Christ" (Acts 10:48). Luke does not always clearly delineate the roles and identities of Jesus and *Yahweh*, but this is not by error but by design. Jason Staples has identified the double use of "Lord, Lord" (*Kyrie, Kyrie*) as specifically addressing *Yahweh*. For Luke, the identity of Jesus is inextricably bound up in God. This will be significant when we answer the questions that we initially raised.

Nomina Sacra

The name of Jesus was treated as divine even in the earliest parts of the New Testament, notably the early letters of Paul, which, by most accounts, predate the finished works of Luke and Acts.[25] The divinity of Jesus, even his heavenly pre-existence, appears to be accepted among Christians thirty years after his Ascension, well within living memory of Jesus. Luke presents a similar Christology, which speaks well of his work being produced close to the time of Paul or later, yet faithfully representing the primitive expressions of the church.

In the earliest extant manuscripts of the New Testament (second to fourth century), the scribes appear to honor this early high-Christology in the use of *nomina sacra* or "sacred names." They abbreviated such words as God (*Theos*) becoming *ths*, Lord (*Kyrios*) becoming *ks*, Christ (*Christos*) *cs*, and Jesus (*Iēsous*) *ic* frequently. They were the earliest attested *nomina sacra* among the texts, some of whom can be dated to AD 200 or earlier.[26] These abbreviated forms consist usually of the first and last letter with a line over the top. These texts are some of the earliest artifacts of Christianity and show what appears to be a deferential reverence for these words. Eleven other abbreviated words began to appear in the texts, but the above four appear early and with greater frequency.[27] Most of these eleven relate in some way to Jesus.

Schuyler Brown identifies these four not only as *nomina sacra* but, more specifically, as *nomina divina*, names for divinity.[28] This Christian deference for sacred names is similar to the avoidance of the Tetragrammaton in Jewish scribal practice and ritual reading and may be the inspiration for the Christian reverence of the name. The *nomina sacra* appear to have come from an earlier practice of revering the name of Jesus because of its close association with the name of God.

Jason Staples notes that the doubled vocative "Lord, Lord" (*Kyrie, Kyrie*) corresponds to *Yahweh, Yahweh* in the Old Testament (e.g., Ps 109:21 [In the Septuagint, the Greek version of the Old Testament, abbreviated LXX) 108:21]; Ezek 37:21; Deut 3:24 of 84 times in LXX). The expression appears as *Kyrie, Kyrie* in the Septuagint and is addressed to God. "*Kyrie, Kyrie*" appears three times in the Gospels at Matt 7:21–22; 25:11 and Luke 6:46 addressing *Jesus*.[29] The Matthean texts present Jesus as the eschatological Lord dispensing final judgment.[30] This doubling of the vocative is not merely emotive or a respectful address.

> It is . . . surely no accident that Matt 7:21–22 involves the first uses of κύριος referring to Jesus in the Gospel after using that term eleven times to refer to God before this passage. The use of the double form for the first application of κύριος to Jesus thus ensures that the reader does not miss the theological implications of that term, signaling that this κύριε is not a rudimentary "sir."[31]

In Luke 6:47 Jesus asks, "Why do you call me 'Lord, Lord,' and do not do what I tell you?" Here the stress is on obedience and judgment is more remotely placed in the following parable of the houses built on rock or sand where safety or ruin is a result of obedience (Luke 6:47–49).

> The Lukan construction of the saying also makes it even clearer than the Matthean examples that the doubling of κύριε does not signal pathos. Indeed, the saying does not occur in the context of emotive dialogue. Instead, Luke 6:46 uses καλέω with direct object and complement (the vocative taking the place of the usual accusative complement), which is a construction for addressing or designating a person by a title or name. That is, the Lukan saying treats κύριε κύριε as a specific metonym or title by which Jesus is invoked: 'Why do you address me as κύριε κύριε and not do what I say?' Coupled with the fact that in the Lukan version Jesus demands the obedience one would expect to be directed towards God (contrast Matt 7:21–22), Luke's treatment of κύριε κύριε as a specific form of address – one that echoes a way to unambiguously represent the divine name in the Greek Bible — is best understood as an application of the divine name to Jesus.[32]

According to Staples, Matthew and Luke use the double *Kyrie* "to represent the Name of YHWH in the Greek texts" and readers of the Septuagint would recognize the expression as such. "Such applications of the name to the exalted Jesus amount to calling him God, a figure to be obeyed and worshipped alongside God the father."[33] Matthew and Luke understand that Jesus himself used the emphatic "Lord, Lord" to refer to himself.

The Name of Jesus in Luke-Acts

We have looked at the blending of the name of God and the name of Jesus; now the name of Jesus on its own will shed much light on our original questions of who is saved and the demands on the Gentile convert. In the Gospel, the angel announces the heaven-given name of Mary's child,[34] he is to be called great, Son of the Highest and the Lord will give him an eternal throne of David (Luke 1:31–33; see also Luke 2:21). Later Elizabeth addresses Mary as "the mother of my Lord" (Luke 1:43); again, we see Lord used for God and Jesus in proximity.

In Luke 9:48, Jesus teaches that if his followers receive a child in his name, they receive him and God. Here power and authority are cloaked in merciful humility. Again, to act in Jesus' name is to act in God's name and will.

When the seventy (two) disciples return they address Jesus as "Lord" (*Kyrie*) rejoicing that the demons are subject to them through Jesus' name (Luke 10:17, see also Luke 9:49–50). His authority and power are extended to others, but he warns against being enamored by power at the expense of one's soul. The name of Jesus reflects the will of Jesus. His power cannot be co-opted. This anticipates Jesus' later warning that there will be imposters who will mislead by presuming upon his name (Luke 21:18).

In Luke's Gospel, the name of Jesus calls for repentance and effects forgiveness of sins (Luke 24:47). John's baptism also accomplished this (Luke 3:3 with Mark 1:4); but the baptism of Jesus also cleanses and empowers through the Holy Spirit (Luke 3:16–18; Acts 1:5, 8).[35] In Acts, baptism in the name of Jesus stands out in contrast to John's and other washings in Judaism. At the beginning of Acts, Jesus himself links baptism with the action of the Holy Spirit and inspired witness (Acts 1:5–8). This baptism, initially in Acts, is not on an occasion of washing in water. Presumably, the disciples had already experienced water baptism at the hands of Jesus and/or the early disciples (John 3:22, 26). This baptism or infilling of the Holy Spirit resulted in the xenoglossic witness on the day of Pentecost (Acts 2:4–11); however, in his following sermon Peter juxtaposes the water baptism in the name of Jesus with the reception of the Holy Spirit: "Repent and be baptized, every one of you in (*epi*) the name of Jesus Christ for the forgiveness of your sins. And you shall receive the gift of the Holy Spirit" (Acts 2:38). Since Jesus is the baptizer in the Holy Spirit (Acts 2:33), it was necessary to baptize the disciples of John in Ephesus in (*eis*) the name of the Lord Jesus to receive the Holy Spirit as did those at Pentecost (Acts 19:5–6). There is a longer time between the baptism of the Samaritans and Spirit reception (Acts 19:14–17).

The prepositions Luke uses in the baptismal formulae, "because of" (*epi*), "into" (*eis*), "in" (*en*) and "upon" or do seem interchangeable;[36] yet the different expressions shed light on the significance of baptism. Ziesler suggests that the use of *epi* could refer to the authority of Jesus in the formula in 2:38.[37] Heitmüller noted that "*eis* (into) the name of" was used in the papyri as a banking term for crediting funds to the account of someone.[38] Thus, the baptizand becomes the property of Jesus.

Others suggest that the origin of the expression is from the Hebrew *lešēm* meaning "into the name of someone" or "in behalf of someone," or as an offering to the "name" as suggested in the Mishnah (m. Zeb 4:6) thus giving it a cultic nuance.[39] In Acts, the baptism is expressed as in the name of Jesus, Jesus Christ, or Lord Jesus Christ (Acts 2:38; 8:16; 10:48; 19:5, see also Pauline practice, Rom 6:3; 1 Cor 1:13; Gal 3:27). For Jews the confession of Jesus as the Christ, the Messiah would be significant; for when Peter calls for his *Jewish* audience to repent and be baptized, he uses the formula "in the name of Jesus Christ" (Acts 2:38).[40] But ultimately, "'Lord Jesus' is the fundamental referent,"[41] for the Jews, it acknowledges the authority of *Yahweh* invested in the risen, ascended Jesus. The overlap between the name of the Lord and that of "Lord Jesus" made this confession crucial. For the Gentiles confessing Jesus as "Lord" would require a major paradigm shift, as we shall see (Acts 9:15).

While there is some reason to consider baptism "in the name of Jesus," or similar variations, as the most ancient, the tripartite baptismal formula, "in in the name of the Father and of the Son and of the Holy Spirit" appears to have an early pedigree as well (Matt 28:19). The Didache or *The Teaching of the Lord to the Nations by the Twelve Apostles* calls for baptism "into the name of Father and Son and Holy Spirit" (7:1, 3).[42] The traditions behind the Didache date back to as far as AD 50–70. Early canonical benediction and other formulations have references to "Father, Son, and Holy Spirit" together (2 Cor 13:13; 1 Cor 12:4–7; 2 Thess 2:13–14). Thus, such triadic groupings had widespread use in the early church. Furthermore, the Didache equates the preferred triune formula to baptism "in the name of the Lord" (comp. 7:1–3 with Acts 9:5). Opinion is divided as to whether "in the name of the Lord" refers to God or to Jesus in Acts 9:5. The Didache does not address Jesus as "Lord" but rather, as *Pais* (Child/Servant 9:2–3 and 10:2–3), so Lord may refer to God, the Father.[43] Given the relative brevity of the document, *Pais* will not bear too much weight as the preferred title for Jesus in the community that penned it. If "in the name of the Lord" refers to Jesus, it demonstrates that the early Christian community, reflected in the Didache, considered both types of baptismal formulae referring to the same God.[44]

Those baptized renounced much of the world order in their repentance, for the convert embraced a new lifestyle in the rejection of the old. Forgiveness now comes through *this* name (Acts 10:43), the name they called upon at their baptism (Acts 22:16). They went into the water as individuals; but came up into a community, to a new allegiance, a new family in submission to the teaching of the apostles (Acts 2:42–47). Invoking the name brings one into a covenant with the Lord in his kingdom and this confession sets one apart from old allegiances (Acts 15:14).

The Name of Jesus and Miracles

The name of Jesus is the primary agent for miracles in Acts (3:6, 16: 4:7, 10, 30; 16:8; 19:11–20; also, Luke 10:17–18). The Holy Spirit also effects miracles; but in Acts, Luke focuses on the role of the Spirit in inspired witness.[45] Jesus delegates the authority, but he is the causative agent in all healings and miracles.[46] Luke stresses the lordship of Jesus, for Jesus even bestows the Holy Spirit. The name cannot be used apart from submission to his lordship, for the name is not a mere lever of magic to be manipulated by anyone. The sons of Sceva attempt to use the sacred name as a mere lever of magic with disastrous results. The demons acknowledge the Person of the name. As a result, many came to believe in Jesus publicly confessing and disclosing their magic practices rendering them ineffective. Magic books were burned and the name of the Lord Jesus was praised (Acts 19:11–20). The reign of Jesus can have no rivals. Further, to accept the name of Jesus is to accept his teachings (Acts 4:12, 18; 5:28, 40–41).[47]

The Name of Jesus and the Gentile Mission: Salvation apart from the Name?

Having examined Luke's understanding of the name of Jesus we can now address our initial questions, the first being, "Must all hear the name of Jesus and his message to be saved or are there godly folk in systems devoid of Christian evangelization?" Frequently, one hears the argument that all religions and worldviews are equally valid and good, and salvation is available in them. Do Peter's words to Cornelius support this: "In every nation anyone who fears him and does what is right is acceptable to him" (Acts 10:34–35a)? Cannot God speak to non-Christians in their own systems? Is not the good in other religions from God (James 1:17)? Does the Christian missionary risk introduce bad Western principles and practices in another society?

Bruce Olson, apostle to the Motilone Indians of Venezuela, came to a culture that internally did not have many of the problems inherent in Western culture. He wondered what the gospel had to offer them and if his presence was corrupting them. On the day a tribe member said he heard the "voice of the tiger" saying that evil spirits would come and take some of their lives. It was then that he knew that the message of Jesus would protect them and that they needed to be delivered from fear.[48] God used Motilone structures and beliefs to communicate his good news. It would appear that every person and people group need something Jesus has to offer. The Jerusalem Council too came to realize that the gospel was transcultural, yet some tenets and practices were non-negotiable (Acts 15). Furthermore, James says that God "looked favorably on the Gentiles, to take *from among them* a people for his name" (Acts 15:14, emphasis mine). He does not intend to leave the Gentile in their former state.

Nowhere is there a "No Trespassing Sign" for God; he can and does invade all domains. Such is the nature of sovereignty. Mark Wilson related an account of his conversion that started in the middle of a Native American peyote cult service: The leader

began to sing a peyote song in Lakota Sioux, "Wakantanka, waonsila yo; Wanikiya, waonsila yo," which means, "God, have mercy on me; Jesus, have mercy on me." Suddenly I heard another inner voice, which I would later identify as the Holy Spirit, also speaking to me, "But *I have* had mercy on you through the death of my son Jesus Christ." I was stunned by this revelation because I had thought the peyote church was the ultimate means to spiritual peace and joy. But doubts had emerged in recent months that had shaken that idea. I now realized that there was no salvation through eating peyote and this so-called sacrament would not lead me to faith and eternal life.

With the conclusion of morning water and the resumption of the service, I stepped outside the church house and looked up into the clear, star-lit sky. "High" on peyote and without an altar call or organ playing "Just As I Am," I thanked God for his mercy on me through Jesus' death. I also told the Lord that I would follow him no matter where that path might lead.[49]

There are numerous accounts of Christophanies to non-Christians before significant exposure to the Christian message. Such visitations are mentioned in Acts. God can meet anybody on any path, but he meets them to direct them to the Way. The Lukan description of the name of Jesus is not merely limited to the lips of missionaries. Given the deliberate overlap of the authority in the name of God and in the name of the Lord Jesus, no one receives such an encounter apart from the name of Jesus, for he is the cosmic Lord. He tells his name (Acts 9:5). The encounter with the divine is never apart from Jesus. The name, that is the authority, compassion, and presence of Jesus, is never apart from any divine act; for it carries the authority, compassion, and presence of the name of the Lord.

What is the state of those who have never heard the gospel message? Are they doomed to eternal loss? God is just, but he is also merciful. In a conversation with Howard Marshall, he suggested that these cases be put on "God's suspense account."[50] As the Eastern Church says, "We know where the Church is, but we cannot be sure where it is not."[51] Some talk of the possibility of the "noble pagan" being spared hell and he/she can be admitted to heaven or relegated to Dante's limbo: "After those who refused choice come those without opportunity of choice. They could not, that is, choose Christ; they could, and did, choose human virtue, and for that, they have their reward."[52]

But rather than speak of a hypothetical possibility, the probability is more pressing, one of eternal loss. All need something from Jesus. According to Luke, Jesus himself has mandated that his message of salvation should be proclaimed to "all nations" through Christian witnesses (Luke 24:46–48).

The second question asks, "What does the name of the Lord Jesus in Luke-Acts say about the mission to the Gentiles?" First, the gospel transcends cultures and the church is cosmopolitan in composition; yet Christ in Gentile cultures affirms, leavens, sanctifies, and prohibits. The incarnation of Jesus demands simultaneously a yes and a no from every tribe and culture. For the Gentile to call upon the "Lord Jesus" at baptism is to embrace his lordship and become his servant. To be baptized in his name is to become the property of Jesus and be offered as a sacrificial offering accepted by God.

Calling Jesus "Lord" in the world of Caesar was a counter-cultural act and potentially deemed as treason. To pray for God's kingdom to come sometimes meant saying "no" to the empire and the petty fiefdom of self: "One must obey God more than man" (Acts 5:29). Christians prayed in the Lord's prayer, three times a day, "Thy kingdom come" (Did. 8:2–3). This, in Roman eyes, was daily dethronement of their divine emperor and a declaration of allegiance to a foreign king. They could pray for the emperor but not to the emperor; blind obedience was not an option.

The Gentile witnessed miraculous power through the name of Jesus that convinced them of the truth. In the sons of Sceva incident, they saw a power that trumped all other supernatural forces. Attempts to manipulate God's power ultimately ended in disaster: with the power came unilateral, non-negotiable sovereignty. One could not participate in God's power while bargaining for favors from lesser spirits; thus, they burned their magic books in Ephesus (Acts 19:19). The Gentile convert adopted a new counter-cultural cosmography, "Jesus is Lord of all" (Acts 10:36). No longer was religion and spirituality a practice of power; but was now a realm of ethics in submission to the ultimately good Sovereign who is to be obeyed, not manipulated. This God is not a mere demon with which to curse one's neighbors. The realm of evil spirits even acknowledges the sovereignty of the Lord Jesus (Acts 19:13–17; Luke 4:33–36, 40).

The good news to the Gentile is once again offered in our day. Jesus offers release from the spirits of materialism, spirits that vainly promise to fill the human spirit with physical things. The Lord of life forbids the death of the unborn as much as *Yahweh* forbade the sacrifice of infants to grim idols for convenience, success, and prosperity (Lev 18:21; Deut 12:30–31; 18:10; see also Did 2:2). He calls for compassion on the destitute. He demands an allegiance that leaves no room for blind obedience to any world government. Again, Jesus offers to exorcise the *mal du siècle* the spirits of postmodernity, if we but bow the knee and say yes to his yes for our life and no to what would destroy it. The West has essentially become Gentile; only the Lord Jesus can save it.

Notes

1. H. Richard Niebuhr, *Christ and Culture* (San Francisco: Harper, 1996).
2. Hans Bietenhard, "ὄνομά," in *Theological Dictionary of the New Testament,* G. Kittel, ed., G. Bromily, trans., (Grand Rapids: Eerdmans, 1972), 5:243.
3. Bietenhard, "ὄνομά," 5:249.
4. "ὄνομα," in Frederick W. Danker, Walter Bauer, William F. Arndt, and F. Wilbur Gingrich, *Greek-English Lexicon of the New Testament and Other Early Christian Literature,* 3rd ed. (Chicago: University of Chicago Press, 2000), 573.
5. For Roman actions against magic and the like, see Fritz Graf, *Magic in the Ancient World,* Franklin Philip, trans. (Cambridge, MA: Harvard University Press, 1997), 236, n.9.
6. Pliny the Elder, *Natural History* 28:19; Tacitus, *Annals* 2:69, 4:22, 52, 12:65, 16:31.
7. Graf, *Magic in the Ancient World,* 201–202.
8. All biblical citations are from NRSV unless otherwise noted.
9. Bietenhard, "ὄνομά," 5:255.
10. H. P. Müller, "קדש/qdš" in *Theological Lexicon of the Old Testament,* Ernst Jenni and Claus Westermann, eds., Mark E. Biddle, trans. (Peabody, MA: Hendrickson, 1997), 3:1104.
11. Müller objects to the notion that God is "wholly other" as proposed by Rudolf Otto, *The Idea of the Holy: An Inquiry into the Non-Rational Factor in the Idea of the Divine and its Relation to the Rational,* J. W. Harvey trans. (London: Oxford University Press, 1943), 25–30. "[T]he experience of the holy as the 'wholly other' presupposes, for the most part, a point of departure in an understanding of the profane that has been suggested only by the absence of the numinous in modern concepts of normalcy," (1104).
12. Note the primordial account of Balaam's attempt to pronounce a curse contrary to the will of the Lord (Num 227–24).
13. A. S. van der Woude, "שם/šēm," in *Theological Lexicon of the Old Testament,* Ernst Jenni and Claus Westermann, eds., Mark E. Biddle, trans. (Peabody, MA: Hendrickson, 1979), 3:1365.
14. M. Schmidt, *Prophet und Tempel: eine Studie zum Problem der Gottesnähe im alten Testament* (Zurich: Evangelischen Verlag, 1948), 93, cited in Bietenhard, "ὄνομά," 5:256.
15. Friedrich Giesberecht, *Die alttestamentliche Schätzung des Gottesnamens und ihre Religiongeschichtliche Grundlage* (Königsberg: Thomas & Oppermann, 1901), 123–26, summarized in Bietenhard, "ὄνομά," 5:257.
16. Albert Marie Besnard, *Le Mystère du Nom* (Paris: Éditions du Cerf, 1962), 37. Translation and italics are mine.
17. Anne Marie Kitz, "The Verb **yahway," Journal of Biblical Literature* 138:1 (2019): 39–62. "[The] aspectual meanings of the two verbal forms yields insight into the divine character behind the name YHVH. The *qal* perfective **yahwī* emphasizes two major features." These are the divinity's essential nature and

his presence, which is "a phase of active divine attendance." It is not a mere statement of existence versus nonexistence. "Rather than highlighting the person of divinity as does the *qal*, the *hiphil* focuses on divine doings. Consequently, 'he causes to be > he creates' illustrates *the enduring process* of divine action that continues to create new forms or reforms what has already been created. . . . Here the emphasis is firmly on the here-and-now and the immediate influences of persistent divine activity in the world." Both aspects are "mutually harmonizing notions designed to articulate humanity's early understanding and experience of the divine that became their God YHWH, whose name, without the vowels, could readily embrace both concepts," 62.

18. A. S. van der Woude, "שֵׁם/šēm," in *Theological Lexicon of the Old Testament*, 3:1366–67.

19. Out of 719 uses in the New Testament, 202 and 203 uses are in the Gospel and Acts, respectively.

20. Darrell L. Bock, *Luke: Baker Exegetical Commentary on the New Testament* (Grand Rapids, MI: Baker Academic, 1996), 1559.

21. Translation mine.

22. Keener, among others, assumes that Peter takes "the name of the Lord" to be referring to Jesus, especially in light of 2:38. Craig Keener, *Acts: An Exegetical Commentary:* Volume 1, *Introduction and 1:1–2:47* (Grand Rapids, MI: Baker, 2012), 920–22 and n.643. Verse 22 starts a distinct section of the speech and is Christological in focus. See Donald Juel, "Social Dimensions of Exegesis: The Use of Psalm 16 in Acts 2," *Catholic Bible Quarterly* 43:4 (1981), 543–56, esp. 544–45; and Barnabas Lindars, *New Testament Apologetic* (London: SCM, 1961), 36–48.

23. Larry Hurtado, *Lord Jesus Christ: Devotion to Jesus in Earliest Christianity* (Grand Rapids, MI: Eerdmans, 2003), 181.

24. Hurtado, *Lord Jesus Christ*, 181, n.44.

25. Hurtado, *Lord Jesus Christ*, 98–153.

26. In the fragment, Rylands Library, ?52, dated as early c. 125, there is reason to believe that the entire original manuscript contained *nomina sacra*. See Charles E. Hill, "Did the Scribe of P52 Use the *Nomina Sacra*? Another Look," *New Testament Studies* 48:4 (2002), 587–92.

27. Larry Hurtado, *The Earliest Christian Artifacts: Manuscripts and Christian Origins* (Grand Rapids, MI: Eerdmans, 2006), 2–4.

28. Schuyler Brown, "Concerning the Origin of the Nomina Sacra," *Studia Papyrologica* 9 (1970), 19.

29. Jason Staples, "'Lord, Lord': Jesus as *YHWH* in Matthew and Luke," *New Testament Studies* 64:1 (2018), 1–19.

30. Some manuscripts have "*Kyrie, Kyrie*" in an eschatological context in Luke 13:25 such as A, D, W, θ, and the Majority Text; while ?75 א, B, L have the single *Kyrie* which N-A/28 and USB/5 follow. The it, lat, syr, and bo witnesses are divided between the options. Some commentators take the longer reading to be a harmonization with the Matthean expressions, but if the double *Kyrie*

stands in the Lukan text, we have yet another eschatological judgment context for *"Kyrie, Kyrie."*

31. Staples, "Lord, Lord," 15.

32. Staples, "Lord, Lord," 18.

33. Staples, "Lord, Lord," 19.

34. In Matthew the angel explains Jesus' name, *Yehoshuah*, "God saves": "for he will save his people from their sins" (Matt 1:21).

35. For more on the absorption of Johannine baptism into the message of Jesus, see James B. Shelton, *Mighty in Word and Deed: The Role of the Holy Spirit in Luke-Acts* (Eugene, OR: Wipf & Stock, 2000), 33–45, esp. 43–45.

36. Lars Hartman, *"Into the Name of Jesus": Baptism in the Early Church, Studies of the New Testament and Its World* (Edinburgh: T & T Clark, 1997), 37. Similarly, in Paul, compare 1 Cor 1:2–3, 15 and 1 Cor 6:11.

37. J. A. Ziesler, "The Name of Jesus in the Acts of the Apostles," *Journal for the Study of the New Testament* 4:2 (1979), 29.

38. Wilhelm Heitmüller, *"Im Namen Jesu": eine sprach- und religionsgeschichtliche Untersuchung zum Neuen Testament, speziell zur altchristlichen Taufe* (Göttingen: Vanderhoeck & Ruprecht, 1903), 100–109, esp. 104–107. Note the use of business metaphors: *in der Geschäftssprache, auf den Nam hinein = auf das Konto.*

39. Heitmüller, *"Im Namen Jesu,"* 113; Hartman, 40–41; Hub van de Sandt and David Flusser, *The Didache: Its Jewish Sources and Its Place in Early Judaism and Christianity* (Minneapolis, MN: Fortress Press, 2002), 284–85.

40. Hartman, *Into the Name of Jesus*, 39.

41. Hartman, *Into the Name of Jesus*, 49.

42. See also Justin, 1 Apol 61:3b. The Didache can be dated from AD 50–150. This ethical and liturgical manual of apostolic instruction was cited by Church Fathers, but an ancient copy was found in Constantinople in 1873.

43. Aaron Milavec, *The Didache: Faith, Hope, and Life of the Earliest Christian Communities, 50–70 C.E.* (New York: Newman Press, 2003).

44. See also van de Sandt and Flusser, *The Didache*, 283–91.

45. James B. Shelton, *Mighty in Word and Deed*, 74–84, esp. 80.

46. The name of Jesus does not take the place of Jesus on earth. Zeisler, "The Name of Jesus in the Acts of the Apostles," 31, 38.

47. Ziesler, "The Name of Jesus in the Acts of the Apostles," 31–32.

48. Bruce Olson, *For This Cross I'll Kill You* (Carol Stream, IL: Creation House, 1973), 65.

49. Mark Wilson, "Conversion Story" and "The Night I Met the Devil," in *The Spirit Said Go: Lessons in Guidance from Paul's Journeys* (Eugene, OR: Wipf & Stock, 2017), 4–6 and 142&–45, respectively.

50. In a conversation at Tyndale House, Cambridge, 1981.

51. Kallistos Ware, *The Orthodox Church* (New York: Penguin, 1997), 308.

52. Dorothy Sayers, trans. *Divine Comedy 1: Hell* (New York, Penguin, 1977); Notes on Canto 9:139.

2.

Only Jesus Is Savior and Lord? How the New Testament Responds to Religious and Political Pluralism

Mark E. Roberts

Abstract

Contrary to the common view today that Christianity is only now facing the challenge of religious pluralism, the New Testament and knowledge of the first-century Greco-Roman world show that the church was born into a world filled with religious competitors. Among these, the New Testament responds to three more than others: Judaism, with its Torah interpretation of the time; the Hellenistic mystery religions, whose relation to earliest Christianity still invites debate; and Roman emperor worship. To all of these, the New Testament speaks in a single voice affirming that only Jesus is Savior of the world and Lord over all lords. But earliest Christians expressed their conviction of the exclusivity of Christ socially and politically with a confident humility that continued the longstanding prophetic response to pagan empires: even they existed under God's authority, and, with the exception of the idolizing of rulers, faithful believers are to "seek the welfare of the city," as Jeremiah directed exiles in Babylon, and not foment violent revolution. The New Testament thus says a clear No to an all-religions-lead-to God religious pluralism while saying Yes to a socio-political pluralism expressed in a God-centered cooperation with non-Christian regimes (exemplified in Luke-Acts) that stops only at idolatry (exemplified in Revelation).

Key words: religious pluralism; sociological pluralism; empire; Christianity and other religions; Jesus Christ — person and offices; Jesus Christ — political and social views; church and state — Rome

A typical attitude today toward Christianity in its relation to other faiths is to assert confidently that in this contemporary world Christianity must descend from its domination in the West and mature by learning how to fit in with the many other faiths and politics in the world. This attitude presumes that before the last century or this, Christianity could exist parochially, barely aware of competing claims of other faiths, naively presuming that it and only its central redemptive figure, Jesus, possessed unique and exclusive powers of salvation. Mature Christianity today should humble itself, accept that God's mercy well overflows the banks of this narrow view about Jesus, and embrace doctrinal and political pluralism fully, agreeing that God saves through others than Jesus Christ.[1]

Mixed within such an attitude are worthy *desiderata*: Christianity should evince humility, because it exists only as an expression of the sheer grace of God; and it should relate with good will toward advocates of other faiths, seeking to understand them as much as it seeks to be understood. But Christianity cannot accept the core imperative within this attitude regarding its core beliefs and, as its founding documents in the New Testament show, it need not dilute its confident confession that Jesus alone is Lord and Christ and Savior of the world. At the same time, this evangel of the arrival of God's saving reign promotes a political pluralism in which followers of Jesus recognize God's delegation of political authority even to governments that do not embrace its gospel, such as the Roman Empire. This recognition prompts a political pluralism that respects God's sovereignty as he determines how "The kingdom of the world [becomes] the kingdom of our Lord and of his Christ, and he shall reign forever and ever" (Rev 11:15 ESV). As this chapter shows, the writers of the New Testament lived in a first-century world populated by various faiths no less than the global village we inhabit today.[2] Did these first-generation apostles and their close co-workers respond to the plural faiths of their day by diluting their confession of Jesus to that of only one among perhaps many through whom persons may be saved?

Let us see. First, we sketch what we know from various sources, biblical and beyond, about earliest Christianity among the religions in the first-century Hellenistic world and what the New Testament says about Jesus among all the first-century deities. Then we look more closely at how specific texts respond more and less directly to the claims of these non-Christian faiths. With conclusions from this doctrinal study, we then consider the way Jesus and writers of the New Testament embraced not a doctrinal but a practical, sociological pluralism in its stance toward the Roman Empire, not rejecting it through violence or non-violence but submitting to its ultimately divine authority, while proclaiming and demonstrating the presence of the greater kingdom of God. This study concludes that the New Testament's evangel of God's saving reign over all of creation rejects fundamental doctrinal pluralism but embraces a between-the-times political pluralism. It arises from confidence in the redemptive sovereignty of God and reserves the "fury of the wrath of God" against idolatrous empires to God himself.

The Church Is Born into a World of Religious Pluralism

Let us first establish that Jesus and the earliest church lived in a world of many religions, of much religious pluralism. Concerning only the Promised Land, throughout the millennia of Old Testament time, the Land was home to people practicing many faiths. The Israelites as a whole were rarely if ever wholly faithful to their delivering God, Yahweh. Recall the many warnings about and rebukes for "going after other gods" expressed throughout the Old Testament. The compromises of many rulers (the worst being Ahab and Jezebel) prompted many rebukes by prophets (such as Elijah, Jeremiah, and Hosea) and led both kingdoms, northern Israel and southern Judah, to being conquered by foreign powers. From the time Judah returned from Babylonia to the time of Jesus under Roman occupation, this ancestral land continued to be populated with many more faiths than Judaism.

Judaism itself was, in the first century AD, made up of factions with varying religious views, among whom we meet in the Gospels Pharisees, Sadducees, Herodians, and zealots, with other groups the New Testament does not mention. An example is the rigorous, separatist Essenes occupying Qumran by the Dead Sea and other locations near Jericho, Jerusalem, and Hebron. Added to these differences within Judaism were the alien cultural and religious influences brought into this region by the extended influence of the Macedonian Alexander the Great. He influenced the world with Greek (Hellenic) culture that blended with local cultures wherever he conquered. His success Hellenizing the world causes historians to name the period following his death the Hellenistic Age. For the Jewish diaspora (Jews living away from their homeland of primarily Judaea and Galilee), in Alexandria, Egypt, Hellenism birthed the Septuagint, the Greek version of the Hebrew Bible, completed about 250 BC (abbreviated as LXX). It was the Bible of many earliest Christians and is quoted often in the Greek New Testament. Hellenism influenced Galilee, Gaulanitis, and the Decapolis (from the Greek *deka,* for "ten," and *polis,* for "city") to the north more, with their larger Gentile populations, than Judea and Jerusalem to the south, which were more Jewish and which observed Torah more scrupulously. Overlying Judaism and Hellenism was the layer of other influences that Roman occupation brought. Much of Roman religion was derived from Greek mythology and its pantheon of deities, but it innovated in transmitting the practice of emperor worship, which originated in the non-Hellenic, longstanding eastern veneration of rulers as deities. Roman emperor worship began with the posthumous veneration by the Roman senate of Augustus Caesar and later emperors who served well, and it continued in the first century by the demand (not endorsed by the senate) of emperors Caligula (who persecuted Jews) and Nero and Domitian (which two persecuted Christians).

In addition, throughout the empire flourished a rather broad basket of cults scholars call mystery religions. These originated in many places — Greece, Egypt, and places farther east — and had distinctive practices making them difficult to classify neatly. Common to many are these features noted by New Testament scholar Robert H. Gundry:

> These promised purification and immortality of the soul and often centered on myths of a goddess whose lover or child was taken from her, usually by death, and later restored. The mysteries also featured secret initiatory and other rites involving ceremonial washing, blood-sprinkling, sacramental meals, intoxication, emotional frenzy, and impressive pageantry by which devotees were supposed to gain union with the deity.[3]

Among the better known are the cults of Eleusis, Mithra, Isis, Dionysus, and Cybele.[4] These pre-date Christianity, and similarities between beliefs of these mysteries and Christianity have prompted some scholars to assert that Christianity borrowed from them. But because most of what we know about the beliefs of these cults comes from the second and later centuries and because such religions were known to borrow from others, while Christianity resisted such assimilation from its beginning, it is more likely the mystery religions borrowed from Christianity.[5] The mysteries emphasize experience more than a system of doctrine that might compare with Christian theology. Edwards writes,

> Most of the cults practiced elaborate and sometimes bloody initiation rites, as well as sacred meals and ceremonies imitating death and rebirth experiences. The purpose of these rituals was to induct adherents into a shared experience and produce a frame of mind that was emotionally gripping. The accent fell on experience. With the exception of Eleusis [a corn cult], Clement of Alexandria [c. AD 150–215] castigated all the Mysteries for channeling that experience through eroticism.[6]

Religion scholar Luther Martin writes about "[t]he experiences of initiates in these rites. . . . The experience induced by the initiatory rites of the Graeco-Roman mysteries can be characterized generally as an emotionally charged sense of disorientation and vulnerability."[7] Thus the secrecy encoded into the term "mysteries" may refer to the religious experience of initiates more than to secret knowledge they were charged not to share.[8]

Closely related to the mysteries was knowledge to be shared, in Gnosticism (derived from a Greek word for knowledge, *gnosis),* a religious expression of Plato's philosophical opposition between ideas, or spirit, and matter.[9] This religious perspective, a hybrid of philosophy and oriental religion, considered spirit (the non-material) good and matter evil, which led to opposite behaviors: 1) asceticism, which denied bodily pleasures because the body, as matter, is inherently evil; and 2) sensualism, which indulged bodily pleasures because the body, as inferior to spirit, was not important. Gnosticism influenced Christianity late in the first century, and New Testament writings such as Colossians respond to gnostic notions that, in full bloom, threatened Christian orthodoxy for several centuries (Col. 2:8–23).[10] Gnosticism shared with the mysteries the gaining of immortality through secret knowledge: doctrines and passwords that, at death, would deliver one's spirit through hostile forces in its celestial journey to heaven.[11]

Along with the syncretistic mystery religions, our sketch of religious pluralism in the first-century world of Jesus and the earliest church concludes with mention of magic. Gundry summarizes:

> Superstition had a stranglehold on most people in the Roman Empire. Use of magical formulas; consultation of horoscopes and oracles; augury or prediction of the future by observing the flight of birds, the movement of oil on water, or the markings on a liver; and the hiring of professional exorcists . . . — all these superstitious practices and many more played a part in everyday life.[12]

Not exactly religions but nevertheless commending specific ways of living valued especially by intellectual elites, philosophies filled out the symbolic world of the time of Jesus and, more so, of the early generations of the church. In Acts 17:18, we meet Epicureans, for whom pleasure — not necessarily sensual — was life's aim, and Stoics, who emphasized duty in a world guided by universal, impersonal, divine Reason. Two other philosophical schools influenced the first-century world, although they are not mentioned in the New Testament: Cynics, the counter-cultural minimalists of the time, who rejected "the popular pursuits of comfort, affluence, and social prestige," and Skeptics, whose thoroughgoing doubt of absolutes nourished relativism, which relativism led them to conform to custom.[13]

From this brief sketch, we can see how much religion and quasi-religion populated the first-century Greco-Roman world of Jesus and the earliest church. New Testament scholar James Edwards focuses our attention on

> Three New Testament images [that] are useful in understanding the interplay of the emerging gospel with the world. One is Jesus sitting on the Mount of Olives opposite the temple in Jerusalem; another is the apostle Paul debating with Greek philosophers beneath the Acropolis in Athens; a third is the same apostle appealing to Caesar in Rome. All three images are historical. All three show a gospel not holed up in the hinterlands but vigorously engaging the power centers of the Jewish, Greek, and Roman worlds.[14]

Words from the missionary and missiologist Lesslie Newbigin conclude this section:

> The world into which the first Christians carried the gospel was a religiously plural world and — as the letters of Paul show — in that world of many lords and gods, Christians had to work out what it means that in fact Jesus alone is Lord. The first three centuries of church history were a time of intense life-and-death struggle against the seductive power of syncretism.[15]

The Gospel Asserts Its Supremacy over All Rivals

We now consider how the New Testament asserts the supremacy of the gospel over its three most important rivals: mystery religions, Judaism, and emperor worship.

Over Mystery Religions

Mystery religions were the weakest of these rivals. They were widespread in the regions Paul visited in his missions from Antioch westward through Asia Minor (modern Turkey) and into Europe,[16] yet only a few New Testament texts seem to engage the mysteries unquestionably. As Greek scholar Bruce Metzger has noted, some seventeen of the terms the mysteries used most commonly are absent from the New Testament.[17] Of those terms common to Paul and the mysteries, religion scholar David Aune writes, "there are what appear to be a number of words and phrases in Pauline vocabulary which seem to have been derived ultimately from the language used to describe aspects of the mystery cults." These terms, which include "wisdom" (1 Cor 1:17–31), "knowledge" (1 Cor 8:1; 13:8), "spiritual person" contrasted with "psychic person," (1 Cor 2:14–16), "to be initiated" (Phil 4:12), "mystery" and "perfect" or "mature" (1 Cor 2:5–6), "unutterable" (2 Cor 12:4), do not appear to be drawn *directly* from the mystery cults but had much earlier passed into the common fund of figurative religious language. In particular instances it appears that Paul actually adopted the language of his opponents in his attempt to refute them (e.g., 1 Cor 2:6–13)." Note important differences between New Testament teaching and the mysteries:

- While Christianity wedded its rites of initiation to a coherent message about God's action in human history in the past, present, and future, the mysteries expressed stories of non-historical deities, stories entered into by rites of initiation but not supported by a body of teaching that covered all of life and pointed to a future certain to the faithful (until some were "annexed by Neo-Platonism in the third century"), as Christianity did from its beginning.[18]

- The mysteries "avoided publicity and proclamation in favor of ineffability," while the gospel was proclaimed publicly, always making Christ "present to save."

- The mythological stories the mysteries told centered on versions of a repeatedly dying and rising god, but the gospel centered on the historical and once-for-all-time event of God's salvation through the crucified, risen, and ascended Son of God.

- "Mysteries attracted adherents, whereas Christianity produced converts."[19] Mysteries adherents participated in ritual experiences aiming at "a quality of experience, a 'high'" in life and might join several mysteries. Converts to Christ, however, experienced conversion into a new life and had to turn away from other ultimate loyalties to God in Christ and his church alone.

- Mysteries gathered for rituals offering individuals "access to the spiritual world" but did not form communities: "the concept of the *ecclesia,* the people of God called out and set apart in the church, had not equivalent in the Mysteries."[20]

Over Torah

Judaism centered on Torah, the five books traditionally attributed to Moses.[21] The word *torah* does not mean "law" in the sense in which we regard criminal or civil law. Instead it means "teaching" or "instruction" and is the subject of the lengthiest of psalms, Psalm 119, from which comes this favorite verse referring to Torah: "Your word is a lamp to my feet and a light to my path" Ps 119:105 ESV. New Testament scholar James Edwards summarizes the high regard with which Jews held Torah:[22]

- Jews regarded it as the "once-for-all exclusive self-revelation of God," concerning which, according to the Babylonian Talmud, doubt about the divine origin of a single verse despised the whole Word of God.[23]

- Rabbis considered Torah one of seven creations pre-existing the world.[24]

- To add or delete a letter from Torah is thought to equal, spiritually, destroying a world.[25]

- Its study is worth more than anything else: In the Talmud God says to David, "Dearer to me is a day when you sit and study the Torah than the thousand burnt offerings which thy son Solomon will one day offer me on the altar."[26]

- Torah brings order to the whole of life, confirming it to God's will and separating Jews "from the rest of the world."

Jesus was an observant Jew, who complied with Torah largely: in dress (Matt 9:20; 14:36); in attending synagogue and otherwise observing Sabbath ("as was his custom," Luke 4:16; Mark 1:21); in finding his mission in fulfilling, not overthrowing, Torah and the prophets (Matt 5:17–19).[27] But he also expressed his authority as the Son of Man, Messiah (Christ), and Son of God by rejecting traditions that distorted or misinterpreted the divine intent of Torah (Mark 7:3–23; 10:1–12). Among these, he rejected traditions about associating with ritually unclean persons ("tax collectors and sinners," Mark 2:15–17), about other religious observances (fasting, for example: Mark 2:18–22), about keeping the Sabbath ("So the Son of Man is Lord even of the Sabbath," Mark 2:23–28; 3:1–6), and about unclean foods ("Thus he declared all foods clean," Mark 7:14–19). Especially in Matthew 5:17–20, Jesus asserts his authority to interpret and apply Torah and the Prophets rightly, without regard for other human authorities. This assertion of authority, including his claim to fulfill the whole of the Hebrew Scripture, is breathtaking and absolute! Such a stupendous claim calls to mind the famous trilemma popularized by C. S. Lewis: Was Jesus a lunatic, a liar, or, as Christians confess, the Lord?[28] To which we should add a fourth possibility, forming a quadrilemma instead: Is he a legend, a fiction created or super-sized by the imagination of Gospel writers?[29] But Jesus' rejection of traditions misusing Torah did not compromise unchanging divine norms, which he expresses in a criterion of righteousness: "unless your righteousness exceeds that of the scribes and Pharisees, you will never enter the kingdom of heaven" (Matt 5:20).[30] His standard was that of the perfect love of the heavenly Father (Matt 5:48).

The Gospels portray Jesus variously but always as superseding Torah and Moses, through whom God gave Torah to his covenant people, and also superseding other prophets, who demonstrated covenant faithfulness and urged God's unfaithful people to repent.[31] Through Jesus the saving reign of God (the kingdom of God or of the heavens) had arrived and God's Torah and covenants were being fulfilled: the end — both as a finality and as the achieving of a purpose or goal — had begun (Luke 16:16; Matt 11:13). In Jesus, the long-prophesied and long-awaited age of Messiah and age of the Spirit had arrived, and new wine called for new wineskins (Mark 2:22). Torah retained high value as God's revelation, as Paul emphasizes in his letters to Roman and Galatian believers, but as much as Torah expressed God's will and holiness and showed a path for righteous living, it lacked the power to save, which only God through Christ can do. And Torah could, as could anything besides God, become an idol separating persons from God and thus enslaving them under its power (Rom 7; Gal 3–4).[32] John's Gospel contrasts Jesus from Torah by identifying only him and not Torah as the living Word of God, who was with God from the beginning and who is nothing less or other than God himself (John 1:1–4). And to Jewish believers raised venerating Torah, the Epistle to the Hebrews declares that Jesus mediates the new covenant "more excellent" than the Torah covenant (Heb 8:6; 9:15; 12:24); and 1 Timothy 2:5 concurs: "there is one God, and there is one mediator between God and men, the man Christ Jesus," not Torah.

How did "locating salvation in Jesus rather than in Torah" affect first-century Jewish believers? In the Gospels Jesus warns his synagogue-attending followers they will be hated, excluded, reviled, and have their names spurned "as evil, on account of the Son of Man" (Luke 6:22). "[T]hree caustic references in the Gospel of John," Edwards writes, "speak of believers in Jesus suffering 'expulsion from the synagogue' (John 9:22; 12:42; 16:2). The Greek word John uses, *aposynagogos*, is unknown in Greek literature outside the New Testament," probably created to refer to "the fate of early Jewish Christians who confessed Jesus."[33]

Synagogue discipline varied from light penalties (a month's suspension) to the most severe, as Josephus says: being cut off from their communities completely, with some starving to death.[34] Such discipline aimed to restore offenders to the community. But *aposynagogos* refers not to discipline but to excommunication.[35] If, as many scholars believe, the Fourth Gospel was finalized near AD 90, its references could be two-fold: to events in Jesus' life and to the cursing of Nazarenes (Christians) in synagogue worship and prayer, which was occurring regularly by that time.[36] Although the Talmud was not completed until centuries after the New Testament, its curse on Christians, among other violators of Jewish norms, undoubtedly arose in the late New Testament period:

> Heretics and apostates and traitors and free-spirits and rejecters of Torah and those who leave the ways of the community and those who deny the resurrection of the dead, and whoever sins and induces others to sin. . . . Hell is bolted behind them and they will be eternally punished in it for all generations.[37]

Earliest Jewish Christians did not seek to separate from Judaism, but some who followed Jesus — not Torah — as their source of salvation suffered the deep loss of membership in their lifelong communities. They did so in a world in which belonging to a community determined one's identity and way of living, a need to belong (and thus submit to that community's norms) not offset by the individualism that has evolved in the contemporary West in which the human need to belong may be met differently.[38] The Christian norm, which conflicts fully with Torah-centered salvation, Paul expresses clearly in a handful of verses Edwards has compiled with comments:

> [T]he gospel was no mere counterpart or epilogue to Torah. Throughout his letters Paul asserts that Jesus Christ fulfills Torah and relegates it to a secondary role. Torah was not sufficient for salvation. It was neither able to forgive sins, nor to make one right with God (Acts 13:38). "We know that a person is justified not by the works of the law but through faith in Jesus Christ" (Galatians 2:16). "But now apart from law, the righteousness of God has been disclosed, and is attested by the law and the

prophets, the righteousness of God through faith in Jesus Christ for all who believe" (Romans 3:21). "For we hold that a person is justified by faith apart from works prescribed by the law" (Romans 3:28).[39]

Jewish Christians, according to Paul, may continue to observe Torah in various ways, but Gentile believers should not adopt Torah observances. And neither Jewish nor Gentile believers may trust in Torah and in their Torah observances for salvation. Salvation God supplies through Christ alone.[40]

Over Caesar Worship

Earliest Christianity conflicted with the Roman Empire as an empire much less than with the emperor cult that began during the first generation of the church. Earlier scholarship asserted that Judaism was specially exempted from various imperial requirements because it had been classed a *religio licita,* an approved religion, and that Christianity benefited from that exemption until it was no longer identified with Judaism. But the phrase *religio licita* seems to originate no earlier than the second century with Christian lawyer, theologian, and apologist, Tertullian; and studies of Roman law find no such empire-wide decree pertaining to Judaism. Instead, it benefitted from the empire's general toleration of, in Emperor Claudius' recollection, Emperor Augustus' "desire that the several subject nations should abide by their own customs and not be compelled to violate the religion of their fathers."[41] The Romans valued ancestral customs and religions: age mattered. Judaism was thus respected for its long history and continued existence "according to their forefathers," and, although its strict monotheism distinguished it from other religions, Rome tolerated other ancestral customs and religion similarly. Before the emperor cult became an issue, the problem for the earliest Christians, especially as they became distinguished from Judaism, was novelty, not antiquity: the Jesus movement could be seen as a wholly new religion. That perception is one reason Luke's account shows that earliest Christianity was rooted in the ancestral traditions and fathers of Israel.[42]

Christian (and Jewish) conflict with the emperor cult followed its rise. At first, emperors such as Julius (100–44 BC) and Augustus Caesar (63 BC–AD 14) were merely venerated without requiring all to participate: Julius was "called a god because of his deeds," after he conquered Britain; Augustus was called by the Latin poet Virgil, in Edwards' words, "the divine child of Jupiter who, as God, would bring peace to the world, govern it with justice and power, vanquish evil, and usher in a golden age."[43] The Empire to the east had a longer pre-imperial history of treating rulers as deities and took even more seriously such descriptions of Augustus. Surprising many Bible readers today, inscriptions there call him "God," "son of God," "noble Benefactor," and (this last applied to nearly all first-century emperors) "Savior of the World."[44] Edwards notes that such veneration was "grandiose acclaim for economic and political accomplishments" already customary in the Greco-Roman world before the rise of the Roman Empire and not required of inhabitants of the empire.[45]

But Emperor Nero (ad 54–68) changed this policy: according to Edwards, he was the first emperor called a god on coinage and the first since Julius Caesar to associate himself with the Roman god Mars by allowing a statue of himself to be placed in Mars' temple. Further, in Boeotia, he was called "lord of the whole world" and by the king of Armenia "master" and "god." Whether or not Nero demanded worship, at least some did worship him, and with him "the emperor cult shifted from an official formality to an intensely personal identification. . . . Nero saw the ideals of the state embodied in himself, and the state as an absolute extension of himself."[46]

But it was Emperor Domitian (81–98) who demanded worship as "Master and God" and punished severely those who refused to worship him. He reigned during the period Revelation was written, and it describes such punishments, even unto death, in 6:9 and 13:15. After Domitian, Edwards writes, "all Roman emperors promoted the emperor cult in earnest"; and, with "very few exceptions, every Caesar from Julius onward called himself 'Savior of the World.'"[47]

Expressed in such lofty titles was the widespread ancient fusion of religion and state such that what we today call religious observances (such as offerings to the city or nation's gods) were not distinguished from what we may today consider merely civil observances (such as the singing of one's national anthem today) and obligations of citizenship. And because across the empire, subject peoples already had their local deities, not to add to the worship of these locals the veneration, or worship, of the supreme ruler of the Roman Empire was believed to threaten the unity and security of the state, to deny the state the loyalty it deserved. Ernst Lohmeyer distills this religion-state unity to its meaning for the emperor cult:

Since the empire was seen as the image of the cosmos or world-order, it was therefore believed to be universal and eternal. As the ruler of the world, Caesar was at the same time lord of the world. This universal state-religion was grounded in the one central thought that the emperor was in some way the incarnation of deity, and that he was the visible, earthly manifestation of the revealed God.[48]

Yet Jews, well known for their ancient monotheistic faith, were exempted from conforming to the emperor cult, at least initially. But the cult targeted Christians, who, by the end of the first century, were seen as distinct from Judaism and were therefore treated the same as adherents to any other non-Jewish religion. Their monotheism and confession that only "Jesus is Lord" conflicted directly with the confession the cult demanded, namely, "Caesar is Lord." Failing to confess Caesar brought on serious consequences, even death. The famous letter from Pliny the Younger to Emperor Trajan in AD 112 describes Pliny's policy of giving Christians three opportunities to rescind their confession of Christ and to confess Caesar's lordship instead. If they refused his offers, he sentenced them to death. In the second century, Polycarp, the bishop of Smyrna, was burned to death at the stake for refusing to hail Caesar as Lord.[49]

Although by most scholars' reckoning most of the New Testament was written by the time Domitian began reigning, it responds to the nascent emperor cult in several texts. The next section shows how the New Testament advocates a between-the-times political pluralism that teaches believers to submit to imperial authority except for those demands that require disobeying God, such as worshiping the emperor. Here we focus on words and phrases in the New Testament that assert the supremacy of Christ over even the empire and emperor:[50]

These assert Christ's supremacy somewhat subtly:

- *The familiar infancy stories of Luke (1–2) express Christ's supremacy over Caesar,* with angelic annunciation, praise, and declaration that the child born in lowly Bethlehem, the city of David — to which his parents traveled because of a Roman decree — is Savior, Messiah, and Lord (2:9–11). While these terms come from the vocabulary of the Hebrew Scriptures and first-century Judaism, their context in this Gospel is also Roman, as Edwards explains:

  The birth of Augustus . . . aroused hopes for peace and good will on earth; and at the birth of Jesus, Augustus presumed to register and control "all the world" (2:1). The angelic host, however, ascribes the authority presumed by Augustus to Jesus — indeed, the *infant* Jesus. In self-adulation Augustus presented himself as "good news," but heaven declares a baby lying in a feed trough as truly "good news of great joy for all the people" (2:10).[51]

- *Matthew's infancy narrative shows all roads do not lead to Rome* and thereby diminishes "the luster of the emperor cult": *Magoi* from the east ("the home court of the Caesar cult") follow the natural revelation of the star not to Rome but to Jerusalem; and from Herod's palace, only the Hebrew scriptures guide them to complete their journey to the Child who is "king of the Jews" (Matt 2:1–12). *In 2 Peter,* "Lord and Savior" occurs five times in three chapters and "firmly remind[s] readers that Jesus, not Caesar, was Lord and Savior" (1:1–2, 11; 2:20; 3:2, 18).

Words and phrases in these texts assert Christ's supremacy more directly:

- *1 Corinthians 8:5–6:* "For although there may be so-called gods in heaven or on earth — as indeed there are many 'gods' and many 'lords' — yet for us there is one God, the Father, from whom are all things and for whom we exist, and one Lord, Jesus Christ, through whom are all things and through whom we exist." Note the Father and "Lord, Jesus Christ" are expressed in parallel with a coordinate conjunction, and this God and Lord is the source and purpose for all that is, not any of the "so-called gods," a direct reference to the many gods along with the divinized emperor. All "believers were created by Jesus Christ and they belong to Jesus Christ, not to Caesar," and "[t]he Caesar-cult, like the powers and authorities in heavenly places (1 Corinthians 15:24; Ephesians 1:21; Colossians 1:13, 16; 2:10, 15) has been subjected to Christ."

- *The Pastoral Letters (1 & 2 Timothy, Titus):* "'savior,' a catchword in the Caesar cult" occurs "unusually often": used of God in 1 Timothy 1:1; 2:3; 4:10; Titus 1:3; 2:10; 3:4. If written by Paul during Nero's reign, when he as "madly promoting himself as god," Paul "would emphasize *God* as the true savior, not Caesar." Terms used for Jesus in 1 Timothy 6:15; 2 Timothy 1:9–10; 4:1; Titus 2:11; 3:4; also Jude 4, include "the *manifestation of God,* the *savior,* the *redeemer,* the *epiphany* of *glory, salvation,* and *hope.* Each of these terms belonged to the official vocabulary of the emperor cult," including this triple ascription to Jesus (in 1 Tim 6:15): "the blessed and only Sovereign, the King of kings and Lord of lords."

- Luke 22:24–26 may be quite confrontational: It contains the only use of the word *euergetēs*, "benefactor," which Edwards notes is "the most frequently employed title for divinized humans, including Caesar" and is, in Luke, "an unmistakable reference to the Caesar cult." The Gospel says, "The kings of the Gentiles lord it over them and those in authority over them are called benefactors. But not so with you."[52]

- The Revelation is most confrontational of all New Testament writings, written probably "during the fierce and bloody persecution of the infant church in Asia Minor" (modern Turkey) during the reign of Emperor Domitian (ad 81–98). Gone from the Empire was any pretense of civil virtue; now clear for all to see was "its idolatrous nature": "the church was battling for its life (Rev 17:14)." Edwards reads Revelation in its immediate context, which portrays the empire as the most concentrated concrete expression of evil: "the accuser of the brothers and sisters (12:10), the devil who had descended in great wrath (12:12) and sits on the throne of Satan (2:13)." The emperor appears "as a brazen whore who fornicated with the nations" on Rome's seven hills (ch 17) and as "two blasphemous beasts (chapter 13); no, a cosmic dragon lurking to devour the newborn child (that is, the gospel) of a celestial woman (the church: 12:1–7)."[53]

- These Christians Revelation "depicts . . . as helpless but not hopeless." As terrible as Caesar's actions may be, God remains sovereign over all of creation (Rev 5:13), and "the victory over the beast — that is, over idolatrous Caesar — has already been won by the blood of the Lamb and the witness of the martyrs (Rev 10:11)." He, Jesus Christ, the Son of God, shall come again as "the Rider on the White Horse" and as the true "King of kings and the Lord of lords" (Rev 19:11–16). He, not Caesar, "is the first and last (22:12), who makes all things new (21:5), and to whom the church prays, 'Come, *Lord Jesus!*' (Rev 22:20)."

The New Testament Embraces a Practical Pluralism toward Human Culture and Government

The preceding sections show that the New Testament confesses the supremacy of Christ over all, with a single voice. This theological certainty about Jesus and the inbreaking of God's kingdom through his ministry could result in many attitudes toward the societies in which believers live and toward governments that do not share but even conflict with this confession and its way of life. How does the New Testament direct believers to live as a tiny minority in the first-century world brimming with religions and governed by an empire that, during the last half of this century, began requiring subjects to obey its law most objectionable to Jews and Christians: namely, the demand that imperial subjects worship its emperor? Christopher Bryan approaches this question by first drawing upon the long experience of Jews under foreign empires.[54]

The Prophetic Tradition Sees All Government as Serving and Accountable to God's Purposes

As God's chosen, Israel's domination by pagans was itself a problem of theodicy, but rather than viewing all such domination as evil to be resisted by all means, Israel expresses instead God's choosing: "a consistent stream of . . . [primarily prophetic] voices, [expresses that] God *chooses* . . . there shall be empires." These include empires of "Egypt (Gen 47:7–10), Assyria (Isa 10:5–6; 37:26–27), Babylon (Jer 25:9; 27:5–6; Dan 4:17), and Persia (Isa 44:24–45:7)." All are said either to be blessed and prosper (Egypt) or "rule over other nations by God's mandate" (the rest). "[A]lways such power is granted within the limits of God's sovereignty. Those who exercise such power are called to obey God's command, for the Lord alone is truly king (Ps 96:10). If they flout that command, they face certain judgment (Ps 2:10–11; Wisd of Solomon 6:1–9)." God through Israel's Scriptures thus affirms human government, including empires that rise, but they are always accountable to him.

A star witness of this stance is Jeremiah and his letter to the exiles in Babylon (Jer 29). Not only does it say Babylon's sovereignty over Israel is God's will but also that God has not forgotten them and they may, in fact, must flourish there, living full lives and, most surprising, "seek[ing] the welfare of the city," even praying to God for it. Bryan quotes Old Testament scholar Walther Eichrodt: "the way in which both the personal longing for revenge and the national desire for retribution are overcome is remarkable, culminating as it does in the formation of a new fellowship with the heathen through intercession."[55]

The divine case against human government, including empire, is not its existence *per se* but its failing to acknowledge its divine reason for existence: namely, under God's sovereignty, to serve those it governs with justice. But when any government disobeys to the point of absolutizing itself and its rulers, it asserts autonomy and commits idolatry, earning divine judgment. Israel expresses this view even toward its own monarchy, epitomized in the prophetic rebuke of king David's gross injustice in his taking of Bathsheba and causing the murder of her husband Uriah (2 Sam 11:27–12:9) for, later, in the words of Isaiah, "the Lord is our judge, the Lord is our ruler, the Lord is our king; he will save us" (Isa. 33:22). David and other disobedient Israelite kings receive judgment no less than empires dominating Israel (Ps 89:32–36). Centuries later, God judges the self-worship of the Babylonian king Nebuchadnezzar by causing him to live as a beast seven years (Dan 4:13–17). But God's faithfulness is the hope not only of his chosen people but also of enemies Egypt, Assyria, and Babylon. Jeremiah tells the exiles to pray for their exilic home, the heathen city (29:7), and God promises grace to Egypt (Isa 19:23–25), welcomes Assyrian Nineveh's repentance (Jonah), and restores even Nebuchadnezzar (Dan 4:34–37), although God will overthrow Babylon to raise up a Persian "messiah," Cyrus, whom God uses to enable his people to return to Judea (Isa 44:24–45:7). God acts for the sake of his people *"through [a] pagan emperor and pagan empire,* called and named by the same word" that made all things. Such an emperor God makes a *"witness to the divine glory,"* so emperor and empire know there is none beside Yahweh.[56]

From this survey, which Bryan extends through the Second Temple period,[57] Bryan turns to Jesus and the New Testament by identifying four possible stances first-century Jews, contemporaries of Jesus and the first Christians, could take toward Roman rule:[58] They could

1. *Accept and cooperate fully with Rome.* First-century examples include Herod's family and most Sadducean priestly aristocrats, and, as the discussion above shows, perhaps also, by analogy, Joseph in Egypt, and Ezra and Nehemiah under Persian rule.

2. *Accept Roman rule but question or challenge some of its actions, nonviolently.* First-century Jewish examples include Jews who protested to Pilate when Roman soldiers' standards were brought into Jerusalem; others who protested emperor Caligula's erecting statues of himself in Jerusalem; and the Jewish philosopher Philo, through his written *Embassy to Gaius.* Old Testament figures

adopting this stance include Esther under Persian and Daniel under Babylonian rule.

3. *Reject Roman rule nonviolently*. Bryan finds no Jewish examples but instead the views of contemporary scholars John Howard Yoder and Richard A. Horsley.[59]

4. *Reject Roman rule violently*. First-century examples include Judas the Galilean, who hectored peers to revolt or be cowards (Josephus, *Wars*, 2.118), also the Sicarii assassinating zealots and those revolting in AD 66.

Because these stances embody as pure types all options along the axes of acceptance and violence, we may ask, Which stance does Jesus take and which the writings of the New Testament?

How Do Jesus and the New Testament Relate to the Roman Empire?

Bryan believes Jesus and the New Testament embody option two, and this chapter agrees.[60] However, some influential New Testament scholars read the New Testament quite differently. They see the language pertinent to empire (discussed in the previous section "Over Caesar Worship") as evidence that Jesus' ministry of the kingdom of God and its reception by the earliest Christians opposed, or directly subverted, the Roman empire and, in various ways, aimed to defeat it. Such scholars include John Howard Yoder,[61] Richard A. Horsley,[62] John Dominic Crossan,[63] and, more popularly, Brian J. Walsh,[64] among others.

Jesus: Render to Caesar and to God

For example, Horsley's *Jesus and Empire* aims to recover the Jesus of his times, not the domesticated and depoliticized Jesus who fits the assumptions of contemporary Western Christianity.[65] Instead, Horsley's Jesus was shaped by and joined the opposition to Roman rule: "For generations before and after the ministry of Jesus, the Galilean and Judean people mounted repeated protests and revolts against the Romans and their client rulers, the Herodian kings and Jerusalem high priests."[66] He pictures first-century society in these regions as fundamentally that of hostile peasants vs. Rome-favored elites. In that ever-conflicted society,

Jesus "pursues the same general agenda in parallel paths: independence from Roman imperial rule so that people can again be empowered to renew their traditional way of life under the rule of God."[67] Jesus' proclamation of the kingdom thus meant rejecting Roman rule.[68] Moreover, Horsley and others claim Paul applies "key imperial language to Jesus" (the empire-pertinent language discussed above), "making [Jesus] into the alternative or real emperor of the world, the head of an anti-imperial international alternative society."[69]

But a reading of the Gospels that presumes neither seething class conflict nor empire language as necessarily anti-imperial, shows Jesus not hostile to the empire, its representatives, or its taxation. Regarding Rome's representatives, a Roman centurion begs Jesus to heal his servant (Matt 8:5–13//Luke 7:1–10), and Jesus does, without hesitation and without any criticism of him, his command, or Roman rule. Instead, Jesus commends this Gentile's faith, which the centurion explains, as Bryan describes it, from his work as "a military agent of imperial rule;" and Jesus predicts that many other Gentiles will join Hebrew patriarchs in the end-time messianic banquet.[70]

Regarding taxation: even though Jews who collected (and extorted) taxes for Rome and clients were viewed by other Jews the same as "sinners" and "prostitutes" (Mark 2:15–16//Matt 21:31–32), Bryan asks if it is not strange that "the gospels do not contain so much as one . . . saying of Jesus that attacks the [taxation] system *as a system*. . . . If independence from Rome and Rome's clients were Jesus' agenda." Indeed, it is strange. Two examples: First, the tax collector "Levi the son of Alphaeus" is the fifth disciple Jesus calls in the Gospel of Mark (2:14).[71] Immediately after his calling, Jesus eats in his house with "many tax collectors and sinners . . . , for there were many who followed him" (2:15), expressing both Jesus' magnetism and his acceptance of them, while prompting others to question his personal purity (2:16). Along with this expression of his favor, Jesus nowhere criticizes Levi's work or urges him to repay those he overcharged (if any). Second, among the most famous of Gospel stories is Jesus' encounter with a "chief of tax collectors," Zacchaeus (Luke 19:1–10). Of its telling, the postcolonial biblical critic R. S. Sugirtharajah is impressed by

the apolitical nature of this encounter. Jesus did not call upon Zacchaeus to give up his profession nor did he request him to work against the system, the very system which had made him rich. Instead, Jesus believed in a person's, in this case Zacchaeus's, ability to transform things from within, beginning with his own change of heart. Jesus's response to an oppressive structure had more to do with personalizing the issue and appealing directly to individuals to act fairly than with calling for a radical overhaul of the system.[72]

Jesus' response to the question about paying taxes to the emperor may best reveal Jesus' stance toward Roman rule (Mark 12:13–17//Matt 22:15–22//Luke 20:20–26). Jerusalem opponents seek to trap Jesus with a politically explosive question: "Is it lawful to pay taxes to Caesar, or not? Should we pay them, or should we not?" Refusing to pay taxes for religio-political reasons was not new: Judas the Galilean in AD 6 had, according to Josephus, "incited his countrymen to revolt . . . [and shamed them] for consenting to pay tribute to the Romans and tolerating mortal masters after having God for their lord."[73] But, as Bryan points out, other Jews, such as Jeremiah and Ezra, had cooperated with a pagan government, including paying its taxes,[74] and Jesus answers the question affirmatively, with greater intensity than it was put to him. His opponents asked about paying, using the word *didõmi*, which refers to giving in contexts that include even being generous.[75] Jesus establishes that it is Caesar's image on his coin and then answers they should pay the poll- or head-tax, but he uses the word *apodidõmi*, which refers to "payment as 'a contractual or other obligation,' or restoration 'to an original possessor.'"[76] Idiomatically, according to Bryan, Jesus implies "Pay up what you *owe!* Give *back* to the Emperor what is his!" Religious Judeans are under Rome's authority, and, as the rest of Jesus' answer asserts, his questioners are also under God's authority, so they must pay — give back — "to God, what is God's," referring, many believe, to the human persons who bear God's image (Gen 1:26).[77]

After Jesus: Submit to Rome until Submitting Requires Disobeying God

These examples show Jesus' relationship with Rome fit the second option above: namely, that he accepts Roman rule but challenges its ultimacy nonviolently as in his answer that Judeans must render to Caesar what belongs to him but to God what belongs to him.[78] A survey of pertinent texts in the remainder of the New Testament will show that Jesus' first followers followed his stance toward Rome. It never compromises its confession of Jesus alone as Savior and Lord of lords, and it guides believers to live as peaceably and honorably as they can under the empire's authority delegated by God.

Paul: Bryan examines several passages in Paul's letters regarding believers' relations with Rome,[79] but for brevity this chapter considers "the only passage we have that *certainly* expresses a Pauline view of the Roman state," Romans 13:1–7.[80] This passage continues the exhortation begun in Romans 12:1ff, appealing to believers to respond appropriately to the "mercies of God" expressed in the preceding chapters 1–11. Most of chapter 12 explicates being a living sacrifice (v. 1) within the believing community, culminating in a call to love (vv. 9–13); and then it attends to relationships with outsiders, those who persecute and those against whom believers must not usurp God's prerogative in vengeance but instead "overcome evil with good" (v. 21).

Then Paul addresses these Roman believers' relationship to the Roman government: "Let every person be subject to the governing authorities. For there is no authority except from God, and those that exist have been instituted by God" (13:1). Bryan notes Paul's writing Romans "when the new emperor, Nero, was regarded with high hopes . . . made it easier . . . to continue" in v. 2, "Therefore whoever resists the authorities resists what God has appointed, and those who resist will incur judgment." Paul portrays authorities as rewarders of those doing good and just punishers of those doing wrong (13:3–4) and twice names them ministers (*diakonoi*) of God. An extensive survey of *diakonos* shows its basic meaning to be "another's representative, agent, or attendant," thus portraying government authorities as bearing "a sacred appointment."[81] Such submission to them entails paying taxes, which is one of the quartet of debts believers owe to government: taxes, revenue, respect, and honor (13:7). Then what is owed seems directed back to life within the church: "love each other," leading to the quotation from Leviticus 19:18: "You shall love your neighbor as yourself" (13:9); but the owing to government and then the direction not to owe anyone except to love them may pull believers' relationship to government itself into the realm of love of neighbor, such that paying taxes and revenues and giving respect and honor express the same love outside the church that 12:9–21 direct within and beyond the church. Favoring this view is the likelihood Paul's exhortation in v. 3, "to do what is good" (Greek, *to agathon poiein*) in order to receive rulers' approval aligns with both Jeremiah's instruction that exiles "seek the good" of their home-in-exile and the contemporary occurrence Bruce Winter notes of the phrase "to do good" (*to agathon poiein*) in a number of inscriptions praising public benefactors. Not all but some believers with means would be able to do good in ways that would honor themselves, the church, and the gospel. This new way of living seems expressed in the conclusion of this chapter: It is time for believers to awaken to a new day in this new life because the completion of the salvation initiated "by the mercies of God" in Christ is "nearer now than when we first believed," and believers are to walk in light (13:11–14). "The laws of the Empire are to be obeyed and Christians are to seek to be good citizens, *not* because life never changes and God's kingdom is only a dream but precisely *because* the new age is already beginning."[82] Thus this discussion of believers' relationship with Roman authorities aligns with the Old Testament prophetic tradition and Jesus' actions, discussed above. None of it promotes rejection of empire but rather promotes obedience and the doing of good works above and beyond merely keeping the law.

Luke-Acts: Without settling debate about the purposes immanent throughout Luke-Acts,[83] including exactly what message about the Roman Empire it sends, we can show the pattern of positive judgments about imperial officials and their actions, which would surely influence the attitude of its readers. Luke's Infancy Narrative brims with language of divine reversals that might prompt readers to expect the work to stand against empire: "he has scattered the proud in the thoughts of their hearts; he has cast down mighty ones from their thrones" (Luke 1:51, 52). But "God and God's action," not Rome, are the center of Luke's narrative, for which Rome is even unnecessary.[84] Now to ways Luke-Acts portrays its protagonist characters in relation to Rome positively:

- *Portraying Judaism as ancient* elicits Roman approval and accounts for Roman toleration of Judaism.[85] *The journey by Joseph and Mary* (who sang of the downfall of the "mighty ones") to Bethlehem (2:1–5) shows them obeying the Caesar's decree, "*identifying* themselves with the Roman Empire." Moreover, Luke shows how Caesar unknowingly advances *God's* agenda, by bringing Mary, through imperial decree, to the place prophesied in Hebrew scriptures for the birth of the messiah. Bryan notes, properly, Luke thus relativizes Caesar's power before God's.[86]

- As discussed sufficiently in the section above "Jesus: Render to Caesar and to God," *Luke includes three episodes accepting Rome's authority*: Jesus' healing the Roman centurion's servant (7:1–10);[87] Jesus' encountering Zacchaeus, a chief tax collector for Rome (19:1–10; unique to Luke); Jesus' replying wisely to the entrapping question about rendering tribute to Caesar (10:19–26). In none of these does he oppose Rome.

- Beyond those already discussed, *Jesus in Luke bypasses other opportunities to oppose Rome, even violently:* In the second temptation, the devil shows Jesus "all the kingdoms of the world" and said, "To you I will give all this authority and their glory" (4:5–7); when arrested, Jesus opposes violence on his behalf and instead heals the cut-off ear of the high priest's servant (22:50–53); and when before Pilate, Jesus answers him without objecting to Pilate's right to question or to judge him (23:1–3). In only Luke, Pilate declares Jesus innocent yet punishes him and ultimately grants the crowd's demand Jesus be crucified. Luke seems to condemn Pilate not for being Roman but for failing to uphold Roman justice — again, no opposition to Rome.[88]

- Unique to Luke is *Jesus' statement of his revolutionary agenda, 4:18–19.* But it neither expresses nor implies a revolt against Rome or Roman interests. Instead, the revolt it incites is of "all in the synagogue," who witness Jesus' showing himself to be a prophet soon rejected because he pronounces God's favor toward Gentiles — not just observant Jews — as part of the Year of Jubilee ("year of the Lord's favor," v. 19). This fulfillment of Isaiah's prophecy could then include Romans, even agents of its empire — hardly a stance of opposition to it.

- *Acts extends the stance toward Rome Luke begins.* It presents positively several "Roman establishment figures" who support the cause of the gospel: Among these it is, after all, a Roman centurion, Cornelius, who marks the advance of a universal gospel to Gentiles (Acts 10), not the merchant Lydia (16) nor Luke the physician, but a military agent of the empire! In the sovereignty of God, the choosing of Cornelius for this pivotal moment in the spread of the gospel merits reflection in discerning the stance of Luke-Acts toward empire. A third centurion in this two-volume work appears at the crucifixion (Luke 23:44–49). At Jesus' death, only Luke's centurion praises God and says "Certainly this man was innocent!" (v. 47; compare Mark 15:39).

- Finally, in Acts, *Paul's Roman citizenship benefits his mission* and shows him not at all slavishly obedient to Rome but acting as an honorable citizen with rights, which he exercises: he denies he has transgressed Jewish law or against the temple or Caesar (v. 8); and he appeals to be judged not by Caesar's tribunal but by Caesar himself, as only a citizen could (25:8–12). Paul's submission to

Rome (Rom. 13) includes actions proper for a citizen, and he "does not hesitate to put even the Emperor himself on the spot."[89]

1 Peter: This epistle coheres with Romans 13 in its stance toward Rome, expressed in 2:11–17. It identifies believers as "elect exiles" and "sojourners" dispersed throughout the empire (1:1; 2:9) but who are already "a chosen race, a royal priesthood, a holy nation," "God's people." They "have been grieved by various trials" (1:6), and the epistle will soon exhort them to suffer fearlessly "for righteousness' sake" (3:8–4:19). Most commentators think these references to suffering "not to persecution by the state but rather to the more intermittent local harassment" from those who note believers' holy living and resent it.[90] An exhortation to holy living (2:11–12) includes doing good deeds nonbelievers may see (2:12). This urging compares with Jesus' words in Matthew 5:16[91] and with Paul's encouraging doing good, not merely living morally but, in the spirit of seeking the welfare of the city, benefitting the public.[92] First Peter does not make explicit the delegation of all authority from God, as does Romans 13:1, but it offers a hierarchy of value: honor everyone, including the emperor; love the brotherhood; but fear only God (2:17). All these exhortations ride on eschatological expectation woven throughout the letter: references to a "salvation ready to be revealed" (1:5), a future "revelation of Jesus Christ" (1:7, 13), and more.[93] The two, doing good and awaiting salvation future, bind together social service and eschatology: It is because of "a greater kingdom that is coming . . . that they are to be . . . good citizens and respectful subjects of Rome."[94]

The Revelation: We might expect the Revelation to shatter the paradigm sketched so far: from Old Testament prophets through Jesus, Paul, and Luke-Acts to 1 Peter, submission to Rome as conduit of divinely delegated authority, an effort to "seek the welfare of the city" by doing good, and thoughts and actions that relativize human authority beneath God's while not resisting it *per se*. Revelation alone in the New Testament visualizes the "fury of the wrath of God the Almighty" against "Babylon" (19:2, 20; 19:15), acknowledged to refer to Rome. But is it empire against which John rails? Revelation 21:24–26 may, in line with the prophetic tradition traced above, visualize empire positively, with nations and their kings bringing "their glory" into the New Jerusalem. Bryan therefore suggests "The object of John's attack is not even the *Roman* Empire . . . but the *worship* of emperor and empire. Above all, John is concerned with *idolatry,*"[95] and his strong opposition to idolatry, not empire, lies at the heart of the prophetic tradition. Revelation 13–19 "opposes the state *perceived as claiming for itself divine honors* and so stands in line with the prophets."[96] Idolatry leads to many other harms: "injustice, exploitation, and abuse," which shall be punished, but the source is not government but idolatry, government absolutizing itself as ancient Nebuchadnezzar did. Moreover, Bryan ventures, had Paul "perceived imperial rhetoric as John did, he would have judged it as John did."[97] And while John does not urge believers to seek the welfare of the city, he also does not urge them to violence, counseling instead not to fear and to "be faithful until death." God, not people, through Christ will cause "Babylon the Great" to fall (18:2), envisioned cosmically as Michael and his angels defeating the dragons and his angels in heaven (12:7–8). Once evil is defeated, John envisions a godly empire, fulfilling "what all earthly empires — David's or Solomon's, Cyrus's or Caesar's — have at their best dreamed of being . . . because it will know its Lord" (21:22–23).[98]

Conclusion

The New Testament proclaims only Jesus is the Savior of the world and the Lord of all lords. It never questions this confession and presents it as the unique good news with the unique power to save all who believe, Jew or Gentile. This New Testament asserts the supremacy of this gospel over its first-century rivals: over the many Hellenistic mystery religions, over Judaism's Torah-keeping as the means of salvation, and over the idolatry of emperor worship. But its rejection of any pluralism regarding the source and giver of salvation — that is, of any view that Jesus is only one among several saviors or only one lord among many rivals to "all authority on heaven and earth" — is accompanied by what this chapter calls an affirmation of political pluralism: Yes, God in Christ is solely sovereign over all, but he has delegated political authority to human institutions from antiquity and continuing into this time between Christ's first and second comings. As this survey has shown of the prophetic tradition vis-à-vis ancient empires we encounter in both Testaments, God works his redemptive purposes through such structures in this fallen world: the decree of Augustus to bring the mother of the messiah to give birth at Bethlehem; the judgments of Sanhedrin, Pilate, and Herod to crucify the Son of glory as atonement for sin; and the benefits of empire and citizenship that help the apostle to the Gentiles spread the gospel throughout much of the Roman empire. The unified witness of the New Testament is that God's people live the gospel of their Savior and Lord graciously in whatever city or empire they find themselves, living obediently, peaceably, and honorably, as much as possible, seeking the welfare of their domiciles and also opposing nonviolently not government *per se* but only its grave transgression of idolatry. In such living they witness to the grace of God and invite others by word and deed likewise to become citizens of the coming kingdom that Christ's return shall consummate.[99]

Notes

1. "We are being told today that the church is facing a radically new situation that it has not faced before, and that it consequently needs a new formulation of the gospel . . . the idea that we are now living in a 'global village' — a multiethnic, multicultural, multifaith world in which it seems simply untenable and perhaps even immoral to believe in one absolute truth against which everything else is to be measured and judged." James R. Edwards, *Is Jesus the Only Savior?* (Grand Rapids, MI: Eerdmans, 2005) 116, chapter seven, "Can the Gospel Compete in a Pluralistic World?"; hereafter Edwards, *Is Jesus*. Much of this study rests on Edwards' chapter.

2. "[T]he hidden assumption . . . is that the gospel arose in the insular world of Judaism in an earlier age of intellectual naiveté, and what was suitable in a simpler age is no longer so in a complex, pluralistic age such as ours. . . . But . . . . this is to assume that the complexity and interdependence of the modern world are unique in history . . . [and that the gospel arose] in a simpler and more naïve world than ours." Edwards, *Is Jesus?* 116, who denies the gospel arose in such a "mythically simple" age.

3. Robert H. Gundry, *A Survey of the New Testament*, 5th ed. (Grand Rapids, MI: Zondervan, 2012), 70.

4. See Jack Finegan, *Myth and Mystery: An Introduction to the Pagan Religions of the Biblical World* (Grand Rapids: Baker Books, 1989), ch. 5, "Greek Religion," and 6, "Roman Religion," 155–215.

5. Gundry, *A Survey*, 70.

6. Edwards, *Is Jesus*, 134.

7. Luther H. Martin, "Aspects of 'Religious Experience' among the Hellenistic Mystery Religions," *Religion & Theology* 12:3–4 (2005) 351. Initiation rites into the cult of Eleusis began with fasting and carried on through the darkness of night, culminating with, "according to Plutarch, . . . an abrupt burst of brilliant light that accompanied the sudden emergence of the hierophant [priest] from the darkness and that further astonished the disorientated initiates (Plu. *Mor.* 8IE; also Hipp. *Haer.* 5.8.40 = ANF 5.3). When the initiates emerged from their

initiatory ordeals of darkness into revelatory light, Themistius concludes, they were 'received into pure regions and meadows, with voices and dances and the majesty of holy sounds and shapes' (Them, in Stob[aeus]. 4)."

8. I do not think the mysteries are significantly comparable with earliest Christianity. Edwards summarizes key differences in *Is Jesus*, 135–139. But attending to religious experience among the mysteries invites consideration of such experience among the earliest Christians and then comparison, more likely contrast, between the two. Some hints at considering such experience among early Christians emerge in the brief discussion of possible New Testament responses to the mysteries.

9. Finegan, *Myth and Mystery*, ch. 7, "Gnostic Religion," 217–258.

10. "Given the date of the available written sources concerning the Gnostic religion (second century AD and later), and the fact that there are many Christian element, it seems probable that the Gnostic movement originated at about the same time as Christianity." But there are reasons to believe a pre-Christian Gnosticism existed, "presumably originating in a syncretistic Hellenistic environment of on the fringes of Judaism," Finegan, *Myth and Mystery*, 219, citing Kurt Rudolph, *The Nature and History of Gnosticism* (San Francisco: Harper & Row, 1983), 52, 276ff.

11. Gundry, *A Survey*, 72–73.

12. Gundry, *A Survey*, 71–72.

13. Gundry, *A Survey*, 73.

14. Edwards, *Is Jesus*, 109.

15. *The Gospel in a Pluralist Society* (Grand Rapids: Eerdmans, 1992), 147, quoted by Edwards, *Is Jesus* 118.

16. "The mystery religions did not appear suddenly in the Mediterranean world during the Hellenistic period, though the period of their greatest popularity appears to have been the first through the third centuries AD religions and the New Testament.

17. Bruce M. Metzger, *Historical and Literary Studies: Pagan, Jewish, and Christian* (Grand Rapids: Eerdmans, 1968), 12, cited by Edwards, *Is Jesus*, 135, note 41.

18. Edwards, *Is Jesus*, 135; on 136, his note 42 cites "Origen's insistence to the pagan critic Celsus that in Jesus God appeared in a true human being, not in a mythological type ([c. AD 248] *Against Celsus* 3.23–25)."

19. Edwards, *Is Jesus*, 137.

20. Edwards, *Is Jesus*, 138.

21. Christopher Bryan identifies these as the core of Judaism before AD 70, uniting its diverse streams: "belief in the one God, acceptance of Torah (the Law), and the Temple": *Render to Caesar: Jesus, the Early Church, and the Roman Superpower* (Oxford; New York: Oxford University Press, 2005), 26, citing Seth Schwartz, *Imperialism and Jewish Society: 200 BCE to 640 CE.* (Princeton and Oxford: Princeton University Press, 2001), 49–74.

22. Edwards, *Is Jesus*, 119.

23. *Babylonian Talmud, Tractate Sanhedrin*, 99a.

24. *Babylonian Talmud, Tractate Pesahim*, 54a.

25. *Babylonian Talmud: Tractate Sotah*, 20a.

26. *Babylonian Talmud: Tractate Shabbath, 30a.*

27. Edwards, *Is Jesus*, 120.

28. *God in the Dock* (Grand Rapids: Eerdmans, 2014), 100–101. Lay Bible student Kyle Barton traces the trilemma through Christian history, beginning with verses in the Gospel of John, at his blog "Conversant Faith," in his post of May 4, 2012, "The History of the Liar, Lunatic, Lord Trilemma," accessed 7 September 2019 at https://conversantfaith.com/2012/05/04/the-history-of-liar-lunatic-lord-trilemma/#ref2.

29. Here is recent scholarship refuting the claim the evangelists fictionalize Jesus by showing instead that the Gospels rest on eyewitness testimony: Craig Keener, *Christobiography: Memory, History, and the Reliability of the Gospels* (Grand Rapids: Eerdmans, 2019); Richard Bauckham, *Jesus and the Eyewitnesses: The Gospels as Eyewitness Testimony*, 2nd ed. (Grand Rapids: Eerdmans, 2017); idem., *Jesus: A Very Short Introduction* (New York, Oxford, UK: Oxford University Press, 2011); Paul Rhodes Eddy and Gregory A. Boyd, *The Jesus Legend: A Case for the Historical Reliability of the Synoptic Jesus Tradition* (Grand Rapids: Eerdmans, 2009).

30. This criterion has led to all kinds of religious rigor, aiming to exceed the scrupulousness and self-denial of these named, by more rigorous religious behaviors, such as long times of prayer and fasting and even lust-fighting self-castration as efforts to surpass their righteousness and measure up to God's. The context shows, however, that the "surpassing righteousness" is that of *agape* love, or what Dallas Willard glosses as "being a really good person" who has "true inner goodness," in his *The Divine Conspiracy: Rediscovering Our Hidden Life in God* (San Francisco: HarperSanFrancisco, 1998), 143. This righteous goodness the heavenly Father expresses by shining the sun and showering rain on both the just and the unjust; and Jesus directs his followers to express that goodness by telling them to love not only neighbors but also enemies (Matt 5:43–48). This love, this generous kindness, expresses the "surpassing righteousness" required of citizens of the kingdom of the heavens more than white-knuckled religious rigor. See "The Rightness of the Kingdom Heart: Beyond the Goodness of Scribes and Pharisees," chapter 5 in Willard, *The Divine Conspiracy*, 129–185.

31. From among many New Testament studies showing this point, see chapter 2, "Jesus: The Prophet Mighty in Word and Deed (Luke 1–24)" in Roger Stronstad, *The Prophethood of All Believers: A Study in Luke's Charismatic Theology* (Cleveland, TN: Centre for Pentecostal Theology Press, 2010). This chapter shows Jesus to be like but greater than Moses (the comparison Stronstad came to understand is most important after writing the book; see his "Preface to the CPT Press Edition"), David (and the category of Royal Prophet), Elijah and Elisha, Isaiah, and various rejected prophets.

32. For a profound analysis of how something truly good, such as Torah, can become idolatrous, see "Destroying the Power of an Idolatrous System of Convictions" in Daniel Patte, *Paul's Faith and the Power of the Gospel: A Structural Introduction to the Pauline Letters* (Philadelphia: Fortress Press, 1983), 281–290. I do not agree, however, with Patte's claim that the intervention of God in Christ is not final, although he does identify God's revelation at the Parousia (the Second Coming) as final, so my quibble may be semantic.

33. Edwards, *Is Jesus*, 122.

34. Edwards, *Is Jesus*, 122, citing Josephus, *Wars of the Jews* 2.143.

35. Edwards, *Is Jesus*, 123, citing H. L. Strack and P. Billerbeck, *Kommentar zum Neuen Testament aus Talmud und Midrasch*, 6 vols. (Munich, 1922–1961), 293–333; Gerhard Kittle and Gerhard Friedrich, eds., Geoffrey W. Bromily trans., *Theological Dictionary of the New Testament* (Grand Rapids: Eerdmans, 1964) *aposynagogos*; Schurer, *History of the Jewish People*; K. L. Carroll, "The Fourth Gospel and the Exclusion of Christians from the Synagogues," *Bulletin of John Rylands Library* 40 (1957/58), 19–32.

36. Edwards, *Is Jesus*, 123, citing Justin, *Dialogue with Trypho* 16; Epiphanius, *Panarion* 29.9.

37. Edwards, *Is Jesus*, 123, citing Strack and Billerbeck, *Kommentar zum Neuen Testament*, 3.230.

38. See Tim Keller, "Our Identity: Alternative to Later Modernity's Story (11/11/2015)," https://youtu.be/Ehw87PqTwKw.

39. Edwards, *Is Jesus*, 121; note 10 adds these pertinent references: Rom 4:5; 9:30–10:4; Gal 3:2; 3:24; Eph 2:8–9; Phil 3:9.

40. This concise statement summarizes what is expressed and implied pertinent to this summary in texts such as these: Rom 14–15; Gal 3–5; Col 2.

41. Ben Witherington, *The Acts of the Apostles: A Socio-Rhetorical Commentary* (Grand Rapids: Eerdmans, 1998), 542, with his note 294: "Josephus himself quotes this very relevant edict in *Ant.* 19, here at 283."

42. Witherington, *The Acts*, 544, lists Luke 3:13; 5:30; 15:10; 22:3, 14; 24:14; 26:6; 28:17. A more important reason is theological: Luke-Acts shows that Jesus himself and the increasingly Gentile movement following him are not apostates and frauds but that they instead fulfill ancient promises and covenants God made with Israel's fathers.

43. Edwards, *Is Jesus*, 124, citing Virgil's *Fourth Eclogue*.

44. Edwards, *Is Jesus*, 124. Note Luke 22:25: "The kings of the Gentiles exercise lordship over them, and those in authority over them are called benefactors."

45. Edwards, *Is Jesus*, 125.

46. Edwards, *Is Jesus*, 126, citing, for Boeotia, A. Deissmann, *Light from the Ancient East*, L. R. M. Strachan trans., (Grand Rapids: Baker Book House, 1978), 354; and for the king, Dio Cassius, *Roman History* 63.14. Edwards here discusses the possibility that reference in Rev 13:8 to the number of the beast (666) corresponds numerically to "the Greek spelling of his name *Neron Kaisar*

(when transliterated into Hebrew script)." If the text refers to Nero, it is evidence he demanded worship in the AD 60s.

47. Edwards, *Is Jesus*, 126, 127.

48. *Christuskult und Kaiserkult* (Tubingen: Mohr/Siebeck, 1919), 17–18, Edwards' translation; *Is Jesus*, 128.

49. Edwards, *Is Jesus*, 127; regarding Pliny, citing H. C. Kee, *The New Testament in Context: Sources and Documents* (Englewood Cliffs: Prentice-Hall, 1984), 44–45; regarding Polycarp, citing *Martyrdom of Polycarp*, 8:2.

50. Edwards discusses these in *Is Jesus*, 128–132.

51. Edwards, *Is Jesus*, 129.

52. Other scholars, however, distinguish between Jesus' rejection of this self-serving use of this honorific title and the prophetic urging that God-followers "seek the welfare of the city" in which they find themselves. Such benefactions need not serve oneself but may please God as they seek to express his goodness. See Christopher Bryan, *Render to Caesar*, 100–101, for whom Jesus' critique here contains nothing "specifically anti-*Roman*"; also Bruce W. Winter, *Seek the Welfare of the City: Christians as Benefactors and Citizens* (Grand Rapids: Eerdmans; Carlisle, Cumbria: Paternoster Press, 1994).

53. Revelation thus condemns the idolatry of the emperor cult, but it is not at all clear it condemns empire *per se*. The next section discusses this important distinction.

54. Bryan, *Render*, 13.

55. Bryan, *Render*, 14, quoting Eichrodt, *Theology of the Old Testament*, vol. 3, John Baker trans. (London: SCM/Philadelphia: Westminster, 1967), 248.

56. Bryan, *Render*, 24; emphasis his.

57. Omitted for brevity in this chapter: *Render*, 26–37.

58. Bryan, *Render*, 34.

59. Bryan, *Render*, 41–42.

60. This topic merits more discussion than this chapter can afford. Those interested will find the sources below representing the anti-empire interpretations of Jesus and the New Testament, along with articles expressing various views, such as D. Downs, "Economics," W. J. Heard and K. Yamazaki-Ransom, "Revolutionary Movements"; and P. Oakes, "Rome," in Joel B. Green et al. (eds.), *Dictionary of Jesus and the Gospels*, 2nd ed. (Downers Grove, IL: InterVarsity Press, 2012).

61. John Howard Yoder, *The Politics of Jesus: Behold the Man! Our Victorious Lamb*, 2nd ed. (Grand Rapids: Eerdmans; Carlisle: Paternoster, 1994), 21–59.

62. Richard A. Horsley, *Jesus and Empire: The Kingdom of God and New World Disorder* (Minneapolis: Fortress Press, 2003) and *Jesus and the Spiral of Violence: Popular Jewish Resistance in Roman Palestine* (Minneapolis: Fortress Press, 1993).

63. John Dominic Crossan and Jonathan L. Reed, *In Search of Paul: How Jesus' Apostle Opposed Rome's Empire with God's Kingdom* (New York: HarperSanFrancisco, 2004).

64. Brian Walsh and Sylvia C. Keesmat, *Colossians Remixed: Subverting the Empire* (Downers Grove, IL: InterVarsity Press, 2004).

65. Horsley, *Jesus and Empire*, 6, cited in Bryan, *Render*, 6.

66. Horsley, *Jesus and Empire*, 35, cited in Bryan, *Render*, 6.

67. Horsley, *Jesus and Empire*, 13, cited in Bryan, *Render*, 6.

68. Bryan, *Render*, 41.

69. Horsley, *Jesus and Empire*, 134; similarly Crossan and Reed, *In Search of Paul*, 10–11; cited by Bryan, *Render*, 83

70. Horsley, *Jesus and Empire*, 46.

71. Also, Luke 5:27; he is called "Matthew" in Matt 9:9.

72. R. S. Sugirtharajah, *Postcolonial Criticism and Biblical Interpretation* (Oxford: Oxford University Press, 2002), 88, cited by Bryan, *Render*, 42–43.

73. Josephus, *Wars of the Jews* 2.118.

74. Bryan, *Render*, 43.

75. Bryan, *Render*, 45.

76. Bryan, *Render*, 45, citing the standard Greek lexicon, abbreviated *BDAG*, and four commentaries in agreement.

77. Bryan, *Render*, 46.

78. Bryan studies the passion narratives of the Gospels in the chapter "Jesus and Empire: The Crucified" and concludes "at no point is Jesus remembered [in the Gospels] as contesting the jurisdiction or authority of *either* of the tribunals that he faces" nor the Sanhedrin's authority over him; and he "acknowledges that Pilate's authority stands within God's providence . . . ([John] 19:11) Rome is under God's judgment, but that is precisely because Rome does not rule without God's fiat." *Render*, 62–63.

79. Bryan, *Render*, for the imperial significance of Jesus' final *parousia* (1 Cor 15:23; 1 Thess 2:19; 3:13, 82–83; for Phil 3:20–4:1, 83–84; for Phil 2:5–11, 85–88; for Phil 3:18–19, 88; for Phil 1:27–30, 89–90. Of Philippians, Bryan concludes "there is no evidence that Paul — or the Philippian Christians — objected to the institution of the Roman state in and of itself or desired to replace it by some other human political institution," 90.

80. Bryan, *Render*, 93.

81. Bryan, *Render*, 79, citing the survey by John N. Collins, *Diakonia: Interpreting the Ancient Sources* (New York: Oxford University Press, 1990), 335.

82. Bryan, *Render*, 81.

83. Accepting this definition of the process of interpreting a text, by literary critic Walter A. Davis: "The task of interpretation is to apprehend the purposive principle immanent in the structure of a literary work which determines the mutual interfunctioning of its component parts. . . . Function, structure, and purpose, in that order, become the primary categories of interpretation: for parts function only by serving a purpose and structure is the process through which purpose is actualized. . . . The critic . . . takes the knowledge of backgrounds and conventions not as a critical conclusion but as a starting point. The task

of interpretation is to discover, through internal analysis, the particular purpose, always potentially new, to which a writer puts the materials, conventions, and generic expectations he derives from his sources." Walter A. Davis, *The Act of Interpretation: A Critique of Literary Reason* (Chicago: University of Chicago Press, 1978), 2, cited in Mark E. Roberts, "Weak Enough to Lead: Paul's Response to Criticism and Rivals in 2 Corinthians 10–13: A Rhetorical Reading" (unpublished dissertation, Vanderbilt University, Nashville, TN, 2003, available through ProQuest Dissertations & Theses Global). Although Davis intends his definition for belletristic works, I find it applicable to more utilitarian, or didactic, works as well, and Luke-Acts expresses a Hellenistic historiography that combines the two: it aims not only to inform and convince but also to please.

84. Bryan, *Render*, 97, also citing commentary by New Testament scholars C. K. Barrett, Luke Timothy Johnson, and Jacob Jervell.

85. Tacitus, *Histories* 5.4–5; Origen, *Against Celsus* 5.25, cited by Bryan, *Render*, 98.

86. Bryan, *Render*, 98–99.

87. Only Luke has Jewish elders praising this imperial representative while pleading with Jesus to help: "He is worthy to have you do this for him, for he loves our nation, and he is the one who built our synagogue," v. 4.

88. So Bryan, *Render*, 101.

89. Bryan, *Render*, 103.

90. Bryan, *Render*, 105, citing commentary by Paul Achtemeier and Donald Senior.

91. "That they may see your good works and glorify your Father who is in heaven"

92. See discussion of *to agathon poiein*, "to do good," in the section above, "(a) Paul."

93. Additionally, their identity as "sojourners and exiles" awaiting "the day of visitation" (2:11, 12); "the end of all things is at hand" (4:7); Christ's glory yet to be revealed (4:13; 5:1); the "chief Shepherd" to appear; the "mighty hand of God . . . at the proper time" to "exalt you"; and "the God of all grace . . . will himself restore, confirm, strengthen, and establish you" (5:4, 6, 10).

94. Bryan, *Render*, 107.

95. Bryan, *Render*, 107.

96. Bryan, *Render*, 109.

97. Bryan, *Render*, 107.

98. Bryan, *Render*, 110.

99. Regrettably, this chapter cannot trace the path from believers' relationship to the state the New Testament expresses to believers' vocation in today's largely Western democracies, in which national constitutions encourage citizens to participate in governance in ways the New Testament does not contemplate. Readers wishing to explore this history with theological reflection may benefit from popular sources, such as these: D. James Kennedy and Jerry Newcombe, *What If Jesus Had Never Been Born?* (Nashville, TN: Nelson, 1994); Jonathon

Hill, *What Has Christianity Ever Done for Us? How It Shaped the Modern World* (Downers Grove, IL: InterVarsity Press, 2005); Francis Beckwith, *Politics for Christians: Statecraft as Soulcraft* (Downers Grove, IL: InterVarsity Press, 2010); Jeremiah J. Johnston, *Unimaginable: What Our World Would Be Like without Christianity* (Minneapolis, MN: Bethany House, 2017); and, more focused on America, Stephen Webb, *American Providence: A Nation with a Mission* (New York: Continuum, 2004), and *Providence: A Journal of Christianity and American Foreign Policy* (ISSN 24713511: www.ProvidenceMag.com). Os Guinness invokes the prophetic tradition discussed earlier when he argues that the Exodus is "the master story of Western freedom and the ultimate regime change in history" and lists in agreement with his claim modern thinkers Daniel Elazar, Michael Walzer, and Rabbi Jonathan Sacks, as well as historical figures such as the Florentine monk Savonarola, Reformers John Calvin, Zwingli, John Knox, Oliver Cromwell, and American figures William Bradford, John Winthrop, Benjamin Franklin, Thomas Jefferson, and Martin Luther King, Jr.: *Last Call for Liberty: How America's Genius for Freedom Has Become Its Greatest Threat* (Downers Grove, IL : IVP Books, 2018), 22.

3.

A New Antinomianism: Universal Salvation and All-Inclusive Grace in Contemporary Charismatic Teaching

Michael McClymond

Abstract

Universalism — or the doctrine of universal salvation — has been a hot topic among Christian writers and readers since the start of the new millennium. While certain early church writers were universalists, mainstream Christian churches (Catholic, Orthodox, and Protestant) rejected their views as unorthodox throughout the medieval and modern era. The present essay surveys the upsurge in advocacy for universalism among evangelical Protestants, and focuses specifically on charismatic authors such as John Crowder, Benjamin Dunn, Francois Du Toit, and Andre Rabe, who combine universalist theology with radical grace or hyper-grace teachings. Generally speaking, these authors are antinomians who hold that God calls Christians simply to believe in Christ, and not to conform to moral or behavioral standards. There is no call to imitate Christ, nor to obey biblical precepts. An analysis of these authors shows two trends. The first is a "Barthian" tendency to affirm that all human beings — whether believers or not — are included in the salvific work of Christ. This view weakens the moral claims of scripture and supports universal salvation. The second is an "esoteric" doctrine that all human beings contain a spark of divinity within them, and perhaps preexisted with God before this earthly life — an idea that also leads to antinominian and universalist consequences. Like other Christians, Spirit-empowered believers are currently faced with a deluge of antinomian and universalist teachings, which all seem to deny that sin carries serious consequences — and, indeed, consequences so serious that they required that Jesus shed his blood for us on the cross. A recovery of the biblical theology of the cross, and a renewed focus on Christ's instruction in discipleship, would thus seem to be a theological imperative for Spirit-empowered Christians today.

Key words: charismatic, universalism, Antinomianism, Karl Barth, grace, law of God, cross of Christ.

Introduction

> We are awakening to our True Selves. The false self — under a false fatherhood of the adversary — has no substance.... We are awaking to our origin — breathed from His very substance, re-created and born anew in Him — the Lamb of God.... He came to awaken humanity to the truth — that we are a divine race.... You are not bound by times and seasons. Your destiny does not hinge on your natural abilities. You are eternal, infinite, immortally woven into His divinity.... Yes, the cosmos has been permanently rewired in the incarnation, death, and resurrection of Jesus Christ. All things have been forever united in the Son of God.... God included you and absorbed the entire created order into Himself.
>
> — John Crowder[1]

Universalism has been a hot topic among Christian writers and readers since the start of the new millennium. The most famous of the recent books might be Rob Bell's *Love Wins: A Book about Heaven, Hell, and the Fate of Every Person Who Ever Lived* (2011). Bell's book became a *New York Times* bestseller and provoked a *Time* magazine cover story during Holy Week that was emblazoned with the question: "What If There's No Hell?"[2] But Bell's book was not alone. Over the last twenty years, a large number of popular books — and a handful of academic titles — have addressed the question of universal salvation. Taking a favorable view of universalism have been: Thomas Talbott, *The Inescapable Love of God* (1999); Randolph Klassen, *What Does the Bible Really Say about Hell?* (2001); Philip Gulley and James Mulholland, *If Grace Is True: Why God Will Save Every Person* (2003); Bob Evely, *At the End of the Ages...The Abolition of Hell* (2003); Kalen Fristad, *Destined for Salvation* (2003); Ken Vincent, *The Golden Thread: God's Promise of Universal Salvation* (2005); Gregory MacDonald [Robin Parry], *The Evangelical Universalist* (2006; 2nd ed., 2012); Carlton Pearson, *The Gospel of Inclusion* (2006); Gerry Beauchemin, *Hope beyond Hell* (2007); Boyd Purcell, *Spiritual Terrorism: Spiritual Abuse from the Womb to the Tomb* (2008); Eric Stetson, *Christian Universalism: God's Good News for All People* (2008); Bradley Jersak, *Her Gates Will Never Be Shut: Hell, Hope, and the New Jerusalem* (2009); Doug Frank, *A Gentler God* (2010); Sharon Baker, *Razing Hell* (2010); and Forrest Church, *The Cathedral of the World: A Universalist Theology* (2010).

During the new millennium's second decade, a plethora of pro-universalist titles appeared, including: Ted Grimsrud and Michael

Hardin, *Compassionate Eschatology* (2011); Charles Gillihan, *Hell No!* (2011); Julie Ferwerda, *Raising Hell: Christianity's Most Controversial Doctrine Put under Fire* (2011); C. Baxter Kruger, *The Shack Revisited* (2012); Heath Bradley, *Flames of Love: Hell and Universal Salvation* (2012); V. Donald Emmel, *Eliminating Satan and Hell: Affirming a Compassionate Creator-God* (2013); Ilaria Ramelli, *The Christian Doctrine of Apokatastasis* (2013); John Kronen and Eric Reitan, *God's Final Victory: A Comparative Philosophical Case For Universalism* (2013); Dennis Jensen, *Flirting with Universalism: Resolving the Problem of an Eternal Hell* (2014); Caleb A. Miller, *The Divine Reversal: Recovering the Vision of Jesus Christ as the Last Adam* (2014); Jean Wyatt, *Judge Is the Savior: Towards a Universalist Understanding of Salvation* (2015); *Christ Triumphant: Universalism Asserted as the Hope of the Gospel on the Authority of Reason, the Fathers, and Holy Scripture* (2015); Robert Wild and Robin Parry, *A Catholic Reading Guide to Universalism* (2015); David Burnfield, *Patristic Universalism: An Alternative to the Traditional View of Divine Judgment* (2016); Ross Marshall, *God's Testimony of All* (2016); Steven Propp, *The Gift of God Is Eternal Life* (2016); David Congdon, *The God Who Saves* (2016); George Hurd, *The Universal Solution* (2017); George Sarris, *Heaven's Doors: Wider Than You Ever Believed* (2017); John Shelby Spong, *Unbelievable* (2018); Ilaria Ramelli and Robin Parry, *A Larger Hope?*, 2 vols. (2019); J. D. Myers, *What is Hell?* (2019); George Hurd, *The Ways of God* (2019); George Hurd, *A Defense of Biblical Universalism* (2019); Peter Hiett, *All Things New: What Does the Bible Really Say About Hell?* (2019); Tim Hodge, *The Gospel of the Restoration of All Things* (2019); Richard Rohr, *The Universal Christ* (2019); and David Bentley Hart, *That All Shall Be Saved* (2019).[3] Universalist books continue to pour off the press at an unprecedented speed.

Though this listing of recent books is no means exhaustive, the range of titles suggests a surge of interest among scholars and laypersons alike. The pace at which new titles are appearing seems to be increasing.[4] In response to the literature just cited, a number of authors have suggested that the current support for universalism, in Christian terms, is biblically and theologically mistaken. Appearing some fifteen years ago was Christopher Morgan and Robert Peterson's edited volume *Hell under Fire* (2004). More recent works that take issue with universalism include Mark Galli, *God Wins* (2011); Brian Jones, *Hell Is Real (But I Hate to Admit It)* (2011); Francis Chan and Preston Sprinkle, *Erasing Hell* (2011); Michael Wittmer, *Christ Alone* (2011); Larry Dixon, *"Farewell,*

Rob Bell" (2011); Ron Sears, *Speaking the Truth in Love — Wins* (2017); Kevin Carmody, *Will Everyone Be Saved?* (2018); and James B. De Young, *Exposing Universalism: A Comprehensive Guide* (2018). Laurence Malcolm Blanchard's *Will All Be Saved? An Assessment of Universalism in Western Theology* (2015) is one of the few theological surveys that takes a critical stance toward universalism.

There are many schools of fish swimming in the universalist pond. A shared belief in universal salvation does not imply any wider agreement on doctrine. As this chapter demonstrates, universalists themselves are in sharp disagreement on God, the Trinity, Christ, human nature, the nature of salvation, and eschatology. The self-described "evangelical universalist," Robin Parry, emphasizes his own Christian orthodoxy, highlights his points of agreement with evangelical Protestantism, and seeks to show that the entire Bible can be interpreted in a universalist way. Yet Parry is an outlier, and most contemporary universalists engage with the Bible in a more limited way than he does.

Universalism in nineteenth-century America appeared in multiple and incompatible forms. Something comparable seems to be happening in the new millennium. An unresolved issue leftover from the nineteenth century was the dispute between restorationist universalists, who believed in postmortem suffering for sins, and the ultra-universalists, who denied that any such suffering was conceivable. Charismatic teacher John Crowder has repudiated the idea of postmortem purgation or a temporary hell as inconsistent with divine grace: "A god who sovereignly burns someone for a thousand years in a pit of demonic, hellish, molestation is only slightly better than one who does it forever....The main problem with this reasoning is that hell becomes viewed as a *purgatory*. A temporary torture chamber to clean you up. Hell doesn't clean you up. Jesus did."[5] In contrast to this, Robin Parry has argued that, "it is legitimate to understand the biblical teaching about hell as compatible with an awful *but temporary* fate from which all can, and ultimately will be saved."[6] Parry mistakenly asserted that his own idea of a temporary hell was, in fact, the *only* Christian universalist teaching before the twentieth century.[7] In the twenty-first century, as in the nineteenth century, the purgationist version of universalism has its advocates, as does the "ultra" version. Clearly, both views cannot be true. On the basis of past experience, it seems unlikely that anyone form of Christian universalism will become so dominant as to displace the others. So a disparity of universalist theologies is likely to remain with us.

Character of the New Millennium Universalist Literature

Popular Christian universalist authors in the new millennium generally come from Evangelical or Pentecostal-charismatic backgrounds. Many of these authors acknowledge that their new universalist faith has taken them beyond the bounds of their earlier faith tradition. Often there is a personal aspect or animus in their writing. For many of these authors, the embrace of universalist theology is a rebellion against fundamentalist religion and an act of personal liberation. In *Spiritual Terrorism*, Boyd C. Purcell writes of the "mixed messages of God's love and justice" during his youth.[8] Thomas Talbott, in *The Inescapable Love of God*, begins by describing his "sheltered childhood" and attendance at a "conservative Christian high school" at which "a good Christian was identified as someone who does not smoke, drink, dance (roller skating was 'iffy'), play cards, or attend Hollywood movies."[9] Carlton Pearson grew up as "a Bible-toting, pew-jumping, devil-thumping Pentecostal" and says that prior to his early twenties "the only world [he] ever really knew...was the small, sequestered world of the Pentecostal denomination [i.e., Church of God in Christ] in which [his] family has been immersed for four generations." He had a sense of being set apart: "We were proud of being the true citizens of the kingdom of God."[10]

Doug Frank's *A Gentler God* is a well-written account of the author's experience within the Protestant evangelical (or fundamentalist) subculture, and the author's reaction against what he now takes to be the narrow, intolerant, judgmental, and fear-inducing character of that subculture. Frank's early life experiences are comparable to those of Purcell, Talbott, and Pearson, noted above. Frank mentions many of the same things: a sheltered childhood, a church background characterized by theological rigidity, a sense of being set apart from others, and encounters with non-Christian outsiders only through evangelism. Frank says: "I grew up in a pastor's home, had a 'born-again' experience in my childhood, spent most of my discretionary time as a teenager in Christian youth programs, graduated from a well-known evangelical college, and, after a brief time-out in a university graduate school, have spent my life as a history professor in evangelical colleges." As an adult, when Frank drove by a road sign that said simply "Trust Jesus," he mentally added the words "Or Else!"[11] For him, such Christian language connoted fear and compulsion — marks of an ex-fundamentalist with a conflicted attitude toward religion, as his lengthy book makes clear. The pattern disclosed in these books suggests that the later turn toward universalism had something to do with the sheltered or even suffocating religious culture that many of the authors experienced in their youth.

One might compare Doug Frank's account with the words of Sharon Baker, a professor of theology who is both a universalist and a critic of traditional atonement theology. At the opening of her book *Executing God* (2013), she writes: "Once upon a time I was a fundamentalist, Southern Baptist and I had God all figured out. I knew it all and delighted in telling people all about God. Men and women flocked to my Bible study classes. They sold cassette tapes in the church narthex, and people bought them....I knew with absolute certainty how God acted and why." The phrase "absolute certainty" bespeaks the rational confidence — or overconfidence — characteristic of fundamentalist Protestantism. Baker goes on to note her faith crisis: "A couple of things happened....Two of my children became very sick with an incurable liver disease, and I went to seminary. All of a sudden I didn't know everything about God anymore." She comments, "I successfully rebuilt my belief system into something new and more forgiving," but "my absolute certainty never returned" and "doubt replaced certainty."[12]

The root-and-branch reevaluation of Christianity that we find among contemporary universalists may also have something to do with the critical voices to which each author is responding. Talbott studied under a college philosophy professor whose argument against an all-powerful and all-loving God triggered a youthful faith crisis. In developing his own arguments, Talbott quotes approvingly from the nineteenth-century skeptic John Stuart Mill and the twentieth-century atheist Bertrand Russell.[13] Universalist author Julie Ferwerda agrees with Bible critic Bart Ehrman that the God of traditional Christianity is a "divine Nazi."[14] Sharon Baker in *Executing God* takes her point of departure from authors who reject the God of the Old Testament and the notion of substitutionary atonement.[15] Generally speaking, today's proponents of universalism pay much attention to the "cultured despisers of religion" and so seek to mediate between traditional faith and its modern critics.[16]

A scrutiny of recent universalist literature shows that there is more at stake in the current intra-evangelical debates than the final scope of salvation, important as that may be. Under the surface, just about everything is up for discussion — for example, what God's character is, how to interpret the Bible, whether the Old Testament is authoritative, what Jesus's death achieved, whether Christians are bound by doctrinal standards and whether the doctrine of hell is proper Christian teaching or just a fear tactic used to scare people into obeying church leaders. Indeed, some of the universalist literature reads more like earlier deistic or skeptical literature than like traditional evangelical literature. Many universalist authors repudiate the notion that fear plays an appropriate role in Christian experience. Typically they reject the God of the Old Testament and are ready to rethink or reject classic evangelical teachings on substitutionary atonement. Toward institutional Christianity in general, some universalist authors have a love-hate attitude or a stance of one-foot-in-one-foot-out.

The remainder of this essay will focus on just one slice of the Evangelical-Pentecostal-charismatic universalism emerging since the start of the new millennium, viz., the charismatic, antinomian universalism of John Crowder and some other authors linked to Crowder.

Charismatic Preachers of Grace, I — Benjamin Dunn

A development of the last decade is the tilt toward universalism among certain Pentecostal-charismatic preachers and teachers. These speakers and authors include John Crowder, Benjamin Dunn, Francois du Toit, and Andre Rabe.[17] The justification for treating these authors as a group derives not only from their parallel teachings but also from their intertwining ministries. Often they have partnered with one another in ministry around the world, and they promote one another's work.[18] While there are variations in their teachings, they all reflect what is popularly called "the grace message." Nevertheless, I attempt to distinguish these figures from one another in what follows. Despite resemblances, one cannot presume that the teachings of one author are found in all the others.[19] The question of "grace" versus "hyper-grace" or "cheap grace" has been a matter of dispute throughout Protestant history. Historic debates invoked the term "antinomianism," understood as the teaching that Christians have no moral obligations to fulfill because faith alone is necessary for salvation. Some of Kruger's and Crowder's teachings — for example, that human beings were already accepted or saved by God before anyone fell into sin — are reminiscent of arguments presented in English Protestantism during the seventeenth century.[20]

The "grace message" should be seen in light of recent developments in the independent charismatic churches. Since the 1990s, the global charismatic movement has often emphasized "dominionism" — an aggressive spiritual and cultural movement to advance Christian social influence, fueled by intense prayer and fasting, bold strategies of evangelism, and practices of spiritual warfare against evil spirits.[21] Rejecting the eschatological pessimism of premillennialism and the gloomy presumption that things must get worse before Jesus returns again, many charismatics embraced postmillennialism and the vision of a restored or "glorious church."[22] Some insist that Christ's earthly reign will be exercised through an elite corps of disciples, led by super-apostles whose authority will exceed that of the first-century apostles.[23] Others, like C. Peter Wagner, have offered less grandiose visions for the future and yet insist that the church must seek to influence all "seven mountains" of human life — namely, business, government, media, arts and entertainment, education, the family, and religion.[24] The "grace message" may be seen as a backlash against this activist mentality in favor of a more quietistic stance. The younger generation is less ready to do battle against the devil and more inclined to rest in the full enjoyment of divine grace.

The stress on grace is associated with joy, happiness, and celebration rather than a lugubrious stress on sin, repentance, and the evils of modern society. Benjamin Dunn quotes selectively from Martin Luther — "The gospel is nothing else but laughter and joy" — and he appeals to wine, drinking, and inebriation as symbols of Christian experience.[25] The language of "drunkenness," "inebriation," and "ecstasy" appears often in the writings of Dunn and Crowder, who are contending with what they take to be legalistic attitudes, moralistic heavy-handedness, and institutional rigidity in the church. In the rhetoric of many contemporary charismatics, the word "religion" connotes everything that is wrong with the church and that causes it to be somber, lifeless, and stultifying. While "religion offers dull, sedative, boring theories," says Georgie Banov, "the real gospel can be nothing less than a radical affectionate enjoyment."[26] Benjamin Dunn's definition of "religion" is wholly pejorative: "External ordinances and disciplines; a form of godliness that does not come from within the heart."[27] By definition, there can be no such thing as "true religion." Religion is always bad. Religion's ordinances, forms, disciplines, and structures are unnecessary and unhelpful. There is a deeply embedded anti-institutionalism in much of the Pentecostal-charismatic world, and the teachers of the "grace message" are generally more strident than others in their utter rejection of and contempt for what they call "religion."

The "grace message" — as we find it in Dunn and Crowder —

is that the church must accept the once-for-all and finished work of Christ on the cross. The grace teachers might accurately be described as antinomian in the sense that they deny that Christians today live under an obligation to obey the moral law.[28] Commandments that must be obeyed reflect "religion" rather than "grace." Dunn writes that "the gospel gives us a life that is no longer stuck in the orbit of moral law."[29] "Law" implies failure, falling short, and guilt, and in contrast to this the Christian believer is liberated from concern with laws and rules. A related motif is usually termed "quietism." The distinctive quietist teaching is that human efforts get in the way of one's relationship with God. Christian quietists call for a kind of holy passivity. As Dunn says, "We can only be the dependent, passive recipients of the gospel. It can only be drunk down and received as a gift."[30] Any summons to exertion or effort in the spiritual life is thus mistaken. Our efforts are the problem, not the answer. Du Toit states, "Any form of striving to become more like Jesus through personal devotion and diligence, no matter how sincere, bears the same fruit of failure and guilt."[31] The implication is that striving and effort play no part in the Christian life. Dunn writes, "I realized that not only are our efforts unnecessary, they are not allowed....We must yield to the ease and effortlessness of the gospel."[32] Fasting from food is something difficult to do, and accordingly, Crowder denies that fasting has value.[33] This teaching may be shocking to charismatics, many of whom (especially during the last decade or two) have gone on ten-, twenty-one-, and even forty-day fasts, partaking only of juice and other liquids, and sometimes water only. For Crowder, though, there is no need to "seek God," because grace is immediate and total. There are no "means of grace," because grace already is. As he states in one of his chapters, "sanctification is not a process."[34]

Crowder and du Toit operate with an implicit canon within the canon in reading the Bible, in which the Old Testament is neglected in favor of the New Testament, and the Pauline Epistles are the crown or apex of divine revelation. Crowder says that Matthew, Mark, Luke, and John are not "the gospel." It is the letters of the apostle Paul that convey the message of grace. Crowder's marginalization of Jesus's moral instruction in the Gospels might raise the question of whether Jesus himself falls short of Crowder's idea of grace — that is, whether Jesus himself was a legalist. It is telling that Francois du Toit's *Mirror Bible* not only leaves out the Old Testament but also omits all of Matthew, Mark, Luke, and John, except for parts of the prologue in John 1:1–18.

This "Bible" consists almost exclusively of heavily paraphrased and reinterpreted portions of the Pauline Letters and some of the general Epistles. Like the Synoptic Gospels, the book of Revelation is entirely absent from the *Mirror Bible*, at least in the present version of this Bible paraphrase.

Among the Charismatic grace teachers, Benjamin Dunn is one who embodies the grace message and yet does not indicate a belief in universal salvation. Like the others, his emphasis is on salvation as a present-time experience rather than as something that believers still await. He defines the word "salvation" as "the spiritual and eternal deliverance granted immediately by God to those who accept his conditions of repentance and faith in the Lord Jesus."[35] The word "immediately" is determinative. Dunn — like the others — does not speak of waiting for final salvation at Christ's return. Salvation is here and now, not there and then. Dunn writes, "In the New Creation language, you won't find longing and wanting. You will find endless praises declaring that the waiting and wanting is over. It's a language and song of blissful fulfillment and ecstatic satisfaction."[36]

Since "the waiting and wanting is over," Dunn seems to be in heaven already. His eschatology is over-realized in the sense that he thinks of the kingdom of God as already present in its full and final form: "The realm people enter then when they become Christians, is a realm that is no longer merely human. They are lifted out of their corrupted condition and into a divine one. They are raised into the humanity that God had in mind when He created us."[37] The new self replaces the old self. The sinner is gone, and someone else is present: "We are new in quality and in kind, and superior to what we were in our fallen state."[38] The stress on "already" rather than "not yet" affects the way in which Dunn construes holiness. He defines "sanctification" as both "Christ himself" and "the divine act preceding the acceptance of the gospel by the individual."[39] Sanctification is already accomplished and completed in Christ prior to any human decision or act of faith. Dunn rejects fear as a motive in the Christian life, saying that, "the gospel leads people to repentance, not because of the fear of eternal punishment, but because of the promise of eternal bliss."[40] Union with Christ is not only a doctrine but also an experience: "This is the ecstasy that the gospel announces. It declares your new reality of mystical oneness with Christ."[41]

Dunn promotes a doctrine of perfectionism — namely, that believers can cease from sin during the present life. For Dunn, mainstream and non-perfectionist Christians have adopted a distorted, or even gnostic, view of the body as something evil. He writes, "Following the idea that the body is evil is the belief that Christians will never be free from sin until they die....If death delivers us from what Christ could not, then death, not Christ, becomes our savior."[42] Salvation cannot be "process-based," because this would lead to "a multi-tiered Christianity, with some holier than others," which is "obviously not the gospel." Instead Dunn insists that "sanctification" or "holiness" is "available freely once for all at the moment of salvation."[43] By implication, there is no process of development in holiness in the Christian life. What is more, the denial that some believers might be holier than others undercuts the biblical teaching on imitation, wherein believers are called to follow the example of eminent fellow believers — and above all to follow and imitate Christ (1 Cor 4:16, 11:1; Phil 2–3; 1 Thess 1:6; Heb 13:7). In general, the grace teachers minimize the idea of *imitatio Christi* (the imitation of Christ).[44] Dunn defines "the offense of the cross" as "the preaching of instantaneous righteousness and union through Christ's cross." He denies that, "Christianity is a struggle" and says that, "the true stumbling block is the ease of the gospel."[45] This is so because most people "are striving for something that is simply a gift."[46]

Charismatic Preachers of Grace, II — Francois du Toit and Andre Rabe

Francois du Toit states that "every human life is...represented in Christ" and "equally included in God's economy of grace" — a theme in Kruger and Crowder too. In du Toit's reasoning, though, it is not easy to tell whether Christ represents humanity or humanity represents Christ. His appeal to the image of the mirror functions in both ways. Christ "gives...reference to our being as in a mirror, not as an example for us, but of us."[47] Du Toit diminishes the distance between Christ and humanity in his teaching that "man pre-existed in the Logic of God."[48] Not only did Christ eternally preexist with God the Father, but so did every human being. Christ's coming functions as a manifestation to us of our own eternal and divine nature. The flesh-and-blood Jesus fades from view. Jesus is less an individual human being and more a reflection of corporate or collective humanity. In rhapsodic language, du Toit stresses the manifestation to humanity of its own true selfhood: "Jesus...did not come as an example for us but of us....He is introduced to us not as

Christ in history, or Christ in outer space, nor even as Christ in a future event, but as Christ in you....Jesus is what God believes about you! Jesus is God's mind made up about the human race! Awake to innocence, awake to oneness!"[49] God acted not because of humanity's sin-ridden state but because of humanity's essential worth: "The lost coin never lost its original value."[50]

The paraphrasing in du Toit's *Mirror Bible* often shifts the meanings in the biblical texts. In the English Standard Version, John 1:12 reads: "But to all who did receive him, who believed in his name, he gave the right to become children of God." In the *Mirror Bible*, this same verse is rendered as: "Everyone who realizes their association in him, convinced that he is their original life and that his name defines them, in them he endorses the fact that they are indeed his offspring, begotten of him; he sanctions the legitimacy of their sonship."[51] One notice that the word "faith" has dropped away in the *Mirror Bible* and is replaced by "realizes." Rather than faith in Jesus, there is salvation by intellectual realization. This paraphrase also changes the historical Jesus into a Christ who is the "original life" of human beings. Christ as Primal Man is a representation of original, eternal humanity. In du Toit's teaching, Christ's function is to reveal myself to me. Self-discovery and God-discovery seem to be essentially the same thing: "To discover yourself in the mirror is the key that unlocks the door to divine encounter."[52] The *Mirror Bible*'s rendering of 2 Corinthians 3:18 makes this clear: "In gazing with wonder at the blueprint likeness of God displayed in human form [i.e., in Jesus], we suddenly realize that we are looking at ourselves! Every feature of his image is mirrored in us!...We are led from an inferior mind-set to the revealed endorsement of our authentic identity. Mankind is his glory!"[53]

Du Toit's themes are paralleled in the literature of ancient gnosis, wherein theophany or Christophany gives way to egophany, the manifestation of the self.[54] Du Toit lays out his theory of humanity's "lost and found" identity as follows:

> Man began in God!...The unveiling of mankind's redemption also reveals our true genesis....We are *another*, from above. We are perfect and complete and lacking in nothing...our natural birth is not our beginning! We come from above! If man did not come from above, the heavenly realm would offer no attraction to him. In our make-up, we are the god-kind with an appetite for more than what bread and the senses could satisfy us with.[55]

This teaching is bona fide esotericism. Human beings come from another spiritual realm but are marooned temporarily within the realm of flesh. Our supernal origin causes us to look toward the sky and pine for our return once again to the heavens. Translated into Coptic, written on a papyrus scroll, and buried in the Egyptian sands, du Toit's sayings might be mistaken for a missing portion of an ancient gnostic library. Du Toit quotes with approval the saying, "The only difference between Christ and us was his understanding of who he was."[56] It is not clear whether du Toit believes that Jesus was uniquely divine or whether Jesus simply revealed the divine nature of all humans.[57]

In the final chapter of his book *Divine Embrace*, du Toit addresses the question of hell. The final page states that everyone is already redeemed, and for this reason "the greatest hell that anyone can face in any age is the torment of the ignorance of their true redeemed identity revealed in Christ as in a mirror."[58] Du Toit interprets hell in this subjective way, yet he makes no statement about whether people do or do not come out of their state of ignorance.

Much like du Toit, the Charismatic preacher and teacher Andre Rabe offers a version of Christian universalism that shows resemblances to the universalism of ancient gnosis. Rabe tells his readers, "You have your origin in Him....Your identity, as God imagined it long before you were born, is displayed in all its purity and beauty by this Word,"[59] for "Jesus...is not ashamed to call you brother because we all have the same origin."[60] This statement raises a question regarding Jesus's eternal preexistence: Is every human being eternal and preexistent with God in the same way that Jesus is often said to be? Rabe saves his most telling statements for the final chapter of *Imagine* (2013), "The Incarnation Continues," which suggests that all human beings are an extension of Jesus's incarnation:

> The same logos [word] that John wrote of — the logos that was in the beginning with God, the logos that became flesh in the person of Christ Jesus — this is the same logos with which we have been enriched. He has enriched us with all of himself! Not just a portion or a fragment, but everything he is has been deposited in you. *The same logos that became flesh in Christ now becomes flesh in you!*...God sees no reason to expect any lesser manifestation of his life in you than in Jesus.[61]

Later we will return to this theme and reconsider Rabe's language regarding "the same logos."

The idea of God as transcendent, writes Rabe, is a reflection of "our natural mind and reasoning," for "a people who are alienated and confused about God...develop philosophies about His unknowability

— or 'transcendence' for the theologically minded."[62] Unlike the God of the Bible and Christian tradition, Rabe's God seems to be wholly immanent. The meaning of "Christ" also hangs in doubt, since Rabe speaks of Jesus's earthly life as the "manifestation of an eternal event": "The life, death and resurrection of Jesus Christ happened within our time, but it was a manifestation of an eternal event. His appearance revealed what has always been true — the mystery hidden for ages and generations was finally made known in our dimension of time and space."[63] But is Jesus eternally born in Bethlehem and forever crucified at Golgotha?

In Rabe's teaching, God's will toward humanity did not change because of Jesus's coming in the flesh. The divine disposition regarding humanity was settled from all eternity. The benefit of Jesus's coming was purely subjective — that is, it changed human attitudes toward God: "Jesus did not come to change the heart and mind of God concerning man, but to change our minds about God. He came to reveal the truth about God and about us and in so doing make us true — genuinely ourselves."[64] In Neoplatonic or gnostic fashion, Rabe refers to evil as something that "has no substance in itself, no eternal significance," and he adds that "evil is the potential by-product of creation — it is everything that God did not create."[65]

For Rabe, God was never alienated from humanity, though human beings may have thought so. Here Rabe's reasoning resembles that of New Thought, which regards evil as illusory and as rooted in false thinking about God and self — an idea found also in Carlton Pearson. Once one's thinking is rectified, then evil disappears, since evil was always an illusion due to distorted thinking. Regarding Christ's atonement, Rabe stresses God's restorative and not vindictive justice: "God's justice is not the selfish desire to satisfy his own offense. God's justice is restorative and healing."[66] More sharply he states, "We continue to subject ourselves to mythical deception when we view the cross of Jesus as the punishment that satisfies God's anger; when we speak of the blood of Jesus that magically satisfies God's blood lust. These are the very fallacies that the cross came to expose."[67] Humanity, not God, was responsible for Jesus's death: "Man is responsible for the death of Jesus, God is responsible for the resurrection of Jesus."[68]

In one of his most revealing passages, Rabe writes, "Man is God's idea. And so when God became man it was the original, authentic idea of man that manifested in the person of Christ — the perfect man. What God always knew to be true of man suddenly burst upon the stage of human history."[69] This statement points to a possible parallel between du Toit's and Rabe's teachings and such early Christian thinkers as Gregory of Nyssa and Maximus the Confessor. Human preexistence within the eternal Son or Word of God is a theme in early Greek Christian authors. For Gregory and Maximus, the "ideal" preexistence of human individuals — that is, as ideas or ideals in the divine mind or intention — was a modification of early Origenism, away from a doctrine of preexisting souls as intelligent, volitional agents. Yet missing from preexistent humanity as du Toit and Rabe conceive it are the ethical and teleological elements that one finds in the Greek fathers. For Gregory and Maximus, Christ in his coming shows us what human beings are called to be. For du Toit and Rabe, it would seem that Christ in his coming shows us what human beings simply are. Without the idea of moral and spiritual striving, so prominent in Gregory and Maximus, any parallel to the Greek fathers is limited in scope. The logic of du Toit's and Rabe's theologies appears to be more gnostic than patristic. The human problem for them is not ethical but cognitive — that many or most people do not know of their own identity in Christ.

On Rabe's premises, it does not seem that anyone can be damned, lost, or separated from God, except to the extent that someone might cling to a false and untrue identity. Rabe states, "To recognize the Lordship of Jesus Christ cannot be separated from recognizing his image and likeness within you. You belong to him because he made you."[70] Relationship to Christ is grounded in God's creation of us rather than in Christ's redemptive work. To be human is already to be connected to God. Our calling is to discover ourselves and to discover God: "Awake to his reality[,] awake to his likeness in you!"[71]

Charismatic Preachers of Grace, III — John Crowder

We turn finally to John Crowder, a self-appointed spiritual troublemaker. He writes that, "in every generation, the Lord appoints a few troublers of Israel to challenge the status quo and awaken his people to the authentic gospel."[72] Reflecting the wilder, untamed side of the independent charismatic movement, Crowder was earlier associated with Todd Bentley, a fiery young evangelist who, prior to his preaching ministry, had been a juvenile offender. In his writings, Bentley reported paranormal experiences, including visions of heaven and encounters with an angel.[73] A 2008 local revival at a church in Lakeland, Florida, led by Bentley, involved reports of miraculous healings and drew the attention of Charismatic Christians around the globe. Crowder expresses high regard for Bentley.[74]

Subsequently, Crowder became known for conducting worship services that drew participants into a kind of spiritual intoxication, not induced by alcohol or drug use but by what Crowder calls "God's drunken glory." Crowder's "Sloshfest" has been held in various locations and was described in 2010 in the British press.[75]

His first two books — *Miracle Workers, Reformers, and the New Mystics* (2006) and *The Ecstasy of Loving God* (2009) — recount many of the most unusual miracles from church history. Included are Catholic saints levitating, Francis of Assisi conversing with animals, and missing limbs being supernaturally restored. Crowder embraces the miraculous phenomena associated with Catholic and Orthodox saints, but rejects the spiritual disciplines (e.g., fasting and monastic routine) generally regarded as integral to the lives of the saints.[76]

Crowder has evolved during the last decade. His first two books were less theological than the more recent *Mystical Union* (2010) and *Cosmos Reborn* (2013). *Cosmos Reborn* cites C. Baxter Kruger and Thomas Torrance, and is the first of Crowder's books to raise explicitly the issue of universal salvation. The final chapter in *Cosmos Reborn* seems to move in a new direction, affirming that human beings are "a divine race" and that "there is a very real eternal aspect" to all of us.[77] Crowder's arguments weave together multiple strands, including a trinitarian inclusion of all humanity in Christ (per Karl Barth, Thomas Torrance, and C. Baxter Kruger) and the esoteric motif of humanity's divine origin and divine nature (per Andre Rabe and Francois du Toit).

Crowder addresses universalism in *Cosmos Reborn* (2013) as well as a ninety-minute online video.[78] Sometimes it is difficult to follow his argument because he begins with strong, bold statements of his position, followed by a series of qualifications. The video states that he intends to "bring more clarity" to the discussion on hell yet adds that he will present no "clean, tidy, theological system." The teaching on hell is tied to "the grace message" or "the finished work of the cross." He sees today a "massive exodus" of "people coming out of the shallow, stagnant, uncreative waters of religion and into the depths of this glorious grace message." Miracles, joy, and God's "benefits package" come from realizing that Christ has already accomplished everything.[79]

Regarding hell, Crowder says that "two seemingly opposite things" appear as a "paradox in scripture." One is "the existence of hell," which

Crowder affirms. The other side is "a very real universal scope of work accomplished on the cross of Jesus Christ."[80] Crowder takes up the theme of predestination, rejects both Calvinist and Arminian views, and favorably cites Karl Barth's teaching on this topic. Generally, Crowder emphasizes God's sovereignty in electing everyone, stating that, "there is no freedom outside of his [God's] will." Human beings have no independent or self-willed existence. Crowder repudiates what he calls the "demonic" and "disgusting idea" of "double predestination, which makes God "much worse than Hitler." Sounding like a number of earlier universalists (e.g., Isaac of Syria, William Law, George MacDonald [*DR* 4.9; 5.9]), he says that for God "there is no such thing as hatred apart from love," since God's "wrath is an extension of...love." Wrath is God's opposition to what destroys human beings, and so "his wrath has always been for you, never truly against you."[81]

Taking a cue from Barth, Crowder states that "it is time we put Jesus Christ right back in the middle of this whole equation." In eternity, God did not make an "arbitrary choice." Jesus Christ is "the elect one...he is the choice of the Father." Election "has always been about the Father's choice for Jesus, and therefore the Father's choice for us." Crowder quotes Barth's summary statement that "election is the sum of the gospel." This implies that Jesus was "the vessel of honor who was also the vessel of wrath" (Rom. 9:22–23) and that "the reconciliation already happened two thousand years ago."[82] He cites 1 Corinthians 15:22 — "In Christ, all will be made alive" — and states that "all means all." He says, "I am not a universalist," yet he concedes, "I do have strong hope in the salvation of all mankind," for Christ "has become our human response to God."[83]

After stating his "strong hope" for universal salvation, Crowder backtracks by admitting, "I just don't know." "This hope in the salvation of all man[kind] is not just permitted, it is commanded," while at the same time "hope cannot verge into dogmatism." Crowder finds the basis for his double-sided attitude in what he takes to be the double-sidedness of scripture. Since "scripture is fluid," one can make a "solid, scriptural case" for "rigid infernalism" and yet also for universalism. The Bible shows an "open-ended tension." He states that salvation must come through Christ — "Jesus is the only door" — and so distinguishes himself from religiously pluralistic universalism. He says that he identifies with Trinitarians like Karl Barth and Thomas F. Torrance, who teach "the inclusion of humanity in the work of Christ." For this reason, Crowder does not "vilify Christian universalists as...heretics."[84]

Drawing on Eastern Christian writers, Crowder states that hell is "not separation from God." Instead "heaven" and "hell" are human terms for what it is like to be in God's presence in two radically different ways. Since there is no escape from God's presence, human beings will necessarily experience either torment or joy. Paradise and hell do not exist from God's standpoint but only from a human point of view. God is a paradise for saints, but God is hell for sinners. Nowhere in scripture do we find that God needed to be reconciled to humanity; instead we find that humanity needed to be reconciled to God. Christ did not cause God to begin to love us, for God always loved us and God has never been opposed to us. Crowder quotes from Isaac of Nineveh (*DR* 4.9), who wrote that sins against love would bring the greatest torment to sinners. Those in hell continue to be the objects of God's love — but are tormented by this love.[85]

Jesus's death is a "black hole" in which all sins and condemnation have vanished. Though there may be torment for those who do not accept Christ, hell is not outside the realm of God's grace. Crowder notes that his views have caused him to look on his fellow human beings in a new way: "Everybody is included in the finished work of the cross. Even unbelievers are included in a hidden way. We can't really use terms any more like outsider versus insider." Crowder now avoids such terms as "saved" and "unsaved" and prefers to speak of "believer" versus "unbeliever." The former group differs from the latter in realizing what Christ has already done for them. Christians may "see unbelievers as insiders who haven't realized their inclusion yet by faith." The "personal encounter" with God, or "altar-call moment," is not crucial for Crowder, and he says, "I was born again two thousand years ago." Unbelievers "are burning" — in the present tense — so long as they do not recognize what God has done for them. In the end, he writes, "we can reject God all we want but you can't make him stop including you." Crowder distinguishes inclusion into Christ (involving everyone) from faith in Christ (involving only believers). Believing in Christ accomplishes nothing as far as inclusion into Christ is concerned.[86]

Crowder rejects purgationism, stating that "hell doesn't clean you up or purge you. Jesus did." Instead, he identifies with Calvinists (e.g., Karl Barth and Thomas Torrance) who reject postmortem suffering or purification as a precondition for heaven. In interpreting Romans 9, Crowder sees Jacob, Esau, Moses, and Pharaoh less as historical figures and more as symbols of human possibilities. Each one of us was Esau, he says, but we can be Jacob. We were Pharaoh but can be Moses. When we read in scripture that God loved Jacob and hated Esau (Mal 1:2–3; Rom 9:13), this means that, "God hates that false self." The vessels of honor and dishonor (Rom 9:22–23) are not separate individuals but "two identities, one true and one false," and so "Jacob represents the true self."[87] This conclusion shifts in a new direction since Crowder earlier insisted that salvation is entirely accomplished for everyone in the person of Christ. In distinguishing a "true self" from a "false self" and ascribing this difference to human faith or decision, Crowder adopts a more human-centered standpoint. His position becomes more moralistic and less grace-based since individuals face antithetical options and must choose to be "Jacob" rather than "Esau."

Always the provocateur, Crowder opens his book *Mystical Union* with the query, "When you think of the cross, do you think of fun? If the answer is 'no' then you have not been taught the cross aright." Because Christ has already done everything, there is a "happy, effortless Christianity" that may "sound scandalous" but is in fact "the gospel."[88] Crowder accepts "the wildest miracles" reported by mystics of the past, though he rejects the spiritual disciplines that mystics practiced: "Ascetic disciplines do not bring us into union."[89] Crowder repudiates the phrase "seeking God," because, he writes, "we are no longer seeking," and "seeking is a pre-Christ action." Instead, there is "enjoyment of the Promise Land [*sic*] that we have entered."[90] In another passage he insists, "Your attempts to get closer to God are the very things that alienate you from grace."[91] He states that believers in Christ are not to model themselves on Christ.[92]

Crowder takes issue not only with Catholic ascetic and mystical teachings but also with the Protestant Reformation, which to his mind did not go far enough in rejecting the Catholic emphasis on good works in the Christian life. Early Protestantism, he argues, went astray in asserting that Christian believers continue to struggle with aspects or remnants of the flesh or "indwelling sin." Crowder declares that "the reformation is not finished" until Christians abolish this notion of the flesh or indwelling sin.[93] He labels Reformation theology as heterodox: "The heresy is this: it is the idea that you, as a believer, still have a sinful nature."[94] That the apostle Paul had "an internal war going on within himself" is "unbiblical hogwash" and "demonic rhetoric."[95] Throughout *Mystical Union*, Crowder insists that the entire Christian life is an exercise of faith in one's already achieved union with Christ.[96] "Your union with Christ," he writes, "is an effortless state of being.

It takes no more work for me than being a natural-born citizen of America....The moment you decide to do something to be holy, you have trusted in yourself, instead of Christ, for salvation."[97] Not only does Crowder negate the Ten Commandments and Old Testament laws, but he also ignores Jesus's instructions in the Gospels on discipleship.[98] Crowder has to ignore much of the apostle Paul's teaching since Paul often spoke of exertion in the Christian life and compared the Christian life to the running of a race that required training and self-discipline so that one might run well (1 Cor 9:24–27).

Crowder's recent work, *Cosmos Reborn* (2013), exhibits many of the same themes as Kruger. Sounding a bit like Barth, Crowder here says, "I am and I am not a universalist."[99] As in his video presentation, Crowder states that "all are included in Christ" and that "it is now impossible to see insiders or outsiders," for "God has clearly reconciled, redeemed and unified all of humanity in himself," and "even the unbeliever is included in Christ in a hidden way."[100] All of humanity thus becomes "church," and telling everyone that they are already included in Christ is the new definition of "evangelism." He reaffirms his rejection of a purgative hell.[101] Such a view would clearly conflict with his radical-grace teaching, in which everything pertaining to salvation has already been accomplished in Christ. Yet *Cosmos Reborn* fails to present a clear-cut position. After commending universalism, he says, "I am a hopeful agnostic" and "I am okay not knowing all the answers."[102] His book recalls Rob Bell's *Love Wins* (2011) in combining expressions of agnosticism regarding the afterlife with rejections of traditional Christian views.[103] Confronting the story of the sheep and goats (Matt 25:31–46), he asks, "Can a goat become a sheep?" His answer is that "we don't really know." He suggests that perhaps "sheep" and "goat" are symbols of two aspects of the human self, so that "the separation of sheep and goats" would be "the separation of individuals from what is false into what is true."[104]

Crowder's motif of two selves moves in the direction of an esoteric rather than a Christocentric version of universalism. In this account, salvation comes as human individuals realize their true rather than false selves. In the final chapter of *Cosmos Reborn*, "The Divinity of Man," Crowder's argument approximates that of Francois du Toit. As human beings, "we pre-existed invisibly in the heart and imagination of God," so "there is a very real eternal aspect about you that goes eternally forward and backward," and "Adam was breathed from the very divine substance." If "dogs produce dogs," he reasons, "what does God produce?" Thus "we are a mirror image of God himself."[105]

Crowder concludes *Cosmos Reborn* with a quasi-gnostic evocation of humanity's awakening knowledge of its eternal origin in God, its divine nature, and its final calling to be eternally united to God:

> We are awakening to our True Selves. The false self — under a false fatherhood of the adversary — has no substance….We are awaking to our origin — breathed from his very substance, re-created and born anew in him — the Lamb of God….He came to awaken humanity to the truth — that we are a divine race….You are not bound by times and seasons. Your destiny does not hinge on your natural abilities. You are eternal, infinite, immortally woven into his own divinity….The entire cosmos has been restored and reconciled to its divine origin….God is not simply bound up in Christ. But rather through Christ, he has bound himself up to the entire created order….Yes, the cosmos has been permanently rewired in the incarnation, death, and resurrection of Jesus Christ. All things have been forever united in the Son of God….God included you and absorbed the entire created order into himself.[106]

In this peroration, Crowder's agnostic and hopeful statements about final salvation give way to an assertive universalism of the gnostic-esoteric sort.

Conclusion — On Comparing Contemporary Universalisms

Popular books in support of universalism may agree on final salvation for all, but they do not necessarily agree on much else. Recent authors differ profoundly in their assessment of Jesus of Nazareth, with Philip Gulley and James Mulholland denying Jesus's unique divinity, while other authors like Robin Parry and C. Baxter Kruger are clearly committed to this central Christian affirmation. Carlton Pearson is akin to Gulley and Mulholland in the minimal role that he assigns to Jesus, and this may be one reason that his universalism is multi- or inter-religious. For Pearson, there are many paths to God, and Jesus is only one of the ways. In contrast to this, C. Baxter Kruger is deeply Christocentric, as is John Crowder. The authors diverge also in their assessments of church history and Christian tradition. Thomas Talbott seems profoundly suspicious of the institutional church, and he seeks to build his universalist theology from the text of the Bible, shorn of past interpretations, together with his own philosophical reasoning from an *a priori* notion of divine love. C. Baxter Kruger operates in a different realm, appealing to Augustine, John Calvin, Karl Barth, and Thomas Torrance, and situating his universalist theology in relation to a number of great Christian thinkers of the past.

We also find major differences among contemporary universalists in their interpretations of the Bible. Gulley and Mulholland largely follow a "canon within the canon" approach, finding fault with the God of the Old Testament and arguing that Jesus embodies a principle of divine love and mercy that offers a key to interpreting the entire Bible. Contrasting with this is John Crowder's exegesis, which diminishes the importance of the New Testament Gospels and instead exalts the Letters of Paul. The four Gospels are "not the gospel" as Crowder sees it, and only the Pauline message of free grace through faith alone is the "gospel." Benjamin Dunn agrees with Crowder in his basic approach to the Bible, which we might call a Pauline antinomianism.

Rob Bell is prone to spiritualizing or allegorical readings of scripture. In the parable of the prodigal son (Luke 15:11–32), the elder brother represents the particularist who wishes to limit salvation just to a few, and so refuses to enter the party and rejoice with the father and the once-erring yet now-returned younger brother. Allegorical exegesis on behalf of universalism goes back to the time of Origen and is prominent in nineteenth-century Anglo-American universalism, and so Bell follows a long line of nonliteralist universalist exegetes. Wholly different is the approach to the Bible taken by Robin Parry (a.k.a. Gregory MacDonald), who seeks to base his universalist conclusions on the Old Testament as well as the New Testament, all literally interpreted. As we showed above, Parry's arguments break down at many places, but the point here is that Parry's hermeneutical principles diverge from those of Crowder, or Bell, or Gulley and Mulholland. Francois du Toit, in his *Mirror Bible* paraphrase, differs radically from Parry's literal exegesis, as du Toit systematically reinterprets the Bible in what might be considered a gnostic-esoteric reading.

Another point of divergence among contemporary universalist authors centers on the contrast between esoteric and Christocentric versions of universalism. Esoteric thought highlights the self's discovery of its own true nature. In coming to a conscious realization of its divine origin or nature, the human self is "saved." The difference between those who are "saved" and those "yet to be saved" lies wholly on the intellectual or cognitive plane. Everyone without exception, whether they realize it or not, is already included in Christ and in all that Christ has accomplished to bring salvation to humanity. So the "saved"/"unsaved" distinction might be construed as a cognitive difference. Yet for the Christocentric universalist, the salvific truth to be understood and realized is not fundamentally a truth about the human self as such but is a truth about Christ — or, perhaps one might say, a truth about the human self in relation to Christ. Kruger is plainly Christocentric, as Crowder was in his earlier writings. By contrast, Francois du Toit's reasoning floats between esoteric and Christocentric motifs without ever clearly resolving itself. Am I saved because of who Christ is or because of who I am — revealed to me by Christ? On the basis of du Toit's and Rabe's writings, it is almost impossible to give a definite answer to this question. Crowder in his later writings shifts away from Barth's or Kruger's views and in the direction of du Toit's and Rabe's esotericism. How Crowder's theology will continue to develop, only time will tell.

A crucial yet unresolved question in contemporary universalism is the issue that was never resolved during the nineteenth century — namely, whether postmortem punishment or purgation is necessary for at least some people before going to heaven. Talbott's and Parry's versions of universalism hinge on postmortem suffering. Parry sees this postmortem suffering as purgative. He looks to Elhanan Winchester and the nineteenth-century Anglo-American restorationists rather than the ultra-universalists as his theological progenitors. Parry also cites Moltmann, asserting that hell was taken away at the cross, although this line of argument is at odds with his consistent emphasis on postmortem suffering as a preparation for the presence of God. Talbott's view on postmortem suffering diverges from Parry's since Talbott argues that God will use increasing levels of pain to bring every human individual finally to make some kind of decision to submit to God. For Talbott, it is not clear if postmortem suffering is simply purgative, or if its point is to force rebel souls to submit themselves to God.

Many more points of contrast might be drawn between the authors surveyed above. As far as theological arguments for universalism are concerned, the only thing that these various "universalisms" have in common with one another is the conclusion that all human beings will finally be saved. The theological positions presented here differ on the following: the nature of God, the doctrine of the Trinity, the proper principles of biblical exegesis, the person of Jesus, the nature of good and evil, the origin and nature of humans, the role of human free will, the significance of Jesus's death on the cross, faith versus effort in the Christian life, and the question of postmortem suffering for sins. Someone today who professes to be a Christian universalist might be asked, "What sort of universalist are you?" since the various types of universalism start from disparate assumptions, offer different arguments, and seem to have little in common with one another.

Today's "evangelical universalists," led by Robin Parry, seek to support their views from the text of the New Testament. Yet the problems with any biblically based univeralism are legion, and they commence with Jesus's attributed teachings in the Gospels. Jesus repeatedly warned of the danger of refusing God's offer of grace and the peril of delaying one's response. Germain Grisez and Peter F. Ryan note that "Jesus would have been dishonest had he tried to motivate people by warnings that were not truthful information about their prospects if they failed to heed his warnings."[107] In response to Parry's *The Evangelical Universalist*, Graham Watts disputes the claim "that universalism offers greater theological coherence" than traditional evangelical theology. It may present "a form of logical coherence," but in light of Thomas Torrance's strident critique, this is "quite different from being theologically coherent."[108]

Derek Tidball offers a number of incisive comments on Robin Parry's views. So-called evangelical universalism, Tidball argues, is "at best...an argument from silence, since scripture nowhere positively states several crucial elements in universalism." He notes that "the accent of the New Testament teaching falls on the significance of this life and the decisions made here, with no hint of a second chance, post-mortem, or of re-education in hell prior to release in heaven." Moreover, "there is no reason to believe that those who were impenitent on earth will become penitent in hell. This is pure supposition. Hell may, indeed, have the reverse effect and harden its residents against God." Regarding the final outcome of God's work, "the triumph of God and the reconciliation of 'all things' are adequately explained in terms of the destruction of evil and of all that opposes him." For this reason, "to say that the reconciliation cannot take place unless enemies are persuaded by re-education to agree with God puts a particular contemporary cultural spin on what we believe must happen."[109] Finally, Tidball inquires into the contemporary Western context and asks whether universalist theology is not a Christian cultural accommodation to the current *Zeitgeist*: "We must ask if the embrace of universalism is not a further example of evangelicals seeking to be civil and of stretching doctrine to accommodate as comfortably as possible to contemporary culture."[110] In light of the ideas presented in this essay, this question seems apt.

Notes

1. This article is adapted from Michael J. McClymond, *The Devil's Redemption: A New History and Interpretation of Christian Universalism*, 2 vols. (Grand Rapids, MI: Baker Academic, 2018), 938–44, 976–97. Used by permission. Epigraph from Crowder, *Cosmos Reborn*, 251, 252, 25, 260, and back cover. See bibliography for complete works cited.

2. The *Time* magazine cover (April 25, 2011) read, "What If There's No Hell? — A Popular Pastor's Best-Selling Book Has Stirred Fierce Debate about Sin, Salvation, and Judgment," while Jon Meacham's article (38–43) bore the title and heading "Is Hell Dead? Rogue pastor Rob Bell's argument about salvation and judgment has Evangelicals in a fury — and a young generation rethinking Jesus." A study guide to Bell's book appeared in 2011 as *The Love Wins Companion*. For an overview of the debates in the wake of Bell's book, see John Sanders's 2013 essay "Raising Hell about Razing Hell."

3. One book suggests that universalism might be true but does not directly assert it: John Noe, *Hell Yes / Hell No* (2011). Two authors support universalism in arguing against atonement theology: Derek Flood, *Healing the Gospel* (2012); Sharon L. Baker, *Executing God* (2013).

4. Also noteworthy is the edited volume by Gregory MacDonald (a pseudonym for British book publisher Robin Parry) that explores the historical lineage of universalist thinking from the early church period to the present time: *"All Shall Be Well"* (2011).

5. Crowder, *Cosmos Reborn*, 148.

6. Gregory MacDonald [Parry], *Evangelical Universalist* (2006), 7.

7. Parry, "Evangelical Universalism," 9: "It is commonly claimed by evangelical critics that universalists do not even believe in hell. In fact, this is simply false. Historically, all species of Christian universalism prior to the twentieth century affirmed a doctrine of hell." It is Parry's claim that is "simply false": in the early nineteenth century, many leaders of the Universalist Church in the USA were ultra-universalists who repudiated any notion of postmortem suffering for sins committed during earthly life.

8. Purcell, *Spiritual Terrorism*, 3. Purcell assesses the Bible according to the feelings it evokes in him: "If an interpretation of the Bible is true it will probably cause you to feel loved by God. If, on the other hand, it causes you to feel fearful of God, it probably is not true. Biblical fear of God...[is] not morbid fear of eternal torture in literal hellfire. Truth will have a ring of authenticity and will resonate with one's spirit that it is correct — 'That just sounds right'" (7).

9. Talbott, *Inescapable Love*, 3.

10. C. Pearson, *Gospel of Inclusion*, 142–43.

11. Frank, *Gentler God*, 17–18.

12. Baker, *Executing God*, 1–2.

13. Talbott, *Inescapable Love*, 1, 23.

14. Ferwerda, *Raising Hell*, 59–60. After quoting the comment on God as a

"divine Nazi" from Bart Ehrman, *Jesus Interrupted*, 276, she comments: "Sadly, I think Bart is right. Without realizing it, the 'god' we have put our hopes in and portrayed to the world is more like Hitler than Mother Teresa. The god we have unwittingly manufactured has feeble hopes for his own children — hopes that are dependent on human free will, and confined to the length of his children's brief, moral lifespans" (*Raising Hell*, 60).

15.   Baker's opening citations in her introduction are from Pfau and Blumenthal, "Violence of God"; J. C. Brown, "Divine Child Abuse?"; J. C. Brown and R. Parker, "For God So Loved the World?" The Pfau and Blumenthal essay consist of correspondence between a student and a faculty member centering on the question, "How can you relate to an abusive God in a positive way?" Brown and Parker offer a feminist theology that rejects the idea of Jesus' death as atoning. For analysis of their views, see Guomundsdottir, "Abusive or Abused?"

16.   Intellectual *mediation* between traditional beliefs and modern critiques was the hallmark of classic Protestant liberal theology, beginning with Friedrich Schleiermacher. The phrase "cultured despisers of religion" derives from his epoch-making work, first published in German in 1799, *On Religion: Speeches to Its Cultured Despisers*. In their attention to religion's "cultured despisers," contemporary universalists are much like the early American universalist Hosea Ballou, whose reading of deist literature (e.g., Thomas Paine, Ethan Allen) shaped the development of his universalist theology.

17.   All of these figures promote their ministries through websites and YouTube videos. Key texts include the following: Crowder, *Miracle Workers*; Crowder, *Ecstasy of Loving God*; Crowder, *Mystical Union*; Crowder, *Cosmos Reborn*; du Toit, *Logic of His Love*; du Toit, *Divine Embrace*; du Toit, *Mirror Bible*; Dunn, *Happy Gospel!*; Rabe, *Imagine*.

18.   John Crowder wrote an endorsement for Benjamin Dunn's *The Happy Gospel!* and there mentioned how they have "partnered closely in ministry." Crowder dedicated his book *Mystical Union* to Dunne. Francois du Toit wrote the foreword to Crowder's most recent book, *Cosmos Reborn*, and the final chapter of *Cosmos Reborn*, "The Divinity of Man," summarizes many of du Toit's themes. Both Andre Rabe and C. Baxter Kruger (whom Crowder regularly cites) wrote endorsements for *Cosmos Reborn*. Francois du Toit wrote the foreword to the second edition of Rabe's *Imagine*. John Crowder wrote an endorsement for du Toit's *Mirror Bible*, as did Mary-Anne Rabe (Andre Rabe's spouse) and C. Baxter Kruger. John Crowder founded a school for ministry, Cana New Wine Seminary, which offered its first classes in summer 2014. The teaching is said to focus on "Finished work of the Cross, Trinitarian Theology, New Covenant Grace, Mystical Christianity, Contemplative Spirituality, [and] Supernatural Experience." The confirmed speakers for 2014 included C. Baxter Kruger, Francois du Toit, Benjamin Dunne, Andre Rabe, and John Crowder. In keeping with Crowder's over-the-top rhetoric, the school is called a "unique seminary for wild-eyed wonder junkies" that "offers a unique marriage of life-transforming, happy theology, woven seamlessly with the intoxicating practice of the presence

of God. A place where you will find doctorate level theologians and mystical ecstatics sharing the same platform. Cana is a drunken seminary" (http://www.cana.co/About_Cana.html).

19. The Singapore-based megachurch pastor, Joseph Prince, offers teachings on grace that are analogous to these other figures. Prince leads New Creation Church, with a reported attendance of thirty-one thousand (as of 2014), and is author of *Destined to Reign: The Secret to Effortless Success, Wholeness and Victorious Living* (2007). See Sahat Sinaga's essay, "Is Joseph Prince's Radical Grace Teaching Biblical?"; Michael Brown, *Hyper-Grace*, with a prompt rebuttal from Paul Ellis, *Hyper-Grace Gospel.*

20. The resemblance is specifically to Tobias Crisp (1600–1643), John Saltmarsh (d. 1647), John Eaton (1575–ca. 1631), and other seventeenth-century Calvinist antinomians. Crisp taught "eternal justification," and his teaching on grace seemed to undercut all moral exertion. See Parnham, "Humbling of 'High Presumption'"; Parnham, "Covenantal Quietism of Tobias Crisp"; Parnham, "Motions of Law and Grace"; Parnham, "John Saltmarsh."

21. See McClymond, "Charismatic Renewal and Neo-Pentecostalism," 43.

22. See Althouse and Waddell, *Perspectives in Pentecostal Eschatologies.*

23. Paul Cain and other 1980s "Kansas City" prophets expressed such ideas, as recounted in Mike Bickle's audio memoir, *Encountering Jesus.*

24. Wagner, *Dominion!*

25. Dunn, *Happy Gospel!*, 39. "Wine is the only thing that can communicate the intense joy and inebriation that fills the heart when salvation's cup is drunk" (Dunn, *Happy Gospel!*, 44). Dunn's reference is to Luther as cited in C. H. Spurgeon's commentary on Psalm 126, in Spurgeon, *The Treasury of David*, 3b:68–82. Dunn's appeal to Luther is one-sided since Luther insisted on preaching God's law as a way of making sinners aware of their guilt.

26. Georgie and Winnie Banov, book endorsement, in Dunn, *Happy Gospel!*, 7.

27. Dunn, *Happy Gospel!*, 33.

28. Sixteenth-century Lutherans debated the so-called third use of the law. The question was whether Old Testament law had a role not only in civil legislation ("first use") and in revealing our need as sinners for God's grace ("second use") but also in living the Christian life ("third use"). Calvinists generally answered yes to the "third use." While some Lutherans denied the "third use," the Epitome of the Formula of Concord (6.2–3) accepted it in the following terms:

> We believe, teach, and confess that the preaching of the Law should be urged not only upon those who have not faith in Christ, and do not yet repent, but also upon those who truly believe in Christ, are truly converted to God, and regenerated and are justified by faith. For, although they are regenerate and renewed in the spirit of their mind, yet this regeneration and renewal is in this life not absolutely complete, but only begun. And they that believe according to the spirit of their mind have perpetually to struggle with their flesh, that is, with corrupt nature, which inheres in us even till death. (Schaff, *Creeds of Christendom*, 1:132)

The Formula of Concord thus justified preaching God's law to Christians on the basis of the continuing presence of the fallen nature or "flesh" in believers, an idea that John Crowder specifically repudiates. During the 1980s, the North American evangelical debate over "Lordship salvation" renewed the discussion on law and grace. The grace emphasis appeared in Charles C. Ryrie, *So Great Salvation* (1989), and Zane C. Hodges, *Absolutely Free!* (1989), while John F. MacArthur's *The Gospel according to Jesus* (1989) argued that Jesus in the believer's life is always both Savior (who gives grace) and Lord (who commands obedience).

29. Dunn, *Happy Gospel!*, 63.

30. Dunn, *Happy Gospel!*, 127.

31. Du Toit, *Mirror Bible*, 10.

32. Dunn, *Happy Gospel!*, 142.

33. Crowder, *Mystical Union*, 142: "Although it is promoted on some of the fanciest web sites and largest conferences today, fasting is two clicks shy of outright gnosticism for a New Testament believer. Fasting does not draw you closer to God." Dunn, like Crowder, is anti-ascetic, and he says that "Christianity is not a fast; it is a festival" (*Happy Gospel!*, 157). Christian penitence is ruled out: "Fasting seems almost always synonymous with sadness and mourning. It implies want and longing. This can in no way be the true expression of Christianity" (160). Crowder and Dunn seemingly have no choice but to reject Old Testament texts (e.g., the books of Nehemiah, Ezra, and Daniel) that made fasting and mourning over sin a deliberate means of spiritual revitalization, and such New Testament texts as Matthew 9:15.

34. Crowder, *Mystical Union*, 57–96.

35. Dunn, *Happy Gospel!*, 31.

36. Dunn, *Happy Gospel!*, 128.

37. Dunn, *Happy Gospel!*, 62–63.

38. Dunn, *Happy Gospel!*, 64. "Everything that we were 'in Adam' has been shattered and destroyed! We have been completely disconnected from the Fall of humanity and its curse….We are not new creatures still under the curse and Fall of man. We are in a new, divinely-lifted condition" (66).

39. Dunn, *Happy Gospel!*, 33.

40. Dunn, *Happy Gospel!*, 41.

41. Dunn, *Happy Gospel!*, 57.

42. Dunn, *Happy Gospel!*, 74. For Dunn and Crowder, "gnosticism" is a term that applies not to their own opinions but rather to those of mainstream Christianity, denying that believers attain perfection during the present life.

43. Dunn, *Happy Gospel!*, 80.

44. Dunn, *Happy Gospel!*, 91–92. Dunn's exposition becomes confusing, because he recognizes the imitation of Christ theme in scripture, yet cannot reconcile it with his notion of radical grace:

The view of Christ for many is that he was as template after whom we should order our lives. They view his work on the cross as their highest example...which they should follow....Yes, of course, he is the perfect example of holy living, but his purpose was not to show us how to live, but to live it out for us — in us and through us....Everything Jesus said and did in his life...should be seen in light of his death. His death on the cross wasn't just a part of his purpose — it was his purpose. (91–92)

This passage raises questions: Why did Jesus preach and teach over several years? Does his earthly life, prior to his death, have enduring significance?

45. Dunn, *Happy Gospel!*, 86–87.

46. Dunn, *Happy Gospel!*, 99.

47. Du Toit, *Divine Embrace*, 12, 161.

48. Du Toit, *Divine Embrace*, 13; "Man began in God; we are not the invention of our parents" (15).

49. Du Toit, *Divine Embrace*, 6.

50. Du Toit, *Divine Embrace*, 7.

51. Du Toit, *Mirror Bible*, 17.

52. Du Toit, *Mirror Bible*, 11.

53. Du Toit, *Mirror Bible*, 123 (paraphrase of 2 Cor 3:18). For another striking change of meaning in paraphrasing, compare the English Standard Version of Rom 9:18 with du Toit's version: "So then he has mercy on whomever he wills, and he hardens whoever he wills" (ESV); "The same act of mercy that he willingly bestows on everyone may bless the one and harden the heart of the other" (du Toit, *Mirror Bible*, 46). Ephesians 2:1 (ESV), "You were dead in the trespasses and sins," becomes "We were in a death trap of an inferior lifestyle, constantly living below the blueprint measure of our lives" (du Toit, *Mirror Bible*, 151). Colossians 2:10 (ESV), "You have been filled in him [i.e., Christ]," is paraphrased as "Jesus mirrors our completeness and endorses our true identity" (du Toit, *Mirror Bible*, 186).

54. For ancient and modern gnostics, salvation occurs through knowledge (Greek *gnōsis*), and the key transition occurs with the self's realization of its own identity — a moment tantamount to rebirth. Marvin C. Meyer states, "The insight that awakens us is within us...and the knowledge that saves us is self-knowledge. In order to be saved, we need to remember, understand, and know our true selves...that is the gospel of gnosis" (*Gnostic Discoveries*, 166). Cyril O'Regan quotes Eric Voegelin's remark that Gnosticism centers on "egophany" (*Gnostic Return in Modernity*, 250n24).

55. Du Toit, *Mirror Bible*, 245.

56. Du Toit, *Logic of His Love*, 31. Du Toit attributes this saying to the early Pentecostal leader John G. Lake (1870–1935).

57. The emergence of gnostic-esoteric thinking among Pentecostal-Charismatic Christians seems to be a recent development, perhaps less than a decade old. Yet Thomas Weinandy finds a gnostic subtext among such late-twentieth-century authors as John Macquarrie, John Hick, Roger Haight, and David Griffin, for whom "Jesus differs from us only in degree and not in kind in that he manifests to a greater degree than we the ever-present God" ("Gnosticism and Contemporary

Soteriology," 258). This means that "Jesus does not establish an entirely new relationship between God and man but makes it possible for the God-man relation, which always was[,] to become more fully actualized" (261). Such views of Jesus are reminiscent of the "Gnostic Redeemer" who "does not change the cosmic blueprint" but "rather makes known what has always been the case" (257). Though these authors differ from the ancient gnostics in not viewing matter as evil, "salvation within these soteriologies similarly consists in coming to know the 'eternally' established and unchanging (and unchangeable) cosmological order," so that "salvation is reduced to and identified with cosmology" (262).

58. Du Toit, *Divine Embrace*, 164.

59. Rabe, *Imagine*, 15.

60. Rabe, *Imagine*, 16.

61. Rabe, *Imagine*, 138–39; emphasis added.

62. Rabe, *Imagine*, 15.

63. Rabe, *Imagine*, 26–27.

64. Rabe, *Imagine*, 56.

65. Rabe, *Imagine*, 35. Rabe's language at this point echoes that of Karl Barth. On God's noncreation of evil, compare the elaborate account of evil as *das Nichtige* (Nothingness) in Barth, *Church Dogmatics* III/1, 289–368. For Barth, evil-as-nothingness is neither Creator nor created — and is thus a metaphysical anomaly.

66. Rabe, *Imagine*, 79.

67. Rabe, *Imagine*, 99–100. Rabe seems to be following René Girard (1923–2015) when he writes, "The cross...exposes the violence of societies build [*sic*] upon sacrificial systems. The principalities and powers of this world, of every culture, began in false accusation escalating to murder. Human societies have violent and deceptive beginnings....Let's first say this: if the cross is the event that God required to satisfy his need for retribution, then it has no revelatory power. That is the story that mythology has always told" (102–3). As Girard argues, in the New Testament writings, one finds a victim god (i.e., Jesus) lynched by a crowd, as in many ancient myths. Yet the biblical recognition of the sufferer's innocence lays a basis for a destruction of the entire sacrificial order. See Girard, *Things Hidden*.

68. Rabe, *Imagine*, 108.

69. Rabe, *Imagine*, 59.

70. Rabe, *Imagine*, 132–33. Other passages likewise emphasize humanity's universal acceptance in Christ. "Receiving Christ is based on the truth that he already 'received,' embraced and reconciled you" (133). "The ascension is the glorification of man to the place and position that He prepared for us — permanent union with Him. All this is of God, He accomplished it without our help and without our permission! It is truth whether we acknowledge it or not" (123).

71. Rabe, On Jesus's divinity, Rabe states: "Jesus not only represents God, he

is God. What he says, God says; what he does, God does" (*Imagine*, 54). Yet other statements to the effect that other persons are not a "lesser manifestation" of the Logos than Jesus was (138–39) suggest that Jesus might be divine but not uniquely so.

72. Crowder, book endorsement, in Dunn, *Happy Gospel!*, 10.

73. Todd Bentley claims to have visited heaven, seen the apostle Paul, and encountered an angel he called "Emma." His books include *The Journey into the Miraculous, The Reality of the Supernatural World*, and *Kingdom Rising*.

74. Crowder refers to Bentley as "a modern-day miracle worker" and says that he personally witnessed Bentley healing the sick: "I have seen Todd…work all manner of healings under the power of the Lord both on the mission field and in conferences in the United States and Canada" (*Miracle Workers*, 228–29).

75. The UK press account reads:

> With sweaty clothes clinging to their backs, some people even pass out. While this could easily be mistaken for a dodgy booze and drug-fueled party, there is something very different about Sloshfest. The revelers are party-loving Christians who don't drink or take drugs — but say their euphoria is down to the power of God and their seeming drunkenness due to "God-ka" and the "yum rum of Heaven." Last weekend around 600 people attended the annual rave-like event — where no alcohol or drugs are available — at the dowdy Dolphin Club in Barry Island, South Wales. Now in its fourth year, it attracts visitors from alternative churches around the UK. (Lowe, "Ravers Who Get High on God")

76. In Catholic teaching, the higher state of union with God generally comes only after a prolonged process of purification. This led to a distinction between "ascetic theology" and "mystical theology":

> Ascetical Theology…is called the *science of the Saints*, and rightly so, because *it comes* to us *from the Saints*, who have taught it more by their life than by word of mouth….The word *"ascetical"* comes from the Greek *askesis* (exercise, effort) and means any arduous task connected with man's education, physical or moral. Christian perfection, then, implies those efforts that St. Paul himself compares to the training undergone by athletes with the purpose of obtaining the victory [1 Cor. 9:24–27]. (Tanquerey, *Spiritual Life*, 2–3)

Mystical experiences derive from supernatural graces that cannot be produced by human striving alone. Yet a deeper prayer life or union with God requires effort (*askēsis*). Unusual phenomena among the mystics, in Catholic thought, are merely epiphenomenal or surface-level manifestations of an underlying process of theosis or progressive union with God. As noted above, Crowder repudiates the idea that union with God is a process or progress and instead maintains that union is total and immediate for all Christian believers.

77. Crowder, *Cosmos Reborn*, 252, 242.

78. Crowder, "Hell Revisited"; Crowder, *Cosmos Reborn*, 155–66. From August 2012 to February 2016, Crowder's YouTube video on hell drew some

38,000 hits.
79. Crowder, "Hell Revisited," 1–2 mins. into the video.
80. Crowder, "Hell Revisited," 4–5 mins. into the video.
81. Crowder, "Hell Revisited," 7–8, 12, 14–19 mins. into the video.
82. Crowder, "Hell Revisited," 20–25 mins. into the video, quoting Barth, *Church Dogmatics* II/2, 13: "The election of grace is the sum of the gospel — we must put it as pointedly as that."
83. Crowder, "Hell Revisited," 34, 79 mins. into the video.
84. Crowder, "Hell Revisited," 33–44 mins. into the video.
85. Crowder, "Hell Revisited," 67–73 mins. into the video.
86. Crowder, "Hell Revisited," 33–44 mins. into the video.
87. Crowder, "Hell Revisited," 72–76 mins. into the video.
88. Crowder, *Mystical Union*, 9.
89. He explains further: "Much of traditional mysticism has been marked by thinly veiled 'works' righteousness....Its focus was often on ascetic practice, prayer, and annihilation of self through meditation or other means to gain reception into God....Let us not drag up any vestiges of that kind of mysticism. In fact, the point of this book is to help you renounce all your own endeavors to find favor with your Father" (*Mystical Union*, 14–15).
90. Crowder, *Mystical Union*, 117–19.
91. Crowder, *Mystical Union*, 133. Crowder also does not believe that marriage takes effort: "I don't believe the religious lies that tell me marriage is hard work" (Crowder, *Mystical Union*, 183). At the end, he states, "Our union is effortless. This does not mean we become idle" (Crowder, *Mystical Union*, 207). There is activity but no exertion.
92. Crowder, *Mystical Union*, 164: "Jesus...did not bring a formula or model for you to repeat. He stepped into your place and bore the bullet that was yours to take."
93. Crowder, *Mystical Union*, 17. He says, "It is a myth that Christians must overcome their flesh" (Crowder, *Mystical Union*, 56). On p. 51, Crowder especially blames Puritan theologian John Owen (1616–83), author of the influential treatises *Of the Mortification of Sin in Believers* (1656) and *Nature, Power, Deceit, and Prevalancy of the Remainders of Indwelling Sin in Believers* (1667). A recent edition of these treatises was published as Owen, *Overcoming Sin and Temptation*.
94. Crowder, *Mystical Union*, 24.
95. Crowder, *Mystical Union*, 43.
96. On the question of why a Christian believer might still sin, Crowder suggests that "maybe you're an unbeliever," or "maybe no one ever told you any of this [i.e., the truth that one is no longer a sinner]" (*Mystical Union*, 40–41). The proper response to every manifestation of sin is *faith*, i.e., believing that one is not a sinner. "Believe you're a sinner; you'll have sin" (Crowder, *Mystical Union*, 41).
97. Crowder, *Mystical Union*, 42.

98. Crowder states: "The gospel is not Matthew, Mark, Luke, and John. The gospel is the good news of Christ's sacrifice for the removal of sinfulness. It is most clearly articulated through the epistles of Paul....Does this sound too Pauline for you? Still, want to mix your grace with law? Law and grace don't mix. Put them together and you get law....Most of the church is still eating a leftover form of Judaism" (*Mystical Union*, 80–81). Quoting Robert Capon, Crowder states that "the Gospels...were written for the sake of the Epistles, not the other way around" (98, citing Capon, *Health, Money, and Love and Why We Don't Enjoy Them*, 32).

99. Crowder, *Cosmos Reborn*, 17. Compare with Karl Barth's comparable statement: "I do not teach it, but I also do not not teach it [sic]." Barth as quoted in Jüngel, *Karl Barth*, 44–45.

100. Crowder, *Cosmos Reborn*, 116–17.

101. "A god who sovereignly burns someone for a thousand years in a pit of demonic, hellish, molestation is only slightly better than one who does it forever....The main problem with this reasoning is that hell becomes viewed as a *purgatory*. A temporary torture chamber to clean you up. Hell doesn't clean you up. Jesus did" (*Cosmos Reborn*, 148). Strictly interpreted, this passage implies ultra-universalism — i.e, that everyone is saved immediately after death.

102. Crowder, *Cosmos Reborn*, 147.

103. Crowder asks, "Is it possible that our concept of a hell-mongering deity is the chief underlying idol of our churches today? Is our Western version of 'Christianity' more akin to Molech worship with a fish on the bumper?" (*Cosmos Reborn*, 127).

104. Crowder, *Cosmos Reborn*, 157–58.

105. Crowder, *Cosmos Reborn*, 241–42.

106. Crowder, *Cosmos Reborn*, 251, 252, 25, 260, and back cover.

107. Grisez and Ryan, "Hell and Hope for Salvation," 612–13.

108. Watts, "Is Universalism Theologically Coherent?" 46.

109. Tidball, "Can Evangelicals Be Universalists?" 29–30. Tidball uses the analogy of a cancer sufferer who is saved not by the "reconciliation" of the cancerous cells to the rest of his body but by their "destruction" (30).

110. Tidball, "Can Evangelicals Be Universalists?" 32. On the contemporary evangelical impetus toward civility, see James Davison Hunter, *American Evangelicalism*, 87–89. In another book, *Evangelicalism: The Coming Generation*, Hunter speaks of a "normative ethic of civility" (47; cf. 33–34, 150–53, 183), according to which the foremost imperative is not to offend — a principle that might help to explain the desire on the part of some evangelicals to downplay or to deny the traditional doctrine of eternal punishment.

4.

Pentecostalism, Primal Spirituality, and Secularism

Allan H. Anderson

Abstract

The growth of Pentecostalism at the end of the twentieth century poses challenges to the theory of inevitable secularization, especially outside the Western world. Scholars like David Martin and Harvey Cox began to point to the significance of Pentecostalism, and its unexpected rapid growth, as running contrary to this theory. The history of Pentecostalism and reasons for its emergence and growth, the exceptionalism of Europe, and the reshaping of religion in the contemporary world, and the cultural flexibility of Pentecostalism are all factors that must be taken into account.

Key words: Pentecostalism, secularization, sociology, church growth

The Rise of "Primal Spirituality"

During the second half of the twentieth century, the most significant changes in the global demography of Christianity have occurred through the growth of Pentecostalism, which began in a series of revival movements at the beginning of the century.[1] Pentecostalism has arguably been the fastest-growing religious movement in the contemporary world and a phenomenon that has to be reckoned with in the debate on secularization. Ironically, most of the growth of what has become Pentecostal and Charismatic Christianity in all its diversity, both inside and outside the older Protestant and Catholic churches, has occurred in the very period when secularization in Europe was at its height and there was a dramatic change in the religious affiliation of ordinary people, as observed by Hugh McLeod and several others.[2] This paper considers the emergence of Pentecostalism at the beginning of the twentieth century and its expansion with reference to the secularization thesis. Stated briefly, this the belief that as humanity becomes more knowledgeable it will no longer need a god or any form of religion. Europe is considered as a case study of how this has happened already, although some scholars argue that Europe is an exception to the rest of the world and that some communities are more susceptible to secularization than others.[3] The unanticipated global expansion of Pentecostalism in the last quarter of the twentieth century continuing into the twenty-first century poses significant questions regarding the role of religion in the contemporary world and challenges the secularization thesis.

Academic studies of Pentecostalism have appeared relatively recently after the early hagiographies written by Pentecostals themselves. Norwegian Lutheran historian Nils Bloch-Hoell was the earliest to publish his historical analysis of Pentecostals in 1964, but it was Walter J. Hollenweger who made the biggest impact on the academic world in the 1970s.[4] Hollenweger and his school of doctoral researchers in Birmingham were intent on portraying Pentecostalism as a revolutionary, ecumenical, and oral missionary movement. Hollenweger essentialized Pentecostalism by describing its witness and narrative theology as benchmarks of what it meant to be Pentecostal. For him, the Pentecostal experience took precedence over theological formulations and therefore, within Pentecostalism testimony was more important than sermons; narrative more significant than dogma.[5] None of the earlier studies directly related the emergence of Pentecostalism to the theories of secularization that were gaining momentum at the time. Social scientists, most notably David Martin, began to do this in the early 1990s.

Hollenweger's approach was followed by more recent scholars, in particular, the well-known Harvard religion professor, Harvey Cox. Author of the widely acclaimed study on the secularization of religion, *The Secular City*, Cox considered the phenomenon of Pentecostalism so significant that he reversed his position on inevitable secularization in his 1995 publication *Fire from Heaven*. There he wrote of Pentecostalism as a manifestation of the "unanticipated reappearance of primal spirituality in our time" that was contributing to "the reshaping of religion in the twenty-first century." His theory of primal spirituality suggested that Pentecostalism had succeeded because it reached into the deep religious consciousness of humanity in a way that traditional religion had not.[6] In the sixties, Cox had thought that there was need of a theology for a post-religious age "that many sociologists had confidently assured us was coming," and he expressed this theology in *The Secular City*.

He later discovered that "it is secularity, not spirituality that may be headed for extinction." Cox admitted that his earlier view might have been wrong and that instead of the "death of God" and the decline of religion, something quite different had taken place. There was now a "religious renaissance" throughout the world, touching every sort of religious expression, a period of renewed religious vitality.[7]

Cox describes the early American Pentecostals "praying that God would renew and purify a Christianity they believed was crippled by empty rituals, dried-up creeds, and the sin of racial bigotry." So "when the fire finally did fall . . . a spiritual fire roared forth that was to race around the world and touch hundreds of millions of people with its warmth and power." These hundreds of millions were not to emerge for almost a century, but the early Pentecostals saw themselves on the edge of a new dispensation. These Pentecostals believed that something had gone wrong with the church after the "original fire from heaven" on the day of Pentecost and that Christianity had degenerated or had "lapsed into writing meticulous creeds and inventing lifeless rituals."[8] The Pentecostal revival, they believed, would be characterized by a worldwide resurgence of faith, and "healings and miracles" that were "a prelude to the second coming of Jesus Christ."[9] The many different ecstatic experiences characteristic of the reports of early Pentecostals (or as Cox puts it, "signs and wonders tumbling out of the pages") were not just an initiation rite, but a mystical encounter in which Pentecostals were convinced that they were already living in a "whole new epoch in history." Cox opined that the essence of Pentecostalism could not be understood through dogma and doctrines but through the experience of God, a "narrative theology whose central expression is the testimony."[10] This was precisely the message that Hollenweger had conveyed thirty years earlier.

However, it was the ground-breaking work of the British sociologist David Martin that set the benchmark for recent studies on Pentecostalism. He dealt with the question of secularization head-on and related this to the growth of Pentecostalism, especially in Latin America, where much of his early fieldwork was conducted.[11]

The Historical and Theological Journey

Pentecostalism has its roots in Pietism, Methodism, and the nineteenth century evangelical and revivalist Holiness and healing movements.

German Pietism, with its emphasis on personal experience or "new birth" by the Holy Spirit and exemplified through Nicolaus von Zinzendorf's Moravians, spread to Methodism through John Wesley and his theological associate, John Fletcher. The personal conversion experience that became the hallmark of Evangelicalism stressed individual decision. It therefore harmonized with the individualism that characterized modernity, in contrast to the monolithic ecclesiastical systems that dominated pre-modern Europe. The early Methodist doctrine of entire sanctification and the possibility of personal spiritual experiences after conversion undoubtedly constituted the spark that ignited the Holiness movement and its direct offspring, Pentecostalism. The Holiness movement radicalized the ideas of Wesley and Fletcher and focused on a personal encounter: a crisis experience of holiness that became known as "baptism with the Spirit." Phoebe Palmer, Charles Finney, William and Catherine Booth, and William Taylor were among its most well-known advocates. The Holiness movement was a reaction to liberalism and formalism in established Protestant churches as a whole. Its main principles were a biblical literalism, the need for a personal, emotional, and individual experience of conversion, and the moral perfection or "holiness" of the Christian individual. The Keswick Conventions that began in the English Lake District in 1875 were another expression of the Holiness movement (although more "Reformed" in orientation), where the emphasis shifted from Spirit baptism as "holiness" or "sanctification" to Spirit baptism as the bestowing of power for a witness to the world and mission. This was the theology of Spirit baptism continued by the Pentecostals, to which they added the practice of spiritual gifts, in particular the gift of speaking in tongues.

Later in the nineteenth century, the healing movement arose in Western Europe and North America mostly within Holiness circles. Its chief proponents included J. C. Blumhardt, Dorothea Trudel, Charles Cullis, John A. Dowie, and A. B. Simpson, among many others. The healing movement was one of the most important influences on early Pentecostalism. The healing movement was another expression of the popular beliefs on the fringes of Evangelicalism out of which Pentecostalism emerged. Former Methodist preacher turned healing evangelist, Charles Parham, who is credited with formulating the doctrinal link between tongues-speaking and Spirit baptism, came from these circles. Like earlier advocates of divine healing, even though they suffered from severe illnesses and many of their missionaries died from tropical diseases, Pentecostals remained unshaken in their conviction that physical divine healing had been restored to the church in the worldwide revival of the last days. Healing and "signs and wonders" were both indispensable ingredients of their message of how the nations would be brought to faith in Christ.

The presence of healing gifts sometimes broke down barriers of gender and race discrimination. One of the earliest healing ministries in North America was that of the African American, Elizabeth Mix. She prayed for healing from an incurable disease of the Episcopalian (later Salvation Army, Christian and Missionary Alliance and finally Pentecostal), Carrie Judd Montgomery. Mix had a formative influence on Montgomery's extensive healing ministry, an influence that Montgomery always acknowledged.[12] For her part, Montgomery taught that healing was part of the gospel of Christ. She began her *Triumphs of Faith* monthly periodical in 1881, which continued for almost seven decades until after her death in 1946.[13] Montgomery's long ministry bridged the Holiness, healing, and Pentecostal movements.

Most of the first Pentecostals came from one or other of these radical evangelical groups. All held a conviction that the second coming of Christ was imminent and that a world-wide revival would usher it in. They were conditioned by a movement reacting to rationalism and secularism; a response to modernity that focused on personal spirituality, emotional release, and divine intervention in human affairs — even if it used modernity's tools to formulate and justify this reaction. By the end of the nineteenth century, the idea grew that there would be a great outpouring of the Spirit throughout the world before the second coming of Christ. It was hoped that this outpouring would happen at the beginning of the twentieth century. Those upon whom the Spirit had fallen were to prepare for this by offering themselves for missionary service. Mission was thereby given a new pneumatological and eschatological dimension that was to become the preoccupation of early Pentecostals. Pentecostalism was missionary by nature; its central experience of the power of the Spirit, which all Pentecostal believers affirmed, was inextricably linked to going out and being witnesses to all nations.[14] This, together with rapid improvements in transportation and communications, and colonial hegemony, facilitated their rapid spread in the early twentieth century into many parts of the world.[15] Add to this the fact that outside the Western world there were hundreds of voluntary mission societies creating a Christian plurality in places like India, China, and British Africa, and the entrance of independent lay

Pentecostal missionaries and native revivalists was neither unexpected nor unusual in these regions, which were those where Pentecostalism has proliferated most.

David Martin writes of the voluntarism and pluralism born in British and American nineteenth-century denominational splits that "rapidly indigenizes in the developing world, partly on account of its astonishing combination of motifs from both black and white revivalism."[16] Pentecostals, like the radical evangelicals they came from, were firm believers in the privatization of religion. For them, because the only "real" Christians were the "born again" ones, the vast majority (whether they attended church or not) were simply not Christians. This is why proselytizing was engaged in without compunction, as well as why comity agreements on the mission fields were largely ignored. Unencumbered by ecclesiastical organizations and "doctrinal purity," Pentecostals relied on their instincts and a raw interpretation of the Bible. Led by the Spirit, they could do whatever they felt he was leading at the time, and they created structures according to this subjective guidance. Similarly, and also because of their ostracism from other churches, Pentecostals remained isolated and within a few years, had corralled themselves into new denominations.

Pentecostalism grew modestly during its first fifty years but gathered pace after that. During the 1950s and after this period of isolation, some Pentecostals began to interact with older churches through such figures as the South African Pentecostal, David du Plessis, who was defrocked by the American Assemblies of God because of his links with and visits to the World Council of Churches, with which American Pentecostals were opposed. However, the efforts of du Plessis and others after him, including figures who rose to international prominence, accelerated the growth of the Charismatic movement in the Western world in the 1960s. Notable work of Charismatic figures during this time included the drug rehabilitation programs of David Wilkerson's Teen Challenge; the television ministry of healing evangelist, Oral Roberts, who left the Pentecostal Holiness Church for the United Methodist Church; the Full Gospel Business Men's Fellowship led by another Pentecostal, Demos Shakarian. Additionally, the entry of singing icons like Pat Boone and Johnny Cash into the movement as well as the publicity accorded the new Charismatic movement with front-page articles in *Time* and *Newsweek* helped fuel the Charismatic movement's visibility during this era.

In 1967, the Roman Catholic Church itself entered the Charismatic movement. Catholics worldwide, especially in countries including the Philippines, India, Brazil, and in many parts of Africa, are now counted in the millions. There are as many Catholic Charismatics in the world today as there are classical Pentecostals. At the end of the 1960s, the Jesus Movement arose in the hippie culture of the USA's West Coast. This too was a reaction to modernity that was sparked off during the sixties revolution, and this movement which appealed to disenchanted hippies was decidedly Pentecostal in orientation.[17] The creation of the Society for Pentecostal Studies in the 1970s and formal dialogue between Pentecostal representatives and the Catholic Church (and later with other ecumenical bodies) led to Pentecostalism being seen for the first time as a reasonably intelligent part of contemporary Christianity that needed to be discovered and better understood.[18]

After the 1980s, the "Pentecostalization" of older churches, especially in Africa and Asia, accelerated while there simultaneously arose a new form of Pentecostalism with a fierce independentism that eschewed denominations and preferred to associate in loose "fellowships." This gave rise to Pentecostal "megachurches" that operate in cities including Lagos, Rio de Janeiro, Seoul, and Singapore, as well as in unexpected European places including Kyiv, Budapest, and Stockholm. Each of these latter three cases is the largest congregation in the country, and in London, the largest congregation is a predominantly Nigerian one.[19] The megachurches form networks of similar churches across the world, and these transnational associations are not only West-South but also South-South and East-South. Contemporary Pentecostalism is very much the result of the process of globalization, and "health and wealth" advocates are as much at home in Lagos and Rio as they are in Tulsa or Fort Worth. The mass media and internet, tourism and pilgrimages to megachurches, voluntarism, and an international economy all transpire to create conditions conducive to the spread of a globally-friendly movement like Pentecostalism.

Facts and Fantasies

Facts and figures on the growth of any global religious movement are notoriously difficult to come by. However, figures on the growth of Pentecostalism are exultingly quoted (especially by Pentecostals themselves), most frequently those of Todd Johnson and associates. According to their estimate, there were almost 694 million "Pentecostals/

Charismatics" in 2019, a quarter of the world's Christian population, projected to rise to over a billion by 2050. Considering that this figure is given at only 61 million in 1970, this is an enormous increase, taking place during Europe's secularization zenith.[20] In fact, the dramatic increase in Pentecostalism is best explained by reference to the three Majority World continents of Africa, Asia, and Latin America. North America had started earlier and made steady progress during the twentieth century, but classical Pentecostalism there, while influential, is not as significant as is sometimes claimed.

A survey conducted in 2007 by the Pew Forum on Religion and Public Life on religious affiliation in the United States found that Pentecostals (including Black Pentecostals) constituted 4% of the total population, part of the 26 percent classified as "Evangelical Protestant Churches," compared to 18 percent "Mainline Protestant Churches," and 24 percent Catholics. Of course, this 4 percent only refers to classical Pentecostal denominations, which includes the Assemblies of God and the Church of God in Christ, the two largest. The historically large denominations, various Baptists and Methodists, had 17 percent and 6 percent respectively.[21] With 16 percent of Americans declaring themselves as unaffiliated to any religious faith and the growing Catholic numbers, the USA is on the verge of losing its Protestant majority.

The European continent as a whole is very different. Although Pentecostals in Europe continued to make modest increases in membership during this period, they remain a small minority in the overall population, constituting fewer than 2 percent of the population in all countries except Portugal, where the vibrant Brazilian faith expression has influenced Pentecostalism. In Portugal, the Brazilian Universal Church of the Kingdom of God is the second-largest denomination after the Catholic Church. The Assemblies of God is well established in Portugal and was started in 1913 by Brazilian missionaries.[22]

David Martin takes issue with the common secularization theories in explaining the "exceptionalism" of Europe and suggests that Pentecostalism is less likely to succeed in the developed world because it "represents the mobilization of a minority of people at the varied margins of that world, whereas in the developing world it represents the mobilization of large masses."[23] He thinks that Pentecostalism flourishes in the United States because of its well-established Protestant pluralism and voluntarism while in Europe, Pentecostalism does not do as well where there is a strong state church. The exception to this is where there is more religious plurality with a significant minority of "free churches" like the Baptists, as is the case in Romania and Ukraine.

Questions of definition arise immediately when one considers what diverse and mutually independent movements are included in the reckoning of numbers.[24] We do not know how many people transfer into Pentecostal churches from older churches, as is certainly the case in Latin America, as well as in Eastern European countries including Romania and Ukraine, where the numbers of classical Pentecostals are greater than in any other European nation.[25] Any attempt at definition will fall short of precision, and it is highly doubtful whether one can ever define Pentecostalism adequately. Nevertheless, it cannot be assumed that there are 694 million "Pentecostals/Charismatics" in the world without further unpacking of what we mean. Only a fifth of this number consists of classical Pentecostals, those with direct or indirect historical links to the 1906–09 revival at Azusa Street in Los Angeles. Nonetheless, about 150 million classical Pentecostals worldwide after one century is still impressive. If we add to this number the many independent churches with a Pentecostal orientation, the Charismatic churches, and renewal movements within older churches, then we have a clearer picture of its magnitude. Global Pentecostalism as we know it today has been formed by long processes of interweaving events that took decades to emerge, but it has become a major component of global Christianity in the twenty-first century.

The decrease in religious affiliation in the so-called Christian West must be seen in light of the rest of the world. It is no accident that the southward shift in Pentecostalism's center of gravity over the twentieth century has coincided with the emergence and expansion of Pentecostalism. Over three-quarters of its adherents live in the Majority World. Worldwide, the numbers of Christian adherents have doubled in the past four decades, from 1.1 billion in 1970 to 2.2 billion in 2010.[26] In Africa especially, numbers of Christians exceeded numbers of Muslims in 1985 for the first time, and Christians are now almost the majority in the African continent, a phenomenon that the late Yale historian Lamin Sanneh described as "a continental shift of historic proportions."[27] There are now over four times as many Christians in Africa as there were in 1970 and almost the same in Asia, while the Christian population of Latin America has almost doubled. So most of this growth has occurred in the global South, where the influence of Pentecostalism is strongest. In contrast, the Christian population of Europe during the same period has increased only by about a quarter and that of North America by about a third.[28]

If we are to do justice to this global shift of Christianity from the North to the South, we must reckon with the contribution of its recent expressions in Pentecostalism. Even if statistics are wildly speculative, no observer of Christianity can deny the significance of Pentecostalism in today's religious landscape. Considering that this movement had a handful of adherents at the beginning of the twentieth century, its growth has been an astounding achievement. Other research corroborates this. The Pew Forum's 2006 research, "Spirit and Power: A 10-Country Survey of Pentecostals" estimated that classical Pentecostals formed 20 percent of the population of Guatemala, 15 percent in Brazil (the largest population of Pentecostals in any country) and 9 percent in Chile. Also impressive are the figures of the African countries of Kenya (33 percent), Nigeria (18 percent) and South Africa (10 percent). With Charismatics and independent churches added in, the figures increase considerably and "Renewalists" approximate half the national populations in Guatemala (60 percent), Brazil (49 percent), Kenya (56 percent) and the Philippines (44 percent).[29] In these countries, Pentecostalism is not only a significant proportion of Christianity, but it is a sizeable chunk of the entire population with enormous socio-political clout.

The many varieties of Pentecostalism have contributed to the reshaping of the nature of global religion and society, and this has important implications. Its adherents are often on the cutting edge of the encounter with people of other faiths, albeit sometimes confrontationally so. The secularization debates have to reckon with the fact that the future of global Christianity is affected by this seismic change in its character. The innovations, challenges, and achievements of Pentecostalism in the Majority World must be taken into account. One need only walk the streets of large African cities like Lagos to see how much Pentecostalism is woven into the fabric of African societies, with evidence of activities everywhere. The contours of the changing nature and demographics of global Christianity and the contribution of Pentecostalism to these features need to be considered by researchers on global religion.

Pentecostalization and Secularization

What is often not as much appreciated is the extent to which Pentecostalism takes on distinctive forms in different contexts. Of all

Christian expressions, Pentecostalism can transpose itself into local cultures and religions effortlessly because of its primary emphasis on the experience of the Spirit and the spiritual calling of leaders who do not have to be formally educated in church dogma. This leads to schism, but it also assists multiplication. The ability to adapt to different cultures combined with incessant evangelism contributes to the growth of Pentecostalism in the present day. Everywhere they are found, Pentecostals see themselves as witnesses for Christ in the power of the Spirit. Evangelism is often their priority, and this is especially true in the Majority World.[30]

In his last work on secularization, David Martin made the point that secularization is a process that is neither inevitable nor an undisputed paradigm, and is subject to differentiation within different social spheres. This social differentiation, where religious and other cultural monopolies are broken, is determined by historical contexts and promotes religious competition and plurality in certain societies while it favors secularization in others. Historical filters producing social differentiation must be taken into account because of these push secularization in different directions.[31] For these reasons, secularization varies enormously in different social groups. Martin considers that the grand meta-narrative of secularization might be "an ideological and philosophical imposition *on* history rather than an inference *from* history."[32] The growth of Pentecostalism in Latin America is an example of the effects of social differentiation, where the dominant Catholic Church was no longer seen as the binding glue of society, especially among the poorer classes. Its monopoly was broken and consequently, Latin American societies became more pluralistic. The reasons for this are complex, but new political factors often made the Catholic Church appear as the religion of the upper classes and foreign to indigenous and mestizo peoples.

The rise of the Charismatic movement in the Western world might also be seen as one result of the privatization of religion in the 1960s when the established churches no longer held monopoly and authority over all things moral and religious. It could be argued that Charismatic Christianity provided a panacea to the spiritual deficit in organized religion and Western society as a whole. Alternatively, as Harvey Cox has put it, not only were people disillusioned with traditional religions in the 1960s but also disappointed by "the bright promises of science and progress." Cox remarks that the "kernel of truth" in the "overblown claims" of the "death of God" theologians was that "the abstract deity of Western theologies and philosophical systems had come to the end of its run."[33] For Cox, the dramatic growth of Pentecostalism seemed to confirm rather than contradict what he had written about the "death of God" theologians in *The Secular City* three decades earlier:

> The volcanic eruption of a Christian movement that relies on the direct experience of the Divine Spirit rather than on archaic creeds and stately rituals seems to corroborate their diagnosis while it completely undercuts their prescription.[34]

The adaptability of Pentecostalism to culture is more easily achieved in those parts of the world where a spiritual universe exists and (for example) healing and the supernatural are regarded as normal experiences. This would also make Pentecostal forms of Christianity more amenable to the United States than in Germany or France. However, the principle of social differentiation means that there will always be groups for whom Pentecostalism is an attractive religious option, even in those countries where voluntarism, pluralism, and freedom of association are limited. There is much more that could be said on the subject. Why has Pentecostalism done well in South Korea while it has made little impact in Japan, where massive neo-Buddhist movements hold sway? China watchers and Chinese scholars themselves observe that the burgeoning new Christian movements there have many Pentecostal features, so that China may soon eclipse Brazil as the country with the most Charismatics, but of a very different nature.[35] There are indeed many reasons for the emergence of this burgeoning movement at the start of the twentieth century, its challenge to secularization theories, and whether it is affected by secularization in some parts of the world, are issues that need further research. This paper has attempted to paint some of the contours of this discussion in the hope that it will stimulate others to continue it.

Notes

1. Allan H. Anderson, *To the Ends of the Earth: Pentecostalism and the Transformation of World Christianity* (New York: Oxford University Press, 2013).
2. Hugh McLeod, *Religion and the People of Western Europe 1789–1989* (Oxford: Oxford University Press, 1997); Hugh McLeod, "The Crisis of Christianity in the West: Entering a Post-Christian Era?" in Hugh McLeod (ed.), *The Cambridge History of Christianity: World Christianity c.1914–c.2000* (Cambridge: Cambridge University Press, 2006), 323–47; Hugh McLeod, *The*

Religious Crisis of the 1960s (Oxford: Oxford University Press, 2010); Callum G. Brown, *The Death of Christian Britain* (London: Routledge, 2001).

3.   David Martin, *On Secularization: Towards a Revised General Theory* (Aldershot: Ashgate, 2005).

4.   Nils Bloch-Hoell, *The Pentecostal Movement* (London: Allen & Unwin, 1964); Walter J. Hollenweger, *The Pentecostals* (London: SCM, 1972).

5.   Walter J. Hollenweger, *Pentecostalism: Origins and Developments Worldwide* (Peabody, MA: Hendrickson, 1997), 18–20.

6.   Harvey Cox, *Fire from Heaven: The Rise of Pentecostal Spirituality and the Reshaping of Religion in the Twenty-First Century* (London: Cassell, 1996), 71.

7.   Harvey Cox, "Foreword," in Allan Anderson and Walter J. Hollenweger (eds.), *Pentecostals after a Century: Global Perspectives on a Movement in Transition* (Sheffield: Sheffield Academic Press, 1999), 7.

8.   Cox, *Fire from Heaven*, 46.

9.   Cox, *Fire from Heaven*, 48.

10.   Cox, *Fire from Heaven*, 58, 68–71.

11.   David Martin, *Tongues of Fire: The Explosion of Protestantism in Latin America* (Oxford: Blackwell, 1990); David Martin, *Pentecostalism: The World Their Parish* (Oxford: Blackwell, 2002).

12.   Kimberley Ervin Alexander, *Pentecostal Healing: Models in Theology and Practice* (Blandford Forum, Dorset: Deo Publishing, 2006), 24–27.

13.   *Triumphs of Faith* 1:1 (Jan 1881): 1, 3–5; Alexander, *Pentecostal Healing*, 151–60.

14.   The central texts were Acts 1:8; 2:4.

15.   Allan Anderson, *Spreading Fires: The Missionary Nature of Early Pentecostalism* (London & New York: SCM and Orbis Books, 2007).

16.   Martin, *On Secularization*, 144.

17.   Allan H. Anderson, *An Introduction to Pentecostalism*, 2nd ed. (Cambridge: Cambridge University Press, 2014), 144–155.

18.   Anderson, *Introduction to Pentecostalism*, 253–258.

19.   Anderson, *To the Ends of the Earth*, 255.

20.   Gina A. Zurlo, Todd M. Johnson, and Peter F. Crossing, "Christianity 2019: What's Missing? A Call for Further Research," *International Bulletin of Mission Research* 43:1 (2019), 96.

21.   http://religions.pewforum.org/affiliations, accessed 9 April 2010.

22.   Anderson, *Introduction to Pentecostalism*, 97.

23.   Martin, *Pentecostalism*, 67–70.

24.   Allan Anderson, "Varieties, Definitions and Taxonomies," in A. Anderson, M. Bergunder, A. Droogers, and C. Van der Laan (eds.), *Studying Global Pentecostalism: Theories and Methods* (Berkeley, CA: University of California Press, 2010).

25.   Anderson, *Introduction to Pentecostalism*, 109.

26.   Todd M. Johnson, David B. Barrett, and Peter F. Crossing, "Christianity 2010: A View from the New *Atlas of Global Christianity*," *International Bulletin*

of Missionary Research 34:1 (2010), 36.

27.   Lamin Sanneh, *Disciples of All Nations: Pillars of World Christianity* (New York: Oxford University Press, 2008), 274–75.

28.   Johnson, Barrett, and Crossing, "Christianity 2010," 36.

29.   Pew Research Center, "Spirit and Power — A 10-Country Survey of Pentecostals," 2008. https://www.pewforum.org/2006/10/05/spirit-and-power/, accessed 30 January 2020.

30.   Anderson, *An Introduction to Pentecostalism*, 210–211.

31.   Martin, *On Secularization*, 58–59.

32.   Martin, *On Secularization*, 19.

33.   Cox, *Fire from Heaven*, 16, 83, 104.

34.   Cox, "Foreword," 7.

35.   Anderson, *Introduction to Pentecostalism*, 150–151.

5.

"And These Signs Shall Follow...": Authenticity and Authentication of the Gospel in the Early Church

Clayton Coombs

Abstract

This study explores the importance of signs in authenticating the declaration of Christ as the only Savior, through a presentation of the 2nd century reception of Mark 16:17–18. Several pieces of evidence from the second century Irenaean tradition are analyzed from a pastoral and practical perspective in order to determine what may be learned for today's Spirit Empowered community. These early sources appear to affirm that the Pentecostal appropriation of the promise of signs is consistent with the teaching of the early post-Acts church. These connections are important because they provide early support in the tradition for Pentecostal preaching and practice, and because they undergird and inform Pentecostal Hermeneutics.

Key words: Irenaeus, signs, authority, doctrine, hermeneutics

Introduction

In Mark 16:17–18, Jesus promised,

> . . . these signs will follow those who believe. In my name, they will cast out demons. They will speak in new tongues; they will take up serpents; and if they drink any deadly thing, it will by no means hurt them. They will lay hands on the sick and they will recover.

This passage is a key text for substantiating the link between the proclamation of the one true gospel and miracles performed in Jesus' name. For this reason, it has been a treasured text, particularly for

113

Pentecostal Christians throughout the twentieth century, who have both the expectation and the experience of the immediacy of God's presence manifested in various ways. On the same grounds, it was also an important text in the Irenaean tradition of the second century, which, like the current Pentecostal movement, represented a time in the history of the church that expected and experienced the moving of the Holy Spirit in miraculous and spectacular ways.[1]

This study represents a small part of a much larger research project on the reception of Mark 16:9–20, the so-called "Longer Ending of Mark." It will focus on the reception of this passage in Irenaeus and the related Hyppolytan material, both of which derive from the second century.[2] There are numerous issues of interest raised by such a study. Some are of a more academic nature; the extent to which pre-fourth century discourse on this passage can aid in establishing the 'original' form of the Markan autograph, the relationship between authorship and authority in pre-critical scholarship, the nascent practice of textual criticism and its relative importance in the era of scribal transmission of the text, the intertextual nature of patristic exegesis, etc. Others are clearly pastoral/ practical in nature, namely, the extent to which supernatural signs like those described in Mark 16:17, 18 occurred at various times in the church's history, the role of signs in authenticating the message of the gospel, and how such subjective evidence should function alongside other more objective sources of ecclesial authority. Since it is impossible to treat any one of these issues in isolation, they are all, in some way, represented in what follows. However, given the context of this consultation, the focus of the present study is practical and pastoral. In particular, inter-related questions will form the framework of this paper, namely, which version of the Gospel of Mark is the author reading; what is his understanding, expectation, and experience of the miraculous gifts of the Spirit; and what can be learned from his approach for contemporary Pentecostalism?

Irenaeus

The single unambiguous citation of the Longer Ending in the corpus of Irenaeus takes up the theme of the fulfillment of Psalm 110. In a section in which Irenaeus is making an argument for the consistency of the New Testament and the Old concerning the oneness of God, and hence the coessentiality of the Word with the Father, Irenaeus cites Mark 16:19 explicitly stating that it comes from the Gospel of Mark:

> Moreover, in the conclusion of the Gospel, Mark says: "Indeed the Lord Jesus after he had spoken to them was received into heaven and sat down at the right hand of God" (thus) confirming what was said by the prophet: "The Lord said to my Lord 'Sit at my right hand until I make your enemies your footstool.'" Therefore God and Father are one and the same, the One who was announced beforehand by the prophets, (and who) was handed down by the true Gospel, whom we Christians desire and love wholeheartedly, the Maker of heaven and earth and all that is in them.[3]

This is part of a larger argument that Irenaeus is making about the essential continuity between the God of Israel, God's promises to Israel through the prophets, and the fulfillment of these promises in the incarnation of Christ. He is refuting the Gnostic claim that Christ represents an essentially different reality and dispensation from what the Jews had received, understood, and worshipped. It is important for him that from the beginning, the gospel confirms what has been said in the prophets.

Of significance for our purposes here is first that Irenaeus' interpretation of the latter part of the Longer Ending as a fulfillment of the prophecy of Psalm 110 is consistent with prior interpretations of the passage.[4] Second, given those prior interpretations, the association between the Psalms passage, which, in addition to predicting Christ's session at the Father's right hand, promised a scepter of authority which can be associated with the proclamation of power (the demonstration of that power being the signs that accompany those who believe), and the end of Mark 16 can perhaps be read in light of other Irenaean material which claims the continuing manifestation of miracles among the churches as proof of their orthodox proclamation of the eternal gospel.

In the *Adversus haereses* between section 2.31.2 and 2.32.4, Irenaeus makes a sustained argument against the magical practices and false miracles occurring among the heretics, particularly the ones belonging to Simon and Carpocrates (*qui sunt a Simone et Carpocrate*).[5] Irenaeus contrasts these false miracles of the heretics with the true miracles that occur amongst the Christians claiming that among the Christians Christ's power to raise the dead, which was continued through the apostles, was still present. He even goes so far as to claim that this happened frequently (*saepissime*) in the Christian community in response to fasting and prayer.[6] The heretics, by contrast, taught that physical resurrection was not even possible and that the concept ought to be understood as a kind of enlightenment experience.[7]

It should be noted that James Kelhoffer sees this passage, which apparently demonstrates Irenaeus' interest in the ongoing manifestation of miracles in the orthodox assemblies, as the exception rather than the rule. He discerns in Irenaeus a "general tendency to *avoid* the miraculous or to discuss miracles only in relation to other points," which for him may at least in part explain Irenaeus' apparent lack of interest in verses 17 and 18 of the Markan ending.[8] In any case, one may certainly counter that Irenaeus' lack of interest in vs. 17–18, far from being evidence of uneasiness about the topic, bears witness to the normativity of the occurrence of miracles in the churches to which Irenaeus related. Indeed, that seems to be his point in the quote above — that miracles *normally* occur. They may be regularly anticipated and literally experienced among the orthodox Christians. The performers of these miracles are not named, which seems to indicate that neither the occurrence of miracles nor those who performed them ought to be considered particularly extraordinary.

But it seems, contra Kelhoffer, that Irenaeus does indeed consider the presence of post-apostolic miracles to be verification of the authenticity of the gospel as preached by the orthodox. Irenaeus is responding to claims that miracles are occurring in the communities of heretics. It is significant in this regard that his defense is not to downplay the importance of miracles, but rather to undermine the veracity of the miracles that occurred in heretical communities. The orthodox have true miracles (even the raising of the dead), and hence the true message. The heretics have "smoke and mirrors" and therefore not the true message. Irenaeus first makes it clear that these so-called miracles were different in kind from Christian miracles (past and present) in that they were illusory and lacking real power. He distinguishes the miracles that occur among the orthodox from those pseudo-miracles occurring in the communions of the heretics on four bases as follows:

> ... who do not do the things that they do by God's power neither in truth nor for the benefit of humans, but rather in mischief and error, by magical evasions and universal deception, thus causing more harm than good to the ones who believe in them. Neither are they able to give sight to the blind, nor hearing to the deaf, nor to drive out all demons, except those which they send from themselves, if they can even do this, nor are they able to cure the weak or the lame or paralytics, or ones who are vexed in any other part of their bodies, just as it turns out has often been done in response to bodily infirmity.[9]

Irenaeus goes on to further claim that they cannot cure injury that results from an accident or call the dead back to life. The implication is that all of these things have been done among the churches that preach the true gospel.

Thus the true miracles are to be distinguished from the false on the basis, first, of the means by which they are accomplished. True miracles are done by the power of God, whereas false miracles are performed merely through magical evasions and universal deception. The true are to be distinguished from the false, second, based on the method. Christian miracles are performed in connection with the truth — that is they are done *in veritate* — whereas the false miracles are done in mischief and error. Third, they are to be distinguished based on motivation. True miracles are performed to benefit people, whereas false miracles do more harm than good because they have the effect of leading people astray. Furthermore, Irenaeus implies a profit motivation among the heretics when he urges that Christians not only perform miracles without charging a fee, but provide from their own resources for the practical needs of those whom they cure.[10]

That the presence of miraculous power substantiates a truth claim is acknowledged by both sides of this argument. The heretics, it seems, attempt to address their lack of real power in two different ways. First, they perform cheap magic tricks and illusions to impress gullible folk. This proves for Irenaeus that they are not miracle workers who follow Christ, but magicians who follow Simon Magus. Says Irenaeus:

> But even if [these magicians] do accomplish something, by means of magic (as I have called it), they strive fraudulently to lead away the unwise; they neither produce fruit nor indeed provide (any) benefit for those in whom they claim to bring about virtues. Instead, they bring young boys and display phantoms that disappear instantly and do not endure even for a moment of time. In this way, they are shown not to be like Jesus our Lord, but Simon the magician.[11]

The second way that these heretics attempt to bridge the gap that exists between their own practices and the legitimate works of power performed by Jesus, his apostles, and faithful followers in Irenaeus' own day was to assert that Christ himself performed miracles in appearance only.[12] In response to this, Irenaeus declares that the miracles Christ performed were, in fact, the sort that had been prophesied of him, thus proving his claims concerning himself. In addition, he again, holds up the miraculous powers that those who were "truly his disciples" enjoyed in Irenaeus' day. Section 2.32.4 is the conclusion to his argument and pertinent to this inquiry. I quote it here in full.

> But if they claim that even the Lord did (miracles) in the same way — by phantoms [that is, in appearance only, by trickery] — we point them to the prophetic books, from which we will demonstrate that all of the things (that he did) were predicted concerning him and most assuredly happened and that he is the only Son of God. And this is why in his name, those who are truly his disciples, who receive grace from him, accomplish (miracles) which benefit the rest of mankind, each one according to the gift that s/he received from him. Indeed some drive out demons most assuredly and truly, with the result that those who have been cleansed from the vile spirits frequently come to faith and are added to the church. Others have foreknowledge of the future and visions and prophetic utterances, others cure those suffering variously with sickness by the imposition of hands, and they are restored to health. Indeed even the dead have been raised, as I have said, and they lived many years among us (after being raised). And what else? It is impossible to specify the number of gifts that the Church receives throughout the whole world from God in the name of Jesus Christ who was crucified under Pontius Pilate, and (which the church) exercises every single day for the help of the nations, neither deceiving any nor extorting any money from them. For just as (the Church) received freely from God, it also ministers freely.[13]

Irenaeus' summary is simple. Jesus did real miracles fulfilling prophecy and thus proving that he is the Son of God. His followers continue to do real miracles, proving by these works and their selfless motivation that they truly are his disciples. What is of particular interest in this summary though is that Irenaeus mentions at least the first and the fifth of the signs in the Mark 16:17–18 list and perhaps also the second. Furthermore, if Irenaeus' mention of foreknowledge, visions and prophetic utterances may be taken as broadly referring to inspired speech — at the very least the same type of phenomenon as the sign of tongues — then these signs are mentioned in the order in which they occur in Mark 16:17–18.[14] It should be noted that for Irenaeus, these phenomena are identified not as "signs" as in Mark, but "gifts" as in 1 Cor 12, 14. In Paul's discussion of the appropriate use of the spiritual gifts in the context of the local assembly, tongues and prophecy are likened and compared based on their usefulness for edifying the body. Both are a form of inspired speech, and like prophecy, the gift of tongues may also edify if it is given with interpretation.

Irenaeus' insistence that the presence of the miraculous authenticates the true Christian message may well be informed by his reception of Mark 16:9–20. Indeed, given his unambiguous citation of Mark 16:19 elsewhere in the treatise, there is no reason to suppose that it is not, whether he intends a reference to the verses here or not. If he does intend the reference, which seems not unlikely, the absence of the third and fourth sign, together with the addition of the other (frankly more impressive) sign, the raising of the dead, indicates that Irenaeus views the list as suggestive rather than exhaustive. "These signs" means for Irenaeus "these sorts of signs." Thus he felt free to substitute the miraculous events of which he was aware, for those which he either felt dubious about or had not personally witnessed — the third and fourth signs. Indeed on this principle, any of God's "gifts," which he identifies these miracles as, may be evidence of true and orthodox Christianity.

It is difficult to say whether Irenaeus interpreted the promise of signs literally because of the miracles that were occurring among the churches in his day, which his account bears witness to, or whether he expected and encouraged miraculous manifestations as a result of his interpretation.[15] What is clear is that Irenaeus expected that literal miracles would bear witness to the Christian truth wherever it was truly found. This is consistent with a literal interpretation of Jesus' promise that signs would follow those who believe in Mark 16:17.

Nevertheless, the pattern that Kelhoffer identifies, the rule to which 2.31–32 appears to be the exception, of avoiding the topic of miracles where possible should not be lightly dismissed. Kelhoffer's broader point stands. Irenaeus does seem intent, despite his insistence on the reality of present-day miracles as a continuity of the ministry of Jesus and the apostles, on diverting attention away from these manifestations to the higher points of doctrine. To substantiate this pattern Kelhoffer points to Irenaeus' mention of the miracle of turning the water into wine in the same *Adversus haereses* 3.11.5, but notes in this case Irenaeus' greater interest in "his argument against the Gnostics that the created order is good."[16] He cites Irenaeus' discussion of apostolic succession in *Adversus haereses* 3.2–5 noting that the miracles that the apostles performed are not mentioned, but only their doctrine.[17] He further notes that Irenaeus' description of Paul's teaching in *Adversus haereses* 4.24.1–2 omits any mention of Paul's miracles.[18] Finally, he traces this tendency in Irenaeus' *Demonstration of the Apostolic Preaching*, "which never refers to miracles performed by Jesus, his followers or those whom Irenaeus deemed heretical."[19]

Kelhoffer's observation raises the question as to why Irenaeus, who bears witness to amazing miracles — the dead even having been raised — and who suggests that the true churches may be known by the occurrence of true miracles, would seek to elevate doctrine and downplay the miraculous. Two reasons for this are immediately apparent. And both of these, in fact, illuminate the question of Irenaeus' reception of the Longer Ending of Mark. The first is the somewhat self-evident observation that in a document such as *Adversus haereses*, Irenaeus' central concern is the refutation of false doctrine. Obviously, the way that he does this is to teach true doctrine. Interestingly in this regard, Schildgen finds that the Gospel of Mark was problematic for Irenaeus. She counts over 100 citations of the Gospel of Mark in the entire treatise, but double the number of citations of Matthew. Schildgen suggests that this was because Mark taught a "low Christology" and that Irenaeus was "[t]hreatened by the gnostic interpretations of Mark."[20] According to her, Irenaeus "sees Mark as less decisive on the divine nature of Jesus than the other Gospels."[21] This is probably at least one reason why in discussing the gospels Irenaeus goes out of his way to (apparently) define the limits of the Gospel of Mark, including the Longer Ending (which, as discussed in the introduction teaches a higher Christology). As I have made clear above, he does this with no other Gospel. Irenaeus' focus on doctrine, then, is necessitated both by false doctrine from without and the potential for incorrect interpretation of scripture from within. In this connection, Irenaeus' reception of the Longer Ending of Mark helped ensure that the second Gospel told the "right" story.

The second reason why Irenaeus might seek to downplay the miraculous and to elevate correct doctrine is to address the very problem to which *Adverses haereses* 2.31.2–2.32.4 is directed, namely the problem of authority. For if the occurrence of miracles was being claimed to legitimate false teaching then the basis for authority lay in the miracles themselves, and hence potentially outside the church of the orthodox. Irenaeus then is in a curious position, which he negotiates masterfully. On the one hand, he must remove the basis of the heretics' authority — the miracles that they claimed were occurring. On the other hand, he had to ensure that the basis for the authority of the orthodox church was not damaged in the process. Irenaeus is of course not writing to the various heretical sects in *Adverses haereses*, but rather to the church about the various heresies that he feels are dangerous to the church. In order to address a heresy which invests such meaning in experience in general, and the experience of the miraculous in particular as the heresy of Simon and Carpocrates evidently did,[22] Irenaeus must first diminish the value of the experiences that the heretics used to impress and deceive their followers, but second, he must remind his readers of the experience of the miraculous and true power of God that was manifested in the churches of the orthodox. However, having done that, Irenaeus seeks to point away from experiences to surer foundations of authority. His goal then appears to be to arm readers with discernment so that when confronted with amazing and apparently miraculous experiences they would not automatically conclude that what they were witnessing was the power of the true God operating, but rather that they would question the nature of the experiences; the method, the motive and the means; to determine if indeed the miracles were "orthodox." Obviously, given the problem of authority which Irenaeus encountered, a text like Mark 16:17–18 was a difficult one to deal with. Irenaeus certainly needs the Longer Ending to conclude Mark's Gospel in a doctrinally satisfactory way, that invests authority in the apostles and finishes with Christ seated at the right hand of the Father providing power to the apostolic church. However, we may understand why though he appears to allude to Mark 16:17–18 in the section discussed above, he may also seek to diminish its importance by substituting promised signs with ones that were actually occurring, and by placing greater emphasis on doctrine than on experience.

Hippolytus

This problem of authority is also evident in the way in which the Longer Ending is handled in the traditions associated with Hippolytus, who was Irenaeus' student according to tradition. The identification of the historical figure of Hippolytus is problematic. Indeed Kannengiesser asserts that "[i]n recent scholarship, Hippolytus is probably the most controversial writer of the early church."[23] Eusebius has little to say about him in the *Ecclesiastical History*. He simply records that Hippolytus authored a number of treatises including Περὶ τοῦ πάσχα, that he was among a company of "learned churchmen" (λόγιοι καὶ ἐκκλησιαστικοὶ ἄνδρες) and that he had some kind of presidency over a church somewhere — though Eusebius is either unable or unwilling to identify both the location of the church and the specific nature of the leadership role that Hippolytus exercised.[24] However, debate now exists over not just what role he played in the church and where, but also on whether there were two or more people by that name.[25] Specifically, the problem seems to be that while history has remembered him as "Hippolytus of Rome," some of the works attributed to him have a distinctly Eastern flavor.[26] The exact identity of the historical Hippolytus is less important to this discussion, however, than is the historical association with this person and the person of Irenaeus of Lyon, and the similarity in the interpretation of the promise that signs will follow those who believe that is evidenced in Irenaeus and in two documents which are associated with Hippolytus that I will establish here.[27] In addition, the precise relationship between the *Apostolic Constitutions* and the *Apostolic Tradition*, both of which I will discuss here, and of which are associated with (if not always definitively attributed to) the person of Hippolytus, is less important than the simple fact that there is abundant evidence that they are indeed related.[28]

Among the works associated with Hippolytus there is a particularly important discussion of Mark 16:17–18 in the *Apostolic Constitutions* that I will examine in some depth. Before this though, I will mention another fairly strong allusion in the *Apostolic Tradition*. It is found in Section 36:

> And everyone who is faithful should try to partake of the Eucharist before they eat anything else. For if they would partake in faith, even though someone should give to them deadly poison, after this it will not prevail against him.[29]

This text is significant to our discussion for at least three reasons. First, it is almost certainly a reference to the fourth sign of Mark 16:17–18, which is entirely absent in Irenaeus. Though the use of the word θανάσιμον, literally a "deadly thing," is the only verbal agreement between the *Apostolic Tradition* and the text of the fourth sign (unless we count the adjective πιστὸς used twice), the conceptual link is unmistakable. The faithful (similar though not identical to the participial πιστεύσασιν in Mark 16:18) are promised protection from θανάσιμον. Second, it evidences what I have been calling a literal interpretation of the sign list, or at the very least of the fourth sign.[30] Third, while Irenaeus considers the first and fifth, and possibly also the second sign (though perhaps, by extension, all five) to be "gifts" hence linking them with 1 Cor 12 and other Pauline passages, Hippolytus interprets the fourth sign, the promise of immunity from poison, to be a consequent benefit of taking the Eucharist. However, as we turn to the next passage (if indeed Hippolytan) it is evident that in addition to the link between the Eucharist and the fourth sign, he not only interprets all five signs literally but also considers all five as gifts, making the link to 1 Cor 12, 14 explicit. It is to this passage that we now turn. I will quote just the text surrounding the reference to the Longer Ending for context, but it will be necessary to trace the whole argument that is being made in this and surrounding sections.

> Our God and Savior Jesus Christ handed down to us the great mystery of piety and called both Jews and Greeks to the full knowledge of the one and only true God, as he himself somewhere said, while he was giving thanks for the salvation of the ones who had believed, "I made known your name to men, I finished the work you gave me," and saying to the Father concerning us, "Holy Father, though the world did not know you, I know you, and these ones knew you." It is suitable that he said to all of us who are mature, concerning the gifts given by him through the Holy Spirit, "And these signs will follow those who believe. In my name they will cast out demons, they will speak with new tongues, they will take up snakes, and if they drink any deadly thing, it will certainly not harm them. They will lay hands on those who are sick and they will get well." These gifts were given first to us apostles (when) we were about to proclaim the gospel to all of creation; thereafter they were ministered to those who necessarily through us had (also) believed, not for the benefit of the ones who exercise them, but rather for the submission of the unbelievers, in order that the miraculous power of the signs might put to shame the ones who the word (alone) did not persuade. For the signs are not for our benefit, but for the benefit of the unbelievers, both Jews and Greeks.[31]

That the primary problem that this document, in general, is dealing with is the problem of authority is evident by its very premise. It purports to be the tradition of the apostles themselves. It is not surprising then that such a tradition evidences reception of the Longer Ending of Mark. For the very authority of the apostles and their successors; the episcopacy of the Church; depends upon their having been witnesses to the risen Christ and recipients of divine power and commission. The short conclusion of Mark, which ends with the fear and failure of the women is inadequate for this purpose and though the other Gospels could indeed fill the gap left by Mark's inadequate conclusion, the presence of Mark in the canon would always provide a resource for those who wanted to believe an unorthodox Christ and hence to form unorthodox groups, as Irenaeus' reception of Mark outlined above demonstrates.

This passage, as in Irenaeus, illustrates a literal reception of the signs, though unlike Irenaeus, all of the signs are mentioned (though this is to be expected, since Mark 16:17–18 is, simply excerpted rather than paraphrased).[32] This passage answers the question of authority by reminding the reader that the apostles were the first to receive the signs. However, it does not limit the operation of these to the apostles alone, though it does make clear that those who subsequently believed and likewise received the signs believed because of the testimony of the apostles. However, the signs were not given for the benefit of those who received them, but rather for the benefit of unbelievers who would through the manifestation of the signs be brought themselves to belief in Christ. The signs are associated with the gifts of the Spirit. Moreover, the explicit link is made, perhaps on account of the second sign, with the discussion concerning the operation of the gift of tongues in the church in 1 Cor 14.[33] By association, the true recipients of all of the signs/gifts — not just the sign/gift of tongues — are not the believers who exercise them, but the unbelievers who may be brought to belief on account of them. Indeed, the *Constitutiones Apostolorum* state that the signs are to shame those whom the preaching of the word alone did not convince. Though not all will believe even on the basis of the signs, but only those of a "good disposition" (εὐγνώμονας).[34] Even the signs can be resisted just as the signs of Moses were resisted by Jannes and Jambres, the plagues were resisted by the Egyptians, and the very miracles of Christ himself were resisted by Annas and Caiphas.[35] Here, we may observe the same kind of hierarchy as we encountered in Irenaeus where the message itself — that is matters of doctrine — is more important than the experience of the demonstration of the power of the word. This should be emphasized. Even where the signs are literally expected and experienced, these alone should not be the basis of one's faith.

The association with spiritual gifts and the link he makes to 1 Cor 14 also allows the author to bring in the discussion concerning spiritual gifts in 1 Cor 12:4–31. Whatever signs are experienced then are the "manifestation of the Spirit" (1 Cor 12:7) that each one experiences, though not everybody will experience the same gift/sign. The author points out that it is not necessary for all to exhibit miraculous gifts, of which, curiously, he names now only three — the casting out of demons, speaking in other tongues and raising the dead. Though this section is clearly expounding Mark 16:17–18, the author, like Irenaeus before him, apparently substitutes the same non-Markan sign into the incomplete Markan list indicating that he interpreted the sign list as open, not closed ("These sorts of things," not just "These things" as in Irenaeus). Though whether this sign is substituted in on the basis of Irenaeus' interpretation or because the operation of this particular miracle had been witnessed by the author of the document, or whether, indeed, the author simply uses hyperbole to make his point (whatever the gift, even if it were raising the dead) is difficult even to speculate about, given the mystery that surrounds the provenance of the document. The miraculous signs then — whatever they may be — are a means of bringing unbelievers to belief. Indeed, it is conversion that is the true miracle, and thus whether or not a believer may manifest miraculous gifts such as speaking in tongues or raising the dead, every believer is a recipient of the "gift" of conversion, the gift of a mind that has turned from polytheism, or from Judaism, and embraced the truth about Jesus, the Son of God. This truth is articulated as follows:

> That by the pleasure of God he was begotten before the ages, was born from a virgin in (this) latter time without intercourse with a man, and that he lived (among us) as a man, without sin having fulfilled all the righteousness of the law, and that by the agreement of God he, the Logos of God endured the cross despising its shame, and that he died and was buried and was raised within three days and after the resurrection, having remained with the apostles for forty days and having fulfilled all his constitutions he was taken up before their eyes to the God and Father who sent him.[36]

This creedal statement is followed by the assurance that the one who has believed these things, has received the gift of God.[37] It is for this reason that any one of those who "works signs and wonders," τις τῶν ποιούντων σημεῖα καὶ τέρατα, must not exalt themselves above any of the faithful/believers (τῶν πιστῶν)[38] who have not been granted these gifts, since both alike have received the one gift that is determinative of salvation, the gift of conversion. That the one who works miracles must not despise the one who does not is substantiated by a number of examples: Moses did not despise Aaron, despite the miracles that God worked through him; Joshua did not despise Caleb and Phineas, despite the sun being caused to stand still at his request; Samuel the prophet, though God spoke through him, did not despise David, the king; Elijah did not despise Obadiah, nor his servant Elisha; Elisha did not despise his servant; Daniel did not despise his fellows; nor did Shadrach Meshach, and Abednego, since they knew that it was by God's power and not their own that they were "accomplishing signs and being delivered from difficulties."[39] The conclusion to be drawn from these examples is that all, despite whatever gifts they may manifest, are equal in Christ, though not all have equal function. Bishops and deacons must not despise those they lead, and the laity must respect those who are over them. For it is God alone who bestows the various offices of the church. The conclusion of these examples is that to manifest miraculous gifts does not equate to any ecclesial authority.

The next section hones in particularly on the gift of inspired speech, amplifying that the prophetic gift specifically does not automatically qualify one for ecclesiastical office.[40] The argument advances along two lines. First, accurately prophesying in no way guarantees that the prophet is of good character or indeed inspired by the true God, at all. Balaam, for example, truly spoke for God, though he did so reluctantly, evidencing his poor character. Caiphas, as high priest, prophesied without his own awareness. Though speaking truly for God, he was not even a believer in Jesus. Furthermore, even the demons could foretell the future and speak accurately about Christ. Thus the false bishops (apparently leaders of heretical movements) run the risk of being exposed and defeated in the same way as the sons of Sceva were. Second, even those who prophesy truly, being inspired by the true God, who are of good character do not qualify themselves by so doing for ecclesial office. For example, though Agabus prophesied, he did not on that account presume to consider themselves among the company of the apostles. The four daughters of Philip (who it seems, according at least to this tradition, all eventually married) did indeed prophesy, but did not by so doing exalt themselves above the natural authority of their own husbands.[41] Having then firmly established this principle, that the operation of miraculous gifts cannot and must not operate outside God-determined authority — the *Constitutiones* moves on to the main point of the eighth book which is the ordination of presbyters.

In conclusion, as we observed with Irenaeus, the *Apostolic Constitutions* bears witness to an environment where miraculous manifestations were both expected, and literally experienced. For that reason, some instruction was needed to govern their use in order to deal with the problem of authority that this created. The somewhat lengthy discussion concerning signs/spiritual gifts does not seek to deprive lay Christians of the operation of miraculous gifts, though it does qualify that the function of signs is to bring the faithless to faith, and therefore, that where unbelief no longer exists, these things are no longer necessary. Rather, the discussion is necessary to establish first, that the operation of gifts does not alone qualify a person for the ecclesial office, and second, and perhaps more importantly, that the non-operation of gifts does not disqualify a person from office. In this way the laity are protected from being drawn away by false signs that do not operate under the correct authority; they are prevented from raising themselves above their God-appointed leaders because of their own charisma; and the bishops are protected from the accusation that since they manifest no miraculous signs, they are not true bishops. While Irenaeus then answers the question of authority created by the continuity of miracles into his time by distinguishing between true and false miracles and by elevating orthodox doctrine as more important than the experience of supernatural miracles, the *Constitutiones* extends this answer by placing the operation of miracles under proper ecclesial oversight.

Implications and Conclusion

What then can be gleaned from the reception of Mark 16:17–18 in the Irenaean tradition of the second century? First, a word about the use of scripture. We, as the worldwide Pentecostal communion, need to embrace and strengthen our roots — scripture, the proclamation of the gospel, and an expectation of the power of the Holy Spirit — rather than capitulating to the (at times almost overwhelming) pressure to "mature" as a movement, lest in the name of "growing up" we lose the childlike simplicity of our faith. We have always preferred the raw heat of God's fire to the dignified complacency of lukewarmness; childlike simplicity with a lived experience of the Spirit to a grown-up faith without evidence of his power. We have, as is often observed, wanted at times for theological depth, often supplanting good theology with any theology, as long as it sounds more sophisticated than what we are accustomed to hearing from the pulpit. In this, we have erred greatly, not because our desire for greater depth is misplaced, but because we have sought in vain for strong theological allies in recent discourse. This has always made us vulnerable to a fundamentalist turn because we have been faced with two equally impossible alternatives; the first to accept a good sounding theology foreign to our experience, and the second to reject "theology" all together on the grounds that it will cost us our Pentecostal soul. The first of these alternatives rightly makes us uncomfortable because foreign theological systems will over time tend to undermine rather than undergird our experience. But the latter is unacceptable because it leaves us vulnerable to all sorts of theological novelty and spiritual pride that will end (and has ended) in isolation, eroded passion, and heresy. But these are not the only alternatives. It is further back that we must reach if we are to find the security of theological allies that both understand and accept scripture the way we do — this ought to be taken as a non-negotiable — and share the experiences that we treasure. The reception of Mark 16:17–18 serves as a great example of this tension between ancient and modern interpretation where we see on the one hand, fundamentalist Pentecostal cults that practice snake handling and poison drinking, and on the other hand, an interpretive tradition almost entirely foreign to the early church, which is more concerned with authorship than authority allowing the question of "authenticity" to drown out the more important questions of contemporary interpretation and usage. The present study is also a small example of a much broader reappropriation that needs to take place of the rich interpretive tradition of the church, which will provide a better anchor for Pentecostal theology to develop than its shallow twentieth century roots.

Second, the presence of spiritual manifestations did (and do) have an authenticating function. However, they were (and are) alone insufficient to authenticate the message of the gospel, since miracles of lesser quality could apparently be done, or at the very least faked by those who did not believe rightly in, or declare rightly about Jesus. However, these lesser or fake miracles could readily be discerned both by their motivation and by their fruit. Healings or miracles performed for fear, manipulation, or financial gain are not evidence of truth rightly believed or preached. The fact that miracles can be faked is a sobering thought, particularly as the proliferation of miracles in the Pentecostal church is (rightly) encouraged and celebrated. There is nothing to be gained by exaggerating the quality or quantity of miracles. Indeed, such exaggeration, insofar as it leads to the enhancement of personal prestige amongst our peers is evidence of the very thing that weakens the authenticating function of signs. Miracles neither derive from nor in themselves enhance or promote the authority of the human vessel that God uses. Both miracles and ecclesial authority are given by God and are not always correlated. To put it bluntly, we should not promote people beyond the level of their character, regardless of the extent to which God's power works through them.

Third, the Irenaean tradition reads both the miraculous gifts of the Spirit of 1 Cor 12 and 14 and the promise of signs that would follow the believing community as broadly referring to the same thing (as, of course, they are), namely, the manifest power of God that is present when the true gospel is preached, and the name of Jesus appropriated by believers. This outpouring of power is a fulfillment of the promise of Psalm 110 that associates Christ's session at the right hand of God to rule with the manifestation of his power.

Fourth and finally, this high view of Christ's kingdom rule accompanied by the promise of his power lead the church both to expect, and to regularly experience signs and wonders. Indeed, miracles were to be expected wherever the message of the gospel was declared and the name of Jesus Christ proclaimed. The early church was clear that the primary purpose of miracles was to cultivate faith and that these were often not necessary where faith in spite of evidence — necessarily a stronger faith — was held. Nevertheless, compassion itself is sufficient motivation for the miraculous both in scripture and in the church. In the same way, the church today should not slacken in its expectation that the manifest power of God will follow the preaching of the word. These signs indeed shall follow those who believe and faithfully declare. And many will be swept into God's kingdom as a result.

Notes

1. It is perhaps ironic that, throughout roughly the same timeframe as the modern Pentecostal movement — that is, since the time of the discovery of the great fourth century Alexandrian codices — a scholarly debate has raged over the position of Mark 16:9–20 in the canon. The consensus goes that since these twelve verses, the so-called "Longer Ending of Mark" is not found at the end of Mark's Gospel in a few important early manuscripts from the fourth century on, its authorship and consequently its relationship to the rest of the Gospel of Mark cannot be established with any certainty. For this reason, the passage has been relegated as secondary, and hence lacking any normative authority by the mainstream of New Testament scholars. As the Pentecostal movement has matured theologically it has deepened its engagement with mainstream scholarship, and as such, Pentecostal appeals to this passage have been rendered virtually mute. This is a great shame. But while there remains a robust minority who contend for the authenticity of these verses by insisting on Markan authorship, what follows in this paper is not an argument for the authenticity of the Mark 16:9–20. Such would merely surrender the home ground advantage to a modernist hermeneutic that seems at times to place a higher exegetical premium on humans than on divine authorial intent. Rather it is an appeal to the authority that these verses exercised over the early church as evidenced by their pre-fourth century reception.

2. Large parts of this chapter are excerpted and adapted from Clayton Coombs, *A Dual Reception: Eusebius and the Gospel of Mark* (Minneapolis: Fortress Press, 2016), 39–75.

3. Irenaeus, *Adversus haereses* 3.10.6 (SC 211:136, 138, lines 193–202). Though the text concerning the ending of Mark is only found in the Latin fragments, James A. Kelhoffer, *Miracle and Mission: The Authentication of Missionaries and Their Message in the Longer Ending of Mark* (Tübingen: Mohr Siebeck, 2000), 170 points out that Theodoret of Cyrus cites the Greek version which confirms the accuracy of the Latin.

4. For this see Coombs, *A Dual Reception*.

5. Irenaeus, *Adversus haereses* 2.31.2 (SC 294:328, lines 47–48).

6. Irenaeus, *Adversus haereses* 2.31.2 (SC 294:326, lines 61–4).

7. Irenaeus, *Adversus haereses* 2.31.2 (SC 294:330, lines 67–9).

8. Kelhoffer, *Miracle and Mission*, 322. Note here the argument from silence. We do not and cannot know that Irenaeus had no interest in vs. 17–18. Nor can we be certain that he never made use of these verses in works no longer extant. We may only speculate about how and why v. 19 which he does cite fits better into the argument that he is making. This Kelhoffer does well (see p. 322, note 165). He suggests that "Irenaeus' selective citations of Mark 1:1–3 and 16:19 in *Adv. Haer.* iii.10.5 reflect the specific purpose of demonstrating that Mark bears witness to important doctrines — namely, the fulfillment of prophecy and the ascension — mentioned elsewhere in the NT." Accordingly, Irenaeus' interest in the LE lies *not* in the miracle traditions which precede and follow 16:19, but rather in the mention of Jesus' ascent to heaven, which accords with passages like Acts 1:9–12 and Eph 4:8. To this, I would only add that this may only be said of "Irenaeus' interest" as evidenced in this section of this treatise.

9. Irenaeus, *Adversus haereses*, 2.31.2 (SC 294:328, lines 49–59).

10. Irenaeus, *Adversus haereses* 2.31.3 (SC 294:330, lines 70–77).

11. Irenaeus, *Adversus haereses* 2.32.3 (SC 294:338, lines 78–86).

12. Irenaeus, *Adversus haereses* 2.32.4.

13. Irenaeus, *Adversus haereses*, 2.32.4 (SC 294:340–342). This section is also attested in Greek in Eusebius, *hist.eccl* 5.7.1–5 (LCL 153:450–4).

14. Note that both the order of the signs and the context preclude the interpretation that Irenaeus has not Mark 16:17–18 in mind, but rather Matt 7:22. In the former passage, as here, the signs are proof of God's genuine presence with the believer. However, in Matt 7:22, where these three "signs" are mentioned (though in a different order), the message is quite different — one should not take security from the presence of these signs, but only from obedience to the will of God. Nevertheless, note also, the curious absence of the third and fourth sign from Irenaeus' discussion (assuming he has Mark 16:17–18 in mind). It may be that Irenaeus chose not to mention these simply because he was not aware of instances where these had occurred, while he was aware of exorcisms, healings and prophetic speech occurring in the churches.

15. To be clear, to infer, as I do, that Irenaeus does indeed "interpret" the sign list is not dependent upon identifying his "miracle list" in 2.32.4 as a citation or Mark 16:17–18. Rather, the inference is made on the basis that he had received and read the entirety of the longer version of Mark and that the logic of his argument in 2.32.4 is consistent with that of Mark 16:17–18.

16. Kelhoffer, *Miracle and Mission*, 322.

17. Kelhoffer, *Miracle and Mission*, 323.

18. Kelhoffer, *Miracle and Mission*, 323.

19. Kelhoffer, *Miracle and Mission*, 323.

20. Brenda Deen Schildgen, *Power and Prejudice: The Reception of the Gospel of Mark* (Detroit: Wayne State University Press, 1999), 53.

21. Schildgen, *Power and Prejudice*, 53.

22. For the emphasis that this heresy placed upon experiences see Irenaeus, *Adverses haereses*, 2.32.2.

23. Charles Kannengiesser, *Handbook of Patristic Exegesis: The Bible in Ancient Christianity* (Leiden: Brill, 2006), 529.

24. Eusebius, *Hist. Eccl.* 6.20.1–2 and 6.22.1, LCL 265:64, 68. The rendering "learned churchmen" is from the English translation on p. 65. Brian Shelton, *Martyrdom from Exegesis in Hippolytus: An Early Church Presbyter's Commentary on Daniel* (Colorado Springs: Paternoster, 2008), 8, who rightly points out that Eusebius' usage of προεστώς diverges from his usual technical designation of the office of a bishop, ἐπίσκοπος raising the possibility that it may be intentionally vague. Note that Jerome, in his *De Viris Illustribus* 61, specifically designates Hippolytus a bishop.

25. Shelton, *Martyrdom from Exegesis*, 7–19, encapsulates this debate well. See also Paul F. Bradshaw, Maxwell E. Johnson, and L. Edward Phillips, *The Apostolic Tradition: A Commentary*, Harold W. Attridge, ed. (Minneapolis: Fortress Press, 2002), 5.

26. The case for Roman provenance is nevertheless strong. Shelton, *Martyrdom from Exegesis*, 25 summarizes well: "Thus, the historical record of Eusebius and Jerome, Prudentius' record of the emperor's persecution on the Tiber, Photius' assertion about his having a protege association with Irenaeus, Hippolytus' burial site on a *via* of Rome, the discovery of a statue commemorating his contribution by his followers, his imperial banishment alongside the Roman bishop and the overall strong association with the Roman church among Patristic writers bear out a Roman livelihood."

27. For the sake of simplicity, I will refer to Hippolytus as the author of the works associated with him. However, the observations made here concerning the reception that these documents evidence is not dependent upon the specifics of their authorship and date.

28. The *Apostolic Tradition* is often attributed to Hippolytus, and the *Apostolic Constitutions* is clearly derived from it. See Marcel Metzger, "Introduction," in *Les constitutions apostoliques*, vol. 1, SC 320 (Paris: Cerf, 1987), 17–18.

29. Hippolytus, *Traditio apostolica* 36.1 (SC 11:118).

30. For an early figurative use of θανάσιμόν see Ignatius, *Epistulae vii genuinae*, 3.6.2. Ignatius' designation of heretical teaching as deadly poison (θανάσιμόν) is picked up by later authors who take the fourth sign figuratively, as the promise of protection from the influence of heretics. For this, see Marcarius Magnes (ref) and Augustine, *Harmony on the Gospels* (ref).

31. *Constitutiones Apostolorum* 8.1.1–3 (SC 336:124–126, lines 1–23).

32. Indeed the text is identical. *Constitutiones Apostolorum* omits the variant καὶ ἐν ταῖς χερσὶν perhaps indicating the reception of an earlier form of the text.

33. *Constitutiones Apostolorum* 8.1.3 (SC 336:126, lines 22–3). The author also links the gift of tongues to the prophecy in Isa 28:11 (see lines 38–40).

34. *Constsitutiones Apostolorum* 8.1.7 (SC 336:128, line 49).

35. *Constitutiones Apostolorum* 8.1.6 (SC 336:128 lines 40–48).

36. *Constitutiones Apostolorum* 8.1.10 (SC 336:130, lines 59–68).

37. *Contitutiones Apostolorum* 8.1.11 (SC 336:130, lines 68–70).

38. *Constitutiones Apostolorum* 8.1.12 (SC 336:130, lines 71–2).

39. *Constitutiones Apostolorum* 8.1.16 (SC 336:132, lines 97–99). Given the citation of Mark 16:17–18 at the head of this section, this is important evidence for understanding the interpretation of the sign list. The third and fourth may well be considered the protection from persecution.

40. There is an implicit association made here between the gift of tongues and prophecy — note that the mention of tongues and exorcism in the previous section (8.1.1, lines 12–13; 8.1.4, lines 30–32 and the mention in this section of prophecy together with exorcism in 8.2.1, lines 1–2). Apparently, tongues is considered here as part of the more general category of prophecy.

41. *Constitutiones Apostolorum* 8.1.2.42–3.

6.

The New Pluralism: The Place of the Christian Church in the 21st Century

Samuel Thorpe and J. Elias Stone

Abstract

This study examines three particular issues with contemporary discourse on the relationship between world religions. First, the authors examine the role that the sovereign nation-state has come to play in determining the "rules of fair play" between the world religions. Second, they identify and evaluate a second driving force behind much of the Western push for "interreligious dialogue;" namely, a guilty Christian conscience for past ill-treatment of other religions. Third, the authors suggest that the tendency for the West to favor intellectual, cultural, or religious traditions other than its own is inconsistent and self-destructive. The authors conclude with some remarks on the unique contributions that Holy Spirit-sensitive Christians can make to the coming years of interreligious dialogue. The Spirit-empowered movement must engage the postmodern world with two emphases: clear and understandable Christian apologetics, and the reality of the experiential relationship with the Holy Spirit.

Key words: pluralism, postmodernism, nation-state, culture, interreligious dialogue

Introduction

The world in its current state of imbalance and cultural chaos presents a unique opportunity for the Spirit-empowered Christian church to make a significant impact. The question is about methodology. How can the church make a difference? What is the message we must present?

The Problem in Brief

One of the main problems that arise when considering Christianity's relationship to a pluralistic world is the definition of "pluralism" itself. In the twentieth century, the term "pluralism" usually meant "religious pluralism" in the sense that all religions were equally valuable, respectable, and meaningful. Christianity was expected to be congenial in its cooperation with other religions. In the twenty-first century, however, there has since come an expanded understanding of the idea of plurality. Now the term not only pertains to religion but includes social, economic, political, and individual worldview. Anyone who does not espouse complete equality of reality, meaning, and participation in social activity, economic resources, political power, or envisioning the world from an empirical, non-religious, scientific perspective is considered a "hater" of other views, one who in extreme denigrates others. Exclusivity in any element is thus inexcusable and must be destroyed or eliminated completely.

The problem that has been commonly pointed out by many Christian (and, particularly, evangelical) commentators is that reality itself is "exclusive" in the sense that there is only one "truth;" that is, only one way that things really are. Often, postmodernism is blamed for its social and epistemic relativism; according to such criticisms, there is no such thing as a meaningful intellectual discussion about the differences in "truths" in a postmodern society. There is a significant element of truth in these claims. However, there is a lot more nuance to the problem than people often recognize.

When contradictory claims compete with one another, one of them may be true, or neither of them may be true, but never under any circumstances can both be true. This is based on Aristotle's logical law of non-contradiction, which undergirds the entirety of the Western philosophical and scientific tradition. Much the same goes for religious metanarrative claims; no two contradictory metanarratives can be true. This has historically put religious thinkers of different traditions at odds with one another as both claim to have insight — of philosophical or revealed nature — into the true nature of things. This is, in large part, why many of the greatest thinkers throughout human history have been religious: their religious convictions compel them to compose holistic interpretations of man, his condition, and his relationship to the spiritual world (if any such world exists).

The contemporary insistence upon acceptance of religious plurality, then, seems a strange thing indeed. It is worth citing Rick Ward at length here:

> It is a common belief today that all religions are basically the same. They may look different — they may differ with respect to holy books or forms of worship or specific ideas about God — but at the root, they're pretty much the same. . . . On the surface at least, it's clear enough that the various religions of the world are different. Theists believe in one personal God; Hindus believe in many gods; atheists deny any God exists. . . . But just the opposite is true! It is on the surface that there is similarity; that is why we can immediately look at certain bodies of beliefs and practices and label them "religion." No, religions are not essentially the same and only superficially different. At their very core, they are drastically different. So, while pluralists might take the religious person seriously, they don't take his or her beliefs seriously.[1]

This description of the true state of religious metanarratives suggests that advocates of the pluralist position are content with acknowledging a system of doctrine that is, in many ways, easily demonstrated to be false: "To our knowledge, no two religions teach the same message or expect the same practices from their followers. . . . Most religious groups teach that their own beliefs and practices are the only true set and that all other faith groups contain some degree of error."[2] At best, this can only be seen as self-deception for the sake of constructing some idea of the meaning of life upon which people will build a set of ethics and acceptable behaviors; a narrative which cannot itself be verified (and is easily demonstrated to be false) and is presented to gullible individuals who crave some notion of purpose for their existence.

It thus seems that many scholars who advocate for pluralism hope (and expect) to eliminate the necessary exclusivity of truth in order to supplant it with an alternative narrative. All we need to do is become educated about the doctrines and practices of all religions, then endeavor to construct "interfaith" partnerships that promote "respect" for everyone's religion.[3] Yet this approach seems so contrary to the overall philosophical trajectory one would expect of the Western world. The Greco-Christian pursuit of truth, evidenced in the Medieval and Enlightenment attempts to arrive at a comprehensive understanding of "the good, the true, and the beautiful" to the exclusion of all alternatives, resulted in a uniquely homogenous value system. Until recently, this homogeneity of values has been evident; in America, at least, there was a time in the nineteenth and early twentieth centuries when a generally "American" worldview, complete with its own set of shared philosophical values, actually existed. Newcomers to the country were expected to adopt these values and bring the best of their respective cultures to the "American melting pot." In the 1960s–1970s, these values, however, were challenged and general support for these "traditional American values" eroded in favor of the pluralist agenda. Why is this?

The answer seems to many to be that society has "evolved" from its previously intolerant and narrow-minded ways. Reardon contends that the "key elements of pluralism include respect for diversity/alternative views, toleration, willingness to learn, curiosity, friendliness."[4] The obvious implication of Reardon's definition is that any view that disagrees with complete tolerance and appreciation of all social worldviews (pluralism) is not friendly, respectful, or learned. Reardon's definition demands that any and all views of life must be accepted with honor, without criticism. Anwaruddin adds to Reardon's idealism the idea that religious pluralism must be taught in schools to eliminate or reduce religious social tensions. He blames religious exclusivity for the "gruesome violence being perpetrated in the name of — or against — religion but also because a sizeable portion of the public has active religious practices and strong religious identifications." Anwaruddin seems to think that if people identify with a religious group, "open-ended conflict and possible anarchy" will inevitably result.[5]

It must be granted that, historically, there are religions that have demanded that "non-believers" must be converted, even by force, or be executed. Christianity and Islam, in particular, have contributed to the commonly accepted notion that religious conflict can often be the bloodiest. Some religions even openly operate with the fear that any "untrue" religious doctrine, if taught and believed by its people, will jeopardize everyone's eternal salvation. But religious identification itself cannot be the main problem. In every culture, which includes social, religious, economic, and political elements, there exist historical and social animosities without reference to religious elements. Some of these stem from purely cultural or ethnic elements, while others can come down to ideological differences. There are multiple factors that create friction between religious groups, not all of which (indeed, most of which) are not even basically religious.

The Pluralist State

The roots of such a pluralistic agenda, it turns out, can be found in the wake of the Reformation in general and, in particular, the Enlightenment. Catholic historical scholar Gavin D'Costa argues in his *Christianity and World Religions* that secular modernity has dictated much of the conceptualization of "religion" in general, and has set the guidelines by which the church must operate in relation to other religious groups. This has, in effect, emasculated Christianity (and "religions" in general) of their power to call humanity into something greater than it currently is:

> "Religion" was an invention of the sixteenth century, and deeply rooted in the work of the Cambridge Platonists; by the eighteenth century it was more a product of the European imagination than an encounter with an alternative form of power and discipline; and by the twentieth century "religion" became a shadow of its pre-modern self precisely because it was allocated a private, not public, role in the political sphere; a role replaced by modernity.[6]

Notably, this results in a depersonalization and demythologization of religion in general, to the extent that it becomes an article of culture: "it might even help things greatly if we scrapped the word "religion" and instead replaced it with "culture" and asked ourselves about a theology of culture, rather than a theology of religions."[7]

Prior to the Enlightenment, there was little to contest the marriage of church and state, as the only real opposition the church faced was Islam, with a few internal skirmishes arising at various points within the church. During the Reformation, however, Martin Luther's proposed "two kingdoms" doctrine began to sever the previously unquestioned ties between church and state: "While God granted coercive power to the secular body . . . the ecclesial body must concern itself purely with the preaching of the word of God."[8] The subsequent "religious wars" that were fought between rival Christian factions "taught" Europeans that religious tolerance was impossible for a society controlled by religion, and that if society was led to bloodshed as a result of religious convictions, then a non-religious government would be more likely capable of dealing with such difficulties in a peaceable and non-violent manner. Thus, secularism was born.

As popularly understood, the secular or "scientific" study of religion came about during nineteenth-century Germany. *Religionswissenschaft* came to be dominated by anthropological and socio-historical perspectives in the hopes of understanding religions both scientifically (on the one hand) and on their own terms (on the other).[9] However, D'Costa argues (with the help of Peter Harrison's *"Religion" and the Religions in the English Establishment*) that it was the Cambridge Platonists, emphasizing "virtue and morality over belief," who paved the way for "the beginnings of comparative religions."[10] The key to this was the dispassionate study of the world religions, which "historically had not yet been achieved." Around the same time, however, deism also became prominent within the academy, maintaining that morality and ethics were the primary substance of religious belief, while "revelation" and the metanarratives they claimed remained nothing but "rubbish."[11] As all religions came to be seen as "equally worthless,"[12] this facilitated a pluralist trajectory within deism, which fused itself into the ethos of *Religionswissenschaft* to produce the contemporary climate of religious study: pluralistic comparative religion.

This, it turns out, is not the whole story. Drawing from William Cavanaugh's *Theopolitical Imagination*, D'Costa argues that the rise of *Religionswissenschaft* was not accidental; in actuality, the emerging field of *Religionwissenschaft* was used as a tool of the modernist liberal attempt to "provide the context for religious plurality where mutual understanding and toleration are possible, without mono-authoritarian religion."[13] While not excusing the violence of Catholic and Protestant Europeans who were genuinely motivated by denominational allegiance, D'Costa argues persuasively that "the driving motor for the wars in Europe was not 'religion,' but rather a new character on the stage . . .: the sovereign nation-state."[14]

Since the sovereign state was a relatively new phenomenon, it had to assert itself in order to both secure its own existence and obtain power with which to control its subjects. This included, among other things, releasing itself from the political clutches of the Catholic Church. To this end, secular modernist liberals spun a narrative about the European wars that placed "institutionalized religion" in a bad light, arguing that "peace in Europe requires the privatization of religion, for there cannot be two public sovereigns."[15] The consequence of this would be the wholesale modernist rejection of state religion and, with it, the subjugation of "religious concerns" to "state concerns." D'Costa maintains that this evidently crucial role of the sovereign state in shaping the definition of "religion" should not be neglected in a Christian consideration of Christianity's relationship to "world religions," particularly as modern democratic states continue to set the rules by which Christians are allowed to play.

D'Costa's work provides significant clarity to the deeper issue that contemporary pluralism poses for the church. Particularly, the insight that the concept of "religion" has always been closely tied to power in the eyes of the state is highly significant. In light of this, modernist critics of religion such as Voltaire and Marx (along with later postmodern thinkers such as Nietzsche and Foucault) should come as no surprise. If the concept of "religion" has always been conceptually defined as "that which is opposed and subject to the state," then contemporary discussion surrounding the concerns of one religion (Christianity) and its relationship to another (say Islam) must be, in turn, subjugated to the concerns of the state. Thus, Christianity cannot come up with its own position on the world religions, particularly if such a position contradicts the aims or concerns of the state.

D'Costa's alternative interpretation of history may seem radical to many readers; it cannot be denied, however, that it makes a great deal of sense out of contemporary discussions about religion and society in general. For example, as D'Costa points out, the effects of this monumental shift in thinking still linger with us today in a substantial amount of political discourse; within the subtext of such discourse, if not explicitly, we hear "religion is a matter of private choice and should not shape the public sphere."[16] Concerns for "civility" often trump concerns for veracity, or freedom of scholarship. Another interesting example would be the work of Alperovitz, who advocates for "pluralism" in the public economic arena, making it a fundamental element for successful community enterprise:

> The key principle is to embed democracy in all these institutions in diverse ways, appropriate to their individual scales. This means envisioning a system that is fundamentally pluralist — and all the richer for it. Indeed, without plural mechanisms of participation in the democratic life of the community and the nation, individual liberty is crippled — only pluralism prevents a certain kind of democratic belonging from becoming mandatory.[17]

The criticism of Western imperialism is one that has become particularly stinging, especially when missionary efforts are accused of destroying (intentionally or otherwise) local cultures. However, Christianity is not simply able to ignore the existence of other world religions; the calling of all Christians is to proclaim the gospel that Jesus is the only Savior. "Go ye therefore and teach all nations, baptizing them in the name of the Father, and of the Son, and of the Holy Ghost; teaching them to observe all things whatsoever I have commanded you" (Matt 28:19,

20). The church's fundamental operational concern, then, must involve evangelism, even to the chagrin of society. It is to this particular issue that Leroy Rouner's article "Theology of Religions in Recent Protestant Theology" is well addressed. Though written in the late 1980s, Rouner's considerations are still of considerable importance, especially since many of the trends that he identifies have only continued to affect the conversation of Christianity's relationship to world religions. First, Rouner points out that the Christian pluralism of his day was in many ways an extension of Protestantism's general concern with its social and cultural surroundings. The existence of other, non-Christian religions of "high moral stature and theological sophistication," Rouner argues, challenges Protestantism in particular because of its awareness of its place in the world. However, unlike Darwinism, another great challenge to Protestant faith which is largely scientific in nature, the challenges brought about by other religions and exemplified by religious pluralism are more about "moral and historical" concerns rather than "factual" concerns."[18] Particularly, Rouner notes two moral challenges that other religions bring to bear upon Christianity. The first is that Christianity's claims to clear and uncontested superiority over other religions have been historically based upon ignorance, while the second is the fact that the Western world was responsible for the colonization and exploitation of the global South.[19]

Interestingly, however, Rouner points out that most of the criticism of the West on these fronts is not from many of those who have been slighted or wronged in these errors. Pulling an example from (more or less) contemporary missions work, Rouner argues that most of the scathing condemnations of missions work in India come not from Indian officials or native Indians themselves, but Western Protestant theologians, who chastise such work for its "triumphalism and social and political collusion with colonialism."[20] Rouner argues that this is indicative that the shift towards "Christian pluralism" is nothing more than an attempt on the part of Christians to salve their consciences for the moral atrocities they have committed in the past. This is all well and good: Christians should feel bad for the way both Christians and the church as a whole has historically treated the other.

The problem for Rouner, however, is that the Christian drive for "moral repentance" leads to an asymmetry in interreligious dialogue. The word "dialogue" in itself implies a two-way street — both parties contributing equally in a mutually beneficial conversation. Yet Rouner points out that most of the initiation and funding comes from Western

Christian groups.[21] This asymmetry seems to betray the fact that the conversation is one-sided, and that Christians have a twofold agenda that they bring to the table of interreligious dialogue: Christianity's primary motivation seems to be to "salve the conscience of post-colonial Western Christians" and solve "the challenge of Pluralism to the Western Christian understanding of God."[22] The result, Rouner argues, is not genuine religious dialogue, but rather a socio-cultural pow wow that enables Christians to feel better about their checkered past with other religions without actually resolving any conflict that may actually exist between the church and other religious groups: "Interreligious dialogue conferences are socially and culturally useful but not yet theologically creative."[23]

This problem in itself would be sufficient for concern, but Rouner argues that the problem goes deeper than that. As a result of the swing towards pluralism, Rouner suggests that "exclusivism" and "pluralism" have swapped their respective roles in Protestantism. Exclusivism, once a commonly accepted "core value" of Protestant theology, has become a problem to work with; conversely, pluralism has evolved from a problem that the church must face to a core Protestant value.[24] Rouner argues that this is largely because of the post-truth society that many Protestants live in today: claims to be the best or only religion "smack of colonialism or ignorance,"[25] neither of which, of course, the church wishes to be seen as.

Additionally, "most Protestant theology also rejects any posited notion of transcendent truth, as begins rather from a historical notion of experiential truth."[26] Rouner, then, suggests that Protestantism (and especially Pentecostalism) has a historical tendency to prioritize experience over other forms of justifying belief, placing modern Protestant theology firmly into a "neoliberal" classification. Not even so radical a thinker as Paul Tillich, Rouner argues, would have "accepted 'experience' as a valid source for our knowledge of God." Tillich certainly argued that experience is a medium for such knowledge; contemporary Protestantism, however, holds experience as its primary source, blurring the line between divine transcendence and immanence. As a result, Rouner argues that Protestantism has shifted away from Christology in general as a "distinctive source for our knowledge of God," turning instead toward a generic God; emphasizing "what we all hold in common" rather than identifying and seriously wrestling with clear differences.[27]

Be this as it may, however, a number of Christians have continued to formulate various doctrines of "Christian pluralism" in an attempt to alleviate societal and political pressures. It must be conceded that Christian pluralism has, in more recent years, evolved into a plethora (one might even say a "plurality") of nuanced formulations of various degrees of attractiveness and internal plausibility. Be this as it may, it would be far from the truth to suggest that the "pluralist" option has been considered viable for historically orthodox Christianity. The gospel of Jesus Christ has historically been specifically and deliberately exclusive: "what universal and emphatic terms does he (Peter) hold up his Lord as the one hope of men!"[28]

There are many biblical passages that clearly indicate the divinity of Jesus Christ and that he is the only route to a relationship with God, particularly in connection to eternal salvation. Hence Jesus is the only Savior of humanity. The real problem with humanity is sin. All humans arrive in the world guilty of sin; we exist in a state of conflict with God and we must be rescued from our slavery to a sinful nature. No other philosophy or religion can achieve the rescue. Jesus, having died for the sins of humanity, is the only sacrifice for sins and his resurrection from the dead demonstrates his accomplished mission, to pay the penalties for our sins against God and each other. "In other words, by raising Jesus from the dead, God has put his seal of approval (as it were) on Jesus' radical personal claims to be the Messiah, the Son of God, and the divine Son of Man!"[29] The scriptures declare:

... how ye turned to God from idols to serve the living and true God; and to wait for his Son from heaven, whom he raised from the dead, even Jesus, who delivered us from the wrath to come (1 Thess 1:9–10).

Neither is there salvation in any other (Jesus); for there is none other name under heaven given among men, whereby we must be saved (Acts 4:12).

Jesus saith unto him, I am the way, the truth, and the life. No man cometh unto the Father but by me (John 14:6).

For the wages of sin is death, but the gift of God is eternal life through Jesus Christ our Lord (Rom 6:23).

Other passages could be cited in support of the claim that Jesus of Nazareth, as God Incarnate, is the only savior (such as John 4:42; Rom 10:1–21, 9; 1 Tim 2:5; Titus 2:13; Heb 1:1–2; 1 John 4:14). Clearly, the Bible asserts that Jesus is God on earth and the only way to find God and attain eternal life. "The gift of God is eternal life. And this gift is through Jesus Christ our Lord. Christ purchased it, prepared it, prepares us for it, preserves us to it; he is the All in all in our salvation."[30] All other religions are false:

> Be ye not unequally yoked together with unbelievers: for what fellowship hath righteousness with unrighteousness? And what communion hath light with darkness? . . . And what agreement hath the temple of God with idols? For ye are the temple of the living God; as God hath said, "I will dwell in them and walk (among) them and I will be their God and they shall be my people" (2 Cor 6:14, 16).

There must be, then, limits to cooperation among members of the Christian church and other religious and philosophical worldviews. There is no truly "inclusive" option for the Christian insofar as "inclusive" means accepting as true other religious metanarrative claims that contradict those of Christianity. People cannot be "saved" through anyone or anything but Jesus Christ. The pluralistic option, then, does not appear to be viable.

Rouner concludes his article by suggesting that the issue of religious pluralism is formative for Christianity. The primary thing, he argues, is that Christians should do everything they can to avoid a negative reaction to their guilt about the past: "A guilty Christian conscience is ostensibly concerned with the authentic life of others, but in fact is self-absorbed, seeking primarily to make amends for past wrongdoing."[31] Christians must accept that Christ's sacrifice has atoned for the sins of the past and be open to the future; the church must offer the world the best solution to the issues the world faces today. Rouner concludes by saying "As interreligious dialogue moves beyond its origins in Christian moral concern to salve its conscience, . . . it will look increasingly to those Christocentric theologies which have developed an open, vulnerable, yet faithful affirmation that God was indeed in Christ, reconciling the world to himself."[32]

The Western Problem

A final concern with regard to Christianity's relationship to the world religions lies in the changing state of Western values in general. Unfortunately, it seems a great deal of scholarly "interreligious dialogue" tends to favor the insights and positions of religious perspectives that are explicitly not Christian (as also hinted at by Rouner's observation of the one-sidedness of interreligious dialogue). Why is this so? As explained above, D'Costa's argument seems to imply that it is because the entire academic concept of "religion" itself has been shaped by both secular modernity and the sovereign state in such a way as to mitigate the role of Christianity in the world. Furthermore, Rouner's insights suggest that guilt over the atrocities of colonialism have compelled both the church and the West, in general, to give other religions an opportunity to join the interreligious discussion as a token of apology.

However, both of these attempted limitations of Christian influence upon the world have left an unintended cultural vacuum, one which has resulted in a Western culture that is devoid of meaning and ultimate significance. As D'Costa points out, the sovereign modern state, in order to secure its existence, stripped "religion" of its ability to make metanarrative claims that would usurp or otherwise threaten the power of the state. The adverse effect of this, however, was that "religious conviction" became a private matter, and such conviction became an invalid justification for public action. Society had no reason to "improve" other than because it forwarded the ends of the state. Bad enough as this may be, the aforementioned Christian guilt over the past has allowed the state to continue to place limitations upon "religious power." All that a modern nation-state has to do to exercise power over the church is an appeal to the "religious" European wars or (more popularly) hold "Christian imperialism" over her head. In these ways, existing power structures can assert power over the church in any way by claiming that it has no right to infringe upon the public square (the definition of which can be adjusted to suit the needs of the state) and by insisting that it cannot do any form of violence towards existing cultures or subcultures (the definitions of which are so vague as to include practically anything). Thus, the church has been muzzled and bound by the West.

Yet this was not always the case. Ever since the time of Constantine until the Enlightenment, virtually all forms of literature, art, and social customs were inspired, in whole or in part, by the Christian church; for a millennium and a half, the Western cultural and intellectual tradition was joined at the hip with Christianity. In fact, the void left by modernism and postmodernism has made many contemporary scholars realize the implicit dependence of the Western world upon Judeo-Greco-Christian values. The problem is that, since the secular modern state was created in opposition to the church, Christianity has since been *a priori* rejected by mainstream scholarship, no doubt in part because a "return" to Christian values would necessarily imply a dramatic change in the power structure of existing sovereign states. As Christianity has been appropriately recognized as the source of "Western values," contemporary progressive secularists have frantically been searching for non-Western cultural systems with which to fill the gap; anything, so the reasoning seems to be, would be better than going "back."

However, contemporary researchers have come to find that cultural values are intensely religious in other parts of the world as well. Thus, the desired "non-Western" cultures that have begun to influence the West are found partially in other, "non-Western" religious systems, with Buddhism and Islam serving as particularly "promising alternatives" to Christianity. Rather than giving up the project and returning to its Western Christian cultural heritage, Western culture, American and European, has begun to appeal to these other cultures to fill the vacuum. Of course, underlying this entire cultural shift is the secularist assumption that, by mixing in cultures from other places, Western culture might become a "tossed salad" culture that accepts and respects all cultures and worldviews as equally truthful and valid. Yet it seems the irony here goes unnoticed: in order to eschew "religious influence" in the West, the West has turned to other "non-Western" cultures, themselves influenced by their own religious traditions. Here, no real "progress" is made; one has simply traded one sort of religious influence for another.

This problem runs so deep that it is even evident in Pentecostal/charismatic literature on world religions. One such example is found in Clifton Clarke's "Dialogue or Diatribe," in which Clarke points out that there is no word for "religion" in many non-Western languages: "for them, religion is not a body of ideas but an act, namely serving God."[33] The same could be said for the West until the Enlightenment, as we have seen from D'Costa. However, the impetus of Clarke's point here is that Western Christian interaction with world religions is often, more than not, based upon its own Christological terms:

> I am struck by the degree in which the discourse has been shaped and informed by Western thought forms and epistemology. The interreligious debate surrounding Christology, for example, is preloaded with the Western presuppositions that have precipitated the ensuing impasse. Christology has been historically shaped and expressed through the vortex of the Western enlightenment tradition. So, part of the stumbling block that has resulted in the impasse within interreligious dialogue is not Christ per se but the Western cerebral conceptualization of him.[34]

Clarke suggests that rather than Christianity investigating other religions on its own terms, the Western church should look to other people groups

(Clarke uses Africans as an example) for examples of expressing their understanding of the world, including "song, dance, proverbs, story, rituals, symbols, and a host of other means."[35] The intuition that Clarke seems to pick up here is that the Western world is somehow culturally deficient in conceptualizing "religion," and Christianity should look to other religions as an example of "lived" or "culturally alive" religion.

It should be noted that Clarke's intuition here is spot-on; the West is indeed at a loss when it comes to truly conceptualizing "religion," but this is because of the particularly sterile definition of "religion" that was put forth by the state in order to control the church and secure its own ends. The problem with Clarke's treatment here is that his perspective is ignorant of the pre-Enlightenment Western tradition. Prior to the invention of the secular modern state, much religious thought in the West was indeed "cerebral," as he puts it, but what made the West special and unique was its complementary mystical or artistic expression of the same "cerebral" truths it discovered. Anyone who studies medieval literature can testify to the rich use of poetry, symbolism, and story that expressed the same metaphysical truths many of the Medieval Christian philosophers exposited in their philosophical treatises. Be this as it may, however, it seems Clarke is ignorant of such cultural treasures, and he is not alone in such ignorance. The real problem, then, is not that the Western church is "culturally deficient" and "unable" to communicate through symbolic and artistic media, as Clarke seems to suggest; rather, it is that the West has, by and large, become both ignorant of and indignant towards its own cultural heritage in favor of adopting a non-Western (read "non-Christian") one. This issue, when compounded with the lens of the D'Costa-Rouner perspective we have elucidated earlier, results in a particularly difficult situation for the church.

Fighting the Many-Headed Hydra

The West's twofold ignorance/indignation of its own Christian heritage, coupled with both the modern secular state's power over the church and Christian guilt over past wrongs, severely limits the church in the number of approaches it can take to the other world religions. Ignoring other religions is out of the question for the following reasons:

- The state needs to interact with other cultures (of which religion is "merely an artifact").

- Christian's past actions towards other religions must be atoned for (presumably by hospitable and charitable interaction with other religions).
- We (the West) "need" them to fill the West's cultural void.

Similarly, any form of hostility towards other religions is equally out of the question, as this is:

- In violation of the state's claim to be the sole power capable of initiating war of any kind.
- Stains the Christian conscience all the more.
- "Regressive" to the "cultural ignorance" of the "Dark Ages."

Violating any one of these three aspects of "fair play" with regard to interreligious interaction is enough to earn severe criticism from all sides. It seems, then, that the only solution left available to the church is to:

- Play by the state's rules in seeking peace and harmony with other world religions, even at the expense of compromising Christianity's metaphysical claims.
- Do absolutely nothing that could be construed as hostility towards other religions for the sake of Christian conscience.
- Accept that other cultures (including their religions) are superior to those of the West and that the West must learn from them in these respects.

In light of these three "requirements" for interreligious dialogue, pluralism indeed seems like the only option. Thus, the problem becomes clear: the church has assented to go along with the whims of the world until she has bound herself into an impossible situation.

Fortunately, however, the church is more than equipped to tackle these difficult and otherwise insurmountable issues. In particular, the Spirit-empowered movement, with its reliance upon the present and active work of the Holy Spirit, may be able to infuse the contemporary academic minefield with an otherwise impossible deftness. With the guidance of the Holy Spirit, those of Pentecostal/charismatic inclinations

may be able to offer insightful and creative solutions to the bind into
which the church has gotten herself.

If such Christians hope to contribute meaningfully to the
"interreligious dialogue" that scholars such as D'Costa, Rouner, and
Clarke (along with other charismatic scholars such as Amos Yong and
Tony Richie) all hope to advance, three things will be necessary to
truly advance the conversation beyond the unspoken limitations that
have been outlined above. In the first place, a broadly applicable
pneumatological approach to the world religions must have a familiarity
with the cultural artifacts that the West can bring to the table. This
provides the artistic epistemological medium that Clarke suggests will
help make interreligious dialogue less "cerebral" and more heartfelt.
Additionally, such a familiarity also prevents the aforementioned
"begging" of other non-Western, non-Christian cultures for help in
filling the cultural vacuum left by secular modernity. Second, the power
struggle of the secular sovereign nation-state, particularly as suggested
by D'Costa and Cavanaugh, will need to be addressed. Only once
Christians understand both the importance and aims of the nation-state
in defining "religion" can they decide whether they will cooperate or
work against the system as has been given to us. Thirdly, the Christian
community must move past its guilt with regard to the ill-treatment of
other religions, historically and even in the present. The church will be
unable to move forward in its relationship with other religions if, at every
mention of the crusades, Christians buckle out of a sense of self-loathing.
As Rouner suggests, Christians must look to Christ for forgiveness, not
those of other religions; once right with Christ, the church will be able to
be in right relationship with the other world religions.

These points, though admittedly quite broad, should serve to help
catalyze the conversation regardless of one's affiliation with the church.
Yet it might be asked, how charismatically-inclined Christians can
uniquely contribute to this conversation. In light of the above points,
a few reflections upon the nature of charismatic theology, in general,
are important. In the first place, charismatics are known foremost for
their emphasis upon the experience of life. This experience enables
the Christian to live in the grace, power, and knowledge that the Holy
Spirit provides to the believer. However, historically speaking, very little
emphasis has been placed upon the lattermost aspect of Spirit-imbued
existence. Only recently have charismatics begun to come to the fore in
contemporary scholarship. To address the issue of the West's ignorance
of or indignation towards its own Christian cultural history, charismatic

scholars can and should continue to foster their newfound scholarship by encouraging historical and cultural research. In so doing, they may unearth the many Spirit-imbued artistic and literary treasures of the Patristics and Medievals; treasures that are simply waiting for the Spirit-sensitive eye to find.

Addressing the concerns raised by the modern secular state's role in the creation of "religion" will be, admittedly, a bit riskier. It seems that one particularly helpful contribution that could be made by the Pentecostal community is their emphasis upon the need for prophecy in the world today. Throughout both the Old and New Testaments, numerous examples can be found where the prophetic office was employed against existing worldly power structures that had set themselves up in opposition to the will of God. If, as D'Costa fears, the modern secular state, complete with its secular modernist ideology, has so enslaved the church by setting the rules by which Christians are permitted to discuss the place of the world's religions in relation to Christ, then perhaps it is time for Spirit-empowered prophecy against such systems. This will, of course, require the assistance of other *charisms* such as the "word of wisdom" and the "discernment of spirits" (such as been well delineated by Yong in his work *Beyond the Impasse*), though such prophetic criticism should not, of course, be ignorant of history or contemporary scholarship. Accordingly, it seems that this need for the prophetic is inextricably bound to the need for Spirit-empowered scholarship.

Finally, it seems especially appropriate that the charismatic emphasis upon the healing power of God can both inform and transform the Christian conscience. With regard to the world religions, it is universally acknowledged that the church has made (and continues to make) a number of mistakes. Whether these mistakes are intentional or not, it is important for the church to recognize the need for forgiveness and reconciliation, which can, ultimately, only come from God. Pentecostals can make a unique contribution by continuing to spread the revealed knowledge that God is a supernatural healer. There is no reason to believe that the same Holy Spirit which is capable of healing individual physical, emotional, and spiritual ailments is unable to bring healing and reconciliation to the church's corporate conscience and Christianity's relationships to other religious groups. As a consequence of this, charismatics should be (and, in many ways, are!) the most enthusiastic to engage other religions in dialogue, because they can and do rely upon the healing and redemptive power of God to turn any previously bad relationship into a most beautiful one.

Conclusion

What response can the Pentecostal/charismatic church make to the efforts of so many people to marginalize religion, and specifically Christianity, in societies around the world? There are two actions that the postmodern Spirit-empowered church must make to speak to the world. First, as in all the history of the church, Christian apologetics and proclamation of the truth of the gospel and the plan of God in scripture must not be diminished. The Christian metanarrative is not a fictional rendition of an attractive myth; it is the literal truth about reality and all people should hear it as such. Christian apologetics is necessary but the church must be aware of the methods that will most effectively address modern issues. "By latest count in 2015, the Library of Congress had well over 160 million items, already a startling increase over the 100 million it counted in 1997. But relative to what circulates on the web, its collections could be described as if not scarce, at least tractable. One data-storage company estimates that worldwide, web data are growing at a rate that jumped from 2.7 billion terabytes in 2012 to 8 billion terabytes in 2015. How are we to keep from being drowned in the data deluge?"[36] In the face of these overwhelming numbers, people tend to retreat to the familiar. What does this mean for cultural elements? Will eventually all cultures blend together in ways that make the historical or traditional disappear and merge into a culture where everyone is alike? Indeed, Rabbi Maller contends that "religious pluralism is the will of God," that God gave us so many religions to test humanity's commitment to "the religion that each of us have been given by God."[37] Then all humans are "brothers" when we obey our individual religious principles and love one another. Grimsrud's view will support Maller. "I suggest that, following Jesus, we should place at the center of this discussion the call to love God and to love our neighbors."[38] However, Jesus did not intend to eliminate the truth and reality of the gospel, the law, or the exclusivity of Christianity. Grimsrud's suggestion will allow people to live and die with false notions of reality and eternity unless we adhere to a universalist view of salvation, which makes all religions essentially meaningless behavioral cultural preferences. Jesus made it clear. "for if ye believe not that I am, ye will die in your sins" (John 8:24). Knowledge and impartation of the truth are essential for all Christian ministry.

"Collective memory — the full scope of human learning, a shared body of knowledge and know-how to which each of us contributes and from which each of us draws sustenance — is the creation of multiple generations across vastly diverse cultures."[39] "What this means for the digital age is that data is not knowledge and data storage is not memory. When distracted — for example by too many bright shiny things and noisy bleeping devices — we are not able to learn or develop strong reusable memories. We fail to build the vital repertoire of knowledge and experience that may be of use to us in the future."[40]

People still must deal with the interpretation of information. What informs this interpretation? Philosophy asks us to indicate what is real, true, and valuable. Culture provides the philosophical driving force to which people retreat when the data "drowning" overwhelms. Each culture in every country answers these questions with their social, economic, political, historical, religious beliefs and practices. If all religions are just the same search for reality and meaning and are equally valid and accurately authoritative for human life and behavior, why do not all people become the same religion, since religious diversity does not matter? Perhaps that is the goal of the "data drowning" phenomenon. Why would there be any cultural resistance to any religious notion if they are all just different ways to reach God?

Second, there is no Pentecostal, charismatic, or Spirit-empowered Christianity without the experience of believers with the Holy Spirit. Spirit-empowered Christianity requires experience, awareness, a real knowledge of Otto's *mysterium tremendum*,[41] a ministry which can only be done in cooperation with the work of the Holy Spirit. People need to be healed; to experience miracles; to come broken to the presence of God in the Holy Spirit and become mended. Otherwise, Christianity wages a war of competing ideas or ideologies. Persuasion of logic then is all the force we have to combat falsehoods and Christianity is no stronger in the reformation of society than civic clubs. Either Jesus is with us in power as he promised in Matt 28:18–20 or he is not. "Truly, truly I say to you, he who believes in me, the works that I do shall he do also, and greater works than these shall he do because I go to the Father" (John 14:12), because we have received the Holy Spirit. For the twenty-first century, the Spirit-empowered church must emphasize Christian apologetics and the personal experience with the Holy Spirit.

It is only by contributing its unique, Spirit-imbued perspective to these issues that the church can hope to overcome the obstacles that have been placed in her way. In the coming years, it may well be that the Pentecostal/charismatic movement will determine the shape of future interreligious dialogue. By God's grace, and with the help of the Holy Spirit, it will only be for the better.

Notes

1. Rick Wade, "Christianity and Religious Pluralism — Are There Multiple Ways to Heaven?" probe.org, 2006, https://probe.org/Christianity-and-religious-pluralism, accessed June 26, 2019.

2. B. A. Robinson, "Which Religion, if Any, is the True One?" *Religious Tolerance*, www.religioustolerance.org/reltrue.htm, accessed June 26, 2019, .

3. Nicole Corea, "Want to be an Ally for People of Different Faiths? What Not to Do," *Aspen Institute*, February 16, 2018, www.aspeninstitute.org/five-mistakes-religious-allies-dont-know-theyre-making, accessed June 26, 2019.

4. Jack Reardon (ed.), "About" *International Journal of Pluralism and Economics Education*, Inderscience Publishers, https://publons.com/journal/47869/international-journal-of-pluralism-and-economics-e, accessed June 26, 2019.

5. Sardar M. Anwaruddin and Ruben A. Gaztambide-Fernandez, "Religious Pluralism in a School Curriculum: A Dangerous Idea or a Necessity?" *Curriculum Inquiry* 45:2 (2015), 147.

6. Gavin D'Costa, *Christianity and World Religions: Disputed Questions in the Theology of Religions* (Chichester, UK: Wiley-Blackwell, 2009), 57–58.

7. D'Costa, *Christianity and World Religions*, 58.

8. D'Costa, *Christianity and World Religions*, 60.

9. D'Costa, *Christianity and World Religions*, 67.

10. D'Costa, *Christianity and World Religions*, 62–63.

11. D'Costa, *Christianity and World Religions*, 64.

12. D'Costa, *Christianity and World Religions*, 65.

13. D'Costa, *Christianity and World Religions*, 68.

14. D'Costa, *Christianity and World Religions*, 74.

15. D'Costa, *Christianity and World Religions*, 74.

16. D'Costa, *Christianity and World Religions*, 75.

17. Gar Alperovitz, "Why Is Pluralism an Important Value for Systemic Design?" *The Next System: Principles of a Pluralist Commonwealth*, May 15, 2017, www.thenextsystem.org/pluralism, accessed June 26, 2019.

18. Leroy Rouner, "Theology of Religions in Recent Protestant Theology," in Hans Küng and Jürgan Moltmann, eds., *Christianity among World Religions* (Edinburgh: T. & T. Clark, 1986), 108.

19. Rouner, "Theology of Religions," 109.

20. Rouner, "Theology of Religions," 109.

21. Rouner, "Theology of Religions," 109.
22. Rouner, "Theology of Religions," 109.
23. Rouner, "Theology of Religions," 110.
24. Rouner, "Theology of Religions," 110.
25. Rouner, "Theology of Religions," 110.
26. Rouner, "Theology of Religions," 110.
27. Rouner, "Theology of Religions," 110.
28. Robert Jamieson, A. R Fausset, and David Brown, *A Commentary, Critical and Explanatory, on the Old and New Testaments* (Grand Rapid, MI: Zondervan, 1984), 177.
29. Michael Gleghorn, "Reasonable Faith — Why Biblical Christianity Rings True," *Probe Ministries*, January 13, 2016, https://probe.org/reasonable-faith-2/?print=print, accessed June 26, 2019.
30. Matthew Henry, *Concise Commentary on the Whole Bible* (Nashville: Thomas Nelson, 1997), 1075.
31. Rouner, "Theology of Religions," 114–115.
32. Rouner, "Theology of Religions," 115.
33. Clifton Clarke and Amos Yong, "Dialogue or Diatribe," in *Global Renewal, Religious Pluralism, and the Great Commission: Towards a Renewal Theology of Mission and Interreligious Encounter* (Lexington, KY: Emeth Press, 2011), 33.
34. Clarke and Yong, "Dialogue or Diatribe," 33.
35. Clarke and Yong, "Dialogue or Diatribe," 34.
36. Abby Smith Rumsey, "The Data Deluge," *The Saturday Evening Post* 289:5 (2017), 46.
37. Allen S. Maller, "Religious Pluralism is God's Will," *The Interfaith Observer*, January 14, 2017, www.theinterfaithobserver.org/journal-articles/2017/1/2/religious-pluralism-is-gods-will, accessed June 26, 2019.
38. Ted Grimsrud, "Christian Faith and Religious Pluralism," *Thinking Pacifism: Reflections on Peace and Faith*, May 8, 2012, www.thinkingpacifism.net/2012/05/08/christian-faith-and-religious-pluralism/, accessed on June 26, 2019.
39. Rumsey, "The Data Deluge," 90.
40. Rumsey, "The Data Deluge," 90.
41. Rudolf Otto uses the Latin phrase *mysterium tremendum* (lit. "tremendous mystery") to describe God. Any theophanic encounter with God, according to Otto, involves an experience of the mysterious "otherness" of God coupled with a "tremendous" impression of God's overwhelming power and majesty. See Rudolf Otto, *The Idea of the Holy: An Inquiry into the Non-Rational Factor in the Idea of the Divine and its Relation to the Rational,* trans. John W. Harvey (Oxford: Oxford University Press, 1936), 5–24.

II

Proclaiming the Uniqueness of Christ in the World

7.

The Uniqueness of Jesus in African Culture: An African Pentecostal Perspective

Emmanuel Anim

Abstract

This paper reflects on the view that "God has not left himself without a witness" (Acts 14:17). This assertion, it is argued, also finds expression in the names and the many attributes of God found in many African societies, such as Ghana, which predates missionary activity and Bible translations. However, as in the case of Cornelius, a devout and God-fearing man (Acts 10), and Lydia of Thyatira (Acts 16:14), and the many religious and devout Jews, the uniqueness of Jesus in salvation history remains a missiological imperative which requires a messenger of the gospel in the power of the Holy Spirit. The vision of achieving a global move of the Spirit will have to take seriously the engagement of the gospel and culture, particularly in the global South where primal worldview or pre-Christian religious categories could serve both as a preparation and a catalyst for the acceptance and spread of the gospel of Christ.

Key words: Holy Spirit, African, Pentecostal, culture, gospel

Introduction

". . . For they drank of a spiritual rock that followed them: and the rock was Christ" (1 Corinthians 10:4).

The belief in the triune God means, where God the Father is, Christ the incarnate Son is present, and the Holy Spirit abides as a bond of fellowship among them. This understanding implies that a Trinitarian fellowship is essentially available to mankind. Thus, the conversion of people and cultures is an invitation to mankind to reconcile with God, through Christ, who makes Christian fellowship possible. And the Holy Spirit empowers the believer to live and act in a manner that is consistent with the opportunity and right to be sons and daughters in God's family. Contemporary African Christianity, which should find Christ within our context, often — and unfortunately — tries to meet him outside of it.

This paper seeks to make the point that the gospel is never brought from "outside" but is always operating within. "And the WORD became flesh" and entered the community (John 1:1–14). The incarnation of Christ is a missiological model. The missionary task of our time, therefore, is to identify the presence of the incarnate Jesus Christ within our cultures and in our lived experiences. This is a call to appreciate what God in Christ is already doing within and among a people and co-labor with Christ to continue the process and ensure through the power of the Holy Spirit that Christ is known, celebrated, and honored in all things. The event of Pentecost, as recorded in the book of Acts, is an indication that God reaches out to all people, at all times, as believers avail themselves to be used by him:

> When the day of Pentecost came, they [the disciples] were all together in one place. Suddenly a sound like the blowing of a violent wind came from heaven and filled the whole house where they were sitting. They saw what seemed to be tongues of fire that separated and came to rest on each of them. All of them were filled with the Holy Spirit and began to speak in other tongues as the Spirit enabled them. Now there were staying in Jerusalem God-fearing Jews from every nation under heaven. When they heard this sound, a crowd came together in bewilderment, because each one heard their own language being spoken. Utterly amazed, they asked: 'Aren't all these who are speaking Galileans? Then how is it that each of us hears them in our native language? Parthians, Medes and Mesopotamia, Judea and Cappadocia, Pontus and Asia, Phrygia and Pamphylia, Egypt and the parts of Libya near Cyrene; visitors from Rome (both Jews and converts to Judaism); Cretans and Arabs – we hear them declaring the wonders of God in our own tongues!' Amazed and perplexed, they asked one another, "What does this mean?" (Acts 2:17–21).

In his explanation of what seemed like an astonishing drama, the apostle Peter quoted the prophet Joel (2:16–21) and explained that what the people had just witnessed was an act of God. God himself had initiated his mission through the disciples who reminded the crowd of God's universal appeal that, "everyone who calls on the name of the Lord will be saved" (Acts 2:21).

That it was God himself who initiated his mission cannot be overemphasized. When the disciples experienced the baptism of the Holy Spirit and were speaking in diverse tongues, they probably had no idea they were ministering to the rest of the community. The triune God was at work, and the disciples were vessels whom God used. The reference to all the nationalities that heard the apostles speak in their mother tongues tells us that God is not a stranger to any people nor culture. From this Pentecost experience, we learn that the effectiveness of the gospel message must take into consideration the language and culture of the hearers, for these important elements give people their sense of identity and allow for meaningful communication.

The narrative in Acts chapter ten also reveals that the Spirit of God is not limited to a particular location, people, or community. That God would reveal himself to Cornelius, a Gentile, was not only a surprise to Peter, but at odds with his worldview, for such a person was "unclean." The fact that Peter still preached the gospel of Christ to the "devout and God-fearing" Gentile reminds us also that salvation in Jesus Christ is not automatic, but requires specific knowledge and understanding as well as a personal acceptance and commitment. This is what we also gather from Acts 16:13–15. In this scripture passage we see the conversion experience and baptism of Lydia, a purple cloth dealer from the city of Thyatira who was "a worshipper of God." Lydia's conversion and baptism occurred after listening to the gospel of Christ from Paul as "the Lord opened her heart to receive Paul's message." Thus, although salvation in Christ is universal in appeal, it exclusively applies to those who accept Christ as their personal Lord and Savior and consciously choose to follow him. Paul Knitter talks about "the ontological necessity of Christ for salvation" meaning that the reality of salvation flows directly from the historical reality of Christ's incarnation and his death on a Roman cross outside Jerusalem. Knitter further draws our attention to the "epistemological necessity of Christ for salvation," meaning that one needs to accept Christ personally and come to know him in order to be saved.[1] This model in the theology of religions is referred to as exclusivism. Exclusivism, as a theological category, has a missiological implication. It follows that believers in Christ have the responsibility to preach this gospel of the kingdom to all people everywhere in the direction and power of the Holy Spirit. Proclaiming Christ and his saving grace should not lead to the proselytization of new converts, but authentic Christians who also reflect the distinctiveness of their given culture. This was the experience on the day of Pentecost.

Thus, evangelization and salvation in Christ should not change us into foreigners or transform us into the image and likeness of an outside culture. Rather, as adopted children of God, we are empowered to transform our cultures and to represent what our cultures should be. In other words, the empowerment of the Holy Spirit must find expression, not only in our individual and personal lives, but more importantly, in the public space, for this is how the father can be glorified and Christ enthroned as Lord and King among our people in the power of the Holy Spirit.

Important questions have been raised regarding early missionary endeavors in Africa. In his classic book, *The Primal Vision: Christian Presence Amid African Religions*, John Taylor argues for the need to discover the footprint of Christ among primal people prior to missionary encounter, and he challenges conventional missionary methods, which tend to be deductive and dogmatic. He criticizes the situation where "the convert is required to listen and obey while the missionary talks and commands." Rather, Taylor suggests that the missionary should recognize and appreciate his status as a guest and create a context in which mutual learning and genuine interaction can take place between himself and the recipients of the gospel. This conversation will provide the platform for integration. After all, the Word became flesh and entered the community (John 1:1–14). To integrate means to come alongside the people, and this is what the incarnation of Christ seeks to do.

The overall objective of this paper is to suggest that Christ has always been active in African cultures. This is a trajectory which could be explored as one means of achieving the vision of Empowered21, which is "that every person on Earth would have an authentic encounter with Jesus Christ through the Power and Presence of the Holy Spirit . . . by Pentecost 2033."[2] The key phrase for me here is, "Authentic encounter with Jesus Christ." If an encounter with Christ is authentic, it must embrace — and transform — the hearer's culture, and this can only happen through the power and presence of the Holy Spirit at work in any given culture.

Africa and Global Christian Mission

Church historians and other scholars have, in recent years, drawn our attention to the exciting growth of the church in the southern continents of Africa, Asia, and Latin America. This growth has major implications for Christian theology.

In 1970, researcher David Barrett boldly predicted that the number of Christians in Africa would reach 350 million by the year 2000. This was from a mere 10 million in 1910.[3] In 2001, Barrett published the second edition of his seminal *World Christian Encyclopedia*, and he estimated the actual Christian population to be 360 million, which was more than he predicted. His classic reference book further illuminated the changing demography of modern Christianity and the massive shift of the faith's center of gravity from the West to the southern continents of Asia, Africa, and Latin America.[4]

In that same period, around the dawn of the new millennium, Andrew Walls and Kwame Bediako were drawing our attention to the fact that not only was Africa practicing the faith, but it was changing it as well. Christianity was becoming a non-Western religion.[5] This assertion was reaffirmed when Philip Jenkins, in his weighty book, The *Next Christendom*, argued that Africa, alongside Asia and Latin America, would define the coming of a new global Christianity by the year 2050. Jenkins observed that the stupendous growth of the church in Africa was principally in the Pentecostal/charismatic strand of Christianity and that these churches were far more traditional, morally conservative, evangelical, and apocalyptic than their northern counterparts.[6] David Barrett and Harvey Cox had previously drawn the same conclusions.[7]

This development forces us to consider the statement by Andrew Walls that theology that matters is theology that comes from where the majority of Christians are.[8] This, by implication, means that the theological reflections coming from the southern continents of Africa, Asia, and Latin America are now the most relevant to the world.

But this leaves us with unfinished business. In the 1950s our attention was drawn to the fact that "there is a sense in which both Christianity and African culture face a crisis."[9] This was taken to mean that the African Christianity that was surfacing all around might not be the real thing. Thus, S.G. Williamson noted, "As every pastor in the church can testify, while the majority of Christians have accepted the church in its outward forms, their inward spirit is still ruled by the attitudes and outlook of the old culture. The two are kept apart, not necessarily because they belong to opposing areas of life, but because men and women desire and expect to keep them apart. . . . It is for the church to think through this problem and proclaim its faith as God's word for Africa."[10] I am of the opinion that this problem is yet to be fully addressed, and the way to address it is to understand that Christ has always been active in African culture — and the gospel brought his footprints to light. Our task as Christian scholars and theologians is to help interpret what this might mean.

What Is the Gospel?

Kwame Bediako rightly observed, "The gospel of salvation which comes in and through Jesus Christ has more to do with the nations and the things which make nations, than is often assumed." He goes on to explain that "we have become so used to regarding the gospel as only concerned with individuals that we are much less alert to its fundamental relationship to those elements and dimensions of our human existence which designate as culture — language, social values, cultural norms, religion, political organization, ethnic identity, technology, arts and craft, and economic activity."[11]

In this regard, the tendency has been to reduce the gospel to a category we regard as purely spiritual with no reference to our culture or way of life. The danger here, Bediako notes, is that Christianity at best becomes only an overlay of an already existing worldview and mentality. However, the aim of the Great Commission is far more than that. It is about "the conversion of cultures, and conversion is not merely an overlay upon our old habits and attitudes and fears, of some regulations and traditions and solutions which do not answer to our needs. That is proselytization, not evangelization. . . . Rather, true evangelization and conversion is turning to Christ all that he finds when he meets us and asking that he cleanse, purify and sanctify us, and all that we are, eliminating what he considers incompatible with him. That is what the Great Commission is about, the discipling of the nations."[12] This position is underscored by Andrew Walls when he observes that every nation "has a pattern of thought and life essentially its own, and this, in the words of Edwin Smith, may be described as 'the shrine of a people's soul.'"[13] Walls explains:

> Within the shrine lie that people's history, its traditions, its corpus of recognized literature (oral or written). If a nation is to be discipled, the commanding heights of a nation's life have to be opened to the influence of Christ; for Christ has redeemed human life in its entirety. Conversion to Christ does not isolate the convert from his or her community; it begins the conversion of the community. Conversion to Christ does not produce bland universal citizenship: it produces distinctive discipleships, as diverse and variegated as human life itself. Christ in redeeming humanity brings, by the process of discipleship, all the richness of humanity's infinitude of cultures and subcultures into variegated splendor of the full grown humanity to which the apostolic literature points (Eph. 4:8–13). This means that the influence of Christ is brought to bear on the points of reference in each group. The points of reference are the things by which people know their identity and know where, and to whom, they belong. Discipling a nation involves Christ's entry into the nation's thoughts,

the patterns of relationships within that nation, the way the society hangs together, the way decisions are made.[14]

Thus Christian mission is about the transformation of people and cultures in the light of God's word. The seed of the gospel must first take root and be nurtured in the context of a given culture in order to transform it from within. This means the gospel must shed light on all cultural elements and judge them accordingly. Such considerations call for an open and honest analysis of all cultural beliefs, practices, and assumptions that inform people's worldviews and attitudes. However, it has often been the case that those who have been the cross-cultural bearers of the Christian faith all too eagerly impose their own priorities and biases upon the people. This was the case in the early church, where the Jewish believers insisted that the non-Jewish converts observe the law and be circumcised. The first church council (Acts 15:1–29) was called to address questions that arose as a result of the missionary activities of the early apostles. The concerns related to gospel and culture: were Jewish regulations meant to thrive in a gentile setting? Thus Paul Hiebert rightly observes, "On the one hand, the gospel belongs to no culture. It is God's self-revelation of himself and his acts to all people. On the other hand, it must always be understood and expressed within human cultural forms."[15] This reveals an abiding tension that exists any time the gospel of Christ crosses different cultures.

Culture may be defined as, "the more or less integrated systems of ideas, feelings, and values and their associated patterns of behavior and products shared by a group of people who organize and regulate what they think, feel, and do."[16] Thus, the Willowbank Report on the Lausanne Congress on World Evangelization had this to say:

> Culture is an integrated system of beliefs (about God or reality or ultimate meaning), of values (about what is true, good, beautiful and normative), of customs (how to behave, relate to others talk, pray, dress, work, play, trade farm, eat, etc.), and of institutions which express these beliefs, values, and customs (government, law courts, temples, or churches, family, schools, hospitals, factories, shops, unions, clubs, etc.), which binds a society together and gives it a sense of identity, dignity, security, and continuity.[17]

Our culture, therefore, "provides us with our fundamental assumptions and beliefs about reality, the nature of the world, and how it works."[18] For this very reason, any effective presentation of the gospel must first touch the cultural assumptions of the people in a relevant and prophetic way.

Hiebert makes the salient point that the gospel must be distinguished from all human cultures. The gospel is a divine relation and not mere human speculation. In this sense, the gospel does not belong to any one culture, but all cultures can serve as vehicles of its message. Without this process, people would have to change cultures to become Christians.

Although the gospel may not be fully understood in any one culture, "all cultures are capable of expressing the heart of the gospel, and each also brings to light certain salient features of the gospel that have remained less visible or even hidden in other cultures."[19] The gospel also has a prophetic dimension and calls all cultures to change. Thus, Richard Niebuhr talks of Christ of culture, Christ against culture, and Christ above culture.[20] In the light of this, Bediako reiterates the "goal of the Gospel is the redemption of cultures, and cleansing of all our cultural forms of life and expression, so that they come to express praise and adoration of the one living God and of our Lord Jesus Christ."[21]

Where Can We Find Jesus in African Culture?

The quest for a relevant Christian theology that takes African culture and identity seriously has often been queried regarding its faithfulness to scripture. This fear is expressed through the catchword "syncretism," and the worry of religious pluralism is also raised. The Christological debate has often centered on the extent to which Christ can be identified with the African as an Elder Brother, Ancestor,[22] or Pro-Ancestor, that is, "Ancestor Par Excellence."[23] Kwame Bediako says this question goes to the heart of the effort to understand Christ authentically in the African world. He argues that,

> accepting Jesus as "our Savior" always involves making him at home in our spiritual universe and in terms of our religious needs and longings. So, an understanding of Christ in relation to spirit-power in the African context is not necessarily less accurate than any other perception of Jesus. The question is whether such an understanding faithfully reflects biblical revelation and is rooted in true Christian experience. For example, the needs of the world require a view of Christ that meets those needs. And so Jesus in the African spiritual universe must not be separated from what he does and can do in that world. The way in which Jesus relates to the importance and function of the "spirit fathers" or ancestors is crucial. ... Ancestors are essentially clan or lineage ancestors. So they have to do with the community or society in which their progeny relates to one another and not with a system of religion as such. In this way, the religious functions and duties that relate to ancestors become binding on all members of the particular group

who share common ancestors. Since the ancestors have such an important part to play in the well-being (or otherwise) of individuals and communities, the crucial question about our relationship to Jesus is, as John Pobee rightly puts it, "Why should an Akan relate to Jesus of Nazareth who does not belong to his clan, family, tribe, and nation?" Up to now our churches have tended to avoid the question and have presented the gospel as though it was concerned with an entirely different compartment of life, unrelated to traditional religious piety. As a result, many people are uncertain about how the Jesus of the church's preaching saves them from the terrors and fears that they experience in their traditional worldview. This shows how important it is to relate Christian understanding and experience to the realm of the ancestors. If this is not done, many African Christians will continue to be men and women, "living at two levels," half African and half European, but never belonging properly to either. We need to meet God in the Lord Jesus Christ speaking immediately to us in our particular circumstances, in a way that assures us that we can be authentic Africans and true Christians."[24]

These concerns, as discussed by Bediako, have often left any attempt of contextualizing the gospel in the African context hanging in the balance. At best, the discussions have been limited to "ivory tower" exchanges among scholars in the academy, while practitioners are left to find their way in the dark. This lack of resolution, I would like to argue, has opened the door for questionable and disturbing theologies of the Spirit by many Pentecostal and Charismatic churches across Africa.

The use of electronic and social media — such as the radio, television, Facebook, and YouTube — have made the situation even worse as such messages easily find their way into homes and onto smartphones. In Ghana, a prophet directed a supplicant to carry a 50kg bag of cement on her head and walk a distance of about two kilometers because she did not follow the prophet's instructions. Another pastor removed the underwear of a lady in the full glare of the congregation as part of the process of deliverance and infilling of the Holy Spirit. In response to these types of activities, the government in Rwanda is orchestrating legislation to require all pastors to have genuine theology degrees before they can open a church, and it is closing down churches that operate in unsafe environments.

Here, we need to ask why the government is forced to act as a corrective to the church. Are we unable to distinguish truth from error? I don't believe that theological chaos is Africa's contribution to world Christianity. I wish to argue that African primal religions, as well as aspects of our culture, provide us with a relevant and useful model to interpret the gospel of Christ to the people and that we can truly know him and offer profound insights to the world.

Because Christ always leaves himself with a witness (Acts 14:17), I believe he left his footprints within the African worldview, culture, and religious experience. Certainly, this evidence must be scrutinized and tested in the light of scripture and the wider Christian fellowship. But we must ask ourselves, why have the African names of God, such as *Onyame* or *Onyankopong* (as known by the Akans of Ghana), *Chinike* (Nigeria), and *Lesa or Leza* (Zambia) found their way into the holy scriptures when the Bible was translated into these cultures? How can the "god" of the pagans translate into the God of our Lord Jesus Christ, who is worthy of worship and adoration?

God in African Thought and Experience

The fact of God's self-revelation may explain the African experience of God and his involvement in the affairs of the people. The high god in some African religions and cultures is an ultimate divinity beyond time, space, or human control.

Andrew Walls makes an important observation that, generally speaking, the story of southern Christianity is a narrative of missionaries discovering that God was at work in primal societies long before they arrived, noting these peoples had given God their own vernacular names. The names of the supreme God were "often associated with the sky, creator of the earth, and moral governor of humanity, having no altars or priesthood, and perhaps no regular worship." More often than not, translators felt comfortable applying those names to the God of the Bible, and they used those names in their Christian liturgies and their sermons about the God of Israel and of the church.

"Where this has happened, the coming of Christianity has not been — as in northern Christian experience — bringing God to the people, so much as bringing him near." No matter how severe the Christian judgment may have been about the religion and life of primal societies, the name of God was in so many instances retained, and this may yet have momentous consequences for the future shape of Christian theology.[25] God is, "the God of the Gentiles also,"[26] in a way that lies outside the experience of Western Christians.[27]

The concept of God in Africa is understood through the meanings of the names and attributes given to him, and these names stem from people's experience of God. Thus, the Akans have the maxim, *obi nkyere abofra Nyame* (no one shows the child that God exists). Children intuitively understand the overwhelming majesty of God.

The Akans designate the supreme being by three important but distinct names: *Onyame, Onyankopong,* and *Odomankoma. Onyame* corresponds to the basic idea of deity. *Onyankopong* describes the supreme being or supreme deity in the sense of a personal religious God, while *Odomankoma* corresponds to a conception of God as the infinite being, the one who is dependable and merciful.

Common to each of these names is the appellation of *Boadee,* which suggests a creator, architect, carver, or inventor. Each of these three names of God recognizes what God can do. Thus, God's self-revelation in the natural world and among his people makes it possible for people to give him a name and to relate to him because the name describes something real about him.

Oluwa is the name given to God by the Yoruba people of Nigeria who identify God as the owner of the sky or the heavens. The Igbos call God *Chukwu,* the Almighty. The Ngombe people of Congo identify God as *Akongo,* meaning the creator of the universe, the molder of men like a potter; whilst the Baganda people of Uganda refer to God as *Katonda,* meaning the creator, protector, and helper. He creates children and molds them in a woman's body. The name *Leza,* for God, is commonly used in East Africa throughout Zambia, Tanzania, and the upper Congo. The name comes from the verb meaning "to cherish" as a mother does her child. *Leza* gives the elements such as the rain and sunshine. Although the source(s) of this identification of God as the Almighty might have come in a limited way to the African people, these local names of God have found their way into the vernacular Bible translations and are at the center of their daily experiences and worship.[28]

Where did these names come from? Certainly, there must have been some experience of God or his deeds before the gospel came. For example, Kofi Abrefa Busia observes that:

> The problem of evil so often discussed in Western philosophy does not arise in the African concept of deity. It is when a God who is not only all-powerful and omniscient but also perfect and loving is postulated that the problem of the existence of evil becomes an intellectual and philosophical hurdle. The Supreme of the African is the Creator, the source of life, but between him and man lie many powers and principalities good and bad, gods, spirits magical forces, witches, to account for the strange in the world. Nature too can have power and even spirits. It must be noted that in farming, fishing, stock raising, and other economic activities, the African shows knowledge of natural causes. . . . When the African offers an egg to a tree, or food to a dead ancestor, he is not expressing ignorance of material substances or natural causes, but he is expressing in conduct a theory of reality, namely that behind the visible substance of things lie essence, or powers, which

constitute their true nature. Those who have read Western philosophy are familiar with such formulations, but because the African does not formulate his problems in terms familiar to the European, or may not even be able to express his awareness in words, his conduct is often grossly misinterpreted.[29]

Busia's observation is most useful as it points us to re-examine not just the essence but also the significance of important elements of African traditional culture such as festivals,[30] pouring of libation,[31] chieftaincy systems,[32] proverbs and *adinkra* symbols as known in Ghana and other West African countries. If the celebration of the Yuletide, a pagan festival associated with the northern winter solstice; and German Ostern, an earlier celebration of an Anglo-Saxon goddess in Europe, could be reinvented and interpreted into Christmas and Easter celebrations, then the same redemption can happen in Africa so that our traditions and cultures can be brought under the feet of Christ.

Conclusion

I have sought to demonstrate that God has not left himself without a witness. By this proposition, I argue that the Logos, who became flesh, also entered the African community ahead of the missionaries' arrival. The evidence of this is clear in the people's experience of God, which afforded them the ability and insight to find a relevant name for God, one which was valid enough to be used in Bible translations in many African countries.

For this reason, we conclude that African theologians and Christians need to understand and appreciate the fact that Christ is no stranger to the African culture and that elements of the gospel lie in our own inner resources to transform us into African Christians in the highest and purest sense. The task, therefore, remains how this experience may best be interpreted and applied in contemporary Christian experience. This, I think, is a unique experience of Christ in African culture that the world is yet to fully realize.

Notes

1. Paul Knitter, *No Other Name? A Critical Survey of Christian Attitudes Towards the World Religions* (Maryknoll, NY: Orbis Books, 1985), 116, Cited in J. N. J. Kritzinger, "The Theological Challenge of Other Religious Traditions," in

Simon Mamela and Adrio Konig, eds., *Initiation into Theology: The Rich Variety of Theology and Hermeneutics* (Pretoria: Van Schaik, 1998), 237.

2.   www.empowered21.com
3.   David Barrett, "AD 2000: 350 Million Christians in Africa," *International Review of Mission* 59 (1970), 39–54.
4.   David Barrett et al., *World Christian Encyclopedia*, 2nd ed. (New York: Oxford University Press, 2001).
5.   Kwame Bediako, *Christianity in Africa: The Renewal of a Non-Western Religion* (Edinburgh: Edinburgh University Press, 1995).
6.   Philip Jenkins, *The Next Christendom: The Coming of Global Christianity* (Oxford: Oxford University Press, 2007), 7–8.
7.   Harvey Cox, *Fire from Heaven: The Rise of Pentecostal Spirituality and the Reshaping of Religion in the 21st Century* (Reading, MA: Addison-Wesley Publishing, 1995).
8.   Andrew Walls, "Towards Understanding Africa's Place in Christian History," in John S. Pobee, ed., *Religion in a Pluralistic Society* (Leiden: Brill, 1976), 183.
9.   S. G. Williamson, "Introduction" (Christianity and African Culture, Accra, Gold Coast, 2nd–6th May 1955), 5.
10.   Williamson, "Introduction," 6.
11.   Kwame Bediako, "What is the Gospel," *Transformation: An International Journal of Holistic Mission Studies* 14:1 (January/March 1997), 2.
12.   Kwame Bediako. "What Is the Gospel," 3.
13.   See, Edwin Smith, *The Shrine of a People's Soul* (London, 1929), cited in Andrew Walls, *The Missionary Movement in Christian History: Studies in the Transmission of Faith* (Maryknoll, NY: Orbis Books, 1996), 50.
14.   Walls, *The Missionary Movement*, 51.
15.   Paul Hiebert, *Anthropological Insights for Missionaries* (Grand Rapids: Baker, 1985), 30.
16.   Hiebert, *Anthropological Insights for Missionaries*, 30.
17.   Lausanne Committee for World Evangelization, *The Willowbank Report: Consultation on Gospel and Culture* (Wheaton, IL: LCWE, 1978), 6–7.
18.   Hiebert, *Anthropological Insights for Missionaries*, 31.
19.   Hiebert, *Anthropological Insights for Missionaries*, 55.
20.   Richard Niebuhr, *Christ and Culture* (New York: Harper and Row, 1951).
21.   Bediako, "What is the Gospel?" 4.
22.   See Charles Nyamiti, *Christ As Our Ancestor: Christology from an African Perspective* (Gweru, Zimbabwe: Mambo Press, 1984).
23.   Benezet Bujo, *African Theology in Its Social Context* (Eugene, OR: Wipf and Stock, 2006), 23–32; 75–144.
24.   Kwame Bediako, *Jesus in Africa: The Christian Gospel in African History and Experience* (Akropong-Akuapem, Ghana: Regnum Africa, 2000), 22–23.
25.   For an important discussion of this see Kwame Bediako, *Theology and Identity: The Impact of Culture upon Christian Thought in the Second Century and Modern Africa* (Oxford: Regnum Books, 1999).

26. See Romans 3:29

27. Walls, *The Missionary Movement*, 71.

28. For further discussions on the subject see, John Mbiti, *Concepts of God in Africa* (London: SPCK, 1969); John Mbiti, *African Religions and Philosophy* (Oxford: Heinemann, 1969); John Mbiti, *Introduction to African Religion* (Oxford: Heinemann, 1975), 40.

29. K. A. Busia, "The African World View," *Présence Africaine*, Nouvelle série 4 (1955), 4.

30. See, for example, Kwame Bediako, *Jesus in African Culture: A Ghanaian Perspective* (Accra, Ghana: Asempa Publishers, 1990).

31. Peter Akwasi Sarpong, *Ghana in Retrospect: Some Aspects of Ghanaian Culture* (Accra-Tema, Ghana: Ghana Publishing, 1974).

32. See Kwabena Opuni Frimpong, *Indigenous Knowledge and Christian Missions: Perspectives of Akan Leadership Formation on Christian Leadership Development* (Accra, Ghana: Son Life Press, 2012).

8.

"God Has Made Him Both Lord and Messiah. . .": An African Perspective on Christology and the Pentecost Day Message

J. Kwabena Asamoah-Gyadu

Abstract

Pentecostalism, as a stream of Christianity, defines itself by appealing to three factors: first, the promise of the outpouring of God's Spirit on all flesh; second, the fulfillment of that promise in Acts 2; and third, the fact that this outpouring of the Spirit can be experienced today. Although the experience of the Spirit lies at the heart of Pentecostalism, the biblical experience of Pentecost pointed to something that was fundamental to the gospel. This is the fact that in Christ, God revealed himself for the salvation of the world. That was the message that Peter was inspired to preach on the day of Pentecost. Thus, although the experience of the Holy Spirit is critical to any definition of Pentecostalism, we miss out on God's agenda if the Christological element is neglected. Centering the Pentecostal message on Christ is critical for the Pentecostal movement in an African context where the message of the movement is often carried away by the attractions of the prophetic and prosperity preaching. These emphases on power, money, signs, and wonders, to the neglect of the more fundamental message of salvation in Christ as Lord distorts the reason for the outpouring of God's Spirit.

Key words: Pentecost, Pentecostal/charismatic, Spirit, Africa, Jesus, Christ

Pentecost has always been discussed in terms of the outpouring of the Holy Spirit. Thus, when the expression "Pentecostal" is used in any Christian context, what comes to mind is the religion of those Christians who claim to have been baptized by/in the Holy Spirit, and as a result, express their spirituality through certain charismatic manifestations and practices. The outpouring of the Spirit of God on the day of Pentecost ensured a certain democratization of charismatic power in which no single church, denomination, or missionary body, could lay claim to the power of God for Christian witness. On that score, African Pentecostals share the same heritage as their counterparts everywhere in the world. Pentecostal/charismatic Christians — whether European, American, or African — value, affirm, and consciously promote speaking in tongues, prophesying, healing, and exorcism, and in their more contemporary forms, even claim the power of the Spirit for wealth creation and upward mobility in life.

What is often missed in our definition of Pentecost is the Christological element. In this chapter, I reflect on the fact that Pentecostal pneumatology only makes theological sense if it is founded on a strong Christology. The point itself is not novel, as we find it both in Frank D. Macchia's *Baptized in the Spirit*, and Ralph Del Colle's *Christ and the Spirit*.[1] In Luke's gospel, for example, Macchia argues that the accent of Spirit baptism is not on *being* in Christ, but rather, "functioning in Christ in the power of the Spirit."[2] Thus, wherever the Pentecostal movement is found, it is expected that the message of Jesus Christ as God's ultimate revelation to the world, would be at the heart of proclamation. This emphasis is particularly critical in twenty-first-century Africa where the statistics seem to suggest that the majority of Christians now live. We argue towards the end of these reflections that Africa was part of the original Pentecostal event and subsequently, in the encounter between Philip the Apostle and the Ethiopian Eunuch, Jesus became the heart of the discussion. Thus, we must discern in the growth of Pentecostal/charismatic Christianity in Africa an opportunity to be consciously Christological in our Christian witness.

The perspective that I offer here is to conduct a systematic exposition of the text in Acts 2, to further support the Christological argument and conclude by relating the study to my African Pentecostal/charismatic context. I argue from the message delivered by Peter on the day of Pentecost that Pentecost and Pentecostalism are defined by something more than just the experience of the Holy Spirit, critical as that experience may be to our identity as Pentecostal/charismatic Christians. The connection between the outpouring of the Spirit and the Christ event is clear in this passage, as indeed it was in Peter's Pentecost day message. Pentecost was a Christological event, and by extension, Trinitarian as well. God poured out the promised Holy Spirit so that Jesus Christ the Son would be known and glorified in the world as Lord and Messiah. Pentecost, theologically speaking then, must always be understood as a Trinitarian event that has everything to do with God's salvation in Jesus Christ. This was what Peter publicly declared when he had to answer a question relating to the name and authority in which a cripple had been miraculously brought back to his feet:

> But Peter and the Apostles answered, . . . [t]he God of our ancestors raised up Jesus, whom you had killed by hanging him on a tree. God exalted him at his right hand as Leader and Savior that he might give repentance to Israel and forgiveness of sins. And we are witnesses of these things, and so is the Holy Spirit whom God has given to those who obey him (Acts 5:29–32).

Although this chapter dwells mainly on the sermon preached by Peter on the day of Pentecost, the text I have here comes from his response to persecutions by the high priest's men following a healing miracle at the Beautiful Gate and the subsequent affirmation of Jesus as Lord as they tried to explain what had happened. Based on my reading of Acts 2, and with particular reference to the sermon Peter preached on the day of Pentecost, this chapter attempts to draw attention to the importance of Jesus Christ to the events of the day. In Peter's own words as he attempted to explain the meaning of Pentecost he noted:

> This Jesus God raised up, and of that all of us are witnesses. Being therefore exalted at the right hand of God, and having received from the Father the promise of the Holy Spirit, he has poured out this that you both see and hear (Acts 2:32–33).

What the crowd was seeing and hearing was a band of disciples of the resurrected Jesus, who, crucified a couple of weeks earlier, was now in glory. True to his word he fulfilled the promise of the Father to his disciples by pouring on them the Holy Spirit. From that point, the message of Pentecost was going to consist of the experience of the Holy Spirit and the witness to Christ as Savior and Lord.

Jesus and Salvation

In the first chapter of Luke, we encounter the prophetic declarations of Zechariah in relation to both the ministries of John the Baptist, and that of Jesus. What is important for our purposes here is what the Holy Spirit inspires Zechariah to prophesy about Jesus:

> Blessed be the Lord God of Israel,
> for he has looked favorably on his people and redeemed them.
> He has raised up a mighty savior for us
>   in the house of his servant David,
> as he spoke through the mouth of

his holy prophets from of old,
that we would be saved from our enemies and from the hand of all who hate us. .
. .
By the tender mercy of our God,
the dawn from on high will
break upon us,
to give light to those who sit in darkness and in the shadow of death,
to guide our feet into the way of peace (Luke 1:68–69, 78–79).

I quote from Luke because we know that in his writings he focuses especially on the prophetic empowerment dimension of the Holy Spirit.[3] "The mighty savior" that God was to raise up for his people was of the house of David, and, as we shall argue from the Pentecost day sermon, this referred to Jesus, the Christ. In other words, these prophecies were consistent with the Davidic ancestry of Jesus and his role as the custodian of salvation. The same Holy Spirit who came upon both Zechariah, and upon Peter at Pentecost, inspired the two men into making prophetic declarations that affirmed Jesus as God's ultimate revelation to the world. The point is that Pentecost exists to testify to the lordship of Jesus Christ. Spirit baptism, in the words of Macchia, "is an empowering calling and gifting for a living witness to Jesus that is the birthright of every Christian as a bearer of the Spirit."[4]

Salvific Promise Fulfilled

Salvation, as far as it relates to our fallen human nature, may be defined as God's rescue mission in Jesus Christ, by the power of the Holy Spirit. The promise of rescue, according to Zechariah's prophecy, was made to the ancestors of the Israelites as part of God's holy covenant (Luke 1:72). The original recipient was Abraham, as named by Zechariah, and the focus was to be rescued for the worship of God in holiness and righteousness forever. It is with this in mind that John the Baptist was to go ahead as the forerunner to "prepare his ways, to give knowledge of salvation to his people by the forgiveness of their sins" so that a new dawn "from on high will break upon" God's people (Luke 1:76–78).

The covenant was one in which God was giving his people a fresh start in their relationship with him. That is why in response to the question regarding whether he was God's messiah or not, John pointed to one that was greater than he: "I baptize you with water; but one who is more powerful than I is coming; I am not worthy to untie the thong of his sandals. He will baptize you with the Holy Spirit and fire" (Luke 3:16–17).

To be baptized with the Holy Spirit and with fire was a declaration not only of cleansing, but also of judgment and empowerment. God the Father fulfilled his promise to pour out his Spirit of cleansing and judgment on all flesh in Jesus the Son, and to empower believers in the ministry of testifying to him as the Christ.

Pentecost as Hearing and Seeing

The point is this: we cannot separate the work of God from the Son and the Spirit. The implications of this sermon for the ministry of the church are profound, for by emphasizing that the same Spirit who empowered Jesus empowers his followers, Luke reminds the body of Christ that it has the same kind of empowerment that Jesus had for his ministry. If that is not evident in our ministry as God's church, then, as Craig S. Keener points out, "it may be because we have failed to recognize the dramatic nature of his gift."[5]

> This Jesus God raised up, and of that all of us are witnesses. Being, therefore, exalted at the right hand of God, and having received from the Father the promise of the Holy Spirit, he has poured out this that you both see and hear (Acts 2:32–33).

On the day of Pentecost, "what did the crowds see and what did they hear?" Arguing from the text itself, the sequence of events was that firstly, having gathered in one place awaiting the Father's promise, "suddenly from heaven came a sound like the rush of a violent wind, and it filled the entire house where they were sitting." Secondly, "divided tongues, as of fire, appeared among them, and a tongue rested on each of them" (Acts 2:2–3). If we understand the coming of the Spirit in terms of the empowering presence of God as promised by Jesus Christ, then the plain meaning of the text is that there was a sudden or forceful rush of wind that was felt, and that simultaneously visibly rested on each person in the waiting room in the form of a tongue of fire. That must have been a very spectacular experience.

Although the crowds may not necessarily have witnessed the initial event of outpouring and infilling, they witnessed the results, because it was the resulting commotion that brought them to the scene. What must have drawn the diversity of crowds of pilgrims towards the meeting place of the then despondent and dejected apostles was what happened next: "All of them were filled with the Holy Spirit and began to speak in other languages, as the Spirit gave them utterance" (Acts 2:4).

It was the spontaneous gibberish of loud voices under the inspiration of the Holy Spirit that brought people around. What this means is that they saw a group of men and women, followers of Jesus, who, having been crucified and who, as his disciples claimed, had suddenly risen from the grave, emerged from their hideout looking vivacious and perhaps even sweating from the heat of the fire that had rested on them. Looking like people who were out of their mind or out of control — for they behaved like people in a drunken stupor — they had started speaking in strange tongues, but which others heard in their own mother tongues. Both the speaking and the hearing were miraculous.

Those observing this strange phenomenon could not help but conclude that it was due to some influence, most likely early morning wine, they guessed. It simply did not make sense otherwise! That was the "seeing" part of the Pentecost event. What was the hearing part then? Pilgrims visiting Jerusalem in the season of Pentecost from "every nation under heaven" (Acts 2:5) gathered in bewilderment "because each one heard them speaking in the native language of each" (Acts 2:6). There are two things about the hearing that "amazed and astonished" the crowd: firstly, those speaking were all Galileans and yet they were understood as speaking in the "native languages" of the hearers. Secondly, what they spoke was divine: "in our own languages, we hear them speaking about God's deeds of power" (Acts 2:11).

"What Does This Mean?"

All who heard the apostles speaking were "amazed and perplexed" and therefore asked what it all meant, for surely there must be a meaning to what was happening. It was out of ignorance that some attributed what was happening in terms of the consumption of new wine. In response, we read from Acts 2:13 that Peter "standing with the eleven, raised his voice and addressed them." The fact that he stood with the eleven meant Peter was going to interpret a collective experience that was of divine inspiration rather than of excessive drinking as some had supposed. In one long sermon, Peter made a direct connection between a prophetic utterance by Joel and the Jesus event. Here I quote Joel's prophecy from Acts 2:17–21:

In the last days, it will be, God declares, that I will pour out my Spirit upon
  all flesh,
and your sons and daughters shall prophesy,
  and your young men shall see visions,
  and your old men shall dream dreams.
Even upon my slaves, both men and women,
  in those days I will pour out my Spirit;
  and they shall prophesy.
And I will show portents in the heavens
    above
  and signs in the earth below,
  blood, and fire, and smoky mist.
The sun shall be turned to darkness
  and the moon to blood,
  before the coming of the Lord's
  great and glorious day.
Then everyone who calls on the name
  of the Lord shall be saved.

We must remember that Peter quoted this passage as part of his response
to the meaning of what the crowd was seeing and hearing on the day of
Pentecost. Some, as we have stated, sneered that the outburst of tongues
in the declaration of the wonders of God had resulted from the intake
of wine by the apostles. Peter was disabusing their minds that any such
thing had happened since it was still about nine o'clock in the morning.
Rather, as he explained, God was working his purposes out by fulfilling
an Old Testament prophecy as found in Joel. Most of the Jews who were
there would immediately have made the connection because they knew
the Hebrew scriptures. What they would have struggled with was the
truth that the Old Testament prophecy actually pointed to Jesus Christ as
Lord.

Jesus of Nazareth: Lord and Christ

This raises a critical issue concerning what we have traditionally pointed
at in terms of Pentecostal distinctives. The focus on the Spirit is not
misplaced, but the fact that the experience ought to point to something
more profound — the revelation of Jesus Christ as Lord and Savior —
of often lost in the argument.[6] This previous knowledge of the scriptures
explains why Peter, immediately after quoting Joel, refers directly to
God's salvation history as fulfilled in Jesus Christ:

You Israelites, listen to what I have to say: Jesus of Nazareth, a man attested to you by God with deeds of power, wonders, and signs that God did through him among you, as you yourselves know — this man, handed over to you according to the definite plan and foreknowledge of God, you crucified and killed by the hands of those outside the law. But God raised him up, having freed him from death, because, it was impossible for him to be held in its power (Acts 2:22–24).

Peter says a number of things about Jesus of Nazareth that were not necessarily new but that people may not have taken seriously. Inspired by the Holy Spirit, Peter was now going to string together events surrounding the incarnation, crucifixion, and resurrection of Jesus. This was to prove that what was being witnessed on the day of Pentecost was a testament to the fact that he was the Christ of God. After all, after the resurrection, Jesus himself had told the apostles that what they would be expected to preach was a message relating to what Peter now talked about: his suffering and resurrection. On the day of Pentecost, the Holy Spirit did indeed descend upon "all flesh." The narration of the events of the day showed clearly that although we have traditionally focused on the Holy Spirit, the third person of the Trinity, when discussing Pentecost, Jesus Christ who was the fulfillment of the Father's promise was very much at the heart of it.[7] Thus, the reason for paying attention to the relationship between Pentecost and Christology lies in the fact that, contrary to what many may have come to believe, the sermon preached by Peter on the day of Pentecost had its foundations and focus on the presentation of Jesus Christ as Lord. In the sermon, Peter talked about the suffering, death, and resurrection of Jesus. Focusing his argument for the lordship of Jesus around the resurrection, he preached that first God raised him up from death, and he was now exalted to God's right hand. Second, that having been exalted, Jesus Christ received from the Father the promise of the Holy Spirit. Third, having received the promise of the Father, it is Jesus who has poured out the Holy Spirit upon God's people.

Luke, who is also the author of the Acts of the Apostles, wrote about this in the gospel that bears his name:

Then he said to them, "These are my words that I spoke to you while I was with still with you — that everything written about me in the Law of Moses, the prophets, and the psalms must be fulfilled." Then he opened their minds to understand the Scriptures, and he said to them, "Thus it is written, that the Messiah is to suffer and to rise from the dead on the third day, and that repentance and forgiveness of sins is to be proclaimed in his name to all nations, beginning from Jerusalem. You are witnesses of these things" (Luke 24:44–48).

If I may begin from verse 48, Jesus reminded the apostles that they were "witnesses" of the things he expected them to preach. What were they witnesses of? They were physically present when he suffered and was raised from the dead on the third day. These were things that had been brought to their attention throughout the ministry of Jesus and clearly stated in response to that eternal Christological question "who do you say that I am?" Those who did not understand the unfolding salvation history of God in Christ had taken Jesus to be one of the prophets, but Peter had a different take on the matter: "thou art the Christ, the Son of the living God" (Matt 16:16). Jesus told Peter that that declaration was not of human but of divine origin.

I submit that it is only by the illuminating power of the Spirit that the things of God are revealed for human understanding. Thus, when in Luke we read that the risen Christ "opened" the minds of the disciples, the scriptures were referring to something that God does by the Holy Spirit. In that respect, Jesus had told the disciples in John that one purpose for which the Holy Spirit was coming upon them would be to reveal to them all that he, Jesus, had taught them. He is the Spirit of truth who brings to human understanding the things of God.

When Peter stood up on the day of Pentecost, therefore, he was revealing spiritual truths to those who already knew what the Old Testament said, but who needed their minds opened just as Jesus had done for the disciples after the resurrection, so that they could come to appreciate the connection between the prophecy of Joel and the developments of Pentecost. This makes Pentecost an ultimately Christological event, for after quoting from Joel, Peter comes to focus on the events surrounding who Jesus was, and affirms his place as God's Messiah. He begins the testimony about Jesus with the words: "Jesus of Nazareth, a man attested to you by God" (verse 22a). How did God attest Jesus to the Israelites? Peter says he did so with "deeds of power, wonders, and signs" (verse 22b).

Jesus Christ and the Deeds of Power

In reading about Jesus from the gospels, these deeds of power, beginning from his conception and later miraculous interventions in various situations dominate the accounts. On one occasion in John chapter 9, when the disciples wondered whether a man's blindness had been due to his own sin or was as a result of a generational curse, Jesus' answer was that the situation existed for the revelation of God's glory. He proved that by opening the eyes of the blind man and through that healing, the man whose eyes had been restored defied the religious authorities of the day and declared Jesus as the Messiah.

Part of the interaction between the man whose eyes were opened and the doubting Pharisees looking to make a case against the messianic claims of Jesus read as follows:

> Then they reviled him, saying, "You are his disciple, but we are disciples of Moses, but as for this man, we do not know where he comes from." The man answered, "Here is an astonishing thing! You do not know where he comes from, and yet he opened my eyes. We know that God does not listen to sinners, but he does listen to the one who worships him and obeys his will. . .&nbnsp;. If this man were not from God, he could do nothing" (John 9:28–33).

In other words, the man argued that Jesus was able to intervene in his situation because he was from God. Much earlier, Jesus had told his disciples about the miracle and the glory of God by noting "he was born blind so that God's works might be revealed in him" (John 9:3). That was the reason for the deeds of power that Jesus performed, that the works of God might be revealed in him as Christ. The signs, miracles, and deeds of power were meant to point to his place as one revealed that we might have life and have it in its fullness and abundance (John 10:10). It was this man "attested to you by God with deeds of power, wonders, and signs" that according to Peter, speaking to the Israelites, was "handed over to you according to the definite plan and foreknowledge of God" (Acts 2:23) to be crucified.

"All Flesh" and "Every Nation Under Heaven"

Pentecost was about the universality of the gospel of Jesus Christ. According to Luke, Jesus told the disciples that "repentance and forgiveness of sins are to be proclaimed in his name to all nations" (Luke 24:47). And indeed "all nations" had gathered in Jerusalem on the day of Pentecost (Acts 2:5). Luke even proceeds to provide a list of the representatives of the nations: Parthians, Medes, Elamites, and residents of Mesopotamia, Judea and Cappadocia, Pontus and Asia, Phrygia and Pamphylia, Egypt and the parts of Libya belonging to Cyrene, and visitors from Rome, both Jews and proselytes, Cretans and Arabs. In the testimony of these representatives "in our languages, we hear them speaking about God's deeds of power" (Acts 2:9–11). In what has come to be known in mission studies as the Great Commission, Jesus instructed his disciples after the resurrection to "Go therefore and make disciples of all nations, baptizing them in the name of the Father and of the Son and of the Holy Spirit" (Matthew 28:19).

In what Bible interpreters normally refer to as the reversal of the curse of Babel, in which languages were confused because people wanted to reach God by human effort, the nations hear about his "mighty works" in their own tongues or languages as he now reaches down in a mighty visitation of the Spirit. It is instructive that in reaching out to the nations the metaphor used for the Holy Spirit is that of a "violent wind" and that he came upon the gathered the disciples as tongues of fire. In Psalm 104 verses 3b and 4, God rides "on the wings of the wind," and he "makes the wind his messengers," and "fire and flame his ministers." Also in Ezekiel 37, which we have looked at in this book, the Spirit of the Lord restores life to very dry bones through violent winds:

> Then, he said to me, "Prophecy to the breath, prophesy, mortal, and say to the breath: Thus says the Lord God: Come from the four winds, O breath, and breathe upon these slain, that they may live." I prophesied as he commanded me, and the breath came, into them, and they lived and stood on their feet, a vast army (Ezekiel 37:9–10).

Although current preaching usually applies this passage from Ezekiel to the need for individual Christians to be revived by the Spirit of God, it originally referred to Israel as a community. That is why at the end of verse 10 it talks in plural terms: "I prophesied as he commanded me, and the breath came, into them, and they lived, stood their feet, a vast army." Right from the beginning of her history, Israel as the covenant people of God, was supposed to be a channel of blessing to every nation. This was clear from the calling of Abram and in fact, his name change to Abraham was so that he would be the "father of nations." God told him:

> And I will make my covenant between me and you, and I will make you exceedingly numerous." Then Abram fell on his face; and God said to him, "As for me, this is my covenant with you: You shall be the ancestor of a multitude of nations. No longer shall your name be Abram, but your name shall be Abraham; for I have made you the ancestor of a multitude of nations. I will make you exceedingly fruitful; and I will make nations of you, and your offspring after you throughout their generations, for an everlasting covenant, to be God to you and to your offspring after you (Genesis 17:2–7).

The communal and global implications of God's covenant with Israel are also found in Exodus 19:5–6, from where we read:

> Now, therefore, if you obey my voice and keep my covenant, you shall be my
> treasured possession out of all the peoples. Indeed the whole earth is mine, but you
> shall be for me a priestly kingdom and a holy nation. These are the words that you
> shall speak to the Israelites.

It is important then to note that these words of the implications of the covenant, starting with Abraham, were directed at "the Israelites" as a nation. Israel had been chosen as a "priestly kingdom and a holy nation" to be mediators of God's covenant with other nations. Critically, it is important to draw attention to the fact that God declares here that "the whole earth is mine" (Exodus 19:5–6). The point then, is that the Pentecostal experience has wider implications between the occurrences in Jerusalem.

Jerusalem only became the central point from which God's Spirit was going to reach not just Jews, but also Gentiles by breaking those ethnic, geographical and generational barriers in order that all who call on his name might be saved. "I will pour out my Spirit upon all flesh," God had prophesied through Joel (2:28) and here on the day of Pentecost, Peter noted how it had all come together on an auspicious festive occasion in which people from across the nations had assembled.

It is important to acknowledge that unlike the historic Christian mission endeavors in which the gospel was said to have been brought by white missionaries into non-Western contexts, Pentecost teaches us a different missionary paradigm. In the Pentecost event, God pours out his Spirit on all flesh. The God of Pentecost was not disdainful of any peoples or cultures as to leave them out of the experience. This is where African Pentecostal/charismatic Christians are called to take the place as equal partners in mission.

A modern-day example of how this plays out may be located in the history of the Church of Pentecost, Ghana's single largest Pentecostal denomination. The origins of this denomination are linked to the work of the Welsh Apostolic Church missionary, James McKeown. However, a closer reading of history indicates that McKeown was only invited by a local Pentecostal group to assist them in work that had already started in the 1920s. McKeown, therefore, came to the then Gold Coast, not to start a new Pentecostal church, but to facilitate the work of one that was already on the ground. According to Keener, the church can spread across cultural barriers only because God's Spirit equips us to speak for him and to experience a foretaste of heaven.[8]

Pentecost and the Resurrection

In telling the story of God's salvation in Jesus Christ under the inspiration of the Spirit at Pentecost, Peter draws attention to the high point of the events as they unfold. Jesus had been crucified at the hands of wicked men, he noted, "But God raised him up having freed him from death, because it was impossible for him to be held by its power" (Acts 2:24). Jesus himself proved that it was impossible for him to be held by the power of death when in the book of Revelation he told John on the Island of Patmos: ". . . Do not be afraid; I am the first and the last, and the living one, I was dead, and see, I am alive forever and ever, and I have the keys of death and Hades" (Rev 1:17–18). In drawing out the implications of the resurrection for what the crowd in Jerusalem was "seeing and hearing," Peter contrasts the positions of Jesus and David after they died. David is supposed to have been referring to the Son of God when he declared:

> I saw the Lord always before me,
>   for he is at my right hand so that I
>   will not be shaken;
> therefore my heart was glad, and my
>   tongue rejoiced;
>   moreover, my flesh will live in hope.
> For you will not abandon my soul to Hades,
>   or let your Holy One experience corruption.
> You have made known to me the ways of life;
>   you will make me full of gladness
>   with your presence (Acts 2:25–28).

Peter argued that these words of hope, although spoken by David, could not have been about himself because "he both died and was buried, and his tomb is with us to this day" (Acts 2:30). According to Peter in making these declarations that include the words "my flesh will live in hope," "you will not abandon my soul to Hades," you will not "let your Holy One experience corruption," and "you will make me full of gladness with your presence," David was speaking prophetically about Jesus Christ. In other words, these prophetic utterances by David, according to Peter's day of Pentecost sermon, were about "the resurrection of the Messiah" (Acts 2:31). "This Jesus," Peter is emphatic, "God raised up, and of that all of us are witnesses" (Acts 2:32). In pouring out his Spirit following the resurrection, Christ also fulfills his destiny to be our Lord. The exalted Christ's bestowal of the Spirit at Pentecost, Macchia points out, is the culminating point of his mission on earth and this, he notes, provides a valuable lens through which to view the Christological import of Pentecost.[9]

The Resurrection and the Outpouring

At this point, it is important to remember that Jesus had referred to the outpouring of the Holy Spirit as something that was going to be in fulfillment of the Father's promise: "And see, I am sending upon you what my Father promised; so stay in the city until you are clothed with power from on high" (Luke 24:49). Therefore, the events of Pentecost, Peter suggests, were not just in fulfillment of an Old Testament prophetic utterance by Joel, but even before Joel, David had also alluded to it. Most importantly, there was a relationship between the resurrection of Jesus and the fulfillment of the promise of the Father. This he outlines in Acts 2:33 when he notes, "Being, therefore, exalted at the right hand of God, and having received from the Father the promise of the Holy Spirit, he has poured out this that you both see and hear."

The Messiah had been enthroned at God's right hand to rule until his enemies become his footstool (Ps 110:1; Acts 2:34–35). These arguments in which Peter connects the resurrection and Pentecost was expected to establish one point and one point only, that Jesus Christ is God's anointed Messiah: "Therefore let the entire house of Israel know with certainty that God has made him both Lord and Messiah, this Jesus whom you crucified" (Acts 2:36).

The message underlying the experience of Pentecost was so that, in having a first-hand experience of the promise of the Father, the disciples and those who come to faith in Jesus might be emboldened to preach him as Lord. Thus, when the crowd was convicted by the message on the day of Pentecost and wanted to know how to respond to it, Peter said to them: "Repent and be baptized every one of you in the name of Jesus Christ so that your sins may be forgiven; and you will receive the gift of the Holy Spirit" (Acts 2:38).

The gift of the Holy Spirit, going by the reiteration of the words of Jesus in Acts 1:8, is to be empowered to serve as witnesses to Jesus as God's Messiah. For many people "speaking in tongues" has become the initial sign of this wonderful experience of the Holy Spirit. There is no point debating whether this sign of the infilling of the Holy Spirit is for every Christian or not. If we continue to dwell on those arguments, the point of the outpouring of the Spirit, which is being empowered by the risen Christ for the work of ministry, would be missed. The important point is to accept that the immediate sign that the Spirit of God had been poured out. The speaking in tongues continues to be an important sign of the experience of the Spirit but, holding that in perspective, to know that the core reason for the outpouring of the Holy Spirit is to know that Jesus was truly raised from the dead and that repentance and forgiveness of sins was to be preached in his name to all nations.

Resurrection and Gifts of the Spirit

It is not only during the day of Pentecost that Peter pointed to the resurrection of Christ as important for explaining the workings of the Spirit of God. Following the surprise that accompanied the healing of the cripple at the gate called Beautiful, Peter again refers to the fact that it is by the name of Jesus, the "Author of life" who they killed and who God raised from the dead, that the man was made whole. "And by faith in his name, his name itself has made this man strong, whom you see and know; and the faith that is true Jesus has given him perfect health in the presence of you all" (Acts 3:14–16). Thus we see Peter, as we have argued above, using the occasion of the performance of a miracle to talk about the death and resurrection of Jesus. It is this same Jesus Christ who had empowered the apostles by his Spirit to witness to the power of his name.

That the outpouring of the Holy Spirit was for Christian empowerment is also seen in the connection that Paul makes between the resurrection and the gifts or graces of the Holy Spirit:

> But each of us was given grace according to the measure of Christ's gift. Therefore it is said,
> "When he ascended on high he made
> captivity itself captive;
> he gave gifts to his people" (Eph 4:7–8).

In Ephesians 4:11, Paul gives us a representative list of the gifts that the risen Christ gave to his people: apostles, prophets, evangelists, pastors, and teachers. In a number of evangelical and charismatic church traditions, these gifts have been in institutionalized as offices that people carry, and into which others may even be promoted when they meet certain denominational requirements. That is not my understanding of how the church is to use the gifts of the Spirit, for in verse 12, Paul states the reason for the granting of the gifts as follows: "to equip the saints for the work of ministry, for building up the body of Christ, until all of us come to the unity of the faith and of the knowledge of the Son of God, to maturity, to the measure of the full stature of Christ."

In other words, the gifts of the Spirit are given to the body of Christ for the work of ministry. Ministry begins with the confession of faith in Christ as Lord and continues with Christian witness in the world, for the formation of a new covenant community, the new Israel of God, in which Jew and Gentile, male and female, menservants and maidservants come to dwell in the kingdom of God in Christ as full members. That which makes this dissolution of national, ethnic, and social differences possible is the Holy Spirit poured out on "all flesh," and with people coming from "every nation under heaven" to experience him, that they may together confess and present Christ as Lord because he was crucified and raised from the dead. To return to Keener's observations, "by citing various passages that identify the Lord with the risen and reigning king, Peter explains that the name of the Lord on whom they are to call is Jesus of Nazareth, God in the flesh."[10]

Conclusion: Refocusing the Message of Pentecost and Pentecostalism

The major emphasis of Pentecost is this: "we witness for Christ, and we depend on God's power to make our witness effective."[11] What has happened in Africa, as in North American Pentecostalism, for example, is that the contemporary Pentecostal movement has, unfortunately, acquired an image that is associated with greed, covetousness, exploitation of the weak and vulnerable, and fake prophetic utterances. The so-called prophetic ministry is so popular in Africa that many Pentecostal/charismatic church pastors have suddenly rebranded their ministries "prophetic." We do not deny the authenticity of the gifts of prophecy that the Spirit endows many with, but the sudden claim by many people that they have been called to operate in that area of ministry raises more questions than answers when it comes to our understanding of the reasons for the outpouring of the Spirit of God at Pentecost. Indeed, Paul is clear in Ephesians 4:11–12 that the reason why some are called to be apostles, prophets, evangelists, pastors and others teachers is to "equip the saints for the work of ministry, for building up the body of Christ."

Contrary to this admonition, a number of self-proclaimed prophetic figures in African Pentecostalism have functioned as the "charismatic Christian" equivalents of traditional diviners and fortune-tellers who exploit the vulnerabilities of a clientele that, in keeping with African worldviews of mystical causality, go around desperately in search of security in life. The prosperity gospel in particular, with its emphasis on material things and money as the prime indicators of God's favor and empowerment, has acquired notoriety for greed that is comparable to the attitude of the servant of the prophet Elijah who pursued Naaman on the blindside of his master to collect money and material things that his master had previously turned down after Naaman's healing from leprosy.[12] The prosperity gospel has left many wondering whether founders of Pentecostal churches with their huge media empires are really in this for pecuniary and other advantages. Some have compared the situation with that of Simon who attempted to pay money to the apostles for the power to impart the Holy Spirit.

On witnessing the apostles imparting the gift of the Holy Spirit through the laying on of hands, Simon put this request to them: "Give me also this power so that anyone on whom I lay my hands may receive the Holy Spirit" (Acts 8:19). In response, he received the sharpest of rebukes from Peter, the lead apostle: "May your silver perish with you, because you thought you could obtain God's gift with money!" (Acts 8:18–20)

The Gehazi-Simon syndrome in which the pursuit of material advantages in ministry and the desire to manifest spiritual power at whatever cost, including "sowing seeds" of money into the lives of charismatic mentors in order to tap into their so-called anointing, is very prevalent in modern Pentecostalism. It is a phenomenon that places much emphasis on the display of spiritual power for personal acclaim and as a tool for numerical growth in ministry within a Christian Pentecostal/charismatic environment that has become very competitive. With these developments, Pentecostalism has been monetized as both members and leaders materialize the gospel for personal gain.

These developments simply undermine the critical message at the heart of the biblical Pentecost. It has contributed to the popular accusation that there is much growth in Christianity in Africa, but little moral impact on a corrupted public sphere. It is very difficult to sit in a contemporary African Pentecostal service of the prosperity preaching type and hear anything about the fundamental truths of the gospel: sin, repentance, judgment, holiness, sanctification, and the consequences of alienation from God in eternal damnation. Contrary to these developments, we learn from the biblical accounts that at every turn the work of the Spirit, beginning from the promise made by Jesus and the events of the day of Pentecost to their interpretation, the messianic truth that Jesus Christ is Lord seems to be the center of the message. It is only in the Spirit that can truly recognize the lordship of Jesus (I Corinthians 12:13). It is only by the Spirit that we can confess Jesus as Lord, because it was from Jesus the risen Lord that the Spirit was bestowed as a living witness to that lordship.[13]

For Africa in particular, it is worth pointing out that Christian growth currently being witnessed on the continent may be God's way of preserving the heart of the message — the lordship of Jesus Christ — for a fresh advance in mission in the Northern contexts where the faith has been in recession since the years of the Enlightenment. In the post-Pentecost experience of Africa, if one may tell the story from the viewpoint of the Ethiopian Eunuch, he was reading a passage about the Suffering Servant in Isaiah, but when the Spirit visited him through the ministry of Philip, the focus was on Jesus Christ: "Then Philip began to speak, and starting with his scripture [that is the Isaiah passage], he proclaimed to him the good news about Jesus" (Acts 8:35).

Even before then, the representative list of nations at the original Pentecost event also included Africans, for among those named, were, "Egypt and the parts of Libya belonging to Cyrene" (Acts 2:10). Thus, Africa was present at the first Pentecost and our representatives were part of the group that testified to the wonders of God in Christ as a result of the outpouring of the Holy Spirit. The message of Pentecost has always been about Jesus Christ and we ought to return to that emphasis.

In conclusion, consider the lesson that Peter brings to the Jews following his short message on the meaning of the cripple healed at the beautiful gate:

> Repent, therefore, and turn to God so that your sins may be wiped out, so that times of refreshing may come from the presence of the Lord, and that he may send the Messiah appointed for you, that is, Jesus, who must remain in heaven until the time of the universal restoration that God announced long ago through his holy prophets (Acts 3:19–21).

All the other experiences associated with these events are meant to make that same point, and it was the message about Jesus Christ that the apostles carried to the world and with which they turned it upside down. The signs of the Spirit granted by God were simply there as confirmation that God was indeed working among his people. Frank D. Macchia put the matter even more succinctly when he notes as follows: "The reign of God comes on us through an abundant outpouring of God's very Spirit on us to transform us and to direct our lives toward Christ like loyalties."[14]

Notes

1. Frank D. Macchia, *Baptized in the Spirit: A Global Pentecostal Theology* (Grand Rapids, MI: Zondervan, 2006); Ralph Del Colle, *Christ and the Spirit: Spirit Christology in Trinitarian Perspective* (Oxford: Oxford University Press, 1994).
2. Macchia, *Baptized in the Spirit*, 14.
3. Craig S. Keener, *Gift Giver: The Holy Spirit for Today* (Grand Rapids, MI: Baker Academic, 2001), 52.
4. Macchia, *Baptized in the Spirit*, 79.
5. Keener, *Gift Giver*, 53.
6. J. Kwabena Asamoah-Gyadu, *The Holy Spirit Our Comforter: An Exercise in Homiletic Pneumatology* (Accra: Step Publishers, 2017), 188–205.
7. See various essays in: I. Howard Marshall and David Peterson, eds., *Witness to the Gospel: The Theology of Acts* (Grand Rapids, MI: Eerdmans, 1998).
8. Keener, *Gift Giver*, 53.
9. Frank D. Macchia, *Jesus the Spirit Baptizer: Christology in the Light of Pentecost* (Grand Rapids, MI: Eerdmans, 2018), 2.
10. Keener, *Gift Giver,* 56.
11. Keener, *Gift Giver*, 58.
12. J. Kwabena Asamoah-Gyadu, *Sighs and Signs of the Spirit: Ghanaian Perspectives on Pentecostalism and Renewal in Africa* (Oxford: Regnum, 2015), 163–176.
13. Macchia, *Baptized in the Spirit*, 110.
14. Macchia, *Baptized in the Spirit*, 116.

9.

Power Encounter in the Proclamation of God's Word

Opoku Onyinah

Abstract

This chapter is about the involvement of the servants of God in the ongoing apparent cosmic battle between the kingdom of God and the kingdom of Satan. The resistance of Satan by God's servants through diverse means leads to confrontation, which is termed as power encounter here. However, the Lord always empowers his servants with the Holy Spirit, who authenticates them in the proclamation of the word through signs and wonders. This study concludes that in all cases, the Lord proves that he is the Supreme Being and does not have a match.

Key words: encounter, darkness, power, confrontation, kingdom

Introduction

Pentecostals joined the Christian front evangelization with the view to preach the gospel to all creation, with the full assurance of the Lord to bless their efforts with signs and wonders. Without any doubts about the authenticity of the conclusion of Mark's gospel, Pentecostals believe that the signs mentioned at the end of Mark's text will follow those who believe. That is, in the name of Jesus, demons will be cast out, believers will speak in tongues, believers will drink poison and it will have no physical effects on them, believers will pick up snakes and they will not be hurt, and believers will place their hands on the sick and they will be healed (Mark 16:18).

Pentecostals believe that those who fail to accept the Lord Jesus will go to hell (literal hell). For this reason, Pentecostals preach with zeal to family members, Muslims, idol worshippers, Hindus, Buddhists, nominal Christians in other Christian denominations, and unbelievers in general. Pentecostals believe that there are two kingdoms — the kingdom of God and the kingdom of Satan. All those people who are not saved are spiritually blind and are in the kingdom of Satan. The gospel is preached to deliver them from darkness, that is, the power of Satan, into the kingdom of God (Acts 26:17–18). Since Satan has kept the unsaved in darkness by his power, it is believed that he will resist the proclamation of the word by all means, to keep the gospel from being preached to unbelievers. For this very reason, the Lord has empowered believers with the Holy Spirit, especially with the baptism of the Holy Spirit, for them to be able to execute the task of the proclamation of the gospel with signs and wonders. The resistance of Satan through diverse means leads to confrontation. This confrontation is what is being referred to here as the power encounter. The coming in of the "Third Wave" and some Charismatics increased people's awareness of power encounters and the supernatural. However, many from the "Third Wave" concentrated their attention on strategies of "spiritual warfare," focusing on territorial and strategic warfare. This approach subtly diverted attention from the power encounter in the proclamation of the word to dealing with obsession and demonization of Christians.[1]

The power encounter is not used here as it used by the third wave theologians, which leads to the engagement of various types of spiritual warfare. It is used here to refer to the ongoing apparent cosmic battle between the kingdom of God and the kingdom of Satan. Throughout the Bible, one of the things that stands out is the encounter that the people of God have with evil powers as they embark on the work of God. This study is about such encounters in the Bible and the tools that the Lord has given to his children to overpower the kingdom of darkness as they work for him. For the purpose of this study, the people of God have been divided into two groups: the people of God in the Old Testament, and the people of God in the New Testament. I will begin by discussing the power encounters that some of the people of God experienced in the Old Testament, and follow with the New Testament. After this, I will discuss the available tools for Christians to engage in the proclamation of the word. Finally, I will interact with some of the criticisms against the Pentecostal stand on the baptism of the Holy Spirit and then draw a conclusion.

Power Encounter in the Old Testament

Right from the creation of the world, there appears to exist a being called, "Satan," or "the devil," who is opposed to God and allied with lesser spiritual beings referred to as "evil spirits," or "demons." This being was able to capture the mind of Adam and Eve to disobey the Lord right from creation. The Lord pronounced judgment on the devil, who was represented by the serpent in Genesis 3. Ever since this period, the Bible indicates that human beings are entangled in this cosmic conflict between the Lord and evil powers and suffer various forms of spiritual and physical attacks, ranging from sickness and misfortune to demonic possession and death. Their main work is to oppose the Lord and his work. Thus, both the Lord and the devil want allegiance from human beings. This scenario is displayed throughout the Bible.

The issue of allegiance was a focus when the Lord delivered the people of Israel from slavery in Egypt. The deliverance of the people of God from Egypt was seen as a power encounter between the Lord and the powers of evil, represented by the gods of Egypt (as seen in the book of Exodus through the book of Numbers). Having delivered the Israelites from slavery, the Lord told them, "You shall not have any other gods before me" (Ex 20:2). The implication is that there are other gods; therefore, he needed the allegiance of those whom he had chosen as his own. The series of miracles in Exodus demonstrates that God is greater than the gods of the Egyptians. In these encounters, both the servants of the Lord and those of the Egyptians appealed to their deities, with Moses and Aaron on one side, and Pharaoh and the Egyptian magicians on the other. From the beginning, Pharaoh's magicians were able to copy some of the miracles that Moses and Aaron performed in the name of the Lord (Ex 7:8–25).

For example, when Aaron (and Moses) threw his staff down in front of Pharaoh and his officials and it became a snake, the Egyptian magicians also did the same thing by their secret arts (Ex 7:10–12).[2] Furthermore, Aaron (and Moses) raised his staff in their presence and struck the water of the Nile River, "and all the water was changed into blood." The Egyptian magicians then did the same things by their secret arts (Ex 7:20–23).

However, eventually, the Egyptian magicians were unable to match up with Moses and Aaron (Ex 8–12). Moses was able to lead and overpower the Egyptians because he had been empowered by the Lord (Ex 3). It is in these encounters that we have the only examples in the Bible of the servants of evil powers copying the demonstration of God's power by his servants in their presence. In addition, these episodes demonstrate that the Lord may allow evil powers to manipulate nature to cause miracles in their deceptive work. The miracles had the crucial purpose of enabling Egypt, Pharaoh, and Israel to know that "I am the Lord" (Ex 6:8, NIV), and that it is the Lord who brings judgment on the gods of Egypt (Ex 12:12). Pentecostals see the episode here as a power encounter.[3]

Another picture of power encounter is the story of Balaam and the people of Israel in Numbers 22–26, 31. From the narrative it appeared that Balaam knew that the God of Israel was the Lord, yet he thought he could manipulate him to curse the people of Israel. As he was constrained by the Lord to do so, he unveiled a very profound truth of the word, "There is no sorcery against Jacob, no divination against Israel" (Num 23:23). However, the people of Israel got involved in idolatry and immorality, which resulted in the death of 24,000 people. This episode shows that the evil one cannot curse the one who is owned by the Lord, or is in the kingdom of God. It is the Lord who disciplines his own. His people should fear to sin against him more than all the roars of the devil.

Power encounter is also demonstrated in the story between Elijah and the prophets of Baal at Mount Carmel (1 Kings 18). Elijah, the man of God, threw a challenge to the prophets of Baal to demonstrate the power of their deities. The purpose was to find out the true God. In the hope of demonstrating the power of their deities, and with full strength, the prophets of Baal were greatly humiliated as they exposed instead the powerlessness of their deities. The servant of God, however, prepared his sacrifice and prayed for the fire of God to consume the sacrifice. The success of this miracle brought the desired result, "When all the people saw this, they fell prostrate and cried, 'The Lord — he is God! The Lord — he is God!'" (1 Kings 18:39). Thus, this power encounter authenticated the authority of the servant of God and led the people to a decision.

Elijah typifies the servant of the Lord who is empowered by the Holy Spirit. Before he was taken up by the Lord, Elijah was requested to anoint three people to take over from him (1 Kings 19:15–18). Many Pentecostals believe that such miracles are real today, and people who are baptized in the Holy Spirit and embark on evangelism are often to be validated by the Lord through the working of signs and wonders. This is well reflected by the assertion of the Church of God theologian, Steven Land, who sees Pentecostalism as the "unseen recovery of the universal call to witness in the power and demonstration of the Spirit in order to carry out the universal mission of the church."[4]

A very typical example of a power encounter is that which was experienced by Daniel with regards to the Prince of Persia (Daniel 10). Daniel was in prayer concerning the plan of God for the people of Israel. He had received a vision he did not understand. As he prayed for the interpretation of the vision, the answer to his prayer was withheld for three weeks. The account indicates that the Prince of Persia resisted a heavenly being who was delegated to bring the answer to Daniel until Michael came to his help. For Pentecostals, this is an example of the cosmic battle behind activities that are carried out on earth. However, the fact that Daniel did not know what was happening, but trusted God in his prayer and received an answer means that believers need to pray and trust God to answer their prayer no matter the type of request.[5]

The discussions so far indicate that the success of these leaders was associated with the power of God upon the lives of God's chosen servants. The Lord had to empower them in order to validate them as his representatives. By such means, the Lord proved that he is the Supreme Being and does not have a match. Thus, Wonsuk Ma, the Korean Pentecostal scholar, argues that "The work of the Spirit in relation to the leaders in God's economy has a twofold function: authentication and empowerment."[6] For Ma, and rightly so, the issues of authentication and empowerment apply to all leaders in the past and the present.[7]

Nevertheless, the Old Testament ends with a sad story concerning the people of Israel. Israel, both the Northern and Southern kingdoms, was taken into captivity. Thus, it appeared that the physical demonstration of God's power through a chosen people had ended, though there was a remnant. The lesson that we gather here, as God told the Israelites, remains. When the people of God remain faithful and obedient to him, the Lord grants them victory. When they disobey him, he disciplines them by delivering them to the evil one (2 Kings 17; 1–23; 2 Chr 36:15–23). Yet, God's heart is always yearning for the repentant ones. Accordingly, the Lord, through his prophets, promised he would anoint servants who would liberate those in captivity, and by that set up his kingdom, which would include the Gentiles (Is 42:1–8, 61:1–2). The Lord, therefore, promised the Spirit that would be poured on all flesh so that everyone will know him, and through that, be empowered to carry out his work (Joel 2:28–29). The New Testament was to fulfill these prophecies.

Power Encounters in the New Testament

The ministry of our Lord Jesus Christ started with an encounter with the devil. This took place after Jesus had been baptized, anointed by the Spirit (empowerment), and validated by the Father as the Son of God, through an audible voice (Matt 4:1–11; 3:13–17). Jesus overcame the devil with the word of God. However, as Luke reports, the devil indicated that he had left him for an opportune time (Luke 4:13). This was a signal that power encounter in the New Testament was going to be even clearer than the Old Testament.

Jesus' announcement that the kingdom of God was at hand takes its special significance from the Old Testament's prophetic expectation that God's rule was coming, and his people would be liberated from satanic domination (Mark 1:15; Luke 4:18–19; Isa. 9:6–11; Isa. 61:1–3).[8] Consequently, Jesus alluded to the expulsion of demons as visible signs of the kingdom of God overpowering the satanic kingdom. In the Beelzebub controversy, for example, Jesus clearly links his casting out of demons with the kingdom of God that is breaking through the satanic kingdom (Matt 12:28). The Parable of the Strong Man implies that the binding and plundering of the strong man, Satan, occurs simultaneously with the coming of the Messiah to inaugurate the kingdom of God (Matt 12:29).

Right from the beginning of his ministry, Jesus encountered a demoniac at the synagogue in Capernaum who shouted at Jesus and claimed to know his person (Mark 1:21–28). This demoniac was frightened at the presence of Jesus and wanted to know if the time for the destruction of evil powers was due. This means Jesus was more powerful than the demoniac. In Jesus' encounter with the man at Gadara, Mark showed that there were thousands of demons in the man but the demoniac was still afraid of Jesus (Mark 5, see also Matt 8:28–34; Luke 8:26–37). Jesus eventually expelled the demons and set the man free. In the other two main narratives of demons in people, Jesus showed that he was more powerful than the demons by setting the captives free from demonization and healing them. These were the Syrophoenician woman's daughter (Matt 15: 21–28; Mark 7:24–30), and the epileptic boy (Mark 9:14–29; Matt 17:14–19; Luke 9:37–45). Several summary reports of Jesus' exorcism and aftermath discourses all show that Jesus was the superman who had power over satanic oppressions (Matt 9:32–34; 12:22–28; Mark 1:32–34, 39; 3:23–27; Luke 11:17–22).

Power encounters continue throughout the rest of Jesus' ministry. He shows in the Parable of the Sower that the devil is the evil one who snatches away the word of God from people's hearts (Matt 13:19). In the Parable of the Weeds, Satan is portrayed as the enemy who seeks to destroy God's people by planting evil among them (Matt 13:25, 38–39). In John's gospel, the Pharisees' desire to kill Jesus is rooted in the desire of their master, the devil (John 8:42–45). Furthermore, Satan enters Judas and prompts him to betray Jesus (John 13:27; Luke 22:3).[9] Jesus was able to do all that he did because the anointing of the Lord was upon him (Luke 4:18–19). Peter confirms in Acts 10:38 that God anointed Jesus of Nazareth with the Holy Spirit and power; that is why he was able to deliver all who were oppressed by the devil.

Additionally, power encounter is painted in the ministries of the apostles, especially in the book of Acts. Satan is directly mentioned in four places as opposing God's work in diverse ways (Acts 5:3; 10:38; 13:10; 26:18). For example, Satan can fill the hearts of believers with evil intent that leads to death. Peter spoke to Ananias, "how is it that Satan has so filled your heart that you have lied against the Holy Spirit?" (Acts 5:3).

When Phillip, a deacon who had been filled with the Holy Spirit, preached the gospel in Samaria and performed miracles in the name of Jesus, evil spirits came out of many, and many paralytics and cripples were healed (Acts 8:6–8). Here, the servant of the Lord was authenticated as demons were being cast out, and those oppressed by the devil were set free. Simon who had been a sorcerer, an agent of the devil, surrendered to the kingdom of God as he saw the power of God demonstrated in the ministry of Philip, and later in the ministry of Peter and John (Acts 8:9–25).

There were two direct power confrontations in Acts. One was between Paul and the slave girl who had the spirit of divination (Acts 16:16–18). This account showed that the servant of God was superior. The other was Paul's confrontation with Elymas who interfered in the preaching of the gospel (Acts 13:4–12). These episodes demonstrated that the servants of the devil were no match for the servants of God. There was a confrontation between "the man who had an evil spirit" and the seven sons of Sceva (Acts 19:13–16), which shows that evil powers know the servants of the Lord and those who are pretenders.

The epistles show that there are still cosmic battles. Paul's terminology of "principalities and powers" (Eph 6:12) indicates an unexplained complexity of the spirit world, which hints at territorial powers (Rom 8:38; 1 Cor 15:24.). The use of the term "archangel" by Paul and Jude implies some degree of angelic hierarchy among the angels of God (1 Thes 4:16; Jude 1:9).[10] However, Paul's letters reveal the conquering of all the principalities and powers in the heavenly realm (Col 2:15; Eph 1:20–22). For him, believers have been rescued from the kingdom of darkness (the adversary), which is dominated by evil forces, and have been transferred into the kingdom of Christ (Col 1:13). Satan (Rom 16:20) is portrayed as the adversary (1 Peter 5:8). Other names given to him include, the devil (1 Peter 5:8), the serpent (2 Cor 11:3), the evil one (Eph 6:16), and the god of this age (2 Cor. 4:4). Satan lives up to his role as an adversary. For example, he tempts, misleads, torments, traps, hinders and deceives Christians (1 Cor 7:5; 2 Cor 12:7; 11:14; 1 Thess 2:18; 3:5; 1 Tim 5:15). Paul himself was given a thorn in the flesh, a messenger of Satan to torment him (2 Cor. 12:7).

The opposing work of the devil and evil powers continues to play a significant role in the New Testament. The authors show that evil stems from the devil who seeks constantly to devour Christians and thwart the will of God (1 Pet 5:8–9; Jam 4:7–10; 1 John 5:18; Rev 12:9). The entire New Testament reveals that evil powers are in rebellion against Christ; they attack the church and operate most effectively through unredeemed humanity (2 Cor 4:4; Eph 6:10–20; 1 Peter 5:8; Rev 12:7–12). Thus, as we live between times of what Christ has done for us already and his second coming, the devil and evil powers are very active in the world, and will remain so until the final consummation when they will be completely subdued.[11]

Therefore, Christians are called upon to resist the devil (1 Pet 5:9; Jam 4:7). Christians can do this by putting on the whole armor of Christ so that they will stand up against "the devil's scheme" (Eph 6:10–18; Is 59:17). Some Pentecostals see in this passage spiritual warfare between Christians and satanic powers.[12] However, the emphasis here is for Christians to know that though defeated, the devil will still fight. What believers need to understand is that Satan's main work is to oppose God, and to achieve this end, he seeks to influence Christians to think and live contrary to the word of God (Job 1–2; 1 Chr 21:1; Zech 3:1–2; Luke 22:31–34). He will use all tricks to deceive Christians, therefore standing (Eph 6:11, 13, 14), that is holding on to your faith and ground, is absolutely essential.[13]

The disciples of Christ were able to overcome the devil because right from the beginning of the book of Acts they were empowered by the Holy Spirit (Acts 2:1–11). It was Peter who had been filled with the

Spirit who preached on the day of Pentecost (Acts 2:22–41) and got 3000 people converted. It was Peter who had been "filled with the Holy Spirit" (Acts 4:8) who was able to stand before the Sanhedrin and preached about the resurrected Christ. It was Paul who was filled with the Holy Spirit who was able to proclaim the word in difficult circumstances (Acts 13–15). Besides the direct power encounters that were experienced in Paul's ministry, he and Barnabas were also indirectly opposed by the devil through Jewish public opposition (Acts 13:50), and jealous Jewish leaders (Acts 13:45). They were often persecuted and sometimes stoned (Acts 14:19). Being filled with the Holy Spirit, the disciples of Christ were able to encounter evil powers at various levels, but proclaimed the word and had results. Thus, the empowerment of the Holy Spirit is absolutely essential in the proclamation of the word.

The Power of the Holy Spirit and His Baptism

Having discussed how the Spirit led the servants of God in their discharge of the ministry of God in both the Old and the New Testaments, this section discusses the important role that the Spirit plays in the contemporary Pentecostal mission.

The Holy Spirit is the motivating force behind all Pentecostal mission activities. The strength of the mission work of Pentecostals is, therefore, attributed to the emphasis it places on the work of the Holy Spirit. The Holy Spirit is considered the one who does the work of missions. He is the one who causes the believer to preach about Christ with the power to heal and cast out demons. He also empowers the believer to live the Christian life. This is reflected in Christian Leonard's records of a conversation that was carried out between Hans Debrunner, a Presbyterian missionary in the Gold Coast, now Ghana, and Pastor James McKeown, a Pentecostal missionary in the same country, "I have only three important messages — One: Jesus Christ and him crucified. Two: the baptism of the Holy Spirit. Three: the power of God to change lives and bring holiness in the Church."[14]

It is believed that it is the Spirit who enables believers to effectively perform the tasks assigned to each believer in Christian ministry. The performance of the tasks is urgent since it is believed that the second coming of Christ is imminent. Therefore, as the Lord empowered his people in the scriptures, so in this generation the Holy Spirit gives supernatural abilities to Christians to proclaim the gospel of Christ with power to cast out evil spirits, the power to heal the sick, and be protected from evil forces.

For Pentecostals, the focal point of the Spirit's work is the baptism of the Holy Spirit. Emmanuel Kinsley Larbi, a Ghanaian Pentecostal Scholar, touches on the crux of the matter when he states that, "the key to the tapping of these unlimited abilities is the *glossolalic* experience, hence the stress on the need for everyone to experience this phenomenon."[15] Once people experience the baptism of the Holy Spirit as initially evidenced by speaking in tongues, they are expected to witness Christ with the power to heal and cast out demons. Thus, people baptized in the Holy Spirit are missionaries wherever they are. This is clearly reflected in the writings of Pentecostal scholars, such as Russel Spittler, William Menzies, and L Grant McClung.[16] Spittler, the North American Pentecostal theologian, writes, "Pentecostal success in mission can be laid to their drive for personal religious experience, . . . the experiential particularism involved in every Pentecostal baptism in the Holy Spirit."[17]

However, sociologists like Paul Gifford adduces the reason for the growth of some Pentecostal churches to "lack of any education requirements, which enables anyone wanting to begin a church to do so."[18] But his argument is weak because if such a requirement were to be the main factor of the growth of a church, then many churches would have grown. Similarly, Paul Pomerville, the Pentecostal missiologist, observes that church growth specialists assign many causes, including the mobilization of the laity, praying for the sick, and aggressive evangelism, to Pentecostal church growth and missions. Nevertheless, Pomerville refutes these and rather lays strong emphasis on the Pentecostal experience of the baptism of the Holy Spirit. He opines, "the Pentecostal experience of individual believers has always been and still is the primary cause of growth of Pentecostal churches."[19]

By putting stress on the baptism of the Holy Spirit, Pentecostals emphasize that the coming of the Spirit on a person's life is the experience that brings the ability to perform signs and wonders in Jesus' name. Thus, it has been a regular feature within the Pentecostal Church's fellowship meetings for people to hear reports of signs and wonders wrought in the power of the Holy Spirit and how evil powers have been defeated in the proclamation of the word.[20] Commenting about the African Pentecostal churches in the diaspora, Gerrie Ter Haar, a Dutch Professor of Religion, observes that they "detect the hand of God in their daily affairs."[21]

The writings of Pentecostal scholars, such as William Faupel, Gary McGee, Steven Land, and C. De Wet all indicate that the emphasis on signs and wonders as part of the Pentecostal evangelistic strategy throughout the world has contributed to the growth of the Pentecostal churches in missions.[22] Consequently, Pentecostalism can be considered as the answer to the clarion call to evangelize in the power of the Spirit to carry out the Great Commission.

The emphasis placed on the need for each person to receive the Holy Spirit also results in spontaneous liturgy, void of rigid order. This is mainly oral and narrative with emphasis on a direct experience of God through the indwelling Holy Spirit. Larbi points out that "formal education is no hindrance, the Holy Spirit enables even illiterates to read and teach the Bible."[23] Accordingly, through the baptism in the Holy Spirit, everyone is involved in worship and knows how to conduct a service. Individuals know from Acts 1:8 that once they are baptized in the Holy Spirit, they have the power to witness about Christ. Pentecostals, therefore, move in power without fear of the devil, and with zeal, proclaiming the gospel and casting out demons.

Pentecostal missiologists globally see this Spirit-baptism resulting in the involvement of the laity in "oral worship" as a contributing factor to the growth of Pentecostal churches. An Assemblies missiologist, Melvin Hodges, contends, "the emphasis which Pentecostals place on the necessity of each individual receiving a personal infilling of the Spirit has produced believers and workers of unusual zeal and power."[24] The effect of this oral liturgy means much of the Pentecostal theology is imported or absorbed from the surrounding culture. This accounts for the absence of any formal education requirements for the ministry of the early Pentecostals. The result of this is indigenous assimilation. It was this sort of indigenous assimilation, exhibiting itself in the lives of African and Asian Pentecostal Christians in the diaspora, which resulted in the establishment of "diasporic" churches in the West. Thus, the Pentecostal power to proclaim the word knows no bounds and fears no power.

Critique of the Pentecostal Concept of Spirit Baptism

Pentecostal emphasis on the baptism of the Holy Spirit, especially regarding *glossolalia,* has not gone unchallenged. McGee remarks that, "critics branded glossolalia as nonsense."[25] Similarly, Harvey Cox, a

North American non-Pentecostal theologian, points to the fact that "the vast majority of psychological or sociological observers classify it [speaking in tongues] as a form of mental aberration."[26] Others claim that almost all cases of *glossolalia* are basically emotional utterances.[27] Closely linked with this criticism is the view that speaking in tongues is the result of hypnotic techniques affecting altered states of consciousness in others. This is heavily based on the belief that the critical mind is by-passed; people are encouraged to accept the supernatural interpretation and detach themselves from the Western rational paradigm.[28] Critical to this view is the work of Steven L. Davies, a professor of Religion in North America. Davies' work constitutes an attempt to contribute to the quest for the historical Jesus, reinterpreting the gospel accounts of healings and exorcisms in the light of modern psychology and anthropology. However, he develops a chapter claiming that Paul delivered his messages orally in order "to effect the induction of spirit-possession in susceptible listeners."[29] Thus, for Davies, Spirit possession, including speaking in tongues, can be understood in reference to discourse productive of hypnotic states.[30]

Nevertheless, some scholars from non-Pentecostal circles admit that Pentecostals (with the *glossolalic* experience) are aggressive in their evangelism. For example, Cox identifies speaking in tongues as an "ecstasy experience" which responds to one of the spiritual crises of our era, which one writer labeled "ecstasy deficit."[31] He observes that the Pentecostals pour their spiritually generated zeal into their work, and continues, "their whole life is a mission...."[32] By this, Cox sees that despite what people say about speaking in tongues, the experience empowers the Pentecostals to dedicate their lives to the mission of God. He sees something, which we can call the demonstration of God's power, in the lives of those who claim to experience the Spirit's baptism.

Although Davies downplayed Spirit-possession in general, his work implicitly reveals that it is Spirit-possession that causes Christianity to grow. He remarks that for Paul, "spirit-possession was the *sine qua non* for Christianity."[33] He recognizes that Paul's criteria for membership in Christianity was Spirit-possession, and that the Spirit is crucial for the Christian life.[34] It must, however, be said that others, represented by a North American clinical psychologist, John Kildahl, consider that the so-called emotional benefits of speaking in tongues do not last long,[35] thus, such scholars may not see any lasting ways through which the Spirit-baptism may enhance the proclamation of the word or missions work.

Regardless of the fact that the Pentecostal emphasis on the Holy

Spirit-baptism, especially regarding *glossolalia*, has been challenged by many scholars, the charismatic renewal worldwide is a confirmation of the impact that the Pentecostal stress on the Holy Spirit has had on Christian missions. McGee, after assessing the work of Father Donald McDonnell, confirms that the Pentecostal stance "has forced the larger church world to reassess the work of the Holy Spirit in missions."[36] Thus, it is an undisputed fact that Pentecostalism has contributed positively to Christian missions through the emphasis on the baptism of the Holy Spirit.

However, the strong emphasis placed on the Holy Spirit, coupled with the idea of the imminent return of Christ which caused the urgency in evangelization and world missions among Pentecostals, caused the Pentecostals to neglect mission theology; there is no reflection on the task, the recipient culture, and the need for special training. Missionaries are sent as the need arises. In addition, sometimes people proclaim the message without giving much thought to the environment in which they proclaim it. Obviously, this is not without repercussions. The repercussion is not power confrontation, but chaos. That this has become a general problem to Pentecostals is highlighted by Klaus D. Triplett, who writes that the Pentecostals concept of "indigenous church must not keep us from the concerted reflection upon whether or not we are allowing authentic indigenous processes to emerge from each culture by the Spirit."[37] Thus, even though Pentecostals believe we have the power to confront the evil one successfully, our lack of conscious effort to contextualize the message within a specific cultural milieu can give way to the devil's attack. Walter Hollenweger observed that there was insufficient attention given to the role of culture as a barrier to the gospel and therefore appealed to Pentecostals for the consideration of intercultural theology.[38] This need still exists within Pentecostalism.

Conclusion

Power encounter has been part of the execution of the work of God. From the Old Testament to the New Testament it has been shown that all the servants of God, in one way or the other, were confronted by satanic powers. However, they overcame them through the power of God, which was evident in their lives and ministries. Similarly, in contemporary times, the Lord has empowered Christians with the Holy Spirit who authenticates them in the proclamation of the word through signs and wonders. The presence of the Holy Spirit, as symbolized by speaking in tongues, in the lives of Pentecostal Christians has been shown to be the motivating force behind every activity that the Pentecostals undertake. Although some scholars have criticized the Spirit-possession of Christians, as claimed by Pentecostals, the experience continues to empower the Pentecostal believers to declare the word of God in power and with zeal. With his empowerment, Spirit-possessed believers can overcome obstacles that come their way in the proclamation of the gospel, leading to the growth of the church.

Notes

1. For some reading on this, see Opoku Onyinah, *Spiritual Warfare: A Centre for Pentecostal Theology Short Introduction* (Cleveland, TN: CPT Press, 2012).

2. Here, Aaron's staff swallowed their staffs showing that the Lord was superior and had no equal.

3. Fred Haltom, "Power Encounters in the Old Testament," in Opal L. Reddin, ed., *Power Encounter: A Pentecostal Perspective* (Springfield, MO: Central Bible College Press, 1999), 93.

4. Steven Land, *Pentecostal Spirituality: A Passion for the Kingdom* (Sheffield: Sheffield Academic Press, 1993), 96.

5. See also Charles Harris, "Encountering Territorial Spirits," in Reddin, ed., *Power Encounter*, 266. The Third Wave theologians see in the passage the need for spiritual mapping before praying against the territorial spirits. However, Daniel did not know what was going on, but only trusted God in his prayer — a good scriptural principle to follow.

6. Wonsuk Ma, "The Spirit of God Upon Leaders of Israelite Society and the Igorot Tribal Churches," in Wonsuk Ma and Robert P. Menzies, eds., *Pentecostalism in Context: Essays in Honor of William W. Menzies* (Sheffield: Sheffield Academic Press, 1997), 301.

7. Ma, "The Spirit of God upon Leaders," 301.

8. Keith Warrington, *Healing and Suffering: Biblical and Pastoral Reflections* (Milton Keynes, UK: Paternoster, 2005), 20–21.

9. Opoku Onyinah, *Pentecostal Exorcism: Witchcraft and Demonology from Ghana* (Blandford Forum, UK: Deo, 2012), 240–244.

10. Onyinah, *Pentecostal Exorcism*, 263–66.

11. Gordon Fees, *God's Empowering Presence* (Carlisle, UK: Paternoster, 1995), 571–574.

12. For discussions on spiritual warfare, see Onyinah, *Spiritual Warfare*, 10–19.

13. Take note of the fact that in the NIV, the term "stand" is mentioned four times in this passage (Eph 6:11–14).

14. Christine Leonard, *A Giant in Ghana: 3000 Churches in 50 Years, the Story*

of James McKeown and the Church of Pentecost (Chichester, UK: New Wine Ministries, 1989), 85. See also Hans W. Debrunner, *A History of Christianity in Ghana* (Accra: Waterville Publishing House, 1967), 325.

15. Emmanuel Kingsley Larbi, "The Development of Ghanaian Pentecostalism: A Study in the Appropriation of the Christian Gospel in the 20th Century Ghana Setting with Special Reference to the Christ Apostolic Church, the Church of Pentecost Etc" (Ph.D. Diss., Centre for the Study of Christianity in Non-Western World, University of Edinburgh, 1995), 248–249.

16. Menzies, in refuting Fee's critique of Pentecostal "doctrine of subsequence" rather, affirms "the purpose of Spirit-baptism is to empower believers so that they might be effective witnesses." Robert Menzies, *Empowered for Witness: The Spirit in Like and Acts* (Sheffield, UK: Sheffield Academic Press, 1994), 235. See also L. Grant McClung, Jr. "Truth on Fire: Pentecostals and an Urgent Missiology," in L. Grant McClung, Jr., ed., *Azusa Street and Beyond: Pentecost Missions and Church Growth in the Twentieth Century* (South Plainfield, NJ: Logos, 1986), 49. McClung stresses the same point that "the outpouring of the Holy Spirit personally into the life of each believer" is the primary cause for church growth.

17. Russel P. Spittler, "Implicit Values in Pentecostal Missions," *Missiology: An International Review* 16:4 (October 1988), 413.

18. Paul Gifford, *African Christianity: Its Public Role* (London: Hurst & Company, 1998), 76.

19. Paul A. Pomerville, *Introduction to Missions: An Independent-Study Textbook* (Irving, CA: ICI University Press, 1987), 100.

20. Opoku Onyinah and Michael Ntumy, eds., *God's Power at Work: Inspirational Testimonies from the Church of Pentecost* (Accra: Church of Pentecost, 2017).

21. Gerrie Ter Haar, *Halfway to Paradise: African Christians in Europe* (Cardiff, UK: Cardiff Academic Press,1998), 45.

22. William D. Faupel, *The Everlasting Gospel: The Significance of Eschatology in The Development of Pentecostal Thought,* (Sheffield, UK: Sheffield Academic Press, 1996), 22; C. De Wet, "The Challenge of Signs and Wonders in World Missions for the Twentieth Century," in *Azusa Street and Beyond: Pentecostal Missions and Church Growth in the Twentieth Century* (South Plainfield, NJ: Bridge Publishing, Inc., 1986), 161; Gary B. McGee "Pentecostals and Their Various Strategies for Global Mission: A Historical Assessment," in Murray A. Dempster, Byron D. Klaus, and Douglas Petersen, eds., *Called and Empowered: Global Mission in Pentecostal Perspective* (Peabody, MA: Hendrickson, 1991), 203–24.

23. Larbi, "The Development of Pentecostalism," 249.

24. Melvin L. Hodges, *The Indigenous Church* (Springfield, MO: Gospel Publishing House, 1953), 132.

25. Gary B. McGee, "Power from on High: A Historical Perspective on the Radical Strategy in Missions," in Ma and Menzies, eds., *Pentecostalism in*

Context, 328.

26. Cox, *Fire from Heaven*, 91.

27. J. Rodman Williams, *Renewal Theology: Salvation, the Holy Spirit, and Christian Living*, vol. 2 (Grand Rapids, MI: Zondervan, 1990), 212.

28. John P. Kildahl, *The Psychology of Speaking in Tongues* (New York: Harper & Row, 1972), 38–39, 54–55; M. J. Cartledge, "Interpreting Charismatic Experience: Hypnosis, Altered States of Consciousness and the Holy Spirit?" *Journal of Pentecostal Theology* 13 (1998), 120.

29. Steven L. Davies, *Jesus the Healer: Possession, Trance the Origin of Christianity* (London: SCM, 1995), 189.

30. Davies, *Jesus the Healer*, 190.

31. Cox, *Fire from Heaven*, 86.

32. Cox, *Fire from Heaven*, 236.

33. Davies, *Jesus the Healer*, 176.

34. Davies, *Jesus the Healer*, 177.

35. Kildahl, *The Psychology of Speaking in Tongues*, 39.

36. Gary B. McGee, "Pentecostal Missiology: Moving Beyond Triumphalism to Face the Issues," *Pneuma* 16:2 (1994), 275–81.

37. B. D. Klaus and L. O. Triplett, "National Leadership in Pentecostal Mission," in *Called and Empowered: Global Mission in Pentecostal Perspective*, 235.

38. Walter Hollenweger, *Pentecostalism: Origins and Developments Worldwide* (Peabody, MA: Hendrickson, 1997), 300.

10.

Towards a Contextual and Effective Engagement of the African Spirit World

Christian Tsekpoe

Abstract

Due to the strong belief in the spirit world in Africa, prophetism has become a dominant feature of Christianity on the continent. Using ethnographic approach of data collection, this chapter discusses how the African Christian engages the spirit world. While on the one hand, the prophetic ministry can be seen as a contextual tool for engaging the African spirit world, on the other hand, it is palpable that this ministry has been used as a tool to manipulate gullible people in society. The chapter identifies that witchcraft accusation has been used as a major factor for interpreting what is considered as life-threatening forces in Africa. An analysis of three different Christian responses from the contexts of Cameroon, Tanzania, and Ghana, shows the acknowledgement of the fact that discussions related to the African spirit world are very complex and require much reflection. Such discussions, however, remain at the academic level and do not seem to impact the grassroots — where the real action is taking place. The chapter therefore proposes the need to enhance collaboration between theological institutions (scholarly research) and grassroots prophets in order to effectively contextualize the engagement of the spirit world in a way that will benefit the church, and at the same time prevent abuses that have been associated with the prophetic ministry.

Key words: Africa, Pentecostal, witchcraft, prophetism, Spirit

Introduction

The belief in witchcraft and demons remains a significant phenomenon in African societies. Whether witchcraft and demons are real or not, the fact is that in Africa, people fear them and take pragmatic actions to protect themselves from what they consider life-threatening forces. While some Western scholars and missionaries have tried to consider the belief in the existence of such spiritual forces as superstitious, African prophets consider almost all misfortunes as emanating from spiritual forces and take pragmatic actions to fight them. Within contemporary Pentecostal Christianity in Africa, the prophetic and deliverance ministry has become prodigious, as its claims to have solutions to all the threats of the spirit forces have attracted large adherents. An assessment of this ministry in Africa can be seen from one angle as contributing to the numerical growth of Christianity in Africa, since many people get converted into the church through their activities. On the other hand, however, some practices within the prophetic/deliverance ministry are seen as a hindrance to effective Christian discipleship on the continent.[1] It is, therefore, imperative for both scholars and church leaders to be concerned about the various Christian responses to the African spirit world and to propose fresh and effective models for engaging the spirit world in ways that can quell abuses and manipulative tendencies within African Christianity, without slowing down the flow of the Holy Spirit. This can be done by appropriating and contextualizing principles and lessons that can be obtained from Jesus' encounters with the spirit world as recorded in the New Testament.

Engaging the Spirit World from an African Perspective

In many African countries, evil spirits emanating from witchcraft and demons are believed to be responsible for many calamities and unexpected circumstances in the lives of individuals, families, and corporate organizations. When confronted with misfortunes such as sudden deaths, miscarriages, infertility in women, impotence in men, failure in business, drought, the outbreak of diseases, and infant mortality, it is perceptibly believed that there is a spiritual cause behind them.[2] It is also believed that spirit forces could inflict material losses on people, make them ignoble through their deeds, as well as being able to read peoples' intentions and work against them. Acts of negligence or carelessness that result in mishaps are mostly ascribed to the works of evil forces. Also, deplorable behavioral practices, such as chronic drunkenness and drug addiction, are sometimes considered as emanating from the schemes of malevolent spirits.[3] Quayesi-Amakye posits, "among Ghanaian Pentecostals, especially in prophetic circles, there is a strong belief that nothing happens accidentally or naturally: there is always a connection between physical evil and supernatural wicked forces."[4] It is believed that these spiritual forces are complex and mysterious and as such, their activities can neither be measured nor subdued by physical and scientific methods. Consequently, scholarly research into issues related to the spirit world is normally considered impotent in the face of spiritual realities. Meanwhile, people live in fear and suspicion, which in some cases leads to witchcraft accusations, promotes divinatory consultation, and in other cases leads to manipulation by those who claim to have insight into the spiritual world.[5] The search for protection from such malevolent forces and seeking spiritual direction as to how to deal with such spiritual and mysterious occurrences permeates all religions in Africa. Thus, both Christians and non-Christians constantly seek pragmatic ways of dealing with the trepidations of the spirit world.

This understanding of the spirit-world partly explains the prevalence of witchcraft accusations in many African countries including Kenya, Congo, Tanzania, Ghana, Angola, Malawi, and South Africa.[6] Over the years, we have been confronted with numerous stories of children (mostly orphans), widows, and old men and women being accused of witchcraft in different African countries. Some of the accused and accusers are Christians or even church leaders. Stephen Rasmussen reports of the accusation of Deborah, a pastor's wife in Tanzania.[7] Robert Priest reports of the accusation of Nzuzi, an elder of a Methodist Church in DR Congo, whose brother is a pastor.[8] Girish Daswani narrates the accusation of the wife of an elder of a The Church of Pentecost in the UK.[9]

In my ministry as a Pentecostal pastor and a lecturer, having interest in the fields of Pentecostal exorcism, witchcraft, demonology, and spiritual warfare, I have been confronted with incidents of witchcraft accusations among Christians, some of which I had the difficult responsibility of helping both the accused and the accuser in managing the spiritual, emotional, psychological, and socio-cultural consequences. On Saturday, February 16, 2019, I was part of a group of leaders from The Church of Pentecost who visited the Gambaga Witches Camp to preach the word of God to the 83 alleged witches kept at that place. We also prayed with them and donated some food items on behalf of The Church of Pentecost, Walewale Area.[10] As at the time of the visit, the oldest alleged witch had spent 35 years at that camp, while the newest arrived at the camp a week before my visit. Conversations with some of the alleged witches revealed different unsubstantiated and pathetic allegations that led to their confinement at the camp. Their individual stories confirmed my assertion that "belief in the reality of the spirit world in Africa does not belong to antiquity. It is a current and ongoing phenomenon, which occupies a significant place in African Christianity."[11] This subject must, therefore, be given the needed attention in order to mitigate the challenges associated with it.

Before my visit to the Gambaga Witches Camp, I attended a national conference on "Witchcraft Accusation in Ghana," on December 10, 2014. The conference was organized by the Ministry of Gender, Children, and Social Protection in Accra and supported by Action Aid Ghana and the Ministry of Chieftaincy and Traditional Affairs. This conference aimed to find ways of integrating the 861 accused witches living in Ghana's six witch camps, back into society. During the discussions at the conference, it became apparent that the six witch camps in Ghana came about as a result of how alleged witches were lynched in some communities without trial. The camps, therefore, serve as a place of refuge, protecting the accused witches. Meanwhile, the conditions at these witch camps are deplorable since the families of such accused persons are not willing to take care of suspected witches. Describing the witch camps in Ghana, John Kirby notes that, "Their mud huts and leaky roofs offer little protection from the torrential rains. The knee-high walls of their compounds deny them privacy and human dignity. Their life lacks the most basic needs: food, water, shelter, and clothing, but most of all, human recognition, companionship, and love."[12] He observes that in most African countries "witchcraft beliefs seem to be the filter through which modern social institutions, including Christianity, are colored, interpreted, given new meanings, and dealt with."[13]

Speaking on "Holistic Overview of Witchcraft Accusations in Ghana" at the conference, Kenneth Agyeman Attafuah, a Barrister-at-Law and Solicitor of the Supreme Court of Ghana shared his mother's story of how she was accused of being a witch. He noted that his mother did not have a child for a long time and when she eventually gave birth, she gave birth to a set of twins (one of whom is himself). She was therefore accused of snatching the eggs of other women, thereby denying them of their biological children. She however, survived the social mistreatment because of her strong personality as well as support from her family and the Presbyterian Church.[14] The role of the family and the Presbyterian Church in supporting this victim is commendable. Sadly, not many people benefit from such support since some of the victims have either been accused by their families or by their churches.

Christian Responses to the African Spirit World

At the initial stages of Christian mission in Africa, exorcism of witchcraft and evil spirits was not a central concern for the mainline mission churches. Rather, Western missionaries in Africa made conscious attempts to expose the deceitfulness of the gods and their priests, explaining witchcraft for example, as superstition.[15] Meanwhile, the African cultures and religions were presented by the missionaries as idol worship and demonic. This resulted in some confrontations between the early missionaries and some traditional Africans. While some Africans accepted the European way of life and rejected everything African, others rejected what they considered as cultural imperialism and the "White man's religion."[16] At this point, it also became clear that the churches were not meeting the holistic needs of the African people. Even though some of the Africans came to believe that their gods were demons, it was also apparent that their fears of spirit forces were not adequately dealt with in the churches. This state of affairs also contributed to ambivalent Christianity in Africa since some people oscillated between both Christianity and traditional African religions. Some charismatic individuals within these mainline mission churches, therefore, emerged claiming to have power over the spirit world. They also claimed to have the ability to cast out demons, heal the sick and prognosticate concerning the future.

Opoku Onyinah hints that the main difference between the Western missionaries and the African charismatic figures (prophets) is that—unlike the missionaries who saw the belief in witchcraft as superstitious and the gods as pagan, and so failed to deal with such issues—the African "prophets" directed their messages against these powers and drove them out through the power of God.[17] The impact of the prophetic ministries as well as the challenges that they posed to the mainline mission churches and the failure of the missionaries to handle them satisfactorily, were to be pictured in the emergence of the African Independent Churches (AICs)[18] and subsequently in the classical Pentecostals churches. Again, the inability of the Classical Pentecostal churches to contain the activities of lay prophets/prophetesses in their churches is similar to schisms that followed the prophetic ministry in the mainline mission churches after the evangelistic activities of prophetic figures like William Wade Harris.[19] To some extent, the activities of lay prophets and prophetesses, as well as prayer camps, were suppressed only for them to reemerge in different forms, including, what Joseph Quayesi-Amakye calls New Prophetic Churches (NPCs).[20]

In contemporary times, the NPCs in Africa represent the most popular and visible prophetic ministries within African Pentecostalism. They usually concentrate on confronting malevolent spirit forces through what they call prophetic declarations, and through what is popularly known as spiritual warfare prayer. Just like the AICs and prayer camps, the NPCs seem to respond to the spiritual needs of the African people at the grassroots level and as a result, attract large followership during their church services. Quayesi-Amakye postulates that,

> Issues of witchcraft are prominent in the theologies of NPC prophetism. Thus, it is impossible to encounter a prophetic figure or service without some reference to the activities of witchcraft. Hence, witchcraft becomes the culprit of evil causality, which demands rejection. The crucial place witchcraft occupies in the socio-religious life of Ghanaians calls for serious scholarly investigation and pastoral attention.[21]

Since witchcraft is considered abhorrent in almost all Ghanaian communities, it naturally becomes the typology for the traditional interpretation of evil that can be negotiated by a prophetic figure. As stated earlier, one of the ways by which the NPCs respond to the fears of the African people is what is called "prophetic declarations." It must be stated that the ubiquity of information technology has been exploited by unscrupulous individuals to take advantage of the unsuspecting in the name of prophetic declarations. Indeed, names of popular Pentecostal pastors have been used pseudonymously to outwit the gullible in prophetic merchandising. A typical media is Facebook, where the pictures of popular African preachers such as Pastor Enoch Adeboye, Bishop David Oyedepo, Archbishop Duncan Williams, Prophet T. B. Joshua, and Prophet Shepherd Bushiri are used to lure people to believe in strange prophetic declarations.

What is worrying about some of these declarations is how they threaten readers of misfortune for failing to share their messages with others on social media. More worrying is how quickly people share such posts, suggesting that large numbers of people probably believe that by sharing these posts, one could be blessed in ways described in the various declarations. For example, one of the declarations in a Facebook post reads: "I am mad at the devil right now and I prophesy to anyone who will share this prayer: no matter the human sacrifices the devil will do this year through car accidents, you and your families will never be victims. Don't take this prophecy for granted. Share it quickly to connect to me." The message was posted on February 9, 2018, at 9:21 am and by February 12 at 11:33, it has been shared by 13,566 people and with 3,900 likes. Again, on February 16, 2018, a post read, "I am crying for those who will ignore this Message. They will miss something Great. Don't joke with this Prophecy! Before 6 pm tomorrow, anyone who shares this prayer will receive a mind-blowing-miracles from God. Just humble yourself and share it. Share quickly and like this page." By February 24, 2018, as many as 11,254 people had shared it and with 2,200 likes.[22]

The examples are ubiquitous, and the pace will not permit the addition of other examples. Many missiological lessons are, however, clear from these observations. First, whether scholars and church leaders agree or not, practicing Christians in Africa have fears that they are dealing with in their own way. Second, the prophetic ministry cannot be ignored in African Christianity since it seems to be responding to the spiritual needs of the ordinary African Christian at the grassroots level. Third, as Onyinah observes about prophetism in Ghana, it is obvious that until the churches have been able to absorb 'prophetism,' into their structure, and offer a theological framework for the operations of healing, exorcism and the prophetic ministries in the African churches, these ministries will continue to be a major problem.[23] It is therefore important to consider Onyinah's suggestion that prophetism, which is an integral part of African religiosity, needs to be contextualized into African Christianity.[24] In an attempt to provide contextual responses to the African spirit world therefore, some Christian organizations and scholars have proposed some models for engaging the phenomenon from different perspectives. Three such examples have been selected for our discussions:

Stephen Rasmussen's Critical Contextual Approach to the African Spirit World: The Case of Tanzania

Concerning the phenomenon of witchcraft in Tanzania, Rasmussen identified some weaknesses in current approaches that are normally used to confront issues of witchcraft in Africa. First is the Western anthropologist or American worldview approach that rejects the existence of such spirits, explaining that sickness is not caused by demons but by germs that cannot be seen with the naked eye. Second is to ignore the issue, as most missionary founded churches do in northwestern Tanzania, explaining that the belief in witchcraft is superstitious, "Do not believe it, talk about it, or seek treatment from healers." The third is to preach within the local worldview and tell amazing stories about witches and spirits to confirm the people's suspicions and increase their fears. Fourth is to preach as African Pentecostals do, explaining that witches exist but Jesus is more powerful than witches, healers, and spirits.[25] Rasmussen gives various reasons for which he considers such approaches to be weak. For example, concerning the approach of the missionary founded churches, he notes that,

> Implicit in some of these statements is an imported cessationist theology, a claim that we have progressed beyond miracles to the rational examination of Scripture. People who attend these churches nevertheless talk about witchcraft every day; they just avoid the subject when in church. Many interpret the silence to mean that Christ cannot handle their sicknesses, spirits, or witches. Therefore, they continue to address them using non-Christian methods. In these churches, even pastors or their families usually call a neo-traditional healer when they are deathly sick.[26]

Rasmussen's observation may not be particular to the churches in Tanzania. Similar observations can be made about the churches in other African countries where church leadership may have their doctrinal position but at the grassroots, church members may behave otherwise when confronted with very confusing situations. He also critiques the African Pentecostal approach that the method may help heal people of physical, psychological, and spiritual problems, but does not attend to the social epidemic of envy and witchcraft accusation in the communities.[27] Agreeing with Paul Hiebert, Daniel Shaw, and Tite Tienou,[28] Rasmussen suggests the use of critical contextualization to diagnose and propose remedies to the challenge of confronting the African spirit world. He narrates his four-day critical contextualization conference in Tanzania as follows:

> We began a four-day critical contextualization discussion on how to respond to those suspected of being witches. Deborah [a pastor's wife who was accused of witchcraft] joined others giving their stories of accusation and persecution as suspected witches. Listening to such unheard stories is one way to shift people's perspectives. Normally, no one believes a woman suspected of being a witch—unless she is giving a forced confession! If she denies being a witch, the village ignores her denial and chases her out of town or kills her without appeal. We then examined the Bible and Tanzanian law. The conference brought together

pastors from the region who were from Catholic, Mennonite, Church of Christ, Africa Inland Church, and Pentecostal backgrounds. Every one of these pastors believed that witches cause harm, and originally many of them believed that killing witches was biblical. They left the conference with an understanding that God loves everyone and commands the church to love them, too. They discovered that God especially loves widows, the poor, orphans, and outsiders—the people who are usually persecuted as witches. Participants in this seminar, in turn, taught four similar seminars in various regions of northwest Tanzania at the end of 2013. They plan to teach more in 2015.[29]

Rasmussen concludes that people will suspect witches to be the source of their problems because they have heard thousands of stories of witchcraft. He, therefore, argues, "to address the root cause, we must change the diagnosis. New experiences and stories can change people's understanding."[30]

This approach may be helpful because it can guide African Christians into understanding God's love for all people, especially widows and orphans. As a result, it can be seen as a contextual Christian response to witchcraft accusations. It is, however, not very clear if the approach is capable of attending to the issue of the causal other[31] or inquiry into the supernatural, which is the root of prophetism in African Christianity. After understanding that widows and vulnerable people are not witches, the African will still want to understand why sudden deaths happen and why a woman should have a miscarriage. They also want to know what to do if someone confesses that he or she is a witch and that she/he drinks human blood and eats human flesh. Rasmussen himself recognizes this gap in his approach to the African spirit world when after a thorough search for resources on the subject of sorcery and witchcraft for six years, he laments that, "I have seen no pastoral theology book that tells you what to do if someone comes to you and says, 'I am a witch. I kill people.'"[32]

A Contextual Theology from the Ground Up: UEM in Cameroon

Claudia Wahrisch-Oblau wrote a report about the actions taken by the United Evangelical Mission[33] (UEM) to address the issue of spirit forces from 2010 to 2014 among member churches in Africa, Asia, and Germany. The report indicates that even though the official stance of the member churches is that the "beliefs in spirits, demons, and witchcraft were superstitions to be overcome by preaching and education," most members of these churches, both villagers and city dwellers, including highly educated ones "believe in spirits both good and evil, in witchcraft and sorcery." These members are afraid that evil spirits may harm them, and as such they go to Pentecostal and charismatic churches or traditional religious practitioners, seeking ways to be protected from these spirit forces or freed from their influences.[34]

It also became obvious to the UEM member churches that "Preaching against witch hunts or education which treats such issues as human rights issues have been shown to have little or no effect. As a result, building their practices and preaching on Pentecostal and charismatic theology and practices, some of the UEM pastors organized deliverance prayers for members. Even though this attracted large numbers of believers, such pastors have been criticized by other pastors and church leadership.[35] Consequently, in February and March 2012, two "Think Tanks" were organized in the Asia and Africa Regions of the UEM with the following objectives:[36]

1. Collect the experiences of member churches with the resurgence of magic, witchcraft and demon beliefs;

2. Collect and evaluate the experiences of UEM member churches with deliverance ministries;

3. Engage in a Biblical and theological discussion about issues of occultism and deliverance (which will have to include discussions about Gospel and culture); and, if possible,

4. Sketch theological foundations and pastoral guidelines for a Protestant way of dealing with magic, witchcraft and demon beliefs.

Wahrisch-Oblau further reports that during the 56th General Synod held in 2012, the Evangelical Church in Cameroon, one of the member churches of the UEM in Africa, made a pragmatic attempt to confront the African spirit world within their context. They decided to "create a ministry of exorcism." They, therefore, put together a committee responsible for bringing out a proposal for effective implementation. The work on the proposal went through a process and was finally approved at the 57th General Synod in March 2014.[37]

This synod also authorized the following process of implementation:[38]

1. Pastors wishing to exercise this ministry had to submit their names

to a newly established National Committee on Healing and Deliverance.

2. The National Committee was to come up with a list of ministers who were authorized to engage in this ministry.

3. The authorized pastors were to attend a training workshop in June 2014.

4. These pastors were to be officially appointed by the General Council of EEC in July 2014.

5. The training workshop in June 2014 was attended by 60 pastors from all regions of the church as well as 42 recent theological graduates now preparing to become pastors.

The outcome of this, according to Währisch-Oblau, is a 48-page document on the ministry of healing and deliverance. She reports that the document laid out practical approaches that can be used as a guide by pastors of the church to respond to issues of healing and deliverance from a Protestant perspective. The document concluded by proposing an approach that listens to clients' spiritual diagnoses closely and takes their spiritual paradigm seriously without giving undue attention to demons and witchcraft.[39] This approach, while identifying the importance of prayer and deliverance, is not oblivious to the fact that some clients may need psychiatric treatment instead of deliverance.[40] This approach suggests that instead of brushing away the belief in the existence of these spiritual forces, the global church will need to be sincere in finding contextual responses to people's spiritual fears.

A Contextualized Local Theology: Ghana's Church of Pentecost Experience

After his research on Pentecostal Exorcism in The Church of Pentecost in Ghana, Opoku Onyinah observes that the African Pentecostals' approach to dealing with the spirit world is in tension with the Bible. First, the approach, which he calls "witchdemonology,"[41] does not recognize the sovereignty of God because proponents present issues of witchcraft and demons as so powerful and tormenting that they can destroy the life of even Christians, until they encounter a 'powerful man of God' or prophet who can intervene. By this, proponents do not understand the supremacy of God who is presented in the Bible as the one true God, having supremacy over all spiritual powers including Satan and his cohorts. Second, proponents of prophetic/ deliverance ministry do not understand the place of misfortune in life. Consequently, they give the impression that all misfortunes originate from the devil while the Bible gives alternative causes. Further, the proponents do not understand the place of suffering in life. Here again, while proponent trace all sufferings to ancestral curses or witchcraft and demonic activities, the biblical concept of suffering indicates that, suffering and death are part of life in this world. They can be natural, they can originate from God, and of course, they can originate from Satan, but under God's supremacy.

Onyinah, therefore, proposes a new approach for Pentecostal exorcism in Africa. This, he thinks will provide, "a contextualized local theology, which serves as a framework for exorcist activities for the churches in Africa."[42] A summary of Onyinah's proposal for the way forward of Pentecostal exorcism has been presented below:[43]

1. The sovereign reign of God over all his creations including Satan, the gods and the demonic, must be emphasized among Christians in Africa. God's sovereign reign over the universe makes little room for the demonic activity to take place. The sovereignty of God is biblical theology, which runs through the whole of the Bible (Ps 115:3; Isa 55:8–9; Mic 4:11–12; Acts 17:24–28; Rom 9:16–25; Heb 6:13–20).

2. African Christians will need to understand the concept of "spiritual warfare." Christians are called upon to put on the whole armor of God so that they can stand up against "the devil's scheme" and resist the devil (Eph 6:10–18; Isa 59:17; 1 Pet 5:9; James 4:7). This should not be understood as a fight between Christians and Satan. It should rather be understood as a transcendental conflict between God and Satan with the human mind as the battleground.

3. The role of exorcism should be seen as part of the means of dealing with a variety of manifestations of evil in human life. In the Gospels, while Jesus sometimes cast out demons, he does otherwise in some cases that appear demonic. This does not mean that exorcism should be pushed to the periphery. If Jesus' exorcism is taken into consideration, then there is no need to set aside a special time or place for the performance of exorcism.

4. Dangerous practices must be discouraged. For example, extracting confessions publicly from self-claimed witches to arrest attention before exorcism. Naïve people may be responsive to suggestive stories and may assume themselves to be possessed. Again, such confessions can put a social stigma on self-claimed witches who may never be accepted in society again. Confession, however, can be done privately.

5. Furthermore, chaining of accused witches, and enforcing long periods of fasting and prayer on clients are quite dangerous practices, since the need for these may be an indication that the exorcists have no authority over the situations or that the problems may be natural and need immediate medical attention.

6. Publicity, either before or after the exorcism, such as writing down clients' information and announcing them publicly or recording the process of exorcism for sale, should be discouraged since they betray the trust and may give the impression that exorcists are using their ministries for money.

Following the Examples of Jesus Christ in Confronting the African Spirit World

The Apostle John tells us that, "The reason the Son of God appeared was to destroy the devil's work"[44] (1 John 3:8b). Although in its context, this scripture refers directly to Jesus' purpose to destroy sin, which is the foundation upon which the devil's work is built, it would be wrong to conclude that the work of the devil precludes demonic activities. Consequently, to engage with the spirit world in any context, there is the need to study Jesus' approach to the spirit world within the Jewish context where he worked and identify lessons that can be extrapolated or contextualized in our contemporary contexts. The Gospels reveal Jesus' numerous encounters with demoniacs and the methods he used to engage their work.[45] Onyinah contends that, concerning the techniques or methods of exorcism, exorcists and deliverance ministers should follow the examples of Jesus Christ. Jesus' main method of exorcism is a simple word of command. The methods should be simple to show trust in the power of Jesus, whose death has given the believer the authority to exercise this kind of ministry. Too many rituals may show a lack of spiritual power on the part of the exorcist and, in a way, the authority, that is, Jesus, to whom he appeals for deliverance. The focus should always be on Christ and what he has done for the world and not on the minister.[46] Since the centrality of Jesus's ministry is crucial in Christian mission, the principles he left behind can teach us valuable lessons as we allow the Holy Spirit to guide us to interpret these principles into timeless lessons for our geographical and generational contexts.

Conclusion

Having identified these methods of engaging the African spirit world from different contexts, it must be acknowledged that discussions related to the African spirit world are very complex and need much attention and reflection. It is also important to notice that concluding that a person's case is demonic or witchcraft needs extra care. Many cases that people consider demonic or witchcraft may be natural issues. This is why it is crucial to make Christ Jesus central in all our attempts to engage the spirit world from any context. If the counselor or pastor has not received discernment or a clear prophetic insight, he/she must explore all possible natural explanations. To contextualize prophetism, Onyinah proposes what he refers to as "prophetic counseling."[47] He explains prophetic counseling as the ability to "divine" in counseling. He argues that:

> Without having prophetic insight into clients' requests and speaking prophetically to them, the sort of counseling being recommended may not be very useful. But when speaking prophetically into the situation the counselor may be able, for example, to assure the client that the problem is physical and that he or she may need to see the doctor, to forgive an offended person, or to ask for an apology. Or that the problem is spiritual, and that, for example, the person may need an exorcism. Or that the problem is both physical and spiritual, and that for example, the person should see the doctor and also pray.[48]

It is also important to heed John's admonishing to test the spirits (1 John 4:1) because failure to test prophetic messages is what gives charlatans opportunities to take advantage of innocent congregations and exploit vulnerable people. More importantly, the role of the Holy Spirit in effecting the work of Christ in the life of the believer must be emphasized. The guarantee of the believers' eternal security in Christ, with all its privileges such as their election, justification, and glorification must be emphasized (e.g., John 3:1–2; Rom 5:8; 8:28–31; Eph 1:3–21). In this case, stress needs to be laid on the purpose of Holy

Spirit baptism to give the believer power for service and strengthen the believer's personality-spirit. The Holy Spirit also gives power to 'be' a witness of Christ and to live the Christian life without fear (Acts 1:8; 11:18; Rom 8:9–16; 1 Cor 14:3; 2 Cor 1:22).[49]

Finally, there is the urgent need for churches and theological institutions to collaborate, providing formal training for both ordained and lay ministers to equip them in handling these complex spiritual issues, within the varying African contexts. It also calls for the need to creatively dialogue with grassroots/ lay prophets and deliverance ministers to reach out to them with theological training programs to equip them with sound biblical teachings in handling spiritual issues. These may minimize some of the excesses that are currently experienced within the prophetic ministries whilst responding effectively to the needs of the grassroots faith seekers in African Christianity.

Notes

1. Opoku Onyinah, *Pentecostal Exorcism: Witchcraft and Demonology in Ghana* (Dorchester: Deo Publishing, 2012); Mookgo S. Kgatle, "The Unusual Practices Within Some Neo-Pentecostal Churches in South Africa: Reflections and Recommendations," *HTS Teologiese Studies / Theological Studies* 73:3 (2017), 1–8.
2. Onyinah, *Pentecostal Exorcism: Witchcraft and Demonology in Ghana*, 47–74.
3. Onyinah, *Pentecostal Exorcism: Witchcraft and Demonology in Ghana*, 47–74.
4. Joseph Quayesi-Amakye, "Coping with Evil in Ghanaian Pentecostalism," *Exchange* 43:3 (2014), 257.
5. Onyinah, *Pentecostal Exorcism: Witchcraft and Demonology in Ghana*, 56–58.
6. Robert J. Priest, "The Value of Anthropology for Missiological Engagements with Context: The Case of Witch Accusations," *Missiology: An International Review* 43:1 (2015), 34.
7. Steven D. H. Rasmussen and Hannah Rasmussen, "Healing Communities: Contextualizing Responses to Witch Accusations," *International Bulletin of Missionary Research* 39:1 (2015), 12–18.
8. Robert J. Priest, "The Value of Anthropology for Missiological Engagements with Context: The Case of Witch Accusations." *Missiology: An International Review* 43:1 (2015), 32–33.
9. Girish Daswani, *Looking Back, Moving Forward: Transformation and Ethical Practice in the Ghanaian Church of Pentecost* (London: University of Toronto Press, 2015), 155.

10. The Gambaga Witches Camp is located in the North-East Region of Ghana. I visited this camp in the company of my wife, Olivia Tsekpoe, Rev. Dr. Daniel Walker (Rector of Pentecost University College) and his wife, Mrs. Irene Walker, Rev. Francis Adu, and few other Pastors of The Church of Pentecost.

11. Christian Tsekpoe, "Contemporary Prophetic and Deliverance Ministry Challenges in Africa," *Transformation: An International Journal of Holistic Mission Studies* 36:4 (2019), 280.

12. John Kirby, "Toward a Christian Response to Witchcraft in Northern Ghana," *International Bulletin of Missionary Research* 39:1 (2015), 19.

13. Kirby, "Toward a Christian Response to Witchcraft," 19.

14. I participated and presented a paper entitled "Protecting the Rights of Alleged Witches at Prayer Centres in Ghana," at the conference. See also Kwesi Tawiah-Benjamin and Anastasia Kaldi, "Report" (National conference on Witchcraft Accusations in Ghana, Accra, Gold Coast, December 10, 2014).

15. Opoku Onyinah, "Contemporary 'Witchdemonology' in Africa," *International Review of Mission* 93:370/371 (2004), 330–345.

16. Onyinah, *Pentecostal Exorcism: Witchcraft and Demonology in Ghana*, 104–107.

17. Onyinah, *Pentecostal Exorcism: Witchcraft and Demonology in Ghana*, 108–11.

18. The names African Initiated Churches, African Instituted Churches or African Indigenous Churches are all used to describe these churches. They are commonly referred to as *sunsum sore* an Akan name, literally meaning "spirit churches." These churches are similar to *Aladura* in Nigeria and South Africa's Zionist churches. See J. Kwabena Asamoah-Gyadu, *African Charismatics: Current Developments within Independent Indigenous Pentecostalism in Ghana* (Leiden: African Christian Press, 2005); Onyinah, *Pentecostal Exorcism*, 112.

19. Onyinah, *Pentecostal Exorcism: Witchcraft and Demonology in Ghana*, 156.

20. Joseph Quayesi-Amakye, "Prophetism in Ghana's New Prophetic Churches," *Journal of European Pentecostal Theological Association* 35:2 (2015), 162–73.

21. Quayesi-Amakye, *Prophetism in Ghana's New Prophetic Churches*, 162–173.

22. PropheticDeclarations, "Prophetic Declarations," *Facebook*. Available at https://www.facebook.com/shares/view?id=1993552090867128#. Accessed on 2 September 2018.

23. Onyinah, *Pentecostal Exorcism: Witchcraft and Demonology in Ghana*, 156.

24. Onyinah, *Pentecostal Exorcism: Witchcraft and Demonology in Ghana*, 268–74.

25. Rasmussen and Rasmussen, *Healing Communities*, 14–15.

26. Rasmussen and Rasmussen, *Healing Communities*, 15.

27. Rasmussen and Rasmussen, *Healing Communities*, 16.

28. Paul Hiebert, Daniel Shaw, and Tite Tienou, "Responding to Split-Level Christianity and Folk Religions," *International Journal of Frontier Missions* 16:4 (2000), 173–82.

29. Rasmussen and Rasmussen, *Healing* Communities,16.

30. Rasmussen and Rasmussen, *Healing Communities*, 16.

31. The belief that evil is always traceable to spiritual forces. See Quayesi-Amakye, "Prophetism in Ghana's New Prophetic Churches," *Journal of European Pentecostal Theological Association* 35:2 (2015), 168; Quayesi-Amakye, *Christology and Evil in Ghana: Towards a Pentecostal Public Theology* (Amsterdam: Rodopi, 2013), 64; Quayesi-Amakye, "Prosperity and Prophecy in African Pentecostalism," *Journal of Pentecostal Theology* 20:2 (2011), 291–305.

32. Rasmussen and Rasmussen, *"Healing Communities,"* 12–18.

33. The United Evangelical Mission (UEM) is a communion of 35 churches in Africa, Asia, and Germany.

34. Claudia Währisch-Oblau, "Meeting a Charismatic Challenge: The Development of Deliverance Ministries within the Protestant Member Churches of the United Evangelical Mission," in *African Pentecostal Mission Maturing*, Lord Abraham Elorm-Donkor and Clifton R. Clarke, eds. (Eugene, OR: Wipf & Stock Publishers, 2018), 178.

35. Claudia Währisch-Oblau, "Towards a Protestant Ministry of Deliverance Experiences, Insights and Reflections from a Process of the UEM Community" (Unpublished Report Presented to the UEM Community 2014), 2–3.

36. Währisch-Oblau, "Meeting a Charismatic Challenge: The Development of Deliverance Ministries within the Protestant Member Churches of the United Evangelical Mission," 182–83.

37. Währisch-Oblau, "Towards a Protestant Ministry of Deliverance," 8–9; Währisch-Oblau, "Meeting a Charismatic Challenge," 184.

38. Währisch-Oblau, "Towards a Protestant Ministry of Deliverance," 8–9.

39. Währisch-Oblau, "Meeting a Charismatic Challenge," 16.

40. Währisch-Oblau, "Meeting a Charismatic Challenge," 16.

41. Onyinah, *Pentecostal Exorcism: Witchcraft and Demonology in Ghana*, 171–72.

42. Onyinah, *Pentecostal Exorcism*, xi.

43. Onyinah, *Pentecostal Exorcism*, 232–89.

44. New International Version.

45. See Jesus' encounter with the man in the Capernaum synagogue (Mark 1:21–28 par Luke 4:31–37); the Gerasenes man (Matt 8:28–34 par Mark 5:1–17; Luke 8:26–37); the Syrophoenician woman's daughter (Matt 15:21–28 par Mark 7:24–30), and the epileptic boy (Mark 9:14–29 par Matt 17:14–19; Luke 9:37–45). See Onyinah, *Pentecostal Exorcism: Witchcraft and Demonology in Ghana* for a detailed discussion on the four main narratives of Jesus' encounter with demoniacs in the Gospels.

46. Onyinah, *Pentecostal Exorcism: Witchcraft and Demonology in Ghana*,

276.

47. Onyinah, *Pentecostal Exorcism*, 268–274.

48. Onyinah, *Pentecostal Exorcism*, 274.

49. Onyinah, *Pentecostal Exorcism*, 278–80.

11.

"No Other Name": Presenting Jesus Christ in Multi-Cultural and Religious Environments

Sylvia Owusu-Ansah and Philip Adjei-Acquah

Abstract

"Salvation is found in no one else, for there is no other name under heaven given to mankind by which we must be saved" (Acts 4:12). Christians are called upon to be witnesses of Jesus Christ in the world. "And this gospel of the kingdom shall be preached in the entire world as a witness to all nations, and then the end will come" (Matt 24:14). This message is a well-known scripture to every evangelical or Pentecostal/ charismatic Christian in West Africa. This paper traces various emphases given to these biblical texts in Christendom and their implications to interreligious relations. How do the various interpretations and emphases promote Christian witness and foster peaceful interreligious relationships or multi-cultural and peaceful coexistence? This paper analyses what theologians have made of the unique claims of Jesus in the context of religious plurality and in relation to the Great Commission.

Key words: gospel, salvation, interreligious, multi-cultural, plurality

Introduction

"There is salvation in no one else, for there is no other name under heaven that is given among men by which we must be saved" (Acts 4:12). This statement was made by the Apostle Peter after the healing of the man at the Beautiful Gate in the name of Jesus. Salvation here implies both healing and reconciliation, or forgiveness of sins. This and other statements portraying the uniqueness and supremacy of Christ have generated heated debates among theologians regarding the place of Jesus Christ and Christianity regarding salvation amidst other religions. John emphasizes Jesus' statements that accord him a unique status, which include, but are not limited to, "I am the way and the truth and the life" (John 14:6); "I am the light of the world" (John 8:12); "I am the gate for the sheep" (John 10:7–9); "I am the good shepherd" (John 10:11); "I am the resurrection and the life" (John 11:25).

In fulfilling the Great Commission, Christians present Jesus to all, including members of other faiths, as the only way to God, and the Savior of humanity. The claim by Jesus concerning his divinity as one with God, "I and my Father are one" (John 10:30, 31), angered the Jews of his day. On two occasions, the hearers of Jesus were offended and wanted to stone him (John 8:54–59). The problem that Jesus encountered in his days as a result of his claim to divinity and exclusive access to God is also prevalent today as the church strives to reach out to the world in obedience to the Great Commission. The church is therefore confronted with the challenge of presenting Jesus Christ as the savior of mankind in a multi-religious world without offending people of different faiths.

This paper addresses the following questions: 1) How best can Christians present Jesus and his exclusive claim to salvation in a multi-religious world? 2) Is the Great Commission still valid in our day? 3) Is the message of the cross and the resurrection of Jesus valid for all people and all generations? 4) How best can the gospel be presented in a way that it does not become a stumbling block to people? To begin, we would like to look at the Christian attitude towards people of other faiths in the past and present concerning the Great Commission.

Christian Attitude toward People of Other Faith — Past Experiences

Two scenarios that I encountered during fieldwork in Ghana and Nigeria aroused interest in probing further into the very important subject of current trends in Christian witness and peaceful co-existence with people of other faiths. In an interview narrating an incident of religious intolerance, Abdurrahman, of the University of Ibadan, mentioned that a young Christian lady entered the mosque at the university campus in a disguise only to begin to preach. After a while, she provocatively shouted out that all the Muslims are lost and would go to hell if they did not accept Jesus Christ as Lord and Savior of the world. She had to be rescued from the angry Muslims present at the mosque on that day.[1] Another incident happened in Ghana at Takoradi when a Pentecostal/

charismatic preacher rose at dawn and began to shout the Islamic morning call for prayer. When some Muslims gathered, he began preaching and insisted that they were all lost and would go to hell.[2] This gentleman had to be rescued from an angry mob.

In his book, *Transforming Mission: Paradigm Shifts in Theology of Mission*, David Bosch underscores what the church's attitude towards people of other faiths has been. In the section on "mission as a witness to people of other living faiths," Bosch pointed out the church's position from Emperor Theodosius' decree of CE 380, which requested all citizens of the Roman Empire to be Christians. This was a further development to "Pope Boniface's bull, Unam Sanctam (1302), which proclaimed that the Catholic Church was the only institution guaranteeing salvation."[3] Again, the Council of Florence (1442) declared hellfire for those not attached to the Catholic Church and the Cathechismus Romanus (1566), and declared the Catholic Church to be infallible.[4] In this era, the Catholic Church proclaimed that there was no salvation outside of the Catholic Church, while the Protestants declared that there was no salvation outside the *word*. Bosch rightly suggests, "In these models, mission essentially meant conquest and displacement. Christianity was understood to be unique, exclusive, superior, definitive, normative, and absolute."[5] During this era, Christianity adopted a hostile attitude toward Islam, which resulted in the Crusades. Consequently, many theologians and Christian leaders have expressed attitudes of intolerance and disregard for other religions, declaring them as heathen. However, with the advent of the Enlightenment came the fading away of this air of superiority of the Christian faith over other religions. Gradually, Christianity was seen to be competing openly with a host of other religions. This has led to the shift of Christianity's relationship with other religions to a more accommodating and tolerant position. It moved from a pure exclusivist position, which regarded the Christian faith as the only true religion, to the fulfillment theology. The fulfillment approach sees Christianity as the fulfillment of other religions.[6] The "Liberal theology of the day accepted the validity of other religions but believed that Christianity was still the best and was sure to outlive them."[7]

Christian Attitude toward Other Religions — The Present

Many who had held a strong exclusivist position have had to change their minds after encounters with pious religious adherents, or after a relationship with people of other religions. Such a change of minds has resulted in the belief that it does not matter what religion one adheres to, what matters is one's commitment and devotion to that religion. However, some Christians hold strongly to the uniqueness of Christ, while others have completely discarded the notion. Theologians and priests like Karl Rahner recognize "supernatural grace-filled-elements in non-Christian religions."[8] Karl Rahner begins his thesis by stating Christianity's claim of superiority and uniqueness, which he affirms without any dispute, but argues further for the validity of the truth claims of non-Christian religions, and finally propounds the theory of anonymous Christians. "Christianity does not simply confront the member of an extra-Christian religion as a mere non-Christian but as someone who can and must be regarded in this or that respect as an anonymous Christian."[9] Raymond Panikkar following a similar thesis speaks of the unknown Christ of Hinduism. Panikkar asserts that Christ is already present and at "work in any Hindu prayer; Christ is behind any Hindu worship."[10] John Hick takes this notion further by claiming that all religions, including Christianity, can be placed on an equal pedestal. None is superior to another. To Hick, Christianity is not the center of all religions, God is. He vehemently denies such superior claims of Jesus to be the Son of God or to be one with the Father, and is against his messianic authority and the doctrine of the incarnation.[11] These positions pose a serious challenge to the traditional Christian faith and traditional evangelism, which makes exclusive claims for Christianity as a means of salvation. The question one may pause and ask is: "What then becomes the fate of the Great Commission given by the Lord Jesus Christ, which engaged the apostles such as Peter, John, Paul, and other disciples such as Philip and Stephen?" One may also question the real goal of evangelism when some Christians theologize that "missionary activity should not focus on enlarging the Christian community. . . . Rather, Christians should 'join hands with' other faith adherents and 'collaborate in proclaiming the importance of religious values in contemporary society.'"[12] The difficulty here is whether adherents of non-Christian religions share the same goal. Bosch attests to the vigor with which other religions propagate their faith, even more than the Christian churches do evangelism.[13] It is indeed true to a large extent that the church is not prepared to face the challenges posed by other religions today.[14]

With the postmodern approach to the theology of religions came the shift and advocacy for a change from ecclesiocentrism to Christocentrism.[15] Karl Rahner, also promoting a shift from ecclesiocentrism to Christocentrism in the theology of religions, believes that "Christianity is the absolute religion," and of "salvation having to come only through Christ," even though he acknowledges "supernatural elements of grace in other religions" deposited through Christ.[16] The relativist position maintained that all religions, despite their differences, had the same goal and would arrive at the same destination.[17] Ernst Troeltsch, for instance, had to finally argue for the validity of all traditional religions unconditionally in *Der Historismus und seine Uberwindung*. Troeltsch states that:

> The great religions might indeed be described as crystallizations of the thought of great races, as these races are themselves crystallizations of the various biological and anthropological forms. There can be no conversion or transformation of one into the other, but only a measure of agreement and mutual understanding.[18]

John Hick, following Troeltsch's tradition, believed that "all religions are different human answers to the one divine reality," and says, "they embody different perceptions which have been formed in different historical and cultural circumstances."[19] Knitter argues against Christocentrism and advocates for theocentrism, emphasizing that Jesus himself had a theocentric view. Knitter suggests "unitive plurality" which he maintains is a new form of religious unity, but different from the notion of "one world religion."[20] He claims that all religions have equal validity and other leaders are comparable to Jesus in their salvific roles. Knitter's position is tilted towards pluralism yet without "mutually exclusive claims or indifference."[21] He maintains each partner in the encounter may hold firmly to their personal experience and truth claims, but none "possesses the final, definitive, irreformable truth."[22] Thus, Knitter's definition of missions is like John Macquarie's, which advocates that Christian mission should not focus on converting members of the other major faiths as they also possess God's saving grace.[23]

Bosch's critique of the above models is that they "seem to leave no room for embracing the abiding paradox of asserting both ultimate commitment to one's own religion and genuine openness to another's, of constantly vacillating between certainty and doubt."[24] Those who oppose the traditional approach to evangelism argue that the traditional approach disregards and overlooks the work of God in other religions. Many who oppose traditional evangelism advocate for interreligious dialogue as a means of creating a cordial relationship between religious groups, however, they maintain that dialogue should exclude attempts to convert or proselytize other believers. We shall now look at the relationship between interreligious dialogue and missions.

Dialogue and Mission

Interreligious dialogue, also referred to as interfaith dialogue, signifies the co-operation, mutual understanding, and respect between people of different faiths. Religious adherents are to stick firmly to their religions while striving to relate cordially with people of other faiths at various levels of human endeavor.[25] Many have proposed interreligious dialogue as a way of reducing the tensions and daily acts of provocation that exists between different religious adherents. Forms of dialogue that have been identified include, dialogue of life — the day to day cordial social interaction between people of different faiths who live as neighbors, meet at workplaces, in the market and elsewhere; dialogue of social actions — people of different religions joining efforts to fight against common social vices and oppression; dialogue of religious experience — sharing religious experiences; and dialogue of theological exchange — scholars who share theological insights from their various faiths. The main aim of the dialogue is to create understanding and foster a good relationship.[26] It is also to reduce elements and attitudes that contribute to tension such as stereotypes, suspicion, and prejudice.

Essential as interreligious dialogue is, does it replace the Christian mission? In describing the place of dialogue in missions, Bosch gives some perspectives of dialogue that are essential to understand the relationship between dialogue and missions. The first perspective is, "to accept the co-existence of different faiths and to do so not grudgingly but willingly."[27] The reality is that Christians everywhere now live or co-exist with people of other faith and this must be accepted as the norm. For the Christian faith to thrive, there is the need for a peaceful co-existence, which is the main aim of interreligious dialogue. As cited by Sustania, the core aim of interreligious dialogue remains to "prevent conflicts, change attitudes and behaviors, build peaceful relations and communities, through reducing tensions and conflicts between religious and other groups in society."[28] Missions cannot prevail in a hostile environment, thus the need for mutual respect for each other's religion.

The second perspective is, "True dialogue presupposes commitment. It does not imply sacrificing one's own position."[29] As posited by Swindler, the partners in the dialogue must be committed both to their faith and the dialogue.[30] The third perspective is, "dialogue (and, for that matter, mission) is only possible if we proceed from the belief that we are not moving into a void, that we go expecting to meet the God who has been preparing people within the context of their own cultures and convictions."[31] He explains that Christians need to give reverence to devotees of other faith, recognizing that everyone depends on the same "mercy, sharing the same mystery" of God.[32] The fourth perspective is, "both dialogue and mission can be conducted only in an attitude of humility," especially for Christians. Particularly, because of the work of grace associated with the cross of Christ.[33] The sixth perspective is:

> Dialogue is neither a substitute nor a subterfuge for mission. They are neither to be viewed as identical nor as irrevocably opposed to each other. It is fallacious to suggest that, for dialogue to be "in," mission has to be "out," that commitment to dialogue is incompatible with commitment to evangelism.[34]

Bosch emphasizes the difference between dialogue and witness, disputing Knitter's declaration[35] that the aim of mission is realized when the proclamation of the gospel has made the Christian a better Christian and the Buddhist a better Buddhist. He adds that Knitter may be describing one of the goals of dialogue, but not of mission.[36] Bosch rightly emphasizes that the church's recognition of its dialogical nature should not be "at the expense of its fundamentally missionary nature."[37] The above positions present a great challenge to traditional evangelism, which aims at presenting the good news that brings salvation to everyone who believes in the Lord Jesus Christ. What is the relationship between the proclamation of the gospel, faith in Jesus, and salvation?

The Gospel and Salvation

In his response to the question he poses, "What is the gospel?" Charles Ryrie explains that Christians should both "preach the word (Acts 13:5), and reason out of the scriptures (Acts 17:2)," as it contains absolute truth.[38] He opines that in as much as Christians "exercise control," they "should not be offensive as to dress, speech, or culture, but the moment we announce the gospel we take on the offense of the cross."[39] Ryrie rightly affirms that the message of the cross is itself offensive and becomes a stumbling block (Gal 5:11), but he emphasizes that the messenger should not be.[40] Ryrie affirms that though repentance and baptism are necessary and important, they do not produce salvation. It is only faith in Jesus Christ that produces salvation. He adds that even commitment to Jesus without faith in him (if that is possible) does not result in salvation.[41] It is essential then to understand the meaning and implications of the term salvation.

The verb form of the noun salvation, "to save," is rendered *yasa* in the Old Testament Hebrew. Its primary meaning is to be preserved from danger or "to remove or seek to remove someone from danger (Ex 2:17; Josh 10:6; Judges 12:2)."[42] It also denotes bringing salvation to the needy and judging the oppressor.[43] In the Old Testament, God is seen as the savior and salvation refers both to:

> Every day, regular types of deliverance – as from enemies, disease, and danger (see 1 Sam 10:24; Ps 72:4) – and to those major deliverances that are specifically interpreted as being a definite part of God's unique and special involvement in human history as well as special revelations of his character and will.[44]

In the New Testament, to be saved (*sozo*) is used with the noun *soteria*. Salvation first implies "material and temporal deliverance from danger, suffering, etc." (Matt 8:25; Mark 13:20; John 12:27).[45] It is also used to denote "the spiritual and eternal salvation granted immediately by God to those who believe in the Lord Jesus Christ" (Acts 2:47; 16:31; Rom 8:24). Again the term implies God's present deliverance from the bondage of sin (Matt 1:21; Rom 5:10; 1 Cor 15:2) and "future deliverance of believers at the second coming of Christ for his saints, being delivered from the wrath of God to be executed upon the ungodly at the close of this age and from eternal doom" (Rom 5:9).[46] In the New Testament, Jesus is presented as the savior of sinners and offers salvation (Luke 2:11; John 4:42; Acts 5:31). Jesus saves from sin and its consequences and delivers from the power of Satan and his oppression. Those who repent and believe in Jesus receive salvation. An example is Zacchaeus, "Today salvation has come to this house" are Jesus' words (Luke 19:9–10). "To those who believed and received God's kingdom/salvation Jesus said, "Your sins are forgiven" or "your faith has saved you" (Mark 2:5; Luke 7:50).

Jesus did not separate the healing of the body from forgiveness of sin. The verb *sozein* means to heal and to save (Mark 1:40–45; 5:33–34).[47] Keener notes that "the term translated saved in Acts 4:9–12 includes making whole."[48] Peter pronounced that there is no salvation in anyone else and there is no other name under heaven given among men through which one should be saved except the name Jesus (Acts 4:12). Paul wrote, Now is the day of salvation (2 Cor 6:2). The writer of Hebrews asked, "How shall we escape if we ignore such a great salvation?" (Heb 2:3).[49] Because of the death and resurrection of Jesus Christ, salvation is a present reality. To proclaim the gospel is to proclaim that salvation is now available through faith in Jesus Christ. It is also a future hope, to be delivered from the wrath to come at the last judgment (Rom 5:9). Peter spoke of salvation to be revealed on the last day (1 Pet 1:5), and in Rev 19:1, it includes all that God will offer his people at the fullness of time in the new heaven and the new earth at the end of the age.[50] With the above definitions of salvation in view, it would be necessary to say that non-Christian religions produce salvation implies faith in Jesus.

It is important to emphasize that Christian witness is still very relevant today as it was in the days of Jesus and the apostles. We would take some time to look at the dynamics of evangelism. The Great Commission given in Matt 28:18–20 has two noteworthy aspects: the command to go, and the promise of companionship. Ray Stedman puts it this way,

> It was never the intention of the Lord that Christians themselves should take over the job of planning the strategy and mobilizing the resources to take the gospel to the ends of the earth. He never intended that we should try to fulfill the Great Commission in our own strength, while He stands by and watches. He is with us always — and we must allow Him to be in charge of his own strategy for reaching the world.[51]

The ever-abiding presence of Christ with the believers in carrying out the Great Commission was because conversion through the gospel is only possible by the Holy Spirit. The apostles were successful because "He worked with them and confirmed the word with signs following" (Mark 16:20).

Christian Witness/Evangelism

Two terms, "to evangelize" and "to witness," are often used by the church to express the mandate that Jesus gave to his disciples before his ascension. The Holman Illustrated Bible Dictionary defines evangelism as, "Active calling of people to respond to the message of grace and commit oneself to God in Jesus Christ."[52] The concept of evangelism is predominantly emphasized in the New Testament in contrast to the Old Testament. However, the idea does appear in the Old Testament (1 King 8:41–45; Ps 22:27–28; Isa 2:2–4).[53] Israel was mandated by God to be a light to the other nations (the Gentiles), as the church of God is also charged to be a light to the world. This signifies that Israel was to point others to the blessings of the almighty God. Israel was to be a blessing and through her, the other nations were to be blessed. It is said that though Israel sought to be blessed, she did not consciously live up to her mandate to be a channel of blessing to other nations.[54] The difference in Israel's mandate was that, whereas Israel was the light for the nations to come and see, the New Testament mandate was to "Go into all the world and preach the Gospel" (Matt 28:19). The New Testament mandate was to be carried out through evangelism.[55]

There are a variety of views and expressions used to define the meaning of evangelism and the dynamics of the concept. Evangelism originates from the Greek term *euangelion* which means "gospel" or "good news." The verb *euangelizo* means "to bring" or "to announce good news" often translated to "preach."[56] It occurs 55 times in the New Testament. Evangelism, therefore, means to preach or proclaim the good news. A witness describes someone who "bears testimony to things seen, heard, transacted, or experienced."[57]

Methods of Evangelism

Elmer I. Towns, discussing a shift in evangelistic strategies, mentions lifestyle evangelism and confrontation evangelism, also known as personal evangelism.[58] While some emphasize lifestyle evangelism as a better option, Elmer suggests that the two can be used together. Lifestyle evangelism deals with how the believer lives his/her daily life among those of other faiths or unbelievers.[59] Much as this is a strategy in evangelism, Jesus expected us to also be confrontational, as we see in the book of Acts. However, in dealing with people of other faiths, the lifestyle of the Christian becomes a good reference point in showing them who Christ really is. The command was to "go" and make disciples of all nations, and this assumes the posture of confrontation.

In arguing for the legitimacy of confrontational evangelism, Elmer I.

Towns asserts that Jesus used confrontation evangelism when he spoke with Nicodemus and Zacchaeus (John 3:3–6; Luke 19:1–8).[60] Confrontational evangelism deals with both the proclamation of the gospel and with spiritual warfare. This is because the devil blinded the eyes of the unbelievers and until they are set free and unfolded, they will not believe the gospel for their salvation (Matt 12:28; 2 Cor 4:3–5). The Apostle Paul, in describing how one can believe the gospel, asked the question, "How can they believe unless they hear" (Rom 10:14). This means that the proclamation of the gospel in evangelism is a critical and integral part, without which mankind cannot believe and be saved.

Towns goes on further to describe front door evangelism and side door evangelism. Front door evangelism is when the church launches out into the community to evangelize.[61] Much of this is done through the confrontational strategy, while side door evangelism is when the members of the church witness and share testimonies with their friends and relatives inviting them to church. Side door evangelism, also known as web evangelism, is more effective and yields greater results than front door evangelism. He purports that the first point of attraction of individuals to be committed to a church is friendship, then spiritual assistance. Much as this style has some merit, it cannot be true that it is the most effective way. For example, in crusade evangelism where we have thousands in attendance, it is the work of the Holy Spirit that brings conviction through the proclamation of the gospel. The evangelist does not have any prior/personal interaction with the audience but there are mass converts to faith in Christ Jesus.

The Apostle Paul used dialogue in his ministry to the Athenians as seen in Acts 17:2; 18:4, 19; 19:9; and 20:7, 9. Paul successfully and progressively engaged his conversation partners in a way that gradually introduced them to his message of salvation. Dialogue allows the partner to ask questions. The appropriateness of each of these proposed methods of evangelism may be considered depending upon the context and the setting. Now how do we proclaim Christ in a multi-religious environment?

The Holy Spirit and Proclamation

The role of the Holy Spirit in missions cannot be over-emphasized. He is the source of power for mission. Jesus Christ, before he ascended to heaven, told the disciples, "I am going to send you what my Father has promised; but stay in the city until you have been clothed with power from on high" (Luke 24:49). Again, it was repeated in Acts 1:8, "But you will receive power when the Holy Spirit comes on you; and you will be my witnesses in Jerusalem, and in all Judea and Samaria, and to the ends of the earth." Luke was referring to the Holy Spirit in 24:29 as the source of power for witness.[62] Missions, after the day of Pentecost experienced in Acts 2, clearly showed that it was the work of the Holy Spirit and not man.

The Holy Spirit is the promise of the Father to all that will believe in his son Jesus, as seen in Acts 2:39, "The promise is for you and your children and for all who are far off — for all whom the Lord our God will call." The Holy Spirit empowers the Christian for the work of evangelism, both lifestyle and confrontational. The success of evangelism, proclaiming Jesus Christ as the only Savior of the world, irrespective of the environment (social or pluralistic religious environment), is through the power of the Holy Spirit.

When the Holy Spirit empowers the believer, the work of witnessing is accompanied by signs and wonders, converting not only non-religious people, but people of other faiths to accept the lordship of Christ. If, through the power of the Holy Spirit, the Jews in Jerusalem who were ardent followers of Judaism cried out, "Men and brethren what shall we do?" then through the same Holy Spirit, people from other faiths can be saved through the proclamation of the gospel of Christ.

Gary McGee typically approached the proclamation of Christ from the Pentecostal perspective. His radical strategy is a pneumatological approach that is founded in the early apostolic era. This approach is based on the Apostles' empowerment by the Holy Spirit before they were able to witness to the resurrection of Jesus (Acts 2:38 and 4:18–31).[63] In proclaiming Christ as Lord and Savior in every environment, the Pentecostals have been seen to be radical and uncompromising in declaring their faith. Anderson describes the first twenty years of Pentecostal mission as chaotic in operation, yet very successful due to their passion and the power of the Holy Spirit at work in them.[64] Anderson pointed out that Pentecostal evangelistic methods were flexible, pragmatic, and astonishingly successful.[65] In contributing to the Pentecostals prowess in evangelistic activities, Miller posits that the sense of urgency that characterized the Pentecostal missiological thrust was a definite argument in Pentecostalism that sustained its existence based on the power of the Holy Spirit. He said,

Azusa Street's greatest contribution was to global missions. Mission was at the very heart of the revival. Seymour and early Pentecostal leaders believed that God was pouring out the "latter rain to empower the church for worldwide witness." They believed that the primary purpose of the baptism in the Holy Spirit was to empower the church to preach the gospel to all nations before the soon coming of Christ.[66]

The above strengthens the opinion that the rapid growth of Pentecostal/ charismatic churches in Africa has been due to its emphasis on the power of the Holy Spirit in missionary works.[67]

The gospel should be proclaimed through the power of the Holy Spirit. In preaching the gospel, there must be signs and wonders. Paul in his letter to the Corinthian church emphasized, "My message and my preaching were not with wise and persuasive words, but with a demonstration of the Spirit's power so that your faith might not rest on [human] wisdom, but on God's power" (1 Cor 2:4–5). In describing the general Pentecostal mission drive McGee opines that consciousness of missions with emphasis on the proclamation of the gospel was what brought about the rapid growth of Pentecostalism. In this vein, mission is a continuation from the past into the future until Christ comes with power and might to destroy finally, Satan and his demonic forces. Until he appears, the gospel should be preached with power and demonstration of the Holy Spirit without any apology to any group of people.[68]

Power encounter has thus become synonymous with the preaching of the gospel. It is always seen as a necessary ingredient in the proclamation of the gospel. It is a pattern of evangelism in the New Testament through the power of the Holy Spirit which confirms Jesus' word in Mark 16:15–20.

Go into all the world and preach the good news to all creation. Whoever believes and is baptized will be saved, but whoever does not believe will be condemned. And these signs will accompany those who believe: In my name, they will drive out demons; they will speak in new tongues; they will pick up snakes with their hands; and when they drink deadly poison, it will not hurt them at all; they will place their hands on sick people, and they will get well.

The concept of power demonstration comes from the belief that there are always powerful evil forces that stand in the way of the salvation of individuals, groups, families, and nations. Signs and wonders are believed to break the hold of the devil and his host of demons over their victims.[69]

The phenomenon of signs and wonders has been deliberately incorporated into the evangelization efforts of Pentecostals/Charismatic churches.[70] Asamoah-Gyadu attests that the growth in Christian ministry, which is the result of conversion, is through the power of the Spirit. This is seen in the numerous healings, signs, and wonders that are seen in the gospel crusade grounds and church services. The church, therefore, becomes the instrument through which the power of God is demonstrated in missions. It is important to note that no missionary activity has been successful without the full control of the Holy Spirit and his power. The multi-religious people will challenge, but the power of the Holy Spirit will convict as it happened on the day of Pentecost.[71] On his part, Cole succinctly puts it thus,

> This book Luke wrote on the expansion of Christianity is not really the Acts of the Apostle, it is really the Acts of the Holy Spirit. The Holy Spirit is mentioned or alluded to by the author fifty-seven times in twenty-eight chapters! When the question is asked, "Who was in control of the growth and expansion of the church?" there is only one answer-the Holy Spirit! Peter was not (Acts 10:19–20). James was not (Acts 15:28). Paul was not (Acts 16:6–10). There is no human leader who orchestrated and organized the growth and expansion of the New Testament church! From a strictly human perspective, this operation was completely out of control![72]

Proclaiming Christ in a Multi-Religious Environment: Trends and Procedures

Proclaiming the gospel of Jesus Christ should not necessarily provoke others or generate strife. Paul did not express his disapproval of the Athenian's multiplicities of idols in an antagonistic way but in a well-ordered, cautiously analytic defense of Christianity (Acts 17:22–23). The unique claims of Jesus did not make him arrogantly disregard others who were not part of his community, but humbly served all who encountered him (Matt 20:28; Mark 10:45). In Jesus' command given to his disciples to fulfill the Great Commission, he said, "All authority in heaven and on earth has been given to me," indicating unqualified authority. Yet, he asked his disciples to learn of his gentleness, humility, and meekness (Matt 11:29). The example of Christ makes arrogance incompatible with the proclamation of the gospel. In an attempt to share the gospel and make converts, we seek to avoid proselytism. Conversion is an inward change resulting in outward transformation, whereas proselytism is simply a change in belief from one faith to another. While proselytism has been associated with coercion, manipulation, and imposition, Christian conversion relies on the grace of God, causing transformation through faith in Jesus, which comes about by the willing commitment of an individual upon hearing the gospel.

Conclusion

We have seen in this paper how different theologians and scholars have handled the subject of salvation throughout the years. They have moved from a strict exclusivist position to inclusivist/relativist, and pluralistic positions. Theologians have often jumped from one end of the ladder to the other end. Those who advocate for a purely inclusivist position deny the supremacy and unique claims of Jesus, without which Christian mission loses its import. Those who hold on to a pure exclusivist position are often seen as portraying attitudes of intolerance and arrogance toward people of other faiths. The conclusion of the matter is: Christians should take Christian mission seriously but should do so in the spirit of Jesus, in compassion, meekness, and empathy.

Christian mission is considered by the Church to be one of the greatest pillars of Christianity because it is a mandate given by the Lord Jesus himself before his ascension. However, this mission has faced various challenges since the inception of the church. The current challenge of the church is how to reconcile her desire to live in peace and harmony with people of other faiths with the mandate to preach the gospel to all people. This notwithstanding, the foundations of our faith should not be compromised at any point in our quest to have a peaceful co-existence with our neighbors and people of other faiths. Through the power of the Holy Spirit, the gospel of Christ can be preached to all mankind, with the emphasis that Christ Jesus is the only Savior of the world, just as the early church and the apostles succeeded in doing through the power of the Holy Spirit.

Notes

1. Interview with Prof. Abdurrahman (University of Ibadan, Nigeria), May 4, 2011.
2. Interview with Father Thaddeus in Tamale, Ghana, September 24, 2009.
3. David J. Bosch, *Transforming Mission: Paradigm Shifts in Theology of Mission* (Maryknoll, NY: Orbis, 2011), 486.
4. Bosch, *Transforming Mission*, 486.
5. Bosch, *Transforming Mission*, 490.

6. Bosch, *Transforming Mission*, 490.

7. Bosch, *Transforming Mission*, 491.

8. Karl Rahner, "Christianity and the Non-Christian Religions," in John Hick and Brian Hebblethwaite, eds., *Christianity and Other Religions: Selected Readings* (Glasgow: Collins, 1980), 61.

9. Rahner, "Christianity and the Non-Christian Religions," 75.

10. Raymond Parnnikar, "The Unknown Christ of Hinduism," in John Hick, & Brian Hebblethwaite, eds., *Christianity and Other Religions* (Glasgow: Collins, 1980), 138.

11. John Hick, "Jesus and the World Religions," in John Hick, ed., *The Myth of God Incarnate* (Philadelphia: Westminster, 1977), 16.

12. Anthony Fernando, "An Asian's View of Jesus' Uniqueness," in Leonard Swindler and Paul Mojzes, eds., *The Uniqueness of Jesus: A Dialogue with Paul F. Knitter* (Maryknoll, NY: Orbis, 1997), 72–23.

13. Bosch, *Transforming Mission*, 487–488.

14. Bosch, Transforming Mission, 488.

15. Bosch, *Transforming Mission*, 492.

16. Bosch, *Transforming Mission*, 92.

17. Paul F. Knitter, *No Other Name? A Critical Survey of Christian Attitudes Toward the World Religions* (Maryknoll, NY: Orbis, 1985), 220, cited in Bosh, *Transforming Mission*, 493.

18. Ernest Troeltsch, "The Place of Christianity among the World Religions," in John Hick and Brian Hebblethwaite, eds., *Christianity and Other Religions* (Glasgow: Collins, 1980), 28.

19. Knitter, *No Other Name?*, 173–175. In Bosh, *Transforming Mission*, 493.

20. Knitter, *No Other Name?*, 173–175. In Bosh, *Transforming Mission*, 493.

21. Bosch, *Transforming Mission*, 494.

22. Bosch, *Transforming Mission*, 494.

23. Bosch, *Transforming Mission*, 494.

24. Bosch, *Transforming Mission*, 494.

25. Leonard Swindler, "The Dialogue Decalogue: Ground Rules for Interreligious Dialogue," *Journal of Ecumenical Studies* 20:1 (1983), 13–15.

26. Philip A. Cunningham and Arthur F. Starr, eds., *Sharing Shalom: A Process for Interfaith Dialogue between Christians and Jews* (New York: Harper Collins, 1998).

27. Bosch, *Transforming Mission*, 495.

28. Sustainia Denmark, *Unlocking Interreligious Dialogue for Sustainable Development* (Copenhagen: Ministry of Foreign Affairs, 2019).

29. Bosch, *Transforming Mission*, 495.

30. Swindler, "The Dialogue Decalogue," *Ecumenical Studies* 20:1 (1983), 13–15.

31. Bosch, *Transforming Mission*, 496.

32. Max Warren, "General Introduction," in Kenneth Cragg, *Sandals at the Mosque, Christian Presence Amid Islam* (London: SCM Press, 1959), 9–10.

33. Bosch, *Transforming Mission*, 496.

34. Bosch, Transforming Mission, 498.

35. Bosch, *Transforming Mission*, 495.

36. Bosch, *Transforming Mission*, 499.

37. Bosch, *Transforming Mission*, 499.

38. Charles, Ryrie, *Basic Theology: A Popular Systematic Guide to Understanding Biblical Truth* (Chicago: Moody, 1999).

39. Ryrie, *Basic Theology*, 388.

40. Ryrie, *Basic Theology*, 388.

41. Ryrie, *Basic Theology*, 388.

42. William Edwy Vine, *Vine's Complete Expository Dictionary of Old and New Testament Words* (Nashville: Thomas Nelson, 1996), 214.

43. Vine, *Vine's Complete Expository Dictionary*, 215.

44. H. D. McDonald, "Salvation," in J. D. Douglas and Merrill C. Tenney, eds., *The New International Bible Dictionary* (Grand Rapids, MI: Zondervan, 1987), 886–887.

45. Vine, *Vine's Complete Expository Dictionary*, 547.

46. Vine, *Vine's Complete Expository Dictionary*, 547.

47. McDonald, "Salvation," 887.

48. Craig S. Keener, *The IVP Bible Background Commentary, New Testament* (Downers Grove, IL: InterVarsity, 1993), 333.

49. McDonald, *"Salvation,"*887.

50. McDonald, "Salvation," 887.

51. Ray C. Stedman, *Adventuring Through the Bible: A Comparative Guide to the Entire Bible* (Grand Rapids, MI: Discovery House, 1997), 545.

52. William G. Schweer, "Evangelism," in Chard Brand, Charles Draper, and Archie England, eds., *Holman Illustrated Bible Dictionary* (Nashville, TN: Holman Bible Publishers, 2003), 518.

53. Schweer, "Evangelism," 518.

54. Gary R. Corwin, Scott A. Moureau, and Gary B, McGee, *Introducing World Missions: A Biblical, Historical and Practical Survey* (Grand Rapids, MI: Baker Academics, 2004).

55. Gailyn van Rheenen, *Biblical Foundations and Contemporary Strategies: Missions* (Grand Rapids: Zondervan, 1996).

56. Schweer, "Evangelism," 518.

57. Dan Laing Stefana, "Witness, Martyr," in Brand et al., eds., *Holman Illustrated Bible Dictionary*, 1677.

58. Elmer L. Towns, "Evangelism: Hot as Ever, but Old Methods are Cooling Off," http://digitalcommons.liberty.edu/towns_articles20, accessed, 10 August, 2019.

59. Joseph C. Aldrich, *Lifestyle Evangelism: Crossing Traditional Boundaries to Reach the Unbelieving World* (Colorado Springs: Multnomah), 1993.

60. Elmer L. Towns, "You Can't Use Old Tools for Today's Job and Be in Business Tomorrow" (paper 9, 1984), http://digitalcommons.liberty.edu/

towns_articles/9.

61. Towns, "Evangelism."

62. James Shelton, *Mighty in Word and Deed* (Peabody, MA: Hendrickson, 1991).

63. Gary McGee, "Power on High: A Historical Perspective on the Radical Strategy in Missions," in Wonsuk Ma and Robert P. Menzies, eds., *Pentecostalism in Context: Essays in Honor of William W. Menzies* (Sheffield: Sheffield Academic, 1997), 317–319.

64. Allan Anderson, *Evangelism and the Growth of Pentecostalism in* Africa (2000), http://artsweb.bham.ac.uk/aanderson/Publications/evangelism_and _the _ growth_of_pen.htm, accessed June 25, 2018,

65. Allan Anderson, *An I ntroduction to Pentecostalism* (Cambridge: Cambridge University Press, 2004).

66. Denzil R. Miller, *Empowered for Global Mission: A Missionary Look at the Book of Acts* (Springfield, MO: Life Publishers, 2005).

67. Charles Agyin-Asare, *It Is Miracle Time* (Accra: Type Company, 1997).

68. Garry McGee, "Power on High: A Historical Perspective on the Radical Strategy in Missions," in Ma and Menzies, eds., *Pentecostalism in Context*, 317–319.

69. Robert Menzies, *Empowered for Witness: The Spirit in Luke-Acts* (London: T & T Clark, 2004).

70. Shelton, *Mighty in Word and Deed.*

71. K. J. Asamoah-Gyadu, "Signs, Wonders, and Ministry: The Gospel in the Power of the Spirit," *Evangelical Review of Theology* 33:1 (2009), 32–46.

72. Neil Cole, "A Fresh Perspective of Paul's Missionary Strategies: The Mentoring for Multiplication Model" (Church Multiplication Associates, 1998), www.cmaresources.org/files/Paulstrategy.pdf, accessed 6 September 2019.

12.

The Spirit-Empowered Church: God's Answer to a Postmodern World: A Sermon

Sakkie Olivier

Abstract

The Western world has seen far-reaching changes in the last couple of decades, and this has given the world a totally different look than a hundred years ago. Big words like postmodernism and universalism have become part of our general vocabulary. The speed at which big cities develop and grow also added to large changes in the way humans have traditionally lived. The church as a role-player in society has also been influenced by all of these changes and must find ways to act on these changes. The purpose of this sermon is to help the church and families deal with these changes and the world as it is today.

Key words: uncertainty, postmodern world, Spirit-empowered, church, family

Introduction

Even in a broken world and uncertain age the Spirit of God continuous to witness to the saving grace found in Jesus as the unique savior of the lost. The Spirit of God is still hovering and as seen in biblical examples we will use, he is ready to show up and empower his people. The Holy Spirit is not obstructed or intimidated by the challenges of the world as it is today. He is supernaturally ready to empower his people, and especially families, to shine as beacons of light and hope in a dark and hurting world.

Scripture Reading

Gen 28:10–22 NKJV

10 Now Jacob went out from Beersheba and went toward Haran. 11 So he came to a certain place and stayed there all night, because the sun had set. And he took one of the stones of that place and put it at his head, and he lay down in that place to sleep. 12 Then he dreamed, and behold, a ladder was set up on the earth, and its top reached to heaven; and there the angels of God were ascending and descending on it. 13 And behold, the Lord stood above it and said: "I am the Lord God of Abraham your father and the God of Isaac; the land on which you lie I will give to you and your descendants. 14 Also, your descendants shall be as the dust of the earth; you shall spread abroad to the west and the east, to the north and the south; and in you and in your seed all the families of the earth shall be blessed. 15 Behold, I am with you and will keep you wherever you go, and will bring you back to this land; for I will not leave you until I have done what I have spoken to you." 16 Then Jacob awoke from his sleep and said, "Surely the Lord is in this place, and I did not know it." 17 And he was afraid and said, "How awesome is this place! This is none other than the house of God, and this is the gate of heaven!" 18 Then Jacob rose early in the morning, and took the stone that he had put at his head, set it up as a pillar, and poured oil on top of it. 19 And he called the name of that place Bethel; but the name of that city had been Luz previously. 20 Then Jacob made a vow, saying, "If God will be with me, and keep me in this way that I am going, and give me bread to eat and clothing to put on, 21 so that I come back to my father's house in peace, then the Lord shall be my God. 22 And this stone which I have set as a pillar shall be God's house, and of all that You give me I will surely give a tenth to You."

Acts 10:1–9, 24, 44–46 NKJV

There was a certain man in Caesarea called Cornelius, a centurion of what was called the Italian Regiment, 2 a devout man and one who feared God with all his household, who gave alms generously to the people, and prayed to God always. 3 About the ninth hour of the day he saw clearly in a vision an angel of God coming in and saying to him, "Cornelius!" 4 And when he observed him, he was afraid, and said, "What is it, lord?" So he said to him, "Your prayers and your alms have come up for a memorial before God. 5 Now send men to Joppa, and send for Simon whose surname is Peter. 6 He is lodging with Simon, a tanner, whose house is by the sea. He will tell you what you must do." 7 And when the angel who spoke to him had departed, Cornelius called two of his household servants and a devout soldier from among those who waited on him continually. 8 So when he had explained all these things to them, he sent them to Joppa. 9 The next day, as they went on their journey and drew near the city, Peter went up on the housetop to pray, about the sixth hour. 10 Then he became very hungry and wanted to eat; but while they made ready, he fell into a trance 11 and saw heaven opened and an object like a great sheet bound at the four corners, descending to him and let down to the earth.

24 And the following day they entered Caesarea. Now Cornelius was waiting for them, and had called together his relatives and close friends.

44 While Peter was still speaking these words, the Holy Spirit fell upon all those who heard the word. 45 And those of the circumcision who believed were astonished, as many as came with Peter, because the gift of the Holy Spirit had been poured out on the Gentiles also. 46 For they heard them speak with tongues and magnify God.

Lessons from Biblical Examples

1. Jacob's Spiritual Empowerment

Jacob, as one of two brothers, came from a family of God's promise, but learned the hard way that relationships are always tough. Being challenged by his elder brother for gaining the first-born blessing in an abnormal way, and having to flee to another country, Jacob was alone, without help and relationship. This is very similar to the world of hurt and broken relationships as seen today. But it is in this situation that God meets Jacob in a very intense, spiritual way. Jacob, as a young man, had an encounter with God through a vision and a wrestling match. This ended in a dream and a promise and made such a lasting spiritual imprint on his life that it carried him through another fourteen years of hardship. He never doubted his faith because he could not doubt the intense spiritual encounter he had experienced. He was supernaturally empowered by the Holy Spirit, and even though he came from broken relationships, we see in his life that there was a brotherly restoration, and he even became the father of twelve sons who were the promised tribes of God's covenant nation.

2. Cornelius and His Family Receive the Holy Spirit

Cornelius was a God-fearing man that carried much authority in the Italian regiment stationed at Caesarea. Living as an immigrant in a foreign nation, he, with his entire household, feared God, and he was known for his charity and prayers. In a miraculous way, God, through his Holy Spirit, brought a divinely appointed meeting together where Peter came to the house of Cornelius and preached the gospel to Cornelius and his whole family and household. How remarkable is this man, that in an age of much uncertainty — where the Roman rulers occupied the Jewish land, and greed, moral decay, idolatry, cruelty, and oppression were the order of the day — had his whole household in a church service learning about Jesus as the unique savior of the world? Then, to put his seal on this joyous occasion, the Holy Spirit fell on all of those listening to Peter and they received the empowerment of the Holy Spirit. God saved the whole family; he anointed the whole family and did it in the midst of a broken and uncertain world.

Characteristics of the World in Which We Live

As a church and as families it is important to understand the realities of the challenges we face today. We live in a society that has changed drastically over the last 120 years and technology, large urban metropolises, high-speed travel, and global interconnectedness have become the order of our day. With these changes, challenges have arisen that harm the family unit. Whereas families are divided into different areas of being occupied each day, technology has changed the way relationships are being done, and postmodern mindsets have highlighted generational gaps. We will now look at some of the major challenges facing our world today, and also highlight some similarities to our biblical examples as used in the introduction.

1. The Crumbling of Social Community

In the modernistic age, community ties were established more easily as churches were built around families, residential areas, and friends. Everybody knew and understood one another socially. The world changed as television, the internet, and mobile technology developed. Children became engaged with their peers through devices and social media even when they were not with their peers. In the cities, many cases exist where both parents have to work to make ends meet, leaving children on their own to navigate through life with a multitude of social technology devices, as well as access to almost any kind of good and bad information, while not being mature enough to deal with it.

The church is thus characterized by a broken social community. Congregations consist of broken families, unmarried single people, divorced people, parents whose teenagers do not attend church or attend another church, teenagers who attend without their parents for whatever given reason, children that get dropped off at children's church by parents who do not attend or who come with their grandparents. The crumbling of social community is visible in the world, and also seen in present-day church life.

There is also a lesson to be learn from Jacob. This is similar to the life of Jacob where he had to flee from his homeland, his family, and his closest relationships. In Bethel, God found Jacob hurting, confused, and alone. But even in this broken season, God, through the supernatural, had an answer for Jacob. Through the supernatural wrestling match, a heavenly vision, and a covenant, Jacob received spiritual empowerment that gave him faith, capacity, and strength to face even larger challenges that followed in his life.

2. Age of Uncertainty

People today are living in the information age. People are bombarded from all sides with information and competing claims to the "truth" or the absence thereof. There is no overarching worldview. The media and the internet, as well as social media, are the instruments of this general explosion, and the crumbling of worldviews. This uncertainty has various negative results as young people face a rise in fear, depression, and eating disorders. Suicide and other destructive tendencies are also on the increase. This uncertainty about the truth makes people question the church and the teachings on religion.

Here is a lesson to be learned from Cornelius. This is similar to the world and environment of Cornelius. He and his household lived in a time of competing claims to the truth. The Romans had their worldview as well as their mythological beliefs, the Jews were fighting the Roman oppression, and seeking freedom to exercise their faith, and in the midst of all this, a new faith arose called Christianity. As an Italian officer, Cornelius would have had first-hand knowledge of all these rivalries and claims to truth, but when he and his household experienced the supernatural empowerment of the Holy Spirit and being redeemed by the only unique savior of the world, Jesus Christ, there was no more confusion. Clarity stepped in with empowerment and they got baptized and became the first gentile family of believers. Hallelujah!

3. Spiritual Hunger

At present, there is a huge spiritual awakening around the world, but much of this awakening is taking place outside of the confines of the church. The postmodern world, with much uncertainty, has mixed spiritual hunger with an experiential hunger that coincides with mistrust in authoritarian institutions, including religious institutions. Spirituality is back in the public sphere, but without a compass or direction. It is seen in the forms of mysticism, new-age religions, gaming, an obsession with darkness and death, especially in teenagers, and growth in the phenomena of self-inflicted pain especially, again, in teenagers. The situation is summed up by a quote from Chris Carter the creator of X-files where he says, "I'm a non-religious person looking for a religious experience."[1]

This brings two big challenges for the church. The first is that people are spiritually hungry, and the second is the spiritual vitality of the church. If the church has spiritual vitality and can give people a solid experience of the Holy Spirit, then people flock to those congregations. Where the Spirit of the Lord is moving in a serious way, based on biblical truth, there is life and freedom that fills the spiritual hunger of those attending. People are looking for a relationship with God that is dynamic and life changing. The young people of today are looking for an experience and not mere talk.

Here is another lesson to be learned from Cornelius. In the life of Cornelius, we can see this spiritual hunger manifest. As an Italian officer, he would have known the Roman religion. Being stationed in Judea he knew Judaism, and yet he sought after God with a spiritual hunger that was not satisfied with known religion. He was thirsting after a living God, a real savior, and when he and his family tasted the empowerment of the Holy Spirit there was no turning back. Once their whole family tasted the living waters of the Holy Spirit, they went through the actual waters of baptism, and found regeneration and rebirth in a very tangible way.

4. Urbanization & Migration

Urbanization is the process whereby big cities and their surroundings become more densely populated whereas rural areas see a decrease in population. More and more people move to urban areas because of the need for healthcare, education, better life, availability of work, larger networks of economic and business infrastructure, political decisions and immigration. Superhighways, cellular and communications networks, impressive architecture and super-fast trains characterize major cities. But urbanization comes with its own sets of problems. A loss of traditional family values, shortage of housing, poverty, easy access to substance abuse products like alcohol, drugs, and narcotics are a few examples. Prostitution and crime become part of everyday living in the less affluent urban areas. Add to this the movement of refugees around the world. Diseases like HIV/AIDS spread more easily. Currently there are more than 12,000,000 aids orphans in the world.[2] All these factors contribute to a world in dire need of a savior.

Here is the third lesson we can learn from Cornelius. He also lived in a time of large-scale movements of people, through conquests of land, conflicts, oppression, and economic reasons. He himself was an immigrant in Judea. But we see in Acts 10 that he was a devout man that had an open heart for the poor. He was an example of being actively involved in his community, and he was commended on this by God. As New Testament believers, we should realize that Spirit-empowerment means that we are active in our communities as shining lights.

5. Postmodernism and Universalism

Postmodernism is a reference to the age after Modernism that is characterized by a resistance to the modern ideals of uniformity. Modernism was the age that developed out of the Renaissance, where the human mind was crowned as the only source for knowing the truth. It was built upon the foundations of hierarchy and absolute trust in science. In the twentieth century, there has been a realization of the shortcomings of science. Aspects such as authority, facts, militarism, and uniformity are now questioned. There is a resistance to the fixed structure and rules of the modern age. The postmodern world has become a kaleidoscope of influences that exist alongside of one another. Different religions, cultures, and political worldviews have come into contact with one another, and even collided, because of increasingly better communication and transport systems. People are living in a global village. Universalism flows from this, as it is the philosophical and theological concept that some ideas and religions have universal application and are inclusive in manner. Add to these worldviews dynamics such as globalism, secularism, homosexuality, and other defining philosophies, and the complexity of the world in which we live and in which our children grow up is even higher. Combine this with television, social media, the internet, and mobile communication, and the world becomes a very small place where everyone is exposed to everyone. This has made the average worldview very grey, where the definition of boundaries between cultures, nations, religions, and philosophies have become minimal.

Here is a lesson from Jacob. The world that he lived in was one of plurality, yet as a young man fleeing from his own brother, he should have been questioning truth and authority. His father explicitly tells him he is not supposed to take wives from the other cultural groups in their areas but has to go find a wife at his uncle in a distant land. In this way, Isaac is trying to protect Jacob from different influences. But it is only when Jacob wrestled with God and had a supernatural experience with the Spirit of God did he find clarity in his heart and mind about what truth really is, and did he find the strength to live his faith in an obedient covenantal way.

Spiritual Answers for Unique Problems

The church finds itself in a world where change rushes forward like a big wave. Therefore, the church must understand its role in this changing world. The church must learn how to communicate the age-old, unchanging truth to a postmodern, urbanized world. This does not imply changes to the message, but it does imply changes to the methods and work-ways. It further implies a strengthening of the work of the Holy Spirit, as the church needs a Spirit-empowered strategy to face the complexity of this age.

The New Testament uses the word *ecclesia* to refer to the church. The word carries the simple meaning of the "called together assembly" with God as the convener and Jesus Christ as the center. The smallest nucleus in which this *ecclesia* should function is the family. This is where the power of the Holy Spirit should operate firstly and foremost, and henceforth be visible in the world. In the impersonal urban situation in which people live, the family and congregation as the body of Christ gives room for an intimate personal faith-relationship with one another and the Lord. The church is not called away from this world, but is called to live within this world in a new way. One of the primary goals of the church in any era is to create a place of true community and fellowship, and to do it in such a way that it reflects the kingdom of God. The community of believers consists of those people, who once were not part of this community, but then came under the conviction of the lordship of Jesus Christ, and out of obedience they embraced the community of believers. They came to this conviction through the working of the Holy Spirit and exposure to the testimony of the body of Christ concerning Christ and his work. The Spirit-empowered church that reflects true community is like the salt of the earth and is as a light on a mountain (Matt 5:13, 14), and in a spiritually hungry world, like water in the desert. Therefore, we will look at ways that believing families can be the salt of the earth and a light on a mountain in this day and age, while referencing our two scriptural examples of Jacob and Cornelius.

1. Renewing of Our Minds

I beseech you therefore, brethren, by the mercies of God, that you present your bodies a living sacrifice, holy, acceptable to God, which is your reasonable service. And do not be conformed to this world, but be transformed by the renewing of your mind, that you may prove what is that good and acceptable and perfect will of God, Rom 12:1–2.

In a postmodern mindset, the church must focus on caring and dialogue instead of authoritarian answers and solutions. This entails a renewal of our minds, methods, and thinking patterns according to the word of God, in a way that includes the whole family and that gives our children access to the word in tangible ways. Paul writes in 1 Cor 9:22 that he "became all things to all men, that he might, by all means, save some." This means that church leaders and parents cannot only lead from an authoritarian foundation, but have to work on a relational and process-orientated approach where renewed thinking goes into the importance of relationship, caring and dialogue.

Here is a lesson from Cornelius. Once his household heard the truth from Peter in a kind, relational way in their own setting, they were open to the work of the Holy Spirit, and came to life-changing faith in Christ. They did not read about this or hear about it through the grapevine. They had a deep spiritual encounter together with a strong relational encounter with Peter that set the whole process moving.

2. Spiritual Vitality through Worship and Music

Postmodern communities are drifting around without religious anchors, yet they have a thirst for spirituality in a variety of ways. The spiritual hunger of the world holds great opportunity for the church because new opportunities for communicating the gospel can be found. To bring the postmodern generation, and especially families and their children, into the church there must be spiritual liveliness. This liveliness can in today's world be greatly enhanced by the correct use of Christian music. Young people today have an exceptional drawing to music and Christian worship music has become a large movement that crosses the bridges that exist over languages, cultures, and generational boundaries, and is a true international communicator of the gospel. An example is when the author leads groups in Israel and has an open-air worship session in Afrikaans, he is always amazed by the number of other language groups that are attracted to the worship and start to take part in their own language. Worship has become an international language, so people know the tunes and therefore take part. Secondly, worship is anointed, and people are attracted to the anointing. We have even seen people from other religions being filled with tears when Jesus as the savior of the world is worshipped in spirit and truth (John 4:24), no matter which language is used. Much of today's Christian music has become a common denominator in drawing families young and old into a similar worship experience that is saturated with the presence of the Holy Spirit, and touches this postmodern generation at a very deep emotional and relational level. At the church pastored by the author, there are regular Sunday night services that focus on worship, prayer and the prophetic. It is always amazing to see how families enjoy these services and the spiritual experience together. Using worship and music as a uniting factor in families holds immense spiritual possibilities.

Here is a lesson from Jacob. The first thing he did after he had an encounter with God was to build an altar and anoint it with oil. This is symbolic of worship (altar) in the presence of the Holy Spirit (oil). Jacob worshipped God and was established in the covenant and purposes of God through this life-changing spiritual experience.

Another lesson from Cornelius. It is evident from scripture that Peter heard the family of Cornelius talking in tongues and "worshipping and praising God" (Acts 10:46). Worship always accompanies the presence of God, and families that pray and worship together receive a special grace of standing together and being seen as lights in this world.

3. The Importance of God's Word

Without a doubt, God's word should be the starting point for a spiritual experience, but the way in which this happens is important. To a generation rejecting absolutism, a message that is inclusive of dialogue, creativity, interaction, illustrations, multi-media, and experience might go a lot further to help people grow in the truth. To experience the word internally it has to touch the whole person. In a world where people are used to full-color stimulation from the media, film, and internet-based entertainment like YouTube, they are looking for a message that will involve their hearts, emotions, and senses. Parents will be wise to understand that they can, through conversation, dialogue, and life experiences, create a Bible-based learning community in their families.

Here is a lesson from Cornelius. He was a remarkable man in that he found a way to draw his whole household into this experience with the Holy Spirit. They all received the gift of speaking in tongues, they were all baptized together, and all came to faith in Christ. For any family, this would have been a productive day of experience and learning.

4. Dealing with Generational Gaps in Families

A generational gap occurs between people from different age groups when each group develops their own set of definitions, values, worldviews, and work methods based on their peers and daily surroundings that clash with that of another age group. This happens because of the changing world we live in. Because of the move from a rural agricultural type of life where everyone was surrounded with more or less the same daily scenery and daily tasks, toward a technologically advanced urban life where everyone goes into their own world daily and returns home at the end of the day, generation and relational gaps develop. Parents and their children find dialogue difficult because they do not share the same daily picture that translates into a worldview anymore.

To bridge this gap of relational and generational withdrawal, the church needs to learn from the example set by God the Father himself. Our heavenly Father took the first step and reconciled the world to himself through his son, Jesus Christ, who was given the ministry of reconciliation. This ministry has now been passed over to us, HIS children (2 Cor 5:17–21). Thus, parents can learn from this and take responsibility and start working on the process of dialogue and communication. True communication starts with listening. Parents should be listening to how their children perceive and understand their world. By stepping into their children's world and trying to understand their world, a parent will begin to win their trust, and proper dialogue will begin to follow. Praying with the children about their needs, fears, and challenges will draw hearts together and in turn, the parent can begin to ask the child to pray with them regarding their challenges, fears, and needs.

Teaching this generation is not only going to happen in a classroom or from a pulpit, but in doing life together in a caring, mentoring way. In this diverse world that drives people apart, families must find common ground that draw them together and enhances their relationship. Doing life together is to find those family traditions and fun things that build the family up. It is furthermore exploring faith together and finding the right church that brings spiritual vitality into the lives of the whole family and not only the parents or children apart. The truth for today is that children should be seen, heard, loved, mentored, understood and cared for in the same way our heavenly Father cares for his children.

Here is a lesson from Jacob. Although his life initially was defined with broken relationships and fleeing from his family, we see how God brought reconciliation as he continued to journey in his covenantal purposes. Firstly, he was reconciled with his brother Esau. Later, he became father of a large household of twelve sons. Even though the sons in this family also had conflicts with each other, Jacob at the end of his life was united with his whole family. Joseph produced a place for Jacob to live in Egypt, where reconciliation met his brothers; and as a family, they prospered under the protection of Joseph as a godly ruler, even in an ungodly Egyptian set-up. Therefore, if families follow Jesus with an open heart for the empowerment of the Holy Spirit, they can see the miraculous, even as they live and journey in an ungodly world.

Conclusion

We have seen from two Biblical examples how God, through supernatural experience and spiritual empowerment, can deeply impact the lives of Jacob, Cornelius, their families and even generations to follow. Jesus Christ as the true and unique savior of the world holds the power through his spirit to enable families, even in this world today, to deeply experience him and find the ability to deeply and intimately know and follow him, even in a confused and broken world.

Notes

1.   Kevin Ward, "Christendom, Clericalism & Church," *Ministry Today* 28 (June 2003),   https://www.ministrytoday.org.uk/magazine/issues/28/330/,   accessed May 6, 2020.

2. UNICEF, "Orphans," June 16, 2017, https://www.unicef.org/media/media_45279.html, accessed May 6, 2020.

13.

Integrating Christianity in the Traditional Religious Milieu: The South African Experience

Dela Quampah

Abstract

Nearly four hundred years after the first Christian missionary contact in Africa, traditional religions and Islam are still active competitors with Christianity in Africa. The response of the early Roman Catholic and Protestant missionaries to African spiritual narratives was one of total disengagement and rejection. However, with the emergence of Pentecostalism in the early twentieth century, a more fertile and symbiotic relationship appears to emerge between the two religious traditions. The outcome is the establishment of prophetic and deliverance ministries that practice exorcisms, healings, and sometimes claim they can foretell the future. Consequently, some of their practices have generated debate regarding morality and human rights abuse. This article reflects on the impact of this Christian and traditional religion interaction to identify possible areas of constructive dialogue and moral progress.

Key words: contextualization, worldview, pneumatological, rituals

Introduction

After almost four centuries of Christian missionary contact, traditional religions and Islam continue to compete vigorously with Christianity in Africa. In such a context, the cross-fertilization of religious ideas and practices is inevitable. The history of Christianity in Africa and its interface with traditional religion is a fascinating one that has engaged scholarly attention from various perspectives. So far, the main school of thought on this Christian-traditional religion interface has labeled the traditional context as *preparation for the gospel*. From 1652, which marks the first missionary contact with South Africa, Christianity has since settled in, and its interaction with African traditional religion has engendered a pneumatically conscious form of Christianity which also depicts elements of traditional religious practices. While an appreciative perspective views this development as relevant contextualization, the critics regard it as syncretism. This article explores the trajectory of over four hundred years' relationship between Christianity and traditional religion in the South African context. I appreciate the traditional religious milieu as one of extreme spiritual consciousness, which, some argue, approximates the first-century Judean context that engendered the gospel narratives. Traditional society in Africa is sensitive to both benevolent and malevolent spiritual forces which compare favorably to angels and demons, respectively. The role of the traditional priest in invoking the favor of benevolent spirits to bless the community or individuals through seances, trances, visions, and prophetic encounters are well documented. This is coupled with their capacity, or so it is believed, to control and regulate the activities of malevolent forces who bring tragedy to the community through exorcisms and pacification rituals. The response of the early Roman Catholic and Protestant missionaries to such spiritual encounters was one of total disengagement and rejection. However, with the emergence of Pentecostalism in the early twentieth century, a more fertile and symbiotic relationship appears to emerge between the two religious traditions. The outcome is the establishment of prophetic and deliverance ministries who practice exorcisms, healings and foretell the future. Some of their rituals, especially in the category referred to as African Independent Churches (AICs), have generated debate regarding morality and abuse. This paper reflects on the impact of this Christianization of traditional religion to identify possible areas of constructive dialogue and moral progress.

The success of any Christian mission endeavor rises or falls with the value and relevance of its theology and promise. And it appears the only theology that would challenge, inspire, and engage meaningfully in the postmodern era should be both pneumatological, and eschatological.

The success of the pneumatological impact in mission theology is revealed in the significant accomplishments of Pentecostals in contemporary missiology. In just about one hundred years of existence, Pentecostalism is acclaimed today as a main role player in world missions, comprising a quarter of the world's Christian population with three-quarters of them living in the developing world.[1] Christian expression in these regions hinges on subjective mysterious encounters that resonate with the traditional religious experiences of Africa, Asia, and Latin America. This strand of the faith is characterized by tangible encounters with the Holy Spirit in audible expressions such as speaking in tongues and prophecy, coupled with super-sense experiences such as visions and dreams, often ascribed to the inspiration of the Holy Spirit. The holistic worldview of such people, which integrates the physical and the spiritual, appreciates Pentecostal Christianity as a religion that responds to their physical needs in healing encounters, as well as material and social blessings, where births and marriages, education, jobs, and travel opportunities are all celebrated as miracles from God. In this regard, it can be said that this strand of Christianity incarnates the gospel in the mundane and routine activities of adherents. This is significantly different from the Western approach that views Christianity mainly as theological concepts and ideas to be debated and accepted or rejected, and applied selectively to limited spheres of life and society. Again, of much significance to Pentecostals, is the idea and practical manifestation of spiritual power confrontations, where the name of Jesus is often invoked in the power of the Holy Spirit in confrontation with the forces of darkness, considered as causal agents of various afflictions, be they cases of demon possession or mild ailments.

What constitutes authentic African theology continues to challenge African theologians in their attempt to realize a consensus on this subject matter. In the 1977 Pan-African Conference of Third World Theologians held in Accra, Ghana, part of the Communiqué attempts to define the shape of African theology, "Our task as theologians is to create a theology that arises from and is accountable to African people."[2] While some African theologians argue that theological concepts from the traditional religious heritage of Africa adequately compete with Christian themes, others suggest that traditional religious ideas are deficient to Christianity. Bediako, for instance, is convinced that understanding Christian soteriology through the African worldview is as biblical and convincing as any other theological perspective.[3] And scholars such as Mbiti and Idowu suggest that the Supreme Being acknowledged by Africans is not different from the God of the Bible. Idowu, arguing on the basis of general revelation, posits that the true God has revealed himself to Nigerians and he is the one they worship.[4] Contrary to this position, Kunhiyop avers, "the beliefs and practices of African traditional religion convey a faint and incomplete understanding of who God is."[5] Taking a middle position between these two extremes, one would suggest that although the theological ideas in African traditional religion may, on occasion, correlate to Christian concepts, the two religions are also significantly different in many dimensions. Therefore, African Christian theologians would have to sift between aspects of traditional culture which converge with the gospel and those at variance with it.[6]

A critical examination of the African religious heritage reveals compelling lessons that can enrich Christian theology and church history. This position is supported by Taylor's view, "The world Church is impoverished and incomplete without the insights that the Logos has been preparing for it in Africa."[7] Furthermore, the current resurgence of Christianity in Africa is attributable, in part, to the similarity and correlation between African beliefs and cultural practices, and the Semitic and pre-Christian European milieus of the Bible.[8] The challenge African theologians face in their attempt to recover the true gospel from its European encumbrances for the African is succinctly captured by Schreiter, "The bitter irony, as African theologians have pointed out, is that African values and customs are often closer to the Semitic values that pervade the scriptures and the story of Jesus than the European Christian values that have been imposed upon them."[9] This makes the Christian message extremely relevant to the mundane challenges of Africa, for instance, the reality of demonic activity in traditional community finds resonance in Jesus' encounter with demonic powers in the Gospels (Matt 9:29–32; Mark 7:24–30; Luke 4:33–37), as well as Paul's response to demon possession in the Book of Acts (16:16–21).

Creative Contextualization

However, with the emergence of Pentecostalism and the so-called African Initiated Churches in the twentieth century, successful attempts have been made at contextualizing, as these Christian denominations respond creatively to the socio-cultural and religious heritage of their communities. In the main, African traditional religions are recognized for their orality of concepts, and lack of systematized theological reflection. This is because such religions view revelation not so much a deposit, but as a perpetual quest that cannot be reduced to a definitive formulation.[10] For the African, religion does not comprise creeds and concepts to be formulated and debated by councils; their religious ideas are forged in the crucible of mundane life, where spiritual forces share in the responsibility of caring for the living community. The African therefore appreciates a holistic or organic view of the cosmos, regarding all things as functioning together in one network, where natural phenomena and the spiritual world blend together in a complex interrelatedness. Therefore, African Pentecostals readily seek succor from their deity for their daily challenges of providing food, shelter, and basic needs, as well as security and protection from evil forces. Consequently, the African concept of salvation is both temporal and eternal. Bolaji contends that African traditional religion functions in a reciprocal relationship by which mankind relies on the deity for the fulfillment of personal and basic needs that are both material and spiritual.[11] And as I have stated elsewhere, "This practicality and pervasiveness of religion in Africa is further enhanced by the idea of mystical causality, or the belief that occurrences in the physical realm are predetermined and influenced by supernatural forces — either benevolent ones such as deities and ancestral spirits, or malevolent ones such as witches."[12]

Various dimensions of the Pentecostal faith smoothly integrate into the fertile traditional religious environment of Africa, where experiencing the reality and manifestation of spiritual powers is preferred to intellectual reflection. This brings into focus Cox's idea of primal piety that characterizes the Pentecostal strand of the Christian faith. He describes primal piety thus:

> This dimension covers the manifestation of the divine purpose or power in mystical experiences such as trance, vision, inspiration, ritual dance, healing, dreams, prophecy, and other forms of religious expression. These irrational forms of religious demonstration are elementary and foundational to the human religious experience. Such approaches to human spirituality are an adequate response to the challenges of modernity, which uses the tools of reason and logic alone to evaluate the human experience. Confirming the idea that other sources of knowledge and experience exist beyond the realm of logic and physical evidence.[13]

Some of those who think the indigenization of Christianity in Africa is syncretistic insist, "The African church is permeated with descriptions of demonic activities that are rooted in the pre-Christian world view and are not consistent with biblical revelation."[14] In the light of the suggestion made above that traditional African cultural practices synchronize very well with biblical culture, Kunhiyop appears to be taking a limited view on the issue. A more comprehensive perspective appreciates the Pentecostal churches' seemingly contradictory approach of continuity and discontinuity. African Pentecostals appear to engage with pristine religious concepts when they affirm the activities of demons, the invocation of curses, and the ascription of tragedy to powers of darkness.

However, this affirmation does not entice them into demon worship or making sacrifices to spiritual powers other than God. Furthermore, some Pentecostals reject traditional rituals that mark the rites of passage of their communities, regarding them as opportunities for demonic influence. In a survey conducted among black African Christians in Soshanguve, a suburb of Pretoria in South Africa, Anderson identified three approaches in responding to traditional rituals and demon consciousness. The first response, which he labels as indifference, is prevalent among educated members of European mission-founded churches, which implies that "the spirit world does not exist and can be safely ignored." The second category, which occurs mainly among African Independent Churches (AICs) and Zionist churches, is one of the accommodation of rituals within the church, ranging from total acceptance of such rituals to limited adoption. The third category, which is dominant among the Pentecostal and Apostolic is defined as confrontation, "where the spirit world is demonized, so that an important part of Christian rituals consists of getting rid of Satan."[15]

In addition, the African religious milieu provides a rich source of imagery that translates the gospel for relevance and effective comprehension for indigenous people groups. It cannot be denied that, "Although the central factor of religious experience is intangible, mysterious, and sometimes unexplainable, its concomitant revelation or message is always communicated through the observable material context within which the encounter occurs."[16] Mission studies have therefore revealed that the indigenization model is effective in translating the gospel message into the idioms and metaphors of the host community.[17] The contextualization and indigenization of Christianity in Africa is most prominently appreciated among the AICs, who, according to Schreiter, "show what a genuinely incultured Christianity might look like in Africa, were inculturation left to Africans alone."[18]

On a continent that is plagued by poverty, instability, wars, famines, and extreme underdevelopment, the hope of eternal redemption intrinsic to the Christian message carries a strong appeal. The relevance of Cox's idea of primal hope in such a context cannot be overemphasized. This refers to the firm millennial belief of the Pentecostals that a totally different world age would soon emerge, offering a promise that transcends any particular human experience; a hope that persists, although other human hopes have failed to materialize.[19]

Hence the appropriation of the gospel among African Pentecostals seems to inspire hope beyond their immediate situation, providing courage to face their myriad mundane problems, and helping them to endure an unfair world order. The AICs in South Africa, for instance, have demonstrated a spirituality that liberated the soul, even though the adherents were physically subjected to the horrors of apartheid. Thus, during the political struggle for liberation from apartheid, a considerable number of Pentecostal-oriented independent churches saw no salvation in the bloody liberation struggle being pursued by political idealists.[20] According to Rossouw, "In a world marked by misery and violence, members can find refuge in these churches — in the domain of the Spirit where healing, conversion, and peace were obtained. In these restless times, the independent churches indeed offer security and harmony."[21]

The first Christian contact with South Africa dates as far back as 1652, with the arrival of the Dutch, and later, the French Huguenots in 1668. Over time the Dutch Reformed Church (known as NGK in Dutch) became the dominant church, but with little concern for the evangelization of the indigenous Africans. The role of the church in racial discrimination is revealed in this statement, "in the very early days at the Cape colony, discrimination practiced between white and black, slave and free person, was ostensibly based more on religion than race."[22] Attempts by George Schmidt (1709–1785), a German Moravian missionary, to evangelize the indigenous *Khoikhoi* from July 9, 1737, were frustrated by the NGK and Dutch political powers who repatriated him in 1744.[23] It was not until 1857 that the NGK initiated efforts to evangelize those of mixed race,[24] who constituted a class of people ranking next to the Europeans on the South African color scale. When in the nineteenth century, evangelism among the indigenous black was gaining grounds, racial tension developed in the church and the synod decided that white and black congregations should worship separately.[25] And this segregation has characterized every Christian denomination in South Africa to date. Reverend Damons' statement made in February 2016 is sad but poignantly true, "The church is the last bastion of apartheid in South Africa."[26]

Pneumatic Christianity in South Africa

Although many scholars trace the progeny of Pentecostalism to the classic Azusa Street event of 1901, it must be acknowledged that spiritual revivalist movements of Pentecostal orientation emerged in Africa much earlier. And many of such movements have crystallized into, for lack of better terminology, what is often referred to as African Independent Churches (AICs). Asamoah-Gyadu thinks this movement emerged for a Holy Spirit revitalization of the "dry denominationalism" of the historic mission churches.[27] In South Africa, this tradition is associated with Zionist and Ethiopian Churches, traceable to as far back as 1892, when a Wesleyan Minister, Mangena M. Mokone, broke away because of racial segregation and led other malcontent Christian leaders to form the Ethiopian Church. A name that was inspired by Psalm 68:31, "Ethiopia shall soon stretch her hands unto God" (KJV), which implies the rise of self-governed churches under African leaders.[28] Many similar churches emerged around this time, and in 1896 in Pretoria, all the independent church leaders met and decided to become affiliated to the African Methodist Episcopal Church of the US, with James M. Dwane being their most influential leader.[29] Later Dwane migrated his congregation to the Anglican Church to form the "Order of Ethiopia." Some of such significant Ethiopian churches relevant to this era include P. J. Mzimba's African Presbyterian Church founded in 1898, which broke away from the United Free Church of Scotland, and Mbiaa Ngidi's Zulu Mbiana Congregational Church, established in 1890.

The advent of classical Pentecostalism in South Africa makes for fascinating reading. Sundkler traces its inception to 1904, which produced Zionist churches associated with John Alexander Dowie's apocalyptic denomination, the Christian Catholic Apostolic Church in Zion, in the United States. The main doctrines of this church were "divine healing," "triune immersion," and an urgent sense of Christ's second coming. However, this denomination was not thoroughly going Pentecostal.[30] It was in 1908 that two Apostolic Faith missionaries, John Lake and Thomas Hezmalhalch from the US, arrived and introduced the baptism in the Holy Spirit to the Zionist churches to make them completely Pentecostal, which birthed the Apostolic Faith Mission (AFM). Initially, the Church was able to accommodate the Black South Africans, Afrikaner Whites, and those of mixed race. By 1919, Afrikaner intolerance led to a split where many of the Blacks left the AFM to form the Zionist churches.[31] Through its sustained evangelistic activities, the AFM was able to attract large constituents of Black, Mixed Race, and Indian people with each cultural group worshipping apart, a situation best captured in Clark's words, "The AFM followed the nationalist emphasis on apartness and by the end of the 1950s consisted of four separate churches: a White (mother) church, and the three daughter churches — a Black, a [Mixed Race] and an Indian."[32]

Another key player in the narrative of South African Pentecostalism is the Full Gospel Church which emerged out of the ministry of George Bowie, who came to South Africa in 1909 as a missionary sent by Bethel Pentecostal Assembly, New Jersey, USA. His ministry began in April 1910 as a Pentecostal mission, which led to the founding of a bilingual church known as The Full Gospel Church of God in Southern Africa in 1951. The church spread quickly among all the races in South Africa, namely Black, White, Indian and Mixed Race. The White community for many years has the oversight of the whole church and all the departments were subject to the Executive Council in Irene, Pretoria. From 1986 all the communities had their own moderators and executive councils, with representation on the general moderator, which constituted 4 associations in one church. Negotiations, however, went on for over sixteen years, when it was eventually agreed that those communities who were willing could unite to become one integrated association within The Full Gospel Church of God. In March 1990, the United Assemblies of the Full Gospel Church of God was constituted, consisting of the majority of the Black, Mixed Race, Indian and a small group of White Community. The church then had two groups instead of four, the White Irene Assemblies and the United Assemblies. Seven years later, on October 9, 1997, the whole Full Gospel Church of God in Southern African united to become one structural organization. Since unification, the church registers about one thousand five hundred ministers, and a total of eight hundred twenty-eight assemblies, with an estimated membership of thirty-five thousand. The structural unification of the church, which formally took place at the Inaugural Conference on October 9, 1997, based on "20 Principles," made the Full Gospel Church of God, South Africa, a non-racial and structurally integrated church.[33]

The ministry of the Assemblies of God (AoG) in South Africa began in 1908, with the arrival of Pentecostal missionaries who worked independently of each other until they began to corporate for fellowship impact. Around 1936, many AoG churches had been planted in South Africa, and although the membership was predominantly black, the church was controlled by expatriate missionaries. The AoG conference of 1938 established the umbrella body that registered the participation and influence of H. C. Phillips, Nicholas Bhengu and James (Jim) Mullan. Nicholas Bhengu worked mainly among the blacks and had a significant ministry that saw thousands of converts made in a short time. By 1959, he had planted 50 assemblies all over South Africa. James Mullan, who was of Irish descent, on his part, worked among the whites, and between 1945 and 1964, established twenty congregations from Cape Town to Zambia and Zimbabwe. The Assemblies of God in South Africa, since the 1970s, have also become segregated along racial lines. By implication, any mission engagement in South Africa today would have to reckon with the composite social structure, and respond sensitively to racial, nationalistic and economic stratification. However, it is also necessary to mention that a significant number of multiracial congregations are emerging in some of the new churches in South Africa.[34]

Neo-Pentecostalism in South Africa

With time, some charismatic individuals founded Neo-Pentecostal denominations, the most significant being the Rhema Bible Church, which was founded in 1979 by Pastor Ray McCauley after he returned from Bible school in the USA. Under the leadership of Senior Pastor Ray McCauley, Rhema was one of the first churches in South Africa to defy Apartheid laws and have non-racial church services, an example of what was to come in the new South Africa. The Rhema Bible College has produced leaders who have also founded churches like the Grace Bible Church, Word Alive Bible Church, and Faith and Power Bible Church, among others. Lately, new strands of Pentecostal ministries have emerged, whose focus is mainly on prophecy and miracles.

African Initiated Churches (AICs) in South Africa

The significant impact of AICs to socio-religious life in South Africa is much appreciated, as they have emerged as the denomination(s) with the largest membership, and continue to grow at such an impressive rate. The AICs numbered over one million in 1936, and by 1970, they had doubled in membership to two million one hundred eighty-eight thousand.[35] The 1996 census figures indicate that the AICs command a following of about 10.66 million people, representing 35.4 percent of all Christians in South Africa. Zion Christian Church, Shembe Church, Ethiopian Catholic Church in Zion, Ethiopian Orthodox Church in South Africa, and the Bantu Peace Holiness Apostolic Church in Zion, among others. Although Asamoah-Gyadu is convinced that the AICs are generally in decline in Africa, he concedes that they are vibrant in

South Africa,[36] where the Zion Christian Church (ZCC), for instance, commands a membership of 4.9 million, emerging as one of the biggest churches on the continent.

The nomenclature and recognition of AICs by mainstream Christianity has undergone a kind of mutation, ranging from outright condemnation as non-Christian, to total acceptance as key players in church history.[37] Although Barret, in 1968, recognized the growth and expansion of the AICs in the last hundred years as unparalleled in the entire history of the church,[38] Strassberger, in 1974, was categorically convinced "that many of the African Independent Churches can hardly be classified as Christian churches."[39] This rejection of AICs by Strassberger should have been measured because, Sundkler's seminal work, *Bantu Prophets in South Africa*, gives clear evidence that many of the AICs emerged as splinter groups from mainstream Christianity, who, if they developed new practices, did not lose their original Christian orientation.[40] With time, researchers began to develop a more appreciative response to these churches, and terminologies such as "Pentecostal-oriented independent churches" was coined by Rossouw,[41] while Anderson refers to them as "Pentecostal-type," all in an attempt to differentiate AICs from classical Pentecostals and Neo-Pentecostals, whose practices, unlike the AICs, appear uncontroversial to mainstream Christianity. The acceptance of traditional rituals and religious practices by some AIC's is the crux of the matter concerning their catholicity. For instance, Sundlker suggests that this engagement of African Christianity with African mores is a kind of syncretism that creates a link back to the past.[42] But others insist that instead of regarding AICs as bridges back to traditional religion, they should rather be acknowledged as emerging churches that are trailblazers to the future of authentic indigenous African Christianity.[43] Kealotswe intimates that, by the middle of the twentieth century, the AICs had firmly established themselves "theologically as genuine expressions of the Christian faith from an African perspective."[44] In my opinion, the orthodoxy debate on AICs should consider the possibility of sanctifying their rituals for acceptable Christian participation, but more importantly, we should focus on the morality of their conduct and practices.

Pentecostalism and Christological Morality

Davies finds the fulfilment of the ethical monotheism of Judaism in

Jesus' ministry and teaching, insisting that the ethical aspirations of the law and prophets are fully accomplished rather than abolished in Jesus' moral discourse.[45] Grenz emphasizes the relational dynamics of Christian ethics over a mere legalistic response to commands. "Jesus knew that inward piety and not outward conformity to the law marks true obedience to God because God's intent focused on establishing relationships."[46] However, restricting Jesus' ethical message to the didactic or teaching passages presents a limited view of the extensive scope of his moral concerns. The moral focus of some of the parables presents us with such piercing ethical assessments that no direct teaching could lend more force. An example of this kind is seen in Jesus' concealed attack on racism in the parable of the Good Samaritan (Luke 10:30–37). In Hays' estimation, "stories form our values and moral sensibilities in more indirect and complex ways, teaching us how to see the world, what to fear, and what to hope for; stories offer us nuanced models of behavior both wise and foolish, courageous and cowardly, faithful and faithless."[47] One area of weakness of Pentecostal theology, and for that matter, its ethics, is the low emphasis it places on Christology. Pentecostal ethicists may, therefore, be challenged by Hays' comprehensive view of Jesus' ethical heritage, which appreciates the total moral significance of his life and ministry by fusing his pronouncements and parables with the complete Jesus narrative of the incarnation, ministry and selfless service, passion, crucifixion, and resurrection.[48]

José Míguez Bonino rejects arguments that Pentecostal faith is Bible-centered; he thinks their focus is basically inspirational, seeking direction to solve mundane problems rather than doctrinal formulations.[49] This overriding concern of appropriating divine power to solve existential problems informs Land's opinion that Pentecostals focus more on the benefits of participating in the divine life than striving for moral uprightness.[50] This perceptive observation of Land's is unfortunately true, as we see the movement's current focus shifting more towards prosperity, success, healing, prophecy, and social security, rather than morality.

Contemporary Challenges

It is suggested that Pentecostals/charismatics appear to be more focused on the benefits of participating in divinity than experiencing the attitudinal change inherent in this relationship. This position is supported by the mantras such as, "African Christianity is a mile wide and an inch deep," and "African Christianity generates more heat than light." These imply that theological concepts that target moral transformation and attitudinal change received less attention compared to success, miracles, and triumphalist ideas. For instance, the favorite text of Pentecostals is Acts 1:8 (NIV), "But you will receive power when the Holy Spirit comes on you, and you will be my witnesses in Jerusalem, and in all Judea and Samaria, and to the ends of the earth." Which is suggestive of empowerment and conquest. Material from the Gospels is selectively applied in the Pentecostal context, with attention frequently directed to miracle narrative rather than teaching material. It is interesting to observe that one text from the teachings of Jesus, which is prominent with Pentecostals, is, "Give, and it will be given to you. A good measure, pressed down, shaken together and running over, will be poured into your lap. For with the measure you use, it will be measured to you." Luke 6:38 (NIV). And the benefits derived from its application are obvious. In many instances, ethical passages such as the Sermon on the Mount and Romans 12 are overlooked for periscopes like the stilling of the storm and the miraculous haul of fish. The impact of this truncated approach to theology is what Miller et al. appropriately lament, "Today there are more churches and more Christians in the world than at any time in history. But to what end? Poverty and corruption thrive in developing countries that have been evangelized."[51] This situation is probably attributable to the cross-fertilization of traditional religious ideas of Africans with Christianity. All the advantages of contextualization notwithstanding, it is evident that if culture is the vehicle of the gospel, culture is also its cross.[52] It is observable that religion permeates every facet of traditional African life, and shrines are regularly consulted for protection and prosperity not only in the hereafter, but more importantly, in the present age. In Gyekye's opinion, traditional religions place unrelenting emphasis on the pursuit and attainment of human wellbeing, and religion is essentially considered "as a means of attaining the needs, interests, and happiness of human beings in this life."[53] Furthermore, it is evident that pneumatic experiences encouraged by Pentecostals such as speaking in tongues, prophecy, spiritual healing, and exorcisms resonate well with indigenous African spirituality.[54]

Theologians such as Bediako,[55] Asamoah-Gyadu,[56] and Mwuara[57] acclaim the contextualization and relevance of the Pentecostal churches in "successfully" engaging with the African worldview. This is confirmed by Mwuara's opinion:

> Pneumatic experiences resonate well with indigenous African spirituality, with its belief in the existence of spiritual forces. But whereas in indigenous spirituality people are subject to the capriciousness of spirit forces, in classical/spiritual AICs [African-Initiated Churches], liberation is experienced through the salvific death of Christ and the power of the Holy Spirit, which it made possible.[58]

Mwuara, however, proceeds to identify the inherent pitfalls in this situation of extreme consciousness of spiritual experience. She explains:

> Some prophet-healers capitalize on the fear of people, who believe that their problems arise from witchcraft and sorcery. . . . This reinforcement of the belief in witchcraft and sorcery (much as we accept it is a reality in Africa) has entrenched this belief. There are people who are unwilling to look beyond these beliefs for the sources of their problems, even when there is a logical explanation to them.[59]

The ethical problem that emerges from this situation is that the obsession with superstition tends to weaken congregation members' sense of responsibility. To reiterate, the African worldview projects a high level of consciousness of spiritual reality; it is often claimed that evil spirits operate variously through witchcraft, dwarfs, ghosts, mermaids, and ancestral curses which work to harm people or impede their progress. In traditional society, it fell to the priests to identify and exorcise people burdened by evil spirits to prevent them from harming the community. Some Pentecostal ministers seem to have taken advantage of these traditional beliefs by specializing in handling the demonic through witchcraft accusations and what is termed "deliverance." We might suppose that with the benefit of formal education and exposure to science and technology, current African Christian leaders would be equipped to respond to these prehistoric societal problems with a balanced spiritual perspective. But the grip of witchcraft and superstition on the consciousness of many Pentecostal leaders directs their ministry to engage in pre-scientific age practices such as witch-hunting; a worrisome development. As Gifford observes, Asamoah-Gyadu is also convinced that some deliverance ministers are merely capitalizing on people's fear of tragedy to manipulate and abuse them.[60]

Deliverance Ministries in South Africa

Among the AICs and a new brand of Pentecostal ministries, which I think should be better classified as Pentecostal Prophetic Deliverance Ministries (PPDM), there are a lot of controversial practices emerging which generate a lot of moral concerns. Some of these practices appear to blend the biblical approach to the use of means in healing with traditional religious methods. So bizarre were certain healing and deliverance methodology used by some prophets that the central government had to intervene with the view to regulate religion in South Africa. Consequently, the government of South Africa has set up the Commission for the Promotion and Protection of the Rights of Cultural, Religious, and Linguistic Communities (CRL Rights Commission). Among the eight mandates, the following resonates with Pentecostal ministries:

1. Investigate and understand further issues surrounding the commercialization of religion and traditional healing

2. Identify the causes underlying the commercialization of religion and traditional healing

3. Understand the deep societal thinking that makes some members of our society vulnerable and gullible on views expressed and actions during religious ceremonies

4. Enquire about the various miraculous claims that are made by religious leaders and traditional healers regarding powers to heal and create miracles.

Some of the stunning practices from the prophetic deliverance ministries, which hit the media headlines provoking such a governmental response, are extremely unusual, such as asking congregation members to eat grass and drink petrol, spraying insecticide on congregation members, asking congregation members to masturbate. Kgatle has written an article on, "The Unusual Practices within Some Neo-Pentecostal churches in Africa," which closely examines some of these bizarre practices.[61] The South African public was stunned when in July 2015, pictures hit television screens and social media, revealing Pastor Penuel Mnguni of End Times Disciples Ministries in Soshanguve, feeding a snake to some of his congregation members. The photos were captioned, "Man of God declared a snake to become a chocolate (chomp) and the congregation ate it. We have the authority to change everything into anything and it will obey because of our authority."[62] In 2014, Pastor Lesego Daniel of Rabboni Centre Ministries outrageously asked his congregation members to drink Petrol at church. He told them, "the petrol had been turned into pineapple juice and persuaded people to line up to take a sip from a bottle of the liquid."[63] The same pastor has asked his congregation members to eat grass on one occasion, and at another time, fed them with flowers, all in the name of deliverance.[64]

On March 16, 2018, about seventy people marched to the offices of the CRL Commission to petition the commission to prevent the abuses being meted out by false prophets to their congregation members. The following press statement was released ahead of the march: "the march is to say 'enough is enough' in regards to sexual abuses, rape, manipulations, deceptions, etc., which many Christians have experienced in the hands of false prophets."[65] Among the marchers were nine women from Klerksdorp (North West) who had been abused financially and sexually by a bishop, with some of them nursing his children.[66] The march, which was organized by Charles Farai, Solomon Ashoms, and Martins Antonio, was captioned #BushiriMustFall. According to Antonio, he was determined to expose Bushiri because the prophet had broken down his marriage by prophesying to his wife that Antonio's mother was a witch, which caused trauma in the family.[67] Prophet Shepheard Bushiri of Enlightened Christian Gathering (ECG) reacted by seeking a court injunction to prevent the march without success.

These extreme cases might not be a fair representation of Pentecostals and their leaders, as many of them lead stable, productive, and responsible lives, worthy of their Christian confession. Nevertheless, one can argue that a single case of abuse at church is one too many. Therefore, a multidimensional approach may be necessary to curb this social menace of Pentecostal abuse. Africa is bedeviled with a hydra-headed situation of socio-economic problems such as extreme poverty, bribery and corruption, conflicts and terrorism, war and economic refugees, HIV/AIDS, Ebola, conflict, abusive political and institutional leadership, slavery and human trafficking, gender inequality, inimical cultural practices, and the church has added one, "Pentecostal prophetic abuse."

Notes

1. Allan Anderson, "Towards a Pentecostal Missiology for the Majority World" (a presentation at International Symposium on Pentecostal Missiology, Asia-Pacific Theological Seminary, Baguio City, Philippines, January 29–30, 2003), 1.

2. Pan African Conference of Third World Theologians, "The Final Communique" in *African Theology en Route*, Kofi Appiah-Kubi and Sergio Torres, eds. (Maryknoll, NY: Orbis Books, 1979), 192.

3. Kwame Bediako, *Jesus in Africa: The Christian Gospel in African History and Experience: Theological Reflections from the South* (Yaounde, Cameroon: Editions Cle, 2000), 22.

4. Bolaji Idowu, *Towards an Indigenous Church* (London: Oxford University Press, 1965), 24–26.

5. Samuel Waje Kunhiyop, *African Christian Theology* (Grand Rapids, MI: Zondervan, 2012), 44

6. D. Crafford, "The Church in Africa and the Struggle for an African Identity," *Skrif en Kerk* 14:2 (1993), 167.

7. John V. Taylor, *The Primal Vision: Christian Presence Amid African Religion* (London: SCM Press, 1963), 33.

8. Robert J. Schreiter, "Jesus in Africa Today" in Robert J. Schreiter, ed., *Faces of Jesus in Africa* (Maryknoll, NY: Orbis Books, 1991), viii.

9. Schreiter, "Jesus in Africa Today," viii.

10. Erasmus, cited in Roland H. Bainton, *Erasmus of Christendom* (Peabody, MA: Hendrickson, 1969), 23.

11. Emmanuel Bolaji Idowu, *African Traditional Religion: A Definition* (London: SCM, 1973), 190.

12. Dela Quampah, *Good Pastors Bad Pastors: Pentecostal Ministerial Ethics in Ghana* (Eugene, OR: Wipf & Stock, 2014), 43.

13. Harvey Cox, *Fire from Heaven: The Rise of Pentecostal Spirituality and the Reshaping of Religion in the 21st Century* (Boston: De Capo Press, 1995), 82.

14. Kunhiyop, *African Christian Theology*, 59.

15. Allan H. Anderson, "Pentecostalism and the Pre-African Spirit World" (a study presented at the European Research Network on Global Pentecostalism Conference, University of Uppsala, Sweden, June 10–11, 2016).

16. Quampah, *Good Pastors*, 32.

17. David Bosch, *Transforming Mission: Paradigm Shift in Theology of Mission* (Maryknoll, NY: Orbis Books, 2008), 421.

18. Schreiter, "Jesus in Africa Today," viii.

19. Cox, *Fire from Heaven*, 82.

20. Pierre Rossouw, *Ecumenical Panorama: A Perspective from South Africa* (Roodeport, South Africa: Transo Press, 1989), 251.

21. Roussouw, *Ecumenical Panorama*, 251.

22. John W. de Gruchy and Steve de Gruchy, *The Church Struggle in South*

Africa (Minneapolis, MN: Fortress Press, 2005), Kindle Locations 330–331.

23. Vincent Anane Denteh, *Revitalizing Mission and Missiology: The Way Forward in the Twenty-First Century* (Mumbai: Quarterfold Printibilities, 2014), 167.

24. De Gruchy, *The Church Struggle in South Africa*, Kindle Location 303. Kindle Edition

25. De Gruchy, *The Church Struggle in South Africa*, Kindle Location 342. Kindle Edition.

26. Rev. Hermy Damons, formerly a senior minister in Rhema Bible Church was interacting with a group of The Church of Pentecost ministerial students at Kempton Park on March 6, 2016.

27. J. Kwabena Asamoah-Gyadu, "'Born of water and of the Spirit': Pentecostal/Charismatic Christianity in Africa," in Ogbu U. Kalu, ed., *African Christianity: An African Story* (Trenton, NJ: Africa World Press, 2007), 341.

28. Bengt G. M. Sundkler, *Bantu Prophets in South Africa* (Oxford: International African Institute, 1976), 39.

29. Sundkler, *Bantu Prophets in South Africa*, 40.

30. Sundkler, *Bantu Prophets in South Africa*, 48.

31. Matthew Clark, "Mission Effort in the Apostolic Faith Mission of South Africa," *Transformation* 26:3 (July 2009), 174–185.

32. Clark, "Mission Effort," 177.

33. See "Our History," Full Gospel Church of God, http://fgcsa.co.za/about-us/our-history, accessed March 15, 2018.

34. David Goodhew, "Growth and Decline in South Africa's Churches, 1960–91," *Journal of Religion in Africa* 30:3 (August 200), 361.

35. Goodhew, "Growth and Decline," 346–369.

36. Asamoah-Gyadu, "Born of Water and the Spirit," 341.

37. Anderson, "Pentecostalism and the Pre-Christian African Spirit World," 6.

38. D. B. Barrett, "The African Independent Churches," in H. Wakelin Coxhill and Kenneth Grubb, eds., *The World Christian Handbook* (London: Lutterworth Press, 1968), 24.

39. Elfriede Strassberger, *Ecumenism in South Africa: 1936–1960* (Johannesburg: South African Council of Churches, 1974), 89.

40. For instance, the first Ethiopian Church in South Africa was founded by a Wesleyan Methodist minister, Mangena M. Mokone, who seceded to form this because of the racial discrimination he had to endure in the Wesleyan Church. See Sundkler, *Bantu Prophets in South Africa*, 9.

41. Roussouw, *Ecumenical Panorama*, 251.

42. Sundkler, *Bantu Prophets in South Africa*, 238–294.

43. D. Crafford, "The Church in Africa and the Struggle for an African Identity" (a presentation at the Symposium on Serving the Independent Churches, Hammanskraal, South Africa, August 1992), 172. See also J. B. Kailing, "Inside Outside, Upside Down: in Relationship with African Independent Churches," *International Review of Mission*, 77 (1988), 38–52.

44. Obed Kealotswe, "The Nature and Character of the African Independent Churches (AICs) in the 21st Century: Their Theological and Social Agenda," *Studia Historiae Ecclesisticae* 40:2 (December 2014), 229

45. W. D. Davies, "Ethics in the New Testament," in George Arthur Buttrick, ed., *Interpreter's Dictionary of the Bible* (Nashville: Abingdon, 1962), vol. 1, 168.

46. Stanley J. Grenz, *The Moral Quest: Foundations of Christian Ethics* (Downers Grove, IL: IVP, 1997), 109.

47. Richard Hays, *The Moral Vision of the New Testament: Community, Cross, New Creation: A Contemporary Introduction to New Testament Ethics* (Edinburg: T&T Clark, 1996), 74.

48. Hays, *Moral Vision*, 74.

49. José Míguez Bonino, "Changing Paradigms: A Response," in *The Globalization of Pentecostalism: A Religion Made to Travel*, Murray W. Dempster et al., eds. (Oxford: Regnum, 1999), 117–18.

50. Steven Jack Land, *Pentecostal Spirituality: A Passion for the Kingdom* (Sheffield: Sheffield Academic Press, 1993), 23.

51. Darrow L. Miller, Bob Moffitt, and Scott D. Allen, *The Worldview of the Kingdom of God* (Seattle: YWAM Publishing, 2005), 13.

52. Quampah, *Good Pastors*, 163.

53. Kwame Gyekye, *African Cultural Values: An Introduction* (Accra: Sankofa, 1998), 14.

54. Philomena Mwaura, "New Religious Movements: A Challenge to Doing Theology in Africa," *Trinity Journal of Church and Theology* 18:3 (July 2003), 8.

55. Bediako, *Jesus in Africa*, 22.

56. J. Kwabena Asamoah-Gyadu, *African Charismatics: Current Developments within Independent Indigenous Pentecostalism in Ghana, Studies of Religion in Africa* (Leiden: Brill Academic, 2004), 17.

57. Mwaura, "New Religious Movements," 8.

58. Mwaura, "New Religious Movements," 8.

59. Mwaura, "New Religious Movements,"16.

60. Interview with J. Kwabena Asamoah-Gyadu, Trinity Theological Seminary, Legon, Accra, June 2, 2009.

61. Mookgo S. Kgatle "The Unusual Practices within Some Neo-Pentecostal Churches in South Africa: Reflections and Recommendation," *HTS Teologiese Studies/Theological Studies* 73:3 (2017), 1.

62. Mpho Raborife, "Pretoria church photos go viral over snake-eating," *News 24*, https://www.news24.com/SouthAfrica/News/Pretoria-church-photos-go-viral-over-snake-eating-20150715, July 15, 2015, accessed May 8, 2018.

63. Ted Thornhill, "First he had his congregation eating grass to make them 'close to God,' now controversial South African preacher makes his flock drink PETROL," *Mail Online*, http://www.dailymail.co.uk/news/article-2794275/first-congregation-eating-grass-make-close-god-controversial-south-african-

preacher-makes-flock-drink-petrol.html, October 15, 2014, accessed May 8, 2018.

64. Stephen Molobi, "Pastor: Grass to Flowers," *Daily Sun*, July 4, 2017.

65. Andre Viljoen, "Christian Group March against False Prophets," *Gateway News*, March 18, 2018.

66. Andre Viljoen, "Christian Group March against False Prophets," *Gateway News*, March 18, 2018

67. Isaac Mahlangu, "Unholy War Over #BushiriMustFall," *Sowetan*, March 12, 2018.

14.

Redundancy in the African Cosmos: Witnessing Jesus Christ as the Only Savior through the Power of the Holy Spirit

Lord Elorm-Donkor

Abstract

Scholars regard the African Pentecostal proclamation of Jesus Christ, which stresses Jesus' power to defeat the activities of evil spirits and set people free, as effective contextualization because it addresses people's felt needs. It is held that for Africans, salvation is not just about a doctrinal belief, but involves actual deliverance from tangible life situations of ill-health, poverty, infertility, famine, drought, etc. This over-emphasis on Jesus Christ as the only reliable power for defeating demonic forces seems to hold many Christians in perpetual fear and never-ending spiritual warfare at the expense of the transforming work of the Holy Spirit for human moral competency. Using the Akan traditional conceptual scheme as an example, this paper argues that good moral relationships with God, physical and spiritual neighbors, and creation, eliminates those spiritual battles as there would be no reason for spiritual attacks. Therefore, instead of Christians overstressing the power of Jesus to overcome evil spirits, they should focus on the transforming power of the Holy Spirit in human hearts, because good relationships deriving from human moral competency will cause redundancy of evil spirits in the African cosmos.

Key words: African, Pentecostals, redundancy, Savior, witnessessing

Introduction

It is now well known that Christian communities that are experiencing continuous exponential growth are those in the global South which emphasize the power and manifestations of the Holy Spirit in their daily practices. In these churches, Jesus Christ is proclaimed as the only Savior through the power of the Holy Spirit against the powers of darkness that militate against human life. For instance, scholars maintain that in many African communities still, there is a strong belief in the incessant evil activities of spirits against the human realm often, causing many misfortunes in people's affairs.[1] People in these places expect from their religions the power to deal with the evil machinations of spiritual entities that manifest as diseases, demonic oppressions, poverty, infertility, etc. Accordingly, most of African Pentecostal witness about Jesus Christ focuses on demonstrating him as the only Savior who overpowers the activities of evil spirits, and sets people free to live a life full of good health and abundant wealth.[2] These Pentecostals use the power of the Holy Spirit to engage in ceaseless spiritual warfare to prove their witness of Jesus Christ as the only Savior. Consequently, there has been an unprecedented growth of Christianity as people are empowered by the Holy Spirit.

However, "It might have been expected that the extraordinary revival of Christianity being experienced across sub-Saharan Africa would have resulted in a public and political life marked by Christian values."[3] But, by and large, the reverse seems to be the case. Political and financial corruption, nepotism, ethnic conflicts, and under-development have remained prevailing features in many African nations and communities. The question is, why is African Pentecostal spirituality not having the desired transformative impact on social morality in African societies?

In this paper, I argue that essentially, many African Pentecostals misdirect the transformative power of the Holy Spirit to fight evil spirits instead of purifying sinful hearts to become obedient hearts that can embody the character of God in all spheres of human existence. I start with a general description of the uniqueness of Jesus, followed by my argument that overemphasis on evil spirits denies African Pentecostals the spiritual resources for authentic personal spiritual growth. I conclude that for the power of the Holy Spirit to transform Christians to realign their moral state and conduct with the character of God to consistently apply godly values in every situation, first, there has to be redundancy[4] in the African cosmos.

Witnessing Jesus as the Only Savior: Reformed and Evangelical Views

A central tenet of protestant Christianity is the stress on personal faith and the experience of Jesus Christ as the only Savior in whom one may have eternal life. The reformers insisted that "the son is better, greater and superior to everyone because in him God has finally and definitely spoken, and the son has finished the cross-work of purification for our sin. . . . [H]e is presented as a unique and exclusive Lord and Savior – the final and perfect self-disclosure of God, our great high priest and conquering king."[5] Evangelicals affirm and protect the uniqueness of Jesus Christ as the central truth of the Christian faith.[6] Although there are differences between fundamentalist evangelicals and ecumenical evangelicals on certain issues, both of these, ecumenical or fundamentalists, are united on the belief in the uniqueness of Jesus Christ.[7]

As far as evangelicals, including Pentecostals, are concerned, eternal life is only achievable through an encounter with Jesus Christ.[8] The Frankfurt Declaration, endorsed by all evangelicals and published in *Christianity Today*, clearly states that "salvation is due to the sacrificial crucifixion of Jesus Christ, which occurred once and for all mankind," and only through participation in faith can this salvation be obtained.[9] Based on Luke 24:47, the emphasis is laid on the universality of sin, and the need for repentance and forgiveness of sins to be proclaimed in the name of Jesus Christ to all nations. This is why for Pentecostals, the proclamation of the gospel in terms of world mission is essential. Pentecostals refer to Romans 10:14–17 to stress the point for missions.

> How, then, can they call on the one they have not believed in? And how can they believe in the one of whom they have not heard? And how can they hear without someone preaching to them? And how can anyone preach unless they are sent? As it is written: "How beautiful are the feet of those who bring good news!" But not all the Israelites accepted the good news. For Isaiah says, "Lord, who has believed our message?" Consequently, faith comes from hearing the message, and the message is heard through the word about Christ (Rom 10:14–17 NIV).

Also, the evangelical declaration in the Lausanne Covenant affirms Jesus as the "only God-man, the only mediator between God and man," for which reason any suggestion that implies that "Christ speaks through all religions and ideologies" must be vehemently contested and rejected.[10]

Thus, for evangelicals, the possibility that one could be saved without believing in Jesus Christ is an aversion.

But it is important to note that in our contemporary globalized world, among Christians generally, some Pentecostals included, there is broader understanding or openness to the inclusiveness of the salvific work of Jesus Christ.[11] In the era of postmodernist thought, the view of Jesus alone as the Savior has been challenged in various ways. Religious pluralism and spiritual hospitality have meant that what once was widely accepted as truth is now being passionately questioned through ideas of pluralism and inclusivism. Don Carson defines pluralism as "The view that all religions have the same moral and spiritual value, and offer the same potential for achieving salvation, however 'salvation' be construed."[12] For pluralists, Jesus is the way God has provided for Christians, and God has made other ways in other religions by which people can get right with God and obtain eternal happiness. In other words, the pluralists believe that through the sacrifice of Jesus Christ on the cross is useful for Christians, it is not required for non-Christians.[13] This view extends further to make Jesus Christ inclusive rather than exclusive. "Inclusivism is the view that all who are saved are saved on account of the person and work of Jesus Christ, but that conscious faith in Jesus Christ is not absolutely necessary: some may be saved by him who have never heard of him, for they may respond positively to the light they have received."[14]

Conversely, for most African Pentecostals, the position remains clear that Jesus Christ is the only Savior because of his uniqueness. African Pentecostals believe that Jesus' taking up of human nature without losing his divinity is important for the signs and wonders that draw many sinners to Christ. Thus, Jesus Christ is unique in that only he was able to take up full humanity without losing his divine nature. In his role as prophet, king and priest, Jesus alone satisfies the requirement for the salvation of humanity. Again, Jesus' work as savior, sanctifier, healer, baptizer in the Holy Spirit, and soon coming king makes him the unique Savior of the world. Generally, Pentecostals believe that it is only through the word of the gospel of Jesus Christ, the signs and wonders, which people encounter as good news that people can be saved by faith, through the grace of God. They believe that, essentially, it is the Holy Spirit that opens people's understanding to get to know Jesus Christ as the Savior of the world.

Moreover, African Pentecostals' focus on the power of the Holy Spirit for evangelism is based on the belief that it is the Holy Spirit who leads people into the saving knowledge of Jesus Christ. Thus, most African Pentecostals believe in the reformed position that, "Apart from the work of the Holy Spirit, who works through the word of the gospel of Christ there is no faith, and no new birth, and no salvation."[15] This makes the Holy Spirit central to God's work of salvation in the world, and African Pentecostals stress the manifestation of the power of the Holy Spirit in all their practices. But how does Pentecostals' stress on the Holy Spirit validate the truth that Jesus is the only Savior? How does it address the socio-political and economic issues in Africa?

Witnessing Jesus as the Only Savior: African Pentecostals

Though African Pentecostals have the same view of Jesus Christ as other Pentecostals elsewhere, their witness of Jesus is intentionally contextualized to address real-life issues as they understand them. In his study of African Christology, Victor Ezigbo notes that any theologian who fails to think contextually and does not take culture and context into account in his or her effort to understand how a people witness to Jesus is in error.[16] He argues cogently that "No Christian community can successfully and meaningfully answer Jesus' question of 'who do you think I am' (Mark 8:29) in foreign thoughts and concepts."[17] Ezigbo explains further that cultures, history, languages, and experiences provide for a people their cognitive framework to interpret and appropriate their encounters with Jesus Christ.[18] Accordingly, although all Pentecostals have the same orthodox view of the person and work of Jesus Christ, African Pentecostals interpret and appropriate this view contextually to make sense of their daily challenges in life.

Extant Christological formulations in Africa insist that Africa should not be burdened with Christological definitions of Western Christianity because the issues those formulations address are not necessarily relevant to African experiences. It is argued that the Christological controversies of the past that were formulated in foreign languages and thought-forms that addressed issues that are not related to the life experiences of Africans.[19] Some scholars propose that Christological formulations should focus on discerning the "reality of Jesus in relation to current issues in the respective contexts."[20] Therefore, it is important to understand what the statement, "Jesus is the only Savior through the power of the Holy Spirit" means to African Pentecostals and how they witness to this truth. Knowing how biblical Christology is applied to daily life experiences of Christians might prove to be a corrective against staid spirituality in other Christian traditions.

Jesus as the Life-Giver

For African Pentecostals, proclaiming Jesus as the only Savior is not just a theological proposition or statement but a real-life experience. J. Kwabena Asamoah-Gyadu argues convincingly that "Pentecostalism is an experiential religion par excellence. . ." and that "Pentecostal churches are thriving in Africa and among African communities in the West primarily because of their emphasis on belief, experience, conviction, and commitment to what the Spirit of God is doing in the world."[21] For these Christians, salvation is not just about a doctrinal belief but involves actual deliverance from tangible life situations of ill-health, poverty, infertility, famine, drought, etc. Thus, the statement "Jesus is the only Savior" means that among all the other religious systems available, Jesus Christ is the only one who brings them the salvation they desire in powerful and concrete ways. Thus, Jesus is seen as the most powerful force that can conquer all other malevolent spiritual forces to protect, deliver, provide, and care for the Christian. Accordingly, the dominant Christological formulation in Africa considers Jesus Christ essentially as a life-giver. While Christ is also seen as mediator, healer, ancestor, and loved one, these are understood as being geared towards life-giving.[22]

In this way, the focus on Jesus as the only Savior tends to emphasize him as the only reliable agent from whom African Christians can draw transcendent power through the Holy Spirit to defeat demonic forces. Jesus is regarded as the only one who brings fulfillment to all the religious aspirations of the African heritage.[23] He is the deliverer who saves people from all inhumane situations and places them in a safer environment where they can enjoy life in full.[24] Also, Jesus is "considered as belonging to the most powerful realm of divinity, the realm of spirit power."[25] He is king, conqueror, protector, supplier, deliverer, and protector of the individual and the community from practical enemies in life.[26] Moreover, very importantly, Jesus is the healer *par excellence*. The African Pentecostal believes whatever Jesus does today is done through the power of the Holy Spirit. They regard the Holy Spirit as the source of God's power, which is given so that personal needs and all other forms of powerlessness can be addressed. Mbiti stated that Pentecostalism helps African Christians to see, know, and experience Jesus Christ as the conqueror over forces such as poverty, witchcraft, sorcery, anxiety, sickness, and death, from which Africa needs liberation.[27] The Holy Spirit also liberates humanity from the oppression of both the spirit world and Western "colonial" forms of Christianity.[28] The power of the Holy Spirit confronts traditional beliefs in witchcraft and provides a substitute for the African deities and all other religious claims. The question of how this view might help to deal with Africa's perennial political and economic crises remains a relevant one.

John Pobee has said in an interview with Diane Stinton that "The test of any cultural construct of the gospel is whether it enables growth, change, and transformation in and into the image and likeness of God through Christ."[29] The question is whether or not African Pentecostal's contextual witness of Jesus as the only Savior engenders real spiritual growth and moral transformation into the image of God. Does this contextual Christology result in the social and political transformation of African societies? To this question, Matthew Ojo has shown that in spite of the massive numerical growth, there is an obvious moral crisis in Africa in the political and socio-economic spheres. He thinks there is distrust in the transformative potential of Christian spirituality in this era more than any other time in post-colonial Christian history, and many people would agree.[30] That is to say, African Christian spirituality is unable to offer a liberating option that would positively impact governance in Africa. Other scholars are curious about how African Christians will meet the challenge of persistent poor governance, various forms of social deprivation, and weak economic performance across the continent.[31] As such, as we celebrate the progress of a vibrant Christianity across Africa, we should also be actively aware that conditions in social and public spheres are way below Christian ideals. But why is it that this enthusiastic, practical, and contextualized Christianity is not making the desired impact of transforming African societies by Christian values and principles?

Before answering the question, it is necessary to state that African Pentecostalism has made a positive impact on African Christianity, and even rejuvenated the historic mission churches. Also, at the individual level, "there is evidence that Pentecostal practices have empowered some individuals to emerge from their misery and self-pity to take advantage of the power available to them through the Holy Spirit, and this has transformed their lives and circumstances, socially, economically and psychologically."[32] However, the understanding and character necessary for a wider social morality is still lacking.

One of the major reasons is that in applying the power of the Holy Spirit to deal with their issues, African Pentecostals over-emphasize the malevolent activities of evil spirits. Inadvertently, they end up enlisting numerous spirit forces in endless spiritual warfare. The never-ending spiritual wars Pentecostals fight force them to channel almost all the spiritual resources they receive from the Holy Spirit into fighting evil spirits. As such, they deprive themselves of the transformative effect of the power of the Holy Spirit for personal growth, morality, and Christian character. The unrelenting effort to fight and overcome evil spirits robs the movement of the productive power of the Holy Spirit — the power needed for making them true witnesses. Although many of these Pentecostals are zealous for the gospel, they mostly take witnessing as a project to be implemented, instead of a complete life of being witnesses. Undoubtedly, overemphasis on the Holy Spirit primarily as a means to overcome the maleficence of evil spirits is a major issue and one of the main reasons for lack of personal transformation that can translate into good governance and socio-political leadership in the African continent.[33]

Another reason, which in fact, is linked to the first, is that African Pentecostals pursue a contextualization that is wrongly premised. This movement rightly deserves the commendations they receive for their efforts to make Christianity relevant to the lived experiences of Africans. But in the process, they start on a wrong premise or basis of the African worldview. Almost uncritically, they believe that every unpleasant life condition: ill health, unemployment, singleness, marital disagreements, draught, poverty, etc., emanates from evil spirits that are always working against human beings. So, the logical thing they do is to fight to overpower these enemy forces so that they can have a more abundant life (John10:10). Using the Akan people of Ghana as a case study, I have argued that the Akan traditional religious view of the causes of evil is different from what Ghanaian Pentecostals have appropriated.[34] In other words, they are providing answers to questions that the traditional scheme does not ask.

Traditional Religious Basis of African Pentecostal Spiritual Warfare

The core of Pentecostal contextualization in Africa is based on the African traditional religious belief that there are wicked spiritual beings who influence human existence in negative ways. Scholars have attested to the fact that when people adopt a worldview that is different from their own, their former worldview persists in their minds, and still influence their beliefs and actions. For instance, in his study of the Kikuyu people of Kenya, Sung Park has shown that Christianity and globalization did not succeed in changing their worldview. According to him, the fundamental worldview assumptions of the Kikuyu still survive in the minds of the Kikuyu "either intact or modified."[35] Charles Kraft also stated that "Even radical paradigm shifts, such as … the introduction of Christianity into previously unevangelized societies, permit a large measure of continuity with antecedent worldview assumptions and the strategies built on them…. Yet many features of the old [worldview] will continue on, often in modified form, into the new."[36] In Africa, the traditional religion (ATR) pervades all aspects of human life and is essential for understanding the contextualized practices of Pentecostals.[37] Although religious expression in Africa may vary from one tribe to the other, the core philosophy of ATR is similar, and there is now an understanding among most African scholars of this religion that in spite of the variations, in essence, ATR is the same.[38]

The continuity of worldviews is a human phenomenon. Throughout the history of Ghanaian Christianity, belief in the power of evil spirits to influence human affairs has persisted. In the 1940s Ephraim Amu showed that this belief was resilient among many Ghanaian Christians of all social status.[39] Later, Mathias Forson studied Ghanaian Methodists and concluded that many Christians believed and understood events of their lives through the prism of the African traditional religion.[40] Opoku Onyinah has confirmed that among Christians, there is still a common belief in malevolent spiritual activities against people.[41] Moreover, Thomas Oduro affirms the point when he states in a recent interview that,

We are surrounded by spirits, and we interpret whatever happens to us in the spiritual realm. And, therefore, we always want somebody who is more powerful than the spirits, to protect us, and lead us through the darkness, and to be our guide and to link us to *Onyankopong*, the Supreme Being. . . . Without him [Jesus] we would have been trying other lesser deities to test their powers, and they may disappoint us. . . . But to know Jesus Christ as someone who created these lesser deities and therefore, more powerful and next to God, makes one rest assured that he does not have to run after gods, and shrines, and fetish priests.[42]

The statement above reveals the religious assumptions of many African Christians and, in this particular case, Ghanaian Christians. Firstly, these Christians believe they are surrounded by spirits in their communities, and every evil that happens in the human realm is interpreted as emanating from the spiritual realm. So, when people are poor, ill, infertile, when there is continuous drought, floods, etc., the spirits are believed to be responsible in one way or the other. It is important to state that in spite of the huge contribution that African Pentecostal Christianity makes to the evangelization of the world, a lot of its witnessing of Jesus Christ has focused on the power of the Holy Spirit to overcome evil spirits in the African cosmos. Thus, both in Pentecostal preaching and prayers, a lot of importance is given to evil spirits.

Onyinah states that preaching and practices of spiritual warfare in contemporary Pentecostalism in Africa give too much focus to Satan than necessary, and give less attention to the word of God, and for that matter, to God.[43] He makes an important statement that highlights the view in this paper that, in witnessing Jesus Christ as the only Savior, spiritual warfare advocates accuse evil spirits of every evil, including poverty in African communities, and spend most of their time praying to demolish the evil powers and render them powerless.[44] By so doing, these Pentecostals "reinforce the 'primitive animistic belief system' that hinders progress and keeps communities and people in servile fearfulness."[45] As Charles Aye-Addo argues, the need to eradicate the nefarious activities of the spirits completely, or render them ineffective, is the foremost concern of most Africans, whether that African resides in the West, East or other parts of the African world.[46] But the question is, how do we eradicate the activities of evil spirits or render them ineffective, since the battle does not seem to be abating?

Ezigbo's statement below is useful to answer this question as it shows that in its current form and strategy, the battle against evil spirits will not stop soon. He states,

The emphases on spiritual warfare perpetuate three quests which are derived from the traditional religion — the quest to understand the relationship between the human and spiritual world, the quest to manipulate, appease or defeat evil agents to attain wellbeing, and the quest to identify a reliable agent through whom they can interpret and appropriate their experience.[47]

The three quests imply that Africans will continue to fear the acts of evil perpetrated against them from the spirit realm and will constantly explore a ceasefire through a reliable agent. Put in another way, the emphasis on spiritual warfare tries to solve the questions: how do we relate to the spiritual realm that we believe exists and impacts our human realm, how do we get the spiritual realm to be always kind to us, and who can help us maintain the desired amicable co-existence? To answer these questions, which I believe are serious ontological questions, we first need to understand what the African traditional conceptions say about the causation of evil. Once the origin or cause of evil is identified it is easier to determine who might be a reliable agent to deal with it.

4.1. The causes of evil and human responsibility for it

Traditional Akans believe that the Supreme Being is wholly good and does not create evil. Kwame Gyekye affirms that evil is the result of human beings and spirits exercising their free will. Likewise, Kofi Busia argued persuasively that the issue of theodicy does not arise in Akan traditional religion because there is a gap between the Supreme Being and humans, which is filled with "…many powers and principalities, good and bad, gods, spirits, magical forces and witches to account for the strange happenings in the world". Evil spirits act on their own initiative to cause evil. But they do so based on their perception of how well or ill human beings treat them. It is good relationships between humans and spirits that ensure people receive constant kindness from their ancestors or deities. On the other hand, immoral deeds by humans cause offense to good spirits and make them withdraw their kindness, subjecting a person or entire communities to the wicked actions of evil spirits. To a large extent, these spirits choose to be evil by their own use of free will prompted by how they feel about their relationship with human beings.

Thus, most evil acts that originate in the spirit realm are regarded as having been caused by human conduct in the physical realm. The most important lesson in this conception is that consistency in good moral conduct is the ideal. To avoid the attacks of the evil forces, people are expected to have good relationships that ensure people do not mistreat each other or act disrespectfully toward the spirits. Basically, it is human action that triggers evil from the spiritual realm.[48] Although there is mutual dependency among humans and spirits, the notion that human beings are ultimately responsible for much of what happens to them and that they can influence the course of events is highly stressed in traditional Akan society.[49] Humans are never passive victims being subjugated by forces external to them. In fact, much of what happens to a person is "regarded as justifiably and predictably proceeding as consequences from his [or her] own precipitating acts."[50] Gyekye states emphatically that evil is seen as proceeding from the desire, conscience, character, and thoughts of humans, and hence is the outcome of the human's free will.[51]

In view of the foregoing, it is clear that African Pentecostal attribution of all misfortune to spiritual causality is not born out in Akan traditional religious conception, which they claim they contextualize the gospel to address. As this is the situation, how should African Pentecostals witness Jesus Christ as their reliable agent, the only Savior who can deliver them from the evil attacks of the spirit realm? This paper proposes that Pentecostal Christians embark on causing redundancy of the evil spirits in the African cosmos so they can channel the power of the Holy Spirit for their personal transformation and social morality.

To explain the idea of redundancy, it is important to restate the case at hand. Firstly, it has been established that the way African Pentecostals contextualize Jesus as the only Savior is based on a wrong premise that evil spirits are on the loose attacking people at will, without any cause, so they need a powerful Savior to protect them. But actually, in the traditional religious scheme it is not the case that evil spirits just cause havoc to their submissive victims arbitrarily. At least from the Akan traditional perspective, human beings have never been passive victims of evil spirits. Instead, it is believed that every evil or misfortune that befell people was triggered by his or her moral misdeeds. Since this is the case, what human beings need is the power to be consistently ethical in their relationships with each other. Once they can maintain consistent moral relationships with other humans and with the spirit realm, the war would be over resulting in massive redundancy in the African cosmos.

Redundancy in the African Cosmos

First of all, it is important to explain the idea of redundancy that is being used here. During the 1980s and 1990s, in Ghana, redundancy was a word every child or dependant dreaded. In those days, the government of Ghana and other African governments launched an Economic Recovery Program (ERP) at the behest of the World Bank (WB) and the International Monetary Fund (IMF).[52] The goal was to reduce government debt by increasing productivity and export. To achieve this goal the government aimed, through the ERP, to direct its economic resources to priority sectors to produce more goods. It was believed that many organizations had more workforces than they needed and that, although huge resources were expended on them, they did not contribute productively to the economy. In other words, large economic resources were being used in sectors that did not make any contribution to the growth of the economy. To prevent wastage of economic resources to increase production, the government used a method called 'redundancy.' It meant that those workers whose roles did not contribute to the growth of the economy did not have any job to perform anymore — they were sacked from their roles to allow for resources to be channeled toward more economically productive activities.[53]

Jesus Christ as the Only Savior of the Sinful Human Heart

J. B. Masinde, a Kenyan pastor, makes an insightful observation about how the world's problems might be solved, arguing:

> When all is said and done, all of us need to find out, where do we begin to tackle the problems of humanity? It's not in the lab, it's not in the streets, it's not in the parliament, it's in our hearts. And the only thing that seems to adequately address the issues of human hearts, whether it's in African heart or a European heart, is the person of Jesus Christ and his teachings. . . . [H]e is the only person who talks about issues of the heart and addresses them in a way that nobody else does.[54]

Pastor Masinde quite rightly identifies the most crucial issue that all human beings have to deal with – the issue of our sinful human heart and how it leads people to conduct their lives in all relationships and interactions in the world. Since beliefs from the traditional worldview persist in the minds of many African Christians, pastors, theologians, and missiologists must understand what these schemes really imply. At least with the Akan conceptual scheme, the responsibility for good relationships is laid on the human being. If humans can live well with each other and with the spiritual realm, then there would be peace, blessing, and flourishing. But because the human heart is deceptive and is the source of all evil, Pentecostals must focus the power of the Holy Spirit on the human heart to get it purified from sinful desires: greed, jealousy, envy, hatred, pride, lust, etc., so an authentic Christian spirituality can emerge and remain. The goal of that new spirituality would be consistent efforts to be like Jesus in all humans' dealings; to love, to forgive, to share with, and to serve other people.

The one thing that is essentially needed is a means for how human beings can live amicably with one another and with their deity. It is clear from the Akan scheme that the spirits become evil and work against human beings only when humans fail in their right relationship with each other, with the ancestors, and with the deities. To stop the evil spirits from unleashing havoc on the human realm, Christians should nurture a Christian lifestyle that is consistent with the values of God. Witnessing Jesus Christ as the only Savior should be about the church transforming every sphere of society by the principles and values of the kingdom of God. It should be about ". . . making believers aware of the dual purpose of God, that we are called to be God's people and sent into the world to transform it."[55] Witnessing Jesus should be about announcing the good news about Jesus Christ to every nation, tribe, and family, and inviting and empowering people to transform their social, economic, and political spheres with Christian values. This should give everyone the opportunity to be saved from whatever situation they are in, whether social deprivation, spiritual bondage, economic stagnation, political incompetence, and other similar predicaments. Transforming every sphere of society means living as a transforming agent in every situation where the moral nature of God is not formed in people's lives.

Christians' Weapon of Spiritual Warfare in Ephesians 6:10–18

Apostle Paul addressed the issue of spiritual warfare in the last chapter of his Epistle to the Ephesians. He listed certain Christian values and principles as the weapons for spiritual battle. Paul's list of weapons shows that the Christian's fight against principalities and powers of darkness is won already in the death of Jesus Christ and that Christians only need to live their lives with the values and principles of God. These are: truth, righteousness, integrity, service, faith, victor mentality instead of victim mentality (salvation), and complete trust in the Holy Spirit with constant prayers. Christians have accepted the truth of revelation, and are now indwelt by the risen Lord, who is, himself, the truth. So, believers have to consistently show a character that springs from the truth. With faith, the believer can extinguish all the destructive devices thrown by the devil. Faith effectively counteracts the danger of any diabolical missiles by neutralizing its effects and prevents it from spreading to other people or places. The faith of believers is supposed to cause them to live productive lives in the hope that God is always with them through the power of the Holy Spirit (2 Cor 5:7). Paul teaches that Christians are not to fear or focus on evil spirits, but to live their lives as victorious people. As they do so, the evil spirits will not have work to do.

Conclusion

This essay discussed how some African Pentecostals witness to Jesus Christ as the only Savior through the power of the Holy Spirit. It is shown that though focus on the power of the Holy Spirit is generally an expectation of all Pentecostals, the presumed brutality of evil spirits in Africa makes Pentecostals there more aggressive in constantly using the power of the Holy Spirit in spiritual warfare. As a result of the over-emphasis on fighting evil powers, the necessary power of the Holy Spirit for personal growth, moral competence, and social transformation is all used on the never-ending spiritual battles. This situation denies African societies the desired transformation that Christianity is expected to bring to their political and economic spheres. The essay has proposed redundancy in the African cosmos, a process by which believers focus their attention to become true agents of transformation whose lifestyles reflect the values and principles of God as seen in Jesus Christ, and leaves no room for evil spirits to attack them, or if even they do, their attacks would be harmless.

Notes

1. Allan H. Anderson, *Spirit-Filled World: Dis/Continuity in African Pentecostalism* (London: Palgrave Macmillan, 2018); and "The Spirit and African Spiritual World," in Vinson Synan, Amos Yong, and J. Kwabena Asamoah-Gyadu, eds., *Global Renewal Christianity: Spirit Empowered Movements, Past, Present and Future* (Lake Mary, FL: Charisma House, 2016), 317; Paul Gifford, *Ghana's New Christianity: Pentecostalism in a Globalising African Economy* (Bloomington, IN: Indiana University Press, 2004); Opoku Onyinah, *Pentecostal Exorcism: Witchcraft and Demonology in Ghana* (Blandford: Deo Publishing, 2012); Opoku Onyinah, *Spiritual Warfare* (Cleveland, TN: CTP Publishing, 2012).
2. See Allan H. Anderson, *Zion, and Pentecost: The Spirituality and Experience of Pentecostal and Zionist Apostolic Churches in South Africa* (Pretoria: UNISA, 2000); Allan H. Anderson, *African Reformation: African Initiated Christianity*

in the 20th Century (Trenton: African World Press, 2001); Allan H. Anderson, "African Initiated Churches of the Spirit and Pneumatology," *Word and World* 23:2 (2003), 178–184; Ogbu Kalu, *African Pentecostalism: An Introduction* (Oxford: Oxford University Press, 2008), chs. 9, 10, 11; Asamoah-Gyadu, *African Charismatics: Current Developments Within Independent Indigenous Pentecostalism in Ghana* (Leiden: Brill, 2005), chs. 5, 6, 7.

3. Kenneth R. Ross and Wonsuk Ma, "Conclusion: Spirituality as the Beating Heart of Mission," in *Mission Spirituality and Authentic Discipleship* (Oxford: Regnum, 2013), 225–227.

4. I have defined and explained the word redundancy as I intend it in this paper in section entitled, "Redundancy in the African Cosmos."

5. Stephen Wellum, *Christ Alone,the Uniqueness of Jesus as Saviour: What the Reformers Taught and Why it Still Matters* (Grand Rapids, MI: Zondervan, 2017), 110.

6. They have used declaration upon declaration to argue against what they consider as liberal theological positions about other religions and evangelization of the world in historical documents such as the Frankfurt Declaration and the Lausanne Declaration.

7. Paul F. Knitter, *No Other Name?: A Christian Survey of Christian Attitudes Towards World Religions* (Maryknoll, NY: Orbis Books, 1992), 78.

8. Knitter, *No Other Name?*, 79.

9. *Christianity Today* 14 (1970), 843.

10. Gerald Anderson and Thomas Stransky (eds.), *Mission Trends:* No.2: *Evangelization* (New York: Paulist Press, 1975), 239–248.

11. See Tony Richie, *Toward a Pentecostal Theology of Religions: Encountering Cornelius Today* (Cleveland, TN: CPT Press, 2013); See also Knitter, *No Other Name ?*, 75–159.

12. D. A. Carson, *The Gagging of God* (Grand Rapids, MI: Zondervan, 1996), 278–279.

13. John Piper, *Jesus: The Only Way to God: Must You Hear the Gospel to be Saved?* (Grand Rapids, MI: Baker Books, 2010), 24.

14. Carson, *The Gagging of God*, 278.

15. Piper, *Jesus: The Only Way*, 44.

16. Victor Ezigbo, "Jesus as God's Communicative and Hermeneutical Act: African Christians on the Person and Significance of Jesus," in Gene L. Green, Stephen T. Pardue, and Y. Y. Yeo (eds.), *Jesus Without Borders: Christology in the Majority World* (Carlisle, UK: Langham Partnership, 2015), 39–40.

17. Ezigbo, "Jesus as God's Communicative," 39.

18. Ezigbo, "Jesus as God's Communicative," 39.

19. Diane Stinton, *Jesus of Africa: Voices of Contemporary African Christology* (Maryknoll, NY: Orbis Books, 2004), 252.

20. Stinton, *Jesus of Africa*, 252.

21. Kwabena Asamoah-Gyadu, "The Promise is for You and Your Children: Pentecostal Spirituality, Mission, and Discipleship in Africa," in Ross and Ma,

Mission Spirituality, 10–29.

22. Laurenti Magesa, *African Religion: The Moral Traditions of Abundant Life* (Maryknoll, NY: Orbis Books, 1997), 24.

23. Lord Elorm-Donkor, *Christian Morality in Ghanaian Pentecostalism* (Oxford: Regnum, 2017), 178.

24. Donkor, *Christian Morality*,178.

25. Donkor, *Christian Morality*, 179.

26. Clifton Clarke, *African Christology: Jesus in Post-Missionary African Christology* (Eugene, OR: Pickwick, 2011), 159.

27. John Mbiti, "Some African Concepts of Christology," in George F. Vicedom (ed.), *Christ and the Younger Churches: Theological Contributions from Asia, Africa, and Latin America* (London: SPCK, 1972), 51–62.

28. Anderson, "African Initiated," 186.

29. Stinton, *Jesus of Africa*, 250.

30. Matthews A. Ojo, "African Spirituality, Socio-Political Experience, and Mission," in Ross and Ma (eds.), *Mission Spirituality*, 59.

31. Ross and Ma, "Conclusion: Spirituality," 226.

32. Donkor, *Christian Morality*, 38. See also Asamoah-Gyadu, *African Charismatics*, chs. 5–7.

33. This point is not about the debate on the relationship between religion and state. The point here is about how a person's religious beliefs shapes his or her character so she or he consistently acts ethically in all political and social relationships.

34. Donkor, *Christian Morality*, ch. 2.

35. Sung Kyu Park, *Christian Spirituality in Africa: Biblical, Historical, and Cultural Perspectives from Kenya* (Eugene, OR: Pickwick, 2013), 152.

36. Charles Kraft, *Anthropology for Christian Witness* (Maryknoll, NY: Orbis, 1996), 436.

37. Park, *Christian Spirituality*, 164.

38. Magesa, *African Religion*, 26; John Mbiti, *African Religions and Philosophy* (Nairobi: East Africa Educational Pub., 2002), 1.

39. Ephraim Amu, "The Position of Christianity in Modern Africa," *International Review of Mission* 29 (1940), 478–489.

40. Mathias Forson, "Split-Level Christianity in Africa: A Case Study of the Persistence of Traditional Beliefs and Practices Among Akan Methodists of Ghana" (PhD. Diss.: Asbury Theological Seminary, 1993), 4.

41. Onyinah, *Pentecostal Exorcism*, 106.

42. Stinton, *Jesus of Africa*, 228.

43. Opoku Onyinah, *Spiritual Warfare: A Centre for Pentecostal Theology Short Introduction* (Cleveland, TN: CPT Press, 2012), 15–18.

44. Onyinah, *Spiritual Warfare*, 15–18.

45. Onyinah, *Spiritual Warfare*, 18.

46. Charles Sarpong Aye-Addo, *Akan Christology: An Analysis of Christologies of John Samuel Pobee and Kwame Bediako in Cconversation with*

Karl Barth (Eugene, OR: Pickwick, 2013), 52.

47. Ezibgo, "Jesus as God's Communicative," 54.

48. Helaine K. Minkus, "Causal Theory in Akwapim Akan Philosophy," in Richard A. Wright (ed.), *African Philosophy: An Introduction* (Lanham: University of America Press, 1984), 140–41.

49. Kwame Gyekye, "The Problem of Evil," in Wiredu and Gyekye (eds.), *Person and Community*, 470.

50. Minkus, "Causal Theory," 140.

51. Gyekye, "The Problem of Evil," 470.

52. E. Gyimah-Boadi, "Economic Recovery and Politics in the PNDC's Ghana," *Journal of Commonwealth & Comparative Politics* 28:3 (1990): 328–343; Richard Sandbrook, *ThePpolitics of Africa'sEconomic Recovery* (Cambridge: Cambridge University Press, 1993).

53. Of course, the ERP came under severe criticism in Ghana for ignoring the economic plight of many people. See Richard Jeffries, "Urban Popular Attitudes Towards the Economic Recovery Programme and the PNDC Government in Ghana," *African Affairs* 91 (1992), 207–226.

54. Stinton, *Jesus of Africa*, 228.

55. Eric Nyamekye, "Possessing the Nations: Equipping the Church to Transform Every Sphere of Society with the Values and Principles of the Kingdom of God" (A keynote address from the Vision 2023 Document of the Church of Pentecost, Gomoa Fetteh, Ghana, January 22, 2019).

15.

Witnessing to Jesus Christ as the Only Savior through the Power of the Holy Spirit: An Asian Experience

Julie C. Ma

Abstract

Key religions such as Hinduism, Buddhism, Confucianism, and pervasive Animism have shaped cultures and worldviews in Asia. In spite of the influence of Western civilization in recent times and of economic developments, distinctive religious beliefs are deeply rooted and have practices widely practiced throughout this vast continent. Therefore, the exclusive Christian claim on Jesus Christ as the only Savior has to negotiate these religious orientations and worldviews. Christianity has often met stiff resistance and sometimes bloody persecution. This study focuses its attention on the Pentecostal impact upon a tribal region of the Philippines, resulting in radical conversions and social impact. This experience is also compared to the author's personal conversion experience to highlight a typical Asian experience with Christianity.

Key words: Buddhism, Shamanism, worldview, religion, ancestral worship

Introduction

In Asia, all the major religions are alive and active. They include Buddhism, Confucianism, Hinduism, and Islam. Besides these, various forms of animism are widespread. They have been deeply embedded in culture and people's lives for millennia. Confucianism was begun around 551–479 BC by Confucius; Buddhism began in the fifth century, and Hinduism began 1500 BC.[1] Islam is the youngest among them. Though Asian societies are rapidly changing due to the impact of increasing secularistic and materialistic trends, they are still intensely rooted in their religious beliefs and practices. Observation suggests that the more they are exposed to secularistic change, the more resolutely they pursue after blessings from their deities. Many Asians still faithfully keep their religious beliefs and practices which have been passed down throughout generations, even though they are living in a very modern society. The pervasive presence of animism continues, influencing established religions. For example,

> Korean Buddhism and shamanism have developed in a close relationship, influencing each other, while at the same time retaining their idiosyncratic characteristics. As attested to throughout its long history, Buddhism has been known for its tolerance toward other religions, particularly in its ability to incorporate shamanism and folk religions into its practice. The case of Korea provides ample evidence to support this notion.[2]

Christianity came to Asian countries in different periods. In the modern era of Protestant mission, several names immediately emerge: In 1793, William Carey went to India, where Marshman and Ward soon joined him. Hudson Taylor started China's in-land mission in 1865. In the following years, many more missionaries, including Roman Catholic, were present in different parts of Asian countries and bore evangelistic fruits. Many of these efforts went beyond other, heavily Westernized, endeavors. A result was that, due to this cultural respect, some Asian churches became indigenized towards "culturally Asian Christianity."[3]

This study will overview the worldviews of several major Asian religions, including animism, to examine the extent of their influence in shaping the perception of Asians and culture. The discussion includes the worldview of the Kankana-ey tribe of the northern Philippines as an example of animists.[4] Despite the differences in beliefs and practices among various animistic groups, there is a set of fundamental common beliefs found among all animists: spirits exist, and they animate the world. The next part will introduce a few cases in which the power of the Holy Spirit was manifested, which functioned as an impactful witness to Christ's supremacy and lordship, as the Savior.

Asian Worldview

A worldview is comprised of assumptions, perceptions, and values. Worldview does not stand on its own, but it coexists with culture, which is external and takes the form of visible expression. Worldview is underneath the external and visible cultural forms. People's behavior is a feature of culture, while people's thinking is in the "level of their worldview." To reveal the "inter-influential nature of the two, a simple illustration may be of help. When a big piece of wood (culture) is thrown into the river, the river water splashes back (worldview) to the surface of the water in and around the area of the wood. These two always go side by side."[5]

Religious beliefs have profoundly shaped the worldview of Asians through many assumptions and perceptions. A person's fundamental assumptions are undisputable. For instance, a tribal group named Hae Enga in India trusts, like any animist, that their ancestor spirits are intensely working in their everyday matters. A tiny boy was sick, and his symptoms pointed to pneumonia. The father thought that the illness derived from the ghost of his mother. Furthermore, villagers assumed that his mother demanded pork. However, the father was not willing to sacrifice a pig. Several days later, the son died. The whole family, as well as the villagers, believed that the boy's mother took his life. It is not because he did anything wrong, but because the spirit's demand was not met. This was the tribe's worldview, and asking if this is correct or incorrect is the wrong question. They instinctively understood that the spirit did it. The mother enjoyed pork during her life; hence, it was believed that her spirit desired pork even after her death. People in the village likely placed a "high value on pigs," and this extended to create an assumption that the spirits favor pigs over other animals.[6] The Hae Enga tribe considers offering a pig to the spirits of more value than selling it.

Collectively, the majority of Asian cultures believe in the existence of spirits and their association in the personal and communal life of the living. Frequently, people experience dread of "attacks from spirits" and "to prevent such attacks by deceased spirits; sacrificial offerings are made."[7] These old assumptions do not simply vanish, even in the middle of rapid societal changes with robust materialistic and secular influences.

In the Chinese *yin-yang* worldview, husbands are regarded as the "sky" and wives as the "earth." In this male-superiority context found throughout most of Asia, what men state is considered more valuable than what women would say. For China, the root of this value is often attributed to the great and powerful influence of Confucianism. A value is deeply biased with people's feelings. It is any notion denoting a "desirable or undesirable state of affairs. The desirable or undesirable position of problems refers to values or what it ought to be."[8] It further describes,

> As an illustration of the desirable and undesirable state, the Hae Enga tribe believes that a husband and his wife should not sleep in the same house, and a woman should not enter a man's house where he is sleeping. The strong concept that men and women should sleep in separate houses leads to a value that men are superior to women. On the other hand, when values are violated, in this case, by a man sleeping in the same house as his wife, mother, or sisters, which seldom goes unnoticed, it becomes an undesirable state of affairs. In such a case, an attempt to make a justified exception, for example, because he is old or weak, reflects another value of the community toward the aged or destitute.[9]

Observing how one educates (often his or her children) is an additional vital way to study certain customary values. In Asia, parents teach their children appropriate behaviors. For instance, bowing one's head to the aged in some cultures displays respect. Waving one's hands to the aged is considered inappropriate. Who checks the appropriateness of behaviors and also how these values are communicated to the next generation discloses the hierarchy of values. Value is related to people's emotional states, and it functions to determine the desirable and undesirable state of problems.

Asian Religious Teachings

In the following sections, teaching and perception of Hinduism, Confucianism, Buddhism, and Animism are discussed.

Teaching of Hinduism

In the absolute notion of Hinduism, Brahman is the beginning, reason, and basis for everything. It is "neutral" and not personal. Indians see numerous characteristics or roles of divinity displayed in a variety of formulas. In the "Vedic hymns,"[10] a god is not wholly perceived in human languages. The gods are the exhibitions of nature or "cosmic forces." Godly terms may be uncountable, but they are all assumed as the "expressions of Brahman." Even though Brahman might have unlimited formulas, it is still viewed as one in the core.[11]

Raymond Hammer postulates on Hindu ethics:

> In classical Hinduism, actions (*karma*) and duty (*dharma*) were the dominant

concepts. *Karma*, as the accumulation of good and evil acts, would influence a person's destiny, but there was no one way to acquire good *karma*. Early in the Veda, there had been the notion of a prevailing moral law (*rita*), of which Mitra and Varuna were the guardians. Humanity had to recognize a divine imperative, and prayer and sacrifice were necessary to maintain the right relationship between the divine and the human. Sin, however, could be either moral or ritual.[12]

Only a perfect ethic is associated with the ability of a person to free themselves from the "cycle of rebirth." It is what the "ascetic" focus of Hinduism points to, as an exercise to pursue "salvation." Hindus are to retain essential ethics, "refraining from killing, stealing, sexual impurity, or the consumption of intoxicants." If they fail to do this, they are unable to attain the vital pureness needed to take them further on the path of *moksha* ("release").[13]

In addition to fulfilling their moral duty, their pledge of dedication to the gods is also required for *moksha*. According to Hindu teaching, the gaining of *moksha* has to do entirely with the gods. Mainly, "grace alone" allows the devotees to achieve *moksha*. It seems that the theology of the Christian God's grace discovers here an outstanding contact point in Hindu thought.[14] Human endeavor is vital in taking the final goal, *moksha*. However, there should be grace from deities to make this complete.

Teaching of Confucianism

Singaporean and Malaysian Chinese, Chinese in China, Korean, and parts of Japanese cultures were formed by Confucian philosophy. Confucianism seeks for impeccable human beings within the sphere of the world. Confucianism is a Latinized name, assigned by the seventeenth-century Jesuit missionaries. *Fu* is the Chinese term for Confucianism. *Fu* literally means scholars with the special meaning of Confucianism from the T'ang dynasty. It also encompasses a broader meaning as an intellectual culture and is commonly considered as philosophy (*chia*). It refers to the basics of "worship, ritual, and sacrifice, which are religious teachings."[15] However, theoretical instruction, which is connected to ethics, is far superior to any other feature of Confucianism.

Confucianism is highly recognized for its ethical teaching, as noted by Confucius (551–479 BC), Mencius (371–289 BC), and Hsun-Tzu (298–238 BC).[16] "Nonetheless, Confucianism gives primary emphasis to the ethical meaning of human relationships, finding and grounding the moral in the divine transcendence."[17] The epitome of Confucianism is Confucius himself. He is considered to be an extraordinary teacher. The foundation of his instruction was the concept of humankind (*Jen*). "As Buddhists emphasize compassion and Christians emphasize love, *Jen* is the ultimate goal of self-transformation" for the Confucian. As Confucius underscored the moral aspect of humanity, "he made it clear that it was Heaven itself which protected him and gave him his message: Heaven is the author of the virtue that is in me."[18]

However, Confucianism also has a distinctive aspect of mysticism:

> It is grounded in religion—the inherited religion of the Lord-on-high, or Heaven. Even the great rationalist Hsun-Tzu sees society founded on the penetrating insight of the sagely mind. Moreover, though Confucianism is less known for its mysticism, the *Book of Mencius*, as well as other works, cannot be fully understood except in the light of mysticism. The *Chung–Yung*, one of the "Four Books," which became the basis for Confucian self-cultivation in the Southern Sung (1126–1279 CE), explicitly states that the sage, having realized true integrity (*ch'eng*), becomes one with Heaven and Earth. Confucian moral metaphysics reaches over into the religious quest for unity with the ground of being.[19]

Confucius showed ethical teachings by his religious consciousness, though he evaded debating the relationship between human nature and the "Way of Heaven." By contrast, Mencius created his whole scheme of beliefs around these two notions. He endeavored to reveal how the very center of the "Way of Heaven," or the "heavenly power of the cosmos," could be human nature. He assumed that, if this human nature could be aptly polished and cultivated, even the ordinary person could be "wise."[20]

Confucianism emphasizes relationships. The "vertical relationship" contains, firstly, filial piety, the utmost of all merits, and the foundation of all decent works. The correct performance of filial piety is the foundation of the five prime relations: "between ruler and subjects, respecting rulers; father and son, respecting and honoring father; husband and wife, obeying husband; brothers, honoring elders; and friends, showing affection, loyalty, and trust. Confucianism teaches ethics in relationships with different levels and groups of people."[21]

In this structure, there is no notion of "horizontal relationship with spirit beings." Confucius and Mencius neither recognized nor repudiated the existence of God and the gods or the immortality of the soul. They were human trainers of ethics and morals. They talked about Heaven (*Tien*) and adored its guard. However, "Neo-Confucianists later cultivated the atheistic idea of *Tai-Chi* (Supreme Ultimate) and *Wu-Chi* (Supreme Ultimateless)."[22]

People may wonder if Confucianism is a religion because there is no concept of gods to worship or honor. On the other hand, it has religious elements: ancestor reverence and rites, though these are not a matter of beliefs but ethics.

> Ancestral worship was first introduced to China at the beginning of the Chou dynasty (1122–325 BCE). It was Confucius (551–479 BCE) who popularized this practice by his teaching on filial piety, decreeing that parents and elders are to be honored and respected while they are alive. This sense of reverence continues after their deaths. The Chinese believe that at death, the soul of the deceased ancestor resides in three places. One part goes to Heaven, the second remains in the grave to receive sacrifices, and the third is localized in the ancestral tablet or shine. The soul has to be assisted as it journeys to Heaven. Hence, at Chinese funerals, elaborate rituals are meticulously carried out to ensure that the soul is amply provided for on its course.[23]

Children are primarily in charge of the well-being of their parents' spirits. The ancestor spirits play an enormously vital part in the existing household, according to Confucian teaching. They are a cause of assistance and defense, and they lead their offspring through an ambiguous future with supervision. This belief strengthens the teaching of filial piety, as people trust the spirits of their ancestors to help them live a useful life. Though Confucianism teaches about many different relationships, the basic one is the relationship between father and son. This teaching, keenly combined with other religions by various groups in Asia, has become a part of more extensive religious traditions.[24]

Buddhism: Understanding Human Suffering

Siddhartha Gautama, the founder of Buddhism, was hugely affected by the instructions of Hinduism. Thus, Buddha was a "reformer of Hinduism, just as Luther was of Roman Catholicism."[25] Siddhartha struggled with the query of how to be free from the sorrow of constant "rebirths." Buddha's unique wish was merely to renew Hinduism, using his innovative methods. His instruction, hence, does present central notions of the traditional Indian religion, namely the doctrine of rebirth and the law of karma.[26]

Buddha[27] discovered significant facts by himself, which became the critical ideas of "Buddhist philosophy." Firstly, existence is suffering. The "knowledge of suffering" says all humanity is desperate and filled with agony. Such teaching says that suffering begins at birth with a variety of problems: old age, illness, worry, ache, anguish, adversity, and other destructive components of life.[28]

Secondly, truth concerns the "origin of suffering," as,

> Suffering and indeed all existence (since they are the same) has its source of desire and ignorance: "But what, O monks, is the noble truth of the origin of suffering? It is that desire (*tanha*) which results in rebirth, that desire bound up with longing and greed, which indulges itself now here, now there; the desire of the senses, the desire to be, the desire to destroy oneself."[29]

Thirdly, truth matters in the destroying of suffering. Suffering must be ultimately sacked and ought not to persist for one's entire lifetime. The crucial lessons of Buddhism are to provide humans with perpetual liberation from suffering. Humans must be freed from the endless cycle of rebirth and dying again (*samsara*), and finally, get into the "blessed condition of *nirvana*."[30] This is a drastically new realm from the visible world, where rebirth and connected *dukkha*[31] will no longer rise again. This is the everlasting territory, the completely "dependable, the true refuge."[32]

Fourthly, truth teaches the way to the abolition of suffering: the honorable eight-fold ways. "Essentially, it is concerned with three things: with morality (right speech, right action, right occupation), with spiritual discipline (right effort, right mindfulness, right composure), and with insight (right knowledge, right attitude)."[33]

During its long history and development, Buddhism has merged with several indigenous spirit-believing religions to a complex degree. Consequently, the intended teachings of Buddha are not clear anymore in people's minds. Numerous gods and spirits were added for the suitability of believers to achieve their desires through the "spirits' trans-empirical power."[34] To further elaborate,

> The film *An Initiation of Shaman*, for instance, clearly shows the convergence of Buddhism and shamanism. It is the story of a woman who was forced to become a shaman not by her own will, but by the desire of spirits. She went through a process of resistance and struggled with the spirits, and this made her life full of misery, as she had no desire to become a shaman. However, she could no longer resist and finally surrendered herself to the spirit. One scene in the movie shows the initiation process of her shaman hood. The spirits in the room were depicted as Buddha, the same Buddha, but with different faces and looks and quite different from the ones that I saw in a Buddhist temple. I immediately noticed a confluence of two religious systems: Buddhism and shamanism. I regularly include this video presentation in

my Folk Religion class to illustrate the point of syncretism as well as the world of the spirits.[35]

Among typical Korean Buddhists, it is entirely suitable to seek a shaman or other religious practitioners for assistance. People frequently look for the assistance of the spirits through mediums (or shamans), for example, to be aware of what would happen in the future. My mother is a typical example. She was a dedicated Buddhist who faithfully went to a Buddhist temple, bringing her children with her for the slightest extenuating circumstance. She was very affected by her mother, my maternal grandmother, who was deeply dedicated to Buddhism. However, my grandmother was also a shaman, playing the role of a medium who could connect the living with dead spirits. When my mother encountered a problem, such as a sickness in the family, she went to a village shaman for his or her help. Often the shaman would come to our house to cast out the evil spirit that was believed to have caused the trouble. She (often it was a female shaman) would dance up and down, while someone played the gong. After that, she ate food prepared by my mother, which had been initially offered to the spirit. I believe the shaman was also a Buddhist who regularly attended the local temple more often than average members did. However, in their daily lives, they were more conscious of the spirit world.

It is worthy to note that Asians had already been wholly orientated to the spirit world when Buddhism came to various Asian countries. Because the fundamental teachings of Buddhism do not include the role of the spirits in everyday life, the prevailing practice of combining animism with Buddhism is not a surprise.

Belief of Animism

The description in this section derives from my own empirical experiences among the Kankana-ey tribe of the northern Philippines.
Animism is defined as:

> A belief in personal spirits and impersonal spiritual forces. Animists also perceive that the spirits and forces have power over human affairs. People who have experienced such spiritual power and influence always seek their help to meet various daily human needs such as healing, success, and decisions for the future. They attempt to manipulate the power of the spirits for a favorable future.[36]

Animistic belief takes seriously spirit beings such as "gods, ancestor spirits, ghosts, nature spirits, and demons in their understanding of the world." The spiritual forces are impersonal powers exposed in diverse ways, such as "magic, astrology, witchcraft, the evil eye, and through sorcerers." In their belief, both organic and non-organic beings intermingle with the human in their everyday lives. "The power of the spirits and the forces can convey evil as well as good."[37]

The Kankana-eys perceive that spirits are beyond the human domain and reside under the earth. They further believe that all human beings have a spirit, which joins with other spirits after they are deceased. These spirits intimately connect with people, intermixing with their lives as though they were living.

This belief indicates that human beings are linked not only with the "creatures of the natural world but also with the beings of the supernatural world." This correlation unavoidably forces animists to get nearer to the spirits, and this explains the "mysteries of human life, such as pregnancy, illness, and death."[38] The Kankana-eys believe that these spirits connect with humans through dreams and omens. Religious practitioners like village priests seek ways to communicate with the spirits through rituals, frequently offering sacrifice.

Case Studies

Radical Conversion of Kankana-eys to Christ

The Kankana-eys have been keeping their traditional religious practices, called *canyao*, from one generation to another. Tribal people believe that their ancestor spirits obtain the power to bless, heal, and meet their needs. Hence, each time they encounter a critical problem, they go to a village priest to consult, and the priest prescribes what they must do. Needless to say, they are instructed to perform a ritual. The priest tells the date, place to perform a ritual, and the kind and number of animals to sacrifice, either pigs, cows or chickens, etc. The Kankana-eys believe that the ancestor spirits are closely associated with them and dwell in their community, and the control of this belief is so rigid that it has withstood outside influence to break the system. Through numerous generations, the Kankana-eys have established these beliefs and practices as part of their life.

The message of God's power was preached and demonstrated among the Kankana-eys by Christian workers and missionaries. God's supernatural power was revealed remarkably, and countless people have turned from their traditional religion to Christ. Some phenomenal accounts which radically drew them to God will be delineated.

In 1948, an American woman missionary Elva Vanderbout and several local workers conducted revival meetings in Tuding, Benguet Province,[39] which continued for a long duration. The Holy Spirit stirred the hearts of the people, and many non-believers accepted Christ as their personal Savior and experienced the baptism of the Holy Spirit. At the end of the meetings, more than 150 were baptized in water. At one time, old and young adults and children shared the testimonies of God's marvelous power which they experienced. Many more surrendered their lives to Christ. They expressed their joy over salvation.[40] In every revival meeting, many were baptized with the Holy Spirit and fire, according to Acts 2:4. It was like old-time Pentecost.

> God's supernatural healing power was displayed in various worship services. One girl eighteen years of age, who had suffered as a deaf-mute for twelve years, was instantly healed. During each morning and night service, the sick lined up to be prayed over for healing.[41] God healed deaf-mutes by the scores; the blind received their sight; and people with paralysis were healed. People suffering from tuberculosis and many other sicknesses were healed. One famous woman in the city was healed of an enormous goiter. It partly diminished when she was prayed for on Saturday night, and when she returned to the Sunday morning service, it had disappeared entirely. A man of twenty-eight years of age, who had been a deaf-mute all his life, was cured instantly one morning.[42] The eight-day salvation and healing revival were marvelous, and countless people came to the Lord, and myriads of sick people were healed.[43]

At another revival meeting, there was a tremendous outpouring of the Holy Spirit, and around forty experienced the baptism of the Holy Spirit. There were numerous exceptional conversions of eminent government officers, such as the deputy-governor of the sub-province, his wife, and their daughter. The mayor of a nearby city had a healing experience; as he shared an amazing testimony, many came to Christ. Such phenomena were acknowledged as the ministry of the Holy Spirit.

My Conversion Experience

My initiation to Christianity was unique. I was raised in a very strong Buddhist-Shamanist family. I grew up in a southern port city where taboos and shamanistic rituals were prevalent. Many people in my area hardly heard the name of the Christian God. The most spiritual member of my family was my maternal grandmother, who was a famous medium or shaman. She was mainly known among her clients for her ability to call up the spirits of the deceased. Being the first grandchild of hers, I became her favorite grandchild. She took me wherever she went. She even took me when she was invited by her client to bring up the spirit of the deceased husband or wife. The invitee prepared a lovely table for the spirit with scrumptious foods, which I enjoyed enormously. However, my grandmother passed away in her 60s, quite an early age. This made me feel miserable and often lonely. Her presence, to me, was exceptional.

My exposure to Christianity was unusual. One day, the English teacher of my high school invited all students to the auditorium without telling us what special occasion it would be. When I entered the auditorium, I had quite an unusual scene unfolded before me. The teacher played a recording of a conversation of a Christian lady with "angels" in her trance-like spiritual state. She was taken to Heaven, seeing many beautiful houses prepared for faithful people of God. As a teenager, it had such a powerful impact on me that I later found myself in prayer in an empty church near my home. I was on my knees on the bare floor and felt tears on my cheeks. Until then, no one taught me how to pray. The ensuing years were filled with battles against the hostility and persecution from the rest of my family for my new-found "foreign" faith.[44] In the following year, I attended a three-day revival meeting in a holiness church in the city, which belonged to the same denomination of the church where I began my Christian walk. A speaker of the revival meeting strongly encouraged us to seek the baptism of the Holy Spirit. With an increasing desire for the spiritual experience, I spent the whole night in the church, praying for the spiritual baptism. Around 3:00 a.m., all of a sudden, my tongue rolled in and began to speak in tongues. Then the wave of the weeping of repentance overcame me, although I did not know what specific sins I was repenting. Then another long period of quietness followed. The Holy Spirit was intimate in this powerful experience.

When my family nearly disowned me due to my new-found faith, I decided to begin a theological education away from home. At the same time, I had a clear sense of calling from the Lord. My faith, similar to that of my husband's mother, developed stronger and bolder in the face of severe hostility and persecution. My faith in God became a wonderful testimony to my immediate siblings, and they all came to Christ, serving the Lord beautifully.

Concluding Remarks

Each religion provides unique teachings based on religious philosophies. However, there are many similarities between Buddhism and Hinduism, mainly because Buddhism was significantly influenced by Hindu teaching and philosophy. The moral teachings of Confucianism are deeply engrained in the lives of people and passed on from one generation to another. Its foundational teachings are filial piety and ancestor veneration. No matter how swiftly people and society change, such beliefs and practices remain for centuries. As discussed above, almost all the major Asian religions share a belief in the spiritual world, and they were influenced by animism or shamanism in varying degrees.

However, when the power of God is manifested extraordinarily, often through healings and miracles, people, who are firmly bound to their traditional religion, turn more readily to Christ. For example, when the Spanish missionaries came to the Philippine mountain area as early as 1610 to introduce the gospel and salvation of God, the tribal people, who were ancestor worshippers (practically animists), rejected them. They burned down a couple of churches built by Roman Catholic priests. In the early 1900s, Protestant missionaries of different denominations came. Their efforts among the mountain tribe yielded only a marginal gain. However, when these same people experienced the overwhelming presence of God and his power through miraculous healing, they were quick to acknowledge his supremacy and bring the entire family to Christ. A village congregation was soon established, and the manifestation of God's power continued. Soon many new churches mushroomed in different mountain regions, and many young people entered Bible colleges with a commitment to serve God.

Although my conversion experience was not so dynamic as those of tribal people, the salvation of all of my siblings testifies to the significance of my testimony. They not only became Christian but also follow the call of God upon their lives. My sister next to me has studied theology and become a minister's wife, serving a church in Korea. My youngest brother is an ordained minister and professor in theological seminary after receiving his advanced degree. He trains students to equip them for the furtherance of God's kingdom.

I desire that the largest continent of Asia (with 4.436 billion people in 2016) longs for the day when the bondage of darkness is broken. Nine of ten Asians still worship ancestor spirits, different spirits, and practice filial piety. The most powerful tool for evangelism is the manifestation of God's love and power.

Notes

1.   Julie C. Ma and Wonsuk Ma, *Mission in the Spirit: Towards a Pentecostal/ Charismatic Missiology* (Oxford: Regnum Books, 2010), 101–107.
2.   Hyun-key Kim, *Syncretism of Buddhism and Shamanism in Korea* (Seoul: Jimoondang International, 2002), xi, 420. See also, *Religious Syncretism: South and East Asians Religions*, https://en.wikipedia.org/wiki/Religious_syncretism. It notes, "Buddhism has syncretized with many traditional beliefs in East Asian societies as it was seen as compatible with local religions. The notable syncretization of Buddhism with local beliefs includes the Three Teachings or Triple Religion that harmonizes Mahayana Buddhism with Confucian philosophy and elements of Taoism, and Shinbutsu-shūgō, which is a syncretism of Shinto and Buddhism."
3.   Ray Porter, *The History of Christianity in Asia*, https://omf.org/blog/2014/07/25/history-of-christianity-in-asia/.
4.   One of fifteen significant tribes in the mountains of northern Luzon, who frequently perform rituals for blessing and healing.
5.   Charles Kraft, *Anthropology for Christian Witness* (Maryknoll, NY: Orbis, 1996), 52.
6.   James Spradley, "Worldview and Values" (Worldview and Worldview Change Class, School of World Mission, Fuller Theological Seminary, 1994), 156. See also Michael Kearney, *World View* (Novato, CA: Chandler & Sharp, 1984), 68–74.
7.   Julie C. Ma, *When the Spirit Meets the Spirits: Pentecostal Ministry among the Kankana-ey Tribe in the Philippines* (Eugene, OR: Wipf & Stock, 2010), 137.
8.   Spradley, "Worldview and Values," 157. See also Paul G. Hiebert, *Anthropological Insights for Missionaries* (Grand Rapids, MI: Baker, 1985), 30–34.
9.   Spradley, "Worldview and Values," 157.
10.   The Vedas are a collection of hymns and other religious texts composed in India between about 1500 and 1000 BCE. It includes elements such as liturgical material as well as mythological accounts, poems, prayers, and formulas considered to be sacred by the Vedic religion.
11.   Raymond Hammer, "Approaches to Truth: The Great Interpreters," in Pat Alexander et al., eds., *Eerdman's Handbook to the World's Religions* (Grand Rapids, MI: Eerdmans, 1994), 183–184.
12.   Raymond Hammer, "Karma and Dharma: Hindu Ethics," in *Eerdman's Handbook*, 190. See also, Gavin Flood, *Hindu Concepts*, http://www.bbc.co.uk/religion/religions/hinduism/concepts/concepts_1.shtml.
13.   Hammer, "Karma and Dharma," 190. See Also, Sunil H. Stephens, "Doing

Theology in a Hindu Context," *Journal of Asian Mission* 1:2 (Jan 1999), 181–203, esp. 185. See also, V. Jayaram, *Hinduism and the Belief in Rebirth*, http://www.hinduwebsite.com/reincarnation.asp.

14. Raymond Hammer, "Concepts of Hinduism," in *Eerdman's Handbook*, 185. See also H. L. Richard, "Evangelical Approaches to Hindus," *Missiology: An International Review* 29 (July 2001), 312–313.

15. Hammer, "Concepts of Hinduism," 185.

16. John Berthrong, "Sages and Immortals: Chinese Religions," in *Eerdman's Handbook*, 248.

17. Berthrong, "Sages and Immortals," 248.

18. Berthrong, "Sages and Immortals," 246. See also, John D. Young, *East-West Synthesis: Matteo Ricci and Confucianism* (Hong Kong: Hong Kong Centre of Asian Studies, University of Hong Kong, 1980), 39.

19. Berthrong, "Sages and Immortals," 246. See also, Ralph R. Covell, *Confucius, the Buddha, and Christ: A History of the Gospel in Chinese* (Maryknoll, NY: Orbis, 1986), 46–48.

20. Berthrong, "Sages and Immortals," 248. See also, Donald Clark, *Culture and Customs of Korea* (Westport, CT: Greenwood Press, 2000), 158.

21. Ma and Ma, *Mission in the Spirit*, 105. See also, Clark, *Culture and Customs of Korea*, 158–159; Don Baker, *Dimensions of Asian Spirituality: Korean Spirituality* (Honolulu: University of Hawaii Press, 2008), 46; Yung Chung Kim, *Women of Korea: a History from Ancient Times to 1945* (Seoul, Korea: Ewha Woman University Press, 1976), 53.

22. Berthrong, "Sages and Immortals," 248.

23. Chua Wee Hian, "The Worship of Ancestors," in *Eerdman's Handbook*, 247.

24. Hian, "The Worship of Ancestors," 249. See also, Yao Xingzhong, *An Introduction to Confucianism* (Cambridge: Cambridge University Press, 2000), 115.

25. Wulf Metz, "The Enlightened One: Buddhism," in *Eerdman's Handbook*, 224.

26. Metz, "The Enlightened One," 224.

27. Metz, "The Enlightened One," 224. See also Ma and Ma, *Mission in the Spirit*, 101–102. Siddhartha Gautama was regarded as Buddha, the initiator of Buddhism, who lived in the sixth century, BCE. His parents named him to mean "he who has reached his goal," and his life story is "shrouded with myths." He was born in about 560 BCE in a village called Lumbini near the boundary between India and Nepal and later passed away at the age of eighty. "One night Maya, the mother of Buddha, had a dream about a white elephant entering her womb. She gave birth to a son, but sadly she died seven days later. This little child was brought up by his mother's sister in affluent and splendorous circumstances. Although he was highly educated in areas of the arts and science, he found that his life did not give him any satisfaction, and he determined to leave that lifestyle and become homeless. He fasted to the point that he lost his

hair. The crucial turning-point before his enlightenment was his awareness of the spiritual and moral vainness of human life and his acceptance of the use of meditation and faith. He taught the public, and people followed him."

28. Drummond, "The Buddha's Teaching," 231.
29. Metz, "The Enlightened One," 232.
30. "In Buddhism as the cessation of all afflictions, cessation of all actions, cessation of rebirths and suffering that are a consequence of afflictions and actions," https://en.wikipedia.org/wiki/Nirvana.
31. Normally translated as "suffering," "pain," or "satisfactoriness" of mundane life, https://en.wikipedia.org/wiki/Dukkha.
32. Metz, "The Enlightened One," 231–32.
33. Metz, "The Enlightened One," 231–32. See also, Sam Littlefair, *What Is Suffering? 10 Buddhist Teachers Weigh In*, https://www.lionsroar.com/what-is-suffering-10-buddhist-teachers-weigh-in/.
34. Ma and Ma, *Mission in the Spirit*, 103.
35. Diana S. Lee and Laurel Kendall, *An Initiation of* Kut *for a Korean Shaman* (videotape; Honolulu: University of Hawaii Press, 1991). See also Ralph R. Covell, *Confucius, the Buddha, and Christ: A History of the Gospel in Chinese* (Maryknoll, NY: Orbis, 1986), 137.
36. Julie C. Ma, "Animism and Pentecostalism," in Stanley M. Burgess, ed., *The Encyclopedia of Pentecostal and Charismatic Christianity* (New York: Routledge, forthcoming).
37. Ma, "Animism and Pentecostalism," 315.
38. Norma Lua, *Fiction in the Traditional Kankanay Society* (Baguio, Philippines: Cordillera Studies Center, 1984), 15.
39. One of seven Provinces in northern Luzon, Philippines.
40. June B Soriano, "Pentecost in the Philippines," *Pentecostal Evangel* (August 1948), 1.
41. Vanderbout, "Salvation-Healing Revival in Baguio City, Philippines," *Pentecostal Evangel* (June 1955), 2–4.
42. Vanderbout, "Salvation-Healing Revival in Baguio City, Philippines," 4.
43. Vanderbout, "Salvation-Healing Revival in Baguio City, Philippines," 4.
44. Some details of my early faith journey are found in "Jesus Christ in Asia: Our Journey with Him as Pentecostal Believers," *International Review of Mission* 94 (2005), 493–506.

16.

Christian Marginality and the Holy Spirit: A Pakistan Encounter

Zia Paul and Rebecca Paul

Abstract

Christians in Pakistan face significant challenges, including discrimination, surveillance, and violent attacks. However, while we pray for relief, we believe that this climate has provided a unique opportunity to proclaim Christ through the Holy Spirit through a lived theology of suffering. This paper details the socio-political history, and current reality of the Christian minority in Pakistan, with special attention given to the courage of both everyday Christians as well as Christian leaders through the power of the Holy Spirit.

Key words: persecution, theology of suffering, Pakistani Christians, evangelism, discipleship

The Socio-Political Background of Christian Minorities in Pakistan

Christians in Pakistan are believed to be descendants of low caste Hindus who converted under the British rule to escape the bondage and discrepancies of the caste system. Some Christians in Pakistan are overwhelming poor, while some have very high caliber jobs in society. The poor are relegated to menial jobs such as cleaners, sweepers, laborers, and farmhands.[1] However, the more privileged ones have made significant contributions to the development of Pakistan: building and running educational institutions, hospitals, and healthcare facilities throughout the country.[2]

In 1971 under the reign of Zulfiqar Ali Bhutto, most of the Christian and missionary institutions and health care centers were nationalized.

Thereafter began the discrimination and victimization of Christians. The 1947 constitution enabled all the non-Muslim minorities like Hindus, Christians, and Ahmadis to enjoyed equal estate as citizens of Pakistan.[3] On August 11, 1947, Muhammad Ali Jinnah (the founder of Pakistan) spoke the following words in the Constituent assembly:

> Hindus would cease to be Hindus and Muslims would cease to be Muslims, not in the religious sense, because that is the personal faith of each individual, but in the political sense as citizens of the state . . . you are free to go to your mosque or any place of worship in this state of Pakistan. You may belong to any religion or caste or creed . . . that has nothing to do with the business of the state.[4]

Thus, this constitution has been amended over the last few decades, and Christians are suppressed and discriminated on the basis of their religion.

The Massacre of Shanti Nagar

In respect to blasphemy allegations, there was an attack on the Christian Community in Khanewal in 1997, when churches were invaded, and the twin towns of Shantinagar and Tibba Colony were demolished over a supposed case of blasphemy. Many observers believe that the police sided with those who had been incited to act against these Christian communities by the local mullahs. The story told that the attack started with a police party that had gone to investigate a case of kidnapping but in the process, they dishonored the Bible. When the residents demonstrated and registered a case against the raiding police party, local Muslims were provoked to react. Torn pages of the Qur'an were strewn around, with the names of supposed suspects. As a result, thirteen churches, seven hundred households, and a number of shops and other properties were demolished to the ground by a ten thousand person-strong mob.[5] Several people were killed, although the police tried to hush up the actual numbers. A one-man inquiry tribunal was established but the report was never published. The HRCP recommended the repeal of Penal Code Section 295–B and C, besides other urgent measures to restore citizenship and security to non-Muslim Pakistanis.

Fifty-seven recent HRCP reports have highlighted the need to repeal discriminatory laws and practices by documenting various incidents of abuse, not only those against minorities and women, but those against poor people in general. The 1999 report records blasphemy cases registered against Christians and Ahmadis, especially that of Ayub Masih in Shantinagar, whom the Multan High Court had sentenced to death. He was released in August 2002 after the Supreme Court quashed the false case instituted against him.[6] This is one of the incidences of prejudice and racial discrimination against Christians. There are many more cases that happen everyday but are not reported.

The Incident of Blasphemy Law in Punjab

Among the abductions, forced conversions, and tantalization of Christian homes and churches, one of the worst cases involved the killing of a Christian couple, Shama and Shehzad, in November 2014 by a mob in the town of Kot Radha Krishna. The couple, who were parents to three young children with the eldest child aged six at the time, was beaten unconscious and thrown into an open furnace shaft after rumors circulated that they had desecrated a Qur'an.[7] There was no serious action taken by the government towards the people who did this injustice, and no relief was provided to the family. The children were emotionally and physiologically affected by the incidence of the brutal killing of their parents before their eyes. Some Christian activists and social workers took a stand against this brutal act but have still not received any justice as of at the time of this writing.

The Peoples Movement and Early Christianity

The Megs Movement started in 1859. The Megs was a term given to the low caste people of the depressed class who lived mainly in the Sialkot and Gujrat districts at that time. They were little above the chuhras who were the sweepers and cleaners. In this movement, a unique work of the Holy Spirit was seen preparing the hearts of the Hindus to accept Christ as their Savior.

Jawahar Masih, a poorly educated person, once stopped by a sugar mill. He started reading the gospel to the laborers there. Soon they developed an interest in the gospel. After eight days, he, along with G. W. Scott, an Indian evangelist from the Ludhiana orphanage, went to Jhandran village. While they were there, three hundred Megs from the village gathered to hear God's word and many were saved that day.[8]

Then came the Chuhra Movement, which began in 1873. Nattu, a convert from Hinduism, witnessed to a colleague named Ditt. At first, Ditt doubted the word of God and his love for humanity through Christ.

But in June 1873, he accepted Christ as his Savior and was baptized. With Ditt witnessing around Sialkot and Gujrat, other conversions were also reported within two months of his conversion. Hence this people's movement led to many conversions.[9]

The people's movement was for the poor and neglected people. The strategy of the missionaries at that time was personal or individual evangelism; which was very successful at first. But failed gradually, as the Muslim and Hindu opposition increased in the early nineteenth century.

The Advent of Missionaries

One of the significant missionaries of the United Presbyterian Church Missions (UPCM) in India and Pakistan is Rev. Andrew Gordon. He went to India with his wife, daughter, and his sister, Elizabeth, in 1854. They arrived in Calcutta by Ship on February 13, 1855. From there they went to Lahore, and then reached Sialkot, their true mission field. In 1856 Pastor Ifrahim Stevenson and Pastor R. A. Hill also came to Sialkot with their wives. They joined Andrew Gordon in the work of evangelism in Sialkot. After this, Elijah Soffit and George Scott were two Indian youngsters who joined Andrew. These two brothers were from Ludhiana European Mission Orphanage and they later became ordained pastors in Sialkot local church. Then, in 1857, the area was struck by the War of Independence; after which Andrew's sister Elizabeth formed an orphanage called Haji Pur Girls Hostel. Two years later she also founded a school for boys. Then finally on October 25, 1857, the first two Hindu converts were baptized. In 1858, two Muslim converts were baptized.[10] The work among the community was slow, but the missionaries were making efforts to learn the local Punjabi language to relate with people better and win more souls for Christ.

By 1863, the UPCM spread throughout Punjab and many Christians spread throughout Southern Punjab.[11] There were other missionaries also arriving; at that time there were Danish and Scottish missionaries. However, there was still a growing opposition towards the missionaries. Due to Andrew's ill health, he went back to his country and died there.

The Assassination of a Missionary Family in Punjab at the Time of Partition

Pastor Hunter Thomas was the first missionary of the Church of Scotland in Sialkot Pakistan. He arrived in Sialkot, crossing the Indus River in October of 1856. He brought along his wife, Jane, and a new convert, Mohammad Ismail. On February 28, 1857, he wrote a letter to the Church of Scotland stating that he was trying to learn the Punjabi language and that he had opened one school for boys and one for girls. There was also a weekly fellowship for new converts, where they were given teachings on growing in faith.[12] During the war of Independence between Pakistan and India, missionaries were told to come to Sialkot Fort if they wanted protection, otherwise, the government would not be responsible.

On the morning of July 9, 1857, Hunter, along with his wife and newborn child, boarded a horse cart to reach the fort, but on their way there, they encountered a criminal named Hurmat Khan, who had broken out of jail. He had a dagger in his hand with which he murdered the whole family. The people around tried to stop him but he went on, killing first the wife, then the child, and then Henry himself.[13] They were left there to die but remained faithful to their Lord. A year after the incident, in 1865, a church was made in remembrance of the sacrifice of Thomas Hunter, named Hunter Memorial Church Sialkot, which still stands there today. The members of that church are scattered all over the world, proclaiming the gospel boldly just like Hunter did. A saying of a church elder proved true, "The blood of the Martyrs is a seed to the church."[14]

The Massacre of All Saints Church in Peshawar

Moving forward to more recent years, the worst massacre took place at All Saints Church Peshawar on September 22nd, 2013. It was a reaction of United States drone bombing on Taliban areas including mosques in Pakistan. The Muslims reacted to it by harming Christians. On Sunday morning of September 2013, two suicide bombers from the Taliban faction did a blast in an Anglican church right in the middle of church service. According to a tally based on information from local officials, eighty-five people were killed and more than one hundred injured, although one doctor who arrived at the scene moments after the blast believes that even more died, but the relatives recovered the bodies before they could be accounted for.[15] Being a minority now, the government has provided security to all big and registered churches of Pakistan for their Sunday services and for special services such as Christmas and Easter.

Present State of Christians

In Pakistan, Christians have to face a lot of discrimination every day: at work, in the society at large, and in politics.

Religious Discrimination

When we talk about Muslim supremacy, we come to know that Muslims have a long-suppressed hatred towards Christians. Because of this, they have a discriminating attitude towards the minorities living in Pakistan. In job placements, Christians are given low profile jobs such as sweeping, garbage collection, and others like that. If a Christian gets a good job, he is bullied by his boss and other co-workers. Sometimes they are forced to change their religion, or are given so much work pressure that they are forced to leave their jobs. Some women are abducted, raped, and either forced to change religion, or used for unlawful purposes. However, some bear the pressure and are successful in their workplace and elsewhere.

Societal and Political Discrimination

When it comes to society, there are factions. There are places where only Muslims live within their respective sects, and there are towns where only Christians live, such as Essa Naghari's and Kuchi abbadi's. In the social sectors Christians are usually accused of blasphemy and other ill moral acts.[16]

Politically speaking, there was a separate electorate for minorities until 2001. Moreover, under the Martial Law of General Pervaiz Musharaf, changes took place in the blasphemy law as well as in the constitution, in which the separate electorate was dissolved and a combined electorate was promoted.[17] But under the new government of Imran Khan, many injustices are being done to Christians in the cabinet and the parliament.[18] The right to speak for the rights of Christians are being usurped, and much more is happening, as the whole system is corrupted.

Massacre of Bethel Memorial Church Quetta 2018

On 16, December 2017, there was a massacre at an Anglican church called Bethel Memorial Church, Quetta, while a Sunday school Christmas program was taking place within the church, fully packed with people. Suddenly, firing was heard right in the middle of the service and all the church gates were closed down. The congregation was told to duck or take refuge in the priest's inner room. Unfortunately, not all could be accommodated in that small room. Soon after, there was a suicide bomb blast at the front gate of the church. This gate was being used by the children to come in and out during their performances. Around fifty people died immediately and many others were injured. Dawn News reported that two terrorists were killed on spot and one was caught wounded. That year's Christmas was considered "Black Christmas" as many were grieving for their lost ones. Some were grieving for their children, some for their parents, and some for the church security people who had died trying to save the rest from a bigger loss. Some mothers still grieve for their children to this day. But ever since the incident occurred, the government of Pakistan has been providing security to churches all over Pakistan every Sunday including special occasions.

The Positive Impact of Injustice on the Christians

Open Field for Evangelism

Quetta is an open field for evangelism these days. But now the people are afraid to evangelize due to fear of being assassinated, or of being threatened by the Islamic militants. Usually, their revenge and anger are felt towards the Americans, who are raging a war against terrorism in Afghanistan. But they retaliate by threatening the Christian communities not to evangelize the Muslims otherwise they would be responsible for the consequences. Some of them have sent threat letters to Christian institutions to stop enrolling Muslims in their schools and institutions. Some have threatened administrations of minority institutions to shut down their institutes or else be prepared for anything like a suicide attack, bombing, firing, etc.[19]

One other significant example is that of Asiya Bibi, a mentally challenged Christian woman who was picking trash and came across some pages of the Qur'an and was accused of blasphemy. Later on, she was thankfully delivered from a death sentence. She made the headlines for quite some time in Pakistan.

Many hopeless people are living in Christian communities who are forced to live in slums, do low profile jobs, and revoke their religion, while some have even been killed due to false accusations of blasphemy. Due to these hindrances, some oppressed masses are living in the interior parts of the country and have not yet heard the gospel.[20] Therefore, we believe Pakistan at this moment is an open field for evangelism for the world, and for the Pakistani church.

Unity in Hard Times

According to James H. Aughey, "The church is not a select circle of the immaculate, but a home where the outcast may come in."[21] This has become true for the Pakistani church amidst all of the persecutions and discriminations the church has gone through. Just like the Corinthian church (1 Cor 12: 25–31), there was a schism in the Pakistani church, but after facing so many troubles, the church has come together for the good. Even the outcasts are now welcomed in the church, and are being taken care of. The hard times have also brought the church leadership together, as church committees have been organized to provide security to churches and Christian communities all over Pakistan.[22] This is a great development on behalf of Christian leadership and the dioceses to join hands in working for the protection of the Christian community.

Existence of Bible School in Quetta

Assemblies of God Bible School (AGBS) is situated in a peaceful and clean area of Railway Housing Society, Quetta. The institute is the result of twenty-nine years of prayer by three sisters, Alice Shevenknek from Canada, Ursula from Germany, and Christine Verma from Pakistan. The fulfillment of this vision has been entrusted to Assemblies of God Church Drigh Road, Karachi, under the supervision of Pastor Zia Paul, by the grace of God and the kindness of the Christine Verma Trust.

The school came into being on March 1, 2005. The purpose of its establishment is to train the leadership of evangelical churches nationwide, particularly that of Sindh and Baluchistan. The logo is "Training for Service."

Right from the inaugural ceremony held in 2015, the Bible school had to face a lot of hurdles. First, there was a letter to the institution from Islamic militants, threatening to close down the institution or else be ready for a great loss. Second, on the first day of classes, there was firing outside the gate to threaten the students and teachers. Then, after a few years, there was a telephonic threat from the Islamic militants to close down the institution and all the teaching, promotion, and practice of a false religion.[23] Despite all this, praise be to God almighty, who has helped sustain this institution for the last fifteen years.

Pastor Zia Paul has diligently been running the Bible school since 2005. This institution is serving as a light in the darkness. The students who get trained here go back to their respective churches and localities, and serve as effective stewards of God's varying grace. Some get healed of physical and spiritual illnesses as they live and study on campus. Others come here for enhancement of the biblical knowledge and spiritual formation. Therefore, we believe that this intuition is like a candle in the dark, where people are enlightened by the grace of God, under the supervision of God-fearing teachers, in order to serve in their respective churches. This institution is equipping leaders and others for effective ministry and evangelism for the glory of God.

Impact of Persecution on the Local Church

On May 16, Pentecostal preacher, Wilson Fazal, left for church and disappeared. He had received prior threats and had evaded a kidnapping just three days earlier. But despite all this, he continued serving the Lord. Jerry Wilson, his eldest son, had reported these threats to the home secretary and senior police officers but to no avail; the threats kept increasing. He and other Christians in Quetta had been receiving threats warning them to stop preaching to Muslims, including a letter from a group called Mahaz-e-Jihad, or "Circumambience of Holy War." (The Voice of the Martyrs has copies of two of these letters.)[24] On May 11, he received a letter from this group saying, "You are an infidel and blasphemer, stop preaching Christianity in schools, hospitals, and churches. Wage war (Jihad) against America." On the following Sunday, Pastor Fazal went to Bashirabad, a suburb in Quetta, to attend a service at

Pakistan Gospel Assembly Church along with his two sons. Thereafter, his sons lodged a report with the police accusing some unknown people of kidnapping their father.[25] Believers across Pakistan were rightfully concerned when he vanished without a trace.[26]

Meanwhile, Asiya Nasir, was a Christian politician holding a seat reserved for minorities by the Islamic Alliance, Muttahida Majlis-i-Amal (MMA). Nasir criticized the government and gave a forty-eight hour deadline for the recovery of the kidnapped preacher. She said that such threats had also been received by principals of various schools run by the Christian community in Quetta. Letters sent to the Christian preacher were circulated among the journalists during her press conference. MMA leaders, including provincial minister, Maulana Faizullah, condemned the incident.[27]

Two days later, on May 18, Pastor Fazal was found safe in Islamabad, the capital of Pakistan. He recalled how he had been taken six hundred kilometers away from Quetta, to the city of Peshawar, where he managed to escape from his captors. He was given electric shocks in the torture cell. He also was beaten up and spat upon. They shaved his head and eyebrows. He said that he called upon the name of Jesus in his misery, and was helped by angels as he managed to escape the torture cell.[28]

Praise be to God, that Pastor Fazal returned to testify of God's goodness, and is safe up until now. He still needs prayers that those responsible for this kidnapping will be found. As believers, we also need to pray that amendments be made to Pakistan's existing blasphemy law, so that the country's citizens, including its children, will be protected from injustice and abuse. May our Lord's mercy and justice prevail, not only in the judiciary system but also in the hearts of the country's militants!

Amid this misery, there was a continuous twenty-four hours prayer meeting going on in the church that Fazal pastored. All the church members fasted and gathered to pray for their pastor. Thankfully he was delivered through their prayers, and this incident greatly impacted their faith, unity, and church discipline. Many who hear his story get saved, and some converts are also attending his church. I believe that the theology of suffering and signs and wonders are more at work these days then testimonies and witnessing.

The Holy Spirit and Evangelism

The Bible says, where two or three gather in his name, he is present in the midst of them (Matt 20:18). So I believe that the Holy Spirit is at work wherever the people of God are present. These days he is at work in people's lives through signs and wonders; miracles are taking place, and many claim to have seen Jesus. People are now seeking the truth for peace and tranquility as Jesus is the only way, the truth, and the light (John 14:6). Everywhere, there are stories of war, political and economic unrest, and social injustices. But there is only one who can provide justice or light to this dark world, and that is Jesus Christ!

The Spirit's Empowerment for Witnessing

In light of the information shared above, there is now a great revival among the Pakistani Christians. Throughout history, Christians have been suppressed as minorities and were afraid to speak for their rights. However, now the scenario has changed. We have Christian activists, NGOs, etc. working for the rights of Christian people. After facing a lot of persecution and suppression, charismatic and Pentecostal churches are now more active in witnessing for Christ. Such as in the case of Pastor Wilson Fazal, where after facing a great trail, he stills goes to rural areas to preach and teach the gospel. He has been beaten many times but he refuses to stop witnessing for the glory and extension of God's kingdom.

Another key person in witnessing is John Mekrani. He is a Sri Lankan missionary who has been living in Pakistan for the last fifty years. He speaks the language, he dresses like the local people, and he has adopted the culture as his own. He is also one of the teachers at Assemblies of God Bible School, Quetta. He is a single missionary and has committed his life to witnessing in rural and unreached areas of Pakistan where even local preachers are afraid to go. He ministers at Makran Coast, an area near Iran and the Afghan border. Every day many Christians and non-residents of that place are killed by locals. He has been imprisoned, beaten, and thrown out of town many times, but he refuses to stop going there. He believes that if he can acquaint them with the gospel their lives would be changed forever. Though now in his late 80's, he is still very active and eager to win souls for Christ.[29] It is encouraging to behold that there are still some missionaries left in Pakistan who are willing to suffer for Christ. I perceive that church as a whole is not as active in evangelism as it should be, and only a handful of believers are out there actively witnessing to the lost.

The Growth of the Church in the Midst of Persecution

As far as church growth is concerned, I believe that the church is growing at a slow pace. In some places, due to lack of unity, the church is not as sticky as it should be: people come and go as a formality. In the case of Pakistan Gospel Assembly, it is not growing rapidly because the pastor is too busy in evangelism. He pays less attention to pastoral care; consequently, many members of the church have been lost.

However, the Catholic, Charismatic, Anglican, and Pentecostal churches are growing due to sound teaching, pastoral care, and in some cases, due to the benefits provided to the poor and needy. If we look at Assemblies of God Church, it is growing and flourishing every day. As far as I have observed, they have trained ministers who guide and lead the flock diligently. Their sermons are theologically equipped to meet the needs of the people. They have times of fellowship where believers pray together and visit the sick.[30] So, that is why I believe these churches are flourishing day-by-day, nevertheless, strong evangelism is lacking. We need to pray that the Lord provides us with Pakistani evangelists, apostles, and missionaries to be sent by the Pakistani church.

The Anglican Church is now focusing on prayer and unity and is slowly growing after facing two major massacres. They have become fearless and are more active in youth evangelism through sports and correspondence courses. Likewise, the Catholic Church is also making progress at a slow pace, and is also weak in evangelism. Their focus is more on theological equipping and spiritual growth of the believers, rather than evangelism to the unreached.[31] Some fathers and nuns are working in rural areas of Pakistan, but it is not that common.

The Salvation Army Church is also doing a great job in Pakistan. They equip men and women for evangelism through various programs and are flourishing by the day. Their strategy is to make a bridge of friendship and then through personal evangelism, win souls for Christ. Sometimes they get caught, and are threatened by the Islamic extremists, but they manage to escape by the grace of God.[32] To conclude, I would say as Pentecostals and evangelicals, we still have a long way to go and should learn from the people who have gone before us. We need to have interaction with the other denomination leaders so that a new strategy can be made to fulfill the Great Commission through evangelism.

Summary

Hence it can be said that time and again, Christians living in various parts of Pakistan have faced trials and tribulations but have not denied their faith. Rather, it has brought them ever closer to God and to each other. Both foreign missionaries and the local church have responded to racial, social, religious, and political discrimination with an unearthly strength imparted by the Holy Spirit. It has enabled Christians to remain steadfast and to grow in faith, love, patience, and unity, and non-Christians to open their hearts to the adherence of the living gospel. However, as long as the earth remains, the principle of seedtime and harvest will remain in force (Gen 8:22). So we are to multiply until the coming of the Lord Jesus Christ (Luke 19:13), whether the days are peaceful or troublesome, through the power of the Holy Spirit.

Notes

1. Irfan Husain, "Minorities at Risk," DAWN.COM, December 22, 2018, https://www.dawn.com/news/1452941, accessed August 26, 2019.
2. Irfan Husain, "Minorities at Risk," DAWN.COM, December 22, 2018. https://www.dawn.com/news/1452941, accessed August 26, 2019.
3. Muhammad Nazeer Kakakhel, "Status of Non-Muslim Majorities in Pakistan," *Islamic Studies* 23:1 (1984).
4. Kakakhel, "Status of Non-Muslim Majorities," 10.
5. See Iftikhar Malik, *Religious Minorities in Pakistan* (London: Minority Rights Group International, 2002), 12, 24.
6. Frederick E. Stock, *People Movements in the Punjab* (South Pasadena, CA: William Carey Library, 1975), 197.
7. Stock, *People Movements*, 200.
8. Allan H. Anderson, *An Introduction to Pentecostalism: Global Charismatic Christianity* (New York: Cambridge University Press, 2013), 305.
9. Roger Karbi and John G. Meadowkraft, *An Introduction to Early Church History: Asia* (Lahore: Open Theological Seminary, 2010), 97.
10. Karbi and Meadowkraft, *An Introduction to Early Church History: Asia*, 102.
11. Stock, *People Movements*, 97.
12. Stock, *People Movements*, 100.
13. Stock, *People Movements*, 106.
14. Stock, *People Movements*, 105.
15. Husain, "Minorities at Risk."
16. "Why Are Pakistan's Christians Targeted?" *BBC News*, October 30, 2018,

sec. Asia, 10, https://www.bbc.com/news/world-asia-35910331, accessed August 26, 2019.

17.   Kakakhel, "Status of Non-Muslim Majorities," 14.

18.   Kakakhel, "Status of Non-Muslim Majorities," 9.

19.   "QUETTA: Preacher in Quetta Feared Kidnapped," DAWN.COM, May 17, 2004, http://www.dawn.com/news/359075, accessed August 26, 2019.

20.   Anderson, *An Introduction to Pentecostalism*, 24.

21.   Anderson, *An Introduction to Pentecostalism*, 25.

22.   Roger Karbi and John G. Meadowkraft, *History of Protestant Christianity in Pakistan* (Lahore: Open Theological Seminary, 2009), 34.

23.   Rebecca Paul, "Interview of Pastor Zia Paul," August 8, 2019.

24.   Rebecca Paul, "Interview of Pastor Wilson Fazal," July 8, 2019.

25.   "QUETTA: Preacher in Quetta Feared Kidnapped."

26.   "QUETTA: Preacher in Quetta Feared Kidnapped."

27.   R. Paul, "Interview of Pastor Wilson Fazal."

28.   R. Paul, "Interview of Pastor Wilson Fazal."

29.   Rebecca Paul, "Interview of Pastor John Mekrani," July 8, 2019.

30.   Rashid Bhatti and Rebecca Paul, "Interview Human Activist Awaish," July 8. 2019.

31.   Bhatti and Paul, "Interview Human Activist Awaish."

32.   Bhatti and Paul, "Interview Human Activist Awaish."

17.

The Challenge of a "Displacing" Secularism: A Tactical Response by Hindu and Christian Traditions in India

Brainerd Prince and Jeffrey R. Thomas

Abstract

Perceptions of secularity vary, but what is common to most is that secularism has or is displacing other ways and traditions of operating and ways of believing, at least as a dominant narrative. Furthermore, a "displacing" secularism cannot function as a neutral mediator between conflicting traditions as secularism's nature as a "displacing" tradition conflicts with secularity's values of individual expressivism. This character of secularity is as strongly present in Indian secularism as it is in other forms in other nations. While it is argued that the secular traditions came to India in three waves, the Indian secular traditions are problematized as positioning themselves as a "mediator of traditions." Based on a case study of Shiksha Rath, it is further argued that secularism is best understood as a tradition similar to other religious traditions, even if it is a dominant tradition in this age. Hindus and Christians in India resist being conformed to secularity through a tactical response that is centered upon a commitment to faithful religious practice, which includes an impulse towards dialogical relationships.

Key words: India, displacing secularism, tradition, tactics, dialogical relationship

Introduction

The question at hand is whether a religious tradition, such as a Spirit-empowered Christian tradition, or even a Hindu tradition in India, can perform in a public sphere that is dominated by a powerful secular tradition. Secularism in its many forms may be characterized in many ways but at the core of these many forms of secularism, there is a common impulse towards displacing any and all other ways of life, including the Spirit-empowered life form.[1] Here we argue that a proper response to a displacing secularism is a subversion of that dominating practice. Using Michel de Certeau's notion of "tactics," we argue that a religious response to secularism must begin with a rejection of practices of displacement and a re-engagement of embodied traditions as a basis for effective dialogue between traditions, in which secularism too is treated as a tradition, one amongst the many other religious traditions. In this paper, we demonstrate how it has been done in the Indian context and showcase it as an example for other contexts which equally experience the displacing power of the secular tradition. We conclude that if secularism is seen as a form of rationality and a social structure of practices, then by historically locating secularism as a tradition, religious traditions such as the Spirit-empowered Christian tradition, or even the multitude of Hindu traditions, can create spaces in which they can not only live out their life forms but also project and promote them in the public sphere.

The Indian Seculars[2]

In contemporary India, the rich get richer, and the poor have a fire in their belly to get rich, but it is the middle class, who have just enough, who continue to dwell in the land of mediocracy. The stories of the rich belong to page three of our newspapers, while the poor and the impoverished make the headlines either because of their drudgery or because of the "turnarounds" they have experienced. From a *chaiwala* prime minister to a clerk's family becoming India's richest business house, India is full of *rags to riches* stories that capture the headlines in our country. There is an equal number of page three stories about the children and the grandchildren of the *kandhani* rich and famous — be it the film families in Bollywood or the dynastic political class — all born with a silver spoon in their mouth. But what about the middle class?

If you want a study of "the great Indian middle class," you will find a thoroughly accomplished job in Pavan Varma's book that goes by the same title. Varma must be remembered for probably being the first to apply the "middle-class" identity marker to the Indian context and for providing some sort of a historical framework for its emergence and growth. But the book is mostly a neo-Marxist critique against the liberalized and globalized emerging class of people known as the middle-class. Varma himself is part of the very class he critiques, often superficially, and without appropriate justification, particularly concerning their "reduced sensitivity to the poor and the legitimization of corruption." He calls them "morally rudderless, obsessively materialistic, and socially insensitive to the point of being unconcerned with anything but their own narrow self-interest."[3] After reading the book, one is left with the idea that the middle class is stuck fulfilling mediocre goals, never to rise above the primal dirt of their existence.

One of the critiques of positions such as Varma's has been that the idea of the Indian middle class is vague. Class is not a clear identity marker. Class has never been an identity marker in the Indian subcontinent. India has all kinds of identity markers, for example, caste, *jati*, tradition, tribe, state, language, or ethnicity, but class is not one of them. This is what happens when we use a category cross-culturally without proper appropriation. If class is not an identity marker, perhaps it is an economic category.

Consider my (Prince's) neighborhood. The so-called middle class seems to be the twenty-odd families that live in the rented flats, wear Western clothes, and send their children to English-medium schools. On the other hand, the owner of the *Kirana* shop who is in his *dhoti* and a vest, not even *kurta-pajama*, and sleeps on the *charpai* outside his shop, and speaks only in Haryanvi, not even Hindi, will never be considered part of the middle-class, although he owns eight of the twenty flats in which the middle-class live! His sons and their families who supply the needs of these families and deposit sacks full of money every day (yes, I have seen them!) will never be called middle-class. Therefore, the eldest brother, Sanjay, rebelled, left the family business, married a girl who had earned a Master's degree and was a teacher by profession, humbled himself to live in one of the flats which they rent out rather than in their village *haveli*, sends his children to an English-medium school, and takes a job. He was willing to do all this, and make the required sacrifice, such as the giving up of the income that the shop and business brought, all for the status of becoming part of the middle-class, even if that meant becoming economically poorer. And yet, would he ever be truly middle-class?

Therefore, in India, if "class" is not necessarily an economic category or a general identity marker, then who are the middle-class in India? We would like to use the language of "tradition" *a la* Macintyre, in trying to answer this question. We would like to propose that the people called the Indian middle-class are those who have opened themselves to a bundle of traditions that can be categorized as "secular traditions." In so doing, they have undergone an intrinsic change in their ontologies, becoming a kind of secular beings. We want to argue that it is these groups of people, these Seculars, who are usually identified as the great Indian middle class.

Three Secular Waves in India

So how did Indians encounter the secular traditions? Primarily in three waves: Firstly, these traditions were brought to India as part of the colonial encounter with the various European nations. Europe has itself been undergoing secularization or getting converted to secularism over the past 500 years. A great book that traces Europe's assignation with secularism is Charles Taylor's *A Secular Age*, a must-read for anyone interested in understanding the great Indian middle-class. Unless we understand the birth and growth of European secularism, we will never have the conceptual tools necessary to understand secular traditions in India. Along with Christianity, secularism too was brought to India by the colonial powers.[4] The religious ideals of secularism come packaged in liberal thought, democratic institutions, capitalist economies, scientific thinking, educational institutions, and the English language.[5]

It is interesting to note, particularly as a student of religion, that Hindu fundamentalists, who are opposed to being colonized by Western Christianity, readily become converts to secularism, without realizing that both Christianity and secularism are siblings and children of Latin Christendom. The language of growth, human rights, and development all belong to secular traditions, which continue the Judeo-Christian worldview, although in an abstracted manner. I (Prince) tell my Hindu brothers and sisters, particularly of the Rashtriya Swayamsevak Sangh (RSS) brand, that if we want to truly fight against foreign religions, then we ought to primarily take on the fight against secular traditions.[6] Christianity in India has minuscule influence and damage in comparison to the catastrophe being brought about to local Indian traditions by secular traditions. Even in the colonial era, it was the secular traditions that made the most radical impact, even if they used Christian missionaries along with company businessmen and the Raj bureaucrats as their carriers.

Secondly, post-independence, as a reaction to colonial capitalism, Nehruvian socialism gained currency in the newly formed Indian State, a secular institution, yet without a well-articulated secular ideology. Nehruvian socialism seemed a good fit for a nation filled with poor citizens who were newborns in the secular tradition. Furthermore, India, as a newborn secular babe, needed the guidance of those who had been older adherents of the secular traditions. India leaned towards Russia and privileged a form of Marxist socialism. No wonder Jawaharlal Nehru University, founded in the sixties, has strong Marxist/socialist leanings. Another reason why socialism was considered a better fit for newborn India is that Hindu society is largely patriarchal and socialism affirms an abstracted form of patriarchy even in its quest for social equality. There is always an elite politburo which governs the majority. This is the blind spot of socialism's egalitarian quest. The national elites soon filled the politburo space in socialist India and the dynastic rule was established. In embracing socialism, Nehru (who, according to a biographer, was called Joe until the age of 26, and whose *Discovery of India* was none other than his personal discovery of India), and his comrades did not realize that they had become "seculars."

In the nineteenth century, secular traditions birthed two children in the West: liberalism that focused on the ideal of freedom, and socialism that followed the ideal of equality. Ultimately it did not matter if India wanted to follow a liberal capitalistic route or the socialist route because underlying both of them was the secular tradition, which was the real powerhouse, pushing itself, expanding, and dominating the post-war world, including India. However, Nehruvian socialism failed in India both theoretically as well as in practice because socialism was an imported tradition, and had no roots in the subcontinent, even if the patriarchal structure offered it a mechanism on which it could operate. Can you think of one Indian thinker who has contributed to social theory at the level of either Marx or the Frankfurt school? Although, in practice, at least in the states of Kerala and West Bengal, there has been a significant influence of socialist ideas and ideals.[7]

It was precisely against Nehruvian socialism that India fought its second battle of independence, and both liberalization and globalization came into being in the India of the nineties. But it was not a battle against the secular traditions, rather against a form of secularism, that is, socialist secularism and its bureaucracy. This left the space open for secularism's "displacement" of local traditions. What the Indian political intellectuals of the eighties and nineties did not realize was the depth to which they had already been colonized by the secular traditions. They were truly already living in the secular age, even if it was as its illegitimate children. Thus, the third wave of secularism that came into the Indian sub-continent was through the so-called globalization and liberalization move that India has made since the early nineties, primarily by the opening up of the Indian economy to foreign investments.

If the first wave of secularism was political as it was colonial, and the second was social in terms of the ideals that India sought to embody in its society, then the third wave was corporate in the domain of business and economy, particularly with the multinational companies coming in, complete with their values and practices. Of course, each of these waves brought in deeper structures and ideologies of the secular traditions and "converted" Indian forms of life. By the time India entered the twenty-first century, it had become deeply secular, particularly India's "middle-class," which numbers over 400 million in the sub-continent.

The ruthlessness of secularism can be seen in how it was able to position its different forms as the only set of options to choose from, while forcefully displacing all other local, native, and indigenous options. We may not be able to go into this clever conspiracy in great detail here, but in the name of an anti-religion rant, Indian socialism played the role of a foot soldier in the secular army and successfully banished anything local, religious and traditional. Of course, being a foot soldier, it completely missed the point that secularism, despite its scientific rationality and holding on to the high horse of reason and critique, is also a religion and a tradition. The point that Gadamer continually made to Habermas in saying that his idea of reflection and critique also belonged to a tradition, even as it opposed tradition. Habermas writes, "Gadamer's prejudice in favor of the legitimacy of prejudices (or prejudgements) validated by tradition is in conflict with the power of reflection, which proves itself in its ability to reject the claim of traditions. Substantiality disintegrates in reflection because the latter not only confirms but also breaks dogmatic forces. Authority and knowledge do not converge."[8] Ricoeur summarizes the Gadamerian position and responds best when he writes, "Critique is also a tradition."[9]

We can apply this to the Indian context: The critique of colonial secularism during and immediately after the independence movement by Indian nationalism came primarily from the tradition of Indian Nehruvian socialism (itself a child of secularism), and the critique of Indian socialism in the nineties came from the tradition of liberal secularism (again a child of secularism). The paradoxical truth of twentieth-century India is that in hopping from the left pedal to the right, India has firmly embedded herself within secular traditions. Thus, the Seculars of India were born and their presence has grown over the decades. They consist of secularized Hindus, secularized Christians, secularized Muslims and so forth, but predominantly of secularized Hindus.

Problematizing Indian Secularism: Secularism as Mediator of Traditions

It has been shown that secular traditions are firmly established in India. More than that though, it has been suggested that secularism is actively displacing local traditions, albeit sometimes covertly. This idea requires a closer look, as understanding the character of secularism is what will enable a proper response.

In exploring liberal secularism as a local tradition that actively seeks to displace others, let us address the question via Charles Taylor and Rajeev Bhargava. Taylor is a significant contributor to the debate on secularism. His inclusion in a discussion of "secularism in India" is important for three reasons. The first, as shown in secularism in India, is connected to Western secularism. As a result, secondly, Taylor's critique of the tradition of liberal secularism is pertinent to the Indian context. And lastly, Taylor is a practicing Catholic Christian. His critique of secularism developed in part from his religious convictions and can indeed inform an Indian Christian response to secularism.[10] Rajeev Bhargava's inclusion here needs little justification. He is a noted Indian political theorist who has contributed significantly to the academic discourse on Indian secularism and its relation to religious and spiritual belonging in India. He currently works for the Centre for the Study of Developing Societies in India. Although, it should be noted that he enters the discourse on secularism in India having a university education from the West, at Oxford. Consequently, he is deeply influenced by Euro-Western liberal thought. Perhaps he speaks as one who has a foot on both sides of the fence.[11]

There are generally two responses to liberal secularism's displacement of local traditions and religions. The first is to argue there is a need for secularism in modern society as a mediating presence between traditions. It is supposed that such a role requires a certain amount of displacement of those traditions. The second response views secularist displacement as detrimental to those traditions and perhaps dangerous to society as well. It is the latter position that is often appealed to as justification for an immediate, if not violent, response to secularity. We will argue that there is a third option. One which allows for the presence of secularism without requiring the displacement of other traditions. This third option is a tactical response, where the idea of tactics is that of Michel de Certeau's spatial theory.

The first position, in support of secularism, is supported by Bhargava's argument for the distinctiveness of Indian secularism.[12] A basic presumption Bhargava attends to is that good ideas last and that when an idea works well we seldom question its value and purpose. Good ideas tend to fade into the background until some crisis forces our assessment of them. Ideas then are much like a public transit system, we don't consider its workings until they fail. Consequently, as Indian secularism is only recently being questioned, he argues that the flaw is not internal to secularism itself but rather to some recent shift in its Indian expression.

A second (two-part) predicate of Bhargava's position is that secularism is not necessarily Western, and that Indian secularity is not modern. He argues that frequently there is a mistaken acceptance of a dichotomous grid dividing the Western modern and the indigenous traditional. And since secularism is often equated with the modern, it is presumed to be Western. Bhargava argues instead, "that something that started out as Western can over time be transformed, and in responding to specific Indian problems and by being nurtured in an Indian context, can become distinctively Indian."[13] Lastly, Bhargava argues that critiques of secularism that presume it is Western give intellectual legitimacy to political attacks on the secular ideal.

Based on these, Bhargava argues for a historical rescue effort of Indian secularism in an effort to recall a distinctive Indian form of the secular ideal. That Indian secularism, Bhargava argues, is not only what India must strive towards in the midst of surging Hindu extremism, but it also can benefit Western nations. There are five pillars of Bhargava's Indian secularism. To quote Bhargava:

> First, its explicit multi-value character. Second, the idea of principled distance that is poles apart from one-sided exclusion, mutual exclusion, and strict neutrality. Third, its commitment to a different model of moral reasoning that is highly contextual and opens up the possibility of multiple secularisms, of different societies working out their own secularisms. Fourth, it uniquely combines an active hostility to some aspects of religion with equally active respect for its other

dimensions. Finally, it is the only secularism that I know that attends simultaneously to issues of intra-religious oppression and inter-religious domination.[14]

A Critique of Rajeev Bhargava: Secularism as a Tradition

Bhargava argues that the connection between Christianity and secularism is largely exaggerated, if not mistaken. Further, he argues that secularism is Western in origin, but that it can no longer be referred to as such. That is, the early and middle phases of the development of secularism as an idea are certainly Western, but since then its institution in nationalism and democracy has been contextualized in different civilizations. Finally, he contends that since Indian secularism, i.e., nationalism and democracy, developed amid deep religious and cultural diversity it is marked by a distinctive active disregard for religion that is not present in Western secularism. This makes it ideal for a mediatorial role between religious and cultural traditions.

Bhargava's position can be critiqued as it assumes the conclusion it then seeks to prove, that secularism is good. Also, Bhargava's conclusion that secularism is an effective mediatorial position between traditions misidentifies secularity as procedural and institutional. This is helpfully explained with Charles Taylor's assessment of secularism as a condition of belief and belonging. In *A Secular Age*, Taylor differentiates between three senses of secularism.[15] The first, what he calls Secularism$_1$ is the often-cited separation of "church and state," the principle that a state should be neutral on matters of religion. Secularism$_2$ refers to trends of decreasing religious and spiritual adherence or practice. Taylor argues that those two concepts are too conceptually thin to assess the various facets of secularism. He proposes in their place a third notion of secularism. Secularism$_3$ refers to a process of change in the conditions of belief, and how these beliefs are practiced. It is this last sense we will look at here.

What are these changing conditions of belief? Taylor identifies a shift, occurring in around 1500–1800 AD, from an enchanted worldview to that of what he calls an immanent frame. The central aspect of the new immanent frame is a change in how people view the world we share. The immanent frame views the world as consisting of a physical world over which we exercise authority through technology, and a human social world accessible through various institutions, i.e., the political, educational, and economic. In the immanent frame, anything beyond the physical and human worlds (meaning religion and spirituality) is open to being accepted, discarded, altered or invented; they are no longer seen to be connected to any deeper "enchanted" meaning. A nation born into the immanent frame or being shaped by its powerful presence exhibits these new conditions of belief.

The second descriptive element of secularism3 is its expression. On this point, Taylor uses an intentionally ambiguous term, "unbundling" to describe the impact of secularity on how we understand identity. He argues that before the changing conditions of belief there was overlap or congruence between the various spheres of belonging. This means that in the various elements of culture, i.e., family, community, region, dress, belief, ritual, etc., there was consistency and a resemblance; they were "bundled." The clearest symbols of this are the beginning and end of life rituals. At one time, for Christians, the baptism of an infant was as much an initiation into the community of faith as it was an acknowledgment of the child as a person and as a citizen. Secularism3, however, evidences an "unbundling" of these identifiers. The markers of identity have shifted away from that sort of traditional image to one of expressive individualism. The symbols of identity in the secular age vary, but they do so within categories we now equate with indicators of status. And a society built on a secular worldview is extremely adept at providing the means for expressing that status as a sense of belonging, for a price.

By conceiving of secularity as secularism3, Taylor has argued against what he refers to as an acultural view of secularity and has instead built a model of secularism as a tradition.[16] As a change in the conditions of belief and as a particular tradition, one of the marks of that secularist tradition is its impulse to displace other traditions. In society, secularism and religion may exist side-by-side, so to speak, but the immanent frame, particularly manifest in the scientific method and technology, leaves no room for an enchanted worldview, and institutionalized secularity leaves no public space for religion.[17]

In this view, we argue that Bhargava takes a few missteps. Two stand out as most significant. The first is one of his predicate statements. Bhargava presumes secularity to be a good idea simply because it has "worked" until recently. The French historian Michel de Certeau has argued that it is our experience of the other that forces our reconsideration of ourselves.[18] So, doubts leveled at secularism are not the result of a recent "feeling" that now secularism doesn't "work."

Rather, secularism is being recognized for what it is, an "other" tradition, and a ruthless one at that. Bhargava's second misstep is in the five points of his Indian secularism. His fourth point is that Indian secularism "uniquely combines an active hostility to some aspects of religion with equally active respect for its other dimensions." This gives us evidence for two conclusions. One, it shows Bhargava himself to be a liberal secular scholar, who views religion in the "unbundled" sense Taylor describes. Religious traditions are simply collections of beliefs and practices that a secular state can choose to retain or discard as they see fit. Two, it advocates a practice of displacing of tradition that is recognized as one of secularity's failings.

In contrast, even as Taylor properly identifies secularism as a tradition and details its challenges to a nation such as India, it fails to account for the particular character of secularism in India. Granted, that is not Taylor's project. Two problems arise from Taylor's position though. The first is that as a primarily descriptive exercise it provides no direction for a path forward. Second, by describing the way that secularism3 has impacted "bundled" traditions and not providing some direction forward he leaves a door open for aggressive counter-displacements such as the sort of extremisms plaguing India today.

Shiksha Rath: Unveiling the Face of Indian Secularism

If we accept secularism as a tradition with an inherent impulse to displace other traditions, we cannot accept secularism as a mediating tradition between others. Let me share a case that illustrates this and identifies the significance of the challenge of a displacing secularism in the Indian context.

In May 2012, initiated by a Non-Government Organization, a group of academics and practitioners discussed the need to equip and facilitate Christian development workers to work effectively and collaboratively with Hindu communities. In 2014 a research team was assembled to explore this problem. The goal of the project was to produce a training manual that would aid Christian development workers serving in multi-faith (primarily Hindu) contexts.[19] It was thought that what was needed was a means for the Christian development workers to preserve the commitment to their own faith identity while making a conscious and intentional investment in understanding other faith communities, particularly Hindu traditions. This thought process was supported by the overall aims of the development project. There was also the possibility that such a means, once developed, could potentially open avenues for legitimately communicating one's own Christian beliefs and practices. The research team decided that the best approach would be to conduct field research on an existing development project.

Shiksha Rath, a holistic child development project in New Delhi, was identified as the first site for research and fieldwork. The main reason for identifying Shiksha Rath as a site for research was precisely because its leadership was aware of the onslaught of secularism in the Indian context and wanted to articulate a Spirit-empowered Christian response, which would be holistic and would not mitigate against the good brought by the secular traditions of development. Shiksha Rath worked amidst a majority Hindu community in North Delhi, although some of the children within the program are from Muslim and Buddhist backgrounds as well.[20] At its inception, the founding leaders of Shiksha Rath sought means for directly establishing a "Spirit-empowered" Christian community. Relatively quickly this was seen to be impossible given the explicit secular demands of the families and community with which they worked. Thus, at the initial stages of Shiksha Rath, the best form of a Spirit-response identified was to primarily listen to the needs of this urban poor community and directly respond to those needs, and in that response show a Spirit-empowered manifestation for authentic long-term impact. This path was chosen rather than an explicit outward manifestation of the Spirit-filled gospel work of evangelism.

Throughout the research, one particular trend was noted above all others. It was evident that matters of religion and local tradition had been subverted or entirely displaced by the secular tradition. Along with the parents who were urban-poor, the children within the program had become Seculars. The first indicator of the trend was discovered in the developing community. Most of the families participating in the program had moved to New Delhi from their villages to pursue better opportunities for themselves. The common theme amongst these families were variations of the need for education as a gateway to financial success. This trend was reinforced by the children in the program. When interviewed, the children (ages 10–12) described the various challenges of life in their community. These included poverty, alcohol abuse, physical abuse, fears of forced marriages, and other general deprivations. In every case, the children shared visions of escaping these problems through securing a good job. When given opportunity *all* the children shared idyllic visions of life consisting of houses, cars, clothing, and technology.[21]

The final indicator was the staff of the development program. Shiksha Rath represented itself as a collaborative, interfaith child development program, focusing on the holistic development of children. However, when questioned regarding the particular challenges and successes of the program, *all* the staff answers focused on educational and familial issues. The most telling response from all interviewees had to do with questions of religion. In spite being a Christian development agency, in every case when asked about the place of religion or the challenges of partnering with people of different religious traditions the standard response was variations of, "We don't talk about religion," and "Religion doesn't matter so long as the children are learning." The impact of these statements is most clearly recognized when it is read in contrast to the views of the representative religions. None of the religious traditions represented hold to such a high view of "institutional education" with such a low view of religious belief and practice. Such a principle is, however, consistent with a secular tradition and its institutions.

What was determined was that the dual demands of belonging within the secular tradition — education and economic status — had displaced religion as informing considerations of "a good life" even within a self-professed interfaith organization, at least in its operations with the urban poor children.[22]

What is the problem in being secularized? The problem is that the majority of Indians, in becoming secular, will only live a mediocre life! Because Indian secularism, like its Western counterpart, includes an active antagonism towards religion. In becoming Seculars, Indians had departed from the narratives, practices, and identity markers that root their lives in a broader and deeper way of being.

If even self-professed interfaith groups are subtly and profoundly secular rather than religious what does this say of Indian society in general? The experience of the Samvada research team as it continued with its project also provides a potential answer to the problem posed by Taylor's assessment of secularism3. The consequence of the "unbundling" of Indian identity in the wake of secularism is identifiable in Bhargava's singling out the rise of Hindu extremism. As secularism increasingly displaces other traditions, the erosion of historical and cultural sources of identity contribute to a crisis of identity. In some cases, the response of those who feel threatened is to, as Taylor suggests, seek a sense of belonging and fullness of life in places that secularism3 has pushed aside. The unfortunate tendency is that in some cases finding belonging and fullness of life in the face of the brute displacing force of secularism3 is thought to be achievable only by a brute response.

This is not to say two things: first, that secular traditions like other traditions, don't have good in them that can benefit India. Secondly, it is not to say that there is no great value that may come from a dialogue of traditions. For example, creative and collaborative dialogue between Hindu, Christian and Secular traditions would have value for each in India, and potentially also in the West. But an uncritical acceptance of secular traditions opens the door for its displacing of other traditions. Meanwhile, a reaction that is too hard towards secularism rejects its educational and technological strengths and has been used to justify extremism. Is there a response that goes beyond these options?

Indian Secular Tradition: A Hindu and Christian Response

This brings us to the question of response. It is here that I want to introduce a cultural theory formulated by the French theorist Michel de Certeau. De Certeau distinguishes between two types of practice: strategy and tactics. These practices, or "ways of operating," constitute the innumerable practices of people as they use the products and conditions that have been organized within sociocultural conditions.[23] There are essential commonalities between these practices. They are social and informed by historical trajectories and connected to locations. De Certeau writes, "Memories tie us to (a) place . . . that's what gives a neighborhood its character. There is no place that is not haunted by many different spirits hidden there in silence, spirits one can 'invoke' or not."[24] Thus, de Certeau argues, social practices are informed and guided if not empowered by a particular "spirit", a "spirit" that embodies the life of a tradition.[25] Although de Certeau's spirit could refer to several influences that build character in a geographical place, an important interpretation of de Certeau's spirit can be the empowering-spirit of Christians, even if it is not limited to it. Then this insight has a huge implication for Indian Christianity because it would mean that only a Spirit-empowered Christian tradition can critique, inform, and guide social practices in a given context. Thus, all efforts towards transforming social practices necessarily need to be Spirit-led, awakening the "hidden spirit" which has been silenced from time immemorial and yet had continually made India too its haunting ground.

Yet, for de Certeau, there is a crucial distinction between strategy and tactics that has to do with the presence or absence of sociocultural power. Practices are strategic where the ability to produce sociocultural conditions are present. Conversely, where such ability is absent, the practice is tactical. The distinction allows for an analysis of different forms of cultural practices occurring in the same place. Strategic practices produce the prevailing conditions and institutions of culture, while, tactical practices are identified as the ways people use or re-appropriate those conditions to bring meaning to a place that is not their own. This has significant relevance to the work of Shiksha Rath, which can be seen as tactical work rather than strategic. It is tactical because it is seeking to manifest a Spirit-empowered life in a secular-dominated context of the urban poor in India.

What does it mean to be a tactical practitioner? Tactics are defined by three positive determinations. First, tactics involve a "way of using" the products of a prevailing order towards ends and references foreign to the system within which the practitioners live. The "way of using" is an imaginative and interpretive event as it requires a creative bridging between sociocultural conditions and a particular context. As we have seen, the prevailing order in India is secularism, and therefore a tactical manifestation of a Spirit-filled life requires Shiksha Rath to involve a "way of using" the secular products towards a Spirit-empowered end, as Shiksha Rath's Spirit-empowered Christian tradition lives within a foreign secular system.

Next, they include "ways of operating" within the place organized by the prevailing tradition that re-appropriate that place to produce within it a different meaning. This idea of "ways of operating" presumes that people will necessarily experience a certain dissonance as they strive to maintain a way of life amid potentially contrary conditions. This dissonance is what was explicitly evident in the research on the work of Shiksha Rath. Even as Shiksha Rath sought to re-appropriate the secular NGO space for the expression of Spirit-led forms of life, it had to equally contend with the prevailing secular tradition; so much so that often its Spirit-led life was made invisible and hidden. Therefore, at first glance, the researchers were unable to detect the Spirit-led motivations and tactics of Shiksha Rath as it had to cope with the prevailing secular tradition.

Finally, these tactical operations are not multiform and fragmentary but are rather constituted by their own logic, a logic that is embedded in a historical way of thinking ordered by tradition, and in our case, by the Spirit-empowered Christian tradition. Tactical practices are often historically informed ways of thinking and acting that approach sociocultural conditions, products, and institutions with a view towards adapting them towards use that incorporates and continues the images and meanings that ground that history. It is concerning this third point of a tactical response where we found the Spirit-led work of Shiksha Rath to be in the early stages.[26]

It has been argued that in a secularized India, the secular tradition as a displacing tradition, is producing the sociocultural conditions. If that is the case, within those conditions religious traditions are the tactical practitioners. Given our understanding of tactical practices, what are Hindu and Christian tactical responses to a displacing secularism? We have shown through the analysis of Shiksha Rath's work how a Spirit-empowered Christian tradition is operating within the predominantly secular context in India. However, we must equally articulate a Hindu response, as India has a majority of Hindu practitioners. With response to secular tradition, both practicing Christians and practicing Hindus are facing the same strategic problems and therefore must offer a tactical response hand in hand.

If the predominant form of practice is that of displacing, then a tactical response is an implicit rejection of any encounter between traditions where there is only imposition of one tradition over the other. Although they work within the field of an established system and though they may be subject to the prescribed forms of that system, they nonetheless, as de Certeau writes, "trace out . . . other interests that are neither determined nor captured by the system."[27] A tactical response to displacing secularism is, therefore, best embodied through re-inhabiting their inherited Hindu tradition, even as they continue their engagement and dialogue with other traditions. We say this not merely to those who identify themselves religiously as Hindus, but to all Indians, irrespective of religion, or caste, or tribe, to get rooted in their "Indianness" or get rooted in "*Hindutva*" which is precisely a translation of "Indianness."[28]

But what is "Indianness"? Is there a single "India" with a singular "Indianness" to which all Indians are to conform? India is a land of a million gods and a thousand rivers. There is nothing singular in India. Even to talk about "India" in the singular is to do violence to Indians. A recent *Times of India* article titled, "Finally, Companies Wake up to a Million Indias," talks about how the corporate world is waking up to the diversity of India and how that should inform their marketing strategies.[29] The companies are, if you remember, part of the third wave of the influx of secular traditions, and are keenly aware that if they are to penetrate and dominate the Indian economic structure, then they have to cater uniquely to the "million Indias" present within India. The "million Indias" refers to the plurality of traditions, castes, and tribes present within India. And Indianness, or *Hindutva*, is the essence of the particular local and historical tradition that one inherits. Therefore, to get rooted in Indianness or *Hindutva* is to get rooted in whatever local or religious tradition in which one is born, perhaps even as Seculars. But remember we had said earlier that all local traditions have suffered loss, therefore, all Indian traditions need to go behind their secular experience and discover their roots while looking forward. These visions and imaginations of being Indian will necessarily vary and be different, and that is going to be the uniqueness of all Indians.

To what purposes is this argument? It is for the purposes of looking around the land in which one has grown and has their being. To understand the local traditions and the communities to which one belongs with a view to reclaim and re-inhabit them. We live in an age of the dialogue of traditions. We cannot ignore secular traditions, nor can we ignore some of the dominant Indian traditions which may not be our own local or religious tradition; and in this dialogue of traditions, we will always be a tapestry.[30]

For Indian Christians, there can be no objection to such a proposal. It allows for the continuation of Christianity in its many forms in India, while at the same time providing the opportunity for the gospel to speak into cultural contexts and critique secularity as well as other traditions. Further, if Christians take seriously the biblical admonition that those who seek "the good" find it, then such an opportunity for the moving of God's Spirit should be welcomed.[31]

Conclusion

Here we have shown how secularism in India has at its core an impulse towards displacing any and all other ways of life. Colonization has resulted in a deterioration of India's culture and the significance of religious belief and practice in the life of many Indians. We critiqued the idea that secularism can have a mediatorial role in Indian culture and argued that a proper response to a displacing secularism is a subversion of that dominating practice. Using Michel de Certeau's notion of tactics it was shown that one potential religious response to secularism is a rejection of practices that eliminate other traditions. This begins with an authentic re-engagement of embodied local and religious traditions as a basis for effective dialogue between traditions. It is guided by a deep alignment of the local and religious traditions with the originating "spirit" that informs and empowers those communities' practices. We have used the term "spirit" thus far to indicate a distinctive character of the Christian tradition that is equated with the Holy Spirit as a divinely empowering presence guiding the practice of Christians. In such a dialogical and Spirit-led environment, Indian Christianity too might find its voice, even if it be in "protesting" against the advances of Indian secularism, through its proclamation of Jesus and in its affirmation of local traditions. For India's Hindus, this allows for a platform from which its deep local history may speak into the pressing needs of Indian society while learning from other traditions, such as Christian and Secular traditions. And within this dialogical space, the "good" of the secular traditions too will have its place without necessitating a displacement of other traditions. Finally, if the space for dialogue is not only a dialogue with secularism but a polyvocal dialogue, it can also be a Spirit-empowered Christian engagement with Hindu traditions.

Notes

1. Craig Calhoun, Mark Juergensmeyer, and Jonathan VanAntwerpren, *Rethinking Secularism* (Oxford: Oxford University Press, 2011), 3.
2. We hold to the idea that Secularism is a tradition in the sense proposed by Alasdair MacIntyre, see *Whose Justice? Which Rationality?* (Notre Dame, IN: University of Notre Dame Press, 1988) and *Three Rival Versions of Moral Inquiry: Encyclopaedia, Geneology, and Tradition* (Notre Dame, IN: University of Notre Dame Press, 1990). As such, in searching for a plural descriptive noun to use to refer to those who follow the Secular tradition we chose "seculars." This adheres to the practice of applying an "s" to the proper noun. For example, those who follow the Hindu tradition are Hindus and those who follow the Christian tradition, Christians. We prefer "seculars" to "secularists."
3. Pavan K. Varma, *The Great Indian Middle Class* (New Delhi: Penguin Books, 1998), 182.
4. For the sake of the brevity, the term Christianity is being used to denote the particular form of Western Christianity Taylor identifies as having been formed alongside and in contrast with secularism. It can be distinguished from Orthodox Christianity and other present expressions of a historical Christianity

(e.g., Egyptian Copts, the Mar Thoma Church).

5.   There is a debate on secular traditions in India. The question is not so much whether or how the secularist tradition came into contact with India, but to what extent that secularism has been translated from the European cultural context. Bhargava argues that this translation has resulted in a unique Indian secularism, in contrast to what Taylor refers to as North Atlantic secularism. See Rajeev Bhargava, "The Distinctiveness of Indian Secularism," in *The Future of Secularism*, T. N. Srinivasan, ed. (Delhi: Oxford University Press, 2006), p. 20–53; and Charles Taylor, *A Secular Age* (Cambridge, MA: Belknap Press, 2007). Another perspective is that of Richard King, "Imagining Religions in India: Colonialism and the Mapping of South Asian History and Culture," in *Secularism and Religion-Making*, Markus Dressler and Arvind-Pal, eds. (Oxford: Oxford University Press, 2011), 37–61.

6.   The RSS is an Indian right-wing, Hindu nationalist, paramilitary volunteer organization.

7.   The French Revolution, a hallmark event of the secular tradition, along with the birth of the American State, provided the three ideals of secular religion — Liberté, égalité, and fraternité. Aurobindo was clever when he rejected both liberalism and socialism founded on Liberté, and égalité respectively and wanted to found the Indian State based on fraternité, as this ideal was mostly ignored in both the Western liberal and socialist states. Aurobindo's idealism was to connect the fraternité of the West with the Advaitic communitarianism of the East. Unfortunately, this Aurobindonian political dream, which might have potentially worked in India, has not yet been properly explored. But yet, in following fraternité, even Aurobindo would have succumbed to the snares of secular traditions that sought to consume the newly formed Indian State.

8.   Jürgen Habermas, *Legitimation Crisis*, trans. Thomas McCarthy (Cambridge: Polity Press, 1988), 170.

9.   Paul Ricoeur, *A Ricoeur Reader: Reflection and Imagination* (Toronto: University of Toronto Press, 1991), 306.

10.   Mahmood Saba, "Varieties of Secularism in a Secular Age," in *Varieties of Secularism in a Secular Age*, Michael Warner, Johnathan VanAntwerpen, and Craig Calhoun, eds. (Cambridge, MA: Harvard University Press, 2009), 282–99.

11.   A discussion featuring these two scholars was hosted by the Australian Catholic University and the Institute for Social Justice in April 2016. The title of the event was "Secularism and Religious and Spiritual Forms of Belonging." Presenters included Rajeev Bhargava, José Casanova, and Charles Taylor. Videos of the session are available online.

12.   Rajeev Bhargava, "The Future of Secularism," in *The Future of Secularism*, T. N. Srinivasan, ed. (Delhi: Oxford University Press, 2006), 20–53.

13.   Bhargava, "The Future of Secularism," 28.

14.   Bhargava, "The Future of Secularism," 29.

15.   Charles Taylor, *A Secular Age*, 1–14

16.   When Taylor uses the term acultural to refer to secularism, he means the

idea that even as secularism developed in the West, it could have or would develop elsewhere if the same conditions were to exist in another cultural setting.

17. Mahmood Saba, "Varieties of Secularism in a Secular Age," 283.

18. Michel de Certeau, *Heterologies: Discourse on the Other*, trans. Brian Massumi (Minneapolis: University of Minnesota Press, 2000).

19. The project was conducted by Samvada Centre for Research Resources (New Delhi, India) under and in partnership with World Vision India (WVI). The finished study and all training materials were produced and provided to WVI to be included in part of their fieldworker training process.

20. The research team from Samvada began with a critical study on three related themes (a) holistic child development, (b) interreligious collaboration, and (c) Christian-Hindu understanding of a child. The first fieldwork was conducted in December 2014, in New Delhi. In light of the challenges and problems identified by the fieldwork, it was decided that the method of action research would be followed, which not only enabled research but also directly facilitated the writing of the training manual within the practical context of a child development project. From April onwards work began with Shiksha Rath intending to enable their development workers to collaborate with the Hindu community whose children attended the programs.

21. Interviews were conducted with the children in the presence of the development workers and with parental consent. An exercise was conducted with the oldest children within the program where they were given a digital camera and tasked with going into the local community to take pictures. They were requested to focus on things or people that felt made life "good" or had personal "significance." The resulting pictures showed images of cars, clothes, homes, and televisions.

22. As a result of the research findings, the training manual was designed to aid development workers in the inclusion of religious perspectives in their programming. More than this, Shiksha Rath staff were led through a guided review of their program to allow the religious traditions of families and workers to structure and inform aspects of the holistic programming. Among other things, this included facilitating the celebration of religious festivals, creative expression, and exploration of religious history and myth.

23. Michel de Certeau, *The Practice of Everyday Life*, trans. Steven Rendell (Berkeley, CA: University of California Press, 1984), 14.

24. de Certeau, *Practice*, 108.

25. As a Jesuit, de Certeau could write that there is the awareness that the core of Christianity consists of in the experience of "there is something more" which is the (S)pirit that gives it its existence. Peter Vandermeersch, "Fragmented Christianity and Elusive Christian Bodies: On Michel de Certeau," in *Spiritual Spaces: History and Mysticism in Michel de Certeau*, Inigo Bocken, ed. (Leuven: Peeters, 2013), 59–75.

26. At the end of the research and subsequent training and reorientation of Shiksha Rath, personnel brought about the creation of space for doing explicit

spiritual activities within their programming. This was done in a mature and wise manner resulting in a significant way to engage the Spirit and be empowered by its presence in their work. Along the lines of Jesus teaching in Luke 12:12 that "the Holy Spirit will teach you at that time what to say" (NIV) the leaders of Shiksha Rath instituted practices of "listening" whereby they could be sensitive to the lives of the people they served instead of being programmatic and directed by organizational objectives.

27. de Certeau, *Practice*, 18.

28. Here we must make an important distinction. We do not presume religion to be something that can be separated from identity, though neither do we wholly equate the two. What we argue is that there is a historically rooted Indian tradition within which Hindu and Christian religion has developed and been appropriated such that they have a distinctive "Indianness." It is this "Indianness" that must be considered as part of a tactical response as much as religion.

29. See https://timesofindia.indiatimes.com/business/india-business/finally-companies-wake-up-to-a-million-indias/articleshow/69790299.cms.

30. It is important to note that in response to the Samvaa findings Shiksha Rath changed their tactics. They have changed the way they "use" approved student curriculum to include explicit introductions and discussion of religious traditions alongside and in contrast with a secular tradition. Further, they have altered their "way of operating" as an educational program to include discourse on the meaning of a "good life" as a structured part of student education based upon the religious traditions of students. This has engendered students to endeavor to engage their own religious tradition while dialoguing openly with and learning from other religious traditions. Parents and staff have been included in these processes.

31. See Acts 7:24–28, "The God who made the world and everything in it is the Lord of heaven and earth and does not live in temples built by human hands. And he is not served by human hands, as if he needed anything. Rather, he himself gives everyone life and breath and everything else. From one man he made all the nations, that they should inhabit the whole earth; and he marked out their appointed times in history and the boundaries of their lands. God did this so that they would seek him and perhaps reach out for him and find him, though he is not far from any one of us. 'For in him we live and move and have our being.' As some of your own poets have said, 'We are his offspring.'" See also Deut 4:29; Prov 8:17; Jer 29:13; Matt 7:7; Luke 11:9.

18.

Fresh Fire, Fresh Wind: Stories of Young African Pentecostals Engaging Secularism in Europe

Harvey Kwiyani

Abstract

This essay is about the growing missional presence of African Christians in Europe. It is informed by my many years of working with African denominations in Europe, in which time I have observed and interviewed several hundred second-generation African migrant Christians about their ministry in Europe. It especially focuses on the circumstances surrounding the emergence of young African Pentecostal Christians in Europe. It begins to assess these young African Pentecostals' missionary potential in Europe, where they must engage secularism in European culture. An attempt is made to debunk the belief that the second-generation migrant Christians will be able to engage in evangelizing Europe in more efficient ways than their parents. In this essay I suggest that this belief is both misguided and dangerous. It is not founded on wishful thinking, to say the least, and only serves to justify the churches' unwillingness to contextualize their forms of Christianity and to engage in multicultural mission in Europe.

Key words: migration, second-generation migrants, secularism, Pentecostalism, mentoring

Introduction

African Christianity continues to rise in Europe. Each new year brings prospects of some more hundreds of African churches to be planted in the cities of Europe, from Athens to Zurich, and every city in-between. Indeed, African Christianity is the growing expression of Christianity in Europe. Generally speaking, where Christianity is said to be growing in Europe, it is usually migrant congregations that are growing.[1] Migrants are fast becoming the most visible Christians in Europe right at the time when both Europe's Christianity and her religious identity are, for various reasons, going through a massive transition. First, since the mid-twentieth century, Christianity has lost its place at the center of Europe's culture and society. The death of Christendom has changed Europe significantly. Indigenous European Christians are disappearing at an alarming pace. Philip Jenkins seems rather cautious when he suggests that, "By 2050, only about one-fifth of the world's 3 billion Christians will be non-Hispanic Whites. Soon, the phrase 'a White Christian' may sound like a curious oxymoron, as mildly surprising as 'a Swedish Buddhist.' Such people can exist, but a slight eccentricity is implied."[2] Jenkins' prophecy has already been fulfilled. Gina Zurlo and Todd Johnson's research shows non-white Western Christians today form around 30 percent of the world's Christian population.[3] Many historic church buildings have been converted to become nursing homes and pubs while many majestic cathedrals now serve as museums. In Britain, a 2016 survey showed that 49 percent of the population identified as non-religious, while Christians are at 44 percent.[4]

Here in Europe, there is already a young generation of Europeans who know nothing of Christianity. They do not know of a time when their ancestors went to evangelize the "heathens" in other parts of the world. They have themselves become the heathens who need to be evangelized. When asked, they can only associate Christianity with the immigrants — the Nigerians, the Koreans, and other non-white people they see giving out tracts on the streets of their cities, carrying Bibles to church on Sunday, or praying vigorously at Friday night vigils. The city of London puts this into perspective for us. Peter Brierley's 2010 research suggested that overall church membership — and attendance — in London is on the increase, and therefore, London churches are growing again as more people are joining the church than those leaving it. In saying so, Brierley confirmed his own earlier argument (made in 2005) that the church in England is "pulling out of the nosedive."[5] However, a closer look at the data reveals that this growth is happening largely in the so-called black-majority churches. Brierley also observed in 2010 that almost fifty percent of the people who attend church in London on any given Sunday were of African and Afro-Caribbean heritage. Newer anecdotal reports are saying that in 2018, more than 60 percent of church attendance in London is black, attending various types of churches in the city.[6] Essentially, people of African and West Indian heritage, who form only 14 percent of London's population, account for 60 percent of church attendance in the city. Most of those will attend an African Pentecostal church. Thus, African Pentecostalism is reshaping London Christianity to a great extent. The future of Christianity in London (and probably Europe) may be very African in nature.

Second, European Christianity today includes people from all parts of the world. Many European Christians today are likely to be of non-European heritage. Many of these will be found in African, Asian, and Latin American churches every Saturday or Sunday right across Europe. Thus, to faithfully count Christians in Europe today, it is necessary to include people of all ethnicities and from all parts of the world living in Europe. Christianity in Europe is no longer a religion of white Europeans only. It is a religion that reflects both its global reach and the current migration trends that bring Christians from all parts of the world to Europe. Indeed, a significant majority of migrant Christians in Europe come from Africa. In some European cities, African Christianity is emerging to be the only type of Christianity visible in town. De-churched Europeans have lost interest in organized religion. In Glasgow, for instance, it seems that Christianity in general is becoming an African religion as many white majority churches close down and African immigrant churches replace them.[7] Of course, migration has brought numerous other religions into the continent that was once the global Christian heartland of the world. Consequently, this changing religious landscape of Europe means that Christianity is just one among many religions that are seeking converts. European Christianity is fast becoming a microcosm of world Christianity, a mosaic of different expressions of Christianity from all parts of the world living together in European countries.

African Pentecostalism in Europe

For centuries, there has always been some form of migration between Africa and Europe. The most documented of these migrations is the Trans-Atlantic slave trade that forced millions of Africans into the diaspora and brought a small number of enslaved Africans to Europe. I concern myself here with contemporary migration that has happened in the aftermath of the collapse of the colonial empires. This is the migration that brings many thousands of Pentecostal Christians from Africa to Europe, those migrant Christians whose children now have to make sense of growing up Pentecostal in a secular world. This migration of African Christians to Europe started in the mid-twentieth century. In the case of Britain, first to arrive were West Indians of the Windrush

Generation.[8] These immigrants brought their own Pentecostal/charismatic-influenced Christianity from the Caribbean Islands. For various reasons, racism being chief among them, these Afro-Caribbean Christians could not stay in British churches. They ended up forming their own West Indian churches in Britain. Many of those churches still exist today, but most of them are past their glory days.

African migration began to accelerate in the 1970s, right after the collapse of European colonization of Africa, and continued until 2005 when it peaked, and then started to decline. The last quarter of the twentieth century is marked by the explosion of both the Pentecostal Christianity in Africa and the migration of Africans to Europe, North American, and other parts of the world. A majority of Africans currently living in the UK migrated between 1991 and 2011.[9] Just like the Afro-Caribbeans did in the 1950s and 60s, African migrants have also brought with them their Christianity and, consequently, have brought many churches with them to Europe. Today it is a well-established fact that the majority of African Christians in Europe identify themselves as Pentecostals. Even those who did not belong to such churches at home find themselves gravitating towards Pentecostal churches in the diaspora. For instance, any directory of black majority churches[10] in Britain will make it evident that African Christianity in Britain is Pentecostal in its outlook and expression. It is not any different in Europe. Outstanding African denominations in Europe include the Redeemed Christian Church of God[11] and the Church of Pentecost.[12] Many other smaller networks of African churches also exist in Europe. From West Africa, we have the Christ Apostolic Church and its sister-denominations, the Apostolic Church of Nigeria, and the Apostolic Church of Ghana, which have many congregations in Britain. The Apostolic Faith Mission is a South African denomination that has congregations scattered around European cities. There are many other Zimbabwean, Congolese, Kenyan, and other clusters of congregations of Africans scattered in Europe. For most of these African Christians in Europe, being a Pentecostal is a significant identity as it distinguishes them from the nominal Christianity they see in European churches and, thus, justifies their sense of call to evangelize Europe. Being a Pentecostal clearly sets them apart from mainline European Christians whom they believe to spiritually dead and whose churches they find lifeless and boring.

Africanizing European Christianity

The growth of African Christianity in Europe is reason enough for optimism when European Christianity has lost millions of followers since the mid-twentieth century. There is a hopeful future for Christianity in a continent that has seen dwindling numbers of Christians for decades. God is bringing to Europe Christians from other parts of the world to renew and reinvigorate European Christianity.[13] Politically, they may be labeled economic migrants, but in God's grand scheme of mission, they are part of the ambassadors, the salt and light that Christ has in Europe in this day and age. Of course, by their sheer numbers, foreign Christians are impacting the religious landscape of Europe in a significant way — Africans have reversed the church decline in London. Many of the largest congregations in Europe are African. The fastest growing and church-planting movements in Europe today are African. Indeed, Walter Hollenweger was right to observe that "British Christians prayed for revival, and when the revival came, they could not recognize it because it was *black*."[14]

Nevertheless, there is great need to be cautious in our optimism. African Christian presence in Europe has not resulted in any significant evangelization of Europeans yet. African churches in Europe are often true to their name; they are African churches both in membership and culture, with a negligibly small number of Europeans in their midst. Many African churches are having great difficulties connecting with Europeans. There are many reasons for this, but one of the main ones, in my estimation, is that a majority of African churches in Europe rather proudly self-identify as Pentecostals or charismatic, when Europeans, generally speaking, are wary of Pentecostalism. There are also many reasons for Europe's skepticism of Pentecostalism. In Britain, I have come to learn that the "excesses" of Pentecostalism (for instance, speaking in tongues and praying for healing and deliverance) go against the values of British culture that loves moderation. Also, Pentecostalism in most Europeans' eyes is grounded in the "health and wealth gospel," a gospel that many European Christians deride. Of course, African Pentecostal pastors leading megachurches in Britain are almost always covered negatively in the media for their flamboyant lifestyles and their preaching of the prosperity gospel.[15] Adding to this, African Pentecostals tend to put a great deal of emphasis on the power and work of the Holy Spirit, which makes sense in the spirit-centered worldview of the Africans. Most Europeans, however, live in a secular post-Enlightenment worldview where spirits (and God) are too far away to be of any relevance to human life. In the language of Charles Taylor, Westerners (including Europeans) live as buffered selves in a world devoid of spirits.[16] The Pentecostal focus on the Spirit and the spirit-world, the belief in a Holy Spirit that acts as God in human life in real and tangible ways, is antithetical to the beliefs of many Europeans, including European Christians. This essentially means that the Africans' Pentecostal identity often hinders their witness to Europeans.

Young African Pentecostals in Europe

Most African churches in Europe have more young people than adults. This is simply because church attendance among Africans is usually a family affair. Parents rarely leave their children at home when they go to church. Most of the young people in these churches are younger than 18 years old and still living with their parents and must attend church even when they do not want to. Consequently, many of these young diaspora Africans stop attending their parents' churches — and any church, for that matter — when they become adults and/or leave their parents' homes. Many will have endured African churches in their teen-years despite not enjoying the services and cannot wait to become independent to choose for themselves whether or not to go to church and, if so, what church to go to. Thus, when compared to those under 18, we find that few young adults between the ages of 18 and 30 years have stayed in African churches.[17] The main reason for this — and this is the crux of my argument — is that young African migrants in Europe are secularizing just as much as young Europeans, the only difference being that they are secularizing later then their European counterparts, doing so after they have left their parents' homes. Only a small percentage of them will keep their faith alive and stay in their parents' churches or find new churches where they can belong.

Part of the reasons for their discontent with their parents' churches, and their subsequent secularization is the frustration of living in two worlds at the same time. Indeed, while they grow up in religious homes and have to follow their parents to church, they are educated, cultured and "civilized" in a Western system whose dominant worldview has not been friendly towards religion for the past few generations. Once these younger Africans step out of their parents' religious homes, they are welcomed into a world where religion is at best kept as a private matter or, at worst, frowned upon. Indeed, unlike the parents whose entire worldview was shaped by religion as they grew up in Africa and were discipled in the public sphere,[18] these young Africans in Europe have minimal access to discipleship. Almost literally, they leave their religion at home when they go to school. Insisting on being religious in the public sphere often brings marginalization and social exclusion. Thus, during their formative years their lives embody the schizophrenic tension of living in a religious home within a secular world. This tension during their formative years may have a long-lasting impact on their lives. They have to learn the delicate art of living in two worlds at the same time. They have to fluently speak both the Pentecostal language of their parents at home and the secular languages of their friends at school in order to belong in both worlds. As religious Africans, they participate in their parents' prayer vigils and long worship services yet, when away from parents, they can be just as secular as any anti-religious Westerner. Many of these migrant children will easily lead worship in church on Sunday and act totally secular on Monday.[19]

Mission and Young African Pentecostals in Europe

Because of the context in which these young Africans are processing their faith, those who stay in the church are usually the ones who have made up their mind to do so. Most of them will have embraced the Pentecostal identity of their parents' Christianity, even though they shape their worship differently. Many of them will have understood that to be a Pentecostal Christian in Europe is countercultural, both in the wider secular culture and in the general non-charismatic inclinations of European Christianity. They will have learned the intricacies of the Pentecostal devotion to Christ through the Spirit and will have taken a fair share of the marginalization suffered by their parents because of their Pentecostal faith in Europe. Yet, they do not mind paying the social price of being the odd ones out in their community, and because of this, they often find themselves involved in the ministry. Like Jeremiah, they have to let out the fire shut in their bones (Jer 20:9). Because of this, we see a young generation of African Pentecostals emerging in Europe. They are very few in number compared to their parents' generation but they are uniquely prepared to serve God in mission in Europe. They understand the shortcomings of their parents' ministries and shape their ministries for a different outcome. However, they also face a unique set of challenges that neither their parents nor their British counterparts have to deal with. Additionally, they lack most of the spiritual and social resources that were available to their parents back in Africa.

These young Pentecostals have grown up in Europe. Many of them were born in Europe. As such, they have been educated in Europe. They think of Europe as home. Culturally, they are more European than they are African. They are fluent in European languages, and indeed, many of them cannot speak any African language at all. When asked where they are from, quite often they say, "my parents are from Africa," thinking of themselves as Europeans and not Africans. Nevertheless, out on the streets of Europe, they are seen as foreigners, immigrants, and black Africans whether they like or not. While they may consider themselves as European as any other European could be, they still face the systemic problems of racial prejudice that their parents encountered. They have to constantly walk the thin line between belonging and rejection. They belong in Europe, and yet at the same time, they are foreigners. They live hyphenated identities; they are Nigerian-British, Ghanaian-British, or Kenyan-British. They embody the true image of resident aliens. As residents, they belong in the European public sphere just like any other Europeans, yet as aliens, they find themselves outside the general spheres of influence in Europe.

As African Pentecostals who have grown up in Europe, they also occupy the tight space between the Pentecostalism of their parents' churches and mainstream European Christianity. On the one hand, the parents have, for the large part, established their ministries and churches at the margins of European Christianity and often have done so intentionally. In general, their parents have grown their ministries in Europe by excluding those of other tribes, nationalities, and ethnicities. They have not connected with other European Pentecostal or mainline European denominations. They have not even connected with African denominations of other nationalities. On the other hand, the younger generation is multicultural in its outlook: anyone can be European, after all. But they have come of age without any good practical models of cross-cultural ministry. They have been discipled in tribally exclusive churches, and have had very little experience of both cross-cultural mission and ministry. They need to learn and discover for themselves how to maintain their faith and, at the same time, share it with their non-African neighbors in Europe.

"We Need Mentors"

In a nutshell, younger generation African Christians in Europe are beginning to play a very significant role in shaping what Europe's religious landscape will be for the next few decades. They carry the burden of preserving not only African Christianity in Europe, but also European Christianity as a whole. However, both their parents (first-generation migrants) and European Christians must help equip and prepare them for the job. As things stand today, they face many challenges that are unique to their generation. For instance, I wonder what it means for them to be European-born African Pentecostals. In addition, how would they contextualize African Pentecostalism to be able to engage European cultures? They are the witness that God has placed in Europe for their generation, thus, they must contextualize whatever form of Christianity they embody if they want to evangelize in Europe. This kind of contextualization is new: both the African Pentecostalism that needs to be contextualized and the religious landscape of Europe for whom the contextualization must be done are calling for something that has not been done before. Indeed, how does a Pentecostal evangelize a people who are suspicious of the works and power of the Spirit?

When we try to understand the situation of young African Christians in Europe, we begin to see why they call for mentoring relationships with leaders who can help them negotiate the two worlds in which they live. Indeed, when I surveyed some 300 young Africans in Europe about what they feel they need most to be effective in ministry, there was a general outcry that they need mentors.[20] This younger generation growing up in the diaspora lacks the communal structures that would support their faith like those their parents had in Africa. The village that should help shape their faith remained in Africa. Their parents are generally not that helpful as they are also struggling to make sense of their own life and faith in the unfamiliar cultures of a post-Christian and secularized West. They cannot guide the faith of their children when they do not understand the challenges that their children face outside their homes. Most first-generation immigrant parents do not know what it is like to be a teenager in a secular world, and thus, find it difficult to disciple their children in a foreign context. Consequently, when I sum up everything that I have heard from the many young diaspora Africans with whom I have spoken in the past 15 years, it boils down to these three words:

"We need mentors." Many of them live in a world that lies *in between* many worlds, and they do so with little relevant guidance among a multiplicity of disjointed worldviews and cultural philosophies. The cost of discipling the younger generation in the individualistic and time-starved consumeristic cultures is often too much for both first-generation immigrants and local European Christians alike. Consequently, many young people in the diaspora grow up feeling isolated and alone, as lonesome figures wandering in the desert, hoping to find good spiritual nourishment along the way, but not knowing where to go. If nothing is done to properly disciple this younger generation of Africans in the diaspora, a generation will be lost (which usually leads to many other generations afterward being lost too).

This plea for mentors highlights three underlying issues. First, most African church leaders are not really doing what they say or think they are doing. Every first-generation African minister I have spoken to in Europe says they are concerned about the faith of their children and are doing everything in their power to make sure that the second generation is properly discipled. However, a majority of the second generation say their parent's style of discipleship is not relevant to them. Second, relevant and effective mentoring and Spirit-empowered discipleship will be critical to the raising of able African younger generations in Europe and must be done by both African and European leaders in collaboration. Third, failure to provide proper discipleship and ministry training to the younger generation means that the impact of African Christianity in Europe will be limited.

Engaging Secularism

There are significant differences in the ways that first- and second-generation African migrants respond to European culture. For most first-generation migrants, secularism is the foundation of an evil system that shapes European culture and that must be pulled down. Many try to steer away from its influences since they do not want to encounter secularism's influences needlessly. The general attitude towards European secularism can be distilled to one sentence: "Beware secular humanism, if you don't beat it, it will beat you." I have heard this counsel repeated hundreds of times in the many African churches both in Europe and in North America. The secular life that shapes many European cultures is diametrically opposed to the spirit-centered religious life of most Africans. Many first-generation African migrants despise secularism and by extension, those who follow it. They generally believe that a life that does not acknowledge God's presence and influence in the world, such as that of most Europeans, is not worth living or emulating. They believe the Psalmist's statement that 'A fool says in his heart, 'there is no God,' or lives like God does not exist as many Europeans do. Thus, secularism is not attractive to African Pentecostals. It is an enemy that needs to be resisted and a stronghold that must be pulled down. Most African migrants in Europe pray fervently that secularism does not take their children away from the faith.

On the other hand, second-generation Africans in Europe have been shaped in a secular culture. Secularism forms the general lens through which they view the world. In keeping with the wider European culture, those of them who are religious confine their religion to a small section of life, leaving a large part of their lives untouched by their faith. In choosing to identify as religious, they are doing something radically countercultural; their generation, both second-generation African migrants and European youths, is secularizing in large numbers in Europe. Unlike their parents, second-generation African Pentecostals in Europe tend to seek (and find) good in European culture. Indeed, secularism hardly bothers them at all. It is their native worldview. Many of them have no other worldview with which to compare it: their parents' African religious worldview hardly looks attractive at all. Consequently, they have found a way to carry on with their religion despite the secularism that surrounds them. Even though they are radical about their faith, they are non-confrontational in their engagement with European secularism.

More important to the argument of this essay, however, is the observation that like their parents' generation, they are also unable to effectively engage European cultures in mission. Their parents used language and worldview as excuses. The second-generation cannot justifiably say that either language or worldview is a problem. We have to look elsewhere for the factors behind the second generation Pentecostals' inability to bridge the gap between their religion and the context. To do so, I have turned to conversations I have had with two young African Pentecostals serving in the ministry in England, Wola and Kweku (not real names).[21]

Wola

Wola is a young African woman in her early twenties. She leads a growing Pentecostal ministry that focuses on evangelizing university students in Birmingham. She was born in Nigeria but migrated to England at the age of four. Her church is of Nigerian origin and its ecclesiology is deeply shaped by a spirit-centered theology and worldview. Her pastor often teaches that all problems are, first and foremost, spiritual problems, and can all be solved by prayer, with the help of the anointing and prophecy. She is often conflicted when she finds herself in situations where prayer seems to go unanswered. Her pastor would tell her to pray more arguing that if she has more faith, all her prayers will be answered. But she knows that sometimes, no matter how much she prays, she receives no answers. Consequently, she tends to avoid situations that could lead to the predicament of unanswered prayer. She told me in an interview:

> I feel that my Pentecostal faith does not prepare me well to deal with situations where what I am trusting God to do does not happen. As a Pentecostal Christian, I want to be able to explain everything in terms of spiritual activity in the world, but this theology often fails to deal with questions that do not need the Spirit for an answer or where the Spirit of God does something I cannot simply explain. In my attempts to minister to my European friends, I find that over-reliance on the spirit puts them off. Very rarely do they respond to miracles at all. Often, what I would recognize as a miracle, they explain away using science and reason. Many of them are logical beings who want their lives to make sense — no surprises. My church has not given me the tools to engage reason at all.

Wola struggles to communicate her Pentecostal faith in a context where the power of the Spirit does not attract the same attention as it did in Africa. Consequently, just like her parents' generation, she is successful in evangelizing fellow Africans. She can connect with other second-generation migrants but always fails to engage non-Africans in evangelism.

Kweku

Kweku is a 25-year old Ghanaian Pentecostal pastor of an African church in the southern part of England. He was born in Britain and has visited Ghana only twice in his entire life, thus he is a real second-generation migrant. His father is a senior leader of a Ghanaian denomination that boasts some two hundred congregations in the UK alone. Kweku is the studious type; he describes himself as a theological nerd. Indeed, in addition to degrees in Mathematics, he also has a bachelor's and a master's degree in theology. His ministry is built on an ability to communicate the word of God in ways that make sense to Europeans. To Kweku, knowledge of the truth (at least as he understands it) is the solution to all human predicament. He admonishes his members not only to know who they are in Christ but also how to make money to excel in this world. His struggle is that, while he can identify with European culture and can minister as any European would, he is not received well among Europeans as well as among Africans. He put it rather succinctly to me in an interview we had in 2015.

> When I minister in my father's church, people say I am too European for them. They love the eloquence with which the word of God is articulated, but they complain that they do not see the passion or the anointing. I understand that for such churches, the word alone without the anointing makes very little impact but I do not know how to talk about the Spirit like they do. I used to be able to "flow in the anointing" but my theological studies took that away from me. I do not despise what I got in return, a sound theological training. But that theology has made me a foreigner among my own people. Worse, when I try to minister among Europeans, I quickly hit the barrier of race. They also do not seem to fully get my theology. Unless I serve as an assistant to a white European minister, there is no way I can fully actualize myself in the ministry.

Kweku embodies the dilemma of contextualization. If he wants to serve cross-culturally, he feels he has to let go of his Pentecostal identity, its theology, and mannerisms. European culture and education has shaped him into a European, he finds it difficult to belong among his own people. However, this is not enough. He needs to negotiate the prejudices that most migrants face, racism being one of them.

Conclusion

The stories of Wola and Kweku depict the two prevalent ways that shape how the second generation is responding to secularism. Some refuse to be influenced by it, while others are subsumed by its worldview. This shows that there is a need for both African and European church leaders to work together to equip and empower young African Christians in Europe. This will help those who, like Wola, learn how to share their faith in ways that Europeans will find relatable. It will also help people like Kweku find ways to keep their identity and while at the same time negotiating the prejudices that make it difficult for foreign Christians to evangelize effectively. The African leaders will disciple them in ways that safeguard their Pentecostal faith, while the Europeans will serve as their cultural interpreters who will show them what works and does not work in Europe. The second generation will have to hold these in a creative tension that enables them to be African Pentecostals while being effective missionaries in Europe. This, I believe, will shape a significant aspect of European Christianity in the next few generations.

Notes

1. Peter W. Brierley, *London's Churches Are Growing!: What the London Church Census Reveals* (Tonbridge: ADBC Publishers, 2013), 3.
2. Philip Jenkins, *The Next Christendom: The Coming of Global Christianity* (New York: Oxford University Press, 2002), 3.
3. Gina A. Zurlo, Todd Johnson, and Peter F. Crossing, "World Christianity and Mission 2020: Ongoing Shift to the Global South," *International Bulletin of Mission Research* 40:1 (2020), 10.
4. NatCen Social Research, "British Social Attitudes 34: Record Number of Brits with no Religion," http://natcen.ac.uk/news-media/press-releases/2017/september/   british-social-attitudes-record-number-of-brits-with-no-religion/, accessed Feb 14, 2020.
5. Peter W. Brierley, *Pulling Out of the Nose Dive: A Contemporary Picture of Church Going, What the 2005 English Church Census Reveals* (Tonbridge: ADBC Publishers, 2006), 1.
6. Brierley, *London Churches*, 3.
7. Sheila Akomiah-Conteh, "The Changing Landscape of the Church in Post-Christendom Britain: New Churches in Glasgow, 2000–2016" (a research paper, University of Aberdeen, 2019).
8. For more on this, see Mike Phillips and Trevor Phillips, *Windrush: The Irresistible Rise of Multi-Racial Britain* (Toronto: HarperCollins Canada, 1998).
9. For more on this subject, see Peter J. Aspinall and Martha J. Chinouya, *The African Diaspora Population in Britain: Migration, Diasporas and Citizenship* (London: Springer, 2016), 12.
10. I use the term "black majority churches" with reservations, which is still quite popular in British literature even though it has serious racial undertones. It seems to be the safest way to categorize all African and Afro-Caribbean churches together. However, it does not account for the differences between the cultural characteristics, the experiences and the histories of the two groups. It is not too dissimilar to the "black church" on the American landscape.

11. The Redeemed Christian Church of God (RCCG) originated in Nigerian in 1952. They have around 1000 congregations in the United Kingdom. For a history of the RCCG, see Stephan Hunt, "A Church for All Nations: The Redeemed Christian Church of God," *Pneuma: The Journal of the Society for Pentecostal Studies* 24:2 (Fall 2002), https://doi.org/10.1163/15700740260388036.

12. The Church of Pentecost is a Pentecostal denomination from Ghana. It has 200 congregations in the UK. For its history, see Robert W. Wyllie, "Pioneers of Ghanaian Pentecostalism: Peter Anim and James McKeown," *Journal of Religion in Africa* 6 (1974), 109–22.

13. Harvey C. Kwiyani, "Blessed Reflex: African Christianity in Europe," *Theologia Reformata* 60:1 (2017), 13–27.

14. Roswith Gerloff, *A Plea for British Black Theologies: The Black Church Movement in Britain in Its Transatlantic Cultural and Theological Interaction with Special References to the Pentecostal Oneness (Apostolic) and Sabbatarian Movements*, Studien zur Interkulturellen Geschichte des Christentums (Frankfurt am Main: P. Lang, 1992), 9.

15. Andrew Brown, "The Prosperity Gospel Makes a Mockery of Christianity," *The Guardian* (London), May 29, 2013, https://www.theguardian.com/commentisfree/andrewbrown/2013/may/29/prosperity-gospel-mockery-christianity, accessed Feb 19, 2020.

16. See Charles Taylor's thesis on the porous and the buffered self in Charles Taylor, *A Secular Age* (Cambridge, MA: Belknap Press, 2007), 37–39.

17. Harvey C. Kwiyani, *Our Children Need Roots and Wings: Equipping and Empowering Young Diaspora Africans for Life and Mission* (Liverpool: Missio Africanus Publishing, 2019), 61.

18. A great deal of their discipleship took place in their youth at school and other charismatic fellowships.

19. Youth workers among diaspora children and teenagers will have to develop new models of discipleship and ministry-training for second-generation children and young adults. The old models that we used in Africa will not work here — the culture is too different; the discipleship needs are too dissimilar and the concerns of the younger generation here too disparate. In the same manner, copying and pasting from Western materials produced by Western youth workers will also not be of much help. Both the cultural contexts and the concerns of British young people will differ immensely from those of migrant youths.

20. This is an ongoing longitudinal research in which I follow the religious lives of young children of African migrant Christians in Europe. I have closely followed 20 of them (12 male and 8 female) for 10 years now but through them I have had access to several hundred young people whom I meet in many youth events in Europe. See Kwiyani, *Our Children*, 80.

21. I have known both Wola and Kweku for five years. I have followed the development of their ministries since 2013 as part of a phenomenological research project exploring the religious lives of second-generation African

migrants in Britain. What I say here about their ministries is no way a comprehensive picture of what they are doing as they seek to be faithful to their calling.

19.

Witnessing to Christ in Eastern Europe: An Assessment of Context

Marcel V. Măcelaru

Abstract

This study offers a summary assessment of Eastern Europe as a context for mission in three steps. A description of the challenges faced by the church during the communist decades is first offered in order to provide a background for some of the contextual realities within which the church operates in the present, which comprises the second part of the chapter. The study concludes with a few suggestions (lessons) for Christian communities and ministries in the region.

Key words: communist oppression of Christians, Christianity in Eastern Europe, Post-1989 Christian witness in Eastern Europe, sustainable ministry

Introduction

One of the stated purposes of the Empowered21 Scholars Consultation for 2018 was to undertake assessments of local contexts within which the witness of the church to Christ's uniqueness takes place. The purpose for which such assessments were encouraged was to identify challenges and opportunities for mission, and eventually to help reformulate the work of Christian communities and ministries in ways that would make them more relevant in the contemporary arena. In light of these, I offer an assessment of the Eastern European context[1] in three chronological, and somewhat autobiographical, steps. Chronological because there is a historical thrust that underlines this evaluation. Autobiographical because the period to which I refer in this article coincides with my lifespan up until now.

I was born and raised to adulthood in a Romanian Pentecostal family during the last two decades of communist Romania. As such, although inevitably influenced by my specific Romanian experience, the assessment provided here can safely be applied to communist Eastern Europe in its entirety. Second, I was trained as a minister in Romania and former Yugoslavia in the period immediately following the fall of Eastern European communism. Therefore, I experienced first-hand much of what will be described below about those years. Finally, as a theological educator now, I am inevitably reflective about directions for mission and the future of the church in my context in Romania, in Croatia, my adoptive country, and implicitly in the larger Eastern European arena within which I serve. Thus, the proposals with which I conclude this study.

The thoughts provided here do not come in a vacuum, for there is a rich body of scholarly evaluations of the Eastern European context that tackle different geographical areas and periods from different perspectives. Reference is made below to several such works, for in addition to my personal understanding of the context, I also take my cue from the experiences others have shared.[2] Among these, I would draw the attention of the reader to three documents I found invaluable in providing a thematic base for my assessment: "The Osijek Declaration of 1991," "The Oradea Declaration of 1994," and "The Osijek Declaration of 1998."[3] Coming out of three gatherings that took place in the region during the first decade after the fall of communism, these documents make reference to the communist oppression of the church in Eastern Europe before 1989, evaluate the post-1989 context of transition toward democratic societies, and project a future for the mission of the church in the region that speaks relevantly even now, more than twenty years later.

Christianity in Communism: The Pre-1989 Context

The beginning of communism in Eastern Europe can be traced back to the summer of 1944 when the Soviet Red Army entered the region in its westward push toward Berlin. The Eastern European territories were freed from Nazi occupation, but at the same time they were turned, one after another, with the help of local communists, into Soviet-controlled communist states. The first to fall completely under communist rule were Albania and Bulgaria (1945), followed by Romania, Poland and Hungary (1947), Czechoslovakia (1948), and the German Democratic

Republic (1949). Thus, a buffer zone was created by Moscow, whose purpose was to deter any other attack coming from the West, and an "Iron Curtain" (an expression first used by Winston Churchill) was now dividing the European continent geographically, as well as politically and ideologically.[4]

One could describe Eastern European communism as a social experiment (albeit a failed one) that aimed to create a classless society within which a utopian dream of a "golden age," ideologically defined along the lines of Marxist economic theories, was relentlessly pursued. Within such a worldview, there was no room for transcendence; as such, religion was regarded a pre-scientific remnant, a proof of obscurantism and, therefore, a hindrance to "true" intellectualism and social development. The consequence was a never-ending opposition to all forms of religion, and in particular, to Christianity.

Freedom of belief was systematically undermined, and as the communist era unfolded, restrictions designed to control all forms of religious manifestation were gradually implemented. The intention behind such actions was evident — to isolate believers and believing communities by making faith an individual, familial, or, at most, a congregational matter. Consequently, any activity that clashed with this strategy was harshly and swiftly dealt with. Evangelism, including the simple act of sharing one's faith with a non-believer, was regarded as a grave political error. Mission and Christian Education were forbidden. Religion was tolerated as an individual practice but was not given space as a social reality. The Marxist charge: "Die Religion . . . ist das Opium des Volkes"[5] was the motto on which the opposition was built, for by demonizing religion and its manifestations, communist authorities justified their anti-religious campaigns.

The communist opposition to Christianity varied in form and intensity from context to context and from period to period: at best, believers were barely tolerated, at worst brutally persecuted. Generally speaking, we can say that restrictions and persecutions were the norms applied by communist authorities against Christian faith and practice in their attempt to control and eventually curb the progress of faith communities. Such restrictions included

- believers, including children and teenagers in schools, were mocked regularly during specially organized public gatherings that they were forced to attend;

- young believers were denied access to higher education;

- believing workers were denied opportunities for professional advancement and therefore better pay;

- unjustified police raids on private and church properties in search of Bibles and other Christian literature were carried out regularly;

- the use of church buildings was controlled and, in some cases, forbidden, a policy that severely restricted communal expressions of worship;

- church properties were confiscated, and church buildings were arbitrarily demolished;[6]

- church gatherings were strictly monitored, and interdictions in terms of worship practices were sometimes applied, to the point that participation in the worship through singing, prayer, Bible reading, preaching, etc. had to be sanctioned beforehand by communist representatives;

- believers, especially pastors and Christian leaders, were permanently monitored, sometimes unjustifiably imprisoned, and if perceived as a political threat, even condemned to years of forced labor.

Needless to say, this is but a summary description of a much harsher history. Accounts of persecutions sometimes became available,[7] but countless stories of oppression that took place throughout Eastern Europe were never told. Furthermore, the list of oppressive actions given above is by no means exhaustive, for the methods through which communists endeavored to control, diminish and eventually extirpate religion from society were variated and numerous.

Of course, as we now know, the communist opposition failed, for not only Christian communities survived the hardships thrown at them, but in some cases, they actually flourished.[8] However, one also cannot deny the effects said opposition had upon Christian communities and individual believers. At least four such consequences come to mind.

First, by confining all religious activities within local church buildings, the communists succeeded in dislocating and disconnecting Christian faith and practice from society. Also, by denying Christian communities the right to active participation in charity and other social activities, the communists managed to make the witness of the church ineffective. Such forced isolation became the ground within which a spirituality of withdrawal, reinforced by escapist eschatologies, flourished, the net result being a socially irrelevant church.

Second, by cutting off the church from the larger (international) body of Christ, the communists eliminated true inter-ecclesial dialogue and cooperation. This led to an underdeveloped ecclesiology, characterized by isolationism and fragmentation, and gave birth to definitions of ecclesial identity that emphasized differences and divisiveness.

Third, by denying the church access to theological education and literature, the communists curbed the theological and spiritual maturity of believers and congregations. Lack of theological knowledge led to uncritical identification with the world and the (unconscientious) adoption of totalitarian and other non-Christian mentalities. The result was confusion in terms of what genuine (gospel-shaped) identity is about and the gradual thinning of the true Christian ethos within communities.

Fourth, the dire opposition to the Christian message, the constant surveillance of Christian leaders, and the unrelenting persecution of the believers have contributed to the propagation of fear and mistrust within and amongst believing communities. This had a negative influence on the cohesion of congregations, for no true sense of *koinonia* is available within an atmosphere of suspicion.[9]

Christianity in Transition(ism): The Post-1989 Context

The collapse of the Marxist-based totalitarian systems that ruled for decades over the eastern part of Europe, and the religious freedom that followed, raised the hope of many in the early nineties that a genuine Christian revival will take place in the region. The immediate reaction from the international Christian community came in the form of hundreds of missionaries and mission agencies that were sent to "bring Christ" to the Eastern European lands. Similarly, evangelical churches from the region, which were previously forbidden to proclaim the gospel and minister to non-believers, engaged in all forms of evangelistic actions, to the point that voices began rising from within the historical churches in the region, accusing local evangelical-protestant Christianity of ineffective proselytism patterned after Western models of mission.[10]

Needless to say, the overall reaction of the people being "evangelized" was not as enthusiastic as expected. The religious scene in Eastern Europe has not changed as dramatically as was hoped for. The long-awaited across-the-board Christian revival announced by many in the early nineties had not come true, and the resurgence of Christianity that took place in some quarters did not succeed in filling the vacuum left by the departure of atheistic ideology.

The realization that no radical change was taking place has prompted many in the churches after 1989 to retort to another utopian view of history, one in which the present is but a transition toward something better. Since the focus on the future makes compromises in the present possible and acceptable, I interpret the current situation as a change from communism to an equally damaging escapist worldview, one I would call "transition(ism)." It is this escapist worldview, I propose, that leads to idleness and lack of will-power within Christian communities to address the urgent issues facing Eastern European societies today. Such a worldview prompts believers and Christian communities to focus all their attention and energy "inwardly," consequently once again making them irrelevant as witnesses for Christ within the public arena of Eastern European societies.

Of course, this is not to say that positive changes did not happen. Numerous examples of ministry intelligence, faithfulness, and divine provision are available throughout the region. For instance, in the past twenty-five years, theological education enterprises in Eastern Europe have progressed outstandingly. In striking contrast with before 1989, when such education was prohibited, most places and Christian denominations in the region have now opened theological institutions of higher education where pastors and Christian workers are trained for ministry.

Also, in terms of positive changes, one needs to mention the significant church growth registered in some quarters and the flourishing of ministries and charities addressing the social and economic needs of Christians and non-Christians alike. Regarding the first, a good example is the Pentecostal movement in Romania, which, according to a government-sponsored study done by the Romanian National Institute of Statistics,[11] has registered a steady growth rate over the years. Thus, if at the census in 1992 Pentecostals were numbering 220,824 adult members, that is 0.97 percent of the total population of Romania, the numbers went up to 324,462 in 2002 (1.50 percent of the population) and 362,314 in 2011 (1.92 percent of the population). In terms of percentages, this translates as 31.7 percent growth over the entire period, with 29.9 percent growth in the first decade and 19.3 percent growth in the second. As I suggested elsewhere,[12] the growth registered was a direct result of a mission strategy that called church members to an outward orientation (person to person social involvement), high moral standards that contrasted the corrupt social norms prevailing in a post-communist society, community cohesiveness accomplished through promoting activities that offered church members the opportunity to interact beyond the worship service (e.g., small Bible study and prayer-groups), continuous, consistent evangelistic and church-planting efforts coupled with long-term financial support of new communities formed, and an emphasis on theological leadership training.

Regarding the second, the data accessed in the preparation of this report shows that, except for a few cases in which charitable ministries were set up as the response of churches or even entire denominations to specific crises,[13] most ministries addressing social needs currently existing in the region have emerged as individual initiatives.[14] Thus, one must admit that the examples given here are isolated cases of positive change that do not define the general situation within Eastern Europe. Such changes are neither available in all geographical areas under scrutiny nor are they taking place within all groups that make up the Christian family in the region. Therefore, when looking at the overall context, several points of concern come to mind:

First, there is a discrepancy in the region between the enormous Western mission investments and the weak outcomes. I suggest that this is a direct result of the fact that many of the missiological enterprises that have flooded the region were wrongly motivated. Some were ideologically-driven; they were a sign of the victory of democracy over communism. Others were money-driven. Western donors, touched by the socio-political changes in Eastern Europe, redirected the focus toward this region regardless the fact that they were neither prepared nor called to minister in a post-communist context. Still others were guilt-driven: the "spiritually and materially wealthy" brethren from the West felt responsible to minister to the "poor nations" from the East. These wrong motivations led to bad mission practices, lack of true cooperation with the indigenous churches and ultimately to an atmosphere of mistrust between indigenous believers and the incoming missionaries, and, therefore, to ineffectiveness.[15]

Second, in spite of massive evangelistic efforts done by indigenous churches, which, as we have seen, have resulted in isolated cases of church growth, there seems to be little change in the general social and moral ethos. Christianity does not seem to have succeeded to fill the ideological vacuum left after the overthrow of communist propaganda. I suggest that this is the result of evangelization done to the detriment of true discipleship. As put by one of the leaders in the region, "we have focused on saving their souls but have neglected their minds." If, in the past, communist ideology was to replace religion, in the post-1989 context the order should have been reversed. The fact is, however, that this has not happened at the rate and to the extent initially envisioned. This, I propose, has had to do with the missional imbalance caused by the heavy emphasis on oral proclamation to the detriment of practical ministry addressing the needs of the people reached.[16]

Third, in spite of impressive developments in terms of availability, theological education in the region has only partially succeeded to raise awareness and fulfill the educational needs of the church. This has to do, I suggest, with the fact that theological institutions in Eastern Europe have been engaged in a catch-up game that did not leave time and space for contextualization and true *metanoia*. In some cases this resulted in the promotion of mission objectives by educational institutions that were at odds with the vision pursued by the churches they were meant to serve, thus making the education offered irrelevant to the community and leaving the schools offering it without the support of their constituencies.[17]

Fourth, barring a few exceptions, there seems to be little concern with leadership development within Christian communities. Most current leadership structures are outdated, based on former communist models. There is little intentional sharing of leadership authority with the younger generation, which in turn leads to leadership ignorance and lack of desire to assume leadership responsibility among young believers. There has also been little emphasis on purposefully identifying and training young men and women to become the next generation of leaders. This has resulted in unpreparedness and lack of leadership structures that would ensure the continuity of long-term ministry plans in congregations and Christian organizations.

Principles of Sustainable Ministry in Eastern Europe: In Lieu of a Conclusion

The future of Christian witness, in Eastern Europe and elsewhere, is and must remain an issue of concern for the church. Gatherings such as Empowered21 are crucial if scholars, church leaders, and ministers are to reflect and plan for change in a holistic way. Furthermore, the findings of such events ought to inform policies and practices leading to positive changes. In this regard, I offer below a few concluding thoughts in seven principles. I believe that they can provide foundations for sustainable missiological practices in Eastern Europe:

1. Congregations and Christian ministries need to adopt a genuine Christian spirituality characterized by high socio-ethical standards as an alternative to a post-communist society plagued by high levels of corruption and showing increased disillusionment with inherited church models and practices. Such spirituality would be biblically based, Christ-centered, and ecumenically sensitive.

2. Congregations and Christian ministries need to develop an excellence-oriented culture of learning as an alternative to the ideologically driven curricula and nepotistic practices of past communist educational systems.

3. Congregations and Christian ministries should promote qualitative ministerial (in the large sense of the word) service, characterized by care for the other and concern for truth, equality, and freedom.

4. Congregations and Christian ministries ought to encourage networking at all levels in order to counteract the reminiscences of a culture of mistrust and suspicion that has ruled the communist Eastern European society for half a century. Such networking would specifically include ecumenical cooperation and interreligious dialogue.[18]

5. Congregations and Christian ministries must increase their involvement in the society at all levels in order to fill the moral and ideological void left by the fall of communism. Such involvement would translate into charitable activities, political action, striving for economic growth (both through investment in businesses and promotion of a Christian work ethic), public promotion of Christian values, participation in education, culture, sports, etc.

6. Congregations and Christian ministries must strive for continuous contextualization of practices, at local and regional levels, in order to maintain the necessary flexibility and dynamism that make individuals and organizations effective agents of transformation.

7. Congregations and Christian ministries should aim to implement methodological innovation in all organizational aspects so that operational rigidity is avoided and institutions remain functional

and effective. Such innovation would consider the personalization of services, technological actualization, the development of non-hierarchical structures of leadership, and the diversification of funding strategies.

Notes

1.   The present study builds on my earlier: "Holistic Mission in Post-Communist Romania: A Case Study on the Growth of the 'Elim' Pentecostal Church of Timişoara (1990–1997)," in *Mission in Central and Eastern Europe: Realities, Perspectives, Trends*, C. Constantineanu, M. V. Măcelaru, A.-M. Kool, and M. Himcinschi, eds., Regnum Edinburgh Centenary Series 34 (Oxford: Regnum, 2016), 333–50.
2.   For the interested reader, the Regnum volume C. Constantineanu, et al., eds., *Mission in Central and Eastern Europe* can serve as an excellent source of information about the region and the period under scrutiny.
3.   See International Fellowship of Evangelical Mission Theologians, "The Osijek Declaration of 1991: Freedom and Justice in Church-State Relations" (a document from INFEMIT Fourth International Conference, last modified May 12, 2009), https://20yearsoffreedom.wordpress.com/2009/05/12/osijek-declaration-1991/; International Fellowship of Evangelical Mission Theologians, "The Oradea Declaration of 1994: Equipping for the Future" (a document from Consultation on Theological Education and Leadership Development in Post-Communist Europe, last modified May 12, 2009), https://20yearsoffreedom.wordpress.com/2009/05/12/oradea-declaration-october-1994/; and International Fellowship of Evangelical Mission Theologians, "The Osijek Declaration of 1998" (a document from Second Consultation on Theological Education and Leadership Development in Post-Communist Europe) published in *Transformation* 16:1 (1999): 1–4.
4.   On the history of communism in Eastern Europe, see Ben Fowkes, *Rise and Fall of Communism in Eastern Europe* (London: Palgrave Macmillan, 1995).
5.   Karl Marx, "Zur Kritik der Hegelschen Rechtsphilosophie," in *Deutsch-Französische Jahrbücher*, Arnold Ruge and Karl Marx, eds. (Paris: Bureau der Jahrbücher, 1844), 71.
6.   Ceauşescu's systematic destruction of church buildings and church properties in Romania is a known example of such persecution. Admittedly, the demolition of church buildings was not always a direct oppressive action taken against a particular faith community. At times, such demolition was simply carried out because the location of the building was included in Ceauşescu's "urbanization" plan, within which tens of thousands of private properties were demolished and replaced with efficiency apartment buildings; the apartments were then rented by the communist government to the families that were left without a home in the demolition process.

7. E.g., Richard Wurmbrand, *Tortured for Christ* (London: Hodder & Stoughton, 2004).

8. For such an example, see Măcelaru, "Holistic Mission in Post-Communist Romania."

9. For instance, in Romania, it is well-known that the communist secret police used infiltrators who posed as church members and collected information on religious communities and individual believers. Unfortunately, many times these "infiltrators" were members of these communities turned "spies," who betrayed their brethren out of fear or for material gain. On these, see further Vasilică Croitor, *Răscumpărarea memoriei: Cultul Penticostal în perioada comunistă* (Medgidia: Succeed Publishing, 2010); Marius Silveşan, *Bisericile Creştine Baptiste din România: Între persecuţie, acomodare, şi rezistenţă (1948–1965)* (Târgovişte: Cetatea de Scaun, 2012–2013); Lucian Turcescu and Lavinia Stan, "Church Collaboration and Resistance under Communism Revisited: The Case of Patriarch Justinian Marina (1948–1977)," *Eurostudia* 10:1 (2015), 75–103; Ciprian Bălăban, *Istoria Bisericii Penticostale din România (1922–1989): Instituţie şi harisme* (Oradea: Scriptum, 2016).

10. On these, see further Mark Elliott, "East European Missions, Perestroika and Orthodox-Evangelical Tensions," *Journal of Ecumenical Studies* 33:1 (1996), 9–20; and Miroslav Volf, "Fishing in the Neighbour's Pond: Mission and Proselytism in Eastern Europe," *International Bulletin of Missionary Research* 20:1 (1996), 26–31.

11. See Institutul Naţional de Statistică, România, "Ce ne spune recensământul din anul 2011 despre religie?," last modified October 31, 2013, http://www.insse.ro/cms/Files/publicatii/pliante statistice/08-Recensamintele despre religie_n.pdf.

12. See Măcelaru, "Holistic Mission in Post-Communist Romania."

13. See, for instance, Antal Balog, *Toward an Evangelical Missiology of Humanitarian Aid Ministry* (Osijek: Evangelical Theological Seminary, 2007), which tells the story of AGAPE, a charity launched by the Evangelical Pentecostal denomination in Croatia to address the Bosnian refugee crisis during the years of the Yugoslav war.

14. See, for instance, Ligia M. Măcelaru and Marcel V. Măcelaru, "Empowering People with Disability to Reach their Full Potential within the Community: The Case of ACAS," in *Mission in Central and Eastern Europe*, 363–71. The study tells the story of ACAS, a charity based in Romania that begun as a simple gesture of compassion. Over the years grew into a flourishing ministry that addresses the needs of children with disabilities and their families, a group that is largely overlooked in "official" charity actions done by churches.

15. On these, see further Davorin Peterlin, "A Wrong Kind of Missionary: A Semi-Autobiographic Outcry," *Mission Studies* 12:2 (1995), 164–74; and Ksenja Magda and Melody J. Wachsmuth, "'Discerning the Body' in Cross-Cultural Relationships: A Critical Analysis of Missional Partnership in Southeastern Europe," *Kairos* 8:1 (2014), 25–43.

16. On mission in the post-1989 context, see further Peter Kuzmič, "Christian Mission in Europe," *Themelios* 18:1 (1992), 21–25.

17. On theological education in the region, its challenges, and possible solutions, see Peter Kuzmič, "A Vision for Theological Education for Difficult Times," *Religion, State and Society* 22:2 (1994), 237–43.

18. On ecumenical networking, note the "conversation" model advanced by Daniel G. Oprean, *Theology of Participation* (Carlisle: Langham, 2019).

20.

Refugee Ministry in the Contrasting Settings of Greece and Germany

John Thompson

Abstract

The refugee crisis in Europe may be one of the most significant opportunities for the spread of the gospel on that continent since the fall of the Iron Curtain. Many churches in Western Europe are engaging these newcomers in holistic ministry. From February to May 2018, seventeen leaders were interviewed from fourteen ministries engaged in refugee ministry in Greece and Germany to explore refugee ministry realities and practices in these two nations with contrasting policies. The research describes the shifting refugee situation, the shifting context, the relationship between these ministries and government, refugee ministry approaches, spiritual openness and the work of the Holy Spirit among refugees, and observations from frontline practitioners.

Key words: refugee ministry, Europe, Greece, Germany, phenomenological study

Introduction

Refugees from the Middle East have flooded into parts of Western Europe from 2015 to the present. The world has watched Europe struggle with the influx of refugees from the Middle East fleeing war, ISIS, and instability. This migration brought millions of Muslims in need into many Western European cities and villages. Europeans have felt both compassion and fear, and they have responded with both generosity and hostility. In this environment, European Christians encounter a tremendous opportunity to love these new strangers now on their doorsteps and to witness for Christ to these primarily non-Christian immigrants. Many Christian communities have displayed sacrificial generosity and love toward refugees. This phenomenological study explored the experience of refugee ministry by Christian ministries and local churches in Greece and Germany. The study sought to discover how Christian ministries were responding to needs and sharing Christ with refugees, as well as church and state dynamics, the spiritual impact of the ministries interviewed on refugees, and what these frontline practitioners had learned about refugee ministry.[1]

Greece and Germany provide unique contexts for exploring ministry to refugees. Greece is now in its eleventh year of the Greek economic crisis and does not have the resources internally to deal with the refugee crisis. Though Greeks have a culture marked by hospitality, they have had to depend on outside funding and resources to provide services to refugees. In contrast, Germany has a robust economy and can provide for the material needs of these new immigrants.

According to those interviewed in Greece, the Protestant believers are doing most of the service to refugees today in that nation. The Orthodox Church is the official state religion and often carries with it nationalistic interests. Consequently, it is more concerned about Greeks than Muslim foreigners. Furthermore, Protestant believers in Greece are ostracized by the Orthodox majority and considered to be members of a sect.

In contrast, Protestants are part of the general culture in Germany. Though evangelicals and mainline Protestants differ theologically, they both are serving refugees with the caveat that evangelicals are interested in both meeting needs and sharing Christ, whereas mainline Protestants (the state-funded Protestant Church in Germany) are primarily interested in meeting the humanitarian and social needs of refugees.

Greece is an entry country for refugees coming to Europe, whereas Germany is a destination country. As a destination country, Germany has received more refugees than any other European nation, recording 44 percent of three million first-time asylum seeker applications in Europe between 2015 and 2017 (1,356,644).[2] Germany opened its doors to refugees for humanitarian reasons and also to bolster its strong economic engine so that future workers would be available for an aging society with a low birth rate. Until just recently, Greece has primarily been a transition country as people entered Europe and headed on to the strong economies in northern Europe.

Greece has 71,200 refugees and migrants as of December 31, 2018. 14,600 were on the islands still (where sea arrivals land) and 56,600 on the mainland. In 2018 alone, there were 50,508 new arrivals (32,494 by sea and 18,014 by land).[3] While refugees in Greece hope to transition on to other countries, many are now beginning to settle into life in Greece, recognizing that it will likely be a multi-year process if it happens at all. Furthermore, the Greek government is recognizing that money is available from the European Union (EU) to take care of refugees, creating opportunities for Greek employment. However, political tension exists. If the government leaders do more for the refugees than for their own people who have suffered for the last decade from austerity measures imposed by the European Union and Germany, they will get voted out of power.

The humanitarian crisis over the past four years for these new arrivals on European soil has been acute. In 2015 alone, over one million refugees arrived in Europe by sea, and 80 percent of these were in Greece and 15 percent in Italy. By the end of December 2015, an estimated 3,700 people had died in the perilous water crossing, with a higher percentage dying in the longer passage from North Africa to Italy. Though the number of water crossings dropped significantly in 2016 and 2017, the number of dead and missing remained high (5,096 in 2016; 3,139 in 2017).[4] In 2015, half of those crossing the Mediterranean were from Syria and were fleeing from the war back home. A quarter of the million were Afghan and Iraqi fleeing conflicts at home as well. [5] At the height of the crisis in October 2015, more than 7,000 refugees arrived each day after weeks of difficult journeys from their country of origin.

Thousands of people a day landed on Greek islands in the summer and fall of 2015, were transported to Athens by ferry, made their way to the city center, and took buses north into central and northern Europe through the Balkan route. In late 2015, however, many countries began to close their borders to refugees causing thousands to get stuck in Greece. Camps sprung up across Greece as well in other parts of Europe. Camp conditions in many locations have been very poor and difficult. Waves of refugees continue to arrive on the Greek islands, overwhelming refugee hotspots on the islands. UNICEF reported in August 2019, the number of unaccompanied refugee minors in Greece exceeded 1,100.[6] This is the largest number since the first part of 2016. Furthermore, overcrowding is overwhelming is these hotspots. The refugee camp on the island of Lesvos has space for 3,000 people, but as of late August 2019, 8,700 people, including 3,000 children, were living at the camp.[7] The needs of refugees materially, financially, socially, and psychologically (given some of the traumatic events they have experienced) can be overwhelming for people trying to help.

The Shifting Refugee Situation

A dramatic shift has occurred in the refugee situation in both Germany and Greece regarding humanitarian assistance. Germany has moved from a humanitarian crisis to the need for assistance in integration. The German government is meeting the humanitarian needs of refugees in most places throughout the country. The German national government desires to integrate refugees into society and the workforce. In much of Germany, camps have been closed, and refugee housing has been disbursed among the German population. However, in the far south, resistance by governing authorities has grown due to anti-immigrant sentiment and the desire to see immigrants return to their country of origin one day.

Throughout the country, government programs have been set up to provide language acquisition followed by job training and placement. However, for refugees to integrate into society, they need friendships with Germans. The government cannot provide friendships. Though the government official in one city has matched German families with refugee families, this is where churches can and are playing a very significant role in some places. Unfortunately, many Germans are not willing to build friendships with refugees and often struggle with fear and political concerns that may prevent friendship engagement.

At the beginning of the crisis, churches and ministries focused on humanitarian assistance, but much of that assistance is now being facilitated by government agencies, while churches and ministries in Germany that are now engaged in refugee ministry see developing friendships and inviting people into their homes and lives at the heart of their ministry to refugees. The days of large gatherings to meet needs have been replaced in many places by small-group gatherings in homes. Because government agencies were meeting the physical needs, attendance at large gatherings dropped significantly, causing churches and ministries to shift to small-group meetings that focused more on friendship and spiritual needs. One ministry leader interviewed summarized the current situation: "It is really about opening two doors: the front door and the door of your heart."

Greece still has some camps, but others have been closed. Much less provision is available from governmental agencies for refugees in Greece than in Germany, which means the needs of refugees are still acute and often are overwhelming for ministries and churches. Some international NGOs are beginning to close and leave, though the needs of refugees are still pressing in many places in Greece. One organization interviewed, for example, no longer operates its centers on the islands, and the center it ran in Athens closed in September 2018.

The material needs can be overwhelming to local ministries and churches serving refugees in Greece. Many local Christian ministries are still providing humanitarian assistance. They are often careful not to be the primary supplier; rather, they try to help connect refugees with agencies that can provide some material support. Those agencies giving weekly groceries have developed databases to ensure a fair distribution. Volunteers and ministries are learning to pace themselves. They often refer to the challenges of burnout and attrition with local volunteers.

Some ministries depend on short-term teams coming to serve refugees. These teams come from other parts of Europe, the United States, or Egypt. The Egyptian volunteers have been very helpful with the language barrier for Arabic speakers. Some are mobilizing immigrants themselves to assist in running programs to serve refugees. More and more, though, ministries in Greece are shifting from the primary focus on humanitarian needs to focus on the social and spiritual needs of refugees.

The Shifting Context

General attitudes toward refugees have shifted, a groundswell of hospitality by Greeks and Germans occurred in the early days of the crisis as desperate refugees flooded through or into their countries. People gave their belongings to help refugees who had lost everything and fled their home country. At first, people were very concerned about the refugees, gave many donated items to help, and felt very empathetic toward the plight of these new immigrants. Unfortunately, over time, feelings have generally changed in both countries toward their new guests. Of course, from the beginning, both countries had minority anti-immigrant constituencies. However, it appears that the attitude of the general population began to shift from empathy to fear and even hostility.

In Greece, the general feeling shifted as other countries closed their borders, which caused refugees to be stuck in Greece. The nation had been enduring its own economic crisis since 2008, and the crisis was in its seventh year and continuing to deepen. The rest of the world did not seem to help, but rather through forced austerity measures, caused the economic pain to be even more profound. When the refugees flooded in, the world took notice and sent resources to help, though they had not helped the suffering Greeks during the previous seven years.

Furthermore, there is a historical root of enmity between Greece and its Muslim neighbors to the east. For eight hundred years, the Byzantine Empire held back the Muslim advance into Europe. But after the fall of Constantinople, Greeks endured life under Ottoman Muslim rule for four hundred years. The Greek Orthodox Church held the Greek language and religion together under this foreign domination and championed liberation. It is the official state church and is very nationalistic. Consequently, the Orthodox Church generally has not done a lot to support the work of caring for Muslim refugees.

Even more importantly, in the twentieth century, the Greek and Armenian genocides occurred in Turkey, and the invasion and occupation of northern Greek Cyprus by Turkey happened in the 1970s. Thus, the history of the Greek people contributes to a feeling of being invaded by Islam and the need to resist the growing presence of Muslims in their land. This feeling is exasperated by the Greek economic crisis and the consequential exodus of Greek youth when they graduate from college to other countries to find jobs. Meanwhile, young Muslim people are immigrating to Greece and have a much higher birth rate than Greeks. These factors foster fear that culture and country demographics will rapidly change.

In Germany, the crimes committed by some refugees in 2016 had a galvanizing effect on many Germans, creating fear and deep concern. Like Greeks, Germans also naturally feel concerned about the long-term impact on German culture. Concern has grown concerning an increase in Islam in Germany that might threaten the historic Christian underpinning or the growing secularism of the German culture. Immigrants represent a significant birthrate differential. Whereas the German birthrate is below population sustainability, immigrant populations will continue to grow if their birth rates remain high and do not adjust to the German norm. Germans sometimes worry about their children possibly marrying these non-Germans from non-European cultures.

The German government is working hard to integrate refugees into society. Unemployment is extremely low, and as Germans retire in the next five years, there will be a growing need for workers. According to one interviewee, 300,000 skilled workers will be needed to replace people retiring in the next five years. Germany saw the refugee situation as an opportunity to fill the growing need for workers in Germany. The country has a robust system for preparing workers for the workplace with apprenticeships and other educational systems to provide technical training and development for the incoming workforce, thus preparing a new generation of workers. However, Germany's economic system works because of the cultural norms wherein people possess an internal orientation to diligence, detail, and precision. The state protects the worker, making it extremely difficult to fire an employee after six months of hire.

Furthermore, the country provides national healthcare and a very generous number of vacation days. This generosity works because the culture contains a deep passion for productivity. Those coming from outside the culture, however, may not have this cultural perspective and may abuse the system. Given these cultural differences, policies designed to provide a safety net and protection to the worker may foster a welfare mentality in those who do not possess the cultural underpinnings that make the system work in Germany. Therefore, the perception is growing among Germans that refugees have come for the money, not the work, and that they are taking excessive advantage of the system designed to help them.

In contrast, Greece is not seeking to integrate refugees into society like Germany is. The economic situation is in stark contrast to their northern counterpart. With high unemployment and young Greeks moving to other countries to find jobs, employment opportunities for refugees in Greece do not exist. Resources are lacking in the country to support refugees, and the Greeks rely on funding from the EU to provide services to the refugee population. Refugees are typically housed in camps with no hope for employment and integration into Greek society. Because the humanitarian need is still acute for refugees in Greece, churches, and ministries, continue to provide some humanitarian help to refugees. However, their overall impact is limited, and refugees are suffering. Nevertheless, while showing love in tangible ways to refugees, Christ is being seen amid an openness to the gospel.

Methodology

This qualitative research was a phenomenological study of refugee ministry in Greece and Germany. The primary research question was how Christian ministries and local churches were responding to needs and sharing Christ with refugees. Additional research questions included: What is the interplay between ministries and government given the political nature of the refugee situation? What is the spiritual impact of the ministries interviewed on refugees? What have frontline practitioners learned about refugee ministry? How were Christians navigating the political environments of their respective countries in working with refugees? What were these frontline practitioners learning about refugee ministry?

The sample consisted of seventeen interviews with leaders engaged in refugee ministry in Greece or Germany. The leaders represented fourteen different Protestant evangelical ministries. Snowball sampling was used to identify ministry leaders engaged in refugee ministry.[8] Each leader interviewed completed a "Refugee Ministry Leader Questionnaire" to provide information about organizational details,[9] outreach activities to refugees, and refugee population in their city and their ministry. Interviews with the leaders were conducted, each interview recorded, coded and later transcribed. All interviews consisted of sixteen questions. Ten face-to-face interviews were conducted in Germany in February 2018, and seven interviews were conducted with ministries in Greece via zoom between March and May 2018. The ministries in Germany were in six cities: Wiehl, Gummersbach, Koln, Heilbronn, Ludwigshafen, and Munich. The ministries in Greece were located in four cities: Athens, Thessaloniki, Serres, and Katerini. All quotes from interviews in this article are anonymous to protect confidentiality.

Results

Refugee Ministry and Government Relations

Both religious and governmental entities serve the poor and seek to protect the downtrodden. Their services to the poor can overlap, although their primary purposes and motivations differ. How do Christian and government organizations interact with one another in the arena of refugee work? Three of the sixteen questions were asked in the interviews to explore this relationship between Christian ministries engaged with refugees and government, both with the national government and the European Union.[10] The relationship between church and state certainly varies among nations across Europe. The historical backdrop of Christendom and the intervening forces of secularism over the past few centuries create a diverse and complex relationship between church and state across the European continent. While Europe is becoming increasingly secular, Greece has an official state church, and in Germany, two national churches receive funds through the state from taxation of members.

The churches interviewed in this project were not state-funded in either of these countries. The non-Greek Orthodox churches in Greece and the free churches in Germany typically have a stronger desire to engage in evangelism, and often this impulse is absent in churches receiving funding from the state. Though not always expressed in church life, the tenets of the Christian religion embrace both serving the needs of the poor (charity) and sharing the message of Christ (evangelism). So, what is the relationship between government entities and those church and ministry representatives that were interviewed?

In many places in Germany, a positive relationship appears to exist between churches and the government in serving refugees. Churches and ministries typically do not feel antagonism from the state. It should be noted that there are two types of churches in Germany, the state churches (both Catholic and Protestant) that receive funding from the state and the free churches that do not receive funds from the government. State-funded churches work with refugees from a social services perspective and do not incorporate teaching about Jesus in their activities. Social service is considered to be an important contribution of these state-funded churches to society. They receive funds for services that they provide to refugees and consequently are prohibited from teaching Christianity in their refugee programs.

Free churches in Germany typically incorporate sharing their faith into their ministry to refugees, whether formally through spiritual programs or informally through friendships. Consequently, they do not receive funding from the state for the work they do with refugees. But because this witness is not forced, they are not prevented from working with refugees in the community, and most of those interviewed saw no conflict between their work with refugees and the government.

German courts often show preference to refugees who have a certificate of Christian baptism. One immigrant congregation reported that they have a solid relationship with the government and work with the judges in their jurisdiction. They provide church attendance records on an asylum seeker to the court to verify the validity of a baptism certificate. This preference to give asylum to those who are Christian has made most ministries wary of the motives of refugees seeking baptism both in Germany and in Greece. Some ministries wait longer to ensure that a real transformation of the heart exists before they baptize.

The huge humanitarian need has contributed to cooperation. Churches and ministries responded to the needs of refugees, and government agencies recognized the good work taking place in the community. For example, the local government in one German town provided the local church with phone numbers for refugees so that the church could contact them to invite them to the programs being offered.

In a northern town in Greece, a local church provided housing for 33 refugees. The United Nations (UN) observed their efforts and proposed that they establish a non-governmental organization (NGO) so that the UN could work with them and provide funding for the housing work to increase its capacity. The church established the NGO, provided housing for 550 refugees in 110 apartments funded by the UN, and served 1650 refugees through this NGO over the past two years.

Sometimes churches or ministries, such as the church in northern Greece, chose to limit their verbal witness to provide a particular service. One free church in Germany was teaching language courses to refugees, but for the refugees to receive an official certificate from the course, the law required it to be a certified course, and thus the church could not share Christ in their language program. This church decided to proceed and be a certified language program, believing that their behavior and the fact that it was housed in the church building would provide a witness. In all of these situations, witness still happens informally through relationships but not formally within the particular program.

Because of the freedom of religion in Europe, "in general, the European Union has no problem when it comes to Christian activities, and the German government generally is favorable to church work among refugees," according to one interviewee. If the ministry is too evangelistic, the government will likely withdraw funding. However, the ministry is not prohibited from being evangelistic if it does not receive public funding.

One interviewee pointed out that state churches sometimes are critical of the free churches based on a different theological perspective. In the early days of the crisis, free churches were mischaracterized as just wanting to share Jesus with people. However, over time other organizations could see that these ministries were helping refugees in their need and showing them love. This idea surfaced in several interviews. Though there was some criticism in the early stages of the crisis, over time, those criticisms faded away as ministries sacrificially served refugees.

Of the six cities in Germany where interviews were conducted, only in Munich did the interviewee report that animosity exists between churches and government regarding serving refugees. Refugees were still in camps in this region, and access was not allowed to those who do anything religious in nature. The negative view expressed in the interview in Munich was the exception to the generally positive views in all the other interviews regarding church or ministry relationships with government entities. The Munich interviewee stated, "Hostile. Overtly hostile."

An example was provided of a group picking up refugees with buses for a barbeque. The workers at the camp yelled at the buses and volunteers demanding that they leave. It was mentioned in the interview that each state in Germany sets its own regulations for the refugees, and in the Munich region, refugees are left in the camps with the hope of sending them back to their home counties. In Munich, there seems to be an antagonism toward Christian groups working with refugees. This feeling was in sharp contrast to all of the other interviews in Germany. It does appear that culturally, there is a stronger anti-immigrant sentiment in southern and eastern Germany.

In both Greece and Germany, the camps are off-limits for any religious activity by groups. One large USA-based Christian NGO was very active in serving on the Greek islands in the registration centers and the camps during the humanitarian crisis. However, they were not allowed to speak about matters of faith in order to serve in that capacity. One interviewee reported that the military controlled the camp he visited in Greece and was opposed to any religious presence. Another interviewee pointed out that often the Greeks employed in the camps are anarchists who are philosophically opposed to religion.

While some Christians face resistance from camp leadership, in some places, they have experienced God-given favor in camps. In Greece, one of the churches interviewed serves in a camp providing humanitarian aid and friendships. They also transport refugees from the camp to their spiritually oriented programs. The situation is changing in both countries as people continue to move out of camps and into local communities. This movement allows freedom and openness for distinctly religious work.

In Greece, the general perspective presented in the interviews was that there is the freedom to minister to refugees outside of the camps.

The greatest opposition seems to come indirectly through the Orthodox Church. The Orthodox Church is called the "prevailing religion" of Greece in the Greek constitution with salaries paid by the government, and it is connected to the Ministry of Education and Religion. The Orthodox Church sometimes appears to leverage its position in the government to make permits difficult for non-Orthodox organizations to obtain.

Furthermore, the Orthodox Church is very concerned with heresy and has an anti-heresy department that sometimes opposes Protestant groups at work in Greece. Protestants, however, are allowed to work with refugees even though the Orthodox Church often makes it difficult for any ministry in Greece that is not Orthodox. Several interviewees noted that the Greek Orthodox Church, apart from a few exceptions, has a nationalistic orientation, is not very welcoming to refugees, has little direct engagement with them, and generally feels refugees should be discouraged from coming to Greece.

According to the Protestant leaders interviewed, most of their interaction is not with the Greek Orthodox Church but rather with governmental refugee agencies. One ministry interviewed serves as an NGO daily at the refugee registration center because the government does not have the staff needed. There is a strong relationship of trust between this group of volunteers and the government. Because they love and serve refugees without a religious agenda, the door is wide open for them. Others note that it is often easier to work with the EU than with the Greek government as the EU is looking for solutions to help refugees, whereas the Greek government is more conflicted in its view of the situation.

Ministry to Refugees

All of the churches and ministries represented in the interviews are engaged in holistic ministry to refugees, serving tangible and spiritual needs. The humanitarian assistance is evidenced in feeding programs (five of the fourteen), food and clothing distribution (six of the fourteen), language classes (eight of the fourteen), housing programs (three of the fourteen), and other specialized services such as legal help, job training, and medical clinics. Every Christian organization interviewed engaged in at least one of these activities and most in multiple services.

A strong emphasis was made on meeting relationship needs as well. Eight out of fourteen have a café ministry or community center. These spaces provide opportunities to spend time with refugees and also provide activities and a place to hold some of the services such as language classes. A number of the interviewees spoke of the importance of friendships with refugees. Without relationships with locals, there will be no integration into the community. Many spoke of friendship being essential for witness. Some spoke of the importance of personal hospitality, such as inviting people into one's home to eat together.

Every leader interviewed expressed a desire to serve the spiritual needs of refugees as well. This service could be structured or organic through friendship. Eleven of the fourteen churches and ministries reported hosting Bible studies for refugees. Some of these are using Al Massira, a twelve-week video series designed for people from Muslim backgrounds starting in the Old Testament and concluding in the Gospels with Jesus. Those using this resource find it very effective in sharing the gospel. The evening format each week includes a meal together, the video, and discussion.

Seven of the fourteen churches and ministries reported having a regular church service for refugees. Some include refugees in their usual church service with translation for refugees, while others developed separate congregations. In some instances, the number of refugees exceeded the number of members in the existing congregation. Unfortunately, when refugees began attending church services, some members left to go to a different church. This loss of some congregants has been one of the costs churches faced when they opened their doors to these foreigners.

Four of the sixteen interview questions were asked to draw out the wisdom and insights these practitioners have gained about ministry to refugees.[11] A prominent theme was the need for patience and longevity in working with refugees. This is emotionally exhausting work. The needs can be overwhelming. Furthermore, building friendships means opening up one's life and inviting others in. Germans and Greeks are busy with their jobs, families, and life responsibilities, leaving little time in their lives for the all-consuming work with refugees. One ministry utilizes university students in their city because young people have more time for relationships. Many use teams from other countries and many are learning to utilize refugees themselves to serve their own community.

Partnering together with other ministries has been an important practice. Out of necessity, churches have teamed up to facilitate a refugee center. Often there are just a handful of people in each church with the commitment to serve refugees. Working with other churches enables a center to be staffed and programs to be offered. Sometimes the partnership is within a city, sometimes within a denomination, and sometimes the partnership is facilitated by an international mission organization. The partnership allows both shared programs and individual programs among member churches or ministries. One non-profit has a community center with daily Bible studies and a weekly discipleship gathering. However, that ministry does not baptize refugees who come to faith in Christ; rather, when they are ready, it funnels them into local churches who then facilitate the baptisms.

Language has been a significant challenge. In Germany, refugees are learning German. Patience is again needed. In Greece, refugees have been reluctant to learn Greek because they are hoping to move to other parts of Europe. In both countries, translators have been important for the work of the ministry.

The need for translation limits what volunteer teams coming from other Western nations can do. However, this has also opened a door of opportunity. Some missionaries serving in Middle Eastern countries who know the language and culture of these refugee populations have returned to Europe for fruitful engagement with refugees. Other missionaries desiring to go to the Middle East have come to work in Germany or Greece as preparation to serve elsewhere.

This crisis seems significant for Egyptian Christians who used to be closed to evangelism because of the centuries of persecution in Egypt. But now, some of these believers are coming to Greece to help engage, translate, and share Christ with refugees. One interviewee talked about an Egyptian Orthodox family who came to their church. The family was opposed to the work they were doing with Muslim refugees. But now the wife is meeting with Muslim women and is requesting that Al Massira be offered for them. Several groups in Greece mentioned that teams from Egypt are coming to serve the refugees for extended periods of time.

Spiritual Openness and the Work of the Holy Spirit among Refugees

Three interview questions addressed the spiritual openness and responsiveness of refugees to Christian witness.[12] The responses were mixed. Contextual factors influence each local setting as to the degree of receptivity to the message of Christ. According to this sample of interviews, the least receptive group seems to be the Yazidis. One organization works with a camp established just for the Yazidis. Because this is a persecuted religious minority in the Middle East, the camp contains many relatives and retains the social networks from their country of origin. For the Yazidis and sometimes for other refugees, religion is one of the few things they still have left in their lives, and therefore their religion provides an anchor in difficult times.

For many, though, arrival in Europe provides an opportunity for a new life and the freedom to explore a new religion. The loving care given by Christians to refugees has been a powerful witness. Refugees often told their new European friends that in their home country, they were told that Christians are bad people. However, when they met Christians in Europe and experienced their compassion, it opened their minds to exploring Christianity. Interviewees in Greece often remarked that they are sowing seeds that might be harvested by others when refugees settle in their destination cities. Stories have been told of refugees arriving in northern Europe and seeking out a church because of the kindness of Christians encountered earlier in their journey.

One key to the increased receptivity of refugees to the gospel has been the work of the Holy Spirit through the supernatural. Some refugees had dreams, visions, or some other supernatural experience on their journey or in their home country that spurred them to seek out Christianity once they arrived on European soil. One interviewee estimated that probably two-thirds of his new, Arabic-speaking congregation had experienced a vision or dream. Often the refugees themselves ask about the Christian faith. Another interviewee provided two reasons for refugees coming to faith in Christ: first, the expression of love through provisions and friendship; and second, numerous visions and dreams. He has heard hundreds of testimonies of visions that included Jesus and/or a white angel. Several interviewees described a specific miracle or healing that was influential in a refugee becoming a follower of Jesus.

Not only has the Holy Spirit been at work among refugees but also among European Christians ministering to refugees. Evangelical and Spirit-empowered churches are working together in local cities, pooling resources together, and volunteering side by side. According to one interviewee, the Holy Spirit is also using this moment to shift ministry from inside the church to outside the church. He estimated that "70–80% of what we are doing in our church now is outside the church." Another church leader shared the story of how the protestant Greek community in his city was founded in 1923 by Greek refugees. Some of their forefathers walked 800 kilometers from the Black Sea in Asia Minor to

Syria, where they were refugees for one year in Aleppo. Now many of the Syrian refugees coming to their city in Greece are from the same location the forefathers of these Greek believers lived as refugees. The Holy Spirit is facilitating an opportunity to reciprocate kindness and love almost a century later.

While some Christian organizations are intentional about sharing their faith and structure ways to do so, others are more organically responsive. They serve, build friendships, and naturally share their faith as God opens doors of opportunity. The opportunities do come as Christians invest in the lives of others. Christians find that most refugees are open to prayer, and sometimes God's miraculous answer to those prayers opens hearts to considering Christ as well.

One of the three interview questions asked about the impact of refugee demographics on receptivity to the gospel. Generally speaking, the Iranians seem to be the most receptive. There has been and continues to be a sovereign move of God among Iranians both inside Iran and among the diaspora. Some interviewees suggested the Syrians and Afghans are open to the gospel, and others felt they are not. Other mitigating factors were at work regarding individualized responses. Regarding gender, some interviewees felt that women are more open because of the freedom for women in Christianity, while others felt women are more closed.

Perhaps one of the most important observations suggested by both a ministry leader in Greece and a ministry leader in Germany is that the key to effective evangelism among refugees is the presence of indigenous believers who are telling their story of transformation through Christ to members of their people groups. Refugees are more open to responding to the Gospel message when national believers from their particular groups, typically converts from Islam, share their faith. Without such believers, the work is very slow with little fruit. However, when Middle Easterners share their faith, there tends to be much fruit.

One European missionary previously lived in Syria, speaks Arabic, and now works in Germany at a refugee community center. He shared that over and over again, he has observed that until the first person comes to faith in Christ, the work is very slow. But once the first one becomes a follower of Jesus and starts sharing the faith in the refugee community, then often many commit their lives to Christ. The German or Greek can share and witness, but when someone from the same culture shares about an encounter with Christ, people in that culture often begin to respond.

In Greece, a ministry that is reaching many immigrants and refugees for Christ puts much emphasis on developing and discipling national workers (believers from the refugee population). The ministry has a whole Farsi team that serves at their Monday night meal. The ministry also has an Afghan believer who leads and preaches at their Wednesday program. Developing these believers to lead has enabled the ministry to grow significantly.

Another ministry in Greece has an Iranian leading daily Bible study with attendance between twenty-five and fifty-five refugees, as well as a weekly discipleship group of twenty persons. They do not baptize new believers but instead introduce them to local churches who then baptize. In just five months (January to May 2018), fifty-five were baptized in local churches who came through these Bible studies.

Conclusion

The last question asked interviewees was the following: "What would you say to ministries, churches, and individual followers of Jesus in Europe about refugee ministry?" The responses were statements of hope. Some expressed the hope and belief that when the crisis dissipates in the future in the Middle East, new refugee believers will return to their home countries to become Christian leaders establishing churches and leading others to Christ. The hope exists that new believers among refugees and immigrants will be witnesses in the future to the ever-growing immigrant populations in Europe. There is also hope that refugee children today will grow up and become followers of Jesus tomorrow. Over half of the ministries reported ministering to refugee children. This is long-term thinking. Loving children today will open doors to the gospel in their lives tomorrow.

Much of the work being done with refugees is planting seeds that will produce a harvest in the future. But the harvest is happening right now as well. This current situation may be the most significant opportunity for the gospel in Europe since the fall of the Iron Curtain and the subsequent harvest in Eastern Europe in the first half of the 1990s. Now in Western Europe, God seems to be facilitating another harvest. One of the most memorable statements in the seventeen interviews was at the end of an interview with a Christian leader in Athens, Greece. In his final words, he declared, "I think this is the most effective place in the whole world to reach Muslims today."

Donald McGavran encouraged practitioners to look for receptive peoples but warned that receptivity in individuals as well as societies "wanes as often as it waxes. Like the tide, it comes in and goes out. Unlike the tide, no one can guarantee when it goes out that it will soon come back again."[13] A window of opportunity is open to serve, bless, and share Christ with refugees in Europe. However, the window of receptivity will likely not remain open for a long period of time. As people settle into their new lives in a new land, their social structures will solidify again, and receptivity will likely wane. Now is the God-given season to live out the great commission with refugees in the West.

Notes

1. The original version of this paper was presented at the 2018 Scholars Consultation of Empowered21 held in Johannesburg, South Africa in May 2018. It was subsequently revised and published in *Great Commission Research Journal* 10:2 (Spring 2019), 30–49. The current study is a substantially revised version.
2. First time applicant table, Eurostat, European Commission, accessed January 21, 2019, https://ec.europa.eu/eurostat/tgm/refreshTableAction.do?tab=table&plugin=1&pcode=tps00191&language=en.
3. Refugees Operation Portal, UNHCR, https://data2.unhcr.org/en/documents/download/67711, accessed January 24, 2019.
4. UNHCR, "Refugees Operational Portal," http://data2.unhcr.org/en/situations/mediterranean?id=83, accessed January 18, 2019.
5. Statistics are from Jonathan Clayton and Hereward Holland, "Over One Million Sea Arrivals Reach Europe in 2015," http://www.unhcr.org/afr/news/latest/2015/12/5683d0b56/million-sea-arrivals-reach-europe-2015.html.
6. UNICEF, "Press release," https://www.unicef.org/press-releases/more-1100-unaccompanied-refugee-and-migrant-children-greece-need-urgent-shelter-and, accessed September 5, 2019.
7. UNICEF, "Press release."
8. The researcher began with personal contacts engaged in refugee ministry as well as those identifiable on the internet. These potential participants were asked to identify other ministry leaders engaged in refugee ministry in their city or nation as well. This method was utilized to identify as many ministries as possible serving refugees.
9. Details consisted of ministry type, denomination, and theological orientation.
10. Questions included the following: "Describe the relationship between government and religious organizations regarding the refugee situation."; "How are ministries and churches navigating the political aspect of refugee work?"; "How are EU and German/Greek laws shaping Christian involvement with refugees?"

11. Questions seven to eleven asked the following: "What have you learned about working with refugees?"; "How do you measure successful ministry to refugees?"; "What are keys to successful ministry to refugees?"; "What are the challenges to refugee ministry, and how have you dealt with those challenges?"

12. Questions twelve to fifteen asked the following: "Describe the spiritual openness of refugees"; "How are refugees coming to faith in Christ?"; "How do refugee demographics (country of origin, gender, and age) impact responsiveness and ministry approach?"

13. Donald A. McGavran, *Understanding Church Growth*, 3rd ed, C. Peter Wagner, ed. (Grand Rapids: Eerdmans, 1990), 180–181.

21.

Witnessing to Christ Among Urban Youths: A Bogota Experience

Richard Harding and Manuela Castellanos

Abstract

Preaching Christ as the only Savior to the next generations has become increasingly difficult in a growing post-modern world where anything is okay, and "All roads lead to salvation." This study looks specifically at the challenges and successes of the ministry of the gospel in Bogota, the Latin American capital city of Colombia. International Charismatic Mission (MCI) has been growing and reaching youth for over thirty years with a great level of success. The unique model of discipleship based around the formation of twelve has seen unprecedented growth and success at bringing Christ to the next generation. This study will focus on the role that family has played, specific strategies used to reach youth, encounter retreat weekends, deliverance, restoration, and leadership.

Key words: G12, MCI, Cesar Castellanos, Encounter, youth, discipleship

Introduction

Why Youth?

The youth are the generation who are going to become the next presidents, leaders, church pastors, evangelists, doctors, teachers, professors, entrepreneurs, etc. We are living in a youth-centered world where everyone is trying to capture the attention and following of the current generation of young people. According to a 2007 study of the *New York Times*, we are exposed to some 5,000 ads trying to capture our attention every day.[1] It is clear that there is a fight going on for the minds and focus of the current youth, but a question needs answering: as a church, what are we doing, and what are we going to do? This process of evaluation and adaptation is something we must begin to carry out if we wish to have any success at preaching the gospel to this next generation.

This study will focus on the work of the International Charismatic Mission (ICM) work with young people over the last 35 years in the capital city of Colombia, Bogota. Kerry Loescher points out that evaluation happens all the time. The problem is that, when informal, it can become "personal" to those involved.[2] That is why formal evaluation that looks through our processes, our ways of working with and preaching to youth are essential if we wish to grow in our ability to preach Christ to the next generation.

When starting this process of evaluation, it is important to look at the broader context within which the church lies. Colombia itself is an interesting case study, with over 78 percent of the young population reporting themselves to be "Christian."[3] Despite this, the same study made by *One Hope* in 2007, revealed that only 25 percent of those interviewed attended youth groups,[4] and only 23 percent were considered to be evangelical; that is confessing that "when you die you will go to heaven because you have confessed your sins and have accepted Jesus Christ as your Savior."[5]

Despite the number of self-identifying Christians among the young people of Colombia, their actual beliefs and behaviors do not necessarily reflect their confession. For example, concerning sexual activity outside of marriage, there was found to be "no statistically significant difference between evangelicals and non-evangelicals in regard to sexual intercourse."[6] There remains, therefore, a great need not only for Christ to be preached as the only Savior amongst young people but continuing discipleship to produce real disciples and not just believers as a statistic.

This is a challenge that has faced ICM, Bogota, and remains a challenge to the current day. How do we effectively engage young people and preach to them the full gospel of Christ as the only Savior in a way that produces not just members or churchgoers, but true disciples of Jesus? This is the key concept that will be investigated in this paper.

Christ as the Only Savior for Today's Youths

We live a society that continues to preach that all roads lead to salvation. This message has found its way into all levels of society, and through the communication of the internet has arrived at every country on earth.

Witnessing among Urban Youths 397

The statistics given in the previous section show that particularly in Colombia, as a representative of a Latin American model, even when our young people confess to believe, their beliefs in Christ do not necessarily produce a biblical change we might expect or desire. In "Growing Young: Six Core Commitments of Churches Effectively Engaging Young People," the following definition of engaging young people is given: "An effective church was defined as one that is involving and retaining young people in the faith of Jesus Christ."[7]

While this addresses the subject of the "engagement" of young people, the definition of this as a simple "retaining young people in the faith of Jesus Christ," only goes so far and is not that easy to measure. What exactly constitutes "retaining young people in the faith"? The study itself focuses on what the church is doing to engage young people, and not necessarily what the young person is doing themselves to engage with Christ and their faith. The question arises: how can we define a young person's commitment to the faith and Jesus Christ to consider them as being "retained" in the faith? Is it that the young person continues to attend church weekly? Is it that they read their Bible regularly or are winning others for Christ?

For the ICM, answering this question has been at the core of missional work within the context of the city. What are we looking for as a response when someone accepts Christ as their Savior? A supernatural encounter with the person of Jesus Christ should produce a desire to want to, in turn, share this faith with others. Unless the new believer has this missionary focus, the real weight of the gospel has not been fully realized. For this reason, ICM Church works with the G12 vision: a vision for both heart and mind that seeks to encourage growth in every level of the church. It is a heart vision, as it grew out of the desire of the primary leader, Cesar Castellanos, to have a multiplying church that has always been driven by a passion for forming leaders that make disciples.[8] This passion permeates all elements of life for a member of ICM Church. It is a mind-vision because it has a specific strategy to allow this work to take place. Elements of this strategy, as well as some of the heart of this vision, will be explained and described in this short study to evaluate the growth within the youth ministry of the church and to explore its effectiveness.

International Charismatic Mission: History and Development

A Brief Overview of the Life of Cesar Castellanos and ICM Church

Over the last thirty years, Colombia as a nation has faced poverty, violence, and many political challenges. Despite all of these difficulties, revival has happened. In the city of Bogota alone, there are more than five churches that have individual congregations of over 20,000 members, International Charismatic Mission being one of these churches. Looking back over the last 30 years since this church was founded, it is clear to see that it has been a work made possible only by God's grace

The story of ICM is better understood by first looking at the life and conversion of the founding pastor, Cesar Castellanos. The story began when he was eighteen years old. Knowing very little about Christ, and having only experienced a Catholic church, he began to study Philosophy. During one of these classes, his professor, an open atheist, began to criticize the Bible directly. The professor claimed to have not only read the Bible but also studied it several times. Upon hearing these words, Castellanos was challenged to think, "If this man who is an atheist has read and studied the entire Bible, perhaps I should consider doing the same? I believe in God, but I've never read a single page of Scripture." That very night, he began to read and study the Bible. About six months later, after having read most of the Old Testament and the four Gospels, he prayed a genuine prayer that would change his life forever: "God, if you are the true God that the Bible says you are, I ask you to come to my living room and meet with me. I'll be waiting for you tomorrow at 8 pm. Amen."[9] The following night, Castellanos had a personal encounter with Jesus Christ. His experience was so powerful and real that he never wavered in his faith and began immediately to preach Jesus Christ to those around him, starting with his own family.

That personal experience led to the foundation and expansion of ICM Church as well as the global G12 movement. At the time of writing, there are over 80 ICM churches across Colombia and over 30 ICM churches worldwide. Besides, there are over 8000 churches connected to the G12 network, and a great many more churches directly impacted and influenced by the G12 movement.[10]

The Importance of Multi-Generational Missions

After seven years of leading the church, Castellanos began to notice how the members of ICM had become relatively passive. Although the church had grown to more than three thousand people, his visionary and focused leadership always believed for and desired more. The reality in the church, however, was that 90 percent of the work, in the area of witnessing and evangelism, relied on just one man, the pastor. In 1990, Castellanos prayed a simple but life-changing prayer: "Lord, give me a strategy so that people will be hungry for your Word, and that the gospel will connect with new people."[11] God's reply came quickly: "If you train twelve people and you are able to reproduce in them the same Christ-like character that is found in you, and if these, in turn, are able to do the same with another twelve and so on, the church will experience unprecedented growth."[12]

Julie Gorman affirms strongly that the "Christian community plays a powerful role in formation."[13] At ICM, the groups of 12 become a community where every member within the church is connected. Within this context of community, spiritual formation is facilitated through intentional discipleship.

Between 1992 and 1993, the work in small groups began to bear exponential fruit. The church had a building with a capacity for 700. After just seven meetings, the building was full, and it was expanded to accommodate twice that number. This enlarged place also quickly filled up, and at the end of 1993, the church decided to rent the city's main indoor arena with capacity for 14,000. The first Sunday was so full that a second meeting was added on the same day. The church quickly grew to five meetings every weekend, a direct result of the strategy of having weekly small group discipleship meetings of 12.

Throughout the scripture, God has revealed himself as the God of Abraham, Isaac, and Jacob (e.g., Gen 26:24; 28:12–15). These passages clearly emphasize how God is a God of generations. This has been a principle that has been understood and put into practice throughout the years of ICM ministry. The goal is for every member of the church to be connected and accountable to a leader. After interviewing more than 300 current leaders, pastors, and active members of ICM, 90 percent of them recognized how having a "father figure" in the ministry played a key role in affirming and establishing their faith in Christ. Many of the leaders referred to their cell leader as a person who became a close mentor and an example that allowed them to find Christ. Moreover, from this interview, the ICM leadership team found that 85 percent of our current leaders and members came to Christ before the age of 25.[14]

A Ministry of Transformation

A key factor that has helped thousands of current ICM members and leaders remain in the church throughout the years has been forming a solid foundation. When the church began, as stated before, it was mostly one man carrying out the workload of the ministry. Counseling sessions were held by the pastor every day from 9 am to 11 pm. However, as the church began to grow, there was a need to do something so that more people could experience this focused time of ministry. In 1988, Castellanos developed a three-day retreat weekend called an Encounter. The aim was to provide a new believer, or a struggling church member, with an opportunity to experience God more fully for themselves, as well as to receive specific and focused ministry to establish a firm foundation for their salvation.[15] These Encounter weekends were usually held somewhere outside the city, where the new believer would leave behind the daily distractions of life and set apart that time to seek God. At the heart of the Encounter was a transformative experience, much like the first message of salvation preached by John the Baptist, a message of repentance or change (Matt 3:2). Castellanos established five specific purposes for the Encounter: to have an assurance of salvation, to receive inner healing, to experience deliverance, to be filled with the Holy Spirit, and to receive a vision.[16]

Looking back at the history of the church, the continued growth and success of ICM has been centered around a distinct ethos of winning souls and making disciples. This ethos was established through strong relationships based on the groups of 12 and staying true to the original call and vision that the church was founded upon.

Challenges in Preaching Christ to the Next Generation in Bogota

The Message and the Means: How ICM has Preached Christ to the Next Generation

For the G12 movement, both the message and the way of transmitting that message has been important, especially when reaching out to youth. In recognition of its significance, the following four channels for reaching youth with the gospel, and helping consolidate that faith, have been developed.

1. *Youth specific meetings.* Many of those coming to Christ first connected with the church in a youth-specific meeting. These take the form of an additional weekend meeting, targeted at youth, focusing on their likes as well as their needs. The current youth service is held at 4 pm on a Saturday to cater for ages between 13 and 25. The youth service currently has an average attendance of 3500 young people with anywhere between 50 to 200 people coming forward to accept Christ.[17]

2. *Cell groups.* Small groups, called cell groups, are a key element to preaching Christ. In the G12 Vision cell model, there are two different types of cell groups. The first is the evangelistic "open" cell groups, where the new person may connect for the first time with the church and find a sense of belonging within the body of Christ. The second is the groups of 12, which are discipleship groups.[18] These groups can be youth-specific but generally contain a range of ages, something essential for young people to grow in spiritual maturity.[19]

3. *Three-day Encounter weekends.* This has been identified as one of the most significant factors in retaining youth after their conversion to Christ, that is, attending a three-day Encounter. Due to the differing needs of people at various stages of their life experience, age-targeted Encounters are offered for youth, with messages focusing on their particular needs.[20] However, the five elements of an Encounter, as discussed above, remain the same for youth and adults alike. This three-day Encounter with Christ has become essential to forming faith that lasts.

4. *Annual Youth Conference.* ICM holds annual G12 conferences worldwide, four of which are based in Bogota, Colombia. The youth conference began out of a desire from Pastor Castellanos to create a context for youth where they could express themselves, feeling a sense of belonging and identity, as well as receiving a message and ministry directed toward their stage in life.[21]

It is important to note that the only youth-specific events carried out by

ICM as a church are the additional youth services, youth Encounters, and the annual conference. The rest is exactly the same for youth as it is for adults. We have inadvertently found that the integration of adults and youth in most contexts has been essential to the development of the faith of the young person.[22]

The Challenges Faced Preaching a Gospel that Bears Fruit

It would be good to emphasize here that the development of the youth ministry in ICM and the outcomes described in this paper have often been a matter of trial and error. There have been plenty of mistakes along the way. ICM is not perfect and doesn't always get things right. However, we have found that dwelling on these "errors" can be counterproductive. Pastor Cesar teaches the importance of a strong positive attitude and the power of words and the confession we make.[23] It is so important to guard our words and confession to see a miracle occur in any area. For this reason, while seeking to learn from mistakes, it is important that we then move on.

Despite this, there is one area that needs to be discussed at this point, regarding the relationship between ICM as a whole church and the "Youth Ministry."[24] In 2004, the church experienced a significant division. There had been phenomenal growth across the church, especially among the female and younger demographics.[25] And there came the point when the youth ministry began to shape its own structure leadership. This development produced what can only be described as a church within a church. There was no real connection between the youth pastors and the senior pastor, but they began to form their sub-vision and sub-culture. This situation came to a head with the departure of the youth pastors and a large part of their leadership team, as well as a great number of young members of the church.

The great danger of youth ministry comes when they are seen as a separate entity leading to a lack of integration between the young people and the rest of the church. The intentions are nearly always good: to provide a relevant, targeted program for church youth. However, the outcome is almost always counterproductive for growing a healthy church with a thriving youth population.

Chap Clark argues, "We must move away from running a program to being a family — from functioning as an institution to living as an organism."[26] We learned this through the difficult division that we went through. The most important thing is to not see youth ministry as an institution; that of being a program of events for young people, but as part of a family. To see it as a place where young people can connect, belong, learn, and feel safe and loved by the wider church family.

After this division and departure, the youth remained segmented in larger gatherings and contexts. However, the cell groups, which were seen as the backbone of the church, began integrating young people into both family contexts and leadership roles. ICM now has over 650 young leaders within the larger leadership team.[27]

The Power of the Universities

The great challenge for many American churches has been to retain young people transitioning from high school to college. In *Adaptive Youth Ministry*, Chap Clark points out that by the time young people in the American church have transitioned from high school to college, a daunting 50 percent will no longer hold to their Christian faith.[28] In Colombia, this does not seem to affect the church for several reasons we have been able to identify.

First, not as many people attend college or higher education. Many go straight into work. In 2017, only 11.3 percent of the population between the ages of 17 and 21 registered for higher education.[29] Secondly, we have found that even those who do attend university remain connected and don't move to a different church. There could be several reasons for this. It could be that the larger network of G12 and ICM churches, with their relational connection, helps to keep young people established in a church with a similar culture and church life. It could equally be that not as many young people travel to other universities to obtain a higher education, but prefer to stay within reach of their family home. Furthermore, the best universities in the country can are in Bogota, the nation's capital. This does not, however, address the challenges faced by young people while on campus and studying in a different context.

A great biblical example of this can be found in the book of Daniel. If we study Daniel 1:3–5, we find how the young people of conquered lands were taken away from their homes and sent somewhere else. Here they were to be trained in the language and literature of the Chaldeans for three years. We see a striking parallel in our current day and age. Young people are often brought into new environments and contexts different from their church setting for several years to study different philosophies, literature, ideas, and even languages. They are often told that what they have learned in church is obsolete and irrelevant for the modern world and culture. In many cases, they are being taught the exact opposite of what they have learned in their church and family settings. It is no wonder that the statistic of young people losing their faith is so high.

The following story illustrates the decision that some of our young people have chosen to make in order to stay true to their faith and calling in God. One pastor's son, for the sake of anonymity, we'll call him James, received an offer from one of the top universities in Colombia to study literature. Right from the outset, he began to feel the external pressure from his lecturers to adopt ideas, mindsets, and values contrary to those he had learned in church and at home. He found himself at odds with his class, often singled out for ridicule and attack due to his strong Christian beliefs. When faced with a reading list that included obscene literate as part of his course, he knew that he had to make a decision. He could either conform to his class and lecturers, with the possibility of damaging his faith and conviction in Christ, at least until he made it through his university course; or drop out, losing the money invested in his education, but keeping his conviction and faith in Christ. He chose the latter, dropped out of his course, and decided that this was not the route for him.

Often, due to external pressures, young people are pushed into higher education in contexts that are not healthy or helpful for their Christian faith. Often parents feel like their children must go to university to be credible. However, this can often be at the expense of their salvation. At ICM, it is clear that higher education is important. However, it is not as important as someone's eternal life and salvation.[30]

Allowing the Spirit to Lead

Visions and Dreams

One of the main principles of ICM is allowing the Holy Spirit to lead. This principle has been central to the development of growth, preaching the gospel, and to having clear dreams, goals, and visions for the church. Solomon aptly stated that without vision, the people perish (Prov 28:18). For nearly a decade during the early years of Castellanos' ministry, he encountered many barriers and shares that he felt as though he was traveling through what appeared to be a desert with no results, no fruit, and only frustration.[31] It was during this time, in 1983, that he came across the teachings of David Yonggi Cho through his book, *The Fourth Dimension*.[32] After having a time of reflection on his teachings of vision, dreams and faith, Castellanos heard the voice of the Holy Spirit speaking to him: "Dream of a big church, because dreams are the language of my Spirit. . . . [T]he church you will pastor is going to be as numerous as the stars in the sky and the sand on the seashore that you will not be able to count it."[33] Exactly one month later, the ICM church was born in the living room of the founding pastors with eight members, most of whom were their family members.[34]

The very nature or DNA of the church was marked by the Holy Spirit as one of faith and conquest, through understanding the principle of visions and dreams. Through this, the Holy Spirit began to bring clarity to what he wanted to do. In the church's first year, Pastor Castellanos felt led by the Holy Spirit to the number 200 and felt a good time would be six months. He shared this goal with the church and encouraged everyone to visualize the church with this many members, as he had done. At the time, there were 30 members, but they all began to write down the number 200 all over there houses, cars, and workplaces.

In just three months, this dream became a reality, and the church grew from 30 members to 200. Through visions and dreams, they began to see the miracle occur; specific prayer requests were answered, and the church began to experience a revival.

Connected

God used the book *The Fourth Dimension* to connect a young pastor to a previous generation, to Pastor David Yonggi Cho. This connection became a key principle to effectively pass the gospel to the next generation. There needs to be a clear connection to the previous generation. Throughout the ages, God has raised key leaders with specific anointing and purpose, but cycles have a beginning and an end. It is in that moment that God raises a new generation to give continuity to the work of the Spirit. In this case, God raised Pastor David Yonggi Cho and gave him the anointing for the cellular movement. Through said movement, God brought a great revival to the nation of Korea.[35] Something ICM has understood is that the anointing God gives to a previous generation has the power to bless the next generation, and certainly, the church in Colombia has been greatly blessed and influenced by the church in Korea. We know that before Israel was to enter the promised land, Moses had to transmit his anointing to a young man called Joshua so that the cycle of conquest could continue. Abraham had to transmit his anointing to Isaac and Isaac to Jacob. Jesus, in the same way, transmitted or passed down his anointing to his church, beginning with the twelve disciples. Pastor Cesar notes that it is through teaching that one generation connects to another.[36] Jesus admonished that to bear much fruit, one must be connected to the vine, that is, Jesus (John 15:5). This is why ICM has made an effort to honor the teachings of Cho and to remain connected to his ministry.

In the same way, this principle can be applied within the church. For a youth ministry to thrive, the leader must understand the principle of being under "the cover of authority." A good example of this would be the story of the prodigal son. The young man rejected his father's authority and left home with the inheritance. The result of this decision was only chaos and pain for the young man (Luke 15:11–32). One of the greatest pitfalls of a thriving young ministry is pride. Remaining faithful to and honoring the authority and spiritual fathers that God has put into place will allow for the work of the Spirit to continue in the next generation.

Directed Training Programs

The Holy Spirit began to bring fresh ideas on how to connect a new generation to the word of God. In the first ten years of the life of the church, as part of the training for discipleship within ICM Church, the members had to go through what was called The Bible Institute. It consisted of different classes such as hermeneutics, the history of the Church, homiletics, and others that might be considered more traditional. However, it was difficult to see the younger generation engaged in these. Furthermore, come the completion of The Bible Institute year, many of those involved in the program stopped doing their cell groups and stopped winning people for the Lord.[37] It was at this moment that the church decided to implement a more practical program to connect new believers to the word of God. In 1988, Castellanos chose *The Navigators Bible Study*, which brought a strong biblical foundation to the young leaders of the church.[38] People began to grow in their knowledge of the Bible. New believers started leading small groups, or cell groups, within their first year of salvation. One young girl, who was studying dentistry, opened her cell group during her training. In the first year, she was able to grow her cell group to more than 30 young people. Today, she is one of the main pastors of ICM Church.[39]

Conclusion

New Ways of Reaching Youth

Today, ICM continues to be very intentional about reaching the younger generations. In 2015, Castellanos approached one of the media team at ICM and encouraged him to begin a project to reach the younger generation through the use of animation. At that moment in time, this idea sounded like something absurd and almost impossible to accomplish for several reasons, not least of all the sheer cost of most projects like this. There was neither any experience nor resources. However, as mentioned above, the DNA of ICM is one of faith, visions, and dreams. The Holy Spirit had been stirring the leader's heart, and the church responded by the same faith in prayerful planning and action. Just three years later, ICM inaugurated the first animation studio in the City of Bogotá, Colombia. There are now more than sixteen people on the animation team working full-time to bring the gospel to younger children, teenagers, and entire families in a fresh and exciting way. More than 600,000 families are reached every week through a project called *Pequeños Heroes* (Little Big Heroes), and Hero Kids.[40]

Four Key Aspects of Winning and Keeping the Next Generation

After a careful review of various aspects of the youth within ICM Bogotá, including a consideration of the strengths and weaknesses of the G12 model, several conclusions can be drawn. There are four main reasons for the numerical growth, the successful retention and discipleship to prepare the ICM youth as committed followers of Christ.

The first is the provision of an opportunity to have a powerful and supernatural encounter with Jesus early on in the believer's walk with God. It takes the form of an Encounter weekend enabling the new Christian to experience and understand the need for genuine repentance and salvation, and to receive freedom and deliverance from the past. The foundations are laid for a lifestyle of ongoing sanctification and discipleship, and the believer is quickly encouraged to develop a meaningful devotional life through prayer and Bible reading.

The second is the church's emphasis on the importance of the family in the ministry. The willingness of the lead pastor to include the younger generation in the style and development of the church has influenced growth within the youth of the G12 Movement. He has never insisted on his own preferences but has encouraged the creativity and input of a younger generation. It has specifically been modeled by his own family, all of whom are involved in full-time ministry in the church. Laudjair and Eline Guerra, the co-ordinators of the G12 Vision in Brazil and pastors in Brazilia, identified this emphasis on families in ministry as being one of the keys to success with the younger generation. Pastor Laudjair explained:

> For me, this is the great difference between G12 and other cell visions. Just as Moses was commanded to make priestly robes for Aaron and his children, Pastor Cesar has included his family as a priestly family. Before entering into G12, I studied various cell visions around the globe until I found G12, and, for me, G12 was completely different. Here I found in this model, the family in the ministry working together. For us, it was clear: the pastor and his wife and children all working together.[41]

The third is the inter-generational nature of all work within the church. As discussed earlier, if a youth group becomes separate and disconnected from the primary pastor and the church's leadership team, there is a danger for the group to become a "church" within the church. Working together across the age groups in most aspects of church life brings a cohesion of vision and purpose.

The fourth and final aspect is an integrated and intentional discipleship structure or discipleship with a cross-generational connection. When connections are fostered across generations in a discipleship setting, there are key opportunities to strengthen the faith of the next generation. Such integration helps the youth to feel valued as having an essential part to play in the mission of the church. It also encourages a sense of belonging, which allows the youth to be closely connected to the church family, church life, and leadership.

These four aspects have been consistent key features in the development and success of ICM. By encouraging and valuing these key principles, the church has been able to continue to win young people to Christ in the nation of Colombia. The example of ICM has shown that it is still possible to connect with the next generation in a rapidly changing world.

Notes

1. Louise Story, "Anywhere the Eye Can See, It's Likely to See an Ad" (Jan 15, 2007), https://www.nytimes.com/2007/01/15/business/media/15everywhere.html, accessed on September 30, 2019.

2. Kerry Loescher, "The Importance of Evaluation" in *Teaching the Next Generations: A Comprehensive Guide for Teaching Christian Formation*, ed. Terry Linhart (Grand Rapids: MI: Baker Academic, 2016), 288.

3. Allen Reesor and Farid Moreno, "Executive Summary for Ministry: Colombia," in *Spiritual State of the World's Children: A Quantitative Study* (Pompano Beach, FL: OneHope, 2009), 14. http://newonehopedemo.wpengine.com/wp-content/uploads/2017/08/Colombia_SSWC_ABY_Ministry-Final-with-Citation1.pdf, accessed on Sept 26, 2019.

4. Reesor and Moreno, "Executive Summary: Colombia," 5.

5. Reesor and Moreno, "Executive Summary: Colombia," 13–14.

6. Reesor and Moreno, "Executive Summary: Colombia," 11.

7. Kara Powell, Jake Mulder, Brad Griffin, and Tyler Greenway, "Growing Young: Six Core Commitments of Churches Effectively Engaging Young People," *Journal of Youth Ministry* 15:2 (Spring 2017), 8.

8. Cesar Castellanos, *The Ladder of Success* (Bogota: G12 Editors, 2008), 19.

9. Cesar Castellanos, *Dream and You Will Win the World* (Bogota: G12 Editors, 2006), 22.

10. Statistics provided by the ICM Missions office, Bogota, Colombia, on Sept 30, 2019.

11. Interview with Cesar Castellanos by the authors, Bogota, Sept 27, 2019.

12. Castellanos, *Dream and You Will Win the World*, 160.

13. Julie Gorman, "Christian Formation," *Evangelical Dictionary of Christian Education*, Michael J. Anthony, ed. (Grand Rapids, MI: Baker Academic, 2001), 135.

14. "Reporte de lideres de celulas, MCI Bogota 2019." A survey carried out by the missions department at ICM Church, Bogota.

15. Castellanos, *Dream and You Will Win the World*, 180.

16. Cesar Castellanos, *ABC of the Vision* (Bogota: G12 Editors, 2019), 137.

17. At this time these youth-specific elements are coordinated and led by the leaders in Pastor Cesar's team of twelve who have the largest percentage of youth, Laudijair Guerra, and his wife, Sara Castellanos, who is also Pastor Castellanos' daughter. This allows there to be a clear connection with the senior Pastor and also a clear leadership for the youth elements of church organization.

18. Castellanos, *The ABC of the Vision*, 158

19. Castellanos, *Dream and You Will Win the World*, 198; Castellanos, *The Ladder of Success*, 115.

20. Cesar Castellanos, *Encounter Messages* (Bogota: G12 Editors, 2016), 34–59, http://g12.es/encountermessages, access on October 25, 2019.

21. For more information on G12 conferences worldwide, https://convenciong12.com/#convenciones-internacionales.

22. This has been identified as a key factor for flourishing youth ministries by several key studies in the United States. For example, Kara Powell, et al., "Growing Young," 22–24.

23. Cesar Castellanos, *Destiny Training: Effective Leadership* (Miami, FL: G12 Editors, 2014), 12–16 explains the four steps to receiving a miracle: promise, visualization, confession, and perseverance.

24. At the time, ICM Church was separated into three different networks: the Men's network, the Woman's network, and the Youth network. See Cesar Castellanos, *The Ladder of Success*, 78.

25. By 2004, the church had grown to 20,000 cell groups and over 100,000 members.

26. Chap Clark, *Adoptive Youth Ministry: Integrating Emerging Generations into the Family of Faith* (Grand Rapids, MI: Baker Academy), 13.

27. ICM has 27 percent of its current leadership team under the age of 30 out of a total of 2412 leaders.

28. Clark, *Adoptive Youth Ministry*, 336.

29. Of the 1,317,000 young people in Colombia in 2017 between the ages of 17 and 21, 487,511 registered for some sort of higher education. Juliana Sanchez, "Universidades ahora tienen menos estudiantes matriculados," dinero.com, 7 March 2019, n.p., https://www.dinero.com/edicion-impresa/pais/articulo/baja-el-numero-de-universitarios-matriculados/267888, access on October 16, 2019.

30. ICM and Pastor Castellanos are currently working on ways to provide this sort of education in a safe environment. These options are available for many Americans but in Latin America there are very few if not any viable options of a faith-based, Spirit-filled higher education.

31. Castellanos, *Dream and You Will Win the World*, 49–56.

32. David Yonggi Cho, *The Fourth Dimension* (Newbury, Fl: Bridge Logos, 1979)

33. Cesar Castellanos, *Pass the Torch to Reach Your Generations* (Bogota: G12 Editors, 2006), 122.

34. Castellanos, *Pass the Torch to Reach Your Generations*, 125.

35. "Yoido Full Gospel Church started with five members at a tent church in Daejo-dong, Seoul on May 18, 1958. It is now the world's largest church through the guidance and work of the Holy Spirit for the past 60 years." http://english.fgtv.com/a01/0101.asp, access on November 28, 2019.

36. Castellanos, *Pass the Torch to Reach Your Generations*, 125.

37. An interview with Cesar Castellanos by the authors in Bogota, Colombia, Sept 27, 2019.

38. This material has since been developed into a series called *Design for Discipleship*.

39. The authors' interview with Cesar Castellanos, Senior Pastor of ICM, Bogota, Colombia, Sept 27, 2019.

40. More information: www.pequenosheroes.com and www.herokids.tv.

41. Authors' interview with Laudijair and Eline Guerra, Senior Pastors of Supernatural Church, Brazilia, Brazil and G12 Coordinators in Brazil, in Bogota, Colombia, August 28, 2019.

22.

Postmodernism, Pluralism, and Pneumiotics: Three Major Influences on the Spirit-Empowered Church

Michael Rakes

Abstract

As culture changes, new questions arise in response. Surrounded by a rapidly changing culture, the church in America finds itself asking new and pressing questions about how to best engage the culture while holding fast to the timeless truth of God's word. For the past thirty years, church leadership in the United States has been discussing the engaging of culture with the truth of Jesus, while becoming increasingly concerned with the growing issues of lack of spiritual vibrancy and depth of roots in those who have given their lives to the Lord. This study seeks to highlight the unique and God-ordained opportunities for Spirit-empowered Christians presented within the West's current culture of pluralism and postmodernism. This paper suggests pneumiotics as a strategy for such engagement. Pneumiotics is a word I created to describe getting to the heart of the issues the church is now facing, through recognizing and pointing to the intimate activity of the Holy Spirit in each believer's life. In this study, I propose that the fields of culture are ripe for spiritual harvest (John 4:35), the American church is in desperate need of renewal, and that pneumiotics can provide a practical solution for these twin issues through pointing to the work of the Holy Spirit in individual lives.[1]

Key words: postmodernism, pluralism, pnuemiotics, North American church, semiotics

Introduction

The impact of culture on the local church in America has been an on-going topic of conversation among those in church leadership positions for nearly three decades. Yet all of the information and talk about culture and ministry, although important, may continue to leave the real threats and opportunities facing the American church unaddressed. Barna states, "There are more than a quarter of a million churches in America that are not highly effective in ministry — roughly nine out every ten churches!"[2]

Soren Kierkegaard's statement made two centuries ago confirms what Barna's research found, "There is no lack of information in a Christian land; something else is lacking."[3] There is a rising vocational agony for some American pastors when it comes to seeing a real transformation in the people that show up at church on Sundays, and they would also affirm Barna's findings.

The mainstream American church at the grassroots is not whole and lacks an overall spiritual vibrancy in its attendees on Monday through Saturday. Obviously, there are exceptions and I hope my own church is one of those, but Kierkegaard's assertion, "something else is lacking," has a growing influence on my thinking daily. The surge of church plants and their explosive growth in some areas of the country only serve to emphasize the underlying unrest in the pews of traditional churches as doctrines and practices are updated and reformed to make way for the new. Yet, many of these once-a-week gatherings may need to make the move from a presentational format on Sundays to an encounter culture that can happen seven days a week.

There have been many voices that have expressed disgust and in some cases anger toward the American church. Aristotle said, "Anyone can become angry — that is easy. But to be angry with the right person, to the right degree, at the right time, for the right purpose, and in the right way — this is not easy." The Spirit-empowered leader knows this:

> The starting point is that the renewal of the church is the work of God and not of man by himself. . . . The church does not renew itself: it is the object of God's work of renewal. . . . What we are looking for, is ways in which local churches can be transformed into expressive witnessing bodies of believers whose very reason to exist is to continue the witness that brought them into existence.[4]

The American church has not made the deep changes needed to communicate to mainstream society. I suggest the "something missing" or the move to a more effective church could be discovered by a deeper look at the way Americans think about life and God. Postmodernism, pluralism, and pneumiotics are three major influences at work in the local church today. Yet, even this sentence is repulsive to the high-energy, go-get-em pastor who is driven to get higher numbers on a Sunday morning. However, a knowledge of these three influences on

Sunday church attenders can be a powerful tool for these leaders. Postmodernism, pluralism, and pneumiotics are more about church health than church growth. Understanding even at a surface level can help leaders elevate their outcomes when it comes to making disciples and forming healthy biblically functioning communities.

Definitions

Postmodernism is an open door. It's an incredible opportunity for Spirit-empowered people to share their God-encounters with their friends because the underlying philosophy of mainstream Americans is that they must be open to all ideas about life and God. Simply put, the job of a Christian, American or not, is to translate the faith to people far from God. The very first assignment of the early church in Acts was that of "translation" (Acts 2).

Pluralism is an unavoidable reality in America. Its main belief is that all gods are to be respected equally. Pluralism compels the community to live in such a way that no one sees his or her god as higher than another's god. Interfaith movements have become a new reality for many pastors in America and left them wondering whether or not to participate at all in the marketplace of ideas.

Pneumiotics is a coined term I developed a few decades ago pointing to the theological and practical correlation between semiotics (a language of signs before vocabularies are formed) and the Holy Spirit. Pneumiotics essentially says that God is always communicating to an ordinary Jesus follower. It is possible for an individual to pick up on personal messages from God in his or her everyday life.

Postmodernism pushes American believers to believe their beliefs and translate their personal stories to their neighbors. Pluralism helps the American believer not confuse patriotism with spirituality. Pneumiotics points to the personal presence of God and offers personalized God moments.

Postmodernism

Even though I was not in your service planning meeting, I can predict fairly well what's going to happen in most churches this Sunday. The service will open with a happy song or two, followed by a couple of sad songs, spilling into a somber, reflective time of prayer; then someone will make announcements (whether live or video) and take the offering; the service will then a shift into the theme for the day, generally presented with slides and visuals, and conclude with an invitation to respond to the message.

Although not in the Bible, this format has become the way Americans do church. Most pastors, including myself, work hard to structure services for maximum impact and make church safer for the newcomer. We do this through predictability and a highly-structured presentational format of the metanarrative of the gospel.

It's true — a predictable service to present the gospel of Jesus to those far from God has been crucial historically. Predictability comes from the modern era as machines began to make all products identical. Entire companies became so good at assimilation they could franchise themselves across the country, allowing people to walk into a restaurant on the East coast and have the exact same experience on the West Coast. But what if Americans have changed? What if they want something more local, more farm-to-table? Something grown locally by a farmer they could trust. The same could perhaps be said about the church.

Your church, whether you're an attendee or leader, has a structure, a social or spiritual construction that shapes how the attendee thinks about God. Leaders may inadvertently be propagating a modernistic idea of a "factory church" rather than being a biblically functioning community. A factory church will produce "clones of god" rather than living breathing disciples on fire with God's Spirit.

Michel Foucault, a French philosopher born in 1926, looked at, among other things, the social structures of humans. From what I read he was not open to faith in God as we would declare it but devoted much of his life to the history of systems of thought. His research on hospital reforms in the second half of the eighteenth century was monumental, and I believe, has implications for our Sunday morning church experiences.

Foucault noticed new hospitals built at the time were constructed in large squares connecting buildings and patients. He argued and proved the way hospitals were constructed demonstrated not only their healthcare philosophy but forced them to do their work in a certain way. He observed hospitals had central observation posts, which changed the relationship between the patient and doctor dramatically. Doctors could avoid unneeded contact with patients by isolating those with contagious diseases into one wing of the hospital and prescribe a general treatment to be administered through nurses and associates.

Foucault subsequently studied nineteenth-century prisons and found they were built along the same motif. In fact, they were eerily similar, only with the addition of guard towers with snipers in them. Just like the patients in the hospitals, the prisoners did not have the view of the entire population, only a few people at a time across from them or beside them.

In both hospitals and prisons, there was no sense of being a part of a greater community for those who were being treated or imprisoned. He discovered only those in power had that kind of view and understanding of "the system." Hospitals were impersonal, set up to treat diseases rather than people. And prisons treated all inmates in mass, eliminating any personal care or attention. [5]

Unfortunately, most pastors I know value growing numerically far above seeing supernatural transformations and wholeness of the people in their care. But those that attend church on Sunday are on a spiritual journey toward a long life with Jesus that is not rooted in their overall moral behavior, but rather in God's Spirit. Growing in their faith is not about information, though they will need some, but rather about transformation.

We may have birthed a generation of pastors out of our seminaries that are more like hospital directors or prison wardens than spiritual leaders or mentors. Most Americans that attend church on Sundays would probably say that they are Christians, but many may not be able to translate their personal faith stories to postmodern people. They've been orientated into a system like a patient or a new prisoner, espousing the ideas and beliefs of the factory church they are a part of, but never able to make the connection of how God wants to use their personal translations of God's grace through their own pains and struggles in this life.

American church leaders need to look deeper at the way they engage with people and not be content just accepting people into a larger general population. We must do the hard work of offering personal ministry to their specific spiritual needs and keep them growing, not just with more information, rather, in their personal interactions with God and other believers.

Postmodernism gives the American church a fresh opportunity to see a transformation in every individual in their churches. Transformed people who leave our parking lots on Sundays have platforms of their own that are not constructed of brick and mortar.

Here are some important observations about postmodernism and Foucault's findings:

- Church buildings were constructed in a presentational way, causing people to watch rather than participate. The physical structure of our churches has a direct impact on the spiritual structure of our faith communities.

- Corporations and companies that survive more than a decade have found a way to position their buildings and factories to be useful rather than their goal.

- Local churches need facilities; no one would argue against that, because gathering together has power and encouragement built into it. However, most church governance systems would struggle to get their minds around building fewer factories and franchises, and instead, constructing spaces that contribute to attendees interacting with God and one another in deeper ways.

- The first multisite gathering of God's people started with the portable tabernacle constructed by Moses (Ex 25–31; 35–40). It was the "dwelling place of God" where ceremonies and memories were planned on the yearly calendar.

- God placed his very presence in the middle of their traveling community. God has still done that through Jesus because his glory is inside the human heart. God's kingdom is now only visible through his people and not edifices.

- American Christians should be sharing their stories as witnesses because our world is now postmodern in its receptivity.

- The architectural construction of offices and sanctuaries actually represents modernism rather than postmodernism. Rick Warren, author and leader of Saddleback Church, often says, "You have to build the people before you build the steeple."[6] I have always taken this to mean that the most important work a pastor does is to make disciples.

- Postmodernism naturally carries an aversion to structure, organizations, and authority, which we can use to our evangelistic advantage. Now that we have coffee shops in our foyers, we should see those spaces as opportunities for the people to embrace and share their own personal translations of God's love to a hurting world.

- Architecture, according to Foucault, elicits by its structure some challenges. The facility may inadvertently send the message that one needs to get on the property to encounter God. This could cause a potential loss of personal intimacy with God outside of a ninety-minute service.

- Leaders must be creative, spending time, staffing, and money in helping people see that God's transformational power can be accessed the other six days of the week leading to naturally supernatural moments of storytelling — the fine art of translation.

- Architecture can turn those on the stage into celebrities of sorts and inadvertently send the wrong message that the people watching have less spirituality and also less spiritual responsibility throughout the week to share their story. But the priesthood of all believers in our postmodern world is the only way forward when it comes to seeing people come to faith.

- Prison wardens and pastors should not have very much in common. The warden can from a distant place of authority make dogmatic announcements across the microphone. Pastoring in the postmodern context must look more like Moses who led the first multi-campus church as they carried with them in a tent the Presence of God moving from one place to another (Ex 25:45–46). Moses was not a warden but told Pharaoh to let the people free that they may worship God as they go on their way.

- The hard truth is we have created services that wait for the "doctor or prison warden" to make their rounds or diagnose their condition from a distance and prescribe three steps toward health. The chairs or pews all face the front where a man (generally not a woman) stands, preaches, performs in a lecture format, speaking down to the uninformed. The priest or person in power delivers powerful pronouncements in well-crafted, intellectually-inspiring phrases of truth which rarely find their way into the practical everyday life of the listener.

Recently our seventy-year-old denominational church has gone through several changes which now poise us to respond to the larger issues surrounding our attendees. We minister to people facing complicated immigration issues and minister to those who are experiencing life below the poverty line. We have created and now launched a volunteer-based chaplains ministry available to the people that attend our services on Sundays.

This fundamental idea of making lay chaplains available to translate their personal stories of transformation in the arena of sexual brokenness, spousal abuse, or infertility, brings the gospel close. This is the work of the church to conduct the "business of God" during the week. The business of God, the product of the kingdom, is understanding how God's story intertwines with your story. The architecture of your facility should not be shaping the way churches do their work. In other words, what are the products of the kingdom? Does the organized church exist to hold worship services on Sundays? These are not simple questions, but we seek to grapple with the higher view of what it means to be God's people at this time and in this place.

Every local church, whether they know it or not, is in conversation with the community and city in which they gather for worship. But the local church is only in conversation with culture as its people interact with the needs of those in their circles of influence. In effect, the disciples we create are in some cases the hiddenness of God to the city, through a corporate body of believers. As they live out the kingdom through their daily lives, the revelation of God's love becomes more and more evident. The presence of an individual or a group of believers that are hidden in Christ is used to overthrow the work of the evil one through the goodness and faithful love of Jesus. Goodness, real virtue, is birthed right at the gates of where you work or live.

Pluralism

Dietrich Bonhoeffer wrote, "To be simple is to fix one's eyes solely on the simple truth of God at a time when all concepts are being confused — distorted and turned upside down."[7] Pluralism has become a glaring reality in the American context. The average church-going person now works alongside others that have passionate beliefs in different gods and reject the message of Jesus. People feel more confident to express their anti-Christ beliefs, which has created a crisis for cultural Christians living and working in the American context.

Pluralism is essentially the agreed upon the idea that all gods are equal. Pluralism demands Christ-followers live in such a way that, when they are in the marketplace, they don't express out loud that Jesus is greater than the gods of their neighbors.

Here are some facts about Pluralism:

- It is the predominant mindset and landscape upon which people in America live.

- The uncomfortable truth is that believers are called to live out their faith in workplaces that have policies that forbid the discussion of people's deepest held beliefs.

- Christians don't believe there are equals with Jesus, but out of our respect for others and God's creation, we listen intently to others in their struggle for truth on the journey.

- Pluralism is growing in its social pressure to force everyday followers of Jesus to reframe their daily interactions at work or after-school functions.

- American pastors are being forced to see the difference between getting a decision for Christ in a weekend service and the actual production or fruitfulness of disciples emerging from that body of believers.

- The vocational danger for American pastors, with its governance oversight usually done by deacon boards, makes growing disciples through people's personal life far less spectacular than having large crowds gather on Sundays.

- Christianity, at its core, is fundamentally opposite of "selfie culture." American Christians and their political and moral beliefs have become the center of their own personal "spiritual" story. The truth is most Americans who think of themselves as Christian have little to no understanding of the greater meta-narrative of God who became sin for them and by his grace redeemed them wholly.

- Despite the prominence of religious believers in politics and culture, America has shrinking congregations, growing dissatisfaction with religious leaders and rising numbers of people who do not think about faith.[8] Chaves wrote in *American Religion: Contemporary Trends*, "Over the last generation there has been a 'softening' that affects church attendance on a regular basis to selecting spouses who have different religions altogether."[9]

- Pluralism forces us to turn our deeply held beliefs into love rather than insults or weapons. We can speak the truth that is differentiated but not divisive.

- Americans are supposed to celebrate the diversity of our nation with all its religions on the landscape of democracy. People of all faiths can continue to come together as Americans and unite to do good things from time to time, and we are compelled to participate in the marketplace precisely because of Jesus. Although we cannot be one with all faiths, we can be respectful of all religions, even those that would pray for the destruction of our own.

These are the challenges that must be grappled with but have always been represented in the biblical text. Moses, Paul, and even Jesus, all ministered in a pluralistic world. There are times for silence as Jesus modeled for us, which helps us see that we are not suspending our beliefs, simply not demanding they take center stage in the middle of the public square. We are trusting that the Holy Spirit is at work in ways in which we cannot see. To be one with Christ not only means unity in friendship but unity in priority and message.

The year was 1996, and we were church planters near all the attractions that draw millions to the city of Orlando every month. My personal trainer, a former Olympic athlete, and her husband became some of our first friends in the city. For several years we worked out five days a week and it immersed me in the world of blended religions. No classification really fits this couple. Part Hindu, part mystical spirituality, and a dose of Jesus-was-a-good-and-holy-man provided the foundation for how they lived, ate, and thought about the more significant concerns of life. This unique couple actually attended our church plant in its infancy and were more generous financially than almost anyone that participated in our services. But there was one major theme that would ultimately cause them not to return. "It's just too much emphasis on Jesus," they would say, "and not enough spirituality." That statement makes complete sense to a majority of Americans. It's rational and leaves room for sincerity and all good people of the earth. It would play well on CNN and is taught by most American mainstream universities. God is god, no matter what you call him, or her, or it. To claim "uniqueness" or to claim to have the truth, therein lies that greatest sin — yea, even blasphemy.

Pluralism allows plenty of room for people to invent, blend, or choose the top ten likable spiritual ideas and frame them in any way they want. Wilfred Cantwell Smith was a Canadian Islamicist, comparative religion scholar, and Presbyterian minister. He was the director of Harvard University's Center for the Study of World Religions. He said,

All the religions have as their core some experience of the Transcendent; that whether we speak of images made of wood and stone or images made in the mind, or even of such an image as the man Jesus, all are equally the means used by the Transcendent to make himself, herself, or itself present to us humans. To claim uniqueness for one particular form or vehicle of this contact with the Transcendent is preposterous and even blasphemous.[10]

Pastors across the United States will meet people just like this not only during the week but in their churches. Americans think of themselves as so in charge of their lives economically, educationally, that they are also now conceiving of God in any particular way they choose. In a very real sense, the spread of Pluralism helps the American pastor see not only the sheep and goats, but the wolves that have moved in among our churches.

Pluralism will force American pastors back to their knees, asking God for the power of the gospel to once again surge in and through their congregations. Jesus did have a conversation in a pluralistic world with the woman at the well in John 4. He heard her views and beliefs and commented about her sincerity, but he also revealed the truth. He told her everything she'd ever done and cut to the core of her humanity.

Pluralism in America will more and more demand a robust demonstration of the power of God at work in the lives of Christ-followers. Pluralism for the church cannot mean that we lay down our faith, but rather seek to embody our faith. If pluralism implies that we are one with all religions, then the death of martyrs and Hebrews 11 are of no consequence to us in the present day. The city where I pastor — Winston-Salem, North Carolina — is rich in the Christian tradition, including the Moravian faith. Would we not be disrespecting those who were burned at the stake for their belief in the Bible and Jesus? Was it not their strong stand against false ideas that led them to those difficult decisions? Were they just narrow-minded, uneducated Bible-thumpers, or was there a deep and profound work of the Holy Spirit in their lives?

Pluralism will eventually force American Christians and their leaders to realize they are living on the edge of a new cultural frontier, as the modernistic culture they've known and provided a landscape for the current wineskins of happy songs and sad songs has changed and demands a new expression of a biblically functioning community. Pluralism will force Americans to embody (incarnate) the truths that have changed their lives, and communicate personal stories of transformation and authentic encounters. This will force American Christians out of hiding and into differentiating moments orchestrated by the Holy Spirit. These changes will happen as Americans are once again empowered by the Spirit.

Pneumiotics

Pneumiotics is a coined term I developed a few decades ago pointing to the theological and practical correlation between semiotics (a language of signs before vocabularies are formed) and the Holy Spirit. Pneumiotics blends the idea that God communicates individually to people, including their surroundings, all for their transformation and empowerment.

We come to understand that when most use the word Spirit-empowerment they mean all the activity of the Spirit. In the early days of Empowered21, when the word "Spirit-empowered" was created, shaped, and deployed for kingdom use, it was to remove the semantic eclipse that had been created with words that had expired culturally. The word "Spirit-empowerment" is serving us well. One dimension of the word that needs much more scholarly work is the assumption that the world in which we live is an open world into which God the Spirit is at work shaping, speaking, and forming God's holy church.

Spirit-empowerment includes the reality that God still speaks. It is about living open, experience-directed, and empowered by God the Spirit. This directly opposes some evangelicals who see a rather closed system of cessationist teachings that emphasize only the work of the Father and the Son. Some evangelicals really squirm over God's Spirit being individualized in any way, and in my estimation, have unintentionally created a weakness in American Christians.

I had the privilege of earning theological degrees from different seminaries from Charismatic, Presbyterian, and Baptist denominations. Those professors and institutions provided a foundation of thought on which to construct my ministry. Each class and degree dramatically shaped how I thought about God and his creation, how the world works, and how we come into any kind of knowledge or experience of God at all. I am so grateful for all of my professors, some famous like R. C. Sproul, and others only famous in heaven. Each had a profound influence on how I think about God and his engagement with humanity.

However, all of my professors could only pass along that which they had been taught from their professors forty years earlier and their own experiences or lack thereof. They taught about God, his nature, and most importantly, the way God acts or does not act in someone's world. I have now come to see that the dominant voice, thought, and structure of thinking coming from all three institutions came out of a period of history known as the Enlightenment. Theological scholars understand that the ground we walk on theologically was radically shaped by that period as the church emerged out of the Dark Ages along with the rest of the world.

To be sure, Augustine and early church theologians, long before the Enlightenment period, were considered and consulted in our theological training; but the predominant training I received centered around this Enlightenment period, the late seventeenth to eighteenth-century mainstream mindset, emphasizing reason, rational thinking, and individualism. The thinkers of this period confronted theology and other fields of study with its skepticism and pushed for evidence.

Perceived allegiance to orthodoxy by the U.S. church has led to less and less spiritual experience in hopes for greater control and objectivity of the faith presentation by many of its leaders. This approach has led to a discipleship in which the follower experiences only cognitive principles, and diminishes both the expectation and capacity of each disciple to experience God for themselves.

In an attempt to project intellectual muscle, the church in the U.S. has intentionally moved away from the vocabulary that speaks of legitimate supernatural experience. This unorthodox theoretical underpinning, the denial of spiritual experiences, leads to lessened expectations of the Trinity's role in providing direction and personal dignity, and degrades the power of renewal available to individuals.

To deny legitimate spiritual experiences is also to deny God's daily communicational intent. Denying communicational intent moves the church as a whole far from a historical faith evidenced in the biblical narratives. Even Martin Luther said,

> Christian faith has appeared to many an easy thing; nay, not a few even reckon it among the social virtues, as it were; and this they do because they have not made proof of it experimentally, and have never tasted of what efficacy it is. For it is not possible for any man to write well about it, or to understand well what is rightly written, who has not at some time tasted of its spirit, under the pressure of tribulation; while he who has tasted of it, even to a very small extent, can never write, speak, think, or hear about it sufficiently. For it is a living fountain springing up unto eternal life, as Christ calls it in John 4.[11]

The self-disclosed revelation of God we call the Bible, is full of thoughts, signs, and moments from an unseen realm toward humanity, and gives us those stories not just to preach from, but as actual examples of a living God at work in the world. The Bible describes some individuals struggling to discern and implement the direction of these thoughts, moments, and signs, and we see the stories of Abraham, Daniel, John the Baptist, as well as Martha, Deborah, and other women play out on its pages. The Spirit in many of those instances seems to be using experiential methods in working to direct the recipients toward dignity or bring renewal to God's people in some way.

Here are some things to think about regarding pneumiotics:

- Stoicism, or no emotion, has become much more acceptable as a viable expression of personal faith, and left the American church with a growing apathy that is eroding the next generations' personal faith in God.

- A functional intellectual Agnosticism has emerged as the mainstream faith for the church of the U.S. culture, especially if it wants to grow numerically.

- Pneumiotics invites us to explore and experience God's supernatural and personal engagement with us.

- Some American pastors, whether formally trained or not, rarely discuss Spirit-empowerment as a personal reality for themselves or their congregants. Most messages emphasize two main biblical themes. The first is grace, fully secured by Jesus, which requires only a mouthing acceptance by the receiver. The second is a trust in God's sovereignty to such a degree that the person disengages from a personal faith altogether, and results in little to no prayer because it will not change anything anyway. They perceive there is no need to pray fervently because whatever is going to happen will happen.

- Postmodernism and Pluralism both raise their ugly heads seemingly confirming what some evangelicals teach continually — that God is watching and working such a big plan that he's not really engaged with anyone's personal struggle or physical ailments. This is the differentiating core value of Spirit-empowered believers and churches around the world.

- Pneumiotics sees God engaged and speaking into our everyday lives and invites us to live wide awake to an open experience directed and energized by the Spirit, centered wholly on the finished work of Jesus.

Jesus prayed often, daily even, not only to be in a relationship but to also be in alignment with the will of God. Jesus prayed and delivered the supernatural regularly in an open universe. The texts describing some of the healings don't appear to be "sovereign as it were" but rather spontaneous, such as the woman with the issue of blood pushed through for a simple touch of his garment. Jesus told those listening to him to have faith.

Intellectualism, for some, keeps God at arm's length distance and exposes many "theologically brilliant" people's discomfort with the vocabulary of the supernatural. What if the ultimate conspiracy theory has been pulled off by the god of this world, as Paul wrote in 2 Corinthians 4:4, and the church emerging from the Enlightenment has taken false comfort in too much sovereignty? What if we live in a more open universe than we have been led to believe and are to engage with God through prayer to see more of God's goodness and glory in the world?

At least two critical understandings emerge if we see a more open universe. First, the God reflected in the Old Testament narratives is more understandable, as the Israelites were supposed to be more and more engaged in trusting God for land acquisition. Their personal obedience was critical to their personal and national history. The second is that we are to engage in personal prayer like Jesus did, taking authority over the demonic affronts in our lives. We are to be passionately expectant in our asking. We ask, we seek, we pray, and we believe, and we watch, and we wait, and keep on knocking until we have a yes or a no. And all of this is done by the power of the Spirit working through our personal lives.

Pneumiotics confirms the fact that God is global in showing his glory and calls for a differentiating people living in all contexts, under all governments, and reaching for eternal things. The kingdom contains within it a built-in diversity of speech and individuality that speaks to the kingdom from different perspectives. The promises of the pouring out of the Spirit start by pushing past cultural differences in the book of Acts and continues to this day.

Pneumiotics calls out the activity of the Spirit in the life of every believer and reveals that it is diverse by God's grand design. This individualization of the Spirit's empowerment in ordinary people births purpose and connects them to a broader new kind of unity in their church and city. This empowerment allows us to be different as God's called-out ones, while maintaining solidarity with the brokenness of humanity within our towns and cities. This demonstrates God's incredible mercy, kindness, and absolute dominion over sin through all kinds of different expressions around the world.

Conclusion

Postmodernism and Pluralism are the best climate for the Spirit-empowered church to thrive and create biblically functioning communities. Spirit-empowered leaders are poised uniquely at this time and place in church history to take the lead theologically and experientially in our weekly expressions of church.

The Spirit absolutely has more creativity in store for the American expression of what it means to be Christ's church than a few programmed happy and sad songs with well-calculated key changes. There is a power that's available to strengthen our diversity and individualized expressions that will model for contemporary seekers an authentic faith in the God of the Bible who gave his only son for the whole world.

Americans should be able to walk into a gathering of believers and immediately tangibly sense the presence of God. They should walk to their cars after the gatherings we call church having been deepened in their faith by seeing the evidence and fruit of God's power in the lives around them.

Every American Christian can avoid the internal pain of feeling like their lives have no purpose or that they aren't important when it comes to influencing the people they care about. They must come to see that they "are the church," and they are far more important to God than they could know.

The conversation by those in church leadership concerning the impact of culture is the right one to have but not so that we retreat in fear or excuses for a lack of ministry effectiveness. The strategies we share between us should contain excitement and creativity available to us by God's Spirit. The something missing that we can sense in the American church is the power of God in our personal lives and ministries. We serve a God not threatened by the American culture, but rather one that enables us to prove that greater is he that's within us than he that's within the world (1 John 4:4).

Notes

1. This study was prepared for an oral presentation in a local church setting.

2. George Barna, *The Habits of Highly Effective Churches: Being Strategic in Your God Given Ministry* (Ventura, CA: Regal, 2001), 18.

3. Fred Craddock, *Overhearing the Gospel* (Nashville: Abingdon, 2002), 38.

4. Visser 'T Hooft, *The Renewal of the Church* (Philadelphia: Westminster, 1956), 90.

5. Michel Foucault, *Power/Knowledge: Selected Interviews and Other Writings* (Brighton, UK: Harvester, 1980).

6. Rick Warren, "Does Your Church Really Need a Bigger Building?" *Pastors.com* February 6, 2015, https://pastors.com/big-buildings/, accessed 20 March 2019.

7. Eberhard Bethge, ed., *Dietrich Bonhoeffer in Ethics* (New York: Macmillan, 1955), 70–71.

8. Mark Chaves, *American Religion: Contemporary Trends* (Princeton: Princeton University Press, 2013).

9. Chaves, *American Religion*.

10. Lesslie Newbigin, *The Gospel in a Pluralist Society* (Grand Rapids, MI: Eerdmans, 1989), 160–61.

11. Martin Luther, *First Principles of the Reformation*, R. S. Grigno, ed., C.A. Buchheim, trans. (London: Clowes and Sons, 1883), 104.

The Gift of Christ's Uniqueness: Postscript

Rebekah Bled

"And there is salvation in no one else, for there is no other name under heaven given among men by which we must be saved" (Acts 4:12 ESV).

Introduction

What is the Spirit-empowered Church's unique contribution and voice in witnessing Christ as the only way, truth, and life, especially in the face of tremendous challenges? This is the question behind the theme of the Johannesburg Scholars Consultation that formed the foundation of this book. This postscript will reflect on this question, beginning with a look at the name of Christ, then using a lens of under-spiritualization, and over-spiritualization. This framework separates purely theological chapters from contextual chapters, and gathers similar challenges faced in specific contextual realities into two categories for the sake of discussion. The proverbial "straight and narrow" of the theme of this book is actually quite wide, when applied to specific contexts across the globe. Therefore, this book does not explore every iteration of proclaiming salvation in Christ alone; it cannot. Even the disciple John wrote that if everything that Jesus did were written down, the whole world could not contain the books it would require (John 21:25). Yet, this book weaves together important and representative stories of witnessing Christ's exclusivity in the face of difficult and specific challenges. God through the Holy Spirit and the global church triumphant is continuously at work drawing all people to himself. This book stands as a testimony to that fact.

Like the crowd in Acts 4 marveling at the courage of ordinary men who proclaimed Christ's exclusivity through the empowerment of the Holy Spirit in the face of persecution, I stand amazed at the courage of today's scholars, who bring windows of clarity in these chapters through the work of the Holy Spirit, in the face of enormous challenges. Tides of doubt and obfuscation from current philosophies pummel against the very foundations of belief in Christ alone. As the infilling and empowerment of the Holy Spirit brought Peter, John, and the other disciples in Acts 4 into conflict with the Sanhedrin, so it may be that the statements of Christ's exclusivity held within these pages may bring thoughts and conversations into conflict. But, it is worth noting that the conflict of proclaiming Christ's exclusivity in Acts 4 was a productive, Spirit-led conflict, as "many who heard the message believed" (Acts 4:4). Christ is indeed the unique Savior, provoking the conversation, question, and perhaps even the conflict so that he may reveal himself within it.

The Unique Name of Christ

While even in Jesus' day there were those who dedicated their lives to the study of scripture, Jesus alone had the authority to fulfill it. When he was a child, this was viewed with amazement by crowds of Jews (Luke 2:46–47). But years later when he was stepping into his ministry as the unique Savior "in the power of the Spirit" (Luke 4:14), a similar audience to that of his childhood visit to the Jerusalem synagogue reacted very differently to him as an adult.

In fact, so enraged were they to hear Jesus claiming to be the fulfillment of scripture that they tried to throw him off of a cliff (Luke 4:14–30). Yet neither the fullness of the Spirit nor the uniqueness of Jesus Christ depends on a crowd's agreement. Throughout the Gospels, Jesus will be shunned and praised, cornered by the religious establishment (Matt 22:15), followed by a throng with a craving that would crush anyone else (Mark 3:7–10), and denied all association by his own disciples (Luke 22:54–62). Christ's fullness does not rest on our reception of him, and this itself is a mercy. Christ gives himself to mankind, not to their whims as their plaything to manipulate and control, but as their hope—the only one who can and will and does make them whole. His uniqueness, his very self, is epitomized in his name.

"And you shall give him the name Jesus" (Luke 1:31), the angel told his mother, Mary, in the annunciation. "Jesus, who consorted with shamed women. Jesus, who is neither orderly nor predictable. Jesus, who with his parents became an immigrant to Egypt when his own country turned inhospitable to him. Jesus, who makes possible our immigration to the Kingdom of God."[1] For her part, Mary understood that this was no ordinary name, and she responds in song, bursting forth in praise to the source of the name (Luke 1:49). If it is true that language shapes reality, as anthropologists have written,[2] then it is noteworthy that the incarnation begins with an announcement of the gift of Christ's name. The name of Jesus Christ shapes our reality, is the very ground on which we stand, and compels us to proclaim (Deut 30:20a; Heb 4:14; 2 Cor 5:14).

Compelled to witness to those who do not yet know the name of Christ, as well as those who have disregarded and misunderstood his name, how do we proceed? This is no small challenge. It requires the careful work of contextualization so that Christ's beloved in each specific context may truly hear and experience him through his Spirit and accept it as their own, entwining their lives with his (Col 3:1–4). Anthropologist, Michael Rykiewich, phrases the question this way: "How can the next group of people (culture, generation) best hear the gospel so that they have a fair chance of responding?"[3]

Witnessing the Name of Christ in Contextual Realities

In the year 2011, I was working at an international church in one of Latin America's most secular countries,[4] leading a fledgling youth group. My group of twenty-six students represented seventeen different nationalities between them. Of these, approximately half came to church without their parents. Adding to this, the parents of my students were mostly highly educated, agnostic expatriates – the "international cultural elite" that sociologist Peter Berger says are one of the "exceptions to . . . a furiously religious world."[5] These students' parents could not fathom why their teenagers wanted to get up and go to church on a Sunday morning. My effectiveness in my part-time job as a youth minister required full-time contextualization as I tried to identify what things made up Hiebert's "excluded middle" issues[6] for sixth graders with hyphenated national identities who came to church alone, in this capital city within the Southern Cone of South America.

Oddly, it was the Christmas pageant that brought the climax of opportunity. At a planning meeting in November, the church leadership had decided that each age group would bring something to the community Christmas celebration. Older people brought stories, traditions and each other. Parents brought exuberant toddlers, food, and their cell phones. And what did the brand new youth group bring? The pastor's wife said they would bring the Christmas pageant.

"Easy enough," I thought, remembering my own career as Mary, Christmas after Christmas as a pastor's daughter in my small-town church in the Midwest of North America. What was there to do, after all, in preparing a Christmas pageant but to assign bathrobes to shepherds one, two and three? However, after the meeting, as I searched "Christmas skits" online, I grew increasingly frustrated. The language of the scripts was that of insiders referencing a known story, commonly agreed upon. That was not our context, nor, therefore, our reality. The reality of our Christmas skit was that while performing this story, many of the students would be experiencing it for the first time. The question was then, how could middle schoolers with various levels of exposure to the story of Christmas tell the story to themselves in a way that they would hear it, even as they performed it in a skit for others?

As I prayed through the skit over the next few days, the answer came, as surprising as it was clear: through the animals. Remembering Balaam's donkey, I wrote a reader's theater style skit in which each student took on the role of a witness to a scene of the story. The grasshopper in Mary's garden, witnessing the annunciation. The termite in Joseph's workshop. The donkey giving Mary a ride to Bethlehem. The mouse in the inn gorging himself on the crumbs dropped by a no-vacancy crowd. The sheep hearing a legion of angels sing. The barn swallow in the stable watching the long-awaited Jesus take his first breath as a baby.

Because on the surface it was a skit about animals, it was disarming. The students fought over who got to be the mouse. They giggled as they played the parts of animals. The parents who had come to see their children perform listened with their guard down because a sixth-grader, especially *their* sixth-grader, imitating a termite is in no way threatening. For my part, I cheered the students on from the back of the room and wanted to weep for the beauty and the silliness and the goodness of God, all manifested at a Christmas potluck.[7] The Spirit blows where it pleases indeed (John 3:8).

Would that every contextualization issue could be as simple as a skit. In reality, however, even the skit was not simple. That very night a student's mother, who had come to watch her daughter in her starring role as a barn swallow, approached me. "My daughter loves it here," she said, with a look of bemusement. "So we have made an agreement. She is allowed to come as long as she stays open-minded. If she starts to become close-minded, she will not be able to come here anymore. I thought you should know that." And so it was that the immediate result of proclaiming the exclusivity of Christ in that moment was a mother's gentle warning that if Christ was not presented as one among options, I would lose the ones I was proclaiming him to.

Brainerd Prince and Jeffrey R. Thomas discuss the awkward tension of witnessing the exclusivity of Jesus with a focus on the inclusion of people who do not yet know him. It can feel awkward, impolite, pushy, and exclusive. In fact, Prince and Thomas report in a conclusion relatable to all who work in a secular, pluralistic context, "It was evident that matters of religion and local tradition had been subverted or entirely displaced by the secular tradition."[8]

On the farthest end of the spectrum of risk, proclaiming the exclusivity of Christ is not simply awkward, it is life-threatening. Pakistani authors, Zia Paul and Rebecca Paul, note without exaggeration the very real stakes of the cost of following, let alone proclaiming, Jesus. Their courageous chapter references the stories of many who have died proclaiming him.[9] We regret that we are not able to highlight more stories of the underground church around the world. Christ's church in these areas stands as an important testimony of the Holy Spirit's activity in the world, drawing all people, in every situation and context to himself. These testimonies are also highly dangerous to share. The editors contemplated another study of this sensitive nature and finally decided not to publish for the sake of the author's safety. While these stories are absent from this book, with the exception of the courageous contribution from Paul and Paul, the stories are not absent from history. We honor the stories we are not able to include.

"Under-Spiritualization" and the Spirit-Empowered Witness

In what may be an over-simplification, the challenges of secularism, pluralism, and Postmodernism can be categorized as challenges of "under-spiritualization." Allan H. Anderson, Sakkie Olivier, Mark Roberts, J. Elias Stone, and Samuel Thorpe are intelligent and thoughtful in their engagement with issues surrounding the exclusivity of Christ in a culture that has already dismissed the conversation as irrelevant.[10] Thorpe and Stone, for example, tackle the questions of the Pentecostal church's voice in secular society, where the state unofficially, but no less effectively, sets the rules of religious engagement.[11] When the apparent rules regarding religious conversation are set like a social straightjacket around the church, insisting that anything can be true as long as nothing is absolutely true, how do followers of Christ proclaim his exclusivity?

Whoever sets the premise wins the argument. Perhaps the importance of experience in Pentecostal Christianity, which runs in the very DNA of Pentecostalism, allows the unique voice of Pentecostal Christianity to subvert secularism's premise, speaking into what might otherwise be a closed circuit of small-storied conversations. "There are calls for a postmodern worldview characterized by some type of holism that integrates humans and the world and takes spiritual needs seriously. But what shape should it take? A number of worldviews compete for the postmodern mind."[12]

Michael Rakes suggests a strategy to begin contextualizing the Spirit-empowered life in conversation with secular, postmodern, and pluralistic culture, noting that the Holy Spirit is continually at work in the daily lives of believers, speaking in intimate, experiential ways.[13] It is the responsibility of those who live by Christ's name to pay attention, because these encounters matter. These stories of individual, often intimate experiences with Christ through the Holy Spirit have credibility within a postmodern and pluralistic culture because they allow each member of the conversation to insert "their truth" in a way that is deeply personal and authentic. The critical difference between the "personal truth" of a believer and that of a non-believer is that a believer's so-called personal truth finds its base in, and therefore points to, the grand metanarrative of Christ's unique love.

A kindred strategy, called three-story evangelism is a model widely used in Youth for Christ mission contexts. Three-story evangelism is a cumbersome tool when in the hands of denominations and strains of Christianity that are primarily intellect-oriented, because three-story evangelism is all about *story*. However, it is possible that three-story evangelism may be a useful tool in the hands of the Spirit-empowered church. The simple framework of your story, my story, and God's story, intersecting in a sort of holy Venn Diagram may help inform and equip, specifically, Pentecostal believers to witness in postmodern and pluralistic contexts. For example, in my own work with Christian teenagers in non-charismatic faith settings, students often struggle to identify their experiences with, and therefore their stories of God. This is a point of tension and even crisis for these students because, in the absence of identification with an experience of the Holy Spirit, they wonder if they have a story with God at all. As they wrestle with the weight of this tension, there is a holy and critical moment of invitation that Pentecostal/charismatic Christ followers are uniquely empowered to offer. The invitation begins and ends in story. Who among Christ's followers are better equipped to offer this invitation then the Pentecostal body of Christ, which, as Allan Anderson notes, has a primarily oral and experiential faith tradition?[14]

If this moment of holy invitation is true in the lives of Christian adolescents, how much more may it be true of adolescents and adults alike in an "under-spiritualized" culture who are not yet walking with Christ? Those who can articulate a genuine personal experience of the power of God through his Spirit at work in the lives they really live are able to use the framework of three-story evangelism to listen to another's story, share their own story, and invite the other into God's grand story. In so doing, they help give shape to an amorphous postmodern worldview that pervades Western culture, both inside and outside the walls of the institutional church.

"Over-Spiritualization" and the Spirit-Empowered Witness

On the other end of the spectrum are challenges of "over-spiritualization." J. Kwebena Asamoah-Gyadu, Lord Elorm-Donkor, Julie Ma, Opoku Oniyah, Christian Tsekpoe, and Dela Quampah, writing on Christianity in animistic and traditional cultures in Africa and Asia, note the grip that traditional religion holds on the hearts and practices of even confirmed believers.[15] As these chapters describe, traditional religion is alive and well alongside Christianity. While in some cases this combination may be syncretistic, in other cases, the root cause is not a lack of allegiance to Christ alone, but a pervasive fear of the spiritual world that stems from an incomplete understanding of Christ. In what may be a shocking sentence to a post-enlightenment reader, Christian Tsekpoe references Opoku Oniyah's work, commenting, "It is believed that these spiritual forces are complex and mysterious and their activities can neither be measured nor subdued by physical and scientific methods. Consequently, scholarly research into issues related to the spirit world is normally considered impotent in the face of spiritual realities."[16]

Given the impotence of scholarly research to speak to issues of the spirit world, as Onyinah states above, it stands to reason that to engage these spiritual realities, Spirit-empowered Pentecostalism—a uniquely experiential strain of Christianity which operates and feels at home in the spiritual realm—is strategically positioned to proclaim Christ's exclusivity over the spiritual realm through his Spirit. As deep calls to deep (Ps 42:7), God's spirit answers the challenge of the spirit world with a promise fulfilled. The enraged dragon from the book of Revelation prowls around to wage war on "those who keep God's commands and hold fast to their testimony about Jesus" (12:17 NIV), but Christ has crushed the serpent's head (Gen 3:15). The dragon does not win.

"Theology and missions never should be separated from each other."[17] The plurality of self-theologizing cultures and countries represented in this book is itself a witness to the unique Savior, Christ Jesus. Christ alone is Lord, and it takes every culture and people group he has created to reveal his Lordship. God has not left himself without a witness (Acts 14:17). In contextualization, we join the Spirit in celebration, highlighting the ways in which he has hidden trails and bridges of himself in each culture.[18]

In bringing challenges and contextualized responses of "over-spiritualization" close through these case studies, a theme emerges regarding the spirit world with a clarity and incisiveness that is almost startling. This theme is that the spirit realm is over-emphasized in African Christianity, to the neglect of the transformation of society. As I read, I am reminded of the instructions to the Israelites in the shadow of Mt Sinai, "You have stayed long enough at this mountain" (Deut 1:6). Asamoah-Gyadu, Elorm-Donkor, Ma, and Onyinah write that in order for society to be transformed, a fuller understanding of Christ's unique power and total salvific work is required. This understanding is often communicated through a power encounter.[19] The point is not that Christ *can* have dominion over the whole spiritual realm, it is that he *does* have dominion. To quote Lawson Stone, "God does not take sides, God takes over."[20] Who the son sets free is free indeed (John 8:36)—and with that freedom, we are called to follow the risen, victorious, Christ in a grounded faith. We follow Christ in seeking the good of the place in which we live (Jer 29:7), trusting that Christ is over, above, behind, below, before, and behind us [21] and will see us through.

Universalism

Interestingly, while up to this point in the discussion there has been a clear categorization of issues under the headings "over-spiritualization" and "under-spiritualization," each of which are delineated along geographical lines, universalism defies these categorical issues and geographies. Universalism seems to an issue of over-spirituality occurring in the West. Michael McClymond describes the Western thirst for universalism, listing as proof no less than forty book titles published in the past twenty years.

Universalism is a term that encompasses an array of theodicies. McClymond focuses on what he calls the "grace message,"[22] noting, "The younger generation is less ready to do battle against the devil and more inclined to rest in the full enjoyment of divine grace. The stress on grace is associated with joy, happiness, and celebration rather than a lugubrious stress on sin, repentance, and the evils of modern society."[23] In this sense, the grace message of Universalism is seductive. It seems to resonate with scriptures that call the believer in Christ to "be still and know" (Ps 46:10), or to be led beside still waters with a restored soul (Ps 23:2). This universalistic grace seems to affirm the work of Christ, rather than boasting in our own efforts—efforts which amount to a pile of reeking garbage anyway (Eph 2:8–9; Isa 64:6). The words of this grace message seem to find root in scripture; and embracing this message seems like the trusting, grace-drenched spirituality that many, especially anxiety-riddled evangelical teenagers and young adults,[24] crave. Is it any wonder that the West is so thirsty?

What does the exclusivity of Christ have to say to those who are hungry for grace and acceptance, and yet feel harried and hassled by what they perceive to be the shrill legalism of religion? How is Christ alone proclaimed in this context in such a way that, on one hand, the proclamation is heard amidst the swirling messages of the universalist cauldron, and on the other, it does not land like a heavy set of rules against those seeking to escape just that?

"Where the Spirit of the Lord is, there is freedom" (2 Cor 3:17) — freedom, because of Christ's exclusivity, not in spite of it, for we worship both in Spirit and in truth (John 4:23). Perhaps Pentecostal believers' experiencing freedom in Christ's *specific* presence can speak to the longing to belong found within those to whom Universalism draws. It is the specificity of Christ that allows us to be uniquely his, and to rest on his specific breast like a weaned child, content to nuzzle against his very own mother (Ps 131:2). For a baby, it is the particularity of the mother which brings calm. As anyone who has held a distraught infant knows, there are times, indeed, whole seasons of life, when no one but their very own mother will suffice. They are not crying for a mother figure, but for their mom. Like infants, may we seek and find our comfort and shelter in Christ's gentle, exclusive, and specific care (Ps 73:28; Is 49:15; 66:13).

Areas of Further Research

Further research is needed for witnessing Christ as the only Savior in specific cultural, socio-economic, and geographic contexts, through a Spirit-empowered lens. In my own experience on a charismatic mission team, our strength of being open to the Spirit's guidance day-by-day also became our weakness, because our lack of structure and the subsequent lack of rigor in paying close attention to our context hampered our witness substantially. It could well be said that we loved the Lord with all of hearts and strength but did not apply our minds to contextualizing our witness (Matt 22:37). We, therefore, used the same methods to witness in Eastern Germany in December that we had used on a Caribbean island in August. What worked in one place was decidedly foolish in another, and it was my team and my folly to assume otherwise. I do believe the foundation of Christ's exclusivity is firmly established through scripture; and theologians through the ages, including James Shelton, Mark Roberts, Clayton Coombs, Philip Adjei-Acquah and Sylvia Owusu-Ansah in this book, solidly reaffirm this. Indeed, the good news is unchanging. However, culture, economic and power systems, and geo-politics continually shift. Therefore, research into contextualizing the message of Christ's exclusivity will always be timely.

How, for example, do Christian pastors and leaders proclaim the exclusivity of Christ in materially impoverished contexts, without dabbling in the prosperity gospel and/or word of faith traditions? In the opposite ditch is the essentially gnostic overcorrection, which proclaims the hope of Christ for the future and ignores the daily reality of suffering in the here and now. Both of these ditches hold enormous temptation when proclaiming Christ's saving power among the poorest fringes of society and are worthy of further inquiry.

On the other end of the spectrum, materialism presents another sizable challenge, insidious in its appeal for autonomy and self-preservation both personally and institutionally. Materialism seems to have a uniquely Western foothold, as Western Christians purchase our way to the narrow gate. Arriving burdened, we look around bewildered as to what to unload to go through the eye of the needle (Mat 19:24), so convinced are we that we have been carrying the Lord's stuff. This syncretistic worship of both God and consumerism is in need of the prophetic voice, calling us out of the Grave of Craving (Num 11:4–34), and into the presence of the only Savior, who alone provides contentment (Phil 4:11–13).

Though we have touched on Latin America with the chapter of Harding-Castellanos on reaching youth and young adults in Bogota,[25] Latin America is a vast continent containing numerous distinct cultures. Further study is needed, for example, on how to contextualize the gospel for the swatch of Central America rapidly losing their working-age male population to gang violence and/or migration.[26] Much further south, in the region of Rio de la Plata, one finds a culture of secularism resembling that of Western Europe and requiring an appropriately unique response.

Harvey Kwiyani has written on the African diaspora in Western Europe with the view that God is strategically sending his witnesses from "New Christendom," to quote Philip Jenkins' famous book,[27] to what we could call "Old Christendom" in Western Europe.[28] The difficulty is how to equip these diaspora missionaries to minister effectively in two worlds. Even Moses experienced anger and a sense of impotence in the face of the pervasive economic injustice his biological people group was the target of, and was ridiculed by a member of the people group he was trying to advocate for (Ex 2:11–15). If this patriarch in the faith had difficulty navigating his two vastly different worlds in his early years, we must acknowledge that today's children, teenagers, and young adults face a swirl of competing commitments and loyalties, worldviews and allegiances. This is especially poignant in diaspora communities where specific practices of faith that define the first generation of immigrants no longer make sense to that generation's children. Kwiyani and others are researching how to equip adolescents in faith that sticks;[29] Sakkie Olivier has spoken to the issue of faith formation in families.[30] It is my conviction that this issue is urgent and more voices are needed. Indeed, one of the fundamental tasks of proclaiming Christ alone is to proclaim him in contextually appropriate, Spirit-empowered and empowering ways to the next generation. "That the next generation might know . . . the children yet unborn, and arise and tell them to their children, so that they should set their hope in God" (Ps 78:6–7 ESV).

The last element to mention this book does not touch on, but that is nonetheless relevant to proclaiming Christ's exclusivity, is environmental stewardship. Two of Adam's first tasks were to care for the Garden (Gen 2:15), and to name the animals in the Garden of Eden (Gen 2:20). I believe we must continue to name the validity of caring for God's good creation as part of holistically proclaiming Christ, both to creation, who are longing for his return (Rom 8:19–23), and neighbors, who are watching for our actions and advocacy to be congruent with the hope we profess.

Conclusion

Christ himself compels us (2 Cor 5:14–15), woos us (Hos 2:14), emboldens us (Ps 138:3), strengthens and sustains us (Isa 58:11), guides us (Ps 38:2) and proceeds us (Is 45:2). He tattoos our names on the palms of his hands (Is 49:11) so that we may write his work on our hearts (Ps 111:19). He calls us his bride, his beloved, his Church. Proclaiming Christ is our great honor and our natural response. Where else would we go but to Jesus? (John 6:68). What could we do but proclaim him? (Jer 20:9).

As Rebecca Paul notes at the conclusion of her chapter, "As long as the earth remains, the principles of seedtime and harvest will be in force (Gen 8:22). So we are to multiply until the coming of the Lord Jesus Christ (Luke 19:13), whether the days are peaceful or troublesome, through the power of the Holy Spirit."[31] So we persevere unto the fullness of our promised hope (Heb 6:10–11), proclaiming Christ and him crucified, through the power of the Holy Spirit, our very lives bearing witness to him (1 Cor 2:2; Ps 138:3; John 15:16).

"The Spirit and the bride say come!" (Rev 22:17).

Notes

1. Lauren Winner, *Wearing God* (New York: HarperCollins, 2015), 107.
2. Michael Ryknkiewich, *Soul, Self and Society* (Eugene, OR: Cascade, 2011), 50.
3. Rynkiewich, *Soul, Self and Society*, 44.
4. Central Intelligence Agency, "The world Factbook; Uruguay," https://www.cia.gov/library/publications/the-world-factbook/geos/uy.html, accessed March 6, 2020.

5. Peter L. Berger, "Secularization Falsified," *First Things: Journal of Religion and Public Life* (February 2008), https://www.firstthings.com/article/2008/02/secularization-falsified.

6. Paul Hiebert, *Anthropological Reflections on Missiological Issues* (Grand Rapids, MI: Baker, 1994), 196–198.

7. David Iaconangelo, "Uruguay Celebrates 'Day of the Family' Instead of Christmas," *Latin Times* December 26, 2013, https://www.latintimes.com/uruguay-celebrates-day-family-instead-christmas-140852, accessed 7 April 2020.

8. See chapter 16.

9. See chapter 15.

10. See chapters 4, 2, and 6 respectively.

11. See chapter 6.

12. Hiebert, *Anthropological Reflections on Missiological Issues*, 224.

13. See chapter 22.

14. See chapter 4.

15. See chapters 8, 9, 10, 12, 13, and 14 respectively.

16. See chapter 10.

17. Gregg Okesson, "Global Expressions of Worship" (a sermon delivered on February 20, 2020 at Asbury Theological Seminary, Wilmore, KY). https://asburyseminary.edu/students/chapel/archive/?service=20200220&campus=ky.

18. See chapter 7. See also Don Richardson, *Eternity in Their Hearts* (Ventura, CA: Regal Books, 1981).

19. See chapters 8, 14, 15, and 9 respectively.

20. Lawson Stone, "Are You Ready to Rumble?" (a sermon delivered on January 15, 2020 at Asbury Seminary, Wilmore, KY), https://asburyseminary.edu/students/chapel/archive/?service=20200115&campus=ky.

21. https://www.worldvision.org/christian-faith-news-stories/reflection-st-patrick-day-prayer

22. See chapter 3.

23. See chapter 3.

24. Rachel Dodd, "Serving Today's Anxious Generation; 5 Ministry Perspectives," *Fuller Youth Institute Blog* February 6, 2020, https://fulleryouthinstitute.org/blog/serving-todays-anxious-generation, accessed March 20, 2020.

25. See chapter 21.

26. Personal Conversation with Cheryl Kuney, Director of Gathering Hearts for Honduras (2018). See also https://www.pewresearch.org/hispanic/2017/12/07/rise-in-u-s-immigrants-from-el-salvador-guatemala-and-honduras-outpaces-growth-from-elsewhere/, accessed 24 March 2020.

27. See chapter 18.

28. Philip Jenkins, *The Next Christendom* (Oxford: Oxford University Press,

2011).

29. See Harvey Kwiyani, *Our Children Need Roots and Wings* (Liverpool: Missio Africanus, 2019).

30. See chapter 12.

31. See chapter 17.

Contributors

Philip Adjei-Acquah is a researcher and lecturer in Pentecostal/ Charismatic Theology and Missions at Central University and Perez University College, Ghana. He is also a minister with the International Central Gospel Church. He serves as a conference speaker and leadership mentor with the passion of empowering the youth. Adjei-Acquah is author of the book *How to Develop the Leader in You* (2015).

Allan H. Anderson is Emeritus Professor of Mission and Pentecostal Studies at the University of Birmingham, England, where he has been since 1995. He is author and editor of many books and articles, the most recent monographs being *Spreading Fires* (2007), *To the Ends of the Earth* (2013), *An Introduction to Pentecostalism* (2004, 2014), and *Spirit-Filled World* (2018).

Emmanuel Kwesi Anim serves as the Director of the School of Theology, Mission, and Leadership at Pentecost University College in Accra, Ghana and is an Associate Minister of the Pentecost International Worship Center. He was formerly Principal of the Pentecost Theological Seminary at Gomoa Fetteh in Ghana. He is a visiting lecturer at the Akrofi-Christaller Institute of Theology, Mission and Culture in Ghana, and the All Nations Christian College in the United Kingdom.

Kwabena Asamoah-Gyadu is Professor of Contemporary African Christianity and Pentecostal/Charismatic Studies and President of Trinity Theological Seminary, Legon, Ghana. He is a member of the Lausanne Theology Working Group and a Fellow of the Ghana Academy of Arts and Sciences.

Rebekah Bled is an ordained minister and a PhD Student in Contextual Theology at Oral Roberts University. She holds a Master of Arts degree in Intercultural Studies and Church Planting from Asbury Theological Seminary, and has served in North and South America as a Youth, College, and Young Adult Minister, as well as in missions with Youth With A Mission in Central America and Western Europe. She lives in Northwest Arkansas with her husband and son.

Manuela Castellanos was born in Bogota, Colombia and grew up in Florida. She graduated in Christian Ministry at Regent University and is currently studying a Masters in Practical Theology at Oral Roberts

University. She is a Pastor at Misión Carismática Internacional (MCI), Bogota, Colombia, where she now lives with her husband and four children. At MCI, she oversees the children's' work, producing children's materials for churches and families. She is also involved in leadership training and pastoral care work.

Clayton Coombs is Academic Dean of Planteshakers College and an ordained minister of Planetshakers Church, a large multi-campus Pentecostal church based in Melbourne, Australia. In addition to a Fortress Press monograph, Clayton has published articles in Pentecostal theology and Greek Philosophy.

Lord Elorm-Donkor is the Principal of Birmingham Christian College, UK. He is also the Director of Training for The Church of Pentecost-UK and a District Minister. His research interests include theological ethics, African Christianity, Mission Studies, Pentecostal theology, Wesleyan theology and the integration of moral traditions.

Richard Harding studied Theology at Durham University, UK. He then oversaw the Global Leadership Training Program for G12 and Misión Carismática Internacional churches worldwide. He is currently leading a project called Hero Kids TV, an animation project for children's animated Christian content, based out of Bogota, Colombia. He is studying a Master's degree in Divinity at Oral Roberts University, and is also one of the lead Pastors at MCI Church, Bogota, Colombia, where he now lives with his wife and four children.

Harvey Kwiyani is a Malawian Missiologist teaching theology at Liverpool Hope University in Liverpool, England. He received his Ph.D. from Luther Seminary in the United States following his research on theological and missiological implications of African immigrant Christianity in the United States. He has written extensively on African Christianity in the diaspora. Among his publications are *Sent Forth: African Missionary Work in the West* (Orbis, 2014) and *Our Children Need Roots and Wings* (Missio Africanus, 2019).

Julie C. Ma serves, as Professor of Missiology and Intercultural Studies at Oral Roberts University, in Tulsa, OK. Previously, she served as a Korean missionary in the Philippines (1981-2006), and as Research Tutor of Missiology at the Oxford Centre for Mission Studies, Oxford, UK. Publications include *When the Spirit Meets the Spirits: Pentecostal Ministry Among the Kankana-ey Tribe in the Philippines* (Peter Lang, 2000). She served as a general council member and executive member of Edinburgh 2010.

Wonsuk Ma, a Korean Pentecostal, serves as Dean and Distinguished

Professor of Global Christianity at Oral Roberts University, Tulsa, Oklahoma. He previously served as Executive Director of the Oxford Centre for Mission Studies, Oxford, UK. He serves as Co-chair of Scholars Consultation, Empowered21.

Michael McClymond is Professor of Modern Christianity at St Louis University, St Louis, Missouri. He previously held teaching or research appointments at Wheaton College, Westmont College, the University of California-San Diego, Emory University, Yale University, and University of Birmingham (UK). An Anglican layperson, he has been a leader in Global Day of Prayer, Habitat for Humanity, and Stepping Into the Light (a substance abuse recovery ministry in St. Louis). He has written many publications that have received numerous awards.

Marcel V. Măcelaru is Professor of Theology at University of Arad, Romania and is the founding President of the Centre for Faith and Human Flourishing in Timișoara, Romania. He is involved with several national and international organizations that advance holistic practices of theological education and Christian mission. His publications include *Mission in Central and Eastern Europe* (2016) a Regnum Edinburgh Centenary Series entry and the special issue on "Christianity and the Refugee Crisis" of *Transformation* journal (2018).

Sakkie Olivier together with his wife and teenage children, serves as Senior Pastor of the Life Christian Foundation congregation in Vanderbijlpark, South Africa. They are also involved in many entrepreneurial endeavors. They host regular conferences at their church in Vanderbijlpark and their ministry house (HisHouse) in George, South Africa. As a family, they are passionate about Spirit-empowered ministry, the new generation of believers, and entrepreneurship, and have a heart for God's unfolding destiny with Israel.

Opoku Onyinah is the immediate past president of Ghana Pentecostal and Charismatic Council, Ghana, and also immediate past chairman of the Church of Pentecost, Ghana, with branches in 102 countries. Currently he lectures at Pentecostal University College, Accra, Ghana. He serves as Co-chair of Scholars Consultation, Empowered21.

Sylvia Owusu-Ansah is a lecturer at Central University, Ghana, and the head pastor of Revival Temple, Perez Chapel International, Accra. Her research interests include missions-related studies, cross-cultural communication, gender studies, interreligious conflict mediation, and dialogue. Among her publications are the book chapters "The Role of Interreligious Collaboration in Conflict Prevention and Peaceful Multi-

Religious Co-Existence: A Case Study of Northern Ghana" (2018) and "Neo-Pentecostalism in Postcolonial Ghana" (2018).

Rebecca Paul ministers with her parents at the Assembly of God Church in Karachi and teaches at the Assemblies of God Bible School in Quetta, Pakistan. She received her graduate education in Pakistan and the Philippines, and is currently pursuing a doctoral degree in the USA.

Zia Paul is Senior Pastor of the Assembly of God Church in Karachi, Pakistan, and has been the Founder and Supervisor of the Assemblies of God Bible School in Quetta and the Assembly of God Secondary School in Karachi, Pakistan. The school's mission is to train the leadership of evangelical churches nationwide. The church also operates ministries to serve women and children. He received his graduate education in the Philippines.

Brainerd Prince is a Research Consultant who tutors, teaches, and trains students at all levels of research. He also designs and executes research tracks for higher education institutions. He undertakes original research projects on various themes for organizations and develops training resources for organizational capacity-building. He is the Founding Director of Samvada Internationaal Research Institute. He is currently working on a book for Routledge titled, *Rethinking Christian Mission in India: Imagining a Hindu Face of Jesus.*

Dela Quampah is Head of the Theology Department at Pentecost University College, and Resident Minister of Pentecost International Worship Centre, Odorkor, Ghana. He was The Church of Pentecost missionary to South Africa from 2015 to 2019. He received his education at the University of Ghana, with Ministerial Ethics as his research focus. His publications include *Good Pastors, Bad Pastors* (2014).

Micheal Rakes is the current Chair of the Board at Oral Roberts University, and serves on the Global Council of Empowered21. Mike and his wife, Darla Rakes, serve as Lead Pastors at Winston Salem First Assembly in North Carolina. They have deep concerns about the spiritual health of the U.S. church and are committed to mobilizing faith communities for God and the good of humanity. His publications include *Slings and Stones* (2015).

Mark E. Roberts is Dean and Professor of Learning Resources at Oral Roberts University. A New Testament scholar by training, he specializes in the literary-rhetorical composition of Luke-Acts and Paul's letters and a related dramatistic approach to biblical interpretation. He has worked also as a pastor, editor and publisher, and musician.

James B. Shelton is Professor of New Testament at Oral Roberts

University and serves as Mentor for the Scholars Initiative for the Museum of the Bible. He is a Director of the ORU Biblical Studies Group, also serving as a fellow for the Foundation of Pentecostal Scholarship and the St. Paul Institute. His publications include *Mighty in Word and Deed: The Role of the Holy Spirit in Luke-Acts* (1991) and "A Commentary on St. Matthew" in *Life in the Spirit Bible Commentary* (1999).

J. Elias Stone is a recent graduate of Oral Roberts University, where he studied philosophy, theology, and mathematics. He enjoys the academic life, discussing his studies and many interests with just about anyone willing to talk about them. Though currently between schools, he intends to pursue graduate study in fields such as Medieval Philosophy and the History and Philosophy of Science in the coming years.

Jeffrey R. Thomas is pursuing a postgraduate study with Middlesex University, London through the Oxford Centre for Mission Studies, on the topic of religious spatiality and secularism. He has conducted research on religion in both India and Canada. He has worked on the training handbooks for Christian development workers on Interreligious Collaboration and on Implementing Development in Faith Contexts. He is a Research Fellow with the Samvada International Research Institute, India.

John Thompson is Associate Professor of Global Leadership at Oral Roberts University. He is President and Founder of Global Equip, an organization that trains leaders in developing nations, and serves as a Billy Graham Center Fellow. Prior to teaching at ORU, he planted a multinational church in Tulsa, Oklahoma, and has served in pastoral and executive director roles.

Robert Samuel Thorpe is Professor of Philosophy at Oral Roberts University since 1990. He received his education from ORU and University of Tulsa with post-doctoral works in Philosophy in two institutions. His recent publication includes *Enigmatic If Not Ineffable* (2019).

Christian Tsekpoe is an ordained minister with the Church of Pentecost, leading the Mission Department at the School of Theology, Mission and Leadership at Pentecost University College, Ghana. He is pursuing a postgraduate program at the Oxford Centre for Mission Studies, Oxford, UK. His research interests include Pentecostal missiology, exorcism, witchcraft and demonology.

Select Bibliography

Adogame, Afeosemime U. *The African Christian Diaspora: New Currents and Emerging Trends in World Christianity.* London: Bloomsbury Academic, 2013.

Allin, Thomas. *Christ Triumphant: Universalism Asserted as the Hope of the Gospel on the Authority of Reason, the Fathers, and Holy Scripture.* Annotations by Robin Parry and Thomas B. Talbott. Eugene, OR: Wipf and Stock, 2015.

Althouse, Peter, and Robby Waddell, eds. *Perspectives in Pentecostal Eschatologies: World without End.* Eugene, OR: Pickwick, 2010.

Anderson, Allan H. "Towards a Pentecostal Missiology for the Majority World." Paper presented at the International Symposium on Pentecostal Missiology. Asia-Pacific Theological Seminary, Baguio City, Philippines, January 2003.

_____. *An Introduction to Pentecostalism.* 2nd Ed. Cambridge: Cambridge University Press, 2014.

_____. *Spirit-Filled World: Dis/Continuity in African Pentecostalism.* London: Palgrave Macmillan, 2018.

_____. *To the Ends of the Earth: Pentecostalism and the Transformation of World Christianity.* New York: Oxford University Press, 2013.

Asamoah-Gyadu, Kwabena J. "'Born of Water and of the Spirit': Pentecostal/Charismatic Christianity in Africa." In Ogbu U. Kalu, ed. *African Christianity: An African Story.* Trenton, NJ: Africa World Press, 2007.

Asamoah-Gyadu, Kwabena J. "Signs, Wonders, and Ministry: The Gospel in the Power of the Spirit." *Evangelical Review of Theology* 33:1 (January 2009): 32–46.

_____. *Sighs and Signs of the Spirit: Ghanaian Perspectives on Pentecostalism and Renewal in Africa.* Oxford: Regnum, 2015.

_____. *The Holy Spirit Our Comforter.* Accra: Step Publishers, 2017.

Aspinall, Peter J., and Martha J. Chinouya. *The African Diaspora Population in Britain: Migration, Diasporas and Citizenship.* London: Springer, 2016.

Aye-Addo, Charles Sarpong. *Akan Christology: An Analysis of the Christologies of John Samuel Pobee and Kwame Bediako in Conversation with Karl Barth.* Eugene, OR: Pickwick, 2013.

Baker, Sharon L. *Executing God: Rethinking Everything You've Been Taught about Salvation and the Cross.* Louisville, KY: Westminster John Knox, 2013.

_____. *Razing Hell: Rethinking Everything You've Been Taught about God's Wrath and Judgment.* Louisville, KY: Westminster John Knox, 2010.

Barna, George. *The Habits of Highly Effective Churches: Being Strategic in Your God Given Ministry.* Ventura, CA: Regal, 2001.

Barth, Karl. *Church Dogmatics.* 14 Vols. G. W. Bromiley and T. F. Torrance, eds. 1942–68. Reprint, Edinburgh: T&T Clark, 1956–69.

Beauchemin, Gerry. *Hope beyond Hell: The Righteous Purpose of God's Judgment.* Olmito, TX: Malista, 2007.

Bediako, Kwame. "What Is the Gospel?" *Transformation: An International Journal of Holistic Mission Studies* 14:1 (1997): 1–4.

_____. *Jesus in Africa: The Christian Gospel in African History and Experience. Theological Reflections from the South.* Yaounde, Cameroon: Editions Cle, 2000.

_____. *Jesus in African Culture: A Ghanaian Perspective.* Accra: Asempa Publishers, 1990.

Bell, Rob. *Love Wins: A Book about Heaven, Hell, and the Fate of Every Person Who Ever Lived.* New York: HarperOne, 2011.

_____. *The Love Wins Companion: A Study Guide for Those Who Want to Go Deeper.* David Vanderveen, ed. New York: HarperOne, 2011.

Bentley, Todd. *Kingdom Rising: Making the Kingdom Real in Your Life.* Shippensburg, PA: Destiny Image, 2008.

_____. *The Journey into the Miraculous.* Shippensburg, PA: Destiny Image, 2008.

451

_____. *The Reality of the Supernatural World: Exploring Heavenly Realms and Prophetic Experiences*. Shippensburg, PA: Destiny Image, 2008.

Bhargava, Rajeev. "The Distinctiveness of Indian Secularism." In *The Future of Secularism*. T. N. Srinivasan, ed. Delhi: Oxford University Press, 2006: 20–53.

Bickle, Mike. *Encountering Jesus: Visions, Revelations, and Angelic Activity from IHOP-KC's Prophetic History*. Audio memoir, 2009. http://mikebickle.org/resources/series/38

Blanchard, Laurence Malcolm. *Will All Be Saved? An Assessment of Universalism in Western Theology*. Milton Keynes, UK: Paternoster: 2015.

_____. *Will All Be Saved? An Assessment of Universalism in Western Theology*. Milton Keynes, UK: Paternoster: 2015.

Bosch, David J. *Transforming Mission: Paradigm Shifts in Theology of Mission*. Maryknoll, NY: Orbis Books, 1991, 2011.

Bradley, Heath. *Flames of Love: Hell and Universal Salvation*. Eugene, OR: Wipf and Stock, 2012.

Bradshaw, Paul F., Maxwell E. Johnson, and L. Edward Phillips. *The Apostolic Tradition: A Commentary*. Harold W. Attridge, ed. Minneapolis: Fortress, 2002.

Brown, Joanne Carlson, and Rebecca Parker. "For God So Loved the World?" In *Christianity, Patriarchy, and Abuse: A Feminist Critique*. Joanne Carlson Brown and Carole R. Bohn, eds. New York: Pilgrim, 1989: 1–30.

_____. "Divine Child Abuse?" *Daughters of Sarah* (Summer 1992): 25–28.

Brown, Michael. *Hyper-Grace: Exposing the Dangers of the Modern Grace Message*. Lake Mary, FL: Charisma House, 2014.

Bryan, Christopher. *Render to Caesar: Jesus, the Early Church, and the Roman Superpower*. Oxford: Oxford University Press, 2005.

Burnfield, David. *Patristic Universalism: An Alternative to the Traditional View of Divine Judgment*. 2nd ed. Charleston, SC: CreateSpace, 2016.

Capon, Robert. *Health, Money and Love . . . and Why We Don't Enjoy Them*. Grand Rapids, MI: Eerdmans, 1990.

Carmondy, Kevin. *Will Everyone Be Saved?* Amazon.Com, 2018.

Carter, Howard. *Questions and Answers on Spiritual Gifts*. Tulsa: Harrison House, 1976.

Castellanos, Cesar. *ABC of the Vision*, Bogotá. Colombia: G12 Editors, 2019.

_____. *Dream and You Will Win the World*. Bogotá, Colombia: G12 Editors, 2006.

_____. *Pass the Torch to Reach Your Generations*. Bogotá, Colombia: G12 Editors, 2006.

Chan, Francis, and Preston M. Sprinkle. *Erasing Hell: What God Said about Eternity, and the Things We Made Up*. Colorado Springs: David C. Cook, 2011.

_____. *Erasing Hell: What God Said about Eternity, and the Things We Made Up*. Colorado Springs: David C. Cook, 2011.

Chaves, Mark. *American Religion: Contemporary Trends*. Princeton: Princeton University Press, 2013.

Church, Forrest. *The Cathedral of the World: A Universalist Theology*. Boston, MA: Beacon Press, 2010.

Clark, Chap, ed. *Adoptive Youth Ministry: Integrating Emerging Generations into the Family of Faith*. Grand Rapids, MI: Baker Academy, 2016.

Clarke, Clifton, and Amos Yong. *Global Renewal, Religious Pluralism, and the Great Commission: Towards a Renewal Theology of Mission and Interreligious Encounter*. Lexington, KY: Emeth Press, 2011.

Colle, Ralph Del. *Christ and the Spirit: Spirit Christology in Trinitarian Perspective*. Oxford: Oxford University Press, 1994.

Congdon, David. *The God Who Saves: A Dogmatic Sketch*. Eugene, OR: Wipf and Stock, 2016.

Constantineanu, Corneliu, Marcel V. Măcelaru, Anne-Marie Kool, and Mihai Himcinschi, eds. *Mission in Central and Eastern Europe: Realities, Perspectives, Trends*. Regnum Edinburgh Centenary Series 34. Oxford: Regnum, 2016.

Coombs, Clayton L. L. *A Dual Reception: Eusebius and the Gospel of Mark*. Minneapolis: Fortress, 2016.

Cox, Harvey, *Fire from Heaven: The Rise of Pentecostal Spirituality and the Reshaping of Religion in the Twenty-First Century*. London: Cassell, 1996.

Craddock, Fred. *Overhearing the Gospel*. Nashville: Abingdon, 2002.

Crowder, John. "About Cana." http://www.cana.co/About_Cana.html

_____. "Hell Revisited–The Jesus Trip." YouTube, August 16, 2012. http://www.youtube.com/watch?v=afloDCTwluY

_____. *Cosmos Reborn: Happy Theology on the New Creation*. Portland, OR: Sons of Thunder, 2013.

_____. *Miracle Workers, Reformers, and the New Mystics*. Shippensburg, PA: Destiny Image, 2006.

_____. *Mystical Union*. Santa Cruz, CA: Sons of Thunder, 2010.

_____. *The Ecstasy of Loving God: Trances, Raptures, and the Supernatural Pleasures of Jesus Christ*. Shippensburg, PA: Destiny Image, 2009.

D'Costa, Gavin. *Christianity and World Religions: Disputed Questions in the Theology of Religions*. Chichester, UK: Wiley-Blackwell, 2009.

De Certeau, Michel. *Heterologies: Discourse on the Other*. Trans. Brian Massumi. Minneapolis: University of Minnesota Press, 2000.

_____. *The Practice of Everyday Life*. Trans. Steven Rendell. Berkeley: University of California Press, 1984.

De Gruchy, John W. *The Church Struggle in South Africa*. Minneapolis: Fortress, 2005.

De Young, James B. *Exposing Universalism: A Comprehensive Guide to the Faulty Appeals Made by Universalists Paul Young, Brian McLaren, Rob Bell, and Others Past and Present to Promote a New Kind of Christianity*. Eugene, OR: Resource Publications, 2018.

Dempster, Murray A., Byron D. Klaus, and Douglas Petersen, eds. *Called and Empowered: Global Mission in Pentecostal Perspective*. Peabody, MA: Hendrickson, 1991.

Dixon, Larry. *"Farewell, Rob Bell": A Biblical Response to "Love Wins."* Columbia, SC: Theomedian Resources, 2011.

Donkor, Lord Elorm. *Christian Morality in Ghanaian Pentecostalism*. Oxford: Regnum, 2017.

Drummond, Richard. "The Buddha's Teaching." In *Eerdman's Handbook to the World's Religions*. Pat Alexander, and Others, eds. Grand Rapids, MI: Eerdmans, 1994.

Du Toit, Francois. *Divine Embrace*. Hermanus, South Africa: Mirror Word, 2012.

_____. *Mirror Bible*. Hermanus, South Africa: Mirror Word, 2012.

_____. *The Logic of His Love*. Hermanus, South Africa: Mirror Word, 2007.

Dunn, Benjamin. *The Happy Gospel! Effortless Union with a Happy God*. Shippensburg, PA: Destiny Image, 2011.

Edwards, James R. *Is Jesus the Only Savior?* Grand Rapids, MI: Eerdmans, 2005.

Ehrman, Bart. *Jesus, Interrupted: Revealing the Hidden Contradictions in the Bible (and Why We Don't Know About Them)*. New York: HarperCollins, 2009.

Ellis, Paul. *The Hyper-Grace Gospel: A Response to Michael Brown and Those Opposed to the Modern Grace Message*. N.p.: Kingspress, 2014.

Emmel, V. Donald. *Eliminating Satan and Hell: Affirming a Compassionate Creator-God*. Eugene, OR: Wipf and Stock, 2013.

Evely, Bob. *At the End of the Ages . . . the Abolition of Hell*. Bloomington, IN: First Books Library, 2003.

Fees, Gordon. *God's Empowering Presence*. Carlisle, UK: Paternoster, 1995.

Ferwerda, Julie. *Raising Hell: Christianity's Most Controversial Doctrine Put under Fire*. Lander, WY: Vagabond Group, 2011.

Flood, Derek. *Healing the Gospel: A Radical Vision for Grace, Justice, and the Cross*. Eugene, OR: Wipf and Stock, 2012.

Foucault, Michael. *Power/Knowledge: Selected Interviews and Other Writings*. Brighton, UK: Harvester, 1980.

Frank, Doug. *A Gentler God: Breaking Free of the Almighty in the Company of the Human Jesus*. Menangle, NSW, Australia: Albatross, 2010.

Fristad, Kalen. *Destined for Salvation: God's Promise to Save Everyone*. Kearney, NE: Morris, 2003.

Galli, Mark. *God Wins: Heaven, Hell, and Why the Good News Is Better than "Love Wins."* Carol Stream, IL: Tyndale, 2011.

Gerloff, Roswith. *A Plea for British Black Theologies: The Black Church Movement in Britain in Its Transatlantic Cultural and Theological Interaction with Special References to the Pentecostal Oneness (Apostolic) and Sabbatarian Movements*. Studien Zur Interkulturellen Geschichte Des Christentums. Frankfurt am Main: Peter Lang, 1992.

Gillihan, Charles. *Hell No! A Fundamentalist Preacher Rejects Eternal Torment*. Santa Barbara, CA: Praeger, 2011.

Girard, René. *Things Hidden since the Foundation of the World*. Stanford, CA: Stanford University Press, 1987.

Graf, Fritz. *Magic in the Ancient World*. Trans. Franklin Philip. Cambridge, MA: Harvard University Press, 1997.

Green, Joel B., et al., eds. *Dictionary of Jesus and the Gospels*. 2nd Ed. Downers Grove, IL: InterVarsity Press, 2012.

Grimsrud, Ted, and Michael Hardin, eds. *Compassionate Eschatology: The Future as Friend*. Eugene, OR: Cascade, 2011.

Grisez, Germain, and Peter F. Ryan. "Hell and Hope for Salvation," *New Blackfriars* 95 (2014): 606–15.

Guinness, Os. *Last Call for Liberty: How America's Genius for Freedom Has Become Its Greatest Threat*. Downers Grove, IL: IVP Books, 2018.

Gulley, Philip, and James Mulholland. *If Grace Is True: Why God Will Save Every Person*. New York: HarperOne, 2003.

Guomundsdottir, Arnfriour. "Abusive or Abused? Theology of the Cross from a Feminist Critical Perspective," *Journal of the European Society of Women in Theological Research* 15 (2007): 37—54.

Gyekye, Kwame. "The Problem of Evil: An Akan Perspective." In *African Philosophy: An Anthology*. Emmanuel Chukwudi Eze, ed. Oxford: Blackwell, 1998: 468–481.

Hagin, Kenneth E. *He Gave Gifts Unto Men: A Biblical Perspective of Apostles, Prophets and Pastors*. Tulsa, OK: Rhema Bible Church, 1992.

Hart, David Bentley. *That All Shall Be Saved: Heaven, Hell, and Universal Salvation*. New Haven, CT: Yale University Press, 2019.

Hartman, Lars. "Into the Name of Jesus" in *Baptism in the Early Church: Studies of the New Testament and Its World*. Edinburgh: T & T Clark, 1997.

Hiebert, Paul. *Anthropological Insights for Missionaries*. Grand Rapids, MI: Baker, 1985.

Hiett, Peter. *All Things New: What Does the Bible Really Say About Hell?* N.p.: Relentless Love Publishing, 2019.

Hodge, Tim. *The Gospel of the Restoration of All Things: A Study in Christian Universalism*. N.p.: M-Y Books, 2019.

Hodges, Zane C. *Absolutely Free! A Biblical Response to Lordship Salvation*. Grand Rapids, MI: Zondervan, 1989.

Hunter, James Davison. *American Evangelicalism: Conservative Religion and the Quandary of Modernity*. New Brunswick, NJ: Rutgers University Press, 1983.

_____. *Evangelicalism: The Coming Generation*. Chicago, IL: University of Chicago Press, 1987.

_____. *The Universal Solution: Presenting Biblical Universalism as the Solution to the Debate between Calvinists and Arminians*. N.p.: TriumphofMercy.Com, 2017.

_____. *The Ways of God: As seen through the Eyes of a Conservative Restorationist*. N.p.: TriumphofMercy.Com, 2019.

Hurd, George Sidney. *A Defense of Biblical Universalism*. N.p.: TriumphofMercy.Com, 2019.

Hurtado, Larry. *Lord Jesus Christ: Devotion to Jesus in Earliest Christianity*. Grand Rapids, MI: Eerdmans, 2003.

_____. *The Earliest Christian Artifacts: Manuscripts and Christian Origins*. Grand Rapids, MI: Eerdmans, 2006.

Husain, Irfan. "Minorities at Risk." DAWN.COM, December 22, 2018. https://www.dawn.com/news/1452941.

International Fellowship of Evangelical Mission Theologians. "The Osijek Declaration of 1998: Second Consultation on Theological Education and Leadership Development in Post-Communist Europe, in the Context of the Kingdom of God and the Kingdoms of the World." *Transformation* 16:1 (1999): 1–4.

Jensen, Dennis. *Flirting with Universalism: Resolving the Problem of an Eternal Hell*. Eugene, OR: Resource Publications, 2014.

Jersak, Bradley. *Her Gates Will Never Be Shut: Hell, Hope, and the New Jerusalem*. Eugene, OR: Wipf & Stock, 2009.

Jones, Brian. *Hell Is Real (But I Hate to Admit It)*. Colorado Springs: David C. Cook, 2011.

Jüngel, Eberhard. *Karl Barth: A Theological Legacy*. Trans. by Garrett E. Paul. Philadelphia, PA: Westminster, 1986.

Kannengiesser, Charles. *Handbook of Patristic Exegesis: The Bible in Ancient Christianity*. Leiden: Brill, 2006.

Karbi, Roger, and John G. MeadowKraft. *An Introduction to Early Church History Asia*. Lahore: Open Theological Seminary, 2010.

Kearney, Michael. *World View*. Novato, CA: Chandler & Sharp, 1984.

Keener, Craig S. *Gift Giver: The Holy Spirit for Today*. Grand Rapids, MI; Baker Academic, 2001.

Kelhoffer, James A. *Miracle and Mission: The Authentication of Missionaries and Their Message in the Longer Ending of Mark*. Tübingen: Mohr Siebeck, 2000.

Kirby, John. "Toward a Christian Response to Witchcraft in Northern Ghana." *International Bulletin of Missionary Research* 39:1 (2015): 19–22.

Klassen, Randolph J. *What Does the Bible Really Say about Hell? Wrestling with the Traditional View*. Telford, PA: Pandora, 2001.

Knitter, Paul F. *No Other Name? A Critical Survey of Christian Attitudes toward the World Religions*. Maryknoll, NY: Orbis Books, 1985.

Kronen, John, and Eric Reitan. *God's Final Victory: A Comparative Philosophical Case for Universalism*. New York: Bloomsbury, 2013.

Kruger, C. Baxter. *The Shack Revisited: There Is More Going on Here than You Ever Dared to Dream*. Foreword by William Paul Young. New York: FaithWords, 2012.

Kunhiyop, Waje Samuel. *African Christian Theology*. Grand Rapids, MI: Zondervan, 2012.

Kuzmič, Peter. "A Vision for Theological Education for Difficult Times." *Religion, State and Society* 22: 2 (1994): 237–43.

Kwiyani, Harvey C. *Our Children Need Roots and Wings: Equipping and Empowering Young Diaspora Africans for Life and Mission*. Liverpool: Missio Africanus Publishing, 2018.

_____. *Sent Forth: African Missionary Work in the West*. American Society of Missiology Series. Maryknoll, NY: Orbis Books, 2014.

Lowe, David. "The Ravers Who Get High on God." *The Sun*, January 21, 2010. http://www.goldminemedia.eu/WP/2011/11/the-ravers-who-get-high-on-god/

Lua, Norma. *Fiction in the Traditional Kankana-ey Society*. Baguio, Philippines: Cordillera Studies Center, 1984.

Ma, Julie C. "Animism and Pentecostalism: A Case Study." In *New International Dictionary of Pentecostal and Charismatic Movements*. Stanley M. Burgess and Eduard M. van der Mass, eds. Grand Rapids, MI: Zondervan, 2002: 315–18.

Ma, Julie C., and Wonsuk Ma. *Mission in the Spirit. Towards a Pentecostal / Charismatic Missiology*. Oxford: Regnum Books, 2010.

MacArthur, John F. *The Gospel According to Jesus*. Grand Rapids: Zondervan, 1989.

Macchia, Frank D. *Baptized in the Spirit: A Global Pentecostal Theology*. Grand Rapids, MI: Zondervan, 2006.

_____. *Jesus the Spirit Baptizer: Christology in Light of Pentecost*. Grand Rapids, MI: Eerdmans, 2018.

MacDonald, Gregory [pseudonym for Robin Parry], ed. *"All Shall Be Well": Explorations in Universal Salvation and Christian Theology from Origen to Moltmann*. Eugene, OR: Wipf & Stock, 2011.

_____. *The Evangelical Universalist*. 1st Ed. Eugene, OR: Wipf & Stock, 2006.

_____. *The Evangelical Universalist*. 2nd Ed. Eugene, OR: Wipf & Stock, 2012.

Măcelaru, Marcel V. "Holistic Mission in Post-Communist Romania: A Case Study on the Growth of the 'Elim' Pentecostal Church of Timişoara (1990-1997)." In *Pentecostal Mission and Global Christianity: An Edinburgh Centenary Reader*. Younghoon Lee and Wonsuk Ma, eds. Oxford: Regnum Books, 2018: 305–22.

MacIntyre, Alasdair. *Whose Justice? Which Rationality?* Notre Dame, IN: University of Notre Dame Press, 1988.

Magda, Ksenja, and Melody J. Wachsmuth. "'Discerning the Body' in Cross-Cultural Relationships: A Critical Analysis of Missional Partnership in Southeastern Europe." *Kairos: Evangelical Journal of Theology* 8:1 (2014): 25–43.

Malik, Iftikhar. *Religious Minorities in Pakistan*. London: Minority Rights Group International, 2002.

Marshall, Howard I., and David Peterson, eds. *Witness to the Gospel: Theology of Acts*. Grand Rapids, MI: Eerdmans, 1998.

Marshall, Ross S. *God's Testimony of All: The Greatest Promise Ever Made*. 2nd ed. N.p.: CreateSpace, 2016.

Martin, David. *On Secularization: Towards a Revised General Theory*. Aldershot: Ashgate, 2005.

_____. *Pentecostalism: The World Their Parish*. Oxford: Blackwell, 2002.

Matarazzo, James M., Jr. *The Judgment of Love: An Investigation of Salvific Judgment in Christian Eschatology*. Eugene, OR: Pickwick Publications, 2018.

Mbiti, John. *Concepts of God in Africa*. London: SPCK, 1969.

McClymond, Michael J. "Charismatic Renewal and Neo-Pentecostalism: From American Origins to Global Permutations." In Cecil M. Robeck and Amos Yong, eds. *The Cambridge Companion to Pentecostalism*, 31–51. Cambridge: Cambridge University Press, 2014.

_____. *The Devil's Redemption: A New History and Interpretation of Christian Universalism*. 2 Vols. Grand Rapids, MI: Baker Academic, 2018.

Meacham, Jon. "What If There's No Hell? A Popular Pastor's Best-Selling Book Has Stirred Fierce Debate about Sin, Salvation and Judgment." *Time*, April 20, 2011: 38–43.

Meyer, Marvin C. *The Gnostic Discoveries: The Impact of the Nag Hammadi Library*. San Francisco: HarperSanFrancisco, 2005.

Miller, Caleb A. *The Divine Reversal: Recovering the Vision of Jesus Christ as the Last Adam*. N.p.: Father's House Press, 2014.

Morgan, Christopher W., and Robert A. Peterson, eds. *Hell under Fire: Modern Scholarship Reinvents Eternal Punishment*. Grand Rapids, MI: Zondervan, 2004.

Moureau, Scott A., Gary R. Corwin, and Gary B, McGee. *Introducing World Missions: A Biblical, Historical and Practical Survey*. Grand Rapids, MI: Baker Academics, 2004.

Myers, J. D. *What is Hell?: The Truth About Hell and How to Avoid It*. Dallas, OR: Redeeming Press, 2019

Nee, Watchman. *The Communion of the Holy Spirit*. New York: Christian Fellowship Publishers, 1994.

Newbigin, Lesslie. *The Gospel in a Pluralist Society*. Grand Rapids, MI: Eerdmans, 1989.

Noe, John. *Hell Yes / Hell No*. Indianapolis: East2West, 2011.

O'Regan, Cyril. *Gnostic Return in Modernity*. Albany, NY: State University of New York Press, 2001.

Onyinah, Opoku. *Pentecostal Exorcism: Witchcraft and Demonology in Ghana*. Blandford: Deo Publishing, 2012.

_____. *Spiritual Warfare: A Centre for Pentecostal Theology Short Introduction*. Cleveland, TN: CPT Press, 2012.

Owen, John. *Overcoming Sin and Temptation*. Kelly M. Kapic and Justin Taylor, eds. Wheaton: Crossway, 2006.

Parnham, David. "John Saltmarsh and the Mystery of Redemption." *Harvard Theological Review* 104 (2011): 265–98.

_____. "Motions of Law and Grace: The Puritan in the Antinomian." *Westminster Theological Journal* 70 (2008): 73–104.

_____. "The Covenantal Quietism of Tobias Crisp." *Church History* 75 (2006): 511–43.

_____. "The Humbling of 'High Presumption': Tobias Crisp Dismantles the Puritan *Ordo Salutis*." *Journal of Ecclesiastical History* 56 (2005): 50–74.

Parry, Robin A. "Evangelical Universalism: Oxymoron?", *Evangelical Quarterly* 84 (2012): 3–18.

Parry, Robin A., and Ilaria Ramelli. *A Larger Hope?: Universal Salvation from the Reformation to the Nineteenth Century*. Eugene, OR: Cascade Books, 2019.

Pearson, Carlton. *The Gospel of Inclusion: Reaching beyond Religious Fundamentalism to the True Love of God and Self*. New York: Atria, 2006.

Peterlin, Davorin. "A Wrong Kind of Missionary: A Semi-Autobiographic Outcry." *Mission Studies* 12: 2 (1995): 164–74.

Pfau, Julie Shoshana, and David R. Blumenthal. "Violence of God: Dialogic Fragments," *Cross Currents* 51 (2001) 177–200.

Powell, Kara, and Chap Clark. *Sticky Faith: Everyday Ideas to Build Lasting Faith in Your Kids*. Grand Rapids, MI: Zondervan, 2011.

Priest, Robert J. "The Value of Anthropology for Missiological Engagements with Context: The Case of Witch Accusations." *Missiology: An International Review* 43:1 (2015): 27–42.

Prince, Joseph. *Destined to Reign: The Secret to Effortless Success, Wholeness, and Victorious Living*. Tulsa: Harrison House, 2007.

Propp, Steven H. *The Gift of God Is Eternal Life: A Novel about Universalism*. Bloomington, IN: iUniverse, 2016.

Purcell, Boyd C. *Spiritual Terrorism: Spiritual Abuse from the Womb to the Tomb*. Bloomington, IN: AuthorHouse, 2008.

Rabe, Andre. *Imagine*. 2nd Ed. N.p.: Andre Rabe, 2013.

Ramelli, Ilaria. *The Christian Doctrine of Apokatastasis*. Leiden: Brill, 2013.

Ramelli, Ilaria, and Robin Parry. *A Larger Hope? Universal Salvation from Christian beginnings to Julian of Norwich*. Eugene, OR: Cascade Books, 2019.

Rasmussen, Steven D. H., and Hannah Rasmussen. "Healing Communities: Contextualizing Responses to Witch Accusations." *International Bulletin of Missionary Research* 39:1 (2015): 12–18.

Reddin, Opal L., ed. *Power Encounter: A Pentecostal Perspective*. Springfield, MO: Central Bible College Press, 1999.

Richie, Tony. *Speaking by the Spirit: A Pentecostal Model for Interreligious Dialogue*. Lexington, KY: Emeth Press, 2011.

Rohr, Richard. *The Universal Christ: How a Forgotten Reality Can Change Everything We See, Hope For, and Believe*. New York: Penguin Random House/Convergent Books, 2019

Rouner, Leroy. "Theology of Religions in Recent Protestant Theology." In *Christianity among World Religions*. Hans Küng, Jürgen Moltmann, and Marcus Lefébure, eds. Edinburgh: T. & T. Clark, 1986: 108-115.

Ryrie, Charles C. *So Great Salvation: What It Means to Believe in Jesus Christ*. 1989. Reprint, Chicago: Moody Press, 1997.

Sarris, George W. *Heaven's Doors: Wider than You Ever Believed*. N.p.: GWS Publishing/Grace Will Succeed, 2017.

Schaff, Philip, and David S. Schaff, eds. *The Creeds of Christendom: With a History and Critical Notes*. 3 Vols. Grand Rapids: Baker Book House, 1931; 1983 reprint.

Schildgen, Brenda Deen. *Power and Prejudice: The Reception of the Gospel of Mark*. Detroit: Wayne State University Press, 1999.

Schleiermacher, Friedrich. *On Religion: Speeches to Its Cultured Despisers*. Ed. and trans. Richard Crouter. Cambridge: Cambridge University Press, 1996.

Sears, Ron. *Speaking the Truth in Love—Wins: A Response to Christian Universalism*. St. Petersburg, FL; Journeyman Press, 2017.

Shakarian, Damos, Elizabeth Sherrill, and John E. Sherrill. *The Happiest People on Earth: The Personal Story of Damos Shakarian as Told to Elizabeth and John Sherrill*. Old Tappan, NJ: Chosen Books, 1975.

Shelton, Brian W. *Martyrdom from Exegesis in Hippolytus: An Early Church Presbyter's Commentary on Daniel*. Colorado Springs: Paternoster, 2008.

Shelton, James B. *Mighty in Word and Deed: The Role of the Holy Spirit in Luke-Acts*. Eugene, OR: Wipf & Stock, 2000.

Sinaga, Sahat. "Is Joseph Prince's Radical Grace Teaching Biblical?" https://independent.academia.edu/SinagaS

Spong, John Shelby. *Unbelievable: Why Neither Ancient Creeds Nor the Reformation Can Produce a Living Faith Today*. New York: HarperOne, 2018.

Spurgeon, Charles. *The Treasury of David*. 3 Vols. Grand Rapids, MI: Zondervan, 1966.

Staples, Jason A. "'Lord, Lord': Jesus as YHWH in Matthew and Luke," *New Testament Studies* 64:1 (2018): 1–19.

Stetson, Eric. *Christian Universalism: God's Good News for All People*. Sparkling Bay Books, 2008.

Sundkler, Bengt G. M. *Bantu Prophets in South Africa*. 2nd Ed. Oxford: International African Institute, 1976.

Talbott, Thomas. *The Inescapable Love of God*. Salem, OR: Universalist Publishers, 1999.

_____. *The Inescapable Love of God*. Salem, OR: Universalist Publishers, 1999.

Tanquerey, Adolphe. *The Spiritual Life: A Treatise on Ascetical and Mystical Theology*. Trans. Herman Branderis. 2nd Ed. New York: Desclée, 1930.

Taylor, Charles. *A Secular Age*. Cambridge, MA: Belknap Press, 2007.

Taylor, John V. *The Primal Vision: Christian Presence amid African Religion*. London: SCM, 1963.

Tidball, Derek. "Can Evangelicals Be Universalists?" *Evangelical Quarterly* 84 (2012): 19–32.

Turner, Max. *The Holy Spirit and Spiritual Gifts: Then and Now*. Carlisle, UK: Paternoster, 1996.

Vincent, Ken. *The Golden Thread: God's Promise of Universal Salvation*. New York: iUniverse, 2005.

Visser 't Hooft, Willem. *The Renewal of the Church*. Philadelphia, PA: Westminster, 1956.

Volf, Miroslav. "Fishing in the Neighbour's Pond: Mission and Proselytism in Eastern Europe." *International Bulletin of Missionary Research* 20:1 (1996): 26–31.

Wagner, C. Peter. *Dominion! How Kingdom Action Can Change the World*. Grand Rapids, MI: Chosen, 2008.

Währisch-Oblau, Claudia. "Meeting a Charismatic Challenge: The Development of Deliverance Ministries within the Protestant Member Churches of the United Evangelical Mission." In *African Pentecostal Mission Maturing*. Lord Abraham Elorm-Donkor and Clifton R Clarke, eds. Eugene, OR: Wipf & Stock, 2018.

Walls, Andrew. *The Missionary Movement in Christian History: Studies in the Transmission of Faith*. Maryknoll, NY: Orbis Books, 1996.

Watts, Graham H. "Is Universalism Theologically Coherent? The Contrasting Views of P. T. Forsyth and T. F. Torrance." *Evangelical Quarterly* 84 (2012): 40–46.

Weinandy, Thomas. "Gnosticism and Contemporary Soteriology." In *Jesus: Essays in Christology*. Ave Maria, FL: Sapientia Press, 2014: 256–65.

Wild Robert, and Robin A. Parry, eds. *A Catholic Reading Guide to Universalism*. Eugene, OR: Resource Publications, 2015.

Willard, Dallas. *The Divine Conspiracy: Rediscovering Our Hidden Life in God*. San Francisco: HarperSanFrancisco, 1998.

Wittmer, Michael. *Christ Alone: An Evangelical Response to Rob Bell's "Love Wins."* Grand Rapids: Edenridge, 2011.

Wyatt, Jean. *Judge Is the Savior: Towards a Universalist Understanding of Salvation*. Eugene, OR: Resource Publications, 2015.

Yao, Xinzhong. *An Introduction to Confucianism*. Cambridge, MA: Cambridge University Press, 2000.

Yong, Amos. *Beyond the Impasse: Toward a Pneumatological Theology of Religions*. Carlisle, UK: Paternoster, 2003.

Zurlo, Gina A., Todd Johnson, and Peter F. Crossing. "World Christianity and Mission 2020: Ongoing Shift to the Global South." *International Bulletin of Mission Research* 40:1 (2020): 8–19.

Name and Subject Index

459

Greece, 376–377, 378–380, 381, 385–386,
390–391
greed, 187–188
Greek language, name concept within, 12
Gregory of Nyssa, 79
Grenz, Stanley J., 268
Grimsrud, Ted, 150
Grisez, Germain, 88
Guerra, Laudjair and Eline, 408
Gulley, Philip, 85, 86
Gundry, Robert H., 34, 35
Gyekye, Kwame, 269, 287, 288

H
Haar, Gerrie Ter, 200
Hae Enga, 297–298
Haji Pur Girls Hostel (Pakistan), 314
Hammer, Raymond, 298–299
Harris, William Wade, 211
Hays, Richard, 268
healer, Jesus as, 282–283
healing. *See also* miracles
authenticating function of, 128
Beautiful Gate cripple, 188
forgiveness from sin and, 233
ministry strategies for, 217
movement of, 102–103
power of, 149
as religious experience, 7
heaven, 82
Heitmüller, Wilhelm, 22
hell, 68, 77, 80–81, 82, 97n101
Hellenistic Age, 33–34
Hellenistic mystery religions, 31
heretics, false miracles of, 115, 116, 120
Hezmalhalch, Thomas, 264
Hick, John, 228, 229
Hiebert, Paul, 163
Hill, R. A., 314
Hinduism, 295, 298–299, 301, 314, 328, 335–341
Hippolytus, 121–127
holiness, 13, 75
Holiness movement, 102–103
Hollenweger, Walter J., 100, 203, 351
holy living, exhortation to, 54
Holy Spirit. *See also* baptism
in the Holy Spirit; Pentecost/
Pentecostalism;
speaking in tongues
Common Call emphasis of, 4
conviction through, 238
criticism of, 201–203
daily practice of, 277
disciples and, 198–199
empowerment by, 159–160, 185
gift exercise through, 8
Jesus and, 11–12, 21, 282–283

as liberator, 283
limitlessness of, 159
metaphor for, 181
missions and, 199, 203, 235–238
necessity of, 151
outpouring of, 184
power of, 199–201, 243
productive power of, 284
as promise fulfillment, 236
prophetic inspiration of, 174
resurrection and, 184–185
revealing power of, 179, 280
hope, Jesus as, 16
hospitals, structure of, 416–417
Hsun-Tzu, 299–300
human hearts, purification of, 289–290
humanism, gospel relevance within, 3
humanity
evil spirits and, 287–288, 290
moral responsibility of, 289
nature of, 300
sin within, 142
suffering of, 301–303
humility, 32
Hurtado, Larry, 17

I
ICM (International Charismatic Mission), 396,
398–405, 406, 407–408, 410n30
idolatry, 54–55, 194
Idowu, Bolaji, 259, 261
Igbo people (Nigeria), names of God of, 167
Imagine (Rabe), 77
IMF (International Monetary Fund), 288–289
immanent frame, 333–334
inclusivism, 280
India
children's conditions within, 336–337
colonization within, 341
economic demographics within, 326–327
education within, 336–337
Hae Enga within, 297–298
Hinduism within, 298–299
identity markers within, 327
"Indianness" within, 340–341, 345n28
middle class within, 326–328
missions work within, 140
secularism within, 326–333
secular traditions within, 328–331, 338–341
socialism within, 328–329, 330
indigenization model, 262
individual decision, 102
The Inescapable Love of God (Talbott), 69
infant baptism, 334
information age, 247
An Initiation of Shaman (film), 302–303
intellectualism, 427

Scripture Index

475

CPSIA information can be obtained
at www.ICGtesting.com
Printed in the USA
LVHW010807211120
672146LV00001B/54